Capital Allowances 2009–10

Capital Allowances 2009–10

Ray Chidell
With Suttons Capital Allowances

a Wolters Kluwer business

Wolters Kluwer (UK) Limited
145 London Road
Kingston-upon-Thames
Surrey
KT2 6SR
Telephone: +44(0) 844 561 8166
Facsimile: +44(0) 208 547 2638
Email: customerservices@cch.co.uk
Website: www.cch.co.uk

This publication is sold with the understanding that neither the publisher nor the authors, with regard to this publication, are engaged in rendering legal or professional services. The material contained in this publication neither purports, nor is intended to be, advice on any particular matter.

Although this publication incorporates a considerable degree of standardisation, subjective judgement by the user, based on individual circumstances, is indispensable. This publication is an aid and cannot be expected to replace such judgement.

Neither the publisher nor the authors can accept any responsibility or liability to any person, whether a purchaser of this publication or not, in respect of anything done or omitted to be done by any such person in reliance, whether sole or partial, upon the whole or any part of the contents of this publication.

Legislative and other material

While copyright in all statutory and other materials resides in the Crown or other relevant body, copyright in the remaining material in this publication is vested in the publisher.

The publisher advises that any statutory or other materials issued by the Crown or other relevant bodies and reproduced and quoted in this publication are not the authorised official versions of those statutory or other materials. In the preparation, however, the greatest care has been taken to ensure exact conformity with the law as enacted or other material as issued.

Crown copyright legislation is reproduced under the terms of Crown Copyright Policy Guidance issued by HMSO. Other Crown copyright material is reproduced with the permission of the controller of HMSO. European Communities Copyright material is reproduced with permission.

Telephone Helpline Disclaimer Notice

Where purchasers of this publication also have access to any Telephone Helpline Service operated by Wolters Kluwer (UK), then Wolters Kluwer's total liability to contract, tort (including negligence, or breach of statutory duty) misrepresentation, restitution or otherwise with respect to any claim arising out of its acts or alleged omissions in the provision of the Helpline Service shall be limited to the yearly subscription fee paid by the Claimant.

© 2009 Wolters Kluwer (UK) Limited

ISBN 978-1-84798-182-0

All rights reserved. No part of this publication may be reproduced, stored in a retrieval system, or transmitted in any form or by any means, electronic, mechanical, photocopying, recording or otherwise, without the prior permission of Wolters Kluwer (UK) Limited or the original copyright holder.

No responsibility for loss occasioned to any person acting or refraining from action as a result of any material in this publication can be accepted by the author or publisher. Material is contained in this publication for which copyright is acknowledged. Permission to reproduce such material cannot be granted by the publisher and application must be made to the copyright holder.

British Library Cataloguing-in-Publication Data

A catalogue record for this book is available from the British Library.

Typeset in-house at Wolters Kluwer (UK) Ltd
Printed and bound in the UK by Hobbs the Printers Ltd

Preface

Few businesses can calculate their tax liabilities without an understanding of capital allowances. These allowances, which provide tax relief for the cost of specified capital assets, are governed by complex rules. Furthermore, different regimes apply for different types of expenditure so that (for example) the rules governing the allowances for the cost of plant and machinery are quite different from those applying to expenditure on the conversion into flats of certain unused commercial properties.

Radical changes to the most commonly claimed allowances – for expenditure on plant and machinery – were made from April 2008. These changes both increased the categories of expenditure that qualify for tax relief and altered the timing at which such relief may be claimed, generally improving the position for smaller businesses but imposing a severe delay in the granting of relief to larger entities incurring higher levels of expenditure. Further changes from 2009 related mainly to allowances for expenditure on cars, including some fairly involved transitional provisions. First-year allowances, having for the most part been abolished in 2008, have also been given a new lease of life, albeit on a temporary basis.

Now that the rules for integral features have started to feature in tax computations, it has also been possible to bring some practical experience to bear on the commentary relating to property that is being bought and sold, including in particular the relative values of integral features and other fixtures in property.

Alongside these plant and machinery changes, the allowances given for industrial and agricultural buildings continue to reduce in value before their final abolition from April 2011. Full details of the transitional arrangements are provided, including the complications relating to enterprise zones.

This edition of the book provides thorough coverage of the changes, illustrated with worked examples. Key developments in relation to plant and machinery allowances include the abolition of the most common first-year allowances and a reduction in the standard rate of writing-down allowances, as well as the introduction of the new concepts of 'annual investment allowances', 'integral features' and 'payable tax credits'. An overview of the changes, with cross references to the fuller coverage, may be found at paragraph 100-150.

All capital allowances within the UK tax system are addressed in detail. With roots firmly in the legislation itself, the book seeks to incorporate relevant case law and HMRC material in relation to every one of the 11 types of allowance. With the help of examples, the intention is that the book will on the one hand provide rapid and accessible guidance for those unfamiliar with particular allowances, and on the other offer comprehensive coverage for the more experienced practitioner.

Allowances for know-how, patents and dredging may be the preserve of the few, and anyone who is not already familiar with Assured Tenancy Allowances can probably remain safely in untroubled ignorance of the topic. Nevertheless, all these topics are explained in detail, each section beginning with an overview to help the reader to gain a rapid understanding of the key issues.

The commentary on the more familiar allowances again begins with an overview, but is then of greater depth. Allowances for plant and machinery are given particularly detailed treatment, reflecting both their complexity and the extent of recent changes.

Few tax topics have generated more case law than the question of what constitutes plant. Textbooks on capital allowances have traditionally taken one of two lines on this issue. Either they have simply included a list of assets that do or may qualify as plant, or they have carried out a case-by-case review of the matter. The problem with the first of these approaches is that a simple list of assets is potentially misleading and also somewhat unhelpful. For example, somebody preparing a tax computation is not very interested in knowing that office partitioning *may* qualify as plant; he wants to know whether, in the particular circumstances, it will do so. The problem with the second approach is that it is not 'user-friendly'; the same individual looking for guidance on office partitions wants to be able to find that guidance without wading through a mass of irrelevant case law. Furthermore, the reader wants to know whether the principles in the case have been modified by statute, HMRC practice or whatever.

This publication has therefore taken a different approach. The A to Z section analyses around a hundred categories of commonly incurred expenditure. For each category, the consistent layout aims to bring together all relevant material on a particular topic. Thus, to continue with the same example of the partitions, the reader will find references to the relevant legislation, to the most directly relevant tax cases, and to appropriate parts of the HMRC manuals. These are followed by a commentary that brings the strands together and draws attention to particular issues that may need to be considered.

Planning tips have been included as appropriate throughout the book, but especially in relation to the treatment of fixtures within property. Major tax planning opportunities arise whenever a commercial property is acquired or refurbished, and pitfalls abound when such property is sold. Several sections of the book are therefore dedicated specifically to these issues, seeking to demonstrate the potential (often unclaimed) for significant tax relief. Once more, that material has been expanded and updated for this edition, now reflecting the greatly increased potential value of fixtures claims in the light of the new rules for integral features.

Unless otherwise stated, all references to legislation are to the *Capital Allowances Act* 2001 (CAA 2001).

The law is stated as at 1 September 2009.

Ray Chidell
Claritax Ltd.
www.claritax.co.uk

September 2009

Foreword

Having contributed to two CCH tax digests earlier in the year we are delighted to have the opportunity to be associated with one of the leading textbooks on capital allowances.

When property is bought (or sold) there are valuable tax-saving opportunities and it has never been more important to identify such opportunities than in the current economic climate. To make the most of the capital allowance savings, however, it is necessary to combine a unique blend of specialist skills, covering expertise both in tax law and in the valuation of plant and property. Our contribution to this book has been to share with Ray Chidell the insights we gain from our daily work on practical valuation matters, so as to complement his detailed tax knowledge.

At Suttons Capital Allowances we work exclusively on capital allowance issues with a portfolio of clients from relatively small owner managed businesses to some substantial household names. We work closely with our clients and (in all cases) their accountants to develop capital allowance opportunities and to implement solutions that achieve all the available tax savings. Our years of experience enable us to handle with confidence all stages of a claim, from the initial identification of an opportunity through the development of the claim itself to the final step of negotiating agreement with HM Revenue and Customs.

We have worked with Ray on a number of different and challenging cases over recent years; his precise and unique insight into the subject has benefitted many of our clients. Ray has in turn used this practical knowledge to improve further what is already an outstanding book on this topic. In the last year, for example, we have been able to give Ray practical insights into how claims for integral features are working out in practice, including in particular the valuation issues relating to such assets. Those insights are now built into the relevant chapters of this book.

Ian Sutton
Suttons Capital Allowances
Telephone: 01905 758 024
Mobile: 07545 696 564
www.suttons-ca.com
Riverside House
River Lawn Road
Tonbridge
Kent
TN9 1EP

September 2009

Contents

Preface	*v*
Foreword	*vii*
Abbreviations	*xvii*
Key Data	*xix*

Introduction and General Provisions   **1**

    Introduction   1

    Claiming capital allowances   7

    Capital expenditure   10

    Timing of expenditure   12

    Chargeable period   16

    Exclusion of double allowances   18

    Capital gains tax issues   19

    Contributions   22

    Miscellaneous issues   24

Plant and Machinery Allowances   **29**

    Introduction and general principles   29

    Giving effect to allowances and charges   30

    Qualifying activities   34

    Qualifying expenditure   42

    Excluded expenditure   53

    Meaning of plant   58

    Annual investment allowances   73

    First-year allowances: availability   88

    First-year allowances: computation   102

    Other allowances and charges   106

    Cars   127

    Cars: old rules   145

    Short-life assets   153

Long-life assets 161

Hire purchase 173

Leasing assets 179

Long funding leasing 210

Ships 238

Mining and oil activities 253

Additional VAT liabilities and rebates 259

Partnerships and succession 262

Anti-avoidance provisions 266

Rent factoring 274

First-year tax credits 275

Fixtures 288

Integral features 312

Plant and machinery: property transactions 325

Newly built property 332

Refurbishing a property 335

Buying a property 337

Selling a property 350

Capital gains tax issues 353

Particular types of property 356

Plant and Machinery: A to Z of Expenditure **361**

A to Z of expenditure: how to use this Chapter 361

Advertising hoardings 362

Aerials 363

Air conditioning systems 364

Alterations to buildings 365

Amusement parks 367

Animals 368

Bicycles and bicycle holders 370

Books 371

Bridges, etc 373

Contents

Briefcases	373
Buildings	374
Bus shelters	377
Cameras	378
Canals	379
Caravans and caravan sites	380
Cars	381
Car parks	382
Car wash apparatus	383
Cash dispensers	384
Ceilings and canopies	384
Central heating, etc systems	386
Clocks	388
Cold rooms	389
Computers	390
Computer software	391
Consumables	393
Containers	394
Counters and checkouts	395
Curtains	395
Décor	396
Demolition costs	397
Designs and patterns	398
Disability Discrimination Act	399
Display equipment	402
Docks (including dry docks)	403
Doors and door handles	404
Dyehouses	405
Dykes, etc	406
Electrical installations and equipment	407
Electricity substations	413

Energy-saving investments 414

Entertaining-related expenditure 414

Fencing 415

Films, tapes and discs 416

Finance costs 417

Fish tanks and ponds 418

Fixtures 418

Floodlighting 420

Floors and flooring materials 421

Football grounds 424

Fridges and freezers 426

Furniture and furnishings 427

Gas systems 428

Gates 429

Golf courses 430

Grain silos 431

Greenhouses 432

Human body 434

Insulation 435

Kennels 437

Land 438

Letter boxes 439

Lifts, escalators and walkways 440

Lighting 442

Loose tools 444

Machinery 445

Milking parlours 445

Mirrors 446

Number plates 447

Panelling 448

Partitions 450

Plant rooms 451

Poultry houses 452

Professional fees and preliminary costs 453

Public address systems 454

Removal costs 455

Reservoirs, etc 455

Roads, etc 456

Safes and strongrooms 457

Sanitary ware 458

Screens 459

Seats 460

Security systems 461

Sewerage 464

Shelves 465

Ships 466

Shop fronts 467

Shutters 468

Silage clamps 469

Slurry storage facilities 470

Spare parts 472

Sports grounds (safety) 473

Stairs 475

Storage equipment 475

Structures 476

Swimming pools 478

Taxi licence plates 479

Telecommunication systems 480

Telephones and fax machines 480

Televisions and videos 481

Temporary buildings 482

Tunnels 484

Wallpaper designs and pattern books   485

Walls   485

Water supplies and water tanks   487

Water towers   489

Windmills   490

Windows   491

Zoo cages   492

Industrial Buildings Allowances   **495**

Introduction and general principles   495

Giving effect to allowances and charges   498

Expenditure on the construction of a building or structure   502

Contributions to capital expenditure   506

Qualifying trades   509

Excluded activities   537

Non-industrial parts of buildings   545

Qualifying expenditure   547

Relevant interest   551

Initial and writing-down allowances   556

Balancing adjustments: principles   574

Anti-avoidance rules   574

Sales treated as being for alternative amount   576

Miscellaneous provisions   579

Qualifying hotels   587

Qualifying sports pavilions   589

Enterprise zones   590

Business Premises Renovation Allowances   **609**

Overview   609

Qualifying expenditure   610

Relevant interest   613

Initial and writing-down allowances   615

Balancing events   616

Additional VAT liabilities and rebate 620

Agricultural Buildings Allowances **623**

Overview 623

Agricultural buildings 628

Qualifying expenditure 632

Relevant interest 634

Allowances and charges 637

Balancing events 640

Other issues 642

Flat Conversion Allowances **645**

Overview 645

Definitions 647

Calculation of allowances and charges 655

Other issues 660

Mineral Extraction Allowances **661**

Overview 661

Definitions 662

Calculation of allowances and charges 673

Other issues 681

Research and Development Allowances **685**

Overview 685

Definitions 686

Calculation of allowances and charges 691

Other issues 694

Know-how Allowances **699**

Overview 699

Definitions 700

Calculation of allowances and charges 702

Other issues 706

Patent Allowances **707**

Overview 707

Definitions   708

Calculation of allowances and charges   710

Other issues   714

Dredging Allowances   **717**

Overview   717

Definitions   717

Calculation of allowances and charges   719

Other issues   722

Assured Tenancy Allowances   **723**

Overview   723

Definitions   724

Calculation of allowances and charges   728

Other issues   733

Case Table   **739**
Legislation Finding List   **743**
Index   **757**

Abbreviations

The following abbreviations may be used in this publication.

ABA	agricultural buildings allowance
AIA	annual investment allowance
ATA	assured tenancy allowance
BIM	Her Majesty's Revenue & Customs Business Income Manual
CA	Her Majesty's Revenue & Customs Capital Allowances Manual
CAA	Capital Allowances Act
CG	Her Majesty's Revenue & Customs Capital Gains Manual
CGT	capital gains tax
CO_2	carbon dioxide
CT	corporation tax
DMG	Her Majesty's Revenue & Customs Decision Makers Guide
ECA	enhanced capital allowances
EIM	Her Majesty's Revenue & Customs Employment Income Manual
ESC	extra statutory concession
EZ	enterprise zone
EZPUT	enterprise zone property unit trust
FA	Finance Act
FCA	flat conversion allowance
FYA	first-year allowance
HMRC	Her Majesty's Revenue & Customs
IBA	industrial buildings allowance
ICTA	Income and Corporation Taxes Act
IRInt	Inland Revenue (now HMRC) interpretation
ITEPA	Income Tax (Earnings and Pensions) Act
LLA	long life asset
MEA	mineral extraction allowance
P&M	plant and machinery
PIM	Her Majesty's Revenue & Customs Property Income Manual
R&D	research and development
RDA	research and development allowance
s.	section
SI	Statutory Instrument
SP	statement of practice
ss.	sections
TCGA	Taxation of Chargeable Gains Act
TMA	Taxes Management Act
VAT	value added tax
WDA	writing-down allowance

KEY DATA

Plant and machinery

10-000   Plant and machinery – overview of allowances

The following is a summary of available plant and machinery allowances, reflecting changes introduced in 2008 and 2009.

Description	Detail	Notes	Commentary
Annual investment allowance	Full relief for first £50,000 (adjusted pro rata for shorter or longer periods).	1. Relief was restricted for periods spanning 1 or 6 April 2008. 2. AIA can cover long-life asset and integral features, as well as standard P&M. 3. Groups and certain other related parties share a single amount.	181-000ff.
First-year allowances (100%) for cars	Cars with CO$_2$ emissions not exceeding 110g/km.	Threshold reduced from 120g/km from 1 April 2008.	185-400ff.
Temporary first-year allowances (40%)	Available for one year from April 2009	Businesses of any size, including landlords (but subject to general exclusions re leasing, etc.)	185-050
Other first-year allowances (100%)	Available for certain energy-saving assets; environmentally beneficial assets; refuelling stations; plant used in ring-fence trades.	Payable tax credits available for company losses created by allowances re energy-saving or environmentally beneficial expenditure.	Energy-saving plant: 185-350. Environmentally beneficial assets: 185-550. Refuelling stations: 185-450. Ring-fence trades: 185-500.
Writing-down allowances (20%)	Standard rate of WDA for assets, including cars but excluding those assets attracting relief at just 10% as below.	1. Reduced from 25% for P&M only from April 2008. 2. £3,000 annual restriction for cars bought before April 2009.	190-250.

Description	Detail	Notes	Commentary
Writing-down allowances (10%)	Reduced rate of WDA applies to certain 'special rate' expenditure, covering long-life assets, integral features, thermal insulation, higher emission cars.	1. Transitional provisions applied for periods spanning 1 or 6 April 2008. 2. AIAs (see above) are available for this expenditure, except cars. 3. Includes higher emission cars bought from April 2009.	Long-life assets: 210-000ff. Integral features: 247-000ff. Thermal insulation: 160-000. Cars: 185-400ff.
Balancing allowances		No change from April 2008.	190-400
Balancing charges		No change from April 2008.	190-500

10-020 Temporary first-year allowances

Temporary first-year allowances at 40 per cent are given for expenditure incurred in the year ended 31 March or 5 April 2010 (for corporation tax and income tax respectively). See 185-050.

See 10-050 re general exclusions.

10-025 Plant and machinery: first-year allowances (CAA 2001, s. 52)

Changes were made to first-year allowances from April 2008. Subject to the general exclusions at 10-050, full 100 per cent allowances are still available for the following types of expenditure incurred by a business of any size. If full FYAs are not claimed, WDA is normally available at 20 per cent on a reducing balance basis.

Nature of expenditure	Authority (CAA 2001)	Notes
Energy-saving plant or machinery	s. 45A–45C	Loss-making companies may claim payable tax credit
Cars with very low CO_2 emissions	s. 45D	Threshold tightened from April 2008
Plant or machinery for certain refuelling stations	s. 45E	

Nature of expenditure	Authority (CAA 2001)	Notes
Plant or machinery (other than a long life asset) for use by a company wholly in a ring fence trade	s. 45F	
Environmentally beneficial plant or machinery	s. 45H–45J	Loss-making companies may claim payable tax credit

10-050 First-year allowances – general exclusions

No first-year allowances are available for a business of any size, for:

- expenditure incurred in the final chargeable period;
- cars (other than those with very low CO_2 emissions);
- certain ships and railway assets;
- long-life assets (other than plant or machinery for use by a company wholly in a ring fence trade, in which case a 24 per cent FYA is available if such expenditure is a LLA);
- plant or machinery for leasing;
- in certain anti-avoidance cases where the obtaining of a FYA is linked to a change in the nature or conduct of a trade;
- where an asset was initially acquired for purposes other than those of the qualifying activity;
- where an asset was acquired by way of a gift;
- where plant or machinery that was provided for long funding leasing starts to be used for other purposes.

See 185-150 for commentary on these exclusions.

Legislation: CAA 2001, s. 46(2)

10-100 Plant and machinery: writing-down allowances (CAA 2001, s. 56)

	From April 2008	Before April 2008
Standard WDAs	20%	25%
Long-life assets	10%	6%
Overseas leasing	10%	10%
Integral features	10%	25% (ie treated as other P&M)
Cars over £12,000	Lower of £3,000 or 20% (but see note)	Lower of £3,000 or 25%

	From April 2008	Before April 2008
Thermal insulation	10%	25% (but restricted to industrial buildings)

The capital allowance treatment of cars changed from April 2009: see 10-300.

10-150 Integral features (CAA 2001, s. 33A)

The following assets are designated as integral features (see commentary at 247-000):

- electrical systems (including lighting systems);
- cold water systems;
- space or water heating systems, powered systems of ventilation, air cooling or air purification, and any floor or ceiling comprised in such systems;
- lifts, escalators and moving walkways; and
- external solar shading.

Expenditure on thermal insulation and long-life assets is also allocated to the 'special rate' pool. Since April 2009, expenditure on higher emission cars has also joined this pool.

10-200 Expenditure unaffected by statutory restrictions re buildings

The restrictions in CAA 2001, s. 21 and 22 (buildings, structures and other assets) do not apply to expenditure in List C at CAA 2001, s. 23. List C, as amended at items 2, 3 and 6 by the *Finance Act* 2008 with effect for expenditure incurred from 1 or 6 April 2008, is as follows:

(1) Machinery (including devices for providing motive power) not within any other item in this list.

(2) Gas and sewerage systems provided mainly:

    (a) to meet the particular requirements of the qualifying activity;

    (b) to serve particular plant or machinery used for the purposes of the qualifying activity.

(3) [omitted by the *Finance Act* 2008].

(4) Manufacturing or processing equipment; storage equipment (including cold rooms); display equipment; and counters, checkouts and similar equipment.

(5) Cookers, washing machines, dishwashers, refrigerators and similar equipment; washbasins, sinks, baths, showers, sanitary ware and similar equipment; and furniture and furnishings.

(6) Hoists.

(7)   Sound insulation provided mainly to meet the particular requirements of the qualifying activity.

(8)   Computer, telecommunication and surveillance systems (including their wiring or other links).

(9)   Refrigeration or cooling equipment.

(10)   Fire alarm systems; sprinkler and other equipment for extinguishing or containing fires.

(11)   Burglar alarm systems.

(12)   Strong rooms in bank or building society premises; safes.

(13)   Partition walls, where moveable and intended to be moved in the course of the qualifying activity.

(14)   Decorative assets provided for the enjoyment of the public in hotel, restaurant or similar trades.

(15)   Advertising hoardings; signs, displays and similar assets.

(16)   Swimming-pools (including diving boards, slides and structures on which such boards or slides are mounted).

(17)   Any glasshouse constructed so that the required environment (namely, air, heat, light, irrigation and temperature) for the growing of plants is provided automatically by means of devices forming an integral part of its structure.

(18)   Cold stores.

(19)   Caravans provided mainly for holiday lettings.

(20)   Buildings provided for testing aircraft engines run within the buildings.

(21)   Moveable buildings intended to be moved in the course of the qualifying activity.

(22)   The alteration of land for the purpose only of installing plant or machinery.

(23)   The provision of dry docks.

(24)   The provision of any jetty or similar structure provided mainly to carry plant or machinery.

(25)   The provision of pipelines or underground ducts or tunnels with a primary purpose of carrying utility conduits.

(26)   The provision of towers to support floodlights.

(27)   The provision of:

    (a)   any reservoir incorporated into a water treatment works; or
    (b)   any service reservoir of treated water for supply within any housing estate or other particular locality.

(28)   The provision of:

Key Data

    (a)   silos provided for temporary storage; or

    (b)   storage tanks.

(29)   The provision of slurry pits or silage clamps.

(30)   The provision of fish tanks or fish ponds.

(31)   The provision of rails, sleepers and ballast for a railway or tramway.

(32)   The provision of structures and other assets for providing the setting for any ride at an amusement park or exhibition.

(33)   The provision of fixed zoo cages.

Items 1–16 of the above list do not, however, include any asset with the principal purpose of insulating or enclosing the interior of a building or of providing an interior wall, floor or ceiling that is intended to remain permanently in place.

10-030   Cars

From April 2009

New expenditure on car purchases goes into the main 20 per cent pool if CO_2 emissions do not exceed 160g/km.

New expenditure on car purchases with higher emissions goes into 10 per cent 'special rate' pool.

Cars with private use go to single asset pool but still attract allowances at 20 per cent or 10 per cent as above, but then adjusted for private use percentage.

Cars with emissions that do not exceed 110g/km continue to attract first-year allowances at 100 per cent.

Cars bought before 1 or 6 April 2009 continue to attract allowances as before.

Leased cars, where lease begins from 1 or 6 April 2009, suffer 15 per cent disallowance of relevant payments if CO_2 emissions exceed 160g/km; otherwise no disallowance.

Before April 2009

Bought cars attract allowances at standard 20 per cent (previously 25 per cent) rate, but cars costing more than £12,000 have annual WDA restricted to £3,000. No restriction on balancing allowances.

Cars with emissions that do not exceed 110g/km (previously 120g/km) attract first-year allowances at 100 per cent.

Permanent disallowance of a proportion of the hire cost of cars where the retail price when new exceeds £12,000.

Other allowances

20-000 Industrial buildings, hotels and sports pavilions; agricultural buildings and structures

These allowances are being phased out. To achieve this, the following percentages are applied to the writing-down allowances that would otherwise be available for industrial buildings, hotels and sports pavilions and agricultural buildings and structures.

Financial year beginning	Tax year	Percentage
1 April 2007 and earlier	2007–08 and earlier	100 per cent
1 April 2008	2008–09	75 per cent
1 April 2009	2009–10	50 per cent
1 April 2010	2010–11	25 per cent
1 April 2011 and later	2011–12 and later	0 per cent (ie no further allowances given)

Where a chargeable period straddles the financial or tax year, the WDA is to be apportioned on a strict time basis.

The restriction applies both to the standard four per cent WDA and to the higher WDA available for some used buildings.

No initial allowances are available.

20-050 Enterprise zones: industrial buildings, hotels, commercial buildings or structures

The following allowances are available for certain buildings in enterprise zones [1](industrial buildings; hotels and commercial buildings or structures[2]):

Date expenditure incurred	Initial allowance	Writing-down allowance
Contract to be made within 10 years of site being included within the enterprise zone (but not expenditure incurred over 20 years after the date of the site being included)	100%	25%

Notes

(1) Areas designated by Orders made under the *Local Government, Planning and Land Act* 1980 or equivalent Northern Ireland legislation.

(2) Buildings or structures used for the purposes of a trade, profession or vocation (but not an industrial building or qualifying hotel) or used as offices; but not a dwelling-house.

Legislation: CAA 2001, s. 281, 298(3), 305ff.

20-075 Enterprise zones

Enterprise zones can be valid for up to 20 years in total (see 320-000). Those that still fall within that 20-year period are as follows:

Statutory instrument	Area	Start date
1989/794	Sunderland (Castletown and Doxford Park)	27 April 1990
1989/795	Sunderland (Hylton Riverside and Southwick)	27 April 1990
1993/23	Lanarkshire (Hamilton)	1 February 1993
1993/24	Lanarkshire (Motherwell)	1 February 1993
1993/25	Lanarkshire (Monklands)	1 February 1993
1995/2624	Dearne Valley (Barnsley, Doncaster, Rotherham)	3 November 1995
1995/2625	Holmewood (North East Derbyshire)	3 November 1995
1995/2738	Bassetlaw	16 November 1995
1995/2758	Ashfield	21 November 1995
1995/2812	East Durham (No. 1 to No. 6)	29 November 1995
1996/106	Tyne Riverside (North Tyneside)	19 February 1996
1996/1981	Tyne Riverside (Silverlink North Scheme)	26 August 1996
1996/1981	Tyne Riverside (Silverlink Business Park Scheme)	26 August 1996
1996/1981	Tyne Riverside (Middle Engine Lane Scheme)	26 August 1996
1996/1981	Tyne Riverside (New York Industrial Park Scheme)	26 August 1996
1996/1981	Tyne Riverside (Balliol Business Park West Scheme)	26 August 1996
1996/2435	Tyne Riverside (Baltic Enterprise Park Scheme)	21 October 1996
1996/2435	Tyne Riverside (Viking Industrial Park – Wagonway West Scheme)	21 October 1996
1996/2435	Tyne Riverside (Viking Industrial Park – Blackett Street Scheme)	21 October 1996
1996/2435	Tyne Riverside (Viking Industrial Park – Western Road Scheme)	21 October 1996

20-100 Business premises renovation allowances

Date expenditure incurred	Initial allowance	Writing-down allowance
On or after 11 April 2007	100%	25%

Legislation: CAA 2001, s. 360Aff.

20-150   Flat conversion allowances

Date expenditure incurred	Initial allowance	Writing-down allowance
On or after 11 May 2001	100%	25%

Legislation: CAA 2001, s. 393Aff.

20-200   Dredging allowances

Date expenditure incurred	Initial allowance	Writing-down allowance
On or after 1 April 1986	Nil	4%

Legislation: CAA 2001, s. 484ff.

20-250   Mineral extraction allowances

Date expenditure incurred	Initial allowance	Writing-down allowance
On or after 1 April 1986	Nil	25%

Legislation: CAA 2001, s. 394ff.

20-300   Research and development allowances

Date expenditure incurred	Initial allowance	Writing-down allowance
On or after 5 November 1962	100%	No provision for WDAs

Legislation: CAA 2001, s. 437ff.

20-350   Patent allowances

Date expenditure incurred	Initial allowance	Writing-down allowance
On or after 1 April 1986	Nil	25%

Legislation: CAA 2001, s. 464ff.

Key Data

20-400 Know-how allowances

Date expenditure incurred	Initial allowance	Writing-down allowance
On or after 1 April 1986	Nil	25%

Legislation: CAA 2001, s. 452ff.

20-450 Assured tenancy allowances

Date expenditure incurred	Initial allowance	Writing-down allowance
1 April 1986 to 31 March 1992	Nil	4%

Legislation: CAA 2001, s. 490ff.

INTRODUCTION AND GENERAL PROVISIONS

Introduction

100-000   Capital allowances: overview

The legislation dealing with capital allowances is a core part of the UK's tax system, with substantial amounts of money at stake. Capital allowances are of relevance to the great majority of businesses operating in the UK, from the largest conglomerate to the smallest business consisting of an individual with a van, a computer or even just a table.

The most familiar allowances are those available for capital expenditure on plant and machinery. For many businesses, however, expenditure on plant and machinery will determine only part of their overall capital allowance claims. Depending on the nature of the business, claims may be made under different rules in respect of any of the following:

- plant and machinery;
- industrial buildings or structures;
- renovation of business premises;
- agricultural buildings;
- flat conversions;
- mineral extraction;
- research and development;
- know-how;
- patents;
- dredging; and
- assured tenancies.

Technically, the allowances are available for both income tax and corporation tax purposes. However, corporation tax relief for expenditure incurred by companies since 1 April 2002 on know-how and on patents will in practice be given instead under the regime applying for expenditure on intangible assets.

The distinction between assets qualifying for the various different types of allowance is not always clear-cut. There may, for example, be an overlap between plant and machinery and industrial buildings. Occasionally it is up to the taxpayer to decide whether to make a claim as plant and machinery on the one hand or as an industrial building or structure on the other, though the phasing out of industrial buildings allowances from April 2008 means that the decision in favour of plant and machinery allowances is now even clearer than it has been in the past.

For businesses carried on in factory or similar premises, the key distinction between the effect of a claim for industrial buildings allowances (IBAs) and one for plant and machinery has in the past been the timing of the tax relief available. The timing difference can be significant and the cash flow implications crucial. Once more, however, the withdrawal of IBAs means that the issue is now more than just one of cash flow.

For businesses carried on in offices, for example, the issue has always been clear cut. If an asset can be shown to constitute plant or machinery then tax allowances may be due. If, on the other hand, the asset is deemed to be part of the building then no tax relief is due at all under the IBA rules (though significant relief may be available for fixtures in a building and, since April 2008, the concept of 'integral features' has further blurred the distinction: see 247-000ff.). There is no doubt that this distinction between the building and the plant within it can lead to borderline cases where the result is not a just one. However, the principles that govern the making of this distinction have been established over decades of legislation and case law. Therefore, the best that somebody carrying on a trade can do is to claim the maximum possible allowances that are due under the system. It is intended that this book will guide readers to that end.

The capital allowances legislation

The legislation governing all the forms of capital allowances listed above is contained in the *Capital Allowances Act* 2001 (CAA 2001), which brings together in one Act the various elements that were once scattered through an earlier consolidated Act and a range of Finance Acts.

The structure of the Act is to include some general provisions at the start (Part 1), and then to have one Part for each type of allowance (Parts 2–10, but including a Part 3A and a Part 4A), followed by two further Parts that are of general application. The Act finishes with four Schedules, now including one for first-year tax credits.

Frequent references are also made in this book to HMRC's *Capital Allowances* manual; such references are designated as (for example) CA 23000, for paragraph 23000 of that manual. Originally written for employees of what was then known as the Inland Revenue, the manual was made public under the Code of Practice on Access to Government Information. It has no legal force but is of immense practical use for businesses and their advisers, in showing how HMRC interprets and applies the statutory rules in practice.

Legislation: CAA 2001

100-100   The function of capital allowances

Broadly, capital allowances provide an equivalent for tax purposes of the depreciation charge shown in accounts. A huge simplification would be achieved if depreciation became an allowable expense in computing profits, but despite some moves to align tax with accounting principles there is no serious prospect of this. The capital allowance legislation gives HMRC, and ultimately the government, far greater control over the calculation of tax liabilities.

The beginnings of the capital allowance system could be said to date back over 100 years. However, the end of the Second World War saw a major reappraisal of the system in the provisions of the *Income Tax Act* 1945. Following the first consolidation of the legislation in the *Capital Allowances Act* 1968, the *Finance Act* 1971 introduced the system as it broadly remains today, albeit subject to some significant changes in the intervening years.

The capital allowance rules have become something of a political football over the years. Thus, various Chancellors have claimed the moral high ground both for increasing the rates of allowances (to encourage investment) and for decreasing them again (to prevent distortions of what is commercially sensible). Since the early 1990s, various first-year allowances have been granted, ie to enhance the rate at which tax relief is given for the expenditure. Many of these were withdrawn in 2008, but that withdrawal was partially reversed, on a temporary basis, in 2009. *Finance Act* 2008 also introduced the concept of the annual investment allowance for most categories of plant and machinery. In March 2007, meanwhile, it had been announced that industrial buildings allowances and agricultural buildings allowances had become anachronistic and were to be withdrawn.

100-150   Major changes to capital allowance regime

Important changes to capital allowances have been made in recent years. The following notes provide an overview of the changes introduced in 2008 and 2009.

First-year allowances (plant and machinery)

The first-year allowances that for many years were given at 40 or 50 per cent were abolished for expenditure incurred after 31 March 2008 (corporation tax) or 5 April 2008 (income tax). See 185-000.

The system of first-year allowances for certain low emission cars was due to come to an end for expenditure incurred after 31 March 2008 (corporation tax) or 5 April 2008 (income tax). See 200-400, however, for details of how the rules have been extended, subject to one change. The rules relating to expenditure on gas refuelling stations have likewise been extended, but again subject to change (see 185-450).

First-year allowances for expenditure on other 'green' technology continue at 100 per cent. Indeed, the value of these allowances has grown in some circumstances as companies may now surrender losses arising from such expenditure in return for a cash payment (see 242-000).

First-year allowances were re-introduced on a temporary basis for expenditure incurred in the year ending 31 March or 5 April 2010 (for corporation tax and income tax respectively): see 185-050. Such allowances are given at 40 per cent.

Annual investment allowance

The concept of the 'annual investment allowance' (AIA) applies to expenditure incurred from 1 April 2008 (corporation tax) or 6 April 2008 (income tax). The AIA gives full tax relief for the first £50,000 of annual expenditure incurred by a business on plant and machinery in its chargeable period. For commentary, see 181-000ff.

The introduction of the AIA coincided with the withdrawal of most first-year allowances (see 185-000) and also with the increase in corporation tax rates for the smallest businesses.

The AIA offers full and immediate tax relief, for all sizes of business, for the first £50,000 of expenditure on plant and machinery in the year. The maximum annual allowance of £50,000 is proportionately increased or reduced if the chargeable period is greater or shorter than one year. In calculating the length of the chargeable period for these purposes, any time before 1 or 6 April 2008 was ignored. Thus a company with accounts drawn up for the year to 31 December 2008 was entitled to an AIA of just £37,500.

Cars and expenditure on 'green' technology continue to be treated separately, but the AIA is available from April 2008 for expenditure on all other plant and machinery, including long-life assets and 'integral features' (see 247-000ff.). Expenditure in excess of the annual £50,000 allowance may attract writing-down allowances (or temporary first-year allowances: see 185-050) in the same accounting period.

Reduction in rate of WDAs for plant and machinery

The rate of writing-down allowances for plant and machinery in the general pool was reduced from 25 to 20 per cent for chargeable periods beginning from 1 or 6 April 2008 (for corporation tax and income tax respectively). A hybrid rate applied for chargeable periods straddling the date of change. Thus, for example, a company with a 31 December year end had a hybrid rate of 21.25 per cent for the year to 31 December 2008, calculated as 91 days at 25 per cent and 275 days at 20 per cent (see 190-250). Periods that are not of exactly 12 months applied the same principle, based on the length of the period before and after the April 2008 change. HMRC have published a 'ready reckoner' for calculating the writing-down allowance for income tax and corporation tax purposes: see www.hmrc.gov.uk/capital_allowances/read-reck-intro.htm for an introduction, and for a link to the ready reckoner itself.

The same rates, and transitional arrangements, apply to single asset pools, such as those for short-life assets. The company with the 31 December 2008 year end will therefore apply the same hybrid rate of 21.25 per cent to its short-life asset pool.

See 190-350 for an illustration of the way the transitional rules worked for periods straddling 1 April 2008.

See also the comments below about the treatment of fixtures (integral features).

The 2008 reduction in the rate of writing-down allowances was for plant and machinery allowances only. Many of the less commonly claimed allowances (eg flat conversion allowances (FCAs) and mineral extraction allowances) continue to have a 25 per cent writing-down allowance (though FCAs, for example, are normally given by way of a full initial allowance). See below for changes to industrial and agricultural buildings allowances.

Long-life assets

The rate of writing-down allowances on long-life asset expenditure increased from six to 10 per cent for chargeable periods beginning from 1 or 6 April 2008 (for corporation tax and income tax respectively). The effect is that LLA expenditure attracts relief at half the rate of most other assets, subject to the question of the annual investment allowance (see 181-000ff.).

See 210-050.

Integral features (plant and machinery)

Since April 2008, expenditure on so-called 'integral features' has been treated separately from most other capital expenditure for the purposes of claiming plant and machinery allowances. Expenditure on these integral features is excluded from the main capital allowances pool and writing-down allowances are given at a 'special rate' of 10 per cent (rather than the standard 20 per cent rate) on the reducing balance of the pool.

See 247-000ff. for commentary on this concept.

Payable tax credits (plant and machinery)

Loss-making companies that have incurred expenditure on certain 'green' technology since 1 April 2008 have been able to claim a cash payment if they are otherwise unable to use their losses against their own profits or those of a group member. The rules are directly linked to the first-year allowances that are given for expenditure on 'energy-saving' plant and machinery or 'environmentally beneficial' plant and machinery. In this way, companies can gain an immediate cash payment rather than carrying losses forward indefinitely in the hope of obtaining relief when profits start to be realised in the future.

See 242-000 for commentary on this concept.

Industrial and agricultural buildings allowances

Since April 2008, writing-down allowances on industrial and agricultural buildings are gradually being phased out, with the final withdrawal of both regimes by April 2011. To prepare the way for final abolition, most balancing adjustments, and the recalculation of writing-down allowances on sale, were effectively withdrawn from 21 March 2007.

Updated commentary re both of these changes is given in the appropriate Chapters.

Introduction

100-200 General interpretation

Parts of assets

References in the legislation to assets (including buildings or structures, plant or machinery, or works) include a part of an asset, unless the context requires otherwise.

A share in plant or machinery is similarly treated but will be accepted as used for the purposes of a trade only so long as the plant or machinery is used for the purposes of a trade.

Legislation: CAA 2001, s. 270, 571

Other material: CA 20080

Sale of property and time of sale

References to the sale of property are taken to include an exchange of property, or the surrender for valuable consideration of a leasehold interest (or, in Scotland, the interest of the tenant in property subject to a lease). References to the 'net proceeds of sale' and to the price include any consideration given for the exchange or surrender. References to capital sums included in the net proceeds of sale include so much of the consideration as would have been a capital payment if it had been a money payment.

HMRC confirms that 'the net proceeds of sale are what the seller receives. They are not what the seller is entitled to receive but is unable to receive. If any part of the agreed sale price ultimately turns out to be irrecoverable ignore it'.

If a company buys assets and satisfies the purchase price by issuing shares then HMRC accepts that the company has incurred capital expenditure and that the purchase price is the value of the shares issued.

References to the time of a sale are to the earlier of the date of completion and the time when possession is given. However, this does not apply for the purposes of research and development allowances.

Legislation: CAA 2001, s. 572

Other material: CA 11540, 12200

Transfers treated as sales

For provisions affecting the following allowances, a transfer of the relevant interest is treated as a sale at market value if it is not in fact a sale. This is subject to any election under CAA 2001, s. 569 (see, for example, the Chapter headed 'Industrial Buildings Allowances', which begins at 300-000), and does not apply if CAA 2001, s. 561 applies (transfer of a UK trade to a company that is resident in another EU member state). The allowances in question are:

- industrial buildings allowances;
- agricultural buildings allowances;
- flat conversion allowances;
- mineral extraction allowances;
- research and development allowances; and
- assured tenancy allowances.

Legislation: CAA 2001, s. 568

Other material: CA 13100

Transfer during formation of SE or SCE by merger

Where certain conditions are met in relation to cross-border mergers, the transfer of a qualifying asset will not give rise to any capital allowance or balancing charge. Anything done to or by the transferor in relation to the asset is treated after the transfer as having been done to or by the transferee, and any necessary apportionment is to be made 'in a reasonable manner'. The rules of ICTA 1988, s. 343 (company reconstruction without change of ownership) are not applied (CAA 2001, s. 561A, as amended by SI 2007/3186).

These provisions applied originally to the *Societas Europaea* ('SE'), a European company created by Council Regulation (EC) No. 2157/2001 of 8 October 2001, where a transfer was made from 1 April 2005. They were extended to apply also to the formation of a *Societas Cooperativa Europaea* 'SCE' from 18 August 2006, and were further extended to all other mergers taking place from 1 January 2007.

The transfer of the 'qualifying asset' must take place as part of the process of a merger to which TCGA 1992, s. 140E (merger leaving assets within UK tax charge) applies (or would apply but for s. 140E(2)(c)). The following conditions must be met:

- the transferor must be resident in the UK at the time of the transfer or the asset must be an asset of a permanent establishment in the UK of the transferor; and
- the transferee must be resident in the UK at the time of the transfer or the asset must be an asset of a permanent establishment in the UK of the transferee immediately following the transfer.

Before the changes made by SI 2007/3186, this last condition referred to the time of formation rather than to the time of the transfer.

Legislation: CAA 2001, s. 561A

Claiming capital allowances

101-000   Need for a claim

No capital allowances are due unless a claim is made in a tax return.

This rule is varied in relation to the following:

- certain special leasing of plant and machinery (CAA 2001, s. 258 and 260(3)(b));
- buildings for miners (CAA 2001, s. 355);
- certain patent allowances for non-trading expenditure (CAA 2001, s. 479);
- special provisions for partnership claims (TMA 1970, s. 42(6) and (7)).

The claim does not have to be for the full amount that could be due, in which case it must specify the lower amount actually claimed. The consequences of claiming less than the full amount of relief vary according to the type of allowance – sometimes it enables greater relief to be claimed in a later year but in other instances there is no chance to catch up and the relief may be lost forever. This aspect is considered in relation to each allowance separately in the Chapters that follow.

In relation to plant and machinery allowances, a key condition for a claim is that the asset must be owned at some time in the chargeable period. If it is discovered in, say, May 2009 that no claim has been made for expenditure incurred five years earlier, it is not possible to re-open that earlier year. However, if the assets are still owned in any part of the year ended on (say) 30 April 2010 then it is open to the business to make a claim for that later period. This commonly arises in practice in cases involving fixtures in property, where a claim is often overlooked when a property is acquired. (Note, however, that any claim for first-year allowances or annual investment allowances must be made for the year in which the expenditure is incurred, so only writing-down or (possibly) balancing allowances will be available in this scenario.)

It may also be possible, in the above scenario, to incorporate the claim in the return for the year to 30 April 2009 or to re-open the return for the year to 30 April 2008, under normal self-assessment principles.

Legislation: CAA 2001, s. 3, 51A(2), 52(2)

Other material: CA 11120ff.

101-100   Time limits

The time limit for making a claim is the normal one for making or amending the return, as follows:

Income tax

For income tax purposes, this is normally 31 January some 22 months after the end of the tax year to which the return relates. As such, for example, a claim for 2008–09 can be made at any time up to 31 January 2011.

Partnerships

Individual partners are not permitted to claim capital allowances – the claim must be made through the partnership return. This can present problems for plant and machinery allowances in particular (in relation, for example, to partner cars). See 120-000 for the treatment of partnership changes.

Other material: CA 11120

Corporation tax

A capital allowance claim for an accounting period may be made, amended or withdrawn at any time up to 12 months after the filing date for the company tax return for the period in question. The time limit is usually two years from the end of the accounting period. When there is an HMRC enquiry, the time limit is extended to 30 days after the conclusion of the enquiry (whether by issue of a notice of completion or a notice of amendment). If the company appeals against the notice of amendment, the time limit is 30 days after the date on which the appeal is finally determined.

Legislation: FA 1998, Sch. 18, para. 82

Extending the time limit

HMRC officers may extend the time limit for making or extending a claim. However, their instructions tell them that they should not do so 'unless circumstances beyond the company's control prevented it from being able to make the claim within the normal time limits'. Various possible circumstances are listed that officers are *not* meant to accept, including oversight or error on the part of the company's officers or its advisers, a change of mind or hindsight (eg showing that a different combination of claims would have been more beneficial). The absence or indisposition of an officer or employee of the company will not be accepted as a reason for a delayed claim unless:

- the absence or illness arose at a critical time which delayed the making of the claim;
- in the case of absence, there was good reason why the person was unavailable at the critical time; and
- there was no other person who could have made the claim on behalf of the company within the normal time limits.

Other material: CA 11140

Interaction with HMRC enquiry powers

A business may have to decide whether or not to re-open an earlier year by making a belated capital allowance claim. In such circumstances, it should be remembered that an amended claim may give HMRC an extended window in which to enquire into the accounts.

> ### Example
>
> Company A bought a commercial property for £1 million during its year to 30 June 2008. It was not aware that a claim could be made in relation to fixtures within the property and so no such claim was made in its return, submitted on 28 April 2009. It becomes aware of

the possibility in December 2009 and calculates that a claim could be made of £150,000 in relation to fixtures in the property. It still owns the property, so it has a choice:

- it is within the time limit to amend the return to 30 June 2008; or
- it can simply include a claim in relation to the qualifying expenditure in its return to 30 June 2009.

Amending the earlier year has cash flow advantages. It also means that, depending on the size of the company, a first-year allowance may be available. (This will not be the case for the later year, as 'any first-year allowance is made for the chargeable period in which the first-year qualifying expenditure is incurred'.)

However, by amending the return, the HMRC officer is given an extended deadline for raising enquiries. Instead of having to do so by 30 June 2010 he may now raise an enquiry 'up to and including the quarter day next following the first anniversary of the day on which the amendment was made'. The quarter days are for these purposes 31 January, 30 April, 31 July and 31 October. So if an amendment to the 2008 return were to be submitted on, say, 15 January 2010, the enquiry window will extend to 31 January 2011.

In booklet SAT 2 (the official guide to self-assessment) HMRC has indicated that 'in most cases any subsequent enquiry will be limited to the area of the return that was amended. But there may be cases in which the amendment is so fundamental to the return that the whole return will be considered for enquiry'.

Legislation: TMA 1970, s. 9A(2)(c), 9ZA(2); CAA 2001, s. 52(2)

Capital expenditure

102-000 Significance

Capital allowances are due only in respect of capital expenditure.

The question of what constitutes capital expenditure is fundamental not only for capital allowances purposes but also for the correct computation of trading profits; it is well established that capital expenditure cannot be deducted in computing profits. Thus, if a consultancy business (for example) earns £10,000 of income and spends £3,000 on stationery, telephone calls and postage and £2,000 on a computer, its taxable profit will be £7,000 not £5,000. Tax relief will be due through the capital allowance system on the cost of the computer but that relief will not necessarily be given all in one go.

There are numerous reasons why capital expenditure is not an allowable deduction. The income tax legislation, the fundamental principles of which also determine the computation of profits for corporation tax purposes, refers to 'the full amount of the profits or gains'. Where there are no statutory rules to the contrary, that 'full amount' is to be calculated on generally accepted accounting principles. Normal accountancy rules do not show a deduction for the direct cost of acquiring a capital asset but instead reduce the profits, where appropriate, through a system of depreciation.

Accountancy principles are reinforced by legislation in the Taxes Acts. ITTOIA 2005, s. 33 provides that no deduction is allowed (for income tax purposes) for items of a capital nature. CTA 2009, s. 53 gives the same rule for corporation tax purposes. In each case, the re-written legislation is simpler than its predecessor provisions, but no fundamental change is intended.

For capital allowances purposes, capital expenditure is defined in CAA 2001, s. 4. As is so often the case, the definition is given in negative terms. See 102-100 for a summary of those rules.

The third layer of rules to prohibit capital expenditure is that established through case law precedents, again discussed at 102-100.

Legislation: CTA 2009, s. 53; CAA 2001, s. 1(1); ITTOIA 2005, s. 33

102-100   Definition

Statutory rules

For capital allowances purposes, capital expenditure is defined in negative terms. Therefore, capital expenditure does *not* include any of the following:

- any amount deductible in calculating the profits or gains of a trade, profession, vocation or property business carried on by the person incurring the expenditure;
- any amount that may, under various specified provisions, be deducted by an employee or office holder from the taxable earnings of an employment;
- any expenditure or sum in the case of which a deduction of income tax falls or may fall to be made under ITA 2007, Pt. 15, Ch. 6 (deduction from annual payments or patent royalties); or
- any expenditure or sum in the case of which a deduction of income tax falls or may fall to be made under ITA 2007, s. 906 (certain royalties etc where usual place of abode of owner is abroad).

Capital expenditure specifically includes 'any contribution to capital expenditure'.

Legislation: CAA 2001, s. 4, 10(1)

Case law overview

The question of what constitutes capital expenditure has been the subject of many disputed legal cases.

A Scottish tax case, that of *Vallambrosa Rubber Co Limited v Farmer (Surveyor of Taxes)*, could be said to have set the ball rolling on establishing a case law definition of capital expenditure. Back in 1910, in the Court of Session, the Lord President felt that the Surveyor of Taxes (the forerunner of the inspector) had misled the commissioners. The Lord President stated:

> 'I don't say that this consideration is absolutely final or determinative, but in a rough way I think it is not a bad criterion of what is capital expenditure as against what is income expenditure to say that capital expenditure is a thing that is going to be spent once and for all, and income expenditure is a thing that is going to recur every year'.

The next case in which the definition was considered in some depth was that of *Atherton v British Insulated and Helsby Cables Limited*. In the House of Lords, Viscount Cave pointed out that there are many cases where a payment may be made once and for all but would still be revenue in nature, rather than capital. He therefore produced the following refinement:

> 'When an expenditure is made, not only once and for all, but with a view to bringing into existence an asset or an advantage for the enduring benefit of a trade, I think that there is very good reason (in the absence of special circumstances leading to an opposite conclusion) for treating such an expenditure as properly attributable not to revenue but to capital.'

A full review of all of the authorities could form a work in itself and is beyond the scope of this book. The HMRC manuals (at BIM 35000 and following sections) contain some reasonably clear guidelines, albeit inevitably with a Revenue slant. Some of the key cases that have gone to the courts are as follows. (This list is far from exhaustive and is given in date order. In each case, an indication is given at the end of whether the case was won by the Revenue or by the taxpayer.)

- *Hancock v General Reversionary & Investment Co Limited* (1918) 7 TC 358 (taxpayer).
- *Mitchell v B W Noble Limited* (1927) 11 TC 372 (taxpayer).
- *Anglo-Persian Oil Co Limited v Dale* (1931) 16 TC 253 (taxpayer).
- *Southern v Borax Consolidated Limited* (1940) 23 TC 597 (taxpayer).
- *Tucker v Granada Motorway Services Limited* (1979) 53 TC 92 (Revenue).

Cases: *Vallambrosa Rubber Co Limited v Farmer (Surveyor of Taxes)* (1910) 5 TC 529; *Atherton v British Insulated and Helsby Cables Limited* (1924) 10 TC 155.

Timing of expenditure

105-000 General rule

Relief by way of capital allowances will not always depend on the timing of expenditure – for IBA writing-down allowances, for example, the key issue is whether the building is in use at the end of the chargeable period. Nevertheless, in many other instances, the question of whether relief is due is determined by the date on which the expenditure was incurred.

The starting point is that capital expenditure is treated as incurred as soon as there is an unconditional obligation to pay it. This is so even though some of the expenditure may not be due until a later date, but see 105-100ff for details of a number of exceptions to the general rule.

The date on which it becomes unconditional is not necessarily the date of the contract itself. In law, a person may in fact become legally required to pay either on delivery or within a prescribed time after the delivery. In such cases, HMRC broadly considers that the obligation becomes unconditional when the asset is delivered (IRInt 54 – *Tax Bulletin* 9). As such, the delivery date is generally the date which triggers the incurring of the expenditure for capital allowances purposes. More recent HMRC guidance (at CA 11700) indicates a rather more complex approach to this issue, however. That guidance distinguishes between a 'promissory condition' (when the condition refers to a term within a contract) and an event upon which the whole contract is conditional. The guidance relating to promissory conditions then distinguishes between the following main categories:

'● **Condition precedent promissory condition**: this term of a contract exists when the performance by one party of his promise is a condition precedent to the liability of the other to perform. Suppose George contracts with Andy for him to repair his car. Under the contract, George promises to pay Andy once he has finished the repairs. George's legal obligation to pay Andy does not become unconditional until he has completed the work.

● **Concurrent promissory condition**: this term of a contract arises if both contracting parties agree that the performance of their respective promises shall be simultaneous. Such conditions typically arise in contracts for the sale of goods where payment is due on delivery. We argue that payment is conditional on delivery and visa versa and thus the obligation to pay becomes unconditional at the time of delivery.

● **Independent promissory condition**: such conditions arise when the parties agree that each party can enforce each other's promise although he, she or it has not performed their own. Suppose that Cass contracts with Oliver for him to build a machine. Cass is required to make payment two months from the date the contract was entered into. Cass's payment is conditional only on the passage of time and is independent of any obligation imposed on Oliver.'

The guidance goes on to consider cases in which there are no specific payment terms:

'Where a sale is made without specifying payment terms, the transaction is governed by Section 28 Sale of Goods Act 1979 which states that "unless otherwise agreed, delivery of the goods and payment of the price are concurrent conditions, that is to say, the seller must be ready and willing to give possession of the goods, and the buyer must be ready and willing to pay the price in exchange of possession of the goods".

This means that the obligation to make payment arises when delivery is made unless there is an agreement specifying some other arrangement.'

The case of *Tower Mcashback LLP1 (and others) v R & C Commrs* was concerned with first-year allowances under provisions that no longer apply. The case is nevertheless of some interest in considering the relationship between CAA 2001, s. 5 (when capital expenditure is incurred), s. 12 (pre-trading expenditure) and s. 50 (disapplication of s. 12 in certain circumstances). The reasoning of the special commissioner was found, by Henderson J in the High Court appeal, to have been incorrect in many respects. In the absence of any finding that the contract was a sham, the only conclusion open to the commissioner should have been that the whole consideration was expenditure on the provision of plant within CAA 2001, s. 11.

Legislation: CAA 2001, s. 5

Introduction

Cases: *Tower MCashback LLP1 (and others) v R & C Commrs* [2008] BTC 805

Other material: CA 11700ff

105-100 Milestone contracts

An exception to the general rule (see 105-000) about the timing of expenditure is for what is known as a 'milestone contract'. HMRC defines a milestone contract as one meeting the following two conditions:

- an asset that is being constructed under a contract becomes the property of the purchaser as it is being constructed; and
- payment becomes due as and when certain stages of the work ('milestones') are completed in a satisfactory way.

HMRC explains that such contracts are often found either in a large-scale construction project of buildings or where major items of plant or machinery are being constructed (such as oil pipelines).

Special rules apply to milestone contracts if all of the following conditions are met:

- capital expenditure is incurred, under an agreement, on the provision of an asset;
- an unconditional obligation arises to pay part of the expenditure as a result of a certificate being given or of 'any other event';
- the giving of the certificate, or other event, occurs within one month after the end of a chargeable period; and
- the asset has become the property of the person who is subject to the obligation to pay before the end of the chargeable period in question (or, under the agreement, the asset is attributed to that person by that time).

Where all four of the above conditions are met in relation to a milestone contract then the expenditure is treated as incurred immediately before the end of the chargeable period in question.

If work under such a contract is certified before the end of a particular chargeable period then the expenditure would be treated as being incurred by that date under the ordinary rules described above. What the special legislation therefore achieves is to bring forward, for capital allowances purposes, the date on which some expenditure is treated as incurred. In this way, a short delay in the certification process will not cause a loss of tax relief for the person who is paying. Nevertheless, if the certification is delayed for more than one month after the end of the chargeable period, then the expenditure will not be treated as incurred until the certificate is given. This is because the obligation to pay will usually only become unconditional once a certificate has been issued.

Legislation: CAA 2001, s. 5(4)

Other material: CA 11800

105-200   Credit period exceeding four months

Under the general rule described at 105-000, it would be possible for expenditure to be treated as incurred for tax purposes long before a payment was actually due. This would arise if there was an unconditional obligation to pay but a long delay in actually making the payment. The legislation therefore addresses circumstances where any part of the payment falls due more than four months after the date on which the obligation to pay becomes unconditional. In such a case, any part of the expenditure falling after that four-month date will be treated as incurred on the date on which the actual payment falls due.

Where, for example, payments are made on a monthly basis then all payments due up to the four-month date will be treated as incurred when the obligation to pay becomes unconditional. The later payments will be treated as incurred on the due date of the payments.

> ### *Example*
>
> AA Clarity Ltd manufactures optical products for the private health industry. It draws its accounts up to 31 March. It pays for the construction of new premises and by 31 March 2010, it has moved into the premises. Under the agreement, however, there is still £200,000 outstanding at that date, of which £40,000 falls due on 30 April 2010 and a further £40,000 at each subsequent month-end.
>
> What expenditure can be taken into account for the year ended 31 March 2010? To determine this, it will be necessary to establish the date on which the obligation to pay became unconditional. The terms of the contract may have specified that this was on completion of the building. Assuming that this was on, say, 16 March 2010 then the payments up to and including the £40,000 due on 30 June will be treated as incurred on 16 March, as they fall within four months of the date on which the unconditional obligation arose. The payments due on 31 July and 31 August will be taken into account in the following accounting period.

Legislation: CAA 2001, s. 5(5)

Other material: CA 11800

105-300   Anti-avoidance

The legislation seeks to prevent the early granting of allowances in situations that have been contrived. If the unconditional obligation to pay is accelerated to 'a date earlier than accords with normal commercial usage' then the amount may not be treated as incurred on that date but rather on the date by which the payment is actually required to be made. This will apply where 'the sole or main benefit which might have been expected to be obtained' from the artificial arrangements would be the acceleration of tax relief.

To determine whether a contract is or is not a normal commercial contract, inspectors are instructed to make a comparison with the normal practice for making contracts for the type of asset in question. They are also advised that they should only apply these anti-avoidance provisions where the amounts involved are substantial.

Legislation: CAA 2001, s. 5(6)

Other material: CA 11800

105-400   Other exceptions

The general rule about the date on which expenditure is treated as incurred, described at 105-000, does not apply to expenditure that is deemed to be incurred as a result of a person incurring an additional VAT liability.

The general rule is also subject to any other provisions that may require expenditure to be treated as incurred on a later date.

Legislation: CAA 2001, s. 5(7)

Chargeable period

106-100   Introduction

Capital allowances are generally given effect in calculating income or profits 'for a chargeable period'. This rule is subject to modification in relation to specific types of capital allowance, as discussed in the appropriate Chapters of this book.

Different definitions of the term 'chargeable period' are given for income tax and corporation tax purposes.

Legislation: CAA 2001, s. 2(1)

106-200   Income tax definition

For income tax purposes, a chargeable period is the same as a period of account, which is in turn defined in accordance with the following principles:

(1) for a person who is entitled to claim an allowance (or who is subject to a charge) in calculating the profits of his trade, profession or vocation, it normally means the period for which the business accounts are drawn up, but:

    (a) if two periods of account overlap, the common period is treated as belonging to the first period of account only;

(b)   similarly, if one period of account is contained within another, the common period is treated as belonging to the first period of account only;

(c)   if there is a gap between two periods of account, the gap is treated as part of the first period only;

(2)   if the period of account exceeds 18 months then it must be broken down into two or more periods, so that the first period begins with the start date; and a new period begins on each anniversary of that date;

(3)   for any other person, a period of account means that tax year running from 6 April to the following 5 April.

Example

Pete sets up as a sole trader on 1 April 2008 and draws his first accounts up to 30 April 2010, a period of 25 months.

For capital allowance purposes, he will have three periods of account, 1 April 2008 to 31 March 2009, 1 April 2009 to 31 March 2010, and 1 April 2010 to 30 April 2010.

Capital allowances for each of the three periods are calculated separately, taking account of purchases and disposals in each period. The total allowances (and balancing charges) due are then aggregated and taken into account in calculating the trading profits of the 25-month period.

Introduction

Legislation: CAA 2001, s. 6

Other material: CA 11510

106-300   Corporation tax definition

Corporation tax definition

For corporation tax purposes, the term 'chargeable period' is synonymous with 'accounting period'.

The term 'accounting period' has its own statutory definition. In practice, a key part of the definition is that an accounting period (AP) can never exceed 12 months. In more detail, the following rules also generally apply:

* A new AP always begins when a company comes into the charge to corporation tax, whether because it becomes resident in the UK or it acquires a source of income or for any other reason;

* A new AP always begins when a company's previous AP comes to an end, unless the company ceases at that point to be within the charge to corporation tax;

* An AP always comes to an end at the company's accounting date;

* An AP comes to an end at the end of any period for which the company does not draw up accounts;

- An AP comes to an end if the company begins or ceases to trade, or if it begins or ceases to be within the charge to corporation tax in respect of its trade (or, as appropriate, in respect of all of its trades);
- An AP comes to an end if the company becomes resident in the UK or if it ceases to be so resident;
- An AP comes to an end if the company ceases to be in administration, and
- An AP comes to an end if the company ceases to be within the charge to corporation tax.

There are exceptions to these rules, as specified in the legislation. These apply, for example, to companies that are being wound up or entering administration, to companies realising capital gains or losses, and in various other specified circumstances.

Legislation: CAA 2001, s. 6(1); CTA 2009, s. 9ff

Other material: ESC C12: accounting periods of retail co-operative societies; CA 11510

Exclusion of double allowances

106-500   Exclusion of double allowances

If an allowance is made under one Part of the *Capital Allowances Act* 2001, then no allowance may be made under any other Part to the same person in respect of the same expenditure (or of any asset to which that expenditure related). This is specifically extended to cover expenditure within a plant or machinery pool where, on a technicality, it might otherwise be possible to argue that such expenditure would not be covered.

This exclusion does not, strictly, apply in relation to know-how or patent allowances. The reasoning behind this was given in the explanatory notes that accompanied the rewritten 2001 Act: 'the nature of patents and know-how is such that it seems unlikely that the subject matter of patent and know-how allowances could in practice lead to claims for double relief'. For companies, expenditure on patents and know-how is in any case now given instead under the regime applying for expenditure on intangible assets.

> ### Planning point
>
> Sometimes there is a choice as to whether to claim under one code or another. For example, a cold store may qualify both under the IBA code and as an item of plant. It is important to make the correct choice because, as HMRC has stated, 'once a choice has been made to claim one type of allowance the taxpayer cannot change to another in later years'. Clearly, this will need particular attention now that IBAs are to be phased out.
>
> Nevertheless, the provision specifically refers to allowances made to the same person. If the cold store has been subject to an IBA claim, but is then sold, there is no reason in principle why the purchaser should not claim plant allowances if the store qualifies as plant and if all other conditions are met. But see the Chapter headed 'Plant and Property', which begins at 250-000 regarding fixtures claims.

A further restriction applies in relation to fixtures (regarding which see 250-000). If *any* person has made a valid claim under any Part of the CAA 2001 except that relating to plant and machinery, then no fixtures claim can be made in respect of the same expenditure.

This restriction does not apply if the earlier claim was for research and development allowances or for IBAs, where, instead, the limits imposed by CAA 2001, s. 186(2) or 187(2) respectively apply – see the Chapters headed 'Research and Development Allowances' (which begins at 525-000) and 'Industrial Buildings Allowances' (which begins at 300-000). (FA 2008, Sch. 27, para. 5) adapts the provisions to take account of the abolition from April 2011 of the IBA rules.

Legislation: CAA 2001, s. 7, 8, 9

Other material: CA 31800

Capital gains tax issues

110-000   Introduction

There are a number of areas where the capital gains tax rules overlap with the capital allowances legislation. It is probably fair to say that there are also numerous common misunderstandings in this area, especially in relation to the interaction of the two sets of tax rules when a property containing fixtures is sold.

110-100   Meaning of 'plant' for CGT purposes

There is no statutory definition of the term 'plant' within the *Taxation of Chargeable Gains Act* 1992 (TCGA 1992). Broadly, the meaning of 'plant and machinery' will follow that given in the *Capital Allowances Act* 2001. However, the restrictions to the definition of plant that are given in CAA 2001, s. 21 and 22 (see the Chapter headed 'Meaning of Plant', which begins at 180-000) do not apply for CGT purposes. This is because both of the sections begin with the words, 'for the purposes of this Act'. In other words, the restrictions apply only for the purposes of the *Capital Allowances Act* 2001 itself. This interpretation is confirmed in HMRC's *Capital Gains* manual.

Other material: CG 76901

110-200   Fixtures

The main circumstances where capital gains tax and the capital allowances rules must be considered in parallel are where property is being bought and sold. This is addressed in the Chapter headed 'Plant and Property', which begins at 250-000. The key point, though, is that a capital allowances claim does not reduce the base cost of a property for capital gains purposes unless the property is sold at a loss.

Example

A company buys a nursing home, paying £100,000 for goodwill, £50,000 for listed fixtures and fittings, and £1.2 million for the property.

It becomes clear that the £50,000 relates entirely to moveable items – beds, tables, chairs, lamps, etc. No previous claim has been made for fixtures in the property. An analysis is carried out and a claim is made and accepted for fixtures, forming part of the property, in the figure of £200,000.

Five years later, the property is sold for £1.5 million. The base cost of the property is £1.2 million, a figure that is not reduced by the £200,000 fixtures claim, even though by definition those fixtures form part of the property. For capital allowance purposes, it will be necessary to agree a transfer value for the fixtures, which can be anywhere between £1 and their cost of £200,000. Thus the vendor may retain all or none of the value of the capital allowances (or a figure somewhere in the middle) but this has no bearing on the computation of the capital gain (whether for capital gains tax purposes as such or for the purposes of calculating a gain that will be subject to corporation tax).

110-300　Chattels and wasting assets

The capital gains tax legislation defines a 'wasting asset' as one 'with a predictable life not exceeding 50 years'. The legislation goes on to say that plant and machinery 'shall in every case be regarded as having a predictable life of less than 50 years'. It follows that the special capital gains tax rules outlined in TCGA 1992, s. 44–47 need to be considered in relation to plant and machinery.

These rules exempt certain wasting assets from capital gains tax altogether, provide that in certain cases no allowable losses can accrue in respect of wasting assets and other circumstances require the cost of a wasting asset to be restricted when calculating the gain.

The following chart summarises the basic considerations:

Chattels and wasting assets

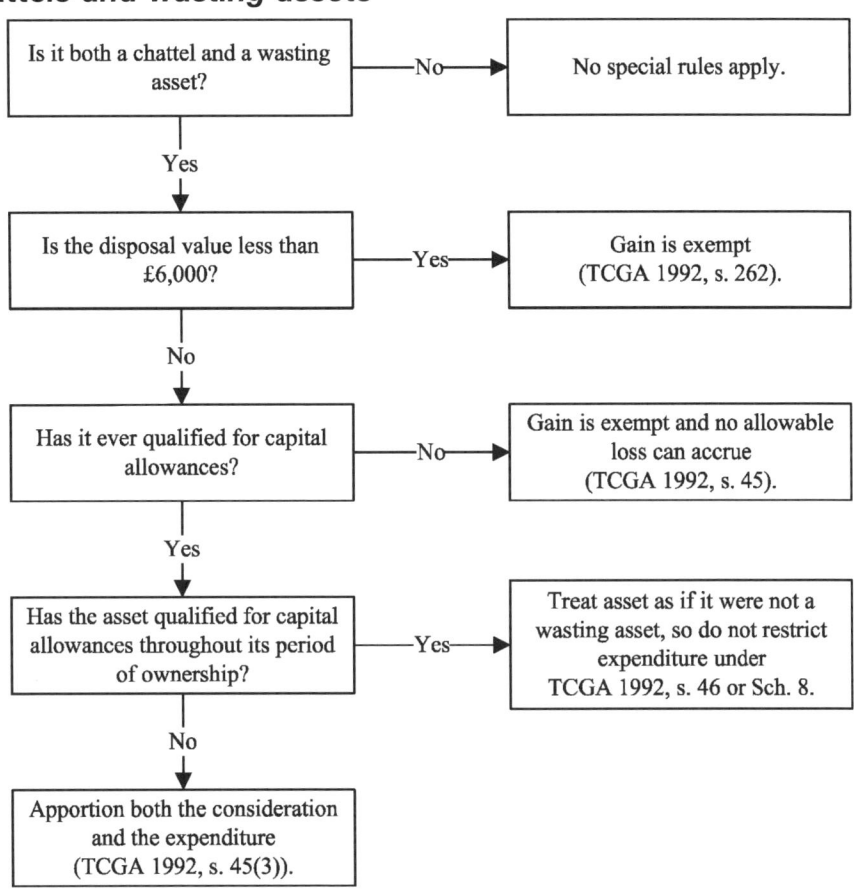

Legislation: TCGA 1992, s. 44(1)

Other material: CG 15450

110-400   Rollover relief

One of the 'relevant classes of assets' for the purposes of rollover relief (relief for replacement of business assets) is 'fixed plant or machinery' that does not already qualify in its own right as a building or other appropriate structure.

In this context, the word 'fixed' is 'a description of the physical state of the asset in the use to which it is put'. In other words, borrowing the wording from the HMRC manuals, 'it is clear that the term is not used in the sense of fixed capital as opposed to circulating capital or fixed assets as opposed to current assets'. The *Capital Gains* manual provides some useful insight into the HMRC interpretation of 'fixed' in this context. Some of these interpretations are questionable. For example, HMRC suggests that the fairground carousel of a travelling showman would qualify as 'fixed' whilst certain shop fixtures and fittings, shelves, counters and moveable partitions would not be treated as fixed plant and machinery where 'although static in function [they] can be moved about without too much difficulty and are intended to be moveable'.

Often, it will be necessary to consider whether an item of fixed plant or machinery has in fact become part of the building, etc. The HMRC guidance indicates that, if so, such an item should then be regarded as an addition to the building rather than as plant and machinery. This can be relevant because of the different treatment of 'depreciating assets' outlined at TCGA 1992, s. 154. For these purposes, it should be borne in mind that any wasting asset is automatically treated as a depreciating asset and any plant or machinery therefore comes within the definition of 'depreciating asset'.

Legislation: TCGA 1992, s. 44, s. 152ff

Other material: CG 60970ff.

Contributions

115-000   Restrictions on allowances

Where some sort of subsidy, grant or contribution is received towards capital expenditure, it may be necessary to restrict the allowances available.

It does not matter whether the subsidy, etc is received, or indeed applied for, after the expenditure has been incurred (see *Cyril Lord Carpets Ltd v Schofield*). A subsidy includes a gift of money but not a loan.

Where insurance or other compensation monies are received 'in respect of an asset which has been demolished, destroyed or put out of use', they are not treated as subsidies or contributions for these purposes.

Legislation: CAA 2001, s. 532ff.

Cases: *Cyril Lord Carpets Ltd v Schofield* (1966) 42 TC 637

Other material: CA 14100

Grants from government bodies etc

It may be necessary to consider whether expenditure is being met by 'the Crown or a government or public or local authority'. Where the grant, etc is received from the Crown or such a public body then the amount received will need to be deducted from the capital expenditure before capital allowances are given. An exception is made for a grant that is made under Northern Ireland legislation and that is declared by the Treasury to correspond to a grant under Part II of the *Industrial Development Act* 1982. This is subject to certain conditions.

The Northern Ireland case of *McKinney v Hagans Caravans Manufacturing Ltd* considered the scope of the expression 'public authority'. The court ruled that it was not a requirement that the body in question should have executive powers over a significant part of the economy.

Five indicators were given by the court, as follows:

(1)   Does the constitution of the body have a public source?

(2)   Does it perform a public service for the wider good of the public?

(3)   Does it have public control and accountability?

(4)   Is there an absence of profit for private individuals?

(5)   Does it have public funding?

Positive answers to the above will tend to indicate that it is a public body for these purposes. The court specifically commented, however, that public funding would not be a necessary qualification but merely a pointer towards classifying the body as a public authority.

Legislation: CAA 2001, s. 534–536

Cases: *McKinney v Hagans Caravans Manufacturing Ltd* [1997] BTC 402

Other material: CA 14100

Grants from other sources

In principle, a contribution made by another person will not have to be deducted from the qualifying expenditure of the recipient unless the person making the contribution can claim tax relief, whether by way of capital allowances or as a trading deduction.

If the person who makes the contribution is not within the charge to tax but, if he had been, would have been able to deduct it in computing his trading profits, then the contribution received must be deducted from the expenditure which qualifies for capital allowances.

If a contribution towards capital expenditure is received from a connected person then the person making the contribution will not be able to claim capital allowances under CAA 2001, s. 538. As a result, it will not be necessary to deduct the receipt from the amount of qualifying expenditure from the point of view of the recipient.

Legislation: CAA 2001, s. 536ff.

115-100   Contribution allowances

In certain circumstances, a person may be eligible for capital allowances where he contributes a capital sum to expenditure on the provision of an asset but where, without this special rule, the expenditure would otherwise have been treated as incurred by somebody else. The legislation refers to the person making the contribution as 'C' and to the other person as 'R'. One condition is that C and R must not be connected persons.

As regards the detailed treatment of contribution allowances under the various capital allowance regimes, see the respective Chapters dealing with those regimes.

Legislation: CAA 2001, s. 537

Miscellaneous issues

120-000   Partnerships and successions

Introduction

Special provisions apply for capital allowance purposes *other than* plant and machinery, research and development and assured tenancy allowances. (As regards equivalent rules for plant and machinery (under CAA 2001, s. 263–267) see the Chapter headed 'Plant and Machinery: Detailed Provisions', which begins at 185-000.)

Concept of succession

Where a person ceases to carry on activities relating to a trade, another person may begin to carry on those activities. The effect on the first person may be such that he is regarded as having ceased a trade, whilst the effect on the second person may be that he is regarded as commencing a trade. On the other hand, either party may be regarded as continuing to carry on the same trade as he did previously, notwithstanding the depletion in its activities or the increase in its activities.

Alternatively, the effect may be that there is merely a change in the persons carrying on a trade or part of a trade: the second person 'succeeds to' the trade (or part) previously carried on by the first person. The second person may carry on the trade (or part) as a separate trade, or as part of a larger trade. Whether there is a succession will clearly depend upon the facts and circumstances.

Partnership changes

Most partnership changes are not, since the introduction of self assessment, treated as a cessation. A change that is not treated as a permanent discontinuance under the terms of the *Income Tax (Trading and Other Income) Act* 2005 is not treated as a cessation for capital allowance purposes (but subject to the comments above regarding plant and machinery, research and development and assured tenancy allowances).

Capital allowances are calculated as if the persons carrying on the trade before and after the transfer of trade were the same persons. In the case of partnership changes, allowances are computed as if the trade, profession or vocation had at all times been carried on by the same person. In the case of company reconstructions, allowances and charges are made to or on the successor as if the predecessor had continued to carry on the trade.

Legislation: ICTA 1988, s. 343(2); CAA 2001, s. 263, 558

Death of a sole trader

When a sole trader dies the business may pass to the surviving spouse (or civil partner). In such a case, capital allowances are to be calculated as if the assets had passed from the sole trader to the surviving spouse (or, as the case may be, civil partner) at open market value.

Other material: CA 15300

Successions

If a succession is treated as a cessation and commencement, capital allowances are calculated as if the assets were taken over by the successor at market value. No initial allowances can be claimed.

If the trade is treated as continuing at the point of succession, capital allowances are calculated as if the successor had always carried on the trade and owned the assets in question.

If the relevant interest in a building, structure or other works is not transferred when the succession takes place, then the successor cannot claim IBA or Agricultural Buildings Allowances (ABA) even if the successor is using the building for the purposes of the trade. This is because the successor does not hold the relevant interest (see the Chapters headed 'Industrial Buildings Allowances' (which begins at 300-000) and 'Agricultural Buildings Allowances' (which begins at 425-000) in that building, etc. In such a case the predecessor can continue to claim IBAs or ABAs if all other conditions are met.

As regards elections in relation to fixtures, see the Chapter headed 'Plant and Property', which begins at 250-000.

Where it is necessary to determine market value, if it is material to the liability of two or more persons, the matter is to be decided by the tax tribunal as if it were an appeal, except that all such persons may appear or make written representations.

Legislation: CAA 2001, s. 559, 564(2)

120-100   Companies not resident in the UK

A company that is not resident in the UK may be within the charge both to corporation tax (on income from one source) and to income tax (on income from another). In this case, any capital allowance to which the company is entitled is given only against the income from the source to which the allowance relates.

Legislation: CAA 2001, s. 566

120-200   Sales treated as being for alternative amount

The legislation uses the heading 'sales treated as being for alternative amount' to cover both an anti-avoidance rule and a tax planning opportunity. The rules apply for the purposes of the following Parts of the *Capital Allowances Act* 2001:

Part 3 – industrial buildings allowances;
Part 3A – business premises renovation allowances;
Part 4 – agricultural buildings allowances;
Part 4A – flat conversion allowances;
Part 5 – mineral extraction allowances;
Part 6 – research and development allowances;
Part 10 – assured tenancy allowances.

Full details are given in the Chapter on IBAs (see the Chapter headed 'Industrial Buildings Allowances', which begins at 300-000) but the overall effect of the legislation can be summarised as follows:

- first, there are tax avoidance rules that require market value to be substituted for actual proceeds where certain transactions are designed primarily to reduce a person's tax liability;
- secondly, there is a requirement to substitute market value for the actual proceeds figure in certain transactions between (broadly) connected parties; and
- thirdly, where there is a transfer between such connected parties, but there is no tax avoidance motive, there is a chance to elect to transfer the relevant interest in an industrial building at such a value as ensures that no balancing adjustment is triggered.

Legislation: CAA 2001, s. 567

120-300   Connected persons

The concept of connected persons is of relevance in various contexts, including the issue of where sales are to be treated as taking place 'for an alternative amount' – see above. The term 'connected persons' is defined at CAA 2001, s. 575 (as amended by ITA 2007 with effect from 6 April 2007). The legislation does not lend itself to simplification, so reference should be made to that definition as required.

Legislation: CAA 2001, s. 575

120-400   VAT capital goods scheme

Introduction and definitions

The VAT capital goods adjustment scheme adjusts the VAT recovered on certain capital items over a period. Input tax is initially recovered in the normal way. Later, that initial recovery is adjusted up (or down) if the taxable use of the item rises (or falls) over a period. The persons most affected are those who are partially exempt from VAT, such as those in banking, finance, insurance and property.

An 'additional VAT liability' is the liability amount which arises by way of an adjustment under any VAT capital items legislation. An 'additional VAT rebate' is the deductible input tax amount which arises by way of an adjustment under any VAT capital items legislation.

The 'VAT capital items legislation' means any Act or instrument which adjusts from time to time the proportion of input tax (as defined in VATA 1994, s. 24) on an asset of a specified description which may be deducted by a person from his output tax (as also defined in VATA 1994, s. 24). The adjustment follows any increase or decrease in the extent to which a person uses the asset for making 'taxable supplies' (as defined in VATA 1994, s. 4(2)) or taxable supplies of a specified class or description over a specified period ('the VAT period of adjustment') applicable to the asset. Such legislation also means any Act or instrument giving effect to the sixth directive, art. 20(2)–(4).

The capital allowances system takes account of these adjustments so that allowances are essentially only given on the cost of the capital item, exclusive of any VAT finally recovered. Generally the rules provide that any reduction in the recovery qualifies for capital allowances in the year the reduction is payable to Customs. Any extra relief is based on the allowances applicable at the time when the use of the asset changed, rather than the allowances applicable at the time the asset was acquired. However, any increased recovery cuts the allowances in the year in which the increase is recoverable from Customs. Thus earlier capital allowances computations require no amendment.

Legislation: CAA 2001, s. 547

Other material: CA 11900

Time additional VAT liability incurred

Any additional VAT liability (or rebate) is incurred (or made) on the last day of the period which is one of the periods making up the 'VAT period of adjustment', and is the period in which the increase or decrease in use which gave rise to the liability or rebate occurs.

The VAT period of adjustment specified under the VAT capital items legislation is the period for which adjustments are made in respect to input tax.

However, the time when any additional VAT liability (or rebate) is incurred (or made) is decided by reference to CAA 2001, s. 549 for the purpose of determining either the

27

chargeable period for which an allowance or charge is made or the amount of that allowance or charge. Section 549 defines the chargeable period in which, and the time at which, the additional VAT liability or rebate accrues, as per the following table:

Accrual of VAT liabilities and rebates

Circumstances	Chargeable period	Time of accrual
The liability or rebate is accounted for in a VAT return.	The chargeable period which includes the last day of the period to which the VAT return relates.	The last day of the period to which the VAT return relates.
The Commissioners of Customs and Excise assess the liability or rebate as due before a VAT return is made.	The chargeable period which includes the day on which the assessment is made.	The day on which the assessment is made.
The relevant activity is permanently discontinued before the liability or rebate is accounted for in a VAT return or assessed by the Commissioners.	The chargeable period in which the relevant activity is permanently discontinued.	The last day of the chargeable period in which the relevant activity is permanently discontinued.

Sometimes only a proportion of any capital expenditure attracts an allowance or charge; for example, where the item's qualifying activity use is less than 100 per cent. In that case, the same proportion of any additional VAT liability or rebate can attract an allowance or charge.

Legislation: CAA 2001, s. 548, 550

Other material: CA 11900

PLANT AND MACHINERY ALLOWANCES

Introduction and general principles

150-000   Plant and machinery: overview

Allowances are available in respect of expenditure on plant and machinery if a person who is carrying on a qualifying activity (see 155-000) incurs qualifying expenditure (see 160-000). If a person carries on more than one qualifying activity then allowances must be calculated separately for each.

The question of what constitutes 'plant' is difficult and often far from clear-cut. The general principles, developed through more than a century of case law, are considered in the Chapter headed 'Meaning of Plant', which begins at 180-000. The treatment of more than 100 commonly-found items is addressed in the Chapter headed 'Plant and Machinery: A to Z of Expenditure', which begins at 260-000.

Important changes to plant and machinery allowances took effect from 1 or 6 April 2008 (for corporation tax and income tax respectively). An overview of all the changes may be found at 100-150.

Relief is generally given in calculating the profits of the trade or other qualifying activity (see 152-100). This means that allowances are calculated, according to the rules described in these Chapters, and are then deducted in calculating the taxable profits of the trade in broadly the same way as other allowable expenses. (This therefore contrasts with an earlier system, under which profits were calculated without regard to capital allowances, and relief for the allowances was given as part of assessing those profits to tax.)

Plant and machinery allowances are given through a system of pooling, whereby most expenditure is merged within a single, ongoing calculation, the value of the pool increasing as new expenditure is incurred but reducing as allowances are given or sale proceeds are received. This is considered in depth beginning at 190-100.

Certain types of asset are not pooled as such (though the legislation uses the illogical term 'single asset pool' (see 190-100)). A third category of assets can be pooled with one another but have to be kept separate from the main pool of expenditure (see 190-100).

For most businesses, capital allowances have, since April 2008 been given mainly by way of an annual investment allowance, giving full relief for expenditure in the year of up to £50,000 (see 181-000). The figure of £50,000 was subject to initial transitional provisions and is only fully available for periods ending on or after 31 March 2009.

Plant and Machinery

However, relief is typically given by means of annual writing-down allowances (see 190-200ff.) for the following types of expenditure:

● expenditure in excess of the annual investment allowance limit;
● assets (such as cars) that do not qualify for annual investment allowances; and
● older expenditure brought forward in a pool.

The general rule before April 2008 was that writing-down allowances for plant and machinery were normally of 25 per cent of the pool value brought down from the preceding computation, but after adjusting for additions and disposals. That figure of 25 per cent reduced to 20 per cent from April 2008, but subject to transitional provisions.

First-year allowances (see 185-000) are given in some cases, depending on the nature of the expenditure. Where available, and subject to one important exception, such allowances are now always offered at 100 per cent, (ie full tax relief in the year in which the expenditure is incurred), though there is an option to accept a lower rate of allowance. Before April 2008, first-year allowances were also given for a much wider range of expenditure, but at a lower figure (typically 40 per cent) and only for small or medium-sized businesses. Where first-year allowances are available, no writing-down allowances are given for the same period. By contrast, the same expenditure may attract both an annual investment allowance and a writing-down allowance in the same period.

The important exception is that first-year allowances were re-introduced on a temporary basis for expenditure incurred in the year ending 31 March or 5 April 2010 (for corporation tax and income tax respectively): see 185-050. Such allowances are given at 40 per cent.

Balancing allowances (see 190-400) or balancing charges (see 190-500) may arise where an asset is sold or otherwise disposed of. Balancing charges can never exceed the total allowances that have been given for the asset in question.

The legislation contains an array of complications, all addressed in the following pages. Key areas of difficulty include the treatment of fixtures (see the Chapter headed 'Plant and Property', which begins at 250-000), the anti-avoidance rules (see various references), short-life assets (see 205-000) and long-life assets (see 210-000).

Legislation: CAA 2001, s. 11

Giving effect to allowances and charges

152-000   Overview

The general rule is that allowances and charges are to be given effect in calculating income (or, for corporation tax purposes, profits) for a given chargeable period. For plant and machinery allowances, this rule is subject to the following provisions, depending on the nature of the qualifying activity.

Legislation: CAA 2001, s. 2(1)

152-100   Trades, etc

The general rule (see 152-000) is specifically reinforced in relation to trades, ordinary property businesses, furnished holiday lettings businesses and overseas property businesses. In each case, allowances and charges are to be given effect in calculating the profits of the trade or business, treating any allowance as an expense and any balancing charge as a receipt of the trade or business in question.

The same principle also applies to professions and vocations.

Legislation: CAA 2001, s. 247–251

152-200   Mines, quarries and other concerns

The general rule (see 152-000) is similarly applied to the various concerns listed below, with allowances and charges treated as expenses and receipts of the concern:

'(a) mines and quarries (including gravel pits, sand pits and brickfields);
(b) ironworks, gasworks, salt springs or works, alum mines or works (not being mines falling within the preceding paragraph) and waterworks and streams of water;
(c) canals, inland navigation, docks and drains or levels;
(d) fishings;
(e) rights of markets and fairs, tolls, bridges and ferries;
(f) railways and other ways;
(g) other concerns of the like nature as any of the concerns specified in paragraphs (b) to (e) above.'

Legislation: CAA 2001, s. 252; ITTOIA 2005, s. 12(4); CTA 2009, s. 39(4)

152-300   Employees

Allowances due to employees, directors and other office holders are given as a deduction from taxable earnings. Balancing charges are treated as additional earnings.

Where an employee wishes to claim capital allowances this should be done as part of submitting his annual tax return. Relief will normally be given in the same way as it would for an expense incurred in the performance of his duties. HMRC accept, in principle, that capital allowances that cannot be set off against the earnings from the employment may, by election, be claimed for offset against other income. However, the HMRC view is that 'such claims will be very exceptional'. No capital allowances are given for cars or bicycles used

Plant and Machinery

by employees for work purposes, relief being given instead by way of approved mileage allowance payments (see 200-500).

Where an employee has claimed capital allowances, a balancing allowance or charge will normally arise on the first of the following events:

(1)   where the individual disposes of the item in question;

(2)   where the employment comes to an end; or

(3)   where the individual permanently ceases to use the item in question in the performance of the duties of the employment.

Where appropriate, any allowance or balancing charge will need to take private use of the asset into account.

See 155-800 for special rules applying to capital allowances claims by directors and employees.

Legislation: CAA 2001, s. 36, 262

Other material: EIM 36890

152-400   Companies with investment business

Where the qualifying activity is managing the investments of a company with investment business (see 155-000), balancing charges are treated as income of the business.

Any allowances are given effect as far as possible by deducting them from any income of the business for the period in question. To the extent that effect cannot be given to the allowances in this way, excess allowances are added to the company's expenses of management for the period and may be carried forward to subsequent accounting periods.

Where allowances or charges are made under other provisions, the investment business capital allowances provisions will not apply (and vice versa) so that there can be no duplication; further, except as noted below, expenditure in respect of which the election is made is disregarded in determining other reliefs and charges.

Legislation: CAA 2001, s. 253; CTA 2009, s. 1223

152-500   Life assurance business

Special rules apply where a company carrying on life assurance business is entitled to allowances (or liable to charges) under the plant and machinery regime. Normally, an apportionment has to be made between basic life assurance and general annuity business, and gross roll-up business and PHI business, though an exception is made in certain circumstances where the company is charged to tax under ICTA 1988, s. 436A (gross roll-up business).

Legislation: CAA 2001, s. 255, 256

152-600   Special leasing

Income tax

Allowances are normally given effect by deducting them from the person's income for the current tax year from any qualifying activity the person has of special leasing of plant or machinery. Any excess may be carried forward against that person's future income of the same description.

If, for the whole or part of the tax year, the plant or machinery in question was not used for the purposes of a qualifying activity carried on by the lessee then the allowance, or a proportionate part of it, is to be given effect by deducting it from the person's current year income from the special leasing of that asset only.

Any balancing charge is treated, for income tax purposes, as assessable income.

Legislation: CAA 2001, s. 258

Other material: CA 29450

Corporation tax

Similar principles apply for corporation tax as for income tax purposes. Allowances are given, and charges made, in calculating the income from special leasing. Once more, there is a restriction where, for the whole or part of the tax year, the plant or machinery in question was not used for the purposes of a qualifying activity carried on by the lessee. In such a case, the allowance, or a proportionate part of it, is to be deducted from the income from the special leasing of that asset only.

These rules also apply to investment assets let by a company for the purpose of its life assurance business.

If an allowance for any accounting period exceeds the amount of income of the class against which it is primarily to be given, the excess may be given against the profits or income of the company, so long as the company remains within the charge to corporation tax, as follows:

(1)   the company can make a claim (within two years from the end of the accounting period) for the excess allowance to be given against the company's profits of the current accounting period;

(2)   if the allowance for which the company has made such a claim cannot be fully allowed

Plant and Machinery

against the profits of the accounting period, any remaining allowance will be set first against the profits attributable to a period immediately before the accounting period for which the allowance is given, equal in length to that period, apportioning accounting periods' profits as necessary. The profits available for set-off are those before any loss carry-back; the total relief for capital allowances under this provision and losses under corresponding provisions must not exceed the proportionate part of the profits relating to the earlier period which is of equal length to that for which the allowances are given; and

(3)   any balance of the allowance still remaining must then be carried forward to succeeding accounting periods and be given against the earliest available income of the specified class until the allowance is fully exhausted.

These rules under (1) and (2) above do *not* apply to investment assets let by a company for the purpose of its life assurance business.

Losses are restricted in certain circumstances where losses arise from a leasing business carried on by a company in partnership and where there are unusual profit-sharing arrangements. The rules apply for accounting periods ending after 5 December 2005 (and in certain cases where the period straddles that date). The effect is that the provisions of CAA 2001, s. 260(3)–(6), as explained above, are disapplied.

Legislation: CAA 2001, s. 19(5), 259–261, 261A

Other material: CA 29450

152-700   Pre-trading expenditure

Where a person who is about to carry on a qualifying activity (see 155-000) incurs expenditure on plant or machinery, that expenditure is deemed to be incurred by him on the day on which he starts to carry on the activity.

Legislation: CAA 2001, s. 12

Other material: CA 23020

Qualifying activities

155-000   Overview

Allowances are in principle available if a person carrying on a qualifying activity incurs qualifying expenditure for the purposes of that activity. Qualifying activities are defined to include the following, but only to the extent that any profits or gains from the activity are (or would be if there were any) chargeable to tax:

(1)   a trade (see 155-100);

(2)   an ordinary property business (see 155-200);

(3)   a furnished holiday lettings business (see 155-300);

(4)   an overseas property business (see 155-400);

(5)   a profession or vocation (see 155-100);

(6)   a concern listed in ITTOIA 2005, s. 12(4) or CTA 2009, s. 39(4) (mines, transport undertakings, etc) (see 155-500);

(7)   managing the investments of a company with investment business (see 155-600);

(8)   special leasing of plant or machinery (see 155-700);

(9)   an employment or office (see 155-800).

Items (2), (4) and (8) are subject to the restrictions in relation to plant and machinery for use in a dwelling-house (see 165-100).

Legislation: CAA 2001, s. 15(1)

Other material: CA 20010

155-100   Trades, professions and vocations

The majority of capital allowance claims for expenditure on plant and machinery are made by those carrying on a trade or other business activity. It is usually clear that such a trade, etc constitutes a qualifying activity.

There is a possible complication within a group of companies. If Company B incurs expenditure at the request of parent company A, it is conceivable that HMRC could argue that Company B was not incurring the expenditure for the purposes of its own qualifying activity. This was touched on in the *Barclays Mercantile Business Finance Ltd v Mawson* case (see 160-000).

Legislation: CAA 2001, s. 15(1)

Cases: *Barclays Mercantile Business Finance Ltd v Mawson* [2003] BTC 81

155-200   Ordinary property business

This is defined to mean any UK property business, other than a furnished holiday lettings business (but see 155-300).

Plant and Machinery

No plant and machinery allowances are given under this heading for plant used in a dwelling house. This, including the non-statutory 'wear and tear allowance', is considered in detail at 165-100.

Legislation: CAA 2001, s. 16, 35

155-300   Furnished holiday lettings business

This is defined to mean a UK property business consisting of the commercial letting of furnished holiday accommodation. The term 'commercial letting of furnished holiday accommodation' is itself defined, with separate statutory provisions for income tax and corporation tax purposes.

The legislation requires all commercial lettings of furnished holiday accommodation that are made by a person or by a partnership or by any body of persons, to be treated as a single qualifying activity for these purposes.

Where accommodation is let such that part of it qualifies as holiday accommodation, then the legislation requires such apportionments to be made 'as are just and reasonable'.

Legislation: CAA 2001, s. 17

Income tax definition

For income tax purposes, the following definitions are applied:

- a letting is a lease or other arrangement under which a person is entitled to the use of accommodation;
- a letting is 'commercial' if the accommodation is let on a commercial basis and with a view to the realisation of profits; and
- a letting is of furnished holiday accommodation if the accommodation is qualifying holiday accommodation (see below) and the person entitled to the use of the accommodation is entitled, in connection with that use, to the use of furniture.

Qualifying holiday accommodation

The above definition raises the further question of what constitutes 'qualifying holiday accommodation', a definition that in its turn throws up yet another concept, that of the 'relevant period' (considered below).

Accommodation is qualifying holiday accommodation if it meets all three of the following conditions:

- during the relevant period, the accommodation must be available for commercial letting as holiday accommodation to the public generally for at least 140 days;
- during the relevant period, the accommodation must in fact be commercially let as holiday accommodation to members of the public for at least 70 days, excluding any period of longer-term occupation; and

- during the relevant period, no more than 155 days must fall during periods of longer-term occupation.

An averaging election is available where the 70-day rule above is not met in relation to a particular property but:

Longer-term occupation

For the above purposes, a 'period of longer-term occupation' is defined as 'a continuous period of more than 31 days during which the accommodation is in the same occupation otherwise than because of circumstances that are not normal'.

Relevant period

The general rule is that the relevant period is the tax year. This is subject to two exceptions.

If the accommodation was not let by the person as furnished accommodation in the previous tax year, then the relevant period is the period of 12 months beginning with the first day in the tax year on which it is let by the person as furnished accommodation.

If the accommodation was let by the person as furnished accommodation in the previous tax year, but is not so let in the following tax year, then the relevant period is the period of 12 months ending with the last day in the tax year on which it is let by the person as furnished accommodation.

Legislation: CAA 2001, s. 17, ITTOIA 2005, s. 323ff.

Corporation tax definition

The corporation tax definition is very similar, but substitutes 'accounting period' for 'tax year' in the definition of relevant period.

Legislation: CAA 2001, s. 17, CTA 2009, s. 264ff

155-400   Overseas property business

This is self-explanatory.

No plant and machinery allowances are given under this heading for plant used in a dwelling house. This, including the non-statutory 'wear and tear allowance', is considered in detail at 165-100.

Legislation: CAA 2001, s. 15(1)(d)

155-500 Mines, transport undertakings, etc

A concern listed in ITTOIA 2005, s. 12(4) or CTA 2009, s. 39(4) (mines, transport undertakings, etc) is a qualifying activity.

See 152-200 for a list of such activities.

Legislation: CAA 2001, s. 15(1)(f)

155-600 Companies with investment business

Managing the investments of a company with investment business is a qualifying activity for the purposes of claiming plant and machinery allowances.

For these purposes, a 'company with investment business' (previously an investment company) is defined in accordance with CTA 2009, s. 1218. Management of such a company is defined as 'pursuing those purposes expenditure on which would be treated as expenses of management within section 1219 of CTA 2009'.

Legislation: CAA 2001, s. 15(1)(g), 18

155-700 Special leasing businesses

'Special leasing' of plant or machinery means the hiring out of the item in question other than in the course of any other qualifying activity.

In these cases, the special leasing begins when the item is first hired out. It comes to an end for capital allowances purposes when the lessor 'permanently ceases to hire out the plant or machinery otherwise than in the course of any other qualifying activity'. There is a final chargeable period if the chargeable period is one in which the taxpayer permanently ceases to hire out the plant or machinery otherwise than in the course of the qualifying activity. The effect of this, which was clarified when the 2001 Act was created under the Tax Law Re-write project, is that there may be a balancing allowance at that point.

There is deemed to be a separate qualifying activity in respect of each item of plant or machinery that is hired out in this way.

No plant and machinery allowances are given under this heading for plant used in a dwelling house. This, including the non-statutory 'wear and tear allowance', is considered in detail at 165-100.

Legislation: CAA 2001, s. 19

Other material: SP 3/91 – Finance lease rental payments

155-800 Offices and employments

Although plant and machinery allowances are in principle given to employees, there are in practice numerous restrictions on the allowances available.

Vehicles and bicycles

No capital allowances are available for cars, other vehicles or cycles funded by an employee; employees who use their own cars for business purposes may only claim tax-free reimbursement from their employers using the fixed rates of 40p per mile for the first 10,000 business miles driven and 25p per mile thereafter. If employees claim a lesser amount (or no reimbursement at all) then they can claim mileage allowance relief on any shortfall. See also 200-500

Legislation: CAA 2001, s. 36(1)(a)

Other material: CA 20015

Other assets used by employees

Expenditure by employees, other than on vehicles, qualifies for plant or machinery allowances only if it is 'necessarily provided for use in the performance of the duties of the employment or office'. This 'necessarily provided' condition is notoriously tight and significantly restricts the ability of employees to claim capital allowances (though the asset does not have to be 'wholly and exclusively' used for the performance of the duties).

In *White v Higginbottom*, a vicar claimed a capital allowance for the cost of a slide projector bought solely for use in his ministry. He argued that the word 'necessarily' in the capital allowance rules should be construed less strictly than in the legislation relating to deductions for employee expenses. He argued alternatively that in a case such as his, there was an element of discretion as to the extent of his duties, and that it could be said objectively that the projector was necessary for his duties as he defined them. It was held, however, that the test of necessity was the same for both sections, and that the fact that the taxpayer could have performed his duties as a vicar without the projector was fatal to his second argument.

Even HMRC recognises that the judgment in that case was erring on the harsh side. Instructions to officers are that they 'should take care when applying this reasoning to situations where the employee's duties are only vaguely defined'. The guidance goes on to state that:

> ' . . . when the equipment purchased represents a more up to date method of carrying out existing tasks which are a necessary part of the duties, . . . the employee can exercise some element of choice in deciding how to go about those tasks without forgoing the entitlement to allowances; in the same way that an employee who undertakes necessary travel in the performance of the duties may choose whether to travel by car or by train.'

Nevertheless, employees can still expect a struggle to establish a worthwhile capital allowances claim. Where significant expenditure is incurred, HMRC may well check

Plant and Machinery

employment contracts or other correspondence, etc between the employer and the director/ employee. The HMRC attitude here is almost that of 'heads I win, tails you lose'. If the employer would be willing to incur the cost then the employee cannot obtain allowances as the item has not been 'necessarily provided' by the employee. Where, on the other hand, the employer is not willing to bear the cost then it may point to the conclusion that the expense is not necessary, a fact which 'will clearly weaken the taxpayer's claim, without being entirely conclusive'.

HMRC will normally accept a claim by an employee if all of the following three conditions are satisfied (though these are not conditions that must be met in every case):

(1)   the employee is paid entirely or largely by results (eg by commission);

(2)   the method by which the employee is to achieve the results is not stereotyped; and

(3)   the employee is required to bear the cost of such equipment performing functions or activities intended to achieve his objective in his employment and that the employer does not provide or pay for such equipment.

It is difficult to understand the legal basis for the first of the above three conditions. Certainly there is nothing in the legislation that states or implies that allowances can only be due to employees who are paid by result. Any inspector putting forward this condition should be challenged as to its basis.

Legislation: CAA 2001, s. 36(1)(b)

Cases: *White v Higginbottom* [1983] BTC 46

Other material: EIM 36550–36730

Particular assets used by employees

Where expenditure is incurred on small items of plant (such as pocket calculators or books other than substantial reference works with a long shelf life) then the HMRC preference is to give a full one-off deduction for the cost, rather than dealing with annual capital allowance claims. HMRC do not normally accept that a briefcase can qualify for allowances.

As regards computers and word processors, the starting position by HMRC is that allowances are not due but it will consider them in appropriate circumstances, particularly if the three points listed above are met.

The HMRC view is that mobile phones paid for by employees will only qualify for capital allowances if the employee has a travelling appointment and his duties require him 'to be in contact, or be able to be in contact with others on a continual basis, for business purposes'.

No allowances are due for assets used for business entertaining (see 165-500).

Legislation: CAA 2001, s. 269

Other material: EIM 36710ff.

Assets used only partly for employment purposes

Where the plant or machinery in respect of which allowances are available for employees is used partly for the purposes of the office or employment and partly for other purposes, allowances may be given but will be reduced to a just and reasonable amount. For the purposes of writing-down allowances, it will be assumed that the machinery or plant is used in a separate qualifying activity, ie it has to be put into a separate 'pool' (see 190-100).

Is it plant?

A particular issue may arise where an asset, other than a machine, is used by a director or employee. HMRC may then seek to deny the item the status of plant: see 180-500.

Overseas earnings

In the case of earnings falling within:

- ITEPA 2003, s. 22 (chargeable overseas earnings for year when employee resident and ordinarily resident, but not domiciled, in the UK); or
- ITEPA 2003, s. 26 (foreign earnings for year when employee resident, but not ordinarily resident, in the UK);

the plant and machinery rules apply to those earnings, or to any other taxable earnings of the employment, 'as if the performance of the duties did not belong to that employment or office'. In other words, if an employee is taxed only on UK-based earnings, he or she will only be entitled to capital allowances for plant and machinery to the extent that it is used in the performance of the UK duties. No capital allowances can be given against general earnings charged on remittance under ITEPA 2003, s. 22 or s. 26.

Legislation: CAA 2001, s. 20(3)

Particular occupations

The HMRC manuals contain specific comments on capital allowances claims by ministers of religion (EIM 60055), insurance agents (EIM 64650), teachers, lecturers and tutors (EIM 70705), and teachers and academics (EIM 70790).

Divers and diving supervisors

In the list at 155-000 above, the term 'employment' does not include an employment where the duties are treated as the carrying on of a trade under ITTOIA 2005, s. 15 (divers and diving supervisors in the North Sea, etc).

Legislation: CAA 2001, s. 20(1)

155-900   Assets used only partly for qualifying activities

Where an asset is used partly for non-business purposes, capital allowances are restricted accordingly (see 190-100). To achieve this, such assets are always allocated to a single-asset pool (see 190-650).

Use by an employee or director will almost invariably be treated as part of that individual's remuneration, and taxed on him accordingly as earnings. From an employing company's point of view, this is not treated as private use. (See 180-500, however, for a possible denial of allowances where plant (but not machinery) is used solely for the private purposes of a director or employee; see also 201-120 for a possible restriction on capital allowances available to either a company or an unincorporated business to take account of personal choice, for example in relation to a very expensive car.)

Legislation: CAA 2001, s. 207

Qualifying expenditure

160-000   General rule

The structure of the capital allowances legislation is potentially misleading. There is a main heading, 'Qualifying Expenditure', for CAA 2001, Pt. 2, Ch. 3. Nevertheless, the 'general rule' is in an earlier part of the Act (CAA 2001, s. 11(4)). This general rule states that expenditure is qualifying expenditure if:

- it is capital expenditure (see 102-000) on the provision (see below) of plant or machinery (see the Chapter headed 'Meaning of Plant', which begins at 180-000) wholly or partly for the purposes of the qualifying activity (see 155-000ff.) carried on by the person incurring the expenditure; and
- as a result of incurring the expenditure, the person owns the plant or machinery.

This definition is then considerably refined, especially in relation to the following types or categories of expenditure:

- buildings, structures and land: see 160-100;
- demolition costs: see 160-200;
- thermal insulation, safety measures, etc: see 261-100;
- integral features: see 247-000ff.; and

- exclusion of certain types of expenditure: see 165-000ff.

The question of whether capital expenditure was incurred 'on the provision of plant or machinery' or on something else was considered in the case of *Barclays Mercantile Business Finance Ltd v Mawson*. Substantial sums of money were at stake and the transactions were complex. The Revenue argued that anti-avoidance case law principles could be invoked to deny capital allowances. Although successful in front of the commissioners and in the Chancery Division, the Revenue lost both in the Court of Appeal and finally, in the House of Lords. It was clear that there was a genuine commercial transaction; the fact that the transaction was structured so that capital allowances could be obtained did not mean that they were therefore to be denied. This was subject only to what is now CAA 2001, s. 215 (restriction on first-year allowances where the sole or main benefit was to obtain allowances).

Legislation: CAA 2001, s. 11(4)

Cases: *Barclays Mercantile Business Finance Ltd v Mawson* [2003] BTC 81

Other material: CA 23000ff.

160-100   Buildings, structures and land

Expenditure on the provision of plant or machinery does not include expenditure on the provision of a building. This concept is fundamental to understanding whether or not many everyday items qualify as plant. See 260-150 for specific commentary on this issue and the Chapter headed 'Meaning of Plant' (which begins at 180-000) for background to the distinction between plant and setting.

Legislation: CAA 2001, s. 21–26

Interest in land

Expenditure on the acquisition of an interest in land is not treated as expenditure on plant or machinery. For these purposes, 'land' is initially defined in accordance with the *Interpretation Act* 1978, Sch. 1, namely to include 'buildings and other structures, land covered with water, and any estate, interest, easement, servitude or right in or over land'. For the purposes of this section, however, the definition is modified so that land does *not* include:

- buildings;
- other structures; or
- any asset so installed or otherwise fixed to any description of land as to become, in law, part of that land (a definition that is similar, but not identical, to the definition of fixtures – see the Chapter headed 'Plant and Property', which begins at 250-000).

Plant and Machinery

An 'interest in land' is defined as per the fixtures legislation (CAA 2001, s. 175 – see 245-100).

Legislation: CAA 2001, s. 24(3)

Building alterations connected with installation of plant and machinery

Where a trader incurs capital expenditure altering an existing building, and the alteration is incidental to the installation of plant or machinery for the purposes of the trade, the expenditure may be treated as part of the cost of that plant or machinery. This is considered in depth at 260-040.

Legislation: CAA 2001, s. 25

Preparing sites to install plant

Capital expenditure on preparing, cutting, tunnelling or levelling land so as to prepare the land as a site for installing plant or machinery is treated as expenditure on an industrial building where plant or machinery allowances or industrial building allowances would not otherwise be available (see 300-650).

Legislation: CAA 2001, s. 273

160-200   Demolition costs

Relief is normally available for demolition costs. Where costs are incurred in demolishing plant or machinery, the tax treatment will depend on whether or not the old plant is replaced. First, however, it is necessary to calculate the net costs of the demolition. The net cost is defined as being the excess of any of the cost of the demolition over any money received for the remains of the old plant or machinery.

Where there are net demolition costs, then these are added to the cost of the new plant if the plant is replaced. If there is no replacement of the plant that is demolished then the net costs are added to the qualifying expenditure for the period in which the demolition is undertaken. If the costs are incurred when a trade ceases then they are added to the qualifying expenditure for the last chargeable period of the trade.

Obviously, it is possible that the disposal proceeds for old plant will exceed the cost of demolition. In that case, the net receipt (including any sale proceeds, insurance receipts or other capital compensation) will be brought in as a disposal value in the ordinary way.

There are special rules applying to demolition costs related to offshore plant or machinery.

Legislation: CAA 2001, s. 26, 163–165

Other material: CA 20070, 22210

160-300   Thermal insulation, safety, integral features, etc

Certain expenditure is treated as qualifying expenditure if it would not otherwise qualify for plant or machinery allowances. The legislation creates a fiction so that allowances are given *as if* the expenditure were capital expenditure on providing plant for the purposes of the trade or other qualifying activity, and *as if* the person incurring the expenditure owned plant or machinery as a result of incurring it. The significance of the highlighted words is that the legislation sidesteps (for example) the requirement for the asset to be owned.

The types of expenditure coming within these special rules are as follows:

- thermal insulation of buildings (previously of industrial buildings only but this qualifying condition was removed by the *Finance Act* 2008) (see 261-100);
- various categories of expenditure on safety at sports grounds (see 160-600);
- expenditure on personal security (see 160-700);
- expenditure, from April 2008, on integral features (see 247-000ff.).

The category of fire safety expenditure (see 160-500) was removed from the list by the *Finance Act* 2008 in relation to expenditure incurred from 1 or 6 April 2008 (for corporation tax and income tax respectively).

The first three items listed above receive this special treatment by virtue of CAA 2001, s. 27. If there is any disposal of assets that have qualified under those three headings then the disposal value is taken to be nil (CAA 2001, s. 63(5)). As such, full tax relief is given to the person incurring the original expenditure, with no relief for subsequent owners. The giving of allowances to integral features as if they were items of plant and machinery is by virtue of CAA 2001, s. 33A(2), and the rule about the nil disposal value does not apply to these.

Legislation: CAA 2001, s. 27, CAA 2001, s. 63(5)

160-500   Fire safety expenditure

The rules regarding allowances for fire safety systems are not as generous as they are often perceived to be and further amendments were made to the rules by the *Finance Act* 2008 in relation to expenditure incurred from 1 or 6 April 2008 (for corporation tax and income tax respectively). The starting point is that fire safety systems are specifically included in the expression of 'building' by virtue of list A, item 6 in CAA 2001, s. 21 and, as such, are initially excluded from qualifying as plant. Some items are immediately then protected from that exclusion. Thus, list C, item 10 provides an exemption for 'fire alarm systems; sprinkler and other equipment for extinguishing or containing fires'. This exemption will therefore

Plant and Machinery

cover, for example, fire blankets as well as fire extinguishers, whether fixed permanently in place or free-standing.

To the extent that fire safety expenditure comes within the categories just listed, it will normally be accepted that such expenditure is on plant or machinery.

In the *Cole Brothers* case, an emergency lighting system was accepted as plant. The cost included cables for the lighting system and separate equipment to control that system.

In the *Wimpy* case, expenditure was incurred on fire-resistant doors and surfaces coated with fire-resistant materials. The commissioners decided that this expenditure did not qualify as plant as it played no part in the trading activities but merely enabled the premises to be used for the company's trade. In the Court of Appeal, the judge felt that the commissioners were entitled to reach this decision. Similarly, a trapdoor and ladder were held in that case not to qualify as plant. The commissioners decided that the expenditure on these items was an alteration to the premises. The judge gave his view that the commissioners were correct to make this finding of fact.

Special rules applying before April 2008

Sometimes, fire safety expenditure will not qualify under general principles. This is when CAA 2001, s. 29 used to come into play, the section applying only where no tax relief was otherwise available for the expenditure. This special rule applied to traders incurring expenditure in taking steps specified in a notice served by a fire authority under the *Fire Precautions Act* 1971, s. 5(4). The notice needed to have been issued on an application for a fire certificate. CAA 2001, s. 29 granted relief and, to avoid possible problems with leases, s. 27 deemed there to be expenditure incurred by the trader as a consequence of which the plant belonged to him. Where necessary, s. 29 took precedence over s. 21. So, for example, a fire door could qualify under s. 29 if its installation was required by law (CA 22230).

A parallel set of rules, also within s. 29, applied in respect of expenditure incurred by a trader in response to a letter or document sent or given to him by the fire authority on an application for a fire certificate under the *Fire Precautions Act* 1971.

Expenditure that qualified under CAA 2001, s. 29 is deemed to have a disposal value of nil, whatever the nature of the event which triggers the disposal (CAA 2001, s. 63(5)).

Changes from April 2008

The provisions of CAA 2001, s. 29, described above, cease to apply for expenditure incurred from 1 April or 6 April 2008 (for corporation tax and income tax purposes respectively). HMRC provided some clarification of these changes in the *Explanatory Notes* issued with Finance Bill 2008. The key points are as follows:

- Most expenditure incurred on fire prevention and safety is deductible as revenue expenditure or under other capital allowances provisions, including expenditure on fire extinguishers, signage, alarms and sprinkler systems.

- CAA 2001, s. 29 provided relief for other expenditure, such as fire escapes and fire doors, that would not otherwise qualify for any tax relief.
- As a result of changes to fire safety legislation, relief was latterly only available to businesses that had not complied with such legislation and that had therefore required penal action by the Fire Authority to remove fire risks.
- It was therefore considered counter-productive to provide relief only to those businesses that had failed to comply with the legislation, and it was felt that the continued provision of relief in such circumstances could even lead to delay in undertaking vital fire safety improvements.

The decision could have been taken to provide tax relief generally for all such expenditure. Instead, the view taken was clearly that businesses have an obligation to meet certain fire safety requirements and that the tax system would therefore no longer be used as an incentive to meet those obligations. As a result, no business can therefore now claim tax relief on the costs of such items as fire escapes and fire doors.

Legislation: CAA 2001, s. 21 (list A, item 6), 23 (list C, item 10), 27, 29 and 63(5)

Cases: *Lupton v Cadogan Gardens Developments Limited* (1971) 47 TC 1; *Cole Brothers Ltd v Phillips* [1982] BTC 208; *Wimpy International Ltd v Warland* [1989] BTC 58 (items 11, 22, 24)

Other material: CA 21010, 21230, 22010–22030, 22230–22260; ESC B16

160-600   Safety at sports grounds

The legislation at CAA 2001, s. 21 and 22 (restrictions re buildings, structures etc) specifically does not apply to certain expenditure on safety at sports grounds. Instead, such safety measures are governed by their own particular rules which provide relief in certain circumstances where no allowance or deduction would otherwise be due.

A number of specialist terms are introduced in the tax legislation, with cross references to Part III of the *Fire Safety and Safety of Places of Sport Act* 1987 and to the *Safety of Sports Grounds Act* 1975.

The importance of this special legislation should not be missed. It is quite conceivable that works on a sports stadium will qualify as to 20–30 per cent under the 'ordinary' rules of what constitutes plant, and that at least as much again will qualify under these special rules.

Reference should always be made to the 'Green Guide' ('Guide to Safety at Sports Grounds') which is the bible for sports ground safety issues. The Guide is the product of years of research into the safety issues at sporting venues and in particular takes account of the lessons learnt from the Hillsborough tragedy of 1989, and from the Taylor report that followed that event. The Guide has no direct statutory force but no sports stadium is likely to be issued with a safety certificate under the *Safety of Sports Grounds Act* 1975 or the *Fire Safety and Safety of Places of Sport Act* 1987 unless the recommendations of the Guide are

Plant and Machinery

followed rigorously. This therefore brings it directly into relevance as far as the CAA 2001 is concerned.

Many HMRC officers are not aware of the existence (never mind the significance) of the Guide and it may well be necessary to educate a local officer to appreciate what is involved.

The extent of the Guide's significance can perhaps be appreciated from a comment in the HMRC manuals on the question of police control rooms which are considered in two different places in the HMRC manuals, at CA 21230 and again at CA 22240. The conclusion is that if the local authority take the view that it has the power to require the installation of a police control room under the provisions of the *Safety at Sports Grounds Act* 1975, then the expenditure will indeed qualify under CAA 2001, s. 30–32. This is so even though 'the construction of a building or structure does not normally qualify' under that section. This principle, if correctly understood and applied, can have a very wide application.

A number of other points are worthy of particular mention.

First, as a general observation, it is clear that if a claim is being made for expenditure not covered by these sections, it will have to satisfy the conditions of CAA 2001, s. 21–33 and of existing case law principles. In this respect, some caution needs to be taken with the *Burnley Football and Athletic* case, where the company failed to obtain capital allowances on the cost of the stand. See in this respect 180-400 for HMRC commentary in the light of that case.

The HMRC manuals contain a specific point about seats and their covers. These cannot, in HMRC's opinion, be covered by the Local Authority Safety Certificate and therefore do not fall within the provisions of the special rules. The manual goes on to say, however, that in any case 'expenditure on seats is likely to qualify as expenditure on plant in the normal way'.

Finally, it should be noted that the plant or machinery is deemed to belong to the person incurring the expenditure and thus satisfies one of the conditions needed for capital allowances to be due. Also, if there is any disposal then the value is taken to be nil.

Cross-reference

The following cross-references may be of particular interest in relation to this category of expenditure.

- Alterations to buildings (260-040)
- Buildings (260-150)
- Cameras (260-200)
- Electrical installations and equipment (260-600)
- Fencing (260-700)
- Fire safety (160-500)
- Floodlighting (260-770)
- Football grounds (260-790)

- Professional fees and preliminary costs (262-240)
- Public address systems (262-250)
- Seats (262-440)
- Structures (262-590)
- Televisions and videos (262-730)
- Walls (262-910)

Legislation: CAA 2001, s. 23, 30–32, 63(5)

Cases: *Brown v Burnley Football and Athletic Co Limited* (1980) 53 TC 357

Other material: CA 21230, 22030, 22240–22260

160-700   Personal security

Special rules apply to expenditure on personal security where all of the following conditions are met:

(1)   a 'relevant qualifying activity' (see 150-000) is being carried on by an individual or partnership (not a company);

(2)   the individual or partnership incurs the expenditure in connection with the provision of a security asset – see below;

(3)   if the special rules did not apply, no tax relief would be due either in calculating the income of the qualifying activity or under the capital allowances legislation;

(4)   the asset is provided or used to meet a special threat to the individual's personal physical security;

(5)   that threat arises wholly or mainly because of the relevant activity; and

(6)   the sole object of incurring the expenditure is to meet that threat.

Only certain assets are able to qualify under this special legislation and, in this respect, the following points are to be noted:

(1)   the asset must be provided to improve *personal* security;

(2)   it must not be a car, ship or aircraft;

(3)   it can be an item of equipment or a structure (such as a wall);

(4)   it must not be a 'dwelling'. HMRC say that 'a flat used as a residence, including a flat above business premises, is a dwelling but a block of flats is not a single dwelling';

(5)   it must not be 'grounds appurtenant to a dwelling' and for these purposes HMRC follow the private residence 'half a hectare' rules (regarding which see TCGA 1992, s. 222 and Revenue manuals at CG 64362).

HMRC list alarm systems, bullet-resistant windows, reinforced doors and windows, and perimeter walls and fences as examples of items that may qualify as security assets.

Plant and Machinery

HMRC have issued guidance on a number of related issues, as follows:

(1) HMRC head office will take the decision as to whether there is a threat to physical security, but the amount of any allowance due will be decided at local level.

(2) The fact that an asset has to be attached to land or a building will not prevent it from being a security asset.

(3) Similarly, the fact that an asset improves the personal physical security of another member of the trader's family or household will not disqualify it, as long as it is also there to protect the trader's own personal physical security.

(4) If an asset is intended solely to improve personal physical security but there is another use for the asset which arises incidentally, then the whole of the expenditure will still qualify for capital allowances. For example, bullet-proof glass may have the incidental effect of keeping the house warm.

(5) On the other hand, if an asset is provided partly to improve personal physical security and partly for other reasons then only the appropriate proportion of the expenditure will qualify for relief. This proportion is defined as 'the proportion of the expenditure attributable to the intended use to improve personal physical security'. This must surely be one of the most bizarre concepts to pin down anywhere in the Taxes Acts. One can hardly imagine an individual at threat from a terrorist organisation telling HMRC that he had installed large bullet-proof windows 75 per cent to prevent a terrorist attack and 25 per cent because he was guaranteed to have low maintenance for 10 years!

Where all of the above conditions are met, the expenditure is treated as if it were on plant or machinery and the asset is deemed to belong to the individual or partnership as a result of the expenditure being incurred. In the event of an asset giving rise to a disposal for capital allowances purposes, the security asset is deemed to be disposed of for nil consideration.

HMRC take a strict line on the interpretation of this special legislation. There will be relatively few cases where HMRC will accept both that there is a genuine personal security risk and that it arises from the nature of the trade. The legislation is a close parallel to that which concerns employees and which is found at ITEPA 2003, s. 377.

That employee-related legislation is discussed in the HMRC manuals at EIM 21811, where HMRC specify that the deduction is for individuals whose work 'exposes them to a very real threat to their physical safety from terrorists, extremists and others who may resort to violence'. A case was heard in 2004 involving the late Lord Hanson. The special commissioner ruled that Lord Hanson was entitled to tax relief under the employment income legislation as there was a special employment-related threat to his personal physical security. The decision was based on a factual finding that Hanson was a potential terrorist target by virtue of his role as executive chairman of Hanson plc. It was also found that the sole object of the company in providing the security services was to meet that threat. (For an in-depth review of the employee tax position, see the book *P11D: Tax-efficient Benefits & Expenses* (produced by the same author and publishers as this book) at section 8.46.)

Legislation: CAA 2001, s. 27, 33, 63(5)

Cases: *Lord Hanson v Mansworth (HMIT)* (2004) Sp C 410

Other material: CA 22270

160-800   Use of an existing asset for a qualifying activity

A person may own an item of plant or machinery for other purposes and only later start to use it for the purposes of a qualifying activity. Where this happens, the person is treated as incurring capital expenditure, referred to as 'notional expenditure', on the item in question for the purposes of a qualifying activity. This is deemed to take place on the date on which it is brought into use for the purposes of that activity. No first-year allowances or annual investment allowances are given in these circumstances, however.

Normally, the amount of the notional expenditure is the market value of the plant or machinery on the date when it is brought into use for the purposes of the qualifying activity. For example, an individual who owns a car starts to carry on a trade. He brings the car into use for the purposes of the trade. Even though he is not incurring expenditure at that time, he will be able to claim capital allowances on the market value at that point.

If an asset has risen in value since the actual expenditure was incurred then capital allowances are only given on the actual expenditure. There are anti-avoidance provisions to prevent the artificial exploitation of this rule (CAA 2001, s. 218 and 224).

Legislation: CAA 2001, s. 13, CAA 2001, s. 38B (*general exclusion* 5), CAA 2001, s. 46(2) (*general exclusion* 8)

Other material: CA 23110

160-900   Use of plant or machinery that was previously under a long funding lease

The long funding lease rules aim to remove tax distortions by transferring entitlement to capital allowances on certain leased plant and machinery from lessors to lessees: see, generally, 240-220ff.

It is possible, of course, that a lessor who has been using an asset for the purposes of leasing it under a long funding lease will retain the asset but start to use it for the purposes of a different qualifying activity. Special rules exist to address the tax issues arising in such a case; in summary, he will normally have been denied tax relief for as long as the asset was used for the purposes of long funding leasing but he may be entitled to relief thereafter. The

Plant and Machinery

rules apply as long as the person in question continues to own the asset, as a result of having incurred capital expenditure on it, at the date of the change.

The person is then treated as having incurred notional expenditure on the provision of the item in question on the day after the cessation of its old use. The asset is treated as if it were a different asset from that previously leased out under the long funding rules. The amount of the notional expenditure is defined as 'an amount equal to the termination amount, determined in accordance with s. 70YG': see 232-250 for a discussion of this issue.

Legislation: CAA 2001, s. 13A

161-000   Assets received as a gift

A person carrying on a qualifying activity (see 155-000) may bring into use for that activity an item of plant or machinery that he has received by way of gift. In such circumstances, he is treated as incurring capital expenditure on the item in question on the date when it is first brought into use for the purposes of the qualifying activity, though no first-year allowances or annual investment allowances are given in these circumstances. The amount of the capital expenditure is the market value of the item in question on that date.

Legislation: CAA 2001, s. 14, CAA 2001, s. 38B (*general exclusion* 5), CAA 2001, s. 46(2) (*general exclusion* 8)

161-100   Shares in plant and machinery

References to an item of plant or machinery include references to a part of such an item, unless the context requires otherwise.

The plant and machinery rules similarly apply to a share in an item of plant or machinery as they apply to a part of plant or machinery. In the case of a share in an asset, the question of whether the expenditure in question is on an asset used for the purposes of a qualifying activity is determined by reference to the use of the asset as a whole.

Legislation: CAA 2001, s. 270, 571(1)

161-200   Abortive expenditure

One of the conditions for obtaining capital allowances on plant and machinery is that as a consequence of incurring the expenditure, the item in question belongs or has belonged to the trader.

A particular issue therefore arises in respect of abortive expenditure. On the face of it, if the acquisition of an asset does not go ahead for any purpose then no allowances can be due as the ownership condition is not met.

Back in 1992, the (then) Inland Revenue issued an 'Interpretation' (IR Int. 10 – February 1992) which helped in many circumstances. According to the HMRC website, that interpretation is 'no longer current' but the effect has since been written into the *Capital Allowances* manual. Essentially, the hire purchase legislation lends itself to this situation and ensures that in many cases relief will be available, as explained in the following extracts from that manual:

> 'The side note to CAA 2001, s. 67 says that it is about hire purchase and similar contracts. However, it is wider than that. In certain circumstances the legislation in Section 67 may apply to abortive capital expenditure incurred on plant or machinery.'

> 'Section 67 ... applies where a person incurs capital expenditure on the provision of machinery or plant for the purposes of the trade 'under a contract providing that he shall or may become the owner of the plant or machinery on the performance of the contract'. Where there is a contract like that Section 67(1)(a) treats the machinery or plant as belonging to the person.

> Abortive expenditure – for example a deposit paid on machinery which is never actually supplied – may be incurred under a contract which provides that the taxpayer shall or may become the owner of the asset on performance of the contract. If so, that expenditure will qualify for PMA because of Section 67(1)(a).'

The above could apply in various circumstances. For example, the buyer may for his own reasons decide not to go ahead with the purchase or the supplier may default for whatever reason.

Legislation: CAA 2001, s. 11(4)(b), 67

Other material: CA 23350, CA 29260

Excluded expenditure

165-000   Plant or machinery for long funding leasing

Expenditure is not qualifying expenditure for the purposes of claiming plant and machinery allowances if it is incurred on the provision of plant or machinery for leasing under a long funding lease, in accordance with the rules in CAA 2001, Pt. 2, Ch. 6A. Allowances are denied in these circumstances to the lessor, but are normally available to the lessee. See 240-220ff. for a discussion of long funding leases generally and 160-700 for details of the rules that apply if an asset that has been used for such purposes starts to be used for the purposes of a different qualifying activity.

Legislation: CAA 2001, s. 34A

165-100   Plant used in a dwelling house, etc

Plant or machinery bought for use in a dwelling house is not allowable in certain cases. Specifically, expenditure on such items is not qualifying expenditure for an ordinary property business, an overseas property business or the special leasing of plant or machinery (see 152-600).

The HMRC manuals define a dwelling house as 'a building, or part of a building, which is a person's home'. The appropriate paragraph goes on to give the following guidance:

'A person's second or holiday home is a dwelling-house as is a flat which is used as a residence. A block of flats is not a dwelling-house although the individual flats within the block may be. A university hall of residence, accommodation used for holiday letting, a hospital, a nursing home or a prison are not dwelling-houses.'

HMRC announced at the end of 2008 (see HMRC Brief 66/08) that they were changing their view of how the legislation applies to student accommodation, on the grounds that 'the provision of student accommodation has evolved since expressing our view'. The new view is that '"communal" areas are not dwelling houses. Areas to which tenants do not have access are also not dwelling houses. However, all other areas are dwelling houses.' The HMRC guidance goes on to give the following example:

'**Example**

A student accommodation block has three floors, each with ten en-suite 'study bedrooms' that are individually lockable. Each floor also has a kitchen and TV room which are for the use of the ten occupants. The building has air-conditioning equipment located in the attic and a boiler located in the basement – only maintenance personnel have access to these areas.

In this example the kitchen and TV room are communal areas and not dwelling houses. The stairs and corridors which give access to other areas are also communal and are not dwelling houses. Tenants do not have access to the roof and attic and so they are not dwelling houses. However, the individual study bedrooms are dwelling houses.'

According to HMRC, 'this view extends to other types of multiple occupancy accommodation, such as those provided to key workers'.

Elsewhere, the manuals make the distinction:

'A lift or central heating system serving the communal parts of a block of residential flats qualifies . . . as it is not part of a dwelling house. A central heating system serving an individual residential flat does not however qualify.'

A non-statutory ten per cent 'wear and tear' allowance, may, however, be available instead, in accordance with ESC B47, which reads as follows:

'FURNISHED LETTINGS OF DWELLING HOUSES – WEAR AND TEAR OF FURNITURE

(1)   Section[s] 35(2), CAA 2001 specifically exclude[s] a claim for capital allowances on plant or machinery let for use in a dwelling house. Accordingly, capital allowances are not due on furniture and furnishings where the income from letting of furnished houses is

assessable under section 260 *Income Tax (Trading and Other Income) Act* 2005 (or Case VI, Schedule D for income tax cases up to 1994–95 and periods before 1 April 1988 for corporation tax) and is outside the scope of Section 503, ICTA 1988 (furnished holiday lettings) and section 327 *Income Tax (Trading and Other Income) Act* 2005.

(2) In practice, an allowance for wear and tear may be made, where capital allowances are not due, by deducting 10% of the net rent received. For this purpose the rent is reduced by any part of the occupier's council tax and water rates which the landlord pays. If the rental includes payments for services which would normally be borne by a tenant and the amounts involved are material, these too should be subtracted before calculating the 10% deduction.

(3) Where the 10% deduction is allowed, no further deduction is given for the cost of renewing furniture or furnishings, including suites, beds, carpets, curtains, linen, crockery, or cutlery. Nor is a further deduction allowed for chattels of a type which, in unfurnished accommodation, a tenant would normally provide for himself (for example, cookers, washing machines, dishwashers).

(4) However, in addition to the 10% allowance, the landlord can also claim the cost of renewing fixtures which are an integral part of the buildings, and which are revenue repairs to the fabric. These are fixtures which would not normally be removed by either tenant or owner if the property were vacated or sold (for example, baths, washbasins, toilets). Expenditure on renewing such items may be treated as expenditure on repairs even though the 10% allowance has been claimed.

(5) As an alternative to the 10% allowance, the actual cost of renewing furniture, furnishings and chattels may be claimed as a deduction. The amount to be allowed is the actual cost of the replacements excluding any additions or improvements, and after deducting the scrap value or sale price of the items replaced. The cost of the original items is not expenditure on renewals and is not allowable.

(6) Whichever basis a taxpayer chooses to adopt should be consistently applied to all furnished properties rented out.

(7) Before 1975–76, when the 10% basis started, there were several bases in common use. [HMRC] will not disturb these so long as the let properties remain in the same ownership. Any properties acquired subsequently should be dealt with on one of the two bases described above.'

Legislation: CAA 2001, s. 35

Other material: CA 20020, 23060; ESC B47

165-200 Accommodation for MPs and others

A more specific restriction applies to Westminster MPs and to members of the Scottish Parliament, the National Assembly for Wales or the Northern Ireland Assembly. Expenditure incurred by such people in or in connection with the use of residential or overnight accommodation will, in certain circumstances, not be qualifying expenditure. The

Plant and Machinery

restriction applies when the accommodation is to enable the individuals concerned to perform their MP, etc duties either at the place where the body sits or at their constituency.

Legislation: CAA 2001, s. 34

165-300   Production animals

If a farmer has made a claim to treat certain animals or other creatures on the herd basis (ITTOIA 2005, s. 111ff. or CTA 2009, s. 109ff.) then such animals, etc (or shares in them) do not count as qualifying expenditure for plant and machinery purposes. Similarly, of course, no claim for capital allowances may be made for animals that are treated as trading stock.

As regards the treatment of animals generally, see 260-060.

Legislation: CAA 2001, s. 38

165-400   Employment expenditure

See 155-800 regarding certain restrictions for employee expenditure.

165-500   Entertaining-related expenditure

Use of an asset for providing business entertainment (or anything incidental to the entertainment) is not treated as use for the purposes of a qualifying activity. Entertainment includes hospitality of any kind provided by a person carrying on a qualifying activity (or by any director or employee) in connection with that qualifying activity.

The restriction does not apply if it is a function of the person's trade or other qualifying activity to provide it, and if it is provided in the course of that activity, either for payment or by way of advertising to the public generally.

The question of whether expenses are incidental to the provision of entertainment was considered in the case of *Netlogic Consulting Ltd v HMRC*, concerning a company which held a function promoting its services to potential clients. The total cost of £2,481 consisted of two separate invoices: one for £1,800 paid to the caterers and another for £681 for room hire. Although the £1,800 was disallowed as an expense of entertaining, the £681 was held to be allowable. The reason given for the decision was that 'the entertainment was incidental to the promotional purpose of the meeting, rather than the hire of the room being incidental to the provision of the entertainment'.

A similar definition of 'business entertainment' was considered in the context of VAT in *C & E Commrs v Shaklee International & Anor*. The taxpayers marketed products through distributors who were not their employees. The distributors received training at meetings, in connection with which they were provided free of charge with food and, when necessary, overnight accommodation. The Court of Appeal held that the supplies of meals and accommodation constituted 'business entertainment'. The provision of free meals and accommodation fell within the term entertainment, and this entertainment was provided in connection with the taxpayers' business. The taxpayers argued that this was not business entertainment because there was a previously established contractual relationship between the taxpayer and the distributors, but this was rejected by the court, which held that the contractual relationship merely emphasised that the meals and accommodation were provided in connection with the taxpayers' business.

Legislation: CAA 2001, s. 269

Cases: *C & E Commrs v Shaklee International & Anor* (1981) 1 BVC 444; *Netlogic Consulting Ltd v HMRC* (2005) Sp C 477

165-600   Life assurance business

No capital allowances, except for plant and machinery, are given for management assets of any life assurance business carried on by a company. A 'management asset of any life assurance business carried on by a company' is defined as an asset that is provided for use, or used, for the management of that business of that company.

Assets held for other purposes by a company that is carrying on a life assurance business are also subject to restrictions. Any capital allowance in respect of an investment asset is treated as referable to the category or categories of business to which income arising from the asset is or would be referable. If the company is charged to tax in respect of its life assurance business under the rules relating to trading income, no allowance in respect of an investment asset is taken into account in calculating the company's profits from that business. Similarly, if the company is charged to tax under ICTA 1988, s. 436A (gross roll-up business), no allowance in respect of an investment asset is to be taken into account in calculating the company's profits from gross roll-up business.

See, also, 152-500 (giving effect to allowances and charges).

Legislation: CAA 2001, s. 544, 545

165-700   Depreciation subsidies

Where subsidies are received to cover depreciation arising from the use of plant and machinery, the expenditure on the asset is not treated as qualifying expenditure. (Before the enactment of CAA 2001, such subsidies were referred to as 'wear and tear subsidies'.)

This restriction does not apply, however, if the sums received are treated as income of the qualifying activity (eg as trading income).

The legislation also uses the term 'partial depreciation subsidy' to describe a payment to a person who has incurred qualifying expenditure for the purposes of a qualifying activity. The payment must have been made in respect of, or to take account of, part of the depreciation of the asset arising from its use for the purposes of the activity. Such a payment is excluded from the definition, however, if it is taken into account in calculating the recipient's profits in relation to the qualifying activity.

Where a person receives a partial depreciation subsidy, allowances are restricted on a just and reasonable basis; expenditure goes into a separate single-asset pool so that this can be achieved.

Legislation: CAA 2001, s. 37, 209–211

Meaning of plant

180-000 Meaning of plant: introduction

There is no definition in the *Capital Allowances Act* 2001 of the word 'plant'. Some types of expenditure are specifically included, for example the cost of thermal insulation for buildings used for qualifying activities and the expense of altering existing buildings in connection with the installation of plant and machinery. These, and other such items, are all subject to their own conditions and in each case the full details can be found elsewhere in this division.

Certain assets are excluded by statute from the definition of plant. All of these items are excluded on the grounds (broadly) that they are buildings or structures or parts thereof. The relevant legislation is fairly convoluted (though less so since the enactment of the *Capital Allowances Act* 2001) and contains an array of exceptions which generally have little in common, other than that they happen to have been the subject of tax cases reaching the courts before the legislation was enacted in 1994.

For the most part, the definition of plant has been left to the courts, where many an intellectual battle has been fought in an attempt to pin down the concept.

The meaning of 'machinery' is a separate issue, which has proved far less controversial, and an item does not need to qualify as both plant and machinery. If it is machinery, then the question of whether it is also plant is irrelevant; it will qualify for allowances if all the other conditions are met (but see 180-500 for assets used by employees). Comments on the meaning of machinery are given at 262-000.

Although the concept of 'plant and machinery' is of interest primarily for income tax and corporation tax purposes, the definition can also be relevant for capital gains tax (see 110-000) and, to a limited extent, for inheritance tax purposes. It is important to note that for these other purposes the meaning of 'plant' will be based on case law definitions only; CAA 2001, s. 21–23 will not apply. Similarly, where expenditure is deemed to be plant (for example building alterations connected with the installation of plant, thermal insulation, computer software, etc) then these deeming provisions apply only for the purposes of the CAA 2001 and do not extend to capital gains tax or inheritance tax legislation.

Legislation: CAA 2001, s. 21–23

180-050   Plants and gardens

In the case of *Cole Brothers Ltd v Phillips*, the judge commented on the origin of the term 'plant' used in the business sense, and made an etymological link with the more general, botanical, sense of the word. The concluding words in the following quotation provide a useful background in the search for a definition:

'I think it worthwhile spending a moment's time in reflecting briefly on what the botanical analogy is. In the field of botany "plant" is used in three quite separate contexts. It can mean a vegetable organism synthesizing its nourishment from inorganic materials by the use of chlorophyll. In this sense an oak tree is a plant, whilst the Matterhorn is not. It can mean a vegetable organism with a soft stem. In this sense a bluebell is a plant, but an oak tree is not. Neither of these senses affords the analogy. But the word can mean a vegetable organism deliberately placed in an artificially prepared setting.

A gardener can say "I am going to dig my flower beds in readiness for my plants" or, "I am going to buy some plants at my garden centre". It is this sense which gives it its analogical meanings, eg in medicine ("an organ transplant"), in crime ("it was planted on me"), or in industry, which is the sense we are now discussing, as the means by which a trade is carried on in an appropriately prepared setting. In each case, the contrast is between the thing implanted, ie the plant, and the prepared setting into which it is placed.'

As will be seen below, this distinction between 'the thing implanted' and 'the prepared setting' is fundamental to the issue of drawing the line between plant and premises.

Cases: *Cole Brothers Ltd v Phillips* [1982] BTC 208

180-100   Plant: a special tax meaning?

After more than 100 years of case law regarding the term 'plant' it ought at least to be clear whether the word is, for tax purposes, to have its ordinary meaning or whether it has developed into a specialist concept. Even over this issue, however, there has been apparent disagreement in the courts. In the case of *Hinton v Maden & Ireland Ltd*, Lord Reid said that it is 'an ordinary English word'. Similarly, Buckley LJ, in *Benson v The Yard Arm Club Ltd*, stated:

'the word "plant" is not a word of art; it must be interpreted according to its ordinary meaning as a word in the English language in the context in which it has to be construed; that is to say, the court of construction must interpret it as a man who speaks English and understands English accurately but not pedantically would interpret it in that context, applying it to the particular subject-matter in question in the circumstances of the particular case.'

Such are the arguments from the 'ordinary English word' camp. The opposition is led by Lord Denning in *Munby v Furlong*:

> 'in this Taxing Statute the courts do not apply the meaning to the word "plant" as the ordinary Englishman understands it. It has acquired by the course of decisions a special meaning in tax cases.'

This view was supported by Lord Wilberforce in *IR Commrs v Scottish & Newcastle Breweries Ltd*, arguing 'as case follows case, and one extension leads to another, the meaning of the word gradually diverges from its natural or dictionary meaning'. The culmination of this argument was perhaps in the *Cole Brothers* case, in which Oliver LJ argued that 'it is now beyond doubt that [the word "plant"] is used in the relevant section in an artificial and largely judge-made sense'. This comment was cited with approval by Lord Hailsham the following year.

On balance it now has to be accepted that the term has developed a technical meaning for tax purposes which extends beyond its natural sense.

Cases: *Hinton v Maden & Ireland Ltd* (1959) 38 TC 391; *Munby v Furlong* (1977) 50 TC 491; *Benson v The Yard Arm Club Ltd* (1979) 53 TC 67; *IR Commrs v Scottish & Newcastle Breweries Ltd* [1982] BTC 187

180-150   Can 'plant' be defined?

Clearly, every time a case concerning the issue of plant reaches the courts, the judges are forced to reach a decision in relation to the particular item in question. However, nobody has yet succeeded in providing a definition to resolve the question in all cases.

The main reason for this is that whether a particular item qualifies as plant depends on the precise use to which it is put and the exact circumstances of the trade, as well as on the nature of the asset itself. Vinelott J provided a picturesque expression of this when he commented in the *Cole Brothers* case that 'the word "plant" is a chameleon-like word which takes its colour from its context'. This both provides the justification for the approach taken by this book and at the same time sounds a note of caution. It provides the justification because this book recognises the danger of simply listing assets that do or do not qualify. Such lists are clearly unable to deal with the issue of the context in which an asset is used. A simple example illustrates this. A boat will normally qualify as an item of plant or machinery in, for example, a transport undertaking. On the other hand, case law shows that when a boat was moored and then used as a floating restaurant it was no longer considered to be an item of plant but merely became the premises for the restaurant business. As the judge said in that case, 'the context of the subject matter which is said to be plant cannot be ignored'.

The approach taken in the A to Z Chapter of this book (see 260-000ff.) is therefore to consider (implicitly or explicitly) the probable applications of each asset, so as to decide whether or not it is likely to qualify as plant in normal circumstances. Even so, and this is where the note of caution is needed, there will be unusual applications for particular items which it is not possible to foresee.

Before turning to consider the guidelines that are available when considering the meaning of the word plant, it is appropriate to provide a warning spoken by Stephenson LJ in the *Cole Brothers* case:

'the more definitions multiply, the less enviable grows the task of HM Inspectors of Taxes ... They may be pardoned for finding anything, or almost anything, to be or not to be plant and may be justified in making any number, or almost any number, of inconsistent concessions and illogical distinctions. It all depends on the circumstances, especially the work of the particular taxpayer, and (I feel bound to add) on how it strikes the particular judges of the question, whether in tax administration or on the judicial bench.'

The task may not be enviable for the tax inspector. However, he does at least have the benefit of hindsight and is able to deal with an established set of facts. The tax adviser, on the other hand, may need to make a decision before any expenditure is incurred as to the likely treatment of that expenditure. For such an adviser, too, the task is fraught with difficulties and grey areas of judgement. It is also worth bearing in mind the attitude which is rarely expressed but which doubtless has played a part in a number of cases. This attitude was stated explicitly by Lord Wilberforce in the *Scottish & Newcastle Breweries* case who said:

'I do not think that the courts should shrink, as a backstop, from asking whether it can really be supposed that Parliament desired to encourage a particular expenditure out of, in effect, taxpayers' money and perhaps ultimately, in extreme cases, to say that this is too much to stomach.'

It should not be assumed that Revenue staff necessarily have clear vision when it comes to the definition of plant. There is evidence of confusion even at Head Office level within HMRC. For example, the Decision Maker's Guide (dealing with tax credits) defines business assets for those purposes. It then says (DMG 35012) that a business asset:

'includes

- buildings;
- plant, machinery;
- vehicles; and
- office equipment.'

Given that vehicles and office equipment will almost invariably qualify as plant, it seems that the latter two categories are superfluous.

Cases: *IR Commrs v Scottish & Newcastle Breweries Ltd* [1982] BTC 187; *Cole Brothers Ltd v Phillips* [1982] BTC 208

180-200 *Yarmouth v France* – the beginnings of a definition

The starting point in the search for a definition of plant is not difficult to find. One case, concerned not with taxation but with compensation under the *Employers' Liability Act* 1880, has been quoted and referred to in nearly every judgment that has considered the meaning of plant. The case in question, *Yarmouth v France*, was heard by the Court of Appeal in 1887. The facts on which the decision was based have ceased to be of relevance but the following short quotation from the judgment of Lindley J has become the cornerstone:

> 'There is no definition of plant in the Act: but, in its ordinary sense, it includes whatever apparatus is used by a business man for carrying on his business – not his stock in trade which he buys or makes for sale; but all goods and chattels, fixed or moveable, live or dead, which he keeps for permanent employment in his business.'

This definition has received judicial approval at the highest level, as by the House of Lords in, for example, the cases of *Maden & Ireland* and of *IR Commrs v Barclay, Curle & Co Ltd*. It was also used as the justification for overturning, after 50 years, the *Daphne v Shaw* decision which had held that a law library was not plant. That the definition is sound is therefore now beyond doubt but it in fact tells us little beyond what is seemingly rather obvious. The contrast with trading stock is uncontroversial, as is the reference to 'fixed or moveable'. (Certainly, the capital gains tax legislation recognises that plant may or may not be fixed, as in the listing of assets that qualify for the relief for replacement of business assets, 'rollover relief'.) The concept that plant may be live or dead has not in practice exercised the courts, though the case itself concerned a horse and in recent times an inspector has been known to accept horses in a riding stable as plant for tax purposes.

The practical importance of the definition can perhaps be said to be threefold:

- that plant is apparatus;
- that it includes 'all goods and chattels'; and
- that it must be kept 'for permanent employment' in the business.

Of these three, the concept of 'permanent employment' is only rarely of significance. In cases where the permanence is in question, the alternative to treating an item as plant is likely to be a deduction as a trading expense. Under the *Finance Act* 1954, however, a special investment allowance was, for a short period, made available. The case of *Hinton v Maden & Ireland* concerned this special allowance. It went all the way to the House of Lords over the issue of whether knives and lasts with an average life of three years were plant. Reference was made to the *Yarmouth v France* definition and the conclusion was reached that:

> 'The reference to permanent employment in the business demands some degree of durability. This, I think, is satisfied in the present case by the life of three years.'

The same case is also relevant for the concept of 'all goods and chattels' in the related matter of whether numerous short-lived small items can qualify as plant. Lord Reid commented that:

'Subject to one point [that of durability], I have no doubt that these knives and lasts are plant in the ordinary sense of the word. It is true that they are numerous, small and cheap. But one trader may have to use a few large articles while another may have to use a large number of small articles.'

Apart from this, however, the significance of 'goods or chattels' has not unduly concerned the courts. In *Jarrold v John Good & Sons Ltd*, it was considered that the reference to goods and chattels 'impliedly excludes the premises in which the business is carried on'. This interpretation was also accepted in *The Yard Arm Club* case and subsequently in *Wimpy International Ltd v Warland*.

Of the different aspects of the *Yarmouth v France* definition, however, it is undoubtedly the reference to 'apparatus used by a business man for carrying on his business' that has given rise to the greatest level of argument in the courts. The contrast has been drawn between the 'apparatus with which' and the 'setting within which' a business is conducted. This dichotomy is, however, an uneasy one, for on occasions the two are not mutually exclusive, albeit now subject to the 1994 legislation (see 180-000). Furthermore, the definition of apparatus has itself given rise to a new problem, the so-called 'functional test' which, in turn, raises a different set of considerations. These concepts are considered at 180-300.

Cases: *Yarmouth v France* (1887) 19 QBD 647; *Daphne v Shaw* (1926) 11 TC 256; *Hinton v Maden & Ireland Ltd* (1959) 38 TC 391; *Jarrold v John Good & Sons Ltd* (1963) 40 TC 681; *IR Commrs v Barclay, Curle & Co Ltd* (1969) 45 TC 221; *Wimpy International Ltd v Warland* [1989] BTC 58

180-250 Apparatus or setting

As mentioned at 180-200 above, the earliest definition of plant came from a case that had nothing to do with tax. Given the significance that the term has developed for tax purposes, there is a small irony in the fact that the next stage in the development of the definition was again in a non-tax case, this time under the *War Damage Act* 1943. The case in question was that of *J. Lyons & Co Ltd v Attorney General*.

The facts and issues are summarised in the headnote to the case, as follows:

'A tea-shop having been damaged by enemy action in 1941, the company owning it claimed a cost-of-works payment ... which included the cost of replacing electric lamps used for lighting the premises, and fittings annexed thereto, as being "plant" or "machinery" ... Held, that the electric lamps and fittings were not part of the apparatus used for carrying on the business, but were part of the setting in which the business was carried on, and, therefore, were not "plant", the subject of compensation within the Act.'

As the key issue to arise is the distinction between setting on the one hand and plant on the other, it is worth looking at the reasoning of the judge.

'In the present case, the question at issue may, I think, be put thus: Are the lamps and fitments properly to be regarded as part of the setting in which the business is carried on or as part of the apparatus used for carrying on the business? The lamps and their fitments are owned by a caterer and used in premises exclusively devoted to catering purposes, but the presence of lamps in this building is not dictated by the nature of the particular trade there carried on or by the fact that it is for trade purposes that the building is used. Lamps are required to enable the building to be used where natural light is insufficient. The actual lamps themselves, so far as the evidence goes, present no special feature either in construction, purpose or position, and, being supplied with electricity from public suppliers, they form no part of an electric lighting plant in or on the hereditament. In my opinion, these lamps are not, in these circumstances, properly described as "plant", but are part of the general setting in which the business is carried on. They would not, I think, in any catalogue of this trader's assets, fall under the heading "machinery and plant", and I hold that the lamps and the fitments in question are not machinery or plant for the purposes of the War Damage Act, 1943.'

The key point to draw out of this ruling is probably the comment that the lamps presented 'no special feature either in construction, purpose or position'. Any such special feature would perhaps have swayed the opinion – the lamps would perhaps no longer have been perceived as 'part of the general setting' but rather as some trade-specific apparatus brought into that setting.

So how has this apparatus-versus-setting distinction survived more than half a century of case decisions? As with all other aspects of the definition of plant, the picture is not clear cut. Certainly, the principle has survived and has received judicial approval over and over again. For example, in the *Cole Brothers* case, Oliver LJ reworked the same formula when he commented as follows:

'At risk of propounding yet a further refinement, it seems to me that the authorities, with one possible exception, demonstrate that the question (however expressed) which the court must ask itself is whether the particular subject-matter under consideration either itself performs, or is a necessary or integral part of that which performs, simply and solely the function of "housing" the business or whether, as its sole function or as an additional function, it performs some other distinct business purpose.'

But the distinction is not always clear-cut. In *Jarrold v Good*, which concerned moveable partitions, the judge considered the reasoning of the *J Lyons & Co* case (see above) and questioned whether the contrast between apparatus on the one hand and setting on the other could always stand scrutiny:

'I do not want to appear to doubt in any way the correctness of that decision on the facts of that case, but it seems to me that the setting in which a business is carried on, and the apparatus used for carrying on a business, are not always necessarily mutually exclusive. Certain fixtures or chattels in certain trades may well represent the setting in which the business is carried on, from one point of view, and apparatus used for carrying on the business, from another point of view. This point is, I think, the same or akin to that made by Uthwatt, J., when he mentioned that the lamps "present no special feature either in construction, purpose or position". In the present case the trade is that of a shipping agent carried on in an office building in the manner set out in the Case Stated. In relation to that trade, as so carried on, it seems to me that these partitions are from one point of view the setting in which the business is carried on, but from another point of view apparatus used for carrying on the business. If one considers the staff engaged in the respective rooms formed by the partitions at any given moment, the partitions, like the floor and ceiling, are the setting in which the staff carry out their duties. But if one considers the Company's policy of office organisation as set out in the Case Stated, then the partitions are fixtures specially designed to enable an appropriate and varying number of employees to perform their duties in an appropriate and varying number of sections, according to the state of the Company's business at the time. It seems to me to be impossible to deny to fixtures possessing this character the title of apparatus used by the Company for carrying on its business. Once this is accepted, the partitions clearly qualify for allowances as plant, notwithstanding that, from another point of view, they may be part of the setting.'

In other words, the judge was accepting the original *Yarmouth v France* reasoning (as the partitions were apparatus they would 'clearly qualify' as plant) but was limiting the application of the *J Lyons & Co* principle of contrasting plant with setting. This limitation was approved in the same case in the Court of Appeal, where Donovan LJ concluded that 'you cannot always answer the question, "Is this plant?" by asking, "Is it part of the setting or not?"'

So is the distinction between apparatus and setting of any continuing value in deciding whether or not an item qualifies as plant? It is tempting to conclude that the courts are saying no more than that the distinction applies except when it does not apply! The Leeds Permanent Building Society successfully went to court to establish that certain decorative screens in their windows were plant. The judge in that case (*Leeds Permanent Building Society v Proctor*) commented as follows:

'In applying that conception of the apparatus used by a business man for carrying on his business, it was found convenient to draw a distinction between the setting in which a business is carried on and the apparatus with which a business is carried on, though subsequent developments have shown that there are overlapping cases where the distinction is not in itself decisive because one object may partake of both characters. Leaving those overlapping cases to one side, that which is the setting in which the trader performs his trade is not plant; the apparatus with which he performs it is plant.'

The conclusion would appear to be that an item may be apparatus or it may be setting or it may be both. For an inspector to show that it is not plant he will need to demonstrate that it is *only* the setting. Even this argument cannot be pushed too far, however, as counsel for *Wimpy International* found. The commissioners had disallowed the cost of shop fronts as plant as 'their principal function is to form a necessary part of the premises'. A Mr Aaronson had argued that this showed that the commissioners had 'misunderstood or misapplied' the functional test. Lloyd LJ in the Court of Appeal considered that argument as follows:

'The question is not, he says, whether the principal function of the shop fronts is to keep out the weather, or whatever, but whether that is their sole function. If the shop fronts have some other business function as well, for example, by capturing attention of the passer-by or by allowing the already captive customer to see out . . . then the shop fronts qualify as plant . . . I cannot accept that it is correct to subject the Commissioners' decision to this sort of linguistic analysis.'

Nevertheless, the principle would seem to remain.

It should be remembered, however, that all of the cases referred to in the above paragraphs predate the 1994 legislation which restricts the definition of plant. For an item to qualify as plant, it will have to satisfy two tests. First, it must be shown that the item in question does not fall foul of the legislation now in CAA 2001, s. 21 and 22. Second, it must be demonstrated that on the case law principles discussed above it is properly treated as apparatus.

A more recent analysis of the distinction between plant and premises was given in the *Wetherspoon* case (considered in greater depth at 262-150). Part of that case concerned the treatment of decorative panelling in a pub. The commissioners took the view that the panelling turned the premises from an unpanelled room into a room that was mainly panelled, but was an unexceptional component of the type of premises (by contrast, for example, to the fixed but not easily removable metal sculpture, that was held to be plant in the *Scottish & Newcastle Breweries* case. Balancing all the considerations, the commissioners concluded that the panelling was more appropriately described as having become part of the premises than as having retained a separate identity. Therefore it did not qualify as plant.

Cases: *Yarmouth v France* (1887) 19 QBD 647; *J. Lyons & Co Ltd v Attorney General* [1944] Ch 281; *Jarrold v John Good & Sons Ltd* (1963) 40 TC 681; *IR Commrs v Scottish & Newcastle Breweries Ltd* [1982] BTC 187; *Cole Brothers Ltd v Phillips* [1982] BTC 208; *Leeds Permanent Building Society v Proctor* [1982] BTC 347; *Wimpy International Ltd v Warland* [1989] BTC 58; *J D Wetherspoon plc v R & C Commrs* (2007) Sp C 657

180-300   The functional test

Alongside the apparatus-versus-setting distinction has developed a further test – that of function. The basic principle is that an item will qualify as plant if it can be shown to be functional within the business. However, this introduces its own complications.

The concept was mentioned in the 1958 case of *Hinton v Maden & Ireland*, where the knives and lasts that were the subject of the case were held to be plant. As the commissioners found, 'the knives and lasts performed an indispensable function in the process of manufacture'.

In the *Barclay, Curle* case, too, it was made clear that the function of the item in dispute needed to be considered, in addition to its inherent nature. 'It seemed to us that what we had to do was to consider the nature and function of the dry dock on the evidence adduced before us'. In the Court of Session in that case, the judge found that 'the dry dock was not "merely the setting" in which the work was carried on. In addition to being the setting it is properly described as "apparatus" performing a function in the work'.

Once the case reached the House of Lords, the function issue was further considered by Lord Reid in the following terms:

'Undoubtedly this concrete dry dock is a structure, but is it also plant? The only reason why a structure should also be plant which has been suggested or which has occurred to me is that it fulfils the function of plant in the trader's operations. And, if that is so, no test has been suggested to distinguish one structure which fulfils such a function from another. I do not say that every structure which fulfils the function of plant must be regarded as plant, but I think that one would have to find some good reason for excluding such a structure. And I do not think that mere size is sufficient.'

The House of Lords judgment was a majority verdict, with two of the five judges dissenting. One of these, Lord Hodson, observed:

'I do not find the argument based on function convincing. No doubt function is a useful test and relevant in considering whether or not a thing is properly described as "plant", but function is not decisive. Whether an item is plant or not depends on all the circumstances of the case.'

The 'function' argument was developed in particular in the early to mid-1970s, where a series of cases wrestled with the concept in an attempt to pin down the all-elusive definition of plant. In the case of *Dixon v Fitch's Garage Ltd*, counsel for the company had sought to argue that the canopy over the forecourt was plant as it was commercially desirable (or even necessary) to have such a cover. The judge would have none of it, however:

'That, to my mind, is an amenity test as distinct from a functional test, and is not a permissible test. The right test is the functional test.'

This can be contrasted with *St John's School v Ward*, where the judge did not want to give any weight to the issue of function:

'In my judgment, it is necessary to find, not the name of the building or its function, but whether the building is in truth a building within which the business is carried on or, to go back to the words of *Yarmouth v France*, whether it is apparatus used by the businessman for carrying on the business.'

The contradiction between the two approaches was perhaps best resolved in the *Wimpy* case, where Fox said:

'It is proper to consider the function of the item in dispute. But the question is what does it function as? If it functions as part of the premises it is not plant. The fact that the building in which a business is carried on is by its construction particularly well-suited to the business, or indeed was specially built for that business, does not make it plant. Its suitability is simply the reason why the business is carried on there. But it remains the place in which the business is carried on and is not something with which the business is carried on.'

A similar conclusion had in fact been reached some years earlier in the *Yard Arm Club* case, where the judge had made the following observation:

'If a chattel, such as a ship or a hulk, only provides accommodation for a business and has the characteristic, and only performs the function, of premises, that chattel does not qualify as plant for the purpose of capital allowances. The fact that a ship or hulk could be used as plant in many businesses does not enable a taxpayer to claim capital allowances for a ship or hulk which performs no function in the business actually carried on by the taxpayer Company, other than the function of premises providing accommodation for that business.'

The same point was well made in the *Cole Brothers* case:

Plant and Machinery

'The question (however expressed) which the Court must ask itself is whether the particular subject-matter under consideration either itself performs, or is a necessary or integral part of that which performs, simply and solely the function of "housing" the business, or whether, as its sole function or as its additional function, it performs some other distinct business purpose.'

So the conclusion to be drawn is that 'function' on its own is of rather limited value. Any asset that meets the 'wholly and exclusively' criterion must by definition have a function within the trade. The question, though, is whether it functions (on the one hand) as the apparatus or (on the other) as the setting of the business. As such, function leads back to the earlier distinction and, ultimately, to the original *Yarmouth v France* definition that continues to underpin every case concerned with the definition of plant.

Cases: *Hinton v Maden & Ireland Ltd* (1959) 38 TC 391; *IR Commrs v Barclay, Curle & Co Ltd* (1969) 45 TC 221; *St John's School v Ward* (1974) 49 TC 524; *Dixon v Fitch's Garage Ltd* (1975) 50 TC 509; *Benson v The Yard Arm Club Ltd* (1979) 53 TC 67; *Cole Brothers Ltd v Phillips* [1982] BTC 208

Other material: CA 21100

180-350   Décor

A further development of the concept has been on the question of decorative assets used in the hotel and similar trades. This is considered under the heading of décor at 260-500. See also 262-150, which is specifically concerned with the treatment of wood panelling in a pub, but which also addresses some general principles about the distinction between plant and premises in connection with expenditure on creating ambience.

180-400   Football League letter

Given the difficulties in determining what is or is not plant, it is very helpful to have from HMRC a list of items that are generally accepted as being plant. The following extract from HMRC Capital Allowances manual gives details of a letter sent by the Revenue to the Football League in January 1991. It is of much wider interest than merely to football grounds. It must be noted that this represents the Revenue view before the enactment of the *Finance Act* 1994, introducing what is now broadly at CAA 2001, s. 21–26 (and obviously long before the introduction of the 'integral features' rules in 2008). Nevertheless, the declared intention of that legislation was to 'leave the present position unchanged':

'Football clubs may incur expenditure on ground improvements in order to implement the recommendations of the Taylor report. The Inland Revenue had discussions with the Football League about what expenditure is likely to qualify for capital allowances. Following those discussions the Inland Revenue sent the Football League a letter on 25 January 1991 indicating what expenditure is likely to qualify. The letter listed as an appendix the sort of assets used by a football club in its trade which would normally qualify as plant or machinery. This is the list.

(1)   Advertising hoardings and perimeter boards which are not simply part of a perimeter fence or other structure.

(2)   Air conditioning plant, fans and ventilation machinery.

(3)   Automatic exit doors and gates.

(4)   Bicycle holders.

(5)   Cameras, televisions, video recorders.

(6)   Cars, coaches and vans.

(7)   Computers, printers, photocopiers, typewriters and cash registers.

(8)   Cookers, fridges, freezers, microwaves, dishwashing machines.

(9)   Crush barriers securely fixed to the ground are not plant or machinery but they may come within the 1975 safety legislation and so qualify under Section 32 CAA2001.

(10)   Electric scoreboards and visual displays.

(11)   Fencing is not plant or machinery but it may come within the 1975 safety legislation and so qualify under Section 32 CAA2001.

(12)   Fire alarm systems, fire extinguishers, sprinkler systems.

(13)   Floodlighting.

(14)   Floor coverings which are not part of the building or structure; for example, carpets (but not tiles which are stuck down).

(15)   Goalposts and certain movable training equipment of a capital nature, for example, a vaulting horse (but not equipment which is part of the premises).

(16)   Heating installations, boilers and water heaters.

(17)   Lifts and hoists.

(18)   Public address equipment – microphones, amplifiers and loudspeakers.

(19)   Racking, shelving, cupboards and furniture.

(20)   Telephones and telephone equipment, for example, private exchanges.

(21)   Toilet sanitary ware, sinks and basins, baths and showers whether for staff or public (but not the mains water supply).

(22)   Turnstiles and spectator counting equipment.

The letter gave some guidance on seats. It said that most modern types of seats are likely to qualify as plant or machinery, both plain plastic tip-up seats and more luxurious types of seat. It makes it clear that seating which is no more than an integral part of the stand will not qualify.

It says that the incidental costs of installing seats, or any other type of plant or machinery, may qualify under Section 25 CAA 2001. It says that expenditure will not qualify as incidental if it creates an essentially new asset such as a stand or a terrace with an entirely new rake. It also says that we would not expect expenditure to qualify as incidental if it is large in proportion to the cost of the plant or machinery being installed.

Remember that not all expenditure incurred by clubs to comply with the requirements of the Football Spectators Act 1989 will qualify for capital allowances. The normal rules will apply.

Plant and Machinery

69

The letter states that expenditure on the fabric of a police control box will not qualify for capital allowances. We have now been advised that some local authorities take the view that they have the power under the Safety at Sports Grounds Act 1975 to require police control rooms to be installed. If that happens the expenditure will qualify under Section 32 CAA 2001.'

Legislation: CAA 2001, s. 21–26

Other material: CA 21230

180-450   Disability Discrimination Act: HMRC guidance

Since 1 October 2004, the *Disability Discrimination Act* has required service providers to make 'reasonable adjustments' to their premises to tackle any physical features that prevent disabled people from using their services. There is nothing in the Capital Allowances legislation to give special treatment to the costs that may result from that Act. However, HMRC have issued (on their website) guidelines on the treatment of such expenditure, recently updated to take into account the 2008 changes. In relation to the question of capital allowances, the guidance contains the following comments:

'**Ramps**

Expenditure on building or installing a permanent ramp to facilitate access by members of the public qualifies only if the work is carried out to an industrial or agricultural building or "qualifying hotel". Relief is given for the expenditure under the IBA code or agricultural buildings allowance ABA code.

Businesses that buy moveable ramps that are not permanently fixed to the building are able to claim PMAs [i.e., Plant and Machinery Allowances] on the cost of the ramp.

Toilets and washing facilities

Minor adjustments, such as changing doors on cubicles from opening inwards to opening outwards, would normally be wholly deductible for tax purposes as revenue expenditure.

The costs of making building alterations to toilets (for example, to widen a doorway to facilitate wheelchair access) are not allowable for tax purposes, unless the building is an industrial or agricultural building or qualifying hotel. In those circumstances, the alteration costs qualify for IBA or ABA capital allowances.

The cost of new sanitary ware installed to comply with DDA requirements qualifies for PMAs. So do the costs of installing the sanitary ware.

Signs

The costs of permanent signage qualify for PMAs.

Expenditure on, say, affixing warning transparencies on glass doors or similar surfaces qualifies for relief as a revenue expense. The use of coloured paint to make things easier to see (by, for instance, painting doors, step edges, or passages in contrasting colours) is allowable in full for tax purposes.

Hand rails

Where businesses replace existing handrails with special handrails to ease access for disabled people, the expenditure would normally be accepted as a repair and would be deductible in full.

Where new handrails are installed for the specific purpose of helping customers with mobility impairments, the cost would constitute capital expenditure but would qualify for PMAs.

Lighting and electrical systems

From 1 April 2008 new expenditure on lighting and electrical systems qualifies for a 10 per cent writing down allowance per annum as integral features. Electrical systems do not include computer, telecommunication, and surveillance systems (including their wiring), nor fire alarm or burglar alarm systems.

If the lighting appears on the Energy Technology Criteria List 100 per cent first-year allowances can be claimed. More guidance can be found in the Capital allowances manual.

Internal and external doors

Usually, doors are considered to be part of the premises and do not qualify for capital allowances. As such, no allowances are due on installing new doors.

But where a door is no longer fit for use, it is likely that the cost of replacing it would qualify for relief as a repair, and so is wholly deductible as a revenue expense.

Quite often simply replacing a traditional door handle with a D-shaped or similar handle enables service providers to provide improved access.

A door handle would normally be an integral part of the door to which it is affixed, with the result that it would not qualify for PMAs. Any replacement of the door handle, however, counts as a repair, and so is allowable as a revenue expense. Some mechanical door handles may not qualify as a repair, where they are actually an improvement over the previous handle, but they could qualify for PMAs as machinery.

Lifts

Where expenditure is incurred on constructing a new commercial building the cost of constructing the lift shaft is not allowable.

However, the cost of installing a lift or replacing an existing lift with a modern lift is considered to be expenditure on an integral feature and qualifies for a 10 per cent writing down allowance per annum. In addition, if incidental to the cost of installing the lift machinery, the costs of installing the lift shaft will also qualify for PMAs. More guidance can be found in the capital allowances manual.

Steps and stairs

Expenditure on knocking down steps and replacing them with ramps is not allowable. However, expenditure on adding fluorescent and coloured strips to the edges of steps, approaching and within business premises, to assist access by visually impaired people, is allowed as revenue expenditure on repairs and maintenance.

Plant and Machinery

Alterations to walls and floors

Alterations to the fabric of a building are not normally allowable for tax purposes, unless the building is an industrial or agricultural building or qualifying hotel or unless the alterations are incidental to the installation of plant or machinery. So any expenditure on making new doorways or widening existing doorways would not normally qualify for relief.

However, repairs to floors, for example, to level out uneven surfacing due to wear and tear over time, is allowable as a revenue expense.

Also, HM Revenue & Customs (HMRC) accept that painting walls or floors in bright contrasting colours, to assist access by visually impaired people, is allowable as revenue expenditure on repairs and maintenance.

Car parks

HMRC accept that expenditure on, for example, redefining parking areas by repainting parking bays to provide wider, designated bays for disabled parking, is a revenue expense, which is allowable in full for tax purposes.

Where the work is more substantial, for example, to include car park resurfacing, then as long as there is no improvement element, the expenditure is allowable as normal revenue expenditure on repairs.

Paths

Normally expenditure on paths or land does not qualify for capital allowances. However there is a distinction between improving and repairing property. While expenditure on improvements generally counts as capital expenditure (which does not normally qualify for allowances) expenditure on repairs is a revenue expense, which is allowable in full for tax purposes.

Thus, where a business incurs expenditure on its paths in order to remove obstacles that could present a danger to the disabled, for example on:

- replacing cracked or uneven paving slabs
- cutting back protruding or overhanging objects, grass or other vegetation

the expenditure is revenue expenditure and is allowable in full.'

Other material: www.hmrc.gov.uk/specialist/disability-act-guidance.htm

180-500 Assets used by directors or employees

There is a potential pitfall where an asset is provided for the private use of a director or employee. In these circumstances, HMRC accept that the asset may be a legitimate part of the remuneration package of the individual concerned (such that a liability on additional earnings will normally arise). However, it may be that the asset will not qualify as plant or machinery.

In practice, as long as the asset is a machine, HMRC instructions to inspectors say that the allowance should be accepted. Examples given include cars, aircraft, yachts, washing machines and dishwashers. However, if the asset is not machinery then it will only qualify for capital allowances if it functions in the trade as plant. HMRC give as examples furniture or paintings provided for use in the director's home. Even though a benefit in kind charge will arise, HMRC view is that the assets are not 'apparatus with which the company's trade is carried on' (see 180-200) and so allowances may be denied.

Other material: CA 27100

Annual investment allowances

181-000 Introduction

Overview

The concept of the 'annual investment allowance' (AIA) first applied to expenditure incurred from 'the relevant date', defined as 1 April 2008 for corporation tax, and 6 April 2008 for income tax purposes.

In essence, the AIA gives full tax relief (similar in effect to a 100 per cent first-year allowance) for the first £50,000 of annual expenditure incurred by a business on plant and machinery. Expenditure must be incurred by a 'qualifying person', defined to mean an individual, a partnership consisting only of individuals, or a company.

Expenditure is said to be 'AIA qualifying expenditure' if it is incurred by such a person and is not subject to any of the general exclusions described at 181-150. The person claiming the allowance must own the plant or machinery at some time during the chargeable period for which the claim is made.

The declared purpose of the AIA is to 'target investment support on all businesses that are investing for growth and help alleviate the cash flow constraints which confront small and growing businesses'. The introduction of the AIA coincides with the withdrawal of most first-year allowances (see 185-000ff.) and also with changes in corporation tax rates.

Legislation: CAA 2001, s. 38A, s. 51A

Scope of the AIA

The AIA offers full and immediate tax relief, for all sizes of business, for (broadly) the first £50,000 of expenditure on plant and machinery in the year (but see 181-050). The AIA is made for the chargeable period in which the expenditure is incurred (but without the benefit of the pre-trading expenditure rules of CAA 2001, s. 12: see 152-700ff.).

Cars and expenditure on 'green' technology continue to be treated separately, but the AIA is available for expenditure on all other plant and machinery, including long-life assets and the new category of 'integral features' (see 247-000ff.). Expenditure in excess of the annual £50,000 allowance may attract writing-down allowances (or first-year allowances: see below and 185-050) in the same accounting period.

Plant and Machinery

Assets provided only partly for business use

Where an asset is provided partly for purposes other than those of the qualifying activity carried on by the person, AIAs may be given to the extent that is just and reasonable in relation to the proportion in which the expenditure was incurred for the purposes of the qualifying activity. So if an asset costs £20,000, and is used one-quarter for private purposes, AIAs can be claimed on £15,000. It would seem to follow, from the way that the legislation is worded, that AIAs can be claimed on other expenditure of up to £35,000 (rather than £30,000).

This interpretation is open to argument, however, and may in any case be contrasted with the position of a trader who buys one asset in the year, costing more than £50,000, and who makes private use of that asset. In that case, the £50,000 would be given first but would then be restricted by reference to the private use. So, if the asset cost £60,000 and was used one quarter for private purposes, AIA would initially be given of £50,000 but this would then be restricted to £37,500.

Writing-down allowances would also be due in the same period, initially calculated as 20 per cent of the remaining £10,000, to give an allowance of £2,000, but then restricted by virtue of the private use to give £1,500.

As such, total allowances would be given in the year of £39,000.

Legislation: CAA 2001, s. 51A(11)(b) and s. 205

Partial depreciation subsidy

If a person is to receive a *partial* depreciation subsidy then AIAs are to be reduced to an amount which is 'just and reasonable'. This does not apply if the subsidy is treated as trading income of the recipient.

Legislation: CAA 2001, s. 210

Other restrictions on relief

The AIA is subject to various 'general exclusions' described at 181-150, and to several targeted anti-avoidance measures (see 181-200 and 181-350).

Restrictions are also made under CAA 2001, s. 217 and s. 241 (additional VAT liabilities – connected persons and contracts where a person may become plant owner). See also CAA 2001, s. 236 with further measures about additional VAT liabilities.

First-year allowances

The legislation specifies that a person may not claim an AIA and a first-year allowance in respect of the same expenditure. When, from April 2008, all remaining first-year allowances were given at 100 per cent, the provision appeared to be simply to remove any possibility of claiming double relief for the same expenditure. Now, with the re-introduction of temporary first-year allowances, the position is more complex than it seems on a quick reading of the legislation: see 185-050.

Legislation: CAA 2001, s. 52A

181-050   Amount of annual investment allowance

The standard maximum amount of the AIA is £50,000, but this figure may be amended by Treasury order.

The figure of £50,000 is proportionately increased or reduced if the chargeable period is greater or shorter than one year. This had important implications for periods of account spanning the introduction of the new relief in April 2008, as explained at 181-400.

Legislation: CAA 2001, s. 51A

181-100   Claiming the annual investment allowance

Subject to various 'general exclusions' (see 181-150), and to various other restrictions (see 181-350), a business may choose which expenditure to include as AIA qualifying expenditure. This will be relevant if costs have been incurred on assets that potentially attract writing-down allowances at different rates.

> ### *Example*
>
> A business spends £40,000 on general plant and machinery and £25,000 on integral features (see 247-000ff.). It will wish to treat the whole of the latter as AIA qualifying expenditure so that the excess £15,000 (£40,000 plus £25,000, less £50,000) can attract allowances at the main WDA rate of 20 per cent rather than at the lower rate of 10 per cent.

A person entitled to the AIA may claim AIA on a reduced amount of qualifying expenditure if desired (perhaps so as to avoid or reduce a future balancing charge). In such a case, however, any remaining allowances given on the expenditure will be by way of writing-down allowances only. This is because the AIA can only be given for the chargeable period in which the expenditure is incurred.

For businesses that rarely, or never, incur more than £50,000 of capital expenditure, the changes represent a welcome acceleration of tax relief. If such a business spends, for example, £20,000 in the year, it can obtain full tax relief for that cost in the year itself, whereas in the past it would have obtained relief on no more than half in the first year, with the balance relieved over an indefinite future period.

For such businesses, the changes also bring considerable simplification – future expenditure will simply be written off in the year in which it is incurred, whether by way of a 100 per

Plant and Machinery

cent FYA for expenditure on green technology or (much more frequently) by way of an AIA. As such, there may be no need to calculate WDAs. The main exceptions will be for cars (which do not qualify for AIAs: see 200-300) and for expenditure brought forward at the time the new rules are introduced. As regards the latter, there are provisions allowing small pools of up to £1,000 of expenditure to be written off, so that they do not need to be carried forward indefinitely (illustrated at 190-275). Apart from this, however, there is no question of carrying forward any unused AIA. If a business starts up in 2009, and spends £10,000 per year on plant and machinery, it will be able to write off the whole amount year by year. If, however, it spends £70,000 in 2012, it will still only be able to claim AIA of £50,000 in that year. The balance of £20,000 will attract writing-down allowances, in principle at 20 per cent per year, on the reducing value. Only when that value falls below £1,000 will it be possible to write the remainder off.

Legislation: CAA 2001, s. 51A

181-150 General exclusions

No AIA is available:

- for the chargeable period in which the qualifying activity is permanently discontinued;
- for cars (as defined: see below);
- for expenditure incurred for the purposes of a ring fence trade in respect of which tax is chargeable under ICTA 1988, s. 501A;
- where the provision of the plant or machinery is connected with a change in the nature or conduct of the trade or business carried on by someone other than the person incurring the expenditure, and the obtaining of the AIA was the main benefit (or one of the main benefits) that could reasonably be expected to arise from the making of the change;
- where existing plant (or plant received as a gift) is brought into use for the purposes of a qualifying activity; or
- where plant that has been provided for long funding leasing is brought into use for other purposes.

The last two exclusions listed immediately above are subject to the rules in CAA 2001, s. 161 (pre-trading expenditure on mineral exploration and access).

Legislation: CAA 2001, s. 38B

Cars (and other vehicles)

As noted above, no annual investment allowances are given for 'cars'.

The definition of a car is given, for capital allowance purposes from April 2009, at CAA 2001, s. 268A, considered in depth at 200-020ff. For such purposes, a car was specifically defined, until April 2009, to include a motorcycle, so no AIAs were given for expenditure on motorcycles. However, this definition was amended, (broadly from April 2009, but see 200-620) to exclude a motor cycle.

More generally, the denial of AIAs for cars means that the distinction between a car and a van gains new significance. Some care is needed, as the definition for capital allowance purpose is not identical to that applying in the context of benefits in kind (see ITEPA 2003, s. 115(1)), but precedents in that context may still be helpful as both definitions use the concept of a vehicle 'of a type not commonly used as a private vehicle and unsuitable' 'to be so used' or 'for such use'.

181-200   Other restrictions on relief

Overview

The annual investment allowance (AIA) rules contain numerous anti-avoidance provisions, the main purpose of which is to prevent artificial multiplication of the £50,000 annual investment limit, though many normal commercial structures (such as groups of companies) are also caught. More specifically, these provisions relate to groups of companies, other companies under common control, qualifying activities under common control, and so on. A further restriction denies AIAs where arrangements have been entered into for a 'disqualifying purpose' (see 181-350).

The headings used below follow those of the legislation, covering five different types of restriction and various related definitions. The term 'company' has the meaning given to it by ICTA 1988, s. 832(1), and thus includes any body corporate or unincorporated association but does not include a partnership, a local authority or a local authority association.

Companies (first restriction)

A company may carry on more than one qualifying activity. Nevertheless, it is only entitled to one AIA in respect of all its qualifying activities in the chargeable period (the 'first restriction'). The company may, however, allocate the AIA to its AIA qualifying expenditure as it sees fit.

Example

A company carries on a trade and an ordinary property business. The company may only use one AIA in total but it may choose to allocate the £50,000 wholly to one or other activity, or it may wish to split the allocation between the two activities.

This general principle is subject to the special rules described below relating to groups of companies generally, to groups under common control, and to other companies that are under common control.

Legislation: CAA 2001, s. 51B

77

Groups of companies (second restriction)

As a general principle, a group of companies has to share a single AIA (the 'second restriction'). The companies may allocate the AIA to the 'relevant AIA qualifying expenditure' (see below) as they see fit.

More specifically, this restriction applies to:

- a company which, in a given financial year, is a parent undertaking in relation to one or more other companies; and
- those other companies.

A company ('P') is treated as a parent undertaking of another company ('C') in any given financial year if P is a parent undertaking of C at the end of C's chargeable period ending in that financial year. For these purposes, the term 'parent undertaking' is defined in accordance with the *Companies Act* 2006, s. 1162.

The 'relevant AIA qualifying expenditure' is the AIA qualifying expenditure incurred by the companies in chargeable periods that end in the financial year referred to above.

This restriction is subject to the rules described immediately below in relation to groups of companies under common control.

Legislation: CAA 2001, s. 51C

Groups of companies under common control (third restriction)

A third restriction applies, allowing just one AIA between the various companies, where – in a given financial year – two or more *groups of companies* are controlled by the same person and where they are related to one another. The companies may allocate the AIA between their 'relevant AIA qualifying expenditure' as they see fit.

The purpose of this restriction was well explained in the technical note issued by HMRC and the Treasury in December 2007:

> 'This section is intended to prevent behavioural changes by businesses seeking to avoid the intent of section 51E. The intent of section 51E, which only applies to companies under common control and not in a group, could be avoided if for each company "P" potentially within the scope of section 51E a new company "C" was incorporated for which the company "P" became the parent undertaking. Section 51D applies where two or more groups of companies are controlled by the same "person" (defined later in section 51F) and the groups are "related" to one another (as defined in section 51G) in such circumstances only a single Annual Investment Allowance is available to be allocated between all members of the groups.'

The 'relevant AIA qualifying expenditure' is the AIA qualifying expenditure incurred by the companies in chargeable periods that end in the financial year referred to above.

For the purposes of this CAA 2001, s. 51D (and of s. 51F and s. 51G), the following definitions apply:

Group of companies

A group of companies is defined to mean:

- a company which, in the financial year in question, is a parent undertaking in relation to one or more other companies; and
- those other companies.

Members of the group

The members of the group of companies are the parent undertaking and the other companies referred to immediately above.

Parent undertaking

A company ('P') is treated as a parent undertaking of another company ('C') in any given financial year if P is a parent undertaking of C at the end of C's chargeable period ending in that financial year. For these purposes, the term 'parent undertaking' is defined in accordance with the *Companies Act* 2006, s. 1162.

Legislation: CAA 2001, s. 51D

Other companies under common control (fourth restriction)

A fourth restriction applies, again allowing just one AIA between the various companies, where – in a given financial year – two or more *companies* are controlled by the same person and where they are related to one another. No further restriction is applied by this rule if the circumstances are already caught by s. 51C or s. 51D.

The companies may allocate the AIA between their 'relevant AIA qualifying expenditure' as they see fit. Once more, the 'relevant AIA qualifying expenditure' is the AIA qualifying expenditure incurred by the companies in chargeable periods that end in the financial year referred to above.

Legislation: CAA 2001, s. 51E

Companies and groups: meaning of 'control'

Both CAA 2001, s. 51D and s. 51E (considered in the paragraphs above) make reference to the concept of control, which is therefore defined for these purposes, as follows:

(1)   a company is said to be controlled by a person in a financial year if it is controlled by that person at the end of its chargeable period ending in that financial year;

(2)   a group of companies is said to be controlled by a person in a financial year if the company which is the parent undertaking is controlled by that person at the end of its chargeable period ending in that financial year;

(3)   in relation to a company that is a body corporate, the concept of control is defined in accordance with CAA 2001, s. 574(2) (see 307-050);

(4)   in relation to a company ('C') that is not a body corporate, control means the power of

Plant and Machinery

a person ('P') to secure that C's affairs are conducted in accordance with P's wishes. This applies whether by means of the holding of shares or the possession of voting power in relation to C or another body, or as a result of any powers conferred by the constitution of C or another body. (The term 'shares' here has the meaning given by the *Companies Act* 2006, s. 1161(2).)

Legislation: CAA 2001, s. 51F

Companies and groups: meaning of 'related'

Both CAA 2001, s. 51D and s. 51E (considered in the paragraphs above) make reference to the concept of companies or groups being 'related', which term is therefore defined for these purposes, as follows.

A company ('C1') is related to another company ('C2') in a financial year if the 'shared premises condition', the 'similar activities condition' or both of those conditions are met in relation to the companies in that year. Where C1 is related to C2 in a financial year, C1 is also related to any other company to which C2 is related in that financial year.

A group of companies ('G1') is related to another group of companies ('G2') in a financial year if in that year a company which is a member of G1 is related to a company which is a member of G2. Where G1 is related to G2 in a financial year, G1 is also related to any other group of companies to which G2 is related in that financial year.

Legislation: CAA 2001, s. 51G

Shared premises

This condition is met in relation to two companies in a financial year if, at the end of the relevant chargeable period of one or both of the companies, the companies carry on qualifying activities from the same premises.

Legislation: CAA 2001, s. 51G(5)

Similar activities

This condition is met in relation to two companies in a financial year if more than half of the turnover of each company for the chargeable period ending in that year is derived from qualifying activities within the same 'NACE classification'. This latter concept is defined to mean

> 'the first level of the common statistical classification of economic activities in the European Union established by Regulation (EC) No 1893/2006 of the European Parliament and the Council of 20 December 2006 (as that Regulation has effect from time to time).'

When the draft legislation for annual investment allowances was published in December 2007, the following definition was given of a company's turnover. However, this definition does *not* appear in the final version of the amended legislation:

'the amount derived from the provision of goods and services within the company's ordinary activities (including any amount which is, or falls to be treated as, a receipt of an ordinary property business, furnished holiday lettings business or overseas property business), after deduction of trade discounts, value added tax and any other taxes based on the amounts so derived'

Legislation: CAA 2001, s. 51G(6), (7)

Qualifying activities under common control (fifth restriction)

The fifth restriction arises where, in a given tax year, two or more qualifying activities meet all of the following conditions:

(1)   they are carried on, at the end of the chargeable period for the activity ending in the tax year, by a qualifying person other than a company;

(2)   they are controlled by the same person (see below); and

(3)   they are related to one another (again, see below).

Where all of these conditions are met, and where the qualifying activities are all carried on by one qualifying person, the person is entitled to just the one AIA. Where the qualifying activities are carried on by more than one qualifying person, those persons are entitled to a single AIA between them in respect of the relevant AIA qualifying expenditure. The person or persons may allocate the expenditure to achieve the best overall tax result. The relevant AIA qualifying expenditure is the AIA qualifying expenditure incurred for the purposes of the qualifying activities in the chargeable periods referred to above.

Legislation: CAA 2001, s. 51H

Qualifying activities: control

A qualifying activity is controlled by a person in a tax year if it is controlled by the person at the end of the chargeable period for that activity which ends in that tax year.

A qualifying activity carried on by an individual is controlled by the individual who carries it on.

A qualifying activity carried on by a partnership is controlled by the person (if any) who controls the partnership, as defined at CAA 2001, s. 574(3) (see 307-050). But where partners who between them control one partnership also between them control another partnership, the qualifying activities carried on by the partnerships are to be treated as controlled by the same person.

Legislation: CAA 2001, s. 51I

Qualifying activities: 'related'

A qualifying activity ('A1') is said to be related to another qualifying activity ('A2') in a tax year if the shared premises condition and/or the similar activities condition is met in relation

Plant and Machinery

to the activities in the tax year. Where A1 is related to A2 in a tax year, A1 is also related to any other qualifying activity to which A2 is related in that tax year.

Legislation: CAA 2001, s. 51J

Shared premises

This condition is met in relation to two qualifying activities in a tax year if, at the end of the relevant chargeable period for one or both of the activities, the activities are carried on from the same premises.

Legislation: CAA 2001, s. 51J(3)

Similar activities

This condition is met in relation to two qualifying activities in a tax year if, at the end of the relevant chargeable period for those activities ending in that tax year, the activities are within the same 'NACE classification' (as defined for the purposes of CAA 2001, s. 51G: see above).

Legislation: CAA 2001, s. 51J(4)

Relevant chargeable period

For the purposes of CAA 2001, s. 51J, the 'relevant chargeable period' is defined, in relation to a qualifying activity and a tax year, as the chargeable period for that activity that ends in that tax year.

Legislation: CAA 2001, s. 51J(5)

181-300   AIA where restrictions apply

As noted at 181-200, there are numerous circumstances in which a single amount of £50,000 is to be shared between more than one tax-paying body or activity. More technically, a restriction may apply where a person is, or persons are, entitled to just a single AIA in respect of relevant AIA qualifying expenditure (CAA 2001, s. 51K).

The way in which the AIA rules operate in these circumstances is already given by CAA 2001, s. 51A(11) but, according to the *Explanatory Notes* to the Finance Bill 2008, the provisions of s. 51K put the matter 'beyond doubt'. Those provisions apply where a restriction is imposed by s. 51B, s. 51C, s. 51D, s. 51E or s. 51H.

The person or persons claiming AIAs are always free to claim them in respect of less than the maximum amount of AIA qualifying expenditure.

Legislation: CAA 2001, s. 51K

General restriction

One key aspect of the rules is to ensure that the provisions of those various sections can never have the effect of increasing the allowances to which a person would otherwise be entitled. The operation of this principle is illustrated with the following example (from the *Explanatory Notes*):

'If a person controlled three companies that were related, and one of the companies with a short chargeable period of 9 months had incurred relevant AIA qualifying expenditure of £60,000, the person would only be able to allocate a maximum AIA of $^9/_{12}$ of £50,000 = £37,500 to that company, even if he had allocated no AIA to the other two companies.'

Legislation: CAA 2001, s. 51K(6)

Total AIA expenditure less than maximum allowance

It is possible that the total of the relevant AIA qualifying expenditure will be less than or equal to the maximum allowance. In this case, the person or persons simply receive an AIA equal to the whole of the relevant AIA qualifying expenditure.

If, for example, there is a simple group consisting of one parent company and one subsidiary, the former spending £10,000 and the latter £30,000, then they may each claim full AIA on the expenditure incurred. There is no question of having to split the £50,000 equally so as to restrict the second company's allowance to £25,000.

Legislation: CAA 2001, s. 51K(2)

Total AIA expenditure exceeds maximum allowance

If the relevant AIA qualifying expenditure is more than the maximum allowance, then the total AIA is restricted to the amount of that maximum allowance (ie typically £50,000: see below). HMRC illustrate this principle with the following example (in the *Explanatory Notes* to the Finance Bill 2008):

'If a person controls three related companies, each with 12-month chargeable periods, and each with relevant AIA qualifying expenditure of £20,000, the person is only entitled to an annual investment allowance of £50,000, which he may allocate between the three companies in any way he sees fit.'

Thus the person may choose to split the £50,000 equally across the three companies, or may opt for another split such as 20-20-10 or 20-15-15.

Legislation: CAA 2001, s. 51K(3), (6)

Maximum allowance: increase for businesses other than companies where s. 51H applies

The maximum allowance is typically £50,000: see 181-050.

Plant and Machinery

A complication can arise where there is a chargeable period in excess of 12 months, and this is addressed at CAA 2001, s. 51K(4) and s. 51M, 51N. The provision is of no relevance to companies as a company's chargeable period can never exceed 12 months.

Legislation: CTA 2009, s. 10(1)(a)

Purpose of legislation

The stated purpose of the provisions (from the *Explanatory Notes* to the Finance Bill 2008) is 'to ensure that where a person controls two or more qualifying activities and one or more of those qualifying activities has a chargeable period of longer than twelve months, the amount of the AIA is not unfairly restricted.' The *Notes* then go on to explain the mechanics of how this is achieved with the following (unedited) text:

'(96) The section works by allowing the person who controls the qualifying activity with the long chargeable period to look back to previous tax years where the activity was being carried on, to determine whether, in those earlier years, there were any relevant unused allowances. The relevant unused allowances are added to the person's entitlement for the current year in order to determine the maximum amount of the AIA available for the long chargeable period. However, this amount is still subject to the overriding cap given by new section 51A (5) and (6).

(97) For example, a person (P) has a newsagents business that he has carried on for many years with a year end of 31 March. In January 2009 he starts a new off-license business and draws his first accounts up to 30 June 2010. The two businesses are related qualifying activities because they fall within the same NACE classification. With respect to the off-licence business, P incurred qualifying expenditure of £100,000 in the eighteen months. With respect to the newsagents business, P incurred qualifying expenditure of £40,000 in the year ended 31 March 2011. Without a special rule P would only be able to utilise an AIA of £50,000 in respect of his related businesses' chargeable periods ending in the tax year 2010–11.

(98) With regard to his business with a long chargeable period, the section allows P to look back to the previous tax years in which that chargeable period fell to see if there was any unused entitlement to an AIA in that or those earlier year or years, which might be added to the 2010–11 AIA.

(99) For example, if in the tax year 2009–10 P had claimed AIA of £10,000 in respect of the newsagent's qualifying expenditure for the chargeable period ending on 31 March 2010, and if he had claimed AIA of £20,000 in the tax year 2008–09 in respect of the newsagents qualifying expenditure for the chargeable period ending on 31 March 2009, the new section would allow:

- A further £40,000 unused allowance (£50,000 less £10,000) from the tax year 2009–10, and
- A further £12,500 in respect of unused allowance (£50,000 less £20,000, but capped at the length of the off-license business's chargeable period falling in the tax year 2008–09, that is, capped at 3/12ths of £50,000 = £12,500).

(100) The total that could be added in the above example is £52,500, giving a theoretical maximum of £102,500, but the absolute maximum is still given by section 51A(5) & (6) – in this case £75,000. So the business can use £52,500 of the earlier years' unused AIA and up to £22,500 of the 2010–11 AIA, leaving £27,500 available for the newsagent business. However, if for example, P allocated £40,000 of the AIA to the newsagents business, then he could only allocate the balance of £10,000 to the off-license business, which might be added to the

£52,500 unused AIA available to this long chargeable period business in relation to earlier years.'

Mechanics of legislation

The legislation applies where a person ('P') controls two or more qualifying activities in a tax year, and where the chargeable period for one of those qualifying activities ('A1') exceeds 12 months.

The effect is that additional AIA, over and above the maximum that would otherwise apply, may be allocated for the purposes of the qualifying activity with the long chargeable period (ie for A1). However, this is still subject to the 'general restriction' given at CAA 2001, s. 51K(6) and discussed above.

The additional amount of available AIA is initially calculated as the aggregate of the amounts of relevant unused allowance for each tax year which:

(1)   falls before the tax year in which the long chargeable period ends; and

(2)   is a tax year in which part of the long chargeable period falls.

The amount of any relevant unused allowance for an earlier tax year is expressed as MA minus AM, where MA is the maximum amount allowed by CAA 2001, s. 51A(5) (ie normally £50,000) and AM is the amount of any AIA made for a relevant qualifying activity controlled by the person in that tax year for the chargeable period ending in that year. A further provision ensures that no amount of relevant unused allowance can be double-counted.

A relevant qualifying activity is any qualifying activity carried on by a qualifying person other than a company which was controlled by P in the previous tax year and related to A1 in that tax year. If A1 was controlled by P in the previous tax year, then A1 is also a relevant qualifying activity. As regards the concept of control, see CAA 2001, s. 51I.

It is possible, of course, that only part of the chargeable period falls in an earlier tax year. In such a case, the amount of the unused allowance is restricted on a time apportionment basis. The legislation uses the formula:

$$\frac{DCPY}{DY} \times MA$$

where

DCPY   is the number of days in the chargeable period that fell in the previous tax year;
DY   is the number of days in the tax year; and
MA   has the same meaning as above (ie the maximum amount (£50,000) specified in new s. 51A(5)).

The result of applying the formula is the capped amount of the relevant unused allowance for the tax year in question.

Plant and Machinery

85

The concept of 'relevant chargeable period' is defined for the purposes of the section by reference to the tax year mentioned in CAA 2001, s. 51M(1)(a). That is the tax year in which s. 51H applies in relation to two or more qualifying activities controlled by a person.

Legislation: CAA 2001, s. 51M

Supplementary provisions

CAA 2001, s. 51N operates where s. 51H applies to a person who controls two or more related activities in a tax year, and more than one of the related activities has a chargeable period in excess of one year. This provision is unlikely to apply often.

Once more, the *Explanatory Notes* to the Finance Bill 2008 are helpful in explaining what is going on here:

> 'The section modifies the rules in new section 51M. For example, returning to the example outlined above in relation to section 51M, assume that P [at the para. numbered as 97 above] had also on 30 November 2008 started a new business of confectioners, spending £50,000 on plant and machinery and drawing the first accounts of the new business up to 30 April 2010. The new section will allow:
>
> - A further £40,000 unused allowance (£50,000 less £10,000) from the tax year 2009–10, to be shared between the two businesses with long chargeable periods; and
> - A further £30,000 unused allowance (£50,000 less £20,000) in respect of the tax year 2008–09, but this must be capped by the length of the chargeable period that falls in that tax year for each of the two businesses. So for the confectioners business, the maximum that could be allocated is $5/_{12}$ths of £50,000 or £20,833, and if that maximum were allocated this would mean that only the unused balance of £9,167 could be allocated to the off-licence. Alternatively, for the off-licence business the maximum that could be allocated is $3/_{12}$ths of £50,000 or £12,500, and if that were allocated, then only £17,500 could be allocated to the confectioner).'

The effect of the legislation is that CAA 2001, s. 51M is applied to each of the qualifying activities where the chargeable period ending in the tax year is longer than a year, but subject to modification where two or more of the qualifying activities – with a relevant chargeable period exceeding a year – were related in a previous tax year. In such a case:

(1) the effect of the formula at s. 51M(8) (see above) is ignored;

(2) section 51M(6) is broadened to apply to all of the qualifying activities with long chargeable periods;

(3) the whole of the unused AIA can be allocated between all of the qualifying activities. However, the allocation in respect of the earlier tax years is capped at the maximum that would have been allowable on a time apportioned basis, up to the last day of each of the tax years prior to the tax year where the long chargeable periods ended, ie at the amount given by the formula at s. 51M(8).

Legislation: CAA 2001, s. 51N

Short chargeable periods

A company or other business may have more than one chargeable period ending in a tax or financial year. In such a case, it is necessary to consider each separate chargeable period independently so as to decide whether or not the related activities conditions are met for the purposes of CAA 2001, s. 51C, s. 51D, s. 51E or s. 51H.

As would be expected, AIA qualifying expenditure of a chargeable period is not relevant AIA qualifying expenditure if the chargeable period is not affected by any of those provisions.

Legislation: CAA 2001, s. 51L

181-350   Further restriction on AIA

No annual investment allowance (AIA) is given where an arrangement is entered into wholly or mainly for a disqualifying purpose. Arrangements are said to be entered into for such a purpose if their main purpose, or one of their main purposes, is to enable a person to obtain an AIA to which the person would not otherwise be entitled. If the allowance has already been given, and such a purpose prohibits the giving of the AIA, then it is to be withdrawn.

According to the guidance material issued jointly by HMRC and the Treasury in December 2007, this restriction 'is aimed at arrangements entered into to access an annual investment allowance where a person would not otherwise be entitled to the allowance'.

Legislation: CAA 2001, s. 218A

181-400   Interaction of FYAs, AIAs and WDAs

As already noted at 181-000, the annual investment allowance (AIA) was introduced from 1 April 2008 for companies and 6 April 2008 for unincorporated businesses that are subject to income tax. To avoid undue repetition, the rules are explained below as they apply to companies.

Expenditure incurred before 1 April 2008 was subject to the rules for first-year allowances (FYAs) as they applied before the changes were introduced (see 185-000ff.). After deducting the amount of the allowance, any balance was carried forward to the following chargeable period.

Subject to the temporary re-introduction of first-year allowances at 40 per cent from April 2009 (see 185-050). Expenditure incurred from 1 April 2008 onwards no longer attracts 40 or 50 per cent FYAs. Instead, the AIA is available. The amount of the AIA depends on the length of the chargeable period and, for this purpose, any period falling before 1 or 6 April 2008 (for corporation tax and income tax respectively) is ignored (FA 2008, Sch. 24,

Plant and Machinery

para. 23). As a result, the maximum AIA is restricted on normal principles (see 181-050). For a company with a 31 December year-end, for instance, the maximum AIA available for the year to 31 December 2008 was £37,500, as there are nine months within the 12-month accounting period that fall in the period beginning on 1 April 2008.

To the extent that the expenditure exceeds the amount on which AIAs can be claimed, the balance is available for writing-down allowances (WDAs) *in the same period*. WDAs in a period spanning 1 April 2008 are given at a hybrid rate, calculated according to the length of the period falling before and after that date. For a company with a 31 December year-end, for example, the hybrid rate will be 21.25 per cent, calculated as 91 days at 25 per cent and 275 days at 20 per cent (see 190-250 and the comments following the example below).

Example

A medium-sized company with a 31 December year-end has a pool value brought down of £60,000. It incurs qualifying expenditure of £20,000 in March 2008 and further qualifying expenditure of £100,000 in November 2008, none of which is on integral features. It can claim allowances for its chargeable period ending 31 December 2008 as follows:

- FYAs of £8,000 (£20,000 × 40 per cent);
- AIAs of £37,500 (£50,000 AIA limit × $^9/_{12}$ months); and
- WDAs of £26,031 (calculated as hybrid rate of 21.25 per cent × (£60,000 brought forward, plus £62,500 excess over AIA limit)).

Total allowances for the year will therefore be £71,531. This compares with £63,000 that would have been available under the old rules (£48,000 FYAs plus £15,000 WDAs).

The legislation introduced in the *Finance Act* 2008 makes it clear that the rate of WDA for periods spanning 1 or 6 April should be calculated on a day-by-day basis. This is illustrated in detail at 190-250 (in relation to income tax: for corporation tax purposes, the same formula is used but with the date of 1 April rather than 6 April). As it happens, the rate calculated using the statutory formula comes out with the same result, for a company with a year ended 31 December 2008, as a monthly apportionment, but this is not always the case.

First-year allowances: availability

185-000 First-year allowances: introduction

As discussed below, capital allowances were for many years typically given (by way of writing-down allowances (WDAs)) at the rate of one-quarter of the reducing value of an item of plant or machinery. The standard rate of WDA reduced from 25 to 20 per cent from April 2008, with a 10 per cent rate applying to certain expenditure.

For various reasons, Parliament has decided that it is appropriate in particular circumstances to allow tax relief at a faster rate. From April 2008, this is normally by way of the annual investment allowance discussed at 181-000ff. Prior to that date, accelerated relief was available only by way of first-year allowances (FYAs). FYAs were not abolished completely from April 2008 but the most common FYAs, giving relief at 40 or 50 per cent for medium or small businesses, were withdrawn from that date. From April 2009, they were re-introduced, but on a temporary basis only. FYAs have been subject to frequent change in recent years, as summarised in the table at 185-010.

For first-year allowances to be available, a person must incur 'first-year qualifying expenditure' and must own the asset in question at some time during the chargeable period (see 106-100) in which the expenditure is incurred. Any first-year allowance is then made for that chargeable period.

Where an asset is provided partly for purposes other than those of the qualifying activity carried on by the person, first-year allowances (FYAs) may be given to the extent that is just and reasonable in relation to the proportion in which the expenditure was incurred for the purposes of the qualifying activity.

Legislation: CAA 2001, s. 52, 205

185-010   First-year qualifying expenditure

The legislation identifies several types of first-year qualifying expenditure, as follows (but subject to the general exclusions at 185-150). The following list takes account of the effect of the *Finance Act* 2008, which formally removed from the legislation certain categories of expenditure. See 185-050, however, regarding the re-introduction of a general first-year allowance, for one year only, for expenditure incurred from April 2009:

Expenditure	Qualifying period	Rate	Authority (CAA 2001)	Comment
Incurred on energy-saving plant or machinery	From 1 April 2001	100%	s. 45A	Still available from April 2008. Payable tax credits available for companies (only) from that date.
Cars with low CO_2 emissions	From 17 April 2002	100%	s. 45D	Extended (with changes) from April 2008.
Incurred on P&M for gas refuelling station	From 17 April 2002	100%	s. 45E	Extended (and expanded) from April 2008.
Incurred on P&M for use in a ring fence trade	From 17 April 2002	24% or 100%	s. 45F	Special rules apply to this type of expenditure.
Incurred on environmentally beneficial P&M	From 1 April 2003	100%	s. 45H	Still available from April 2008. Payable tax credits available for companies (only) from that date.

Each of the above categories is considered in this Chapter.

As regards additional VAT liabilities and rebates, see 238-000.

In *Ensign Tankers (Leasing) Ltd v Stokes (HMIT)*, the House of Lords steered a middle course between disallowing all first-year allowances for the negatives of films which were regarded as plant in connection with film-making (and alleged to result from a tax avoidance scheme) and allowing the whole amount claimed. Their Lordships held that only the expenditure which came out of the taxpayer's own resources was allowable. The balance of film production costs, borrowed from the producer, to whom it was immediately returned, was a self-cancelling transaction to which the principle of *WT Ramsay Ltd v IR Commrs* applied.

Legislation: CAA 2001, s. 39

Cases: *WT Ramsay Ltd v IR Commrs* (1983) 54 TC 101; *Ensign Tankers (Leasing) Ltd v Stokes (HMIT)* [1992] BTC 110

Other material: CA 23100ff.

Categories of expenditure removed by the Finance Act 2008

The most important categories of expenditure that ceased to apply from April 2008 were the standard 50 and 40 per cent first-year allowances given to small and medium-sized businesses.

Expenditure incurred for Northern Ireland purposes has not attracted special allowances since 12 May 2002 but was only formally removed from the capital allowances legislation in 2008.

Certain ICT expenditure incurred by 31 March 2004 attracted 100 per cent allowances. Again, these rules were only formally removed from the capital allowances legislation by FA 2008.

185-050   Temporary re-introduction of first-year allowances

Most first-year allowances were abolished from April 2008. As a result of pressures on businesses arising from the 'credit crunch', and of the desire to encourage businesses to spend money to lessen the effects of the recession, a general first-year allowance was re-introduced from April 2009 (FA 2009, s. 24).

The temporary allowances are given at 40 per cent and apply to expenditure incurred in the year ended 31 March or 5 April 2010 (for corporation tax and income tax respectively). For this purpose, the rule in CAA 2001, s. 12 (pre-trading expenditure) is not applied, so a person incurring expenditure in February 2009 and starting to trade in May 2009 would not be eligible to claim the first-year allowances.

The expenditure must not be 'special rate expenditure' (see 247-150).

The usual general exclusions (see 185-150) apply to these temporary allowances as they do to other first-year allowances. However, general exclusion 6 (plant or machinery for leasing) does not prevent expenditure from qualifying if it is provided for leasing under an excluded lease of background plant or machinery as defined at CAA 2001, s. 70R. The effect of this is that property lessors will be entitled to claim the first-year allowances on certain expenditure on plant or machinery in the property to be let. If, for example, a property lessor incurs expenditure on installing computer networking facilities incidental to the occupation of the building then such expenditure will qualify for the temporary allowance. (This is on the assumption that the expenditure is not special rate expenditure which would mean, for example, that the expected useful economic life would be less than 25 years.)

Interaction with annual investment allowances

A business may claim AIAs and FYAs in the same period. This intention was confirmed in the April 2009 Budget press release BN04:

> 'Businesses incurring expenditure in excess of the AIA cap that would normally be allocated to the main pool and qualify for a 20 per cent WDA in the 12 month period beginning on 1 April 2009 and 6 April 2009 will now be able to claim a 40 per cent FYA instead.'

For example, take a company with accounts drawn up to 31 December. It spends £42,000 in March 2009 and a further £15,000 in September 2009, all of which is on assets qualifying for unrestricted capital allowances. The company will first use up its £50,000 AIA allowance. It has excess expenditure in the year of £7,000 and first-year allowances can be claimed at 40 per cent, so £2,800, leaving £4,200 to carry forward to the next year.

If the company had instead spent £52,000 in March 2009 and £5,000 in September 2009, it will be able to claim £50,000 AIA, writing-down allowances at 20 per cent on £2,000 and first-year allowances on £5,000. This is because the expenditure incurred before 1 April 2009 does not qualify for the temporary first-year allowance.

This may all seem surprising in view of the wording of CAA 2001, s. 52A, which clearly states that a person may not claim an AIA and a FYA in respect of the same expenditure. The solution seems to lie in the interpretation of 'the same expenditure'. If a business spends £60,000, the correct interpretation seems to be that the £50,000 qualifying for AIA and the £10,000 qualifying for FYAs are not the same expenditure, even though they may be on the same asset. And where s. 58(4A)(a) refers to AIA qualifying expenditure *in respect of which the allowance is made* (italics added here for clarity), the expenditure to which it refers must again be capped at £50,000. On this basis, the additional £10,000 would be unaffected by the restriction in that subsection.

185-100   Enhanced capital allowances

The term 'enhanced capital allowances' (ECAs) is often applied to expenditure under the following headings:

Plant and Machinery

- energy-saving plant or machinery;
- low emission cars; and
- environmentally beneficial plant and machinery.

Although the capital allowances legislation does not use the term, there is some logic in it: all three categories relate to environmentally conscious expenditure and all offer businesses of whatever size the chance to gain full tax relief in the year in which the expenditure is incurred. Nevertheless, different rules apply and the best approach is to recognise the overlapping concepts but to apply the legislation on a case-by-case basis. Each category is therefore dealt with under its own heading in the following paragraphs.

The mechanics of claiming ECAs may represent unfamiliar territory for accountants and tax advisers. Under the energy-saving rules, for example, manufacturers need to register their products for inclusion on the Energy Technology List. The government website, *www.eca.gov.uk*, contains details of how to go about this. To be included, products must normally meet the scheme's published energy-efficiency criteria, though separate conditions are imposed for certain product types (including lighting).

Care is needed since, as the website states, 'it is the purchaser's responsibility to check with the manufacturer which of their products meet the criteria'. The end-user or his adviser therefore needs either to receive formal assurance from the supplier or to go to the same website. It is then possible, under 'product search', to choose (for example) to search for lamps. The site lists many thousands of items (and their manufacturers) that qualify under the energy-saving scheme. If the business wants to buy from a particular manufacturer, it can select that name, but often that will not be necessary.

Other material: CA 23135

Hiring and leasing of assets qualifying for enhanced allowances

The question of whether enhanced allowances are available for 'energy-saving' or 'environmentally beneficial' plant and machinery can be complex. Exclusions from first-year allowances generally are considered at 185-150 immediately below. As far as these two categories of asset are concerned, the position may be summarised as follows:

- Generally speaking, expenditure on plant and machinery for leasing or letting on hire, does not qualify for FYAs.
- An amendment was made in 2003 so that the exclusion did not apply to the schemes for first-year allowances for environmentally beneficial technologies.
- A further amendment was made in 2006 to remove the availability of first-year allowances for spending on energy-saving or environmentally beneficial technologies for leasing (but this amendment did not affect low emission cars qualifying under CAA 2001, s. 45D).
- But the denial of first-year allowances does not apply to 'background' plant and machinery, within the meaning of CAA 2001, s. 70R (see 231-050).

In each case, the changes were effected by amendments to CAA 2001, s. 46.

Evaluation of enhanced capital allowances

An evaluation of the effectiveness of the whole scheme of enhanced capital allowances was published in May 2008, by 'HM Revenue & Customs with HM Treasury & Defra'. It is referred to as HMRC 'Research Report 54' and may be viewed online at www.hmrc.gov.uk/research/report-54.pdf.

185-150   General exclusions from first-year allowances

Certain exclusions prevent expenditure from qualifying for first-year allowances, regardless of the heading under which such allowances might otherwise have been given. First-year allowances will *not* be available on any of the following:

(1)   expenditure incurred in the chargeable period in which the qualifying activity is permanently discontinued;

(2)   expenditure on a car (but see 200-400) (CAA 2001, s. 268A);

(3)   expenditure on certain ships (CAA 2001, s. 94);

(4)   expenditure on railway assets (CAA 2001, s. 95);

(5)   expenditure which is only saved from being long-life asset expenditure by the transitional provisions of CAA 2001, Sch. 3;

(6)   expenditure incurred on the provision of plant or machinery that is to be leased, defined to include the letting of a ship on charter or of any other asset on hire (see below);

(7)   where the provision of the plant is connected with a change in the nature of the trade, etc carried on by someone else and where the obtaining of the first-year allowance would be a main benefit that could reasonably be expected to arise from that change (see an illustration at CA 23110);

(8)   where an asset used for other purposes starts to be used for the purposes of a qualifying activity (see 160-700);

(9)   where plant is received by way of gift (see 160-700); and

(10)   where plant or machinery that has been used for long funding leasing starts to be used for other purposes (see 240-220ff.).

Hiring or leasing

The question (item (6) above) of what is meant by hiring or leasing can raise some difficult points of practice. A classic example might be a business that supplies scaffolding to the building trade. Is this the provision of an asset on hire (no first-year allowances due) or is it the provision of a service?

The Revenue issued guidance on this matter in the summer of 2003, following the non-tax case of *Baldwins Industrial Services plc and Barr Ltd* (TCC December 2002). In that case,

93

the hire of a crane with a driver was held to be a contract for a supply of plant and labour. HMRC therefore now accept that 'the supply of plant or machinery with an operator, by a business, is the provision of a service and not mere hire'. For these purposes, HMRC will interpret 'the supply of plant or machinery with an operator' as applying where 'the operator remains with the equipment during its use and [where] it will be operated by him or her alone save for exceptional circumstances. It is not sufficient for the plant or machinery to be delivered or installed by the hire company. For example, the delivery and installation of a generator would not be regarded as the provision of a service but the supply of a digger with a driver would be so regarded'.

HMRC goes on to say that it will now accept that the provision of 'building access services' by the scaffolding services will be more than mere hire (but the simple supply of scaffolding poles, etc for use by others will not qualify).

The general exclusion for leasing does not apply to cars with low CO_2 emissions (see 200-400).

In the case of energy-saving or environmentally beneficial plant or machinery, the exclusion is sometimes disapplied. This is the case where the plant is provided for leasing under an excluded lease of so-called 'background' plant and machinery, within the meaning of CAA 2001, s. 70R.

Landlords

The general exclusion does not prohibit completely the claiming of first-year allowances by landlords: see 185-050.

Legislation: CAA 2001, s. 46(2)

Cases: *Frazer (HMIT) v Trebilcock* (1964) 42 TC 217

185-250   Expenditure incurred by SMEs

Expenditure under this heading no longer qualifies for first-year allowances if incurred on or after 1 April 2008 (for corporation tax purposes) or 6 April 2008 (for income tax) (but see 185-050).

Expenditure incurred by a small or medium-sized enterprise could previously count as first-year qualifying expenditure as long as it was not within the general exclusions. In other words, this was a general type of first-year allowance available for all but the largest businesses. First-year allowances given under this heading were generally at 40 per cent. However, this increased to 50 per cent, for small enterprises only, for expenditure incurred in various periods.

There was a specific exclusion for expenditure on a long-life asset (see 210-000).

Legislation: CAA 2001, s. 44, 52; FA 2007, s. 37

Other material: CA 23160

185-350   Energy-saving plant and machinery

Overview

See the general comments at 185-100 regarding enhanced capital allowances for various types of environment-friendly expenditure.

First-year allowances are available at a rate of 100 per cent on expenditure on plant and machinery which falls into the category of 'energy-saving' (see below). An equivalent relief is given for 'environmentally beneficial plant and machinery' which covers various types of water-related technology (see 185-550). Both of these types of allowance continue to be available after April 2008 (ie despite the withdrawal of most other first-year allowances from that date). Indeed, the value of these allowances is in some cases increased from 1 April 2008 as loss-making companies may from that date claim payable tax credits based on this type of allowance. These credits are discussed at 242-000ff.

Expenditure on energy-saving plant and machinery qualifies for first-year allowances as long as it is not within the general exclusions identified at 185-150. Allowances under this heading are not restricted to small or medium-sized enterprises, and are given at 100 per cent. (The general exclusion re leasing does not apply if the asset is provided for leasing under an excluded lease of background plant or machinery for a building.)

To qualify, the plant or machinery in question must meet certain energy-saving criteria specified by the Treasury. These criteria need to be met either when the expenditure is incurred or on the date the contract is entered into for the provision of the plant. This means that expenditure, not treated as qualifying when the contract is entered into, may nevertheless qualify if the list is suitably amended by the time the expenditure is incurred. This latter date is determined by CAA 2001, s. 5 (generally, as soon as there is an unconditional obligation to incur it, but see 102-000). The Product List contains those products in the technology classes that have been accepted as meeting the published water-saving standards. Neither the product nor the installation normally needs to be separately certified, though each installation *does* need to be certified for efficient membrane filtration systems, which (according to HMRC guidance) are usually tailor-made for a particular application.

If only certain components of an item of plant meet the energy-saving criteria then the normal apportionment rules do not apply. Instead, the Treasury will specify the amount that will qualify under this heading for first-year allowances.

Plant and Machinery

Products on the published Product List may be incorporated into other items of plant or machinery. In this case, it is necessary to identify the proportion of the expenditure incurred that qualifies for 100 per cent FYA, using tables included as part of the Product List. These specify the deemed expenditure qualifying for first-year allowances to be attributed to a particular product when incorporated into other equipment. The balance can still qualify for ordinary capital allowances.

Legislation: CAA 2001, s. 39, 45A–C, 52

Other material: CA 23140

What qualifies as 'energy-saving plant or machinery'?

The criteria that must be met if plant or machinery is to qualify as 'energy-saving' are set out in the *Capital Allowances (Energy-Saving Plant and Machinery) Order* 2001, as amended on various occasions.

The plant or machinery is energy-saving plant or machinery if:

(1)   it falls within a technology class specified in the Energy Technology Criteria List;

(2)   it meets the energy-saving criteria set out in that List; and

(3)   in the case of plant or machinery falling within any of the specified technology classes, it is of a type that:

   (a)   is specified in, and has not been removed from, the Energy Technology Product List; or
   (b)   has been accepted for inclusion in the Energy Technology Product List.

The Energy Technology Criteria List and the Energy Technology Product List are published by the Secretary of State for the Environment, Food and Rural Affairs. The lists are updated each summer by the Secretary of State for the Environment, Food and Rural Affairs on that date. Reference should be made to the official 'Enhanced Capital Allowances' website (www.eca.gov.uk) for full details of qualifying technologies.

Expenditure on qualifying technologies only qualify if the particular product has been approved, whatever the energy-saving qualities of the items in question. Expenditure incurred on a technology that is subject to the issue of a certificate can qualify for the enhanced allowances even if it was incurred before the certificate was issued. However, no claim can be made until certification has been given.

Legislation: CAA 2001, s. 45A–C; *Capital Allowances (Energy-Saving Plant and Machinery) Order* 2001 (SI 2001/2541)

The technology classes referred to in (3) above are specified at SI 2001/2541, as amended from time to time.

Lighting, pipework, CHP

The above does not, however, represent a full list of the qualifying technologies. Three other types of technology are specifically subject to different criteria, namely lighting, pipework insulation and combined heat and power (CHP) technology. Details of the special criteria are given in the dedicated www.eca.gov.uk website referred to above.

According to HMRC guidance, 'combined heat and power equipment (CHP) can be used to recycle what would otherwise be waste heat to provide hot water and/ or generate electricity.' The plant which falls in the combined heat and power class must be installed to provide heat and power to clearly identified end users, and certified as Good Quality by the CHPQA programme (known as the Qualifying Power Capacity; see www.chpqa.com). This type of plant must also carry a certificate of energy. It was announced at the time of the March 2008 Budget that the qualifying criteria for CHP will be revised to ensure that the category includes 'all the necessary equipment to enable such facilities to use solid refuse waste as a fuel'.

Similar rules apply to plant or machinery 'comprising a component based fixed system falling within the technology class "automatic monitoring and targeting equipment"'. Expenditure qualifying under the CHP heading is restricted if it fails to meet the Threshold Quality Index Criterion for CHP. The certificate of energy efficiency specifies the amount of the restriction, based as a percentage of the costs of the equipment.

Not all lighting has qualified as plant and machinery in the past. However, general lighting systems are brought within the definition, as 'integral features', for expenditure incurred from April 2008 (see 247-000ff.).

Legislation: CAA 2001, s. 45B; SI 2001/2541

Revocation of certificate

A certificate may be revoked (presumably by the person who originally issued it). If this happens, the revocation is retrospective in that the certificate is treated as if it had never been issued. Any tax computations made on the understanding that a valid certificate had been issued will have to be amended accordingly. If:

- a person has submitted a tax return on the basis of a valid certificate in respect of certain plant or machinery; and
- that person then discovers that the tax return is incorrect because the certificate has been revoked,

then that person must notify HMRC of the required amendment to the tax return within three months of the day on which the error came to light.

Example

Jack's tax return for the year ending 5 April 2008 is prepared on the basis of an entitlement to a 100 per cent first-year allowance in respect of plant or machinery subject to a certificate under CAA 2001, s. 45B.

Plant and Machinery

> The tax return is submitted on 7 October 2009. On 29 November 2009, the certificate is revoked. Jack learns of this on 24 March 2010 and realises immediately that the tax return is therefore incorrect.
>
> Jack must therefore notify HMRC of any required adjustment by 23 June 2010.

TMA 1970, s. 98 allows a penalty to be served on any taxpayer who does not provide a timely notice correcting a tax return following the revocation of a certificate. Penalties are £300, with additional daily penalties of £60.

Legislation: CAA 2001, s. 45B(5)

Apportionments

Normally, if expenditure on plant or machinery needs to be apportioned because two or more items are bought in a single purchase, an apportionment is made by virtue of CAA 2001, s. 562(3), which provides for a 'just and reasonable apportionment' for both the seller and buyer. However, that section is disapplied for energy-saving equipment.

In the case of some (but not all) of the classes of technology specified above, a component of the overall product may qualify for first-year allowances in its own right (ie even though the product as a whole does not so qualify). The Energy Technology Product List specifies the amount for each qualifying component. That amount is the maximum expenditure on the component that can qualify for 100 per cent first-year allowances under the energy-saving rules. So, if only one component is on the Treasury order, then the amount qualifying for 100 per cent first-year allowances under the energy-saving rules will be the lower of:

- the amount actually incurred for the whole item of plant or machinery; and
- the amount specified in the Product List.

Any actual expenditure in excess of the specified amount will qualify for plant or machinery allowances in the usual way, but not for 100 per cent first-year allowances by reason of the energy-saving rules.

Similarly, if two or more components are on the Product List, then the maximum amount qualifying for 100 per cent first-year allowances under the energy-saving rules is the sum of the relevant amounts specified by the Treasury order.

The legislation does not appear to provide for any apportionment rules to apply if the Product List does not specify an amount for each qualifying component (even though the general rules in CAA 2001, s. 562(3) are disapplied by virtue of CAA 2001, s. 45C(5)).

Legislation: CAA 2001, s. 45C, 46(1); SI 2001/2541, reg. 5

185-400   Cars

The general rule is that no first-year allowances are available for cars. Although one of the 'general exclusions' (see 185-150) preventing first-year allowances relates to cars and another relates to assets used for leasing, these restrictions are removed for certain low CO_2 cars (see 200-400).

Other material: CA 23153

185-450   Gas refuelling stations

Full 100 per cent allowances are available for expenditure qualifying under this heading that is incurred in the period to 31 March 2013 (extended by the *Finance Act* 2008 from 31 March 2008). No relief is due if the expenditure falls within one of the general exclusions (see 185-150). The restriction on leasing expenditure does not apply in this case, but the detail of this was altered for expenditure incurred from 1 April 2006.

The expenditure must be on plant that is 'unused and not second-hand'. The asset must be installed at a gas refuelling station, defined to mean 'any premises, or part of premises, where vehicles are refuelled with natural gas, biogas [for expenditure incurred from 1 April 2008] or hydrogen fuel'. The premises do not need to be open to the public and could therefore include, for example, a station maintained for his own use by the operator of a fleet of lorries.

Expenditure qualifying under this heading is on plant or machinery installed at a gas refuelling station 'for use solely for or in connection with refuelling vehicles with natural gas biogas [for expenditure incurred from 1 April 2008] or hydrogen fuel'. This is defined to include any storage tank for natural gas, biogas or hydrogen fuel, any compressor, pump, control or meter used in connection with refuelling vehicles, with natural gas, biogas, hydrogen gas or natural fuel, and any equipment for dispensing the gas or fuel to the fuel tank of any mechanically propelled road vehicle.

The legislation, as amended from April 2008, defines biogas as 'gas produced by the anaerobic conversion of organic matter and used for propelling vehicles'. The *Explanatory Notes* to the 2008 Finance Bill described it as 'a non-fossil fuel substitute for natural gas'.

Legislation: CAA 2001, s. 45E, 46(5)

Other material: CA 23155

185-500   Ring-fence trades

This is a specialist area relating to petroleum revenue tax. It relates to expenditure incurred by companies wholly for the purposes of a trade of extraction of oil or gas in the UK or UK

Plant and Machinery

Continental Shelf (a 'ring-fence' trade) which is subject to the supplementary charge under ICTA 1988, s. 501A for ring-fence trades.

Full 100 per cent allowances are available for certain plant and machinery. Enhanced 24 per cent allowances are also given for certain long-life asset expenditure under this heading. The standard rate of writing-down allowance, reduced to 20 per cent for most plant and machinery from April 2008, remains at 25 per cent.

First-year allowances are clawed back unless the plant or machinery is used, and used exclusively, for the purposes of a ring-fence trade for a period of at least five years from the date on which the expenditure was incurred. There are statutory reporting requirements where the person making the return becomes aware that it is incorrect as a result of the application of this rule.

Legislation: CAA 2001, s. 45F–G, 52, 56(1A)

Other material: CA 23157

185-550   Environmentally beneficial plant and machinery

First-year allowances are available at a rate of 100 per cent on expenditure on new plant and machinery that falls into the category of 'environmentally beneficial'.

The relief mirrors that for 'energy-saving plant or machinery' (see 185-350 and the general comments at 185-100), including a section on restrictions applying to certain leased assets. Both of these types of allowance continue to be available after April 2008 (ie despite the withdrawal of most other first-year allowances from that date). Indeed, the value of these allowances is in some cases increased from 1 April 2008 as loss-making companies may from that date claim payable tax credits based on this type of allowance. These credits are discussed at 242-000ff.

The term 'environmentally beneficial plant and machinery' is used for certain water technology products. The idea is that the cash flow advantage of accelerated allowances should encourage businesses to invest in technology that either saves water or improves water quality.

No allowances are due for used or second-hand plant or machinery or for long-life assets. According to HMRC, however, equipment will not cease to qualify due to the 'unused and not second-hand' rule solely because it is held as trading stock, is in the course of construction, or is in operation only for commissioning, testing or training.

First-year allowances for environmentally beneficial plant or machinery are available to all businesses of whatever size or location, in contrast to some of the other types of first-year allowances, which were generally restricted to small or medium-sized enterprises.

Expenditure must be on plant or machinery that is 'unused and not second hand'. It must not be long-life expenditure and must not be ruled out by any of the 'general exclusions' discussed at 185-150.

The statute authorises the Treasury to make such orders as appear appropriate 'to promote the use of technologies, or products, designed to remedy or prevent damage to the physical environment or natural resources'. The Treasury is also permitted to require allowances to be given, in certain cases, only where a 'certificate of environmental benefit' is in force. Rules specify by whom such a certificate may be issued and the consequences if it is ever revoked. Revocation of the certificate imposes an obligation on a taxpayer who has claimed allowances to make an amended return within three months of becoming aware that the certificate was incorrect.

Legislation: CAA 2001, s. 45H

Other material: CA 23135; www.hmrc.gov.uk/capital_allowances/eca-water-pt2.htm

Meaning of 'environmentally beneficial plant or machinery'

The term 'environmentally beneficial plant or machinery' is defined by the *Capital Allowances (Environmentally Beneficial Plant and Machinery) Order* 2003, as amended.

In accordance with that Order, the plant or machinery is energy-saving plant or machinery if:

(1)   it falls within a technology class specified in the Water Technology Criteria List;

(2)   it meets the environmental criteria set out in that List; and

(3)   in the case of plant or machinery falling within any of the specified technology classes, it is of a type that:

   (a)   is specified in, and has not been removed from, the Water Technology Product List; or
   (b)   has been accepted for inclusion in that List.

The Water Technology Criteria List and the Water Technology Product List are updated each summer by the Secretary of State for the Environment, Food and Rural Affairs.

The technology classes referred to in (3) above are specified in the *Capital Allowances (Environmentally Beneficial Plant and Machinery) Order* 2003 (SI 2003/2076), reg. 3, as amended from time to time.

The lists are updated on a regular basis as technology develops. The detailed categories of qualifying expenditure within each broad heading also change periodically; according to HMRC guidance, these sub-lists are reviewed monthly. Reference should be made to the appropriate website (www.eca.gov.uk) for full current details.

Wastewater recovery systems

For expenditure on efficient membrane filtration systems for the treatment of wastewater for recovery and reuse, first-year allowances are only available under these provisions if a relevant certificate of environmental benefit is in force. The same restriction applies to efficient wastewater recovery and reuse systems.

These provisions are contained in the *Capital Allowances (Environmentally Beneficial Plant and Machinery) Order* 2003 (SI 2003/2076), in art. 5 as amended from time to time.

Legislation: CAA 2001, s. 45H; *Capital Allowances (Environmentally Beneficial Plant and Machinery) Order* 2003 (SI 2003/2076)

Other material: CA 23135

Environmentally beneficial components of plant or machinery

Special rules address the case in which qualifying plant or machinery is part of a larger item of plant or machinery that does not qualify for the 100 per cent allowance. If figures are specified in the Treasury Order for one or more components then the amounts qualifying for first-year allowances under this heading are restricted to those figures. If payments are made in instalments then the proportion of each instalment qualifying for first-year allowances is equal to the proportion that the total qualifying expenditure bears to the whole expenditure incurred on the plant and machinery.

The normal apportionment rules of CAA 2001, s. 562(3) are disapplied where the special rules apply to environmentally beneficial components of plant or machinery.

Legislation: CAA 2001, s. 45J

Other material: CA 23135

First-year allowances: computation

187-000   Calculating first-year allowances

Having established that a person is entitled to a first-year allowance, such an allowance will be made for the chargeable period in which the first-year qualifying expenditure is incurred. For expenditure incurred from April 2009, the computation would be on the following lines.

Example

A business with a value brought forward in its main pool of £20,000 incurred expenditure on a new asset costing £10,000 and sold an old asset for £1,000. Assuming that the new asset qualified for a 40 per cent first-year allowance, the computation may be presented as follows:

	£	£
Value brought forward		20,000
Additions	10,000	
Disposals		(1,000)
	10,000	19,000
First-year allowance (40%)	(4,000)	
Writing-down allowance (20%)		(3,800)
	6,000	15,200
Transfer to carry forward	(6,000)	6,000
Value carried forward	Nil	21,200
Total allowances due for period = £7,800		

Legislation: CAA 2001, s. 52(1)

Other material: CA 23110ff.

187-050   Claiming reduced first-year allowances

A person who is entitled to a first-year allowance may choose to claim the allowance in respect of only part of the first-year qualifying expenditure. This can be advantageous by preventing a balancing charge. The point is illustrated below in relation to expenditure incurred before 6 April 2008.

Example

A business qualifying for first-year allowances under the rules applying before 6 April 2008 had a pool written-down value brought down of £1,000. Suppose that in the year in question where 40 per cent first-year allowances were due, it disposed of an asset from the pool for £2,000 (being less than the original cost of the asset) and bought a new van for £10,000. There were no other transactions in the year.

If full first-year allowances were claimed then the allowances due would have been as follows:

	£
Value brought down	1,000
Disposal proceeds	(2,000)
Balancing charge	1,000
Cost of van	10,000
First-year allowance	4,000
Value carried down	6,000

In this case, the net allowances due would have been calculated as £3,000 (£4,000 writing-down allowances less £1,000 balancing charge); in net terms, the balancing charge absorbed part of the first-year allowance.

Plant and Machinery

Suppose, however, that the first-year allowance had been restricted in relation to one-tenth of the cost of the van, ie £1,000. Such a restriction was (and still is) permitted under CAA 2001, s. 52(4). This proportion of the expenditure was then treated as normal expenditure qualifying for writing-down allowances. (Section 58(5) refers to a first-year allowance being made in respect of an amount of first-year qualifying expenditure and shows that writing-down allowances can be claimed on any first-year qualifying expenditure on which no first-year allowance is made.)

The revised position was then as follows:

	£
Value brought down	1,000
Additions with no first-year allowances	1,000
Disposal proceeds	(2,000)
Balancing charge	Nil
Cost of van	10,000
Less: as above	1,000
	9,000
First-year allowance	3,600
Value carried down	5,400

The total net allowances due in the period would in this case have been £3,600, an improvement of £600 over the position where first-year allowances were claimed in full. This was, of course, a timing difference only but nevertheless there was a real cash flow advantage.

The Revenue used to confirm explicitly the availability of this approach in their manuals at old CA 2060 ('when the taxpayer chooses not to take a first-year allowance, expenditure can go straight into the pool and cover a disposal value from another asset which might otherwise create a balancing charge'). The current manual is not quite so explicit but the principle is confirmed in the example at CA 23110.

If no allowance at all is claimed in respect of particular expenditure, the opportunity to claim a first-year allowance is permanently lost; the expenditure is added to the pool and writing-down allowances only may be claimed in later years. The legislation states that 'any first-year allowance is made for the chargeable period in which the first-year qualifying expenditure is incurred'.

Legislation: CAA 2001, s. 52

Other material: CA 23110

187-100   FYA where asset bought and sold in same year

An asset may be bought and sold in the same year, as a result of which the issue arises of how to deal with the disposal proceeds: should they be set against the first-year allowance or should they go into the main pool?

Example

A trader who draws accounts up by the calendar year had a pool value brought forward of £11,000 at 1 January 2008. The only capital allowance transactions related to an asset that was bought in January for £1,200 and sold in September for £1,000. First-year allowances were available at 40 per cent as the expenditure was incurred before 6 April 2008.

It might be thought that the disposal should somehow be offset against the acquisition cost, giving a net £200 on the first-year allowance pool and a writing-down allowance of £2,750 on the main pool. However, this appears to be incorrect (though there are no official guidelines on the point).

The legislation does not recognise such a thing as a first-year allowance pool (though the author has seen an inspector of taxes arguing for one). The answer seems to lie in CAA 2001, s. 58(5)(a) and 58(6), which make it apparent that the balance of the first-year expenditure may exceptionally be allocated to the main pool when there is a disposal in the year of acquisition. On this basis, the trader may claim a first-year allowance of £480 and transfer the balance of £720 to the main pool in the same year. The balance of the main pool is then £11,720 less disposal proceeds of £1,000, to leave a net figure of £10,720 on which a writing-down allowance may be claimed at the transitional rate applying for the year.

187-150   Partial depreciation subsidies

If a person is to receive a *partial* depreciation subsidy (see 165-700 and 200-050) then first-year allowances are to be reduced to an amount which is 'just and reasonable'. This does not apply if the subsidy is treated as trading income of the recipient.

Legislation: CAA 2001, s. 210

Other material: CA 27500

Other allowances and charges

190-000   Other allowances and charges: introduction

Overview

The *Capital Allowances Act* 2001 uses two key concepts to determine the amount of any entitlement to capital allowances or liability to balancing charges: 'available qualifying expenditure' (AQE) and 'the total of any disposal receipts to be brought into account' (TDR).

The legislation then says, simply enough, that if AQE exceeds TDR then a writing-down allowance or balancing allowance will be due for the period in question. If the reverse is true then there will be a balancing charge for the period.

The principles apply equally to any single asset pools, any class pools and the main pool; see 190-100 for details as to how pooling operates. The only exceptions to the above are in respect of overseas leasing allowances (see 220-200) where restrictions are applied in certain cases and special rate cars anti-avoidance provisions (CAA 2001, s. 104F: see 200-520.

The allowance given where AQE exceeds TDR will always be a writing-down allowance except in the final chargeable period, when it will be a balancing allowance. The term 'final chargeable period' is in turn defined at 190-600. As regards first-year allowances, see 185-000.

Legislation: CAA 2001, s. 55

Reducing balance – old 25 per cent rate

The 25 per cent writing-down allowance, that applied for many years, was reduced to 20 per cent from April 2008, albeit subject to transitional rules. In principle, the allowance is given on the reducing balance of the pool.

From April 2008, writing-down allowances become less common but, in a sense, more complex. To begin with, therefore, the following examples look at the rules as they applied before the changes introduced in April 2008, and for a business that was not entitled to any first-year allowances. Suppose that such a business incurred expenditure of £16,000 in year one and that there are no other assets on which capital allowances are being claimed. In such a case, the full £16,000 would not have been written off over four years. Instead, the position would have been as follows:

Year 1	£
Additions	16,000
WDA (25% of £16,000)	(4,000)
Value carried forward	12,000

Year 2

WDA (25% of £12,000)	(3,000)
Value carried forward	9,000

Year 3

WDA (25% of £9,000)	(2,250)
Value carried forward	6,750

(and so on ad infinitum)

Legislation: CAA 2001, s. 55

Other material: CA 23200ff.

Reducing balance – lower rate from April 2008

The rate of writing-down allowance reduced from 25 per cent to 20 per cent in relation to chargeable periods that began from 1 or 6 April 2008, and was subject to transitional provisions for periods spanning those dates. The above example would look as follows in relation to a 20 per cent rate:

Year 1	£
Additions	16,000
WDA (20% of £16,000)	(3,200)
Value carried forward	12,800

Year 2	
WDA (20% of £12,800)	(2,560)
Value carried forward	10,240

Year 3	
WDA (20% of £10,240)	(2,048)
Value carried forward	8,192

(and so on ad infinitum)

In practice, it is likely that the new expenditure would be covered by annual investment allowances or would be subject to a claim for a first-year allowance.

190-100   Pooling

Most businesses spend substantial amounts of money on plant and machinery, ranging from computer equipment to cars and other vehicles or to sophisticated electrical systems and many items which are specific to the trade in question. Clearly, it would be impractical to produce separate tax computations to claim relief on every individual item. For this reason the legislation provides for a 'pooling' system which enables most expenditure to be dealt with in a single computation.

Plant and Machinery

The broad principle is therefore that expenditure has to be pooled for the purpose of calculating a person's entitlement to writing-down allowances and balancing allowances and any liability to balancing charges. If the same person carries on more than one qualifying activity (see 155-000), a separate pool (or set of pools) is required for each activity.

The legislation provides for a main pool but also for 'single-asset pools' and 'class pools'. Certain assets are stated to belong to the single-asset or class pools and all other expenditure is allocated to the main pool.

Single-asset pools

As the name suggests, such pools may contain expenditure relating to only one asset. Items in the following categories must go into a single asset pool (and no other items may do so);

- expensive cars bought (broadly) before April 2009 – see 201-040;
- short-life assets (CAA 2001, s. 86 – see 205-000);
- ships (CAA 2001, s. 127 – see 235-000);
- items used partly for non-trade purposes (CAA 2001, s. 206 – see 190-600);
- assets where a partial depreciation subsidy has been received (CAA 2001, s. 211 – see 200-050); and
- plant and machinery contribution allowance payments (CAA 2001, s. 538 – see 115-200).

Legislation: CAA 2001, s. 54(2)

Other material: CA 23210

Class pools

These are required for special rate expenditure (CAA 2001, s. 104C) (previously for long-life assets: CAA 2001, s. 101) and for assets used for overseas leasing (see 220-200). From April 2008, expenditure on thermal insulation, on integral features and on long-life assets is allocated to a 'special rate pool', normally with the effect that allowances are given at 10 per cent rather than at any higher rate (CAA 2001, s. 104C). Higher emission cars also go into the special rate pool from April 2009.

Where appropriate, separate class pools must be kept for overseas leasing on the one hand and for special rate expenditure on the other. Within the special rate pool, however, expenditure on the various assets is merged in a single ongoing computation.

Legislation: CAA 2001, s. 54(4), (5), 101, 107

Other material: CA 23210

190-200   Writing-down allowances

Normal rule

The normal rule is that the writing-down allowance is 20 per cent of the amount by which the AQE exceeds the TDR (see below for a definition of these terms). This figure of 20 per cent was reduced from 25 per cent, broadly from 1 or 6 April 2008 (for corporation tax and income tax respectively) but subject to transitional rules as explained at 190-250.

Example 1

A business has expenditure brought down from the previous period of £20,000. An asset is sold for £6,000 and a replacement is bought for £10,000. For simplicity, it is assumed that the business is not entitled to any annual investment allowance (probably because that allowance has been fully allocated to a connected business: see 181-200).

AQE will be £30,000 and TDR will be £6,000. Therefore, the allowance available is 20 per cent of the net figure of £24,000, so £4,800. The balance of £19,200 is carried forward to the following period of account.

If first-year allowances are claimed at 40 per cent, however, they will be given separately (£4,000). AQE will in that case be just £20,000 and the writing-down allowance will be calculated on a net figure of £14,000, giving an allowance of £2,800. Total allowances will therefore be £6,800, with £17,200 carried forward.

Example 2

A trader has a value brought down from year one of £100,000. He incurs expenditure in year two of £25,000. He sells an asset in the year for £5,000 (which is less than the cost of the asset). Assume that no first-year allowances or annual investment allowances are due. His computation for year two is as follows:

	£
Unrelieved qualifying expenditure brought forward	100,000
Additional qualifying expenditure	25,000
Available qualifying expenditure	125,000
Total disposal receipts	(5,000)
	120,000
Writing-down allowance (20%)	24,000
Unrelieved qualifying expenditure carried forward	96,000

Legislation: CAA 2001, s. 56

Modification of the normal rule

The normal rule is modified in various circumstances, as follows:

- in the case of special rate expenditure, where the rate is restricted to 10 per cent

Plant and Machinery

(previously, for long-life assets only, six per cent) (CAA 2001, s. 102 – see 210-000). This category includes integral features (CAA 2001, s. 104D – see 247-000ff.);

- in the case of certain assets used for overseas leasing, where the allowance is restricted to 10 per cent (CAA 2001, s. 109 – see 220-200);
- if the qualifying activity is carried on for part only of the chargeable period then the amount is proportionately reduced;
- a person claiming a writing-down allowance may choose to reduce the allowance to a specified amount. This could be beneficial, for example, where a full allowance would reduce the level of profits of a sole trader to the point where his personal allowances would not be fully used. By restricting the amount of allowances claimed, the trader may be able to make better use of the higher allowances that will be available in future years. For a company, it may well be appropriate to restrict relief claimed to make use, for example, of group relief;
- no writing-down allowance is given in the final chargeable period (as defined below);
- if the chargeable period is more or less than a year then the figure of 20 per cent is proportionately increased or decreased, and
- in the case of qualifying expenditure incurred wholly for the purposes of a ring fence trade in respect of which tax is charged under ICTA 1988, s. 501A, in which case the rate is 25 per cent (CAA 2001, s. 56(1A)).

For periods of account spanning 1 or 6 April 2008, a hybrid rate is used.

Example 3

The facts are as in example 2 above but the company carrying on the business has an accounting period of just nine months. In this case, allowances are calculated as follows:

	£
Unrelieved qualifying expenditure brought down	100,000
Additional qualifying expenditure	25,000
Available qualifying expenditure	125,000
Total disposal receipts	(5,000)
	120,000
Writing-down allowance (20% × 9/12)	18,000
Unrelieved qualifying expenditure carried forward	102,000

Legislation: CAA 2001, s. 56

Basis periods

A little care is needed when considering the interaction of these rules with the for determining the taxable profits of a sole trader or partner for any given period.

Example 4

Take, for example, a sole trader who has always drawn up accounts to 31 December each year, most recently to 31 December 2007. Suppose that he then draws accounts up to 30 September 2008.

For income tax purposes, his basis period for 2008–09 will be the period from 1 October 2007 to 30 September 2008, with an accrual of overlap relief for the period from 1 October 2007 to 31 December 2007, as this period has been 'taxed twice'. This is on the assumption that the sole trader chooses, and is able, to meet the conditions in ITTOIA 2005, s. 217.

As far as capital allowances are concerned, he will have a short period of accounts to 30 September 2007, so his writing-down allowances for that period will be restricted to $9/12$ths of what they would otherwise have been. Nevertheless, the capital allowances still merge in with the other deductions from the trading profits. Therefore, his tax liability will be on:

(1)   one-quarter of the profit net of capital allowances for the year to 31 December 2007; plus

(2)   the whole of the profit net of reduced capital allowances for the period to 30 September 2007.

A company can never have an accounting period in excess of one year (CTA 2009, s. 10(1)(a)). Under self-assessment, however, it is possible for an individual sole trader or a partnership to have a chargeable period of more than 12 months (but not more than 18 months) (CAA 2001, s. 6(6)).

Where the period of accounts does exceed 12 months then an increased writing-down allowance is made accordingly.

Example 5

The facts are as in Example 2 above except that the business is carried on by a sole trader in the course of a 15-month period. In this case, allowances are calculated as follows.

	£
Unrelieved qualifying expenditure brought down	100,000
Additional qualifying expenditure	25,000
Available qualifying expenditure	125,000
Total disposal receipts	(5,000)
	120,000
Writing-down allowance (20% × 15/12)	30,000
Unrelieved qualifying expenditure carried forward	90,000

Legislation: CAA 2001, s. 56

Other material: CA 23220

Plant and Machinery

190-250   Writing-down allowances: transitional rules

In principle, the rate of writing-down allowances for expenditure incurred on plant and machinery is reduced from 25 to 20 per cent with effect from 1 April 2008 (corporation tax) or 6 April 2008 (income tax). For the chargeable period that spans that April 2008 date, however, it is necessary to calculate a hybrid rate of WDA. The legislation requires this rate to be worked out on a daily basis, to two decimal places, rounding up in all cases. The hybrid percentage ('x') is given by the formula:

$$x = \left(25 \times \frac{BRD}{CP}\right) + \left(20 \times \frac{ARD}{CP}\right)$$

where:

BRD   is the number of days in the chargeable period before 6 April (or 1 April) 2008;

ARD   is the number of days in the chargeable period on or after 6 April (or 1 April) 2008; and

CP   is the total number of days in the chargeable period.

So if a sole trader draws accounts up to 31 December 2008, for example, the calculation will be as follows:

$$x = \left(25 \times \frac{96}{366}\right) + \left(20 \times \frac{270}{366}\right)$$

and the WDA figure to be used is therefore 21.32 per cent.

HMRC have published a 'ready reckoner' for calculating the writing-down allowance for income tax and corporation tax purposes: see www.hmrc.gov.uk/capital_allowances/read-reck-intro.htm for an introduction, and for a link to the ready reckoner itself.

190-275   Small pools

For the great majority of businesses, most *new* expenditure on plant and machinery (but excluding, for example, cars) will be relieved by way of the annual investment allowance (AIA) (see 181-000ff.). Most businesses, though, will have pools of expenditure brought forward from times before the new rules were introduced. This is where the new concept of a 'small pool' (introduced by the *Finance Act* 2008) will eventually simplify future capital allowance computations. Once the value of the pool has reduced to the 'small pool limit', it will be possible to write off the whole remaining balance in one go, by way of a special writing-down allowance. The small pool limit is set at the disappointingly low figure of £1,000, however, which means that many businesses will need to retain small and diminishing pools for many years.

The £1,000 threshold is applied to the pool value brought down, as adjusted for additional qualifying expenditure and total disposal receipts in the year. If, for example, there is a value of £1,100 brought forward then this in itself is too high to benefit from the small pool rules.

However, if there were also disposal proceeds in the year of £120 then this would take the value down to £980, and the whole amount could be claimed by way of a special writing-down allowance in the year.

Example

A sole trader draws up her accounts to 31 December. She has a pool value brought down at 1 January 2008 of £1,400 and she incurs no expenditure on plant and machinery in the following few years.

Her WDA percentage for the year is 21.32 per cent, as calculated above. As such, she will claim WDAs of £299 for 2008–09, giving a pool value carried down of £1,101. In the following year, WDAs will be given (at a straight 20 per cent) of £221, with £880 carried forward. In the year after that, WDAs can be claimed – under the small pool provisions – of the whole amount of £880. The sole trader will then never again need to claim WDAs on her main pool unless her expenditure exceeds £50,000 in the year or she buys an asset (such as a car) that does not qualify for AIAs.

For an example illustrating the interaction of writing-down allowances, first-year allowances and annual investment allowances, see 181-400.

The rules relating to small pools apply to the main capital allowances pool and to the special rate pool. They do not apply, for example, to short-life assets. They first applied in relation to chargeable periods that began from 1 or 6 April 2008 (for corporation tax and income tax respectively).

Legislation: CAA 2001, s. 56A; FA 2008, s. 81(5)

190-300   Interaction of first-year allowances and writing-down allowances

Where first-year allowances are claimed then no writing-down allowance is given in the same period for the same expenditure, but see 185-050 for details of why this is not quite as restrictive as it seems. Writing-down allowances are given in the ordinary way for expenditure brought forward.

Example

The facts are as in Example 2 at 190-200 (and the period is one of 12 months). In this case, though, a 40 per cent first-year allowance was due. The allowances would be calculated as follows:.

Plant and Machinery

	£	£
Unrelieved qualifying expenditure brought down	100,000	
Additional qualifying expenditure		25,000
Total disposal receipts	(5,000)	
	95,000	25,000
FYA (40%)		(10,000)
WDA (20%)	(19,000)	
	76,000	15,000
	15,000	
Unrelieved qualifying expenditure carried forward	91,000	

Total allowances due for the year will be £29,000.

As regards the interaction of FYAs, AIAs and WDAs, see 181-400ff.

Legislation: CAA 2001, s. 56ff.

190-400   Balancing allowances

A balancing allowance can only be obtained in the 'final chargeable period' as defined (see 190-600). For the main pool or for a special rate expenditure pool (or, before April 2008, long-life asset pool), this only arises when the qualifying activity is permanently discontinued. For single-asset pools (including, for example, short-life assets) the disposal will itself trigger the final chargeable period for capital allowances purposes.

The results can be surprising. Taking the main pool as an example, the important point to note is that a balancing allowance does not arise merely because all the assets in the pool have been sold. The position is complicated, however, by the changes introduced from April 2008 and the following example applies to periods before those changes, but with a note at the end explaining the implications of those changes.

Example

Winston is a window cleaner who has never owned any plant or machinery. He buys a second-hand van for £2,000 and uses it exclusively for the purpose of his window-cleaning trade. The following year he regrets his decision and sells the van for £1,000. His capital allowances position will be as follows, calling the year of purchase year one and ignoring possible first-year allowances:

Year 1	£
Value brought forward	Nil
Additions	2,000
WDA	(500)
Value carried down	1,500

Year 2

Sale proceeds	(1,000)
	500
WDA	(125)
Value carried forward	375

Year 3

WDA	(94)
Value carried down	281

(and so on ad infinitum)

He will thus continue to obtain capital allowances for as long as he carries on trading, with the writing-down allowance reducing each year. It will be seen that the tax relief therefore lags behind any accounting treatment of the asset concerned. The way around this disadvantage may be to make a short-life asset election (see 205-000), or to use the van for occasional private journeys. In either of these cases, the van will need to go into a single-asset pool and the disposal will then (if appropriate) trigger a full balancing allowance.

Changes from April 2008

The above example is left in place as it remains of relevance for periods before April 2008. However, the position would now be different in a number of ways.

First, the cost of the van would almost certainly be subject to a claim for an annual investment allowance.

Secondly (if, for the purposes of illustration, Winston forgot to claim such an allowance), the rate of any WDA would now be at 20 per cent instead of 25 per cent.

Thirdly, the 'small pool' rules would now operate to ensure that the entire balance could be written off once the value of the pool reduced below £1,000 (as illustrated at 190-275).

Legislation: CAA 2001, s. 55(4)

Other material: CA 23240ff.

190-500   Balancing charges

Unlike the balancing allowance (for details of which see 190-400), a balancing charge can arise at any time. It will arise if the disposal value to be brought into account exceeds the qualifying expenditure (brought forward plus expenditure in the year). In statutory terms, a person will be liable to a balancing charge in any period, including the final period, if TDR exceeds AQE. The charge will be the amount of that excess. See 190-600ff. for definitions of these terms.

Looking back at the example at 190-400, what would the position have been if the sale proceeds in year 2 had been £1,700? In that case, the disposal value would exceed the total qualifying expenditure that is left of £1,500 and a balancing charge of the excess £200

Plant and Machinery

would be made in year 2. There would then be no value to carry forward at the end of year 2 and no further capital allowances computations would be needed. (It should be remembered that if he had sold the van for £2,500 then the sale proceeds for capital allowances purposes would be £2,000 as they cannot exceed the cost to him of the asset. He would therefore suffer a balancing charge in year two of £500 so as to wipe out the allowance he had received in year one.)

Legislation: CAA 2001, s. 56(6)

Other material: CA 23240

190-600   Definitions

Introduction

For the purpose of calculating allowances and charges some key terms need defining, as follows:

- final chargeable period (see 190-650);
- available qualifying expenditure (AQE) (see 190-700); and
- total disposal receipts (TDR) (see 190-750).

190-650   Final chargeable period

This concept is important to determine the timing of any balancing adjustments. The meaning varies according to the type of pool in question, and is variously defined as follows:

- for the main pool, and for the special rate expenditure pool (or, before April 2008, the long-life asset pool), it is the chargeable period in which the qualifying activity is permanently discontinued;
- for a class pool under CAA 2001, s. 107 (overseas leasing – see 220-200) it is the chargeable period 'at the end of which the circumstances are such that there can be no more disposal receipts in any subsequent chargeable period'. Presumably in practice this means the first such chargeable period;
- for a single-asset pool, it is defined as the first chargeable period in which any disposal event within CAA 2001, s. 61(1) occurs, as outlined at below.

There are various exceptions to this last definition, as follows:

(1) a period is not a final chargeable period merely because the item in question starts to be used partly for purposes other than those of a qualifying activity (206(4) and (formerly, in relation to cars, CAA 2001, s. 77(1));

(2) it is not a final chargeable period when the four year cut-off period comes to an end for a short-life asset pool (CAA 2001, s. 86(2) and 87(2) – see 205-000);

(3)   special rules apply for a single ship pool (CAA 2001, s. 132(2)).

Legislation: CAA 2001, s. 65

Other material: CA 23270

190-700   Available qualifying expenditure

Available qualifying expenditure (AQE) is defined to include two elements:

(1)   qualifying expenditure that is allocated to the pool for the period in question; plus

(2)   unrelieved qualifying expenditure brought forward in the pool from the preceding chargeable period.

Various elements go to make up the concept of qualifying expenditure and the key sections of the legislation are as follows:

- the initial definition of 'qualifying expenditure' is given in CAA 2001, s. 11(4) (see 160-000);
- the rules dealing with the allocation of qualifying expenditure to any particular pool are given in CAA 2001, s. 58 (see below);
- the concept of unrelieved qualifying expenditure brought forward from an earlier period is addressed at CAA 2001, s. 59 (see below);
- various types of expenditure that are specifically included in, or excluded from, the concept of available qualifying expenditure are listed (respectively) at CAA 2001, s. 57(2) and (3) (see below).

In determining whether particular expenditure can be added to a given pool for any given period, the following exclusions need to be noted:

- if an amount of expenditure has been taken into account for an earlier chargeable period, it cannot be allocated to a pool for a subsequent period (though, to the extent it has not been exhausted, it will be brought forward under separate rules);
- qualifying expenditure cannot be allocated to a pool before the cost has been incurred;
- it cannot be allocated to a pool for any given chargeable period unless the person in question owns the plant or machinery at some time in that period;
- any annual investment allowance (AIA) qualifying expenditure is allocated to the appropriate pool(s) but the AQE is then reduced by the amount of that expenditure (see below);
- any amount of expenditure on which first-year allowances have been claimed in the year must be excluded; and
- any amount on which first-year allowances have been claimed for an earlier period must be limited to the balance left after deducting the first-year allowance.

Plant and Machinery

The treatment of AIA may seem puzzling – adding expenditure to the pool but then immediately deducting it again. The purpose of this provision is to ensure that disposal proceeds are properly allocated on any future disposal of the asset that has attracted AIAs.

Legislation: CAA 2001, s. 57–58

Other material: CA 23230

Unrelieved qualifying expenditure

A person will have unrelieved qualifying expenditure to carry forward to a subsequent period if, for the earlier period, the available qualifying expenditure exceeds the total of any disposal receipts.

If a writing-down allowance is made for the period then the amount to be carried forward will be AQE minus TDR minus the writing-down allowance given for the period. If there was no writing-down allowance in the period in question then the unrelieved qualifying expenditure carried forward will simply be AQE minus TDR. In each case, AQE includes unrelieved qualifying expenditure brought forward from an earlier period.

No unrelieved qualifying expenditure can ever be carried forward from a final chargeable period.

Legislation: CAA 2001, s. 59

Amounts specifically to be included in qualifying expenditure

A person's available qualifying expenditure in a pool for a chargeable period also includes any amount allocated to the pool for that period under any of the following provisions (CAA 2001, s. 57(2)):

- CAA 2001, s. 26(3) (net costs of demolition – see 260-510);
- CAA 2001, s. 86(2) or 87(2) (allocation of expenditure in short-life asset pool – see 205-000);
- CAA 2001, s. 111(3) (overseas leasing: standard recovery mechanism – see 220-200);
- CAA 2001, s. 129(1), 132(2), 133(3) or 137 (provisions relating to operation of single ship pool and deferment of balancing charges in respect of ships);
- CAA 2001, s. 161C(2) (decommissioning expenditure incurred by person carrying on trade of oil extraction);
- CAA 2001, s. 165(3) (abandonment expenditure incurred after cessation of ring-fence trade);
- CAA 2001, s. 206(3) (plant or machinery used partly for purposes other than those of the qualifying activity – see below); or
- CAA 2001, s. 211(4) (partial depreciation subsidy paid – see 200-050).

Amounts specifically to be excluded from qualifying expenditure

A person's available qualifying expenditure does *not* include any expenditure excluded by any of the following (CAA 2001, s. 57(3)):

- CAA 2001, s. 8(4) or 9(1) – rules against double relief;
- CAA 2001, s. 166(2) – transfers of interests in oil fields: anti-avoidance;
- CAA 2001, s. 185(2), 186(2) or 187(2) – restrictions where other claims made in respect of fixture – see the Chapter headed 'Plant and Property', which begins at 250-000;
- CAA 2001, s. 218(1), 224(1), 228(2), 242(2) or 243(2) – general anti-avoidance provisions – again, see 220-500.

There are also special rules (CAA 2001, s. 220 – see 220-500) determining the allocation to particular chargeable periods of expenditure incurred on plant or machinery for leasing under a finance lease (CAA 2001, s. 57(4)).

190-750   Total disposal receipts

Although the legislation uses the concept of 'the total of any disposal receipts' (which it abbreviates to 'TDR') there is no definition of this term. However, there is a definition of 'disposal receipt'. In other words, disposal receipts are converted to TDR simply by an arithmetic process rather than by any sleight of legislation.

In most cases, the disposal value for capital allowances purposes will simply be the sale proceeds. The position can be more complex, however, and even in the rewritten legislation of CAA 2001, the sections dealing with disposal events and disposal values need to be considered with some care. An outline of the structure of the legislation is as follows:

(1) a 'disposal receipt' is defined as a disposal value that a person is required to bring into account (CAA 2001, s. 60(1));

(2) the most common disposal values, together with the disposal events that trigger them, are listed at CAA 2001, s. 61 (see below);

(3) a 'general limit' on the amount of disposal value that has to be brought into account is defined at CAA 2001, s. 62 (see below);

(4) certain cases where a disposal value is taken into account, but where that value is actually nil, are listed at CAA 2001, s. 63 (see below);

(5) a particular circumstance where no disposal value needs to be brought into account is given at CAA 2001, s. 64 (see below);

(6) a further example of where no disposal value needs to be taken into account is given at CAA 2001, s. 264(3) (a disposal between members of an ongoing partnership);

(7) a wide range of additional circumstances where a disposal value may need to be brought into account is then listed at CAA 2001, s. 66 (see below);

(8)   a disposal value may need to be brought into account by virtue of FA 1997, Sch. 12, para. 11 (Finance Lease or Loan: Receipt of Major Lump Sum);

(9)   finally, the legislation recognises that a disposal value may need to be brought into account in accordance with 'any other Enactment'.

Whenever the legislation requires a disposal value to be brought into account this is referred to as a 'disposal event'. If, after qualifying expenditure has been allocated to a pool, there is more than one disposal event in respect of the item of plant or machinery in question, then a disposal value has to be brought into account only on the happening of the first event.

Special rules deal with deferred balancing charges for shipping and two additional VAT rebates.

Disposal events

Subject to the complications outlined above, the following are listed as the main events that will require a person to bring a disposal value of plant or machinery into account:

* if the person ceases to own the plant or machinery;
* if he loses possession of it in circumstances where 'it is reasonable to assume that the loss is permanent';
* if plant or machinery that has been used for mineral exploration and access is abandoned by the person at the site where it was in use for that purpose;
* if the plant or machinery ceases to exist, whether because it has been destroyed, dismantled or otherwise;
* if it starts to be used wholly or partly for purposes other than those of the qualifying activity (where it is partly used, restricted allowances will still be available);
* if the plant or machinery begins to be leased under a long funding lease (see 240-220ff.); or
* if the qualifying activity is permanently discontinued.

The legislation then quantifies the disposal value to be taken into account in relation to each disposal event, as below.

Legislation: CAA 2001, s. 61

Disposal values – normal rules

The amount of the disposal value to be brought into account 'depends on the disposal event'. Each event is dealt with in turn in the following paragraphs. Where appropriate, an apportionment of a transaction may need to be made between different types of asset, (eg buildings and plant).

The sale of plant or machinery

The great majority of disposals of plant will fall under this heading. As would be expected, the basic rule is that if machinery or plant is sold then the disposal value equals the net proceeds of that sale (but see below if the disposal is not at market value). There is no definition of 'net proceeds' but a commonsense approach means that it is the amount of proceeds after deducting any costs of sale.

The legislation does say that in addition to these net proceeds there must be brought in any insurance received for any event that has affected the price obtainable on the sale of the plant or machinery. Similarly, any other capital compensation received for the same reason must be brought into account.

Legislation: CAA 2001, s. 61(2)

Other material: CA 23250

The sale of plant or machinery other than at market value

There is a general principle that where plant or machinery is sold below its market value then it is necessary to bring in the market value figure. There are, however, certain exceptions. If the disposal gives rise to a charge to tax as earnings from an employment – for example because it is given to an employee or sold to him at less than its market value – then only the actual proceeds (if any) need to be brought into account. This is the case even if no tax is actually payable by the director or employee because of the £30,000 exemption applying to certain payments on the termination, etc of an employment.

Similarly, market value does not have to be substituted if the buyer can claim capital allowances on the asset as plant or machinery or under the research and development allowance rules (though this exemption does not apply if the buyer is a dual resident investing company connected with the seller, as defined in ICTA 1988, s. 839). This is the case even if the buyer and seller are connected with each other. Note that whilst there is no right of election in these circumstances to transfer assets at tax written-down value, the parties can agree an actual proceeds figure that achieves this effect. This is subject to HMRC's right to impose a 'just and reasonable apportionment' in certain circumstances – see the Chapter headed 'Plant and Property', which begins at 250-000.

If the asset is sold for more than its market value then there is nothing in the legislation to restrict the proceeds figure to the market value (see below, however, for the restriction of proceeds by reference to the historic cost of the asset).

The demolition or destruction of the plant or machinery

If the plant or machinery is totally demolished then three elements need to be added together to produce the proceeds figure for capital allowance purposes:

- the net proceeds of sale of the remains of the machinery or plant; plus
- any insurance payment made in respect of the demolition or destruction; plus
- any other compensation which is capital in nature and received in respect of the demolition or destruction.

121

The permanent loss of the plant or machinery

An asset may be lost even though it has not been demolished or destroyed. The obvious example is if it is stolen. In this case, the principle is identical to that under the above heading (demolition or destruction) except that there will obviously not be any sale proceeds for the remains of the machinery or plant.

Abandonment of plant or machinery used for mineral exploration

At the end of a period of mineral exploration, a business may abandon plant or machinery on-site because it is more expensive or dangerous to move it than to leave it behind. In these cases, the disposal value equals any insurance money received in respect of the abandonment plus any other compensation that is capital in nature and that is received in relation to the abandonment.

Commencement of the term of a long funding finance lease

In relation to leases whose inception is on or after 13 November 2008, the disposal value is the greater of the 'qualifying lease payments' and the market value of the plant or machinery at the commencement of the term of the lease (FA 2009, s. 64 and Sch. 32). The term 'qualifying lease payments' is defined to mean the minimum payments under the lease (including any initial payment) but excluding the following:

(a) so much of any payment as, under generally accepted accounting practice, falls (or would fall) to be treated as the gross return on investment in respect of the lease,

(b) so much of any payment as represents charges for services, and

(c) so much of any payment as represents qualifying UK or foreign tax (within the meaning of s. 70YE) to be paid by the lessor.

For earlier periods, the disposal value was an amount equal to that which would be recognised as the lessor's net investment in the lease if accounts were prepared in accordance with generally accepted accounting practice. See generally 230-000ff.

Commencement of the term of a long funding operating lease

The disposal value is an amount equal to the value of the plant or machinery at the commencement of the term of the lease.

The permanent discontinuance of the qualifying activity

It may be that the trade, or other qualifying activity, is brought to an end before any of the above events. If the permanent discontinuance is followed by one of the events outlined in the above paragraphs then the disposal value is still the amount specified for whichever event duly occurs. Thus, if the trade ceases and the asset is then sold, the proceeds will be calculated on the basis of the first of the above headings.

Any other event

If a disposal value needs to be brought into account, but none of the events envisaged in the preceding paragraphs has taken place, then the open market value is to be brought into account as the disposal value.

Disposal values – special cases

In addition to the circumstances outlined above, CAA 2001 s. 60(1)(b) requires a disposal value to be taken into account in accordance with numerous provisions listed in CAA 2001, s. 66. Section 66 reads as follows (as amended from April 2009):

'66 List of provisions outside this Chapter about disposal values

The provisions of this Part referred to in section 60(1)(b) are:

Section 68	hire-purchase, etc: disposal value on cessation of notional ownership
Section 70E	long funding leases: disposal events and disposal values
Sections 72 and 73	grant of new software right: disposal value
Sections 88 and 89	short-life assets: disposal at under-value or to connected person
Section 104E	special rate expenditure: avoidance cases
Sections 108, 111 and 114	overseas leasing: disposal values in various cases
Sections 132 and 143	ships: ship used for overseas leasing, etc; attribution of amount where balancing charge deferred
Section 171	oil production sharing contracts: disposal values on cessation of ownership
Sections 196 and 197	fixtures: disposal values on cessation of notional ownership and in avoidance cases
Section 208	effect of significant reduction in use of plant or machinery for purposes of qualifying activity
Section 208A	cars: disposal value in avoidance cases
Section 211	effect of payment of partial depreciation subsidy
Section 222	anti-avoidance: limit on disposal value
Sections 228K to 228M	disposal of plant or machinery subject to lease where income retained
Section 229	hire-purchase: disposal values in finance leasing and anti-avoidance cases
Sections 238 and 239	additional VAT rebates.'

Legislation: CAA 2001, s. 62–64

Other material: CA 23250, 23260

Restrictions on disposal value

There are various circumstances where the disposal value is limited, is nil or does not need to be brought into account at all.

Legislation: CAA 2001, s. 62–64

General limit

As a first principle, the disposal value to be brought into account can never exceed the cost incurred on the asset by the person concerned.

> ### Example
>
> A trader buys an asset for £20,000. The asset goes into the main pool of expenditure and allowances are given over a period of three years. The asset is no longer manufactured and is badly needed by a particular business which therefore offers £30,000 to obtain it. The disposal value to be brought into the first trader's accounts will be restricted to £20,000. The vendor may have to pay capital gains tax (or corporation tax) on the gain.

This rule is modified where the person making the disposal acquired the plant or machinery in a transaction with a connected person. Sometimes there will have been a series of such transactions between connected persons. In such a case, the amount of the disposal value is restricted to 'the amount of the qualifying expenditure on the provision of the plant or machinery incurred by whichever party to the transaction, or to any of the transactions, incurred the greatest such expenditure'.

> ### Example
>
> Bill and Ben are brothers operating two separate transport businesses. Bill buys a lorry for £50,000. Ben is in financial difficulty and Bill duly sells the lorry to Ben for £5,000. In due course, Ben sells it at arm's length for £10,000.
>
> If the transaction between Bill and Ben had not been between connected persons then Ben's disposal proceeds would be restricted to the £5,000 he had paid for the lorry. As it is, however, the restriction is the £50,000 originally paid by Bill. As such, Ben must bring into his capital allowances computation the full amount of proceeds of £10,000.

The above provisions can also be modified where one or more additional VAT rebates have been made in respect of original expenditure. In such a case, the amount of the disposal value is normally limited to the amount of the original expenditure reduced by the total amount of any additional VAT rebates accruing in respect of that expenditure. The position is actually slightly more complex than this, as outlined in full at CAA 2001, s. 239.

Cases where the disposal value is nil

There are several circumstances where an event constitutes a disposal but the value is nil. In some cases, this will produce a balancing allowance.

(1) Where a person disposes of plant or machinery by way of gift in circumstances that produce a tax charge as earnings of an office or employment. This will typically arise where a director is leaving a company and is allowed to keep his company car. If he had been paid a £10,000 bonus then this would normally be an allowable expense for the employer. If, instead, he takes his car which is valued at £10,000 then it is proper that the employer should still obtain tax relief. This is achieved by bringing in a disposal value of nil.

The disposal value in these circumstances is nil even if the director or employee concerned pays no tax because of the exemption applying to certain compensation and termination payments (ITEPA 2003, s. 403(1)). The point is confirmed at CA 23250.

The nil disposal value applies only where the asset in question was a gift. HMRC make the following observation in this respect:

> 'If an employer transfers an asset to an employee and claims that the disposal value is nil, you should check that the transfer is really a gift. A gift is a transfer from one person to another for no consideration ... This means that a transfer that is a gift cannot have been made wholly and exclusively for the purposes of the trade and ICTA 1988, s. 74 (1)(a)[see ITTOIA 2005, s. 34 and CTA 2009, s. 54] will prevent a Case I deduction ...
>
> An employer cannot be entitled both to a Case I deduction and to have a disposal value of nil on the transfer of an asset to an employee. If the employer has claimed a Case I deduction, the transfer must have passed the wholly and exclusively test. If it has passed the wholly and exclusively test, it cannot have been for no consideration and so it cannot have been a gift. In that case the employer is required to bring a disposal value to account in the capital allowance computation.'

(2)   The disposal value is also treated as nil where the person carrying on the activity gives the plant or machinery to:

(a)   a charity (within ICTA 1988, s. 506);

(b)   various heritage bodies and museums (as listed in ICTA 1988, s. 507(1)); or

(c)   a designated educational establishment (within the meaning of ITTOIA 2005, s. 110 or CTA 2009, s. 106).

Gifts of plant or machinery to bodies within (a) to (c) above will only have a nil disposal value where they are made by somebody carrying on a trade, profession, vocation, furnished holiday lettings business, UK property business or overseas property business.

The special treatment does not apply to holders of an office or employment, to investment companies, to businesses involved in special leasing of plant or machinery or to concerns listed in CTA 2009, s. 39(4) (mines, transport undertakings, etc.).

The disposal value for gifts to bodies within (a) to (c) above will not be nil if the donor or a connected person receives a benefit which is attributable to the gift – see ITTOIA 2005, s. 109 and CTA 2009, s. 108 (and CAA 2001, s. 63(4)).

(3)   The disposal value is also to be taken as nil where the expenditure was only deemed to be incurred on plant or machinery by virtue of CAA 2001, s. 27(2), covering thermal insulation of buildings, various expenditure connected with safety at sports grounds and certain personal security expenditure (see 160-000). The category of fire safety expenditure was removed by the *Finance Act* 2008.

Cases where no disposal value needs to be brought into account

If none of the qualifying expenditure has been taken into account for the purposes of claiming capital allowances, then no disposal value needs to be brought into account when it is disposed of. For these purposes, a person takes expenditure into account in a claim in a tax return, in an amendment to a tax return or in any other claim under the plant and machinery legislation. (A technicality arises where a 100 per cent first-year allowance is given as the

Plant and Machinery

expenditure never features in a pool as such and a strict reading of CAA 2001, s. 64(1) might lead to the conclusion that no disposal event could therefore occur. The point is resolved by s. 58(6) and (7), which ensure that a balance is transferred across to the main pool 'even if the balance is nil (because of a 100% first-year allowance)'.)

The above rule is modified where there have been connected party transactions. In this case, it will be necessary to bring a disposal value into account if any connected party has been required to bring a disposal value into account. HMRC illustrate this with the following example:

> 'Sam and Dave are connected. They are both musicians. Sam buys an electric guitar for £15,000 and brings it into use for his business. He decides to get a better one and so he sells the electric guitar to Dave for £7,000. Dave can claim [plant and machinery allowances] on the guitar and so Sam's disposal value is £7,000.
>
> Dave then decides to change to an acoustic guitar and so he does not add the expenditure to his pool and sells the electric guitar for £12,000. Dave has to bring a disposal value of £12,000 to account and he can treat the £7,000 as qualifying expenditure.
>
> The guitar was bought by Sam for £15,000 and sold by Dave for £12,000 – a net loss of £3,000, which is the overall result. Sam has expenditure £15,000 and disposal proceeds £7,000 while Dave has expenditure of £7,000 and proceeds £12,000.'

190-850   Private use restriction

Where there is private use of an asset by a business proprietor, allowances are restricted accordingly. The most common example of the private use restriction is probably in relation to the car owned by a sole trader or the cars owned by a partnership and driven by its partners. A restriction is made to all types of allowance (first-year, writing-down, balancing) and balancing charges are also restricted as appropriate.

Take, for example, a sole trader who buys a car in July 2009 for £18,000, with emissions of 170g/km. Allowances are first calculated at 10 per cent (because the car has emissions in excess of 160g/km: see 200-100) to give an allowance for the first year of £1,800. If it is agreed that the car is used one third for private purposes then the actual allowance given will be restricted accordingly, to £1,200. In calculating the balance to carry forward in the special rate pool, however, the full amount of £1,800 must be deducted.

Legislation: CAA 2001, s. 207

Cars

200-000   Introduction and overview

Introduction

The tax rules granting relief for business expenditure on cars were changed quite radically from April 2009.

The underlying principle has always been that a business should gain tax relief - at some stage - on the amount by which the value of a car has fallen over the period of ownership. If, for example, a business buys a car for £20,000 and sells it three years later for £7,500, then it will be able to reduce its taxable profits by £12,500 (albeit subject to a likely private use adjustment if the car is not owned by a company). What the tax system does not do, though, is to give tax relief on a timescale that mirrors commercial depreciation; rather, it contains its own fairly complex rules to determine the timing of the tax deductions.

The changes applying from April 2009 relate almost entirely to the timing of that tax relief. In the past, the main factor that determined the speed at which relief could be gained was the cost of the car: more expensive cars were discouraged by slowing down the percentage of relief that could be given in the early years. Now, the rate of relief is determined primarily by the level of engine emissions, the idea being to encourage businesses to buy cars that are more fuel efficient and that therefore have a less damaging environmental impact.

Considering that they are concerned primarily with the timing of tax relief, the changes to the legislation applying from April 2009 are more complex than might be imagined. For this reason, this commentary has been split into two discrete parts. The current rules are shown first and the older rules are then given separately, starting at 201-000.

Although the changes broadly apply from 1 or 6 April 2009 (for corporation tax and income tax respectively), the commencement and transitional provisions are also quite involved and these are considered at 200-620.

Summary of new rules

Key features of the rules introduced from April 2009 are as follows:

- The former concept of 'expensive' cars is abolished and the rate of tax relief instead depends on the level of the vehicle's CO_2 emissions.
- Qualifying expenditure incurred from (broadly) 1 or 6 April 2009 (for corporation tax and income tax respectively) is normally allocated to one of the two main pools for plant and machinery. Expenditure on 'main rate cars' (broadly, those with emissions of up to 160g/km: see 200-100) goes into the main plant and machinery pool, attracting allowances at 20 per cent. Cars with higher emissions attract allowances at just 10 per cent in the 'special rate' pool.
- Cars with private use are kept in a single asset pool but the rate at which allowances are given is still determined by reference to the same emission principles.

- For cars bought before April 2009, allowances are normally calculated according to principles applying up to that date, though the transitional provisions are quite complex: see 200-620.
- Car leases that began before 1 or 6 April 2009 broadly continue to be subject to the former rules. For new leases of vehicles above the 160g/km threshold, a flat rate disallowance is made, calculated as 15 per cent of 'relevant payments'. New cars with lower emissions will suffer no disallowance.
- Certain hire cars (eg taxis) that were formerly exempt from the restrictions for expensive cars are from April 2009 subject to the new rules. Conversely, motor cycles were previously classified as cars for capital allowance purposes but are excluded from the definition from April 2009 (see 200-020).
- The 100 per cent first-year allowance for cars with very low emissions continues unchanged.

Comparison with old rules: slower tax relief

As noted above, the normal rule is that expenditure incurred from April 2009 is allocated either to the main plant and machinery pool or to the special rate pool, and attracts allowances at either 20 or 10 per cent accordingly.

Compared with the system applying before April 2009, the pooling of cars in this way may have a short-term advantage (as annual writing-down allowances are no longer capped at £3,000). However, the amended rules represent a significant cash-flow cost in the longer term as there will be no balancing allowance on sale of the vehicle, even if is the only item in the main or special rate pool (see 190-400). This will be disadvantageous for most cars but the change is especially severe for cars with higher emissions.

Example

A company director drives a company car with emissions of 170g/km. The vehicle is bought in Year 1 for £40,000 and sold in Year 4 for £18,000. Under the old rules, the company would obtain tax relief on £3,000 in each of years one to three, and £13,000 (by way of balancing allowance) in year four.

Under the rules now applying, the company will initially be slightly better off, but will lose out badly when the car comes to be sold. Allowances will not be calculated separately for the car but will effectively be £4,000, £3,600, £3,240 and (adjusting for the sale proceeds) £1,116. The loss on the car is £22,000 but only just over half of that loss has attracted tax relief by the time the car comes to be sold. The rest of the relief will be obtained over an indefinite future period.

200-020   Definition of 'car'

The capital allowance definition of 'car' now covers any 'mechanically propelled road vehicle' except:

- a motor cycle;

- a vehicle of a construction primarily suited for the conveyance of goods or burden of any description, (eg a van, but see 200-040); or
- a vehicle of a type not commonly used as a private vehicle and unsuitable for such use (eg a police car, but see 200-060).

The definition is similar (but not identical) to that used for the purposes of determining benefits in kind on company cars. As a result, some of the case law that has helped to hone the definition in that area of the legislation may be applied equally to the capital allowance definition.

Legislation: CAA 2001, s. 268A

Motor cycles

The exclusion of motor cycles was a change introduced from April 2009. This means that motor cycles are now treated for capital allowance purposes like any other asset, rather than being subject to the special rules applying for cars. One effect of this is that annual investment allowances are now available for motor cycles, whereas this was not previously the case. See 200-620 for transitional rules applying around April 2009.

In this context, the term 'motor cycle' has the meaning given by the *Road Traffic Act* 1988, s. 185(1). As such, it is defined as 'a mechanically propelled vehicle, not being an invalid carriage, with less than four wheels and the weight of which unladen does not exceed 410 kilograms'.

Legislation: CAA 2001, s. 268A(2)

200-040   Conveyance of goods or burden

As noted in the definition given at 200-020, a vehicle will not be treated as a car if it is 'of a construction primarily suited for the conveyance of goods or burden of any description'.

This condition will mainly exclude vans, pick-up trucks and heavy-goods vehicles, though in practice, it is not always clear what constitutes a van in any particular case. A key point is that the test is one of construction rather than the use to which the vehicle will be put. This principle was explored in the case of *Morris v R & C Commrs*, where a 'motorhome' was held to be a car, even though it was in fact used for transporting goods. The judge emphasised that the construction of the vehicle was what counted and not the use to which it was in fact put. On the facts found, the motorhome was of a type commonly used as a private vehicle.

Cases: *Morris v R & C Commrs* [2006] BTC 861

Estate cars

HMRC view is that estate cars are not 'primarily suited for transporting goods' and that such vehicles are therefore cars rather than vans. For employment income purposes, though,

Plant and Machinery

HMRC do say that estate cars may nevertheless come within the exemption if they 'have been permanently and substantially modified to change their construction'.

Other material: EIM 23020

Off road vehicles

Luxury off road vehicles, and four wheel drive recreational vehicles, are normally treated as cars for the purposes of the benefit in kind rules and the same principles will apply to classify them as cars for capital allowance purposes. The HMRC view is that such vehicles are not designed primarily for carrying goods or burden (and there is nothing about them that makes them unsuitable for private use).

Other material: EIM 23044

Pick-up trucks

There can be areas of doubt over such vehicles as double cab pick-up trucks. In the area of employment tax law, where the same principle applies, HMRC take the view that such trucks are suitable for private use (see below) but that it is more difficult to determine whether they are of a construction primarily suited for the conveyance of goods or burden. HMRC make the general observation that:

> '[Pick-up trucks] present us with a challenge in terms of establishing the predominant purpose of construction ... as on the surface many of them appear to be equally suited to convey passengers or goods. However, when all factors relating to their construction are taken into account, a number of vehicles within this category do have a predominant purpose of carrying goods or burden.
>
> It follows from the above that it is not possible to come up with a single categorisation for all double cab pick-ups. Nor is it possible to give a blanket ruling on any particular makes, as the standard vehicle may have been adapted in the factory, by the dealer, or once acquired. So each case will depend on the facts and the exact specification during the period when the vehicle is made available for private use.'

As a pragmatic approach (which is, however, open to possible challenge as there is no specific statutory authority for it), HMRC interpret the legislation in line with the definitions used for VAT purposes. The practical effect of this is explained as follows:

> 'Under this measure, a double cab pick-up that has a payload of 1 tonne (1,000kg) or more is accepted as a van for benefits purposes. Payload means gross vehicle weight (or design weight) less unoccupied kerb weight (care is needed when looking at manufacturers' brochures as they sometimes define payload differently).
>
> Under a separate agreement between Customs and the Society of Motor Manufacturers and Traders (SMMT), a hard top consisting of metal, fibre glass or similar material, with or without windows, is accorded a generic weight of 45kg. Therefore the addition of a hard top to a double cab pick-up with an ex-works payload of 1,010 kg will convert the vehicle into a car (net payload reduced to 965 kg). Under this agreement, the weight of all other optional accessories is disregarded. HMRC has also adopted this treatment.'

Other material: EIM 23045

200-060   Not commonly used as a private vehicle and unsuitable to be so used

As noted in the definition given at 200-020, a vehicle will not be treated as a car if it is 'of a type not commonly used as a private vehicle and unsuitable for such use'. As such, there are two separate tests, both of which have to be satisfied if the vehicle is to fall outside the definition of 'car' for capital allowance purposes:

- it must be of a type not commonly used as a private vehicle; *and*
- the vehicle must be unsuitable to be so used.

(There is a possible argument in relation to the second condition. The accepted reading seems to be that the vehicle must, in itself, be unsuitable to be used as a private vehicle. An alternative reading is that the vehicle must be of a type that is unsuitable for such use.)

HMRC accept that the following types of vehicle are 'not commonly used as a private vehicle': fire engines, agricultural tractors, buses, back-hoe loaders, diggers. Strictly, it is still necessary to consider whether they are unsuitable for use as such, though it is thought that all of the listed vehicles will also meet that second condition without any problem.

By contrast, HMRC comment that:

> 'A vehicle that in itself is not of a common model because there are not very many of them, for example a luxurious sports car, is still of a type of vehicle that is commonly used as a private vehicle and suitable for that use. The type in that instance is a sports saloon.'

Legislation: CAA 2001, s. 268A

Other material: EIM 23041

Types of vehicle

Once more, it can be helpful to consider the HMRC guidance in relation to employment tax issues, as many of the concepts are identical. In considering the issue of the type of vehicle, for example, HMRC have commented that 'a vehicle which has been modified in some way can be a different "type" from one which has not been modified'.

The mere fact that a car is usually kept loaded with goods or equipment will not take it outside the definition if simple unloading would make it suitable for private use. Similarly, painting a car (e.g. as an advertisement) is not sufficient to establish a different type of vehicle. HMRC accept that any of the following may change the 'type' of vehicle:

- adding fixed flashing blue lights (*Gurney (HMIT) v Richards*);
- fitting dual controls, for example on a driving school vehicle (*Bourne (HMIT) v Auto School of Motoring (Norwich) Ltd*); or
- fitting a loudspeaker or a roof-top sign (e.g. for a taxi or driving school) on top of a car.

Plant and Machinery

In *Gurney v Richards*, for example, the judge held that 'a vehicle which is altered so that, without being reconverted, it cannot be used lawfully on a road by a member of the public ... cannot be said to be of a type commonly used as a private vehicle ... '.

However, even though such alterations may change the nature of the vehicle, HMRC go on to warn that 'even if a vehicle has been modified so that it is of a different type, it will not necessarily follow that the vehicle is not a car'. In other words, if it can be successfully established that the vehicle is of a type not commonly used as a private vehicle then it must be considered whether the second half of the test can also be satisfied, by demonstrating that it is unsuitable to be so used.

Cases: *Bourne (HMIT) v Auto School of Motoring (Norwich) Ltd* (1964) 42 TC 217; *Gurney (HMIT) v Richards* [1989] BTC 326

Other material: EIM 23040

Unsuitable for private use

In the *Gurney v Richards case*, the judge recalled an earlier definition of 'suitable' as meaning 'fitted for, adapted or appropriate for'. The case concerned a fire officer's car which was equipped with a flashing light and with emergency equipment. Under the Road Traffic Acts, the car (being fitted with a flashing light) could not lawfully have been used by any member of the public.

The quotation given above in fact continued so as to link the issue of 'type' with that of 'suitability'. More fully, therefore, the judge decided that 'a vehicle which is altered so that, without being reconverted, it cannot be used lawfully on a road by a member of the public ... cannot be said to be of a type commonly used as a private vehicle, nor ... can it be described as suitable for such use'. Even though the individual concerned could legally have driven the car, it was not suitable for use by members of the public generally and therefore fell outside the definition of 'car' for tax purposes. HMRC acknowledge that a vehicle will be unsuitable for private use if ordinary members of the public are legally barred from driving it.

Other material: EIM 23042

Summary

As noted above, HMRC like to analyse the two sub-conditions separately. If a vehicle is 'of a type not commonly used as a private vehicle', HMRC will look separately at the question of whether it is also 'unsuitable for such use'. That is, strictly, the correct statutory approach. Nevertheless, the case law precedents (and, dangerous though it is in the field of taxation, common sense) suggest that the two conditions are very closely linked.

In relation to emergency vehicles, HMRC specifically accept that 'where a vehicle that would otherwise be treated as a car for car benefit purpose is an emergency vehicle because it has blue flashing lights and/or audible warning devices, then you can accept that it is of a type not commonly used as a private vehicle and unsuitable to be so used'.

Other material: EIM 23043

200-080   Taxis

The special rules relating to 'qualifying hire cars' were abolished from April 2009. It follows that most new taxis are therefore now treated exactly as any other cars, with allowances determined according to emission levels.

The treatment of black cabs (or 'taxicabs') and limousines is less clear cut. It is understood, but only unofficially, that at least some HMRC officers take the view that these vehicles are not commonly used as a private vehicle and are unsuitable for such use. If this is correct then they will not be treated as cars for these purposes. The practical effect of this will be that annual investment allowances will be available (but also, for example, the temporary first-year allowances given for the year beginning in April 2009).

There is, in fact, an indirect statutory authority for this view. The rules giving first-year allowances for low emission cars can be found at CAA 2001, s. 45D. That section contains its own definition of 'car' to be used for the purpose of those rules alone. The definition (s. 45D(8)) states that the term is to be defined in accordance with CAA 2001, s. 268A (the new general definition for capital allowance purposes), 'except that it ... includes a reference to a mechanically propelled road vehicle of a type commonly used as a hackney carriage'. That suggests, at least, that a distinction may be made between a type of car used as a private vehicle and a type used as a taxicab. Technically, it is then also necessary to consider the condition about whether such a vehicle is unsuitable for private use.

200-100   Main rate cars

Rate of allowances

The rate at which writing-down allowances are given depends on whether or not the car is a 'main rate car'. In simple terms, a main rate car will be added to the main plant and machinery pool (and will therefore attract allowances at 20 per cent) but any other car will go into the special rate pool, where allowances are given at just 10 per cent.

A 'main rate car' is defined as including three categories of vehicle:

- any car first registered before 1 March 2001;
- a car with low CO_2 emissions (as defined for these purposes: see below); or
- a car that is electrically propelled.

Legislation: CAA 2001, s. 104AA

Low CO_2 emissions

For the purposes of this definition, a car has low CO_2 emissions if it meets both of the following conditions:

- when the car is first registered, it is so registered on the basis of a qualifying emissions certificate; and

Plant and Machinery

- the applicable CO_2 emissions figure in relation to the car does not exceed 160g/km.

The Treasury may ('from time to time') alter the figure of 160g/km, and any order to this effect 'may contain transitional provision and savings'.

In the great majority of cases, it will be easy to determine whether or not the car has emissions of more than 160g/km. Nevertheless, the legislation does contain numerous technical definitions: see 200-600.

Legislation: CAA 2001, s. 104AA(2)

200-200   Writing-down allowances

General principle

Before April 2009, most business cars (specifically, those costing more than £12,000) were allocated to a single asset pool and allowances were therefore computed on a car-by-car basis. This principle no longer applies and the general rule is now that cars are pooled with other expenditure for the purposes of calculating writing-down allowances.

Main rate cars

If a car is a 'main rate car' (broadly with emissions not exceeding 160g/km, but see 200-100), and if there is no private use of the vehicle (i.e. by a sole trader or member of a partnership) then the cost of the car is added to the main plant and machinery pool and allowances are given accordingly. There are no special rules to determine the treatment of such cars as they are not needed: in simple terms, the legislation has removed the requirement (formerly the first item at CAA 2001, s. 54(3)) to allocate these cars to a single asset pool.

Where there is private use of the main rate car, the car must be allocated to a single asset pool (CAA 2001, s. 206: see, generally, 190-600). The rate of allowance will still be the same (20 per cent) but this will then be subject to an adjustment to reflect private use.

> ### Example
>
> John is a sole trader. He buys a car for £20,000 in May 2009. The car has emissions of 135 g/km.
>
> John estimates that one half of his use of the vehicle is for business purposes.
>
> He initially calculates allowances for the year of £4,000 (£20,000 at 20 per cent), but he then reduces this figure by half to reflect his private use. The allowances available are £2,000 and the value carried down to the next period of accounts is £16,000 (as he still deducts the whole of the £4,000).

Legislation: CAA 2001, s. 206

Other cars

If the car is not a main rate car (as defined: see 200-100) and if there is no private use, the cost of the vehicle will be added to the special rate pool, together with expenditure on long-life assets, integral features, etc. Allowances will be given accordingly (ie normally at 10 per cent of the reducing balance of the pool).

200-300   Annual investment allowances

As noted at 181-150, no annual investment allowances (AIAs) are given for 'cars' (general exclusion 2 at CAA 2001, s. 38B).

The term 'car' was specifically defined, until April 2009, to include a motorcycle, so no AIAs were given for expenditure on motorcycles. However, the definition was amended, broadly from April 2009, to exclude a motorcycle: see 200-020). It follows that AIAs are available for expenditure on motor cycles from (broadly) 1 or 6 April 2009 (for corporation tax and income tax respectively).

More generally, the denial of AIAs for cars gives greater significance to the distinction between a car and a van, a point brought out at 200-040.

Legislation: CAA 2001, s. 268A

200-400   First-year allowances

General rule

The general rule is that no first-year allowances are available for cars.

Legislation: CAA 2001, s. 46(2)

Exception

An exception is made for a car that is 'electrically propelled' or that has 'low CO_2 emissions'. Both of these are technical terms with their specific definitions, discussed below.

A full 100 per cent first-year allowance is available for expenditure on such cars with very low carbon dioxide emissions. To qualify for these first-year allowances, the car must be bought by 31 March 2013 and must be 'unused and not second-hand'. HMRC accept that this condition is met 'even if it has been driven a limited number of miles for the purposes of testing, delivery, test driven by a potential purchaser, or used as a demonstration car'.

Legislation: CAA 2001, s. 45D

Other material: CA 23153

Electrically propelled

An electrically-propelled vehicle is one that is propelled solely by electrical power. The power must be derived either from a source external to the vehicle or from an electrical storage battery that is not connected to any source of power when the vehicle is in motion (CAA 2001, s. 268B).

Low emissions

A car is said, for these purposes, to have low CO_2 emissions if it meets two conditions:

(1)   at the time of first registration, the car must have been registered on the basis of a 'qualifying emissions certificate' (see 200-600); and

(2)   the applicable CO_2 emissions figure (again, see 200-600) in relation to the car must not exceed 110g/km.

Legislation: CAA 2001, s. 45D(2)

Tax effect

Where the conditions are met, 100 per cent first-year allowances are available for such vehicles. This principle was not changed from April 2009, though the definitions were altered to fit with the new structure of the legislation.

Although the first-year allowances are given at 100 per cent, the question of pooling can still be relevant when considering how to deal with the disposal proceeds of such vehicles. Unless there is private use, expenditure on cars with low CO_2 emissions is allocated to the main pool. It follows that any disposal proceeds will not automatically give rise to a balancing adjustment.

Other material: CA 23153

200-500   Employees

Employees are not permitted to claim capital allowances on privately owned cars used for business purposes. Instead, they can claim mileage allowance relief under ITEPA 2003, s. 231 (or tax-free mileage allowance payments from the employer under ITEPA 2003, s. 229).

There was no change to this principle from April 2009.

Legislation: CAA 2001, s. 36

200-520   Anti-avoidance re special rate cars

Purpose and conditions

Allowances for higher emission cars are now given at a rate that is much slower than the actual rate of commercial depreciation. Anti-avoidance measures are therefore in place to try to prevent the exploitation of loopholes. One of these measures is entitled 'special rate cars: discontinued activity continued by relevant company', and is concerned to counter the generation of artificial balancing allowances. The purpose of the rule was explained as follows in the *Explanatory Notes* to Finance Bill 2009:

> '... to prevent the artificial generation of balancing allowances by groups of companies who engineer the cessation of a group company's business of providing cars, only for another company in the group to continue a similar activity.'

The rule therefore applies where all of the following conditions are met:

Expenditure

The company must have incurred expenditure on a car other than a main rate car and been required to allocate it to a special rate pool.

Discontinuance

The qualifying activity carried on by the taxpayer must have been permanently discontinued.

Nature of activity

The nature of that activity must have been, or included (other than incidentally), the activity of making cars available to other persons.

Related activity of group company member

At some time in the period of six months after the taxpayer's qualifying activity is permanently discontinued, the qualifying activity of a 'group relief company' must consist of or include (other than incidentally) the making of cars available to other persons. The concept of the 'group relief company' is defined as follows:

(a)   a company to which group relief under Chapter 4 of Part 10 of ICTA would be available (on the making of a claim) in respect of balancing allowances surrendered by the taxpayer in the taxpayer's final chargeable period, and

(b)   a company to which such relief would be available (on the making of a claim) in respect of balancing allowances surrendered by a company within paragraph (a).

Balancing allowance

The final condition is that (were it not for this anti-avoidance rule):

- the company would be entitled to a balancing allowance in the special rate pool, and
- that balancing allowance would be greater than the total of any balancing charges less any balancing allowances in any other pools (treating this as a figure of nil if the other balancing allowances exceed the balancing charges).

Plant and Machinery

Example 1

There is a balancing allowance in the special rate pool of £100,000. Taking all the other plant and machinery pools together, the discontinuance of the business also generates a balancing charge of £170,000 and other balancing allowances of £50,000.

The condition is not met (so the anti-avoidance rule does not operate). The balancing allowance of £100,000 on the special rate pool (which is the target of the anti-avoidance measure) does not exceed the net balancing charges of £120,000 on the other pools.

Example 2

There is a balancing allowance in the special rate pool of £100,000. Taking all the other plant and machinery pools together, the discontinuance of the business also generates a balancing charge of £80,000 and other balancing allowances of £120,000.

The condition is this time met (so the anti-avoidance rule does operate). The other balancing allowances of £120,000 exceed the balancing charges of £80,000 so the net figure is taken as nil. Thus the balancing charge of £100,000 on the special rate pool exceeds that figure of nil.

Legislation: CAA 2001, s. 104F

Effect of legislation: company with discontinued activity

Where all the conditions are met, the balancing allowance that the company would otherwise be entitled to for the special rate pool will be limited to the net balancing charges (i.e. after deduction of any balancing allowances) on the other pools.

Example 3

There is a balancing allowance in the special rate pool of £100,000. Taking all the other plant and machinery pools together, the discontinuance of the business also generates a balancing charge of £80,000 and other balancing allowances of £25,000.

The condition for the anti-avoidance rules to apply is met as the special rate balancing allowance of £100,000 exceeds the other net balancing charges of £55,000. As such, the company still suffers its balancing charges of £55,000 but can claim balancing allowances of that same figure on the special rate pool. Therefore £55,000 of the special rate balancing allowance can be claimed, but the remaining £45,000 is disallowed.

Effect of legislation: group relief company

Where the balancing allowance has been restricted as above, the other group relief company (or 'relevant company': see below) is treated as incurring an equivalent amount of (notional) special rate expenditure. This applies whether or not the relevant company in fact owns cars that were previously owned by the other company. The expenditure is treated as incurred on the day after the end of the first company's final chargeable period.

To avoid the claiming of writing-down allowances by both companies for the same period, it may be necessary to apportion expenditure, as spelt out in the *Explanatory Notes*:

'when the ceasing company's penultimate chargeable period and the period in which the relevant company is treated as acquiring the expenditure overlap, the expenditure acquired is apportioned so that writing down allowances cannot be claimed by the relevant company for the overlapping period.'

The relevant company is the group relief company. However, if there is more than one such company then the original company may nominate which group relief company is to be treated as the relevant company for these purposes. The original company must make such a nomination within six months from the end of its final chargeable period, failing which HMRC will make the nomination.

200-540   Anti-avoidance: disposal values: connected parties

Where a car attracts allowances at the lower 'special' rate, it will still be held in a single asset pool if there is private use of the vehicle. The legislation seeks to prevent the artificial generation of balancing allowances for such cars.

The rule applies where allowances are already restricted under CAA 2001, s. 217 or 218 (restrictions on allowances for connected party transactions: see, generally, 205-300).

In such a case, the disposal value to be brought into account is the market value of the car at the time of the disposal event, restricted to the cost incurred (or treated as incurred) by the person disposing of the vehicle. The person acquiring the car is then treated as having incurred capital expenditure on it of an equal amount.

Legislation: CAA 2001, s. 208A

200-600   Definitions

The capital allowances legislation contains numerous definitions in relation to cars.

Car

For detailed consideration of the definition of 'car', see 200-020.

Legislation: CAA 2001, s. 268A(1)

Main rate car

The concept of 'main rate car' is critical for determining the manner in which allowances are given and is considered in detail at 200-100.

Legislation: CAA 2001, s. 104AA

Plant and Machinery

Motor cycle

The definition of 'motor cycle' is given by reference to s. 185(1) of the *Road Traffic Act* 1988: see 200-020.

Legislation: CAA 2001, s. 268A(2)

Electrically propelled vehicle

An electrically-propelled vehicle is one that is propelled solely by electrical power and where that power is derived either from a source external to the vehicle or from an electrical storage battery that is not connected to any source of power when the vehicle is in motion.

Legislation: CAA 2001, s. 268B

Qualifying emissions certificate

For the purposes of the plant and machinery rules, a vehicle's 'qualifying emissions certificate' is defined to mean either an 'EC certificate of conformity' (see below) or a 'UK approval certificate' (again, see below) which specifies:

(a)   in the case of a vehicle other than a bi-fuel vehicle, a CO_2 emissions figure in terms of grams per kilometre driven, or

(b)   in the case of a bi-fuel vehicle, separate CO_2 emissions figures in terms of grams per kilometre driven for different fuels.

Legislation: CAA 2001, s. 268C

EC certificate of conformity

This term is defined as 'a certificate of conformity issued by a manufacturer under any provision of the law of a member State implementing Article 6 of Council Directive 70/156/EEC, as amended'.

Legislation: CAA 2001, s. 268C(4)

UK approval certificate

This term is defined as a certificate issued under:

(a)   s. 58(1) or (4) of the *Road Traffic Act* 1988, or

(b)   Article 31A(4) or (5) of the *Road Traffic (Northern (Ireland) Order* 1981 (SI 1981/154 (N.I. 1)).

Legislation: CAA 2001, s. 268C(4)

Applicable CO_2 emissions figure

The definition of this term depends on whether or not the vehicle is a bi-fuel vehicle.

Definition applying to bi-fuel vehicles

If the qualifying emissions certificate specifies more than one CO_2 emissions figure in relation to each fuel, the applicable figure is the lowest CO_2 emissions (combined) figure specified.

In any other case, the applicable figure is the lowest CO_2 figure specified by the certificate.

Legislation: CAA 2001, s. 268C(3)

Definition applying to all other vehicles

For all vehicles other than bi-fuel vehicles, the applicable CO_2 emissions figure is the CO_2 emissions figure specified in the qualifying emissions certificate. But if the certificate specifies more than one such figure, then the applicable figure is the figure that is specified as the CO_2 emissions (combined) figure.

Legislation: CAA 2001, s. 268C(2)

Bi-fuel

A bi-fuel vehicle is defined as one that is capable of being run either by both petrol and road fuel gas, or by both diesel and road fuel gas.

Legislation: CAA 2001, s. 268C(4)

Petrol

Petrol has the meaning given by Article 2 of Directive 98/70/EC of the European Parliament and of the Council.

Legislation: CAA 2001, s. 268C(4)

Diesel

For these purposes, diesel is any diesel fuel within the definition in Article 2 of Directive 98/70/EC of the European Parliament and of the Council.

Legislation: CAA 2001, s. 268C(4)

Road fuel gas

Road fuel gas is for these purposes defined by reference to the definition in ITEPA 2003, s. 171(1). As such, the term means 'any substance which is gaseous at a temperature of 15°C and under a pressure of 1013.25 millibars, and which is for use as fuel in road vehicles'.

Legislation: CAA 2001, s. 268C(4)

Plant and Machinery

200-620   Transitional and commencement provisions

Complicating factors

Broadly, the amended capital allowance rules relating to cars apply from 1 or 6 April 2009, for corporation tax and income tax respectively. However, transitional rules are needed to deal with cars that were already owned before those dates and with cars that were ordered but not yet owned. Also, anti-avoidance rules aim to combat arrangements under which cars would be treated as bought before April 2009, even though the vehicles are not in fact delivered until many months later. Another issue to be addressed is that of the rules that deem certain expenditure to be acquired on particular dates (see, generally, 105-000).

To address these various matters, the legislation introduces a series of 'relevant dates' and the concepts of 'new expenditure' and 'old expenditure'.

Relevant dates

The legislation defines three different relevant dates:

- The first relevant date is 1 April 2009 (for corporation tax purposes) or 6 April 2009 (for income tax).
- The second relevant date is 1 August 2009 (corporation tax) or 6 August 2009 (income tax).
- The third relevant date is 1 April 2014 (corporation tax) or 6 April 2014 (income tax).

(The August dates are for anti-avoidance purposes and are linked to the four-month rule at CAA 2001, s. 5(5): see 105-200.)

New and old expenditure

The term 'new expenditure' is defined as follows:

- expenditure incurred on or after the first relevant date; and
- expenditure incurred before that date where the agreement for the provision of the vehicle was entered into after 8 December 2008 and - under that agreement - the car is not required to be made available before the second relevant date.

(The significance of 8 December 2008 is that that is the date on which HMRC published their 'technical note' concerning the new tax rules.)

Any expenditure that is not 'new expenditure' is termed 'old expenditure'.

Legislation: *Finance Act* 2009, Sch. 11, paras. 26 to 28

Date of agreement

For these purposes, an agreement in entered into on the date on which the following conditions are met:

- there is a written contract for the provision of the car;

- the conditions in the contract (if there are any) have been met, and
- no contractual terms remain to be agreed.

In other words, if a contract becomes unconditional after 8 December 2008, and the car is to be made available only from the start of August 2009, then the expenditure is treated as new expenditure even if it was in fact incurred before April 2009.

Legislation: *Finance Act* 2009, Sch. 11, para. 27(3)

General rule

The general rule is that the new capital allowances provisions apply to all new expenditure (as defined above). If a business buys a car on, say, 16 April 2009 then this is clearly new expenditure and the capital allowances are calculated on the new basis. But this does not cover a disposal in, say, July 2009 of a car that was bought in May 2008: the purchase did not constitute new expenditure and separate rules are therefore needed to determine the treatment of such a vehicle.

Legislation: *Finance Act* 2009, Sch. 11, para. 28(1)

Cars already owned at April 2009

Many familiar provisions relating to capital allowances for cars are repealed from April 2009. However, the repeals do not have effect in relation to old expenditure (as defined above) until the first chargeable period that begins on or after the third relevant date (1 or 6 April 2014: see above). The provisions to which this principle applies are the following:

- CAA 2001, s. 74: single asset pool for cars costing more than £12,000.
- CAA 2001, s. 75: restriction of annual writing-down allowance to £3,000.
- CAA 2001, s. 76: restriction where part of expenditure is met by another person.
- CAA 2001, s. 77: adjustment where car used partly for other purposes (including especially private use).
- CAA 2001, s. 78: effect of partial depreciation subsidy.

For example, a company drawing accounts up to 31 December owns a car that was bought for £40,000 in October 2007. The car will have been allocated to a single asset pool so that writing-down allowances could be restricted to £3,000 per year. That treatment will continue, and the newer capital allowances rules will be ignored, as long as the car is disposed of before 31 December 2014.

If the car is still owned at 1 January 2015 (the first day of the first chargeable period that begins on or after the third relevant date) then the unrelieved old expenditure is carried forward to the main plant and machinery pool at that time (whatever the level of vehicle emissions). The value to be transferred into the main pool will be £16,000 (original cost of £40,000, less eight annual writing-down allowances, each restricted to £3,000).

Legislation: *Finance Act* 2009, Sch. 11, paras. 28(2), 31

Plant and Machinery

Inexpensive cars

The above rule, requiring the remaining value to be transferred to the main pool from the third relevant date, only applies to old expenditure where the car cost more than £12,000. A purchase of a car for £10,000 (for example) in May 2008 will have been added to the main plant and machinery pool where its identity will have been lost. No adjustment will be needed in 2014 or 2015 for such cars.

Cars with private use

A car may be allocated to a single asset pool because there is non-business use of the vehicle (whether or not it also cost more than £12,000). In such a case, there is no transfer of value to the main pool in 2014 or 2015. Instead, allowances will continue to be calculated indefinitely on the old basis.

Legislation: *Finance Act* 2009, Sch. 11, para. 31(3)

Anti-avoidance rules

The new rules relating to disposal values in avoidance cases (CAA 2001, s. 208A: see 200-540) only apply to disposals of cars where the expenditure on the car was new expenditure. They would not, for example, apply to the disposal of a car in June 2009 that had been acquired a year earlier.

CAA 2001, s. 79 (certain anti-avoidance disposal rules) continues initially to have effect for old expenditure on a car or motor cycle. The provision will cease to apply only for chargeable periods beginning on or after the third relevant date (see above).

Legislation: *Finance Act* 2009, Sch. 11, paras. 28(2), 29(2)

Mixed new and old expenditure

It is technically possible that part of the expenditure on a car might be treated as new expenditure and part as old. In such a case, the expenditure is notionally split as if it were incurred on two separate but identical vehicles (cars or, possibly, motor cycles). Allowances are then given accordingly and, when the vehicles is disposed of, the proceeds are to be apportioned on a just and reasonable basis.

Legislation: *Finance Act* 2009, Sch. 11, para. 30

200-700   Car hire restrictions

Where cars costing more than £12,000 were leased, a proportion of the leasing costs was – under rules applying to April 2009 – permanently disallowed. The disallowance was calculated by reference to half of the excess of the retail price when new over £12,000. For example, a car with a retail price of £20,000 had relief restricted to 80 per cent of the leasing costs.

For car leases entered into from (broadly) April 2009, the £12,000 threshold ceases to apply. Instead, a restriction may be made by reference to the car's CO_2 emissions.

200-980   Vehicle scrappage scheme

At the time of the 2009 Budget, the government announced the introduction of a temporary scheme to encourage the scrapping of old cars and vans. The scheme came into operation on 18 May 2009 and broadly offers a discount of £2,000 where a person scraps a vehicle (car or light van) first registered before the end of August 1999, and buys a brand new vehicle. The £2,000 consists of two subsidies, one from the government and the other from the vehicle manufacturer.

HMRC have confirmed the tax treatment for capital allowance purposes (R&C Brief 31/09):

* the old vehicle is scrapped, and therefore has no disposal value. The two subsidies do not constitute disposal receipts for capital allowance purposes; but
* the purchaser can only claim capital allowances on the net cost, after deduction of the subsidies.

Cars: old rules

201-000   Introduction

As noted at 200-000, the tax rules granting relief for business expenditure on cars were changed quite radically from April 2009. The following paragraphs explain the rules as they applied before those changes.

Transitional rules apply for up to about six years, and in certain cases the older rules will continue to apply indefinitely to certain vehicles. These transitional provisions are explained in detail at 200-620

201-020   Definition of 'car'

Car

The definition of car before April 2009 (given at former CAA 2001, s. 81) was similar (but not identical) to that used for employee tax issues (benefits-in-kind, etc.). The definition has changed slightly from April 2009, mainly to exclude motor cycles which were specifically treated as though they were cars until April 2009.

A car was defined for capital allowances purposes as a mechanically propelled road vehicle other than one that was:

* of a construction primarily suited for the conveyance of goods or burden of any description, (eg a van); or

Plant and Machinery

145

- of a type not commonly used as a private vehicle and which is also unsuitable for such use, (eg a police car).

See 200-020ff. for detailed consideration of the above conditions.

201-040   Purchase of expensive cars

Main principle

The rules described in the following paragraphs apply to cars bought before 1 or 6 April 2009 (respectively for corporation tax and income tax). See 200-620 for details of transitional provisions.

Until the changes described at 200-000 came into effect in April 2009, special rules applied to cars costing over £12,000. The writing-down allowance to be made for such cars was capped at £3,000 per year. This figure of £3,000 was to be increased or reduced proportionately if the chargeable period was more or less than a year. There were exceptions for certain electric vehicles and cars with very low carbon dioxide emissions. Qualifying hire cars (see 201-180) were not affected by the £12,000 restriction.

Example

A car was bought by a limited company for £26,000 and used for business purposes, including the private use of one of the directors. It was sold in the third year for £9,500.

Allowances were due as follows:

		£
Year 1	Cost	26,000
	Allowance	3,000
		23,000
Year 2	Allowance	3,000
		20,000
Year 3	Proceeds	9,500
	Allowance	10,500

As such, it can be seen that the restriction caused a timing delay on the giving of the allowances, but that eventually they were due in full. Indeed, the fact that expensive cars went into their own single asset pools generally meant in practice that a balancing allowance was obtained sooner than would otherwise have been the case.

This position was in contrast to the rules then applying to expensive cars that were hired where there was a permanent loss of tax relief. The effect of this disparity was that the hiring of cars became increasingly unattractive from the tax point of view as the retail price of the vehicle increased. Hired cars costing slightly over £12,000 may have had VAT advantages sufficient to offset the lost relief but for cars costing more than say £15,000 or £16,000, the permanent loss of tax relief often counted heavily against hiring.

Complications

There were four circumstances under which the £3,000 (or adjusted figure) could be further limited, as follows:

- where part of the expenditure was met by somebody else (see 201-060);
- where the car was used partly for purposes other than those of the qualifying activity, (eg it was used privately by a sole trader or partner (see 201-100); but use by a director or employee was treated as use for the purposes of the qualifying activity);
- where the car was clearly much more expensive and luxurious than would be necessary for the purposes of the qualifying activity (see 201-120); and
- where the person carrying on the qualifying activity received a 'partial depreciation subsidy' (see 201-140).

First-year allowances

As now, the general rule before April 2009 was that no first-year allowances were available for cars.

An exception was (as it still is) made for cars with very low carbon dioxide emissions, and electric cars, that were bought new. Where the conditions were met, 100 per cent first-year allowances were (and are) available for such vehicles. See 200-400 for further details.

Cars that qualify for 100 per cent allowances by virtue of this rule were also exempt from the £12,000 'expensive car' rules as described above.

Legislation: CAA 2001, s. 46(2)

201-060   Expenditure partly met by another person

There is a general rule for capital allowances purposes that restricts capital allowances to the extent that the cost of an asset is met (directly or indirectly) by a public body or by somebody else. There are exceptions to this rule for contributions made by somebody other than a public body which do not in themselves qualify for tax relief. There are also exceptions for certain Northern Ireland regional development grants and for some insurance and compensation monies.

Legislation: CAA 2001, s. 532ff

Recipient of contributions

Therefore, where a restriction is required because of a contribution by someone else, the annual writing-down allowance was not to exceed (former CAA 2001, s. 76):

$$£3,000 \times \frac{E - X}{E}$$

147

where

E   equalled the capital expenditure incurred on the provision of the car; and
X   was the amount of expenditure excluded by virtue of CAA 2001, s. 532.

The figure of £3,000 was adjusted for chargeable periods lasting more or less than a year.

Tax treatment of contributor

If a contributor towards capital expenditure was entitled to writing-down allowances by virtue of CAA 2001, s. 538 (contribution allowances for plant and machinery) then his entitlement would be calculated as follows:

$$£3,000 \times \frac{C}{E}$$

where

C   was the amount of the contribution; and
E   was the amount of capital expenditure incurred on the provision of the car.

Once more, the £3,000 figure was increased or reduced as appropriate if the chargeable period was not of exactly 12 months.

Employee contributions

To reduce the benefit in kind charge on a company car, an employee may contribute an amount – normally up to £5,000 – towards the cost of buying the car. Tax relief is then given by virtue of ITEPA 2003, s. 132.

An employee is not able to claim capital allowances in these circumstances so it follows that the employer could still claim capital allowances on the full cost of the car, without deduction for the employee contribution.

201-100   Use for private or other purposes

If a car was used privately, then the capped figure of £3,000 was further adjusted to take account of that private use (former CAA 2001, s. 77). Similarly, any balancing allowance or balancing charge would be adjusted.

The reduction was to be made on a basis that was 'just and reasonable having regard to the relevant circumstances'. The legislation specifically stated that these circumstances particularly included 'the extent to which the car is used in that chargeable period for purposes other than those of the qualifying activity'. In practice, it was normal to make the calculation on the basis of business and private mileage in the year.

When an employer provides a car for an employee (or director) no restriction is made for private use as, in these circumstances, any such private use will be dealt with by way of a

P11D benefit in kind. This is therefore conceptually different from the VAT treatment of cars used by employees.

In calculating the amount of unrelieved qualifying expenditure carried forward, any reduction for private use was to be disregarded. In other words, the full amount of £3,000 was written off the tax value of the car but only a part of the £3,000 was allowed in the tax year.

Example

A partnership bought a car costing £20,000 in year one. It was eventually sold for £5,000 in year five. Private use of the car was agreed as being 25 per cent throughout. Allowances were due as follows:

	£	
Year 1	20,000	
WDA (max)	(3,000)	× 75% = £2,250
	17,000	
Year 2		
WDA (max)	(3,000)	× 75% = £2,250
	14,000	
Year 3		
WDA (max)	(3,000)	× 75% = £2,250
	11,000	
Year 4		
WDA (20%)	(2,200)	× 75% = £1,650
	8,800	
Year 5		
Disposal proceeds	(5,000)	
Balancing allowance	3,800	× 75% = £2,850
Value carried down	Nil	

It will be seen that over the lifetime of the asset the total allowances given amounted to £11,250. This represented the cost to the business of £15,000 (£20,000 cost less £5,000 proceeds) less private use of 25 per cent which was permanently disallowed.

Although the allowance was restricted to £3,000 a year, a full balancing allowance (or, as the case may be, a balancing charge) was made as soon as the vehicle came to be disposed of, though this would again be adjusted for any non-business use. Thus, whilst the early allowances may have been given more slowly for expensive cars, allowances may still ultimately have been received sooner than they would have been if the expensive cars had been included in the main pool.

201-120   Very expensive cars

If a car was of a quality that was clearly disproportionate to the requirements of the trade, etc. then HMRC could impose a further restriction on the capital allowances available. Such

Plant and Machinery

a restriction would be in addition to any private use restriction and would be based on the principle of 'personal choice'. The statutory authority for the deduction was former CAA 2001 s. 77 which permitted the inspector to restrict the allowances to an amount that was 'just and reasonable having regard to the relevant circumstances'.

The application of this restriction was made by reference to the case of *G H Chambers (Northiam Farms) Ltd v Watmough* (1956) 36 TC 711, but was only applied where there was 'blatant incongruity' (CA 23530) between the type of car and the nature of the business – HMRC gave the example of 'Pedro the fisherman' who used a £150,000 Rolls Royce, though HMRC had certainly been known to apply the rule in less extreme cases.

Before applying any such restriction, HMRC would look at the size and type of car, the nature of the business and the extent of business use. Inspectors were also instructed to compare the cost of the car with the business turnover and profits.

No personal choice restriction was imposed if business use of the car was substantial.

If a personal choice restriction was made, this would be imposed after any restriction for private use. Take, for example, a car that was bought by a sole trader for £100,000 and that was used 80 per cent for private purposes. Assume that it was agreed that there should be a one-third personal choice restriction. The first writing-down allowance calculation might have been calculated as follows:

	£	
Cost	100,000	
WDA	(3,000)	(before restrictions)
Carried forward	97,000	

WDA actually allowed:

	£
As above	3,000
less private use	(2,400)
Initially allowed	600
Personal choice	(200)
Allowance given	400

The above calculation concerned an unincorporated business. HMRC sometimes sought to apply the principle in the case of expensive company cars provided for directors or employees of a large company (CA 27100). However, it is not at all clear that this approach could be justified, for the following reasons:

- the statutory justification for a restriction applied when the car was 'used partly for purposes other than those of the qualifying activity' (former CAA 2001, s. 77(2));
- the HMRC manual (at CA 27100) instructed Inspectors that they should 'accept that expenditure incurred by an employer in providing an asset for a director's or employee's

private use as part of a remuneration package, thus giving rise to liability under ITEPA, is incurred wholly and exclusively for the purposes of the qualifying activity'.

If, on the basis of this wording, the only use of the car can be seen to be for the purposes of the qualifying activity then it would seem to follow there could be no restriction under former CAA 2001, s. 77. HMRC are known to have backed down from a Commissioner hearing based on this argument. Nor was there any apparent injustice in this; it is self-evident that what is 'just and reasonable' where there is no tax charge on the director or employee is not the same as what is 'just and reasonable' where there is such a charge.

201-140   Partial depreciation subsidy

Sometimes a person carrying on a qualifying activity would receive a sum to take account of part of the depreciation of the car. If the sum received was not taken into account as income of the recipient, or as part of the profits of any qualifying activity he carried on, then the capital allowances were to be adjusted 'to an amount which is just and reasonable having regard to the relevant circumstances' (former CAA 2001, s. 78). Any such reduction was ignored when determining the amount of unrelieved qualifying expenditure carried forward.

201-160   Inexpensive cars

For cars bought from 1 or 6 April 2009, the concept of 'expensive' or 'inexpensive' has ceased to be relevant. All cars now have their capital allowances determined according to the level of carbon dioxide emissions (see 200-000ff.).

For earlier periods, cars costing less than £12,000 were treated in the same way as any other asset and normally held in the main plant and machinery pool. However, if there was private use – by a business proprietor, not a director or employee – then inexpensive cars still needed to go into a single asset pool, in the same way as any other asset used partly for private purposes.

201-180   Qualifying hire cars

Some of the capital allowance rules for cars, as the rules applied before April 2009, did not apply to 'qualifying hire cars' (see below). Specifically, such vehicles:

- did not need to be allocated to a single asset pool (former CAA 2001, s. 74(2)(a));
- did not have annual writing-down allowances restricted to £3,000 (former CAA 2001, s. 75(1));
- did not suffer the restriction on part of the hire cost (ITTOIA 2005, s. 48(1) and CTA 2009, s. 56(1)); and
- were not affected by former sections: CAA 2001, s. 76 (expenditure partly met by another person); s. 78 (partial depreciation subsidy for cars), or s. 79 (anti-avoidance).

The fact that a car was a qualifying hire car did not, however, change the rules about first-year allowances – they remained unavailable for such vehicles (except for those with very

Plant and Machinery

low carbon dioxide emissions – see now 200-400). The concept was abolished from April 2009 (subject to the transitional provisions applying to cars already owned) so taxis are now treated in the same way as other vehicles.

Definition

A qualifying hire car (former CAA 2001, s. 82) was one that was 'provided wholly or mainly for hire to, or the carriage of, members of the public in the ordinary course of a trade'. To qualify, the vehicle also had to meet at least one of the following conditions.

(1)   The car was not normally on hire to, or used for the carriage of, the same person (or connected persons) for 30 or more consecutive days or for 90 or more days in any 12-month period.

(2)   The car was provided for hire to a person who himself used it wholly or mainly for hire to (or for the carriage of) members of the public in the ordinary course of the trade. In this case, that onward hiring also had to meet the first condition above.

(3)   The car was provided wholly or mainly for the use of a person in receipt of various special allowances or supplements, as below:

    (a)   a disability living allowance under:

        (i)   the *Social Security Contributions and Benefits Act* 1992, or
        (ii)   the *Social Security Contributions and Benefits (Northern Ireland) Act* 1992,

        because of entitlement to the mobility component; or

    (b)   a mobility supplement under a scheme made under the *Personal Injuries (Emergency Provisions) Act* 1939; or

    (c)   a mobility supplement under an Order in Council made under *Social Security (Miscellaneous Provisions) Act* 1977, s. 12; or

    (d)   any payment appearing to the Treasury to be of a similar kind and specified by them by order.

From April 2009, however, taxis are treated in the same way as other cars and the concept of the qualifying hire car disappears.

201-200   Employees

As under the newer rules, employees were not permitted to claim capital allowances on privately owned cars used for business purposes. Instead, they were entitled to claim mileage allowance relief under ITEPA 2003, s. 231 (or tax-free mileage allowance payments from the employer under ITEPA 2003, s. 229).

Legislation: CAA 2001, s. 36

201-220   Anti-avoidance

Anti-avoidance rules applied where a car was disposed of in a transaction which fell within CAA 2001, Pt. 2, Ch. 17 (connected parties, sale and leaseback, sole or main purpose transactions). In these cases, the disposal value was restricted to the open market value of the asset or the capital expenditure incurred on the asset in question by the person disposing of it, whichever was less (former CAA 2001, s. 79(2)).

The acquirer was then treated as having incurred expenditure equal to the disposal value on provision of the asset (former CAA 2001, s. 79(3)).

See 200-620 for details of transitional provisions.

Short-life assets

205-000   Short-life assets: introduction

Use of the short-life asset legislation is voluntary. The rules allow a person, if he so chooses, to make an election. Where this is done, the effect is to accelerate capital allowances on certain assets that are scrapped or sold at a low value within approximately four years from the date of their purchase. In practice, use of short-life asset elections will normally now be restricted to larger businesses incurring substantial expenditure, as most smaller enterprises will instead claim immediate tax relief by way of annual investment allowances (see 181-000ff.).

Some care is needed as, in particular circumstances, it is possible that the effect of making an election will be the reverse of what is intended and will actually be to slow down the overall rate at which allowances are given. This may happen if an asset is sold within the first four years or so for more than its tax written-down value.

The only effect of making an election is one of timing. Most assets which are the subject of a capital allowances claim go into the main pool. In broad terms, the effect of this is that tax relief is given each year on 20 per cent of the reducing balance (using the rates applying from April 2008). Thus, an asset costing £1,600 will attract allowances of £320 (£1,600 $\times$ 20 per cent) in the first year.

In the second year, the allowances due will be £256 (£1,600 less £320 already given, to leave £1,280, at 20 per cent = £256). In year three, the allowance will be £205 and so on. Because of the effect of pooling, allowances may continue to be given on an annual basis even after an asset has been scrapped.

The effect of making the short-life asset election will be to ensure that the total allowances given *over the period for which the asset is held* are (normally) exactly equal to the net cost of the asset to the trader, calculated as the original cost less any disposal proceeds. Thus, an asset costing £1,600 in year one which is sold for £200 in year three will attract total

Plant and Machinery

allowances over the three-year period of £1,400. This is therefore more favourable than the total allowances of £781 given in the ordinary way as above (£320 + £256 + £205), even though the remaining £619 of allowances would eventually be due anyway.

Short-life assets are held in a single asset pool and the 'small pool' rules (see 190-275) do not apply to short-life assets.

Legislation: CAA 2001, s. 83ff.

Other material: CA 23610ff.

205-050 Conditions

The conditions for a short-life asset election may be summarised into three rules, as follows:

(1) qualifying expenditure must have been incurred on plant and machinery;

(2) treatment as a short-life asset must not be prohibited; and

(3) the person incurring the expenditure must make a valid election.

Each of the above three conditions is now considered in turn.

Qualifying expenditure

This is defined at CAA 2001, s. 11(4) but subject to various other conditions (see 160-000). In essence, it is necessary to demonstrate that capital expenditure has been incurred on plant or machinery that is to be used for the purposes of a qualifying activity.

Legislation: CAA 2001, s. 83

Other material: CA 23620

Cases where short-life asset treatment is ruled out

Short-life asset treatment is denied in various circumstances, as follows.

(1) Where an asset that has been used for other purposes is brought into use for the purposes of a qualifying activity, or where plant or machinery received by way of gift is used for such a purpose.

(2) Where plant or machinery that has been provided for long funding leasing (see 230-000) starts to be used for other purposes.

(3) Where plant or machinery is hired out otherwise than in the course of any other qualifying activity ('special leasing').

(4) Where the item concerned is a car (defined, until April 2009, to include a motor cycle). However, this rule does not catch a vehicle if it is a 'hire car for a disabled person' (see below). Before April 2009, the exemption applied to certain cars hired

out to persons receiving disability allowances or similar payments (as defined at former CAA 2001, s. 82(4)).

(5) For any special rate expenditure (or, before April 2008, for expenditure on a long-life asset (see 210-000)). Once more, this rule does not catch a vehicle if it is a 'hire car for a disabled person' (see below).

(6) For any plant or machinery provided for leasing. Two exceptions are given in the legislation, however, as follows:

(a) a 'hire car for a disabled person' (see below));
(b) plant which is provided for leasing but which within (normally) a ten-year period will be used for certain qualifying purposes (as defined at CAA 2001, s. 122–125).

(7) For certain plant or machinery used for overseas leasing (within CAA 2001, s. 109 – see 220-200) and which qualifies only for a ten per cent writing-down allowance.

(8) For plant or machinery leased jointly to two or more persons at least one of whom is not resident in the UK (such that CAA 2001, s. 116 applies).

(9) For ships.

(10) For expenditure incurred on an asset provided or used only partly for a qualifying activity.

(11) For expenditure on an asset enjoying a partial depreciation subsidy (under CAA 2001, s. 211) (see 165-700).

Legislation: CAA 2001, s. 84

Hire car for a disabled person

This concept is defined to mean a car that is 'provided wholly or mainly for hire to, or the carriage of, disabled persons in the ordinary course of a trade'. A 'disabled person' is for these purposes defined to mean a person in receipt of any of the following:

(a) a disability living allowance under -

(i) the Social Security Contributions and Benefits Act 1992, or
(ii) the Social Security Contributions and Benefits (Northern Ireland) Act 1992, because of entitlement to the mobility component,

(b) a mobility supplement under a scheme made under the Personal Injuries (Emergency Provisions) Act 1939,
(c) a mobility supplement under an Order in Council made under section 12 of the Social Security (Miscellaneous Provisions) Act 1977, or
(d) a payment that appears to the Treasury to be similar to those mentioned in paragraphs (a) to (c) and that is specified by order made by the Treasury.

Legislation: CAA 2001, s. 268D

Plant and Machinery

Electing for short-life asset treatment

An election for such treatment is irrevocable. Once made, an HMRC officer is required to make 'such assessments and adjustments of assessments' as are required to give the election effect.

The election needs to specify:

- the plant or machinery that is the subject of the election;
- the amount of qualifying expenditure incurred on that item; and
- the date on which the expenditure was incurred.

For corporation tax purposes, the time limit for an election is two years from the end of the relevant chargeable period. For income tax purposes, the time limit is 'the normal time limit for amending a tax return', ie 31 January some 22 months after the end of the tax year in which the relevant chargeable period ends.

For these purposes, the relevant chargeable period is the chargeable period in which the qualifying expenditure was incurred or the first such period if the expenditure was incurred in more than one chargeable period.

Example

John, a sole trader, incurs expenditure of £10,000 during his accounts year ended 31 December 2008. Thus, the period of accounts ends in the tax year 2008–09. The time limit for making an election for treatment as a short-life asset will be 31 January 2011.

Legislation: CAA 2001, s. 85

205-100   Effect of making a short-life asset election

Once an election is made, then a balancing adjustment will be made on the basis of the ordinary capital allowances rules if the asset is disposed of within approximately four years. This is because qualifying expenditure on a short-life asset is (in theory – but see 205-350) always allocated to a single-asset pool.

Example

A business with qualifying expenditure of £160,000 brought forward buys a computer system costing £24,000 in year 1. In year 4 it is scrapped. No other assets are bought or sold in the period in question. The annual investment allowance has been fully absorbed by another company in the group (explained at 181-200ff.).

Without a short-life asset election the position is as follows (assuming writing-down allowances at 20 per cent throughout):

Main pool	£
Value brought forward	160,000
Additions	24,000

	£
	184,000
Year 1 WDA	(36,800)
Value carried forward	147,200
Year 2 WDA	(29,440)
Value carried forward	117,760
Year 3 WDA	(23,552)
Value carried forward	94,208
Year 4 WDA	(18,842)
Value carried forward	75,366

With no election, the total allowances given over the four-year period amount to £108,634.

If an election is made, the position is as follows:

	Main pool £	SLA pool £
Value brought forward	160,000	–
Additions	–	24,000
	160,000	24,000
Year 1 WDA	(32,000)	(4,800)
Value carried forward	128,000	19,200
Year 2 WDA	(25,600)	(3,840)
Value carried forward	102,400	15,360
Year 3 WDA	(20,480)	(3,072)
Value carried forward	81,920	12,288
Year 4 WDA	(16,384)	
Proceeds		Nil (asset scrapped)
Balancing allowance		(12,288)
Value carried forward	65,536	Nil

With the election, the total allowances given over the period amount to £118,464, an increase of £9,830.

Plant and Machinery

The legislation defines a 'four-year cut-off', meaning the fourth anniversary of the end of the chargeable period (or first chargeable period) in which the qualifying expenditure was incurred on the provision of the short-life asset (but see 205-150).

There will be a 'final chargeable period' (see 190-600) if the asset is disposed of before the four-year cut-off (see below), and this will trigger a balancing adjustment.

If the asset is still held at that date then it ceases to be a short-life asset and the value is transferred to the main pool for the first chargeable period ending after the four-year cut-off date. The appropriate pool is normally the main pool, but will be the special rate pool in relation to a car that is not a 'main rate car' (ie, broadly a car bought from April 2009 with emissions in excess of 160g/km, but see 200-100).

To gain a fuller understanding of the position three points need to be considered.

(1) The effect of a short-life asset election is one of timing only. The increased allowances of £9,830 in the above example will eventually be offset by reduced allowances in future years. The carried forward value of £65,536 is therefore exactly £9,830 less than the figure of £75,366 where no election is made.

(2) The timing benefit of £9,830 all arises in the year of disposal (year four in the example). All that is happening is that a full balancing allowance is being given in that year instead of the standard 20 per cent writing-down allowance.

(3) By looking at the position at the start of the disposal period it can be seen (in this case, too late – the time limit for the irrevocable election has passed) whether or not the election will be beneficial. In the example, the brought forward value of the short-life asset is £12,288. As long as the asset is sold for less than 80 per cent of this figure then the election will prove beneficial. If it is sold for more, the election will be disadvantageous.

Legislation: CAA 2001, s. 84ff.

205-150   Short-life assets: four-year cut-off

Corporation tax

For a company, the position is as follows (CAA 2001, s. 86(3)). In accordance with CAA 2001, s. 6(1)(b) a chargeable period of a company is its accounting period. The relevant chargeable period means the accounting period in which the qualifying expenditure is incurred. The question is therefore whether a disposal value has to be brought into account for any accounting period ending on or before the date four years after the end of the accounting period in which the expenditure was incurred.

This will normally mean that the disposal value has to be brought into account in any of the four accounting periods following that in which the expenditure was incurred. However, if the company has a change of accounting date then care is needed. To qualify, the chargeable period must then *end* on or before the fourth anniversary.

Example

A company incurs expenditure on a short-life asset during its accounting period ended 30 April 2006. It then has accounting periods ending on the following dates:

30 April 2007
31 December 2007
31 December 2008
31 December 2009
31 December 2010

The fourth anniversary of the end of the accounting period in which the expenditure was incurred falls on 30 April 2010. The accounting period ending 31 December 2009

---

therefore ends 'on or before the fourth anniversary', whereas the accounting period ended on 31 December 2010 does not. As such, the short-life asset election will only have any effect if a disposal value is brought into account in the accounting period ended on 31 December 2009 or in any earlier period.

Legislation: CAA 2001, s. 86

Income tax

For income tax purposes, a chargeable period means a period of account which for a trader is defined to mean 'a period for which accounts are made up for the purposes of the trade'. For other qualifying activities, it means a tax year. There are certain complications in relation to overlapping periods and periods where there is an interval, as well as periods of account lasting more than 18 months: see 190-200 for further details. As for corporation tax, it is necessary to identify the fourth anniversary of the end of the period of accounts and to determine whether a disposal value is brought into account by that fourth anniversary.

Legislation: CAA 2001, s. 6

205-200   Short-life assets to be used for leasing

There are special rules relating to assets that have achieved short-life asset status on the basis that they will be provided for leasing but will then be used for a qualifying purpose. If the asset starts to be used otherwise than for a qualifying purpose then it ceases to be a short-life asset and is transferred to the main pool.

Legislation: CAA 2001, s. 87

205-250   Disposals for less than market value

For the purposes of the short-life asset calculation, market value normally needs to be substituted if an asset is disposed of for less than its true value. This will not apply if there is a charge to tax as earnings from an employment (or if there would be such a charge but for the £30,000 exemption). Similarly, it will not apply if an election is made in respect of a disposal to a connected person (see 205-300 below).

Legislation: CAA 2001, s. 88

205-300   Connected persons

As noted at 205-250, a disposal of a short-life asset will normally be made at market value if an asset is disposed of for a lower figure. Where the disposal is to a connected party, however, an election may be made which allows the acquiring party to step into the shoes of the party making the disposal. The rule only applies if the disposal is within the four-year cut-off period.

Plant and Machinery

The two connected persons may elect that the sales should be treated as taking place at the written-down value of the asset concerned, (ie for an amount equal to the available qualifying expenditure in the single-asset pool). If they do so elect, then the normal connected persons disposal rules (CAA 2001, s. 217 and 218) and the sale and leaseback provisions (CAA 2001, s. 222–225) do not apply.

Where such election is made it must be given to an officer of Revenue & Customs within two years of the end of the chargeable period in which the disposal takes place.

Irrespective of any such election, the buyer is treated as though he had made a short-life asset election in respect of the asset concerned; the original time limit for a future disposal of the asset (approximately four years – see above) applies from the original start of that period. In other words, the transaction between the connected persons is ignored as far as establishing the time limit is concerned.

Legislation: CAA 2001, s. 89(7)

205-350   Practical issues arising

A number of practical difficulties arise in relation to short-life assets. Often, these matters come about because of the difficulty in tracking numerous similar assets.

The Revenue therefore issued a Statement of Practice addressing many of these matters: SP 1/86 – Capital allowances: machinery and plant: short-life assets.

HMRC will in practice accept that a short-life asset pool may contain a group of assets. Where assets are held in large numbers, inspectors are instructed to accept 'computations which give the correct statutory result, and do not abuse the short-life asset provisions'. Normally, a separate short-life asset pool would be created each year and proceeds are to be treated as relating to the earliest period for which a short-life asset pool is in existence for the type of asset concerned. HMRC illustrate this with the following example:

'Example

Alice runs a restaurant and, every year, buys glasses to use in the business. She agrees with her inspector that the glasses have an actual life of three years and that nothing is received for the remains.

She spends £1,200 on wine glasses in the year ended 30 June 2002 and makes a SLA election. She can make a single capital allowance calculation for that expenditure of £1,200 and claim a balancing allowance in the year ended 30 June 2006 based on a disposal value of nil. None of the glasses bought in the year ended 30 June 2002 should still exist by then because they have an actual life of 3 years and Alice will not have received anything for the remains.

If Alice spends £1,500 on glasses in the year ended 30 June 2003 and makes another SLA election, that expenditure is put into a separate pool.

If in the year ended 30 June 2006 Alice sells the broken glass for recycling for £50 and the £50 is not treated as a trading receipt, then it should be treated as disposal proceeds.

If the disposal proceeds cannot be tied to any particular acquisition, then they should be treated as disposal proceeds of the earliest period for which a short-life asset pool is in existence.

If the broken glass cannot be related to any particular acquisition of glasses, the £50 should be treated as disposal proceeds of the pool for the expenditure of £1,200 incurred in the year ended 30 June 2002.'

Changes from April 2008

In practice, the introduction from April 2008 of the annual investment allowance (see 181-000ff.) will mean that few businesses will need to consider short-life asset elections for expenditure incurred from that time.

Other material: CA 23640

Long-life assets

210-000   Introduction

The long-life asset legislation was introduced to slow down the rate at which capital allowances can be given for certain plant and machinery which is likely to have a long useful life. For certain types of asset, allowances are given at 10 per cent rather than 20 per cent (and still on a reducing balance basis).

Since April 2008, the rules for long-life assets have been grafted onto the rules for integral features. Collectively, the assets are all now badged as 'special rate expenditure'.

210-050   Effect of applying the long-life asset legislation

The mechanics of computing allowances for long-life assets are as follows:

- expenditure on long-life assets is excluded from the main pool and is instead held in a class pool (the 'special rate expenditure pool' (or, before April 2008, the 'long-life asset pool')), or a single-asset pool;
- the special rate expenditure pool continues for as long as the qualifying activity continues, irrespective of whether any of the assets in the pool remain (CAA 2001, s. 65(1)(b)): in some cases, only a small proportion of the expenditure will have been allowed for tax purposes even after the asset has been sold;
- writing-down allowances are given on the reducing balance basis at a rate of 10 per cent (but six per cent before April 2008) rather than the standard 20 per cent (even if the long-life asset is in a single-asset pool); and
- no first-year allowances are normally available.

The effect on the relief available used to be drastic but is less so since the changes introduced by the *Finance Act* 2008. At a rate of 25 per cent, more than half of the expenditure will have been written off after three years; at 20 per cent, that is achieved in the

Plant and Machinery

fourth year; at 10 per cent, in the seventh year, and at the rate of six per cent, it would take 11 years to write off about half of the cost.

Assets leased overseas normally qualify for writing-down allowances at a special ten per cent rate. Where these are long-life assets then the expenditure is to be added to the special rate expenditure pool (previously the long-life asset pool) rather than the pool for assets leased overseas. In the past, the effect was that these assets too would have their allowances restricted to the rate of six per cent, but this distinction has now gone. In certain circumstances, allowances are prohibited.

Legislation: CAA 2001, s. 41(1), 44(2), 65(1)(b), 101, 102, 110, 114

210-100   Businesses affected

When the Explanatory Notes for the *Finance Bill* 1997 were published, the Revenue expressed the view that 'the new rules will in the main apply only to companies that invest heavily in long-life assets. The rules are subject to *de minimis* exclusions which will ensure that most or all small and medium-sized enterprises are not affected'. It is important to note, however, that there are no exclusions as such for particular types or sizes of business.

The only exclusions are for certain categories of expenditure and for businesses which, in any given year, spend less than a specified figure on long-life assets. It is therefore possible that a medium-sized business, for example, would not normally need to be concerned with the long-life asset rules but that it would suddenly need to consider them if it made a more substantial investment in a particular year.

Furthermore, an asset can never lose its long-life status. A business spending under £100,000 on assets may therefore have to claim restricted allowances if purchasing second-hand equipment that has already been classified as a long-life asset.

210-150   Definition of long-life assets

A long-life asset is defined as plant or machinery that, if new, can reasonably be expected to have a useful economic life of at least 25 years. If it is not new then it is necessary to look back at the time when it was new to see whether at that time it could reasonably have been expected to have a useful economic life of at least 25 years. The word 'new' is defined to mean 'unused and not second-hand'.

There is also a definition of 'useful economic life'. This is defined as the period beginning when the asset is first brought into use by any person for any purpose and ending when it is no longer used or likely to be used by anyone for any purpose as a fixed asset of a business.

The above definitions give rise to all sorts of issues and complications which are discussed below. It is important to bear in mind, however, that there are particular circumstances where the rules are *not* applied, even though the assets come within the above definition.

Assets that would otherwise fall within the long-life asset rules may be excluded either because of the nature of the asset itself or because the business spent relatively little on long-life assets in the period in question. Each of these issues is considered below.

Legislation: CAA 2001, s. 91

Other material: CA 23700ff.

One large asset or many small ones

The question will often arise of whether a large asset should be treated as a single item of machinery or plant or whether it can be divided into separate items each to be considered on its own merits. This can be relevant for long-life asset purposes in applying the 25-year rule. If there is one large machine, for example, it may well be that the machine will have a useful life of more than 25 years. If the business can demonstrate, however, that the machine is really made up of four entirely separate component parts then it may be possible to show that it is reasonable to expect that some or even all of those parts will be replaced within the 25-year period. Thus, if the machine is broken down into its component parts, it might be possible to argue that each separate part is outside the long-life asset rules.

Not surprisingly, HMRC look closely at this issue. In the August 1997 *Tax Bulletin*, they explained their view as follows:

'You should use the concept of the entity or entirety as developed by the Courts in cases about whether expenditure on a replacement part is allowable as expenditure on a repair in deciding what is the whole of the item of plant or machinery. You should not accept that the 25 year test can be applied to part of an item of plant or machinery if the cost of replacement of that part without improvement would be allowable for Case I purposes as a repair to the plant or machinery as a whole.'

As their justification for this, HMRC quote CAA 2001, s. 571(1) which provides that any reference to plant or machinery must be construed as including a reference to part of any plant or machinery.

The point was made to HMRC that CAA 2001, s. 92(1) (previously s. 38A(4)) appeared to allow expenditure to be broken down in this way. That section was omitted by the *Finance Act* 2008 but previously the subsection allowed expenditure in certain circumstances to be split so that part was subject to the long-life asset rules and part was not. The HMRC view, however, was that the subsection 'only applies where parts of the expenditure are treated differently under a subsequent provision of CAA 1990, section 38C, D or (the transitional provisions) in section 38H'. These provisions are now broadly at CAA 2001, s. 97–100, and Sch. 3, para. 20. HMRC made reference to the cases of *Brown v Burnley Football and Athletic Co Limited* and *Cole Brothers Limited v Phillips*. Each of these cases considers the concept of the 'entity', the former in relation to the calculation of trading profits and the latter specifically in relation to capital allowances.

The above comments in respect of splitting the cost of an asset do not apply if expenditure is incurred on an improvement to existing plant or machinery. In such circumstances, HMRC

Plant and Machinery

apply the 'useful economic life' test by reference to the improvement, looking at the period from when the improvement is first used until it ceases to be used. Obviously, if it comes to form part of the existing machinery or plant then the remaining expected life of that existing machinery or plant is likely to form a maximum remaining life for the improvement.

It follows from this that the original machinery or plant may be in a long-life pool whilst the costs of improvements go into the main pool (or vice versa). In such a case, any apportionment (for example, on a sale) should be made on a 'just and reasonable' basis in accordance with CAA 2001, s. 562(3).

HMRC give an example in their manuals of a printing press which initially has an expected working life of 30 years. They say that if, after 25 years, there is a major refurbishment which extends the expected working life of the press to 20 years from the refurbishment then the capital expenditure on that refurbishment will not be caught by the long-life asset rules as it will have a useful economic life of just 20 years.

Where an item is installed as a fixture in a building or structure then HMRC accept that the 'economic life of the building or structure will not necessarily determine the useful economic life of the machinery or plant' (*Tax Bulletin*, August 1997). So if a lift with a 20-year life expectancy is installed in a factory with an expected life of 50 years, the lift will not be a long-life asset (CA 23720).

Legislation: CAA 2001, s. 91

Cases: *Brown v Burnley Football and Athletic Co Limited* (1980) 53 TC 357; *Cole Brothers Limited v Phillips* [1982] BTC 208

Other material: CA 23720

The meaning of 'use'

Given that the useful economic life has to be measured from the time when the machinery or plant is first brought into use by any person, it is necessary to know what 'brought into use' actually means.

Again, HMRC has given guidance on this, indicating that:

- the asset will not be treated as being in use for as long as it is held as trading stock rather than as a fixed asset; and
- if it is constructed by a business for its own use then the period of use will not be deemed to have begun until the asset is actually brought into use for the purposes of the trade in question.

In considering whether the useful economic life of the item is likely to be 25 years, account should be taken of the way in which the machinery or plant is likely to be used in that business and, if it is likely to be sold in working order within the 25-year period, by any subsequent owner.

Where the machinery or plant is bought new and is unlikely to be sold on, other than as scrap at the end of its use in that business, HMRC will normally accept the economic life for accounting purposes as equating to the useful economic life for tax purposes 'unless it is clearly not reasonable' (*Tax Bulletin*, August 1997).

In the *Tax Bulletin* the Revenue indicated the type of evidence they would consider in order to make a decision on the likely useful economic life of an asset. They would expect, where necessary, to obtain details of 'design specifications, investment appraisals and experience with other similar machinery or plant'. They say that, for reasons of confidentiality and otherwise, they would not normally make a direct comparison with a claim by another business but, on the other hand, they might well 'have regard to general trends of claims by other taxpayers where similar machinery or plant is likely to be used in a similar way'.

Other material: CA 23720

Second-hand assets

A number of issues arise in relation to second-hand assets.

The starting point when a second-hand asset is bought is to consider what was a reasonable expectation of the useful economic life of the asset when the machinery or plant was new. That is what determines the treatment of the asset throughout its life, however many times it is sold, irrespective of any subsequent changes to the expected life.

Take, for example, an asset bought by trader A in the belief that it had a useful economic life of 40 years. It is possible that, because of some advance in technology, it becomes clear after just ten years that the asset will need to be scrapped within a further five years. Nevertheless, the first trader must treat it as a long-life asset.

If he sells it at the ten-year point, the purchaser must continue to treat it as a long-life asset even though it is by then clear that the total useful economic life of the asset will be considerably less than 25 years.

The rules work both ways, however. If the life of the asset is properly determined when it is new as being less than 25 years then it cannot subsequently become a long-life asset. HMRC indicate that they would consider themselves bound 'by a decision by the inspector, after consideration of the facts, that an asset was not long-life'. The trouble with this is that, under self-assessment, there will be relatively few cases in which the inspector will have specifically considered the facts.

Legislation: CAA 2001, s. 91, 103

Practical implications

The above rules put an onus on the purchaser of a second-hand asset to establish from the vendor whether the asset has been previously treated as a long-life asset. HMRC say that

Plant and Machinery

they would expect the purchaser to make suitable enquiries where the asset bought is 'of a type that is likely to have been treated as a long-life asset'.

The other possibility for a purchaser, however, is that the asset has received standard 25 or later 20 per cent writing-down allowances, (ie it has not been treated as a long-life asset), but on a proper consideration of the facts only 10 per cent (or, previously, six per cent) allowances should have been given. In such circumstances, the purchaser of the second-hand asset may find that allowances are gained much more slowly than had been anticipated, possibly with serious cash-flow implications.

Whilst the long-life asset legislation is still relatively new, it will often be the case that a second-hand asset is purchased from somebody who had not treated it as a long-life asset simply because it originally predated the legislation.

The effect of this was previously summarised by the Revenue (at old CA 3048), as follows:

'The long-life asset legislation does not apply to second-hand assets if allowances were given at 25 per cent to the first owner under the rule in section 38H(1) CAA 1990 and to each subsequent owner under the rule in section 38H(2). But if the asset is sold to a person who does not claim capital allowances, for instance if it is purchased on trading account, the long-life asset legislation may then apply to any subsequent owner.'

Section 38H CAA 1990 is found in updated form in CAA 2001, Sch. 3, para. 20.

HMRC apply the long-life asset legislation to an imported second-hand asset if it was reasonable to expect that the asset would have a useful economic life of at least 25 years when it was new, even if the remaining life when it is imported is less than 25 years.

Other material: CA 23750

210-200   Excluded assets

Certain assets are specifically exempted from the rules, however long they are likely to last and however much expenditure was incurred by the business. The legislation exempts certain fixtures, cars, ships and railway assets. Each of these is now looked at in detail. (As regards greenhouses, see 210-500.)

Legislation: CAA 2001, s. 93–96

Fixtures

A fixture is defined for these purposes, as for other capital allowance purposes, in accordance with CAA 2001, s. 173(1). It is an item of plant or machinery 'that is so installed or otherwise fixed in or to a building or any other description of land as to become, in law, part of that building or other land'.

There is no general exemption for fixtures, but the long-life asset rules do not apply to expenditure on plant or machinery that is either a fixture in, or is provided for use in, a building used wholly or mainly as a dwelling house, retail shop (as defined), showroom, hotel or office, or which is used for purposes ancillary to the purposes of such a building.

Those familiar with the IBA rules will immediately recognise the categories of building just referred to; the buildings are listed in the IBA rules as those which do not normally qualify for industrial buildings allowances (see the Chapter headed 'Industrial Buildings Allowances', which begins at 300-000). In their Explanatory Notes to the *Finance Bill* 1997, the Revenue commented that 'plant and machinery in dwelling houses, retail shops, showrooms, hotels and offices ... are wholly excluded from the rules on *de minimis* grounds'. In determining the degree of use of a building as a dwelling-house, etc HMRC will generally accept that the 'wholly or mainly' test is satisfied if at least 75 per cent of the building, measured on a reasonable basis, for instance by floor area, is used for purposes within the list. This is a slightly less stringent test than that applying for IBA purposes.

The term 'retail shop' has a wider meaning for capital allowances purposes than it would have in ordinary English usage. It is defined to include 'any premises of a similar character where retail trade or business (including repair work) is carried on'. In other words, if the public have regular access to the premises then they are likely to qualify as a retail shop – bad news for IBA purposes but good news when considering long-life assets. See 302-600 for a fuller discussion of the meaning of 'retail shop'.

Legislation: CAA 2001, s. 93

Other material: CA 23730

Ships

For expenditure incurred before 1 January 2011, expenditure on the provision of 'a ship of a sea-going kind' is outside the long-life asset rules if certain conditions are satisfied. Broadly, it is necessary to show that the ship is not an offshore installation in connection with mineral workings and that it is not used primarily for sport or recreation. There is no registration or weight requirement.

Legislation: CAA 2001, s. 94

Other material: CA 23730

Railway assets

The long-life asset rules do not apply to expenditure incurred before 1 January 2011 on the provision of railway assets that are provided wholly and exclusively for the purposes of a railway business. The concepts of 'railway asset' and 'railway business' have specific definitions in the legislation. A railway asset is defined as follows:

'(a) A locomotive, tram or other vehicle or a carriage, wagon or other rolling stock designed or adapted for use on a railway;

(b)   Anything which is, or is to be, comprised in any railway station, railway track or light maintenance depot or any apparatus which is, or is to be, installed in association with such a station, track or depot.'

HMRC provide the following further guidance in this respect:

'The definition of a railway includes a tramway or other system of guided transport. Railway assets are locomotives, rolling stock, tracks, stations, light maintenance depots, signalling equipment, power supplies and other associated apparatus. A railway business is a business or the part of a business which provides a public service of transporting goods or passengers by means of a railway in the UK or the Channel Tunnel.

Expenditure on the provision of a railway asset for use (whether by the owner or by a lessee) wholly and exclusively for the purposes of a railway business is excluded from long-life asset treatment. Expenditure which involves a benefit to a non-railway business may satisfy the wholly and exclusively condition if the benefit is incidental (see BIM 42135), for instance an electricity generator to supply power to a railway system which also incidentally supplies power to shops on railway stations.

Parts of a station which are intended to be used to a material extent for other purposes are likely to fail the wholly and exclusively condition but may come within the shops and offices exclusion instead.'

Legislation: CAA 2001, s. 95

Other material: CA 23730

Cars

The long-life asset rules do not apply to the provision of a motor car, as defined for capital allowance purposes (CAA 2001, s. 96). (The definition of 'car' included, until April 2009, a motor cycle. That definition was changed but s. 96 was amended from the same date so that motor cycles are still excluded from the long-life asset rules. See, generally, 200-000ff..) In practice, few vehicles will in any case have a life expectancy when new of more than 25 years.

Legislation: CAA 2001, s. 96

210-250   Expenditure limit not exceeded

The long-life asset rules do not apply to expenditure where the total expenditure on long-life assets does not exceed £100,000 in the chargeable period. This figure is increased or reduced for chargeable periods that are not of 12 months.

Broadly, this limit applies to an individual, to a partnership or to a group of companies. The rules vary slightly according to who is incurring the expenditure, as detailed below. The limit does not apply to trusts or partnerships with companies.

Certain types of expenditure cannot benefit from the £100,000 limit and so will be within the long-life asset rules anyway. Such items do not, however, count towards the £100,000 limit as far as the treatment of other expenditure is concerned. Expenditure subject to this special rule is:

- expenditure on the provision of a share in plant or machinery;
- expenditure which is treated as being on plant or machinery by virtue of CAA 2001, s. 538 (allowances in respect of contributions to capital expenditure); or
- expenditure which is on plant or machinery to be used for leasing, whether or not the leasing is in the course of a trade.

To illustrate these principles, HMRC give the following example in relation to a sole trader who draws her accounts up to 31 December each year:

> 'Janis draws up her accounts to 31 December each year. Her spending in 2003 on long-life assets is £90,000 on a machine to be let and £80,000 on a machine for use in her manufacturing business. The long-life asset rules apply to the £90,000 but not to the £80,000 as that is below the de-minimis limit.'

Particular rules apply to determine when expenditure is treated as incurred for capital allowances purposes. Where, under a contract for the provision of plant or machinery, the expenditure is deemed to be incurred in more than one chargeable period, all of the expenditure under that contract is nevertheless treated for the purposes of the long-life asset provisions as being incurred in the first chargeable period in which any of the expenditure is incurred. (This applies only for the purposes of determining the £100,000 threshold. The allowances themselves are given in the usual way.)

Legislation: CAA 2001, s. 97–100

Other material: CA 23740

Individuals and partnerships

For individuals and partnerships, a period of account may be more or less than 12 months. Where this is the case, the limit of £100,000 is to be proportionately increased or reduced.

The limit only applies if the individual (or, in the case of a partnership, at least half of the partners) can be said to devote substantially the whole of his or their time to carrying on the qualifying activity. In accordance with the HMRC interpretation of a similar expression in the retirement relief rules, this is likely to mean a minimum of some 30 hours per week on average.

The purpose of this 'full-time' rule is, according to the *Explanatory Notes* produced by the Revenue when the Finance Bill was published, 'to ensure that the effect of the *de minimis* limit is not multiplied through application to separate trades carried on by the same persons and to different partnerships with common members'. In the case of a partnership, it is of course possible that the members of the partnership will change over the course of the period. HMRC explain that the condition would still be satisfied 'if the chargeable period is

Plant and Machinery

169

made up of sub-periods throughout each of which the trade is carried on full time by at least half the members of the partnership in that sub-period, although the number of partners and the identity of the partners working full time may differ between sub-periods'.

HMRC illustrate this with the following example:

> 'David, Stephen and Graham are farming in partnership. Neil and Jackson join the partnership half way through the chargeable period. David and Graham work full time on the farm up to the change. David, Graham and Jackson work full time after the change. The condition is satisfied as 2 out of 3 partners in the first half and 3 out of 5 in the second half work full time.'

The £100,000 threshold is not available to a partnership if any member of that partnership is not an individual.

Legislation: CAA 2001, s. 99(2)

Other material: CA 23740

Companies

Similar but not identical rules apply to ensure that companies can also benefit from a £100,000 threshold.

The rules for companies refer to expenditure incurred in a 'chargeable period'. This is defined to mean an accounting period of a company. As an accounting period can never exceed 12 months, it follows that the £100,000 can never be increased for a longer period but, where the accounting period is shorter than 12 months, it is to be reduced pro rata.

Where the company has one or more associated companies then the £100,000 (or reduced figure as above) is to be spread equally between all the companies in question. Thus, if there is one associated company, each one has a limit of £50,000. If one company spends £60,000 and the other spends £30,000 then the £60,000 cannot benefit from the *de minimis* threshold, even though the total spent by the companies is below £100,000. The £30,000 will be treated as below the threshold and therefore outside the long-life asset rules.

For these purposes, the definition of associated companies is that given by ICTA 1988, s. 13. Broadly, two companies are associated at any time if one has control of the other or both are under common control. The term 'control' is to be interpreted in accordance with ICTA 1988, s. 416. An associated company which has not carried on any trade or business at any time in the accounting period is disregarded, but a company is treated as associated even if it is only associated for part of the accounting period. Similarly, two or more associated companies have to be counted even if they are associated for different parts of the accounting period.

Legislation: CAA 2001, s. 6, s. 98(3); CTA 2009, s. 10(1)(a)

210-300   Anti-avoidance

Later claims

If an asset is treated as a long-life asset then it must continue to be so treated even if its ownership changes. The only exception will be if, for the new owner, it comes within the categories of assets that are exempted from long-life treatment (certain fixtures, ships, railway assets and cars). According to the HMRC manuals, the effect of the rule is to avoid the need to reconsider the life of the asset once it has been determined that it is long-life.

Instructions to inspectors are that they should only expect somebody to establish whether a second-hand asset was treated as long-life in the hands of the previous claimant if it is an asset of a type that is clearly likely to have been so treated or if 'it is reasonable to expect that the information will be readily available to the taxpayer' (and the manual gives examples of sales between connected persons, sales of a business as a going concern or a sale and lease back).

Legislation: CAA 2001, s. 103

Other material: CA 23750

Disposal value of long-life assets

Since April 2008, the disposal value of all 'special rate' assets, including long-life assets, has been determined by CAA 2001, s. 104E. This is covered under the heading 'Disposal value: anti-avoidance rules' at 247-150.

Very similar legislation governing the disposal value of long-life assets was previously given at CAA 2001, s. 104.

Legislation: CAA 2001, s. 104, 267A

Other material: CA 23770

210-400   Aircraft

The treatment of jet aircraft as long-life assets was originally considered in a Revenue Interpretation in June 1999, but that is now marked as superseded by CA23781. Guidance originally issued in *Tax Bulletins* in April 2000 and December 2003 is similarly marked as having been superseded.

The Revenue, being unable to reach agreement with the British Air Transport Association as to the treatment of jet aircraft, offered a compromise. Under the agreement, groups of companies can deem the cost of a jet aircraft to fall into two equal halves, one attracting long-life asset allowances at the reduced rate and the other attracting full writing-down

Plant and Machinery

allowances at the standard rate. Particular conditions apply and when these are not met HMRC will start 'with the presumption that the aircraft will normally be a long-life asset'.

HMRC has indicated that a further formal agreement is impracticable for aircraft outside the terms of the BATA Agreement due to 'the wide variety of type and the even wider variety of use' of aircraft. Nevertheless, the Revenue have provided a 'broad indication of how, in general, we will handle the application of the legislation' to various different types of aircraft. This is considered at CA 23782.

The various agreements regarding aircraft were originally to run to the end of 2003, but were then extended for a further five years. As at July 2009, however, the wording of the HMRC manual still stated that the agreement runs 'until 31 December 2008, and will then be reviewed'.

Other material: CA 23781

210-450   Printing equipment

The Revenue issued guidance in *Tax Bulletin* 57 on whether printing equipment is to be treated as a long-life asset, but this is now superseded by guidance at CA 23790. The broad principle is now that HMRC will accept that 'modern printing equipment purchased new and unused is unlikely to have an expected useful economic life of 25 years of longer. This means that it will not be a long life asset.' Specifically, this will normally apply to pre-press equipment, to printing presses as such and to finishing equipment (for folding, cutting, binding, etc).

The same treatment will not necessarily apply to second hand equipment (as explained in greater detail in the HMRC guidance).

210-500   Greenhouses

The Revenue agreed with the NFU that certain sophisticated greenhouses that qualify as plant would not be treated as long-life assets but the agreement only covered expenditure incurred up to 31 December 2005 'because designs and technology will not stand still'. There is a warning, however, that 'if glasshouses are developed before then which have a useful economic life exceeding 25 years, they will necessarily be outside this agreement'. The guidance was not, however, updated and the wording remained well into 2009.

Other material: CA 23785

Hire purchase

215-000 Introduction

For capital allowances to be available on plant and machinery, the person incurring the expenditure has to own the asset in question as a result of incurring it. To achieve this in cases of hire purchase, plant or machinery subject to a hire purchase contract is deemed to be owned by the person incurring the capital expenditure, and not by any other person. This rule applies at any time when the person is entitled to the benefit of the contract so far as it relates to the asset in question.

Hire purchase may be considered synonymous with lease purchase.

To come within this special treatment, there are three fundamental conditions:

(1) The person carrying on a qualifying activity (or a corresponding overseas activity) must incur capital expenditure on the provision of plant or machinery for the purposes of that activity.

(2) The expenditure must be incurred 'under a contract providing that the person shall or may become the owner of the plant or machinery on the performance of the contract'.

(3) For contracts finalised on or after 1 April 2006, the contract is treated as a finance lease, or would be so treated if the lessee prepared accounts but does not in fact do so (as, for example, in the case of a lessee who is an employee).

The addition of the reference to a corresponding overseas activity is (according to the *Explanatory Notes* to the 2006 Finance Bill) intended to 'secure that hire purchase contracts with non-residents are treated in the same way as contracts with residents in comparable circumstances'.

A lessee may be prevented from claiming allowances because of the third condition above (requirement that the contract should be a finance lease). In such a case, the lessor is also prevented from claiming allowances. According to the *Explanatory Notes* to the 2006 Finance Bill, 'this result is reasonable as such circumstances will only occur where the contract has been artificially structured to gain a tax advantage that was not envisaged when section 67 was originally enacted and the lessee will be entitled to relief for all his expenditure'.

Ordinary hire purchase contracts, with a nominal option fee payable to acquire the asset at the end of the lease, will be accounted for as finance leases and will therefore not be affected by the *Finance Act* 2006 change.

There is also a special rule about when the expenditure is treated as incurred. Once the asset is brought into use for the purposes of the activity, the person is treated as having incurred all the capital expenditure in respect of the asset that he will be incurring under the contract from that time on. HMRC illustrate this with the following example:

Plant and Machinery

'Bob enters into a contract on 24 May 2001 to buy a computer from Robbie. He pays £5,000 on 24 May 2001 when he enters into the contract and then there are 5 payments of £1,000 at yearly intervals. He brings the computer into use on 4 July 2001. Bob is treated as owning the computer from 24 May 2001 onwards, the date of the contract, and Robbie is treated as ceasing to own it. Bob can claim PMAs on the initial payment of £5,000 then. He can claim PMAs on the 5 payments on £1,000 each of which he has still to make when he brings the computer into use on 4 July 2001.'

The legislation relating to long funding leases (see 230-000ff.) does not apply to hire purchase contracts.

Legislation: CAA 2001, s. 11(4)(b), 67

Other material: CA 23310

215-100   Disposal values

If somebody then ceases to be entitled to the benefit of the contract relating to the asset, and does not at that time acquire actual ownership of the asset, then he is treated at that time as ceasing to own it.

In such a case, the disposal value will depend on whether or not the asset has been brought into use for the purposes of the qualifying activity.

If it has not been brought into use then the disposal value will be the total of any capital sums that the person receives (or is entitled to receive) 'by way of consideration, compensation, damages or insurance money in respect of his rights under the contract or the plant or machinery'.

If the plant or machinery has been brought into use then the disposal value will be as above but increased by the amount of any capital expenditure which is treated as having been incurred but which has not in fact been incurred.

Certain anti-avoidance rules apply if the person carrying on the qualifying activity assigns the benefit of the contract to somebody else and allowances to the assignee need to be restricted under CAA 2001, Pt. 2, Chapter 17 (anti-avoidance).

Legislation: CAA 2001, s. 68

215-200   Fixtures

The hire purchase rules as outlined above do not apply to fixtures, regarding which see 245-000.

If somebody has been treated as owning plant or machinery under the hire purchase rules, but the asset in question then becomes a fixture without the person being treated as owner of the plant or machinery, then he is treated for the purposes of the hire purchase rules as ceasing to own the plant when it becomes a fixture.

For these purposes, a fixture is defined to be any item of plant or machinery 'that is so installed or otherwise fixed in or to a building or other description of land as to become, in law, part of that building or other land'. Specifically, it includes boilers or water-filled radiators installed in buildings for the purposes of heating space or water.

Legislation: CAA 2001, s. 69, 173(1)

215-300   Plant and machinery provided by lessees

Special rules apply, which have a bearing on both the lessor and a lessee, where all the following conditions are met:

- under the terms of a lease or tenancy, a lessee is required to provide plant or machinery; and
- he therefore incurs capital expenditure for the purposes of a qualifying activity which he is carrying on; and
- the asset is not a fixture; and
- the lessee does not own the asset in question.

Where these conditions are met, the lessee is deemed to be the owner of the plant or machinery for as long as it continues to be used for the purposes of the qualifying activity. If the lease comes to an end, the lessee is not required to bring a disposal value into account.

In certain circumstances, the lessor will be required to bring into account a disposal value. This will apply if all the following conditions are met:

- the plant has been used for the purposes of the lessee's qualifying activity until the lease ends; and
- the lessor holds the lease in the course of a qualifying activity; and
- when the lease comes to an end, or at any time thereafter a 'disposal event' (see 190-600) occurs in respect of the plant or machinery; and
- at that time, the lessor owns the plant or machinery 'as a result of the requirement under the terms of the lease'.

Where the above applies, the lessor will bring the disposal value into account for the chargeable period in which the disposal event occurs.

There are rules to determine which pool of expenditure suffers the disposal event. The pool in question will be the one that would be applicable in relation to the lessor's qualifying activity if:

- the expenditure incurred by the lessee had in fact been qualifying expenditure incurred by the lessor; and

- if that expenditure were allocated to a pool for the chargeable period in which the disposal event occurred.

Legislation: CAA 2001, s. 70

Diminishing shared ownership

Legislation was introduced in 2005 and 2006 to clarify the tax treatment of certain 'alternative finance arrangements', designed to be compliant with Shari'a law, which prohibits the payment or receipt of interest. The legislation was mainly concerned with the income tax treatment of amounts paid or received in place of interest.

In March 2007, HMRC published a 'Brief' in response to questions about the capital gains and capital allowances implications of one particular alternative finance arrangement, the diminishing shared ownership arrangements or 'diminishing musharaka'. Such an arrangement involves a financial institution and the intended buyer jointly purchasing an asset. Each acquires a share in the title to the asset in proportion to their contribution to the purchase price. Subsequently, the buyer acquires a greater share in the title to the asset as and when he makes payments to the financial institution over an agreed period. The financial institution will grant a lease to the buyer in respect of that part of the asset which the buyer has not yet acquired, in return for a rent.

As far as capital allowances are concerned, the Brief makes the following points:

'Section 67 CAA 2001 was amended in Finance Act 2006 to ensure that where, as in DSO arrangements, there are two or more agreements then the agreements have to be viewed as parts of a single contract for the purposes of section 67 CAA 2001.

We therefore consider that where DSO arrangements are entered into for assets that qualify for plant and machinery allowances then the buyer (lessee) is entitled, once the plant or machinery is brought into use, to claim plant and machinery allowances on all of the future capital payments to be made under the arrangements. No other person can claim allowances on these assets.'

Other material: HMRC Brief 26/07

Alternative finance investment bonds

Legislation was introduced in FA 2009 (s. 123 and Sch. 61) with effect from 21 July 2009. The measure is not primarily concerned with capital allowances but the following extract from the *Explanatory Notes* to FB 2009 explains the effect:

'The position of alternative finance bond-holders will be clarified to ensure that [stamp duty land tax] does not arise on the acquisition or transfer of an alternative finance bond certificate. The originator should also be able to claim any [capital allowances] on the asset during the term of the bond.'

215-400   Software

Where a person carrying on a trade incurs capital expenditure on a right to use or otherwise deal with computer software, the expenditure is treated as having been incurred on the provision of plant or machinery for the purposes of the trade. As long as the person is entitled to the right, the plant or machinery will be treated as his.

Where capital expenditure is incurred on computer software which does not constitute plant or machinery – for example, software transmitted electronically from the owner to the person who incurs the expenditure – the software is treated as plant or machinery for capital allowances purposes.

Expenditure on computer software may be subject to a short-life asset election (see 205-000).

Legislation: CAA 2001, s. 71

Disposals

The granting of a right to use or otherwise deal with computer software for a capital sum is treated as a disposal of plant or machinery, and a disposal value brought into account accordingly. This does not apply where an event defined in CAA 2001, s. 61(1)(e) or (f) occurs first, ie if machinery, etc begins to be used wholly or partly for non-trade purposes, or if the qualifying activity is permanently discontinued.

The disposal value to be brought into account is as follows:

- if the consideration for the grant is not wholly in money but equals an open market money value, or if any consideration is less than the open market value, then the value is the market value of the right granted at the time of the grant (subject to the two exceptions below);
- in other circumstances the value is the net proceeds to the grantor plus any insurance monies, compensation or other capital payments.

If the grant gives rise to a charge to tax as earnings from an employment – for example because it is made to an employee free of charge or at less than its market value – then only the actual proceeds (if any) need to be brought into account. This is the case even if no tax is actually payable by the director or employee because of the £30,000 exemption applying to certain payments on the termination, etc of an employment.

Similarly, market value does not have to be substituted if the grantee can claim capital allowances on the asset as plant or machinery or under the research and development allowance rules (though this exemption does not apply if the grantee is a dual resident investing company connected with the seller, as defined in ICTA 1988, s. 404). This is the case even if the buyer and seller are connected with each other.

Plant and Machinery

Where there is a series of grants of leases in respect of the same software, the aggregate consideration received is taken into account for the purposes of limiting any capital allowances balancing adjustment.

Legislation: CAA 2001, s. 72, 73

Other material: CA 23250

Computer software – extracts from Tax Bulletin

The distinction between revenue and capital expenditure on software is not always straightforward. The following is the text of a Tax Bulletin article from November 1993 concerning the tax treatment of computer software (IR Int. 55). On the HMRC website itself, this article is now said to be 'superseded by BIM 35800 onwards'. Reference to the Business Income Manual, however, shows that the article is still current: it is reproduced in full at BIM 35810 and the instruction to HMRC officers still states that 'computer software expenditure … should be dealt with along the lines of the article in Tax Bulletin 9F (November 1993)'.

'Software acquired under licence

This is the way that nearly all off-the-shelf software is acquired nowadays. The treatment of expenditure of this nature depends on the form the consideration for the licence takes.

Regular payments akin to a rental

Payments of this kind are revenue. The timing of deductions will be governed by correct accounting practice which normally requires the rentals to be spread over the useful life of the software in accordance with the fundamental accruals concept in Statement of Standard Accounting Practice No. 2. (What is correct accounting practice is ultimately a question of law but the courts are heavily influenced by current generally acceptable practice.)

Lump sum

The first question to be asked here is whether the licence is a capital asset in the trade of the licensee. In broad terms a licence is a capital asset if it has a sufficiently enduring nature. This approach has to be applied by reference to the function of the licensed software in the context of the licensee's trade. Very often the expectation will be that the software will function as a tool of the trade for a period of several years. On the other hand, the benefit to be obtained by the licensee in question may be sufficiently transitory to stamp the payment as revenue even though the licence granted is for an indefinite period.

No simple rule of thumb covering every business situation can be successfully devised but, in any event, where software is expected to have a useful economic life of less than two years Inspectors will accept that the expenditure is revenue. In these circumstances the timing of the deduction will depend on the correct accounting treatment in the same way as it does for regular payments.

Where the licensed software functions as a capital asset of the licensee's trade capital allowances on plant and machinery will be due under CAA 1990, s. 67A (now s. 71 CAA 2001). This will be the case whether or not the software comes in a corporeal medium (such as on "floppy discs") separate from the licensee's computer hardware. A short-life asset election may be made where appropriate. Computer software is not defined for capital allowances purposes and therefore has its normal meaning which is wide and covers both programs and data (for example books stored in digital form).

Equipment acquired as a package

Often computer hardware and the licence to use software are purchased as a package for a single payment. In these circumstances the expenditure between hardware and software should be apportioned. Capital allowances under the ordinary plant and machinery rules will be due on the expenditure attributable to the hardware. The treatment of the balance of the expenditure, attributable to the software licence, will depend on the considerations described above. Where, however, both the hardware and software are acquired on capital account and the expenditure all goes into the general machinery and plant "pool", apportionment will not in practice be necessary.

Software owned outright

Most widely marketed software is licensed to users and not sold to them outright. But some, particularly larger, concerns may develop their own software. The treatment of expenditure on software acquired outright follows the same principles as those governing the treatment of licensed software. In particular, where the expenditure concerned (including salaries of in-house computer professionals) is capital or revenue again depends on the economic function of the software in the trade in question as it does for licences acquired for lump sums.'

Leasing assets

220-000   Leasing assets: introduction

Capital allowance rules on leasing are complex and have developed over many years.

For the treatment of assets leased in the UK, see 220-100. For the treatment of assets leased outside the UK, see 220-200. See 241-800 for details of certain restrictions placed on allowances available to finance lessors by the two Finance Acts of 1997.

Leasing will sometimes amount to a trade, in which case the loss relief provisions are more generous, particularly in the ability to carry back such losses. Whether a leasing trade is being carried on is a question of fact but the following factors should be borne in mind:

- a trade is more likely to exist if there are more than just a few transactions and where there is more than one lessee;
- a specific leasing organisation dealing with and controlling the letting will indicate a trade; and
- leasing transactions which form part of a trade tend to specify a profit structure throughout their terms (ignoring the tax benefits derived from the allowance).

The question of whether or not a leasing trade was being carried on was considered in *Barclays Mercantile Industrial Finance Ltd v Melluish (HMIT)*. A finance leasing company purchased a master print of a film from the production company and leased it back to an associate of the producer. That associate distributed the film by granting licences to other

Plant and Machinery

affiliates to it in their respective territories. It was held, by the High Court, that the licences were not leases and the distribution company used the film for a non-leasing trade.

Leasing generally takes the form of a finance lease (or 'full payout lease') or an operating lease. In the case of the former, the asset leased is not expected to have any residual value at the end of the lease. In other words, the leasing agreement is merely a method of providing capital for the lessee of the asset. In the case of an operating lease, the asset will generally retain some of its value at the end of the lease, and either be sold or re-let by the lessor. This type of leasing provides a longer-term investment for the lessor as well as a source of capital for the lessee; accordingly the lessor normally retains a greater interest in the maintenance of the asset during the lease.

Cases: *Barclays Mercantile Industrial Finance Ltd v Melluish (HMIT)* [1990] BTC 209

Tax avoidance

The tax benefits, as opposed to commercial benefits, of leasing have diminished with the withdrawal of first-year allowances.

While 100 per cent first-year allowances were available, there was considerable scope for using leased assets as a 'tax shelter', and as a result the question arose as to whether leasing transactions could fall within the *Ramsay* principle as enunciated by the House of Lords in *Furniss v Dawson*. The Institute of Chartered Accountants in England and Wales sought confirmation from the Revenue that leases with a tax motive as well as being based on sound commercial principles were not within the 'new approach'. In a letter dated 20 September 1985 the Revenue gave the following reply:

> 'Perhaps it would be helpful to make two preliminary points. First, straightforward commercial leasing transactions – no doubt the vast majority – and especially those involving hire and operating leasing, are unlikely to be called into question by *Ramsay*; and second, the phasing out of accelerated depreciation may in any event reduce the extent in practice to which *Ramsay* needs to be considered in the context of leasing.
>
> As you say, leases, or arrangements involving leasing, may very well not be straightforward. Where this is so and just like any other complicated transaction, it may be necessary for the Revenue to make sure in appropriate cases that it understands precisely what is happening before being satisfied that claims to allowances or reliefs are validly based – especially where the claims are large.
>
> Against this background we would be concerned for example about arrangements which have the appearance of a finance lease but where there are doubts about whether a person claiming capital allowances is genuinely at risk for the financing of the activity or has actually incurred the capital expenditure concerned; where it appears that no earnings (or substantially none) flowing from the investment on which allowances are being claimed will materialise in the United Kingdom; where the lessee has directly or indirectly financed the lessor's expenditure; where there is doubt about whether expenditure has been incurred for the purposes of the claimant's trade; and generally where a composite transaction appears artificially to have been structured so as to bring it within the provisions, about claiming allowances, of the Finance Acts. In one or more of these areas it is possible that *Ramsay* could apply to the particular arrangements – certainly it is not possible to say that it would not apply.'

The last paragraph of the Revenue's reply should now be read subject to the statutory measures targeted at the problems of finance leasing which were introduced in 1997. These are discussed at 220-500.

Cases: *Furniss v Dawson* [1984] BTC 71

Changes in accounting practice for equipment leasing

Following the issue of the Statement of Standard Accounting Practice on 'Accounting for Leases and Hire-purchase Contracts' (SSAP 21) by the Accounting Standards Committee of the six major accountancy bodies in the UK and Ireland in August 1984, there was some confusion as to who was entitled to claim capital allowances on leased equipment. This was because the standard required a lessor under a finance lease to show the lease in his business accounts in the same way as a loan made by him, rather than as a fixed asset subject to depreciation, and it required the lessee to capitalise the lease, showing it in the balance sheet both as an asset and as an obligation to pay future rentals.

To clarify these issues, the Revenue issued the following press release on 27 October 1986:

'1. The Inland Revenue today confirmed that the 1984 statement of Standard Accounting Practice on leases and hire-purchase contracts (SSAP21) did not alter the tax position: lessees are not entitled to obtain capital allowances in respect of leased plant or machinery.

2. The lessor, by incurring the capital expenditure and retaining ownership of the assets will normally be entitled to capital allowances.

This continues to be so even where leased machinery is capitalised in the lessee's accounts.

3. Following discussions with the Inland Revenue the Equipment Leasing Association is recommending to its members that new leases should include a clear statement of the tax position, ie, that irrespective of the accounting treatment adopted, the lessee is not entitled to capital allowances on leased equipment.'

Lease purchase

Lease purchase transactions are similar in nature to hire-purchase, ie the lessee of the asset obtains immediately the use of the asset, and at some time in the future also acquires ownership. Provided the lessee does have an ultimate right to acquire the asset, capital allowances will be given to him, rather than to the lessor.

See the Chapter headed 'Fixtures', which begins at 245-000 for discussion of allowances available to lessors of equipment which becomes a fixture in a building belonging to a third party.

220-100   Assets leased in the UK

Plant and machinery leased in the UK qualifies for standard writing-down allowances, whether or not they were leased in the course of a trade. If leased in the course of a trade, they form part of the general plant and machinery pool. If leased otherwise than in the course of a trade or any other qualifying activity, they are treated as leased in the course of a separate trade ('special leasing') and are separately pooled, as discussed at 155-700.

Where a lessee, tenant or potential lessee has incurred capital expenditure on certain plant or machinery which he is required to provide under the terms of the lease, etc the asset may be treated as belonging to him so as to enable him to obtain allowances. In actual fact, it will normally belong to the lessor (who will not be entitled to allowances if he does not incur expenditure), except in relation to certain fixtures provided under leases entered into on or after 12 July 1984 otherwise than in pursuance of an agreement made before that date.

For the purposes of establishing the disposal value, the capital expenditure on providing the asset is treated as having been incurred by the lessor and not by the lessee once the lease has ended, etc. If the lessee has incurred the expenditure in point, the provisions relating to subsidies and contributions may apply (see 115-000).

Legislation: CAA 2001, s. 70

220-200   Overseas leasing

Overview

Extensive special rules apply to overseas leasing. The principle behind the rules is 'to ensure that leases of plant or machinery to lessees with little or no connection to the UK are not tax subsidised' (CA 24010). Following the introduction of the long funding leasing rules, however, the legislation concerning overseas leasing is being phased out. Specifically, no account is taken of any lease finalised (as defined) on or after 1 April 2006, when determining whether plant or machinery is used for overseas leasing. The following paragraphs are therefore subject to that overriding change.

The effect of the legislation is to reduce the rate of capital allowances for most plant and machinery leased outside the UK to ten per cent. Certain assets are protected from this reduced rate of allowances, but in other circumstances even the ten per cent allowance is withdrawn.

The restriction applies to expenditure incurred on the provision of plant or machinery that at any time in the 'designated period' is used for overseas leasing that is not 'protected leasing'. The 'designated period' is normally the period of ten years beginning when the plant or machinery is first brought into use (but see 220-300). 'Protected leasing' is broadly short-term leasing, although a wider definition applies to certain ships, aircraft and transport containers (see below).

Legislation: CAA 2001, Pt. 2, Ch. 11

Other material: CA 24010

Definition

Overseas leasing (previously 'foreign leasing') means the leasing of plant or machinery to a person who:

- is not resident in the UK; and
- does not use the asset exclusively for earning 'profits chargeable to tax', whether from a trade carried on in the UK or by virtue of CTA 2009, s. 1313(2) (non-residents' exploration or exploitation activities); or in relation to the use of an asset for leasing under a lease entered into before 16 March 1993, for the purposes of a qualifying activity carried on in the UK or its territorial seas.

The definition is, however, now subject to the phasing-out provisions referred to under 'Overview' above.

For these purposes, profits that are exempt under a double tax treaty are not treated as chargeable to UK tax.

A lease includes a sub-lease and every hire (including ship chartering) is regarded as leasing.

Legislation: CAA 2001, s. 105

Detail

Special provisions generally apply (but see below) where plant or machinery is, at any time within a period normally equal to ten years after it is first brought into use, or within the period of the lessor's ownership if shorter (the 'designated period': see 220-300), leased to a person who:

- is not resident in the UK; and
- does not use the asset exclusively for earning 'profits chargeable to tax', whether from a trade carried on in the UK or by virtue of CTA 2009, s. 1313(2) (non-residents' exploration or exploitation activities); or in relation to the use of an asset for leasing under a lease entered into before 16 March 1993, for the purposes of a qualifying activity carried on in the UK or its territorial seas.
- Profits in respect of which relief may be available under a double taxation agreement are *not* 'profits chargeable to tax' for these purposes.

HMRC (now) take the view that CAA 2001, Pt. 2, Ch. 11 applies where any lessee or sub-lessee meets the conditions in CAA 2001, s. 105(2), (3), 109(2) and is not protected leasing.

Protected leasing is 'short-term leasing' (see 220-300) or where a ship, aircraft or transport container is leased and used for a 'qualifying purpose' by virtue only of the extension for certain such assets. In these circumstances, the special rules do not apply and the usual pooling arrangements and writing-down allowances apply instead. The claim for the normal allowance must be accompanied by a certificate setting out the description of such 'protected leasing', the identity of the lessee and the assets in point.

Plant and Machinery

The overseas leasing rules also exclude a proportion of expenditure corresponding to the degree to which a jointly leased asset is used for a non-leasing trade, the profits from which will be chargeable to income tax or corporation tax (see below).

Legislation: CAA 2001, s. 105(3), (4), 106(1)–(2), 109(2), 118

Pooling

In relation to overseas leasing, allowances in respect of the relevant expenditure are calculated separately from the main plant and machinery pool and, except as mentioned below, any other pool. Each asset is treated as if it were pooled with other such assets, (ie other overseas leasing assets). The expenditure on such assets is included in a class pool (the overseas leasing pool).

This pooling arrangement does not override those special provisions which provide for each asset to be treated individually (as single asset pools), though the restrictions on allowances, etc below then apply equally to those individual assets.

Legislation: CAA 2001, s. 107(1), (2)

Allowances and charges

A writing-down allowance is available at ten per cent of the excess of 'available qualifying expenditure' for the period (AQE) over 'total disposal receipts value to be brought into account for that period' (TDR) (see 190-600), in respect of the overseas asset pool and in respect of expenditure on overseas leasing in single asset pools. Different rules apply if the chargeable period in point is the 'final chargeable period' for the overseas leasing pool or if the lease is a 'lease disqualified from any allowances'.

The ten per cent rate is proportionately reduced or increased if the chargeable period is less or more than 12 months or reduced if the qualifying activity has been carried on for only part of the period.

Where a writing-down or balancing allowance has been made and, in the 'designated period', the plant or machinery is used for overseas leasing which is not protected leasing, the allowance may be recovered (see below).

Legislation: CAA 2001, s. 102, 109

Final chargeable period

The 'final chargeable period' for the overseas leasing pool means the chargeable period at the end of which the circumstances are such that there can be no more disposal receipts in any subsequent chargeable period.

Unless the lease is a 'lease disqualified from any allowances' (see below), a balancing allowance is given for the period equal to the excess of the 'available qualifying expenditure for that period' (AQE) over the 'total disposal receipts to be brought into account for that period' (TDR) (see 190-600), in respect of each of the separate overseas leasing pools, or a balancing charge is made for the period equal to any corresponding shortfall.

Legislation: CAA 2001, s. 56(6), (7), 65(4), 109(1)

Transactions between connected persons or persons under common control

There are special provisions relating to transactions between connected persons or persons under common control (see 235-500), successions to trade (see 240-000) and tax-structured transactions (sole or main benefit test: see 220-500). In particular, where the asset is disposed of to a 'connected person':

- the disposal value to be brought into account in the separate 'overseas leasing pool' will be equal to the open market value or, if less, the capital expenditure incurred on the provision of the vehicle by the person disposing of it; and
- the person acquiring it will be treated as having incurred on its provision capital expenditure equal to that disposal value.

The above rules do not apply if the disposal occurs on the occasion of a change in the persons carrying on the qualifying activity which either falls within ICTA 1988, s. 343(1) (company reconstructions without change of ownership) or in relation to which either Condition A or Condition B is met where (CAA 2001, s. 108, 577):

- Condition A is that at least one person who carried on the activity immediately before or immediately after the change was within the charge to income tax in respect of that activity, and at least one person who carried on the qualifying activity before the change continued to carry it on after the change.
- Condition B is that all of the following sub-conditions are met:

  - the qualifying activity was carried on in partnership both immediately before and immediately after the change;
  - a company that was within the charge to corporation tax in respect of the activity carried it on immediately before or immediately after the change, and
  - at least one company which carried the activity on before the change continued to carry it on after the change.

Legislation: CAA 2001, s. 108, 577(1)

Recovery of excess relief: reduction in rate of allowances

Special rules apply where an asset, which has been included in the pool of qualifying expenditure eligible for 'normal writing-down allowances', comes, in the 'designated period' (see 220-300), to be used for overseas leasing (other than protected leasing). The term 'normal writing-down allowances' means specifically allowances where the 10 per cent restriction does not apply.

In the chargeable period in which the event occurs:

- a balancing charge is made on the person to whom the asset then belongs of an amount (the 'excess relief') equal to the excess of allowances already given at the 20 (or 25) per cent rate plus any first-year allowance made over the sum of the writing-down allowances to which the lessor would have been entitled at the 10 per cent rate. Reference to the giving of an allowance is effectively to the falling due of the allowance, ie irrespective of whether it can be offset against profits, etc (CAA 2001, s. 577(3)); and
- the written-down value of the asset at the end of the period in question, (ie the expenditure less the allowances given to date, as above) must be brought into account as a disposal value in respect of the pool of assets in point, thereby removing the asset from the remaining pool of qualifying expenditure.

See, however, ICTA 1988, s. 768 where trading losses are disallowed in connection with a change in ownership of a company.

In the *next* chargeable period, the lessor is treated as incurring expenditure in respect of the overseas leasing pool or the single asset pool in point equal to the sum of the balancing charge and the disposal value recovered above. Writing-down allowances at ten per cent will then be available and balancing adjustments will be made in the usual way as if the asset had always been used for the purposes of such trade.

For the purpose of the calculation of normal allowances (and therefore the written-down value), the asset in question is treated as if it were the only asset on which the lessor had been given allowances.

Example

This example is based on the rates of allowance applying since April 2008, and ignores transitional figures.

In the course of a trade, Len leases an asset to Ed, who uses it for qualifying activity purposes. The asset cost Len £40,000 and is a general asset (not special rate expenditure, for example, a car). The balance brought forward on Len's main pool is £53,121. One year later, Ed becomes non-resident and begins to use the asset for a qualifying activity carried on outside the UK. In that chargeable period a balancing charge arises as follows:

Allowances given:		£
Year 1 (20% × £40,000)		8,000
Year 2 (20% × £32,000)		6,400
		14,400
Allowances now due:	£	
Year 1 (10% × £40,000)	4,000	
Year 2 (10% × £36,000)	3,600	(7,600)
Balancing charge		6,800

The written down value of the asset (£40,000–£14,400) is brought into account as a disposal value in respect of the main pool so as to remove the effect of the asset on the pool.

	General pool	Separate pool
Year 1	£	£
Balance brought forward	53,121	
Capital expenditure incurred	40,000	
Qualifying expenditure	93,121	
Writing-down allowance at 20%	(18,624)	
Balance carried forward	74,497	
Year 2	£	£
Balance brought forward	74,497	
Capital expenditure incurred	–	
Qualifying expenditure	74,497	
Writing-down allowance at 20%	(14,900)	
Balancing charge		6,800
Disposal value brought into account	(25,600)	25,600
Balance carried forward	33,997	32,400
Year 3	£	£
Balance brought forward	33,997	32,400
Writing-down allowance at 20%/10%	(6,800)	(3,240)
Balance carried forward	27,197	29,160

Note: In the chargeable period shown as Year 3 Len will be treated as incurring qualifying expenditure in respect of the overseas leasing pool of £6,800 + £25,600 = £32,400. Len will thereafter be entitled to writing-down allowances at ten per cent per annum.

Legislation: CAA 2001, s. 111, 126

Notice of requirement to reduce entitlement to allowances

The occasion requiring the step down to ten per cent allowances also brings about a requirement for the lessor to give written notice to HMRC specifying the identity of the lessee and the assets to which it relates. Notice must be given within three months after the chargeable period in which the asset is first leased as mentioned above. However, if at the end of the three months the lessor does not know and could not reasonably be expected to know of the use, he must give notice within 30 days of becoming aware of it.

This timing can lead to anomalies. If the lessor becomes aware of the overseas leasing two months and 28 days (say) after the end of the chargeable period, then the notice still falls due at the end of the third month. However, a lessor who becomes aware four days later (say) will be given 30 days after becoming so aware.

Penalties will fall due for non-compliance under TMA 1970, s. 98.

Legislation: CAA 2001, s. 119, 126(2)

Plant and Machinery

187

Where the asset was acquired from a 'connected person' (see 120-200), the recovery of excess relief extends back to the allowances given to the earlier owner (or, in a series of such disposals, any of the earlier owners). In such a case, the excess relief is calculated by reference to the original expenditure, ignoring the interim disposal proceeds and adjusting the allowances which have actually been made to withdraw (in a just and reasonable manner) the effect of any balancing adjustments. However, the extension does not apply if the transaction (or any of the other transactions) was effected on the occasion of a change in the persons carrying on the qualifying activity which either falls within ICTA 1988, s. 343(1) (company reconstructions without change of ownership) or in relation to which either Condition A or Condition B is met where (CAA 2001, s. 112):

Condition A is that at least one person who carried on the activity immediately before or immediately after the change was within the charge to income tax in respect of that activity, and at least one person who carried on the qualifying activity before the change continued to carry it on after the change.

Condition B is that all of the following sub-conditions are met:

- the qualifying activity was carried on in partnership both immediately before and immediately after the change;
- a company that was within the charge to corporation tax in respect of the activity carried it on immediately before or immediately after the change, and
- at least one company which carried the activity on before the change continued to carry it on after the change.

If any of the above connected persons could have taken a normal writing-down allowance but chose not to, with the effect that a balancing allowance is made to any of them instead, the clawback and pool addition applies to such allowance with the necessary modifications.

Where the asset in point is a ship, the clawback of excess relief and its addition to the overseas leasing pool or single asset pool in point takes precedence over the writing-down allowance postponement rules. As such, the postponed allowance may not be claimed in the period in question or thereafter, but that amount is added to qualifying expenditure in respect of the appropriate pool in the next period.

Legislation: CAA 2001, s. 112, 113

Expenditure disqualified from any allowances

In certain circumstances, no writing-down or balancing allowances at all are available in respect of assets leased outside the UK. This is where an asset is used for a non-qualifying purpose within the 'designated period' (see 220-300), and any of the following applies:

- there is more than a year between any two consecutive due dates for payment under the lease;
- any payments other than periodical payments are due under the lease (or under any agreement which might reasonably be construed as being collateral to the lease);

- monthly payments under the lease are variable for any reason other than changes in tax or capital allowance rates, inter-bank loan interest rates or insurance premiums;
- the lease exceeds or is for a period capable of exceeding 13 years; or
- the lessor, or anyone 'connected' (see 120-200) with him, may become entitled to receive any payment (other than insurance proceeds) which is referable to the value of the assets at or after expiry but is determinable before expiry of the lease.

If an asset becomes such an asset, any allowances previously given (and not recovered by operation of the excess relief provisions above) are clawed back by a balancing charge made on the person to whom the asset then belongs for the chargeable period in point and a disposal value equal to the previously unrelieved expenditure must be brought into account. This has the overall effect of negating any previous allocation of the expenditure on the asset to the pool in question.

Allowances are treated as given when they fall due, irrespective of whether they can be offset against profits, etc. In determining such allowances it is assumed that the asset in question is the only one on which the lessor has received any allowances. This circumvents problems of calculations involving any pooling of expenditure.

Where the asset was acquired from a connected person, the balancing charge extends back to allowances given to the earlier owner (or, in a series of such disposals, any of the earlier owners). In such a case, the excess relief is calculated by reference to the original expenditure, ignoring the interim disposal proceeds and adjusting the allowances which have been made to withdraw (in a just and reasonable manner) the effect of any balancing adjustments. However, the extension does not apply if the transaction (or any of the other transactions) was effected on the occasion of a change in the persons carrying on the qualifying activity which either falls within ICTA 1988, s. 343(1) (company reconstructions without change of ownership) or in relation to which either Condition A or Condition B is met where:

Condition A is that at least one person who carried on the activity immediately before or immediately after the change was within the charge to income tax in respect of that activity, and at least one person who carried on the qualifying activity before the change continued to carry it on after the change.

Condition B is that all of the following sub-conditions are met:

- the qualifying activity was carried on in partnership both immediately before and immediately after the change;
- a company that was within the charge to corporation tax in respect of the activity carried it on immediately before or immediately after the change, and
- at least one company which carried the activity on before the change continued to carry it on after the change.

Legislation: CAA 2001, s. 115(1), (3); CAA 2001, s. 577(3)

Plant and Machinery

Notice of change of use to non-protected leasing

The owner of the plant or machinery is required to give a notice to an officer of HMRC if:

- expenditure on plant or machinery has qualified for either a first-year allowance or a normal (25 or 20 per cent) writing-down allowance; and
- the plant or machinery is subsequently used during the designated period for overseas leasing which is not protected leasing.

The notice must specify:

- the non-resident lessee; and
- if the notice is given by reference to a chargeable period, all items of plant or machinery (if more than one) relevant to that period.

The notice must be given within three months of the end of the chargeable period in which the plant or machinery is first used for overseas leasing which is not protected leasing. If the lessor does not know (and cannot reasonably be expected to know) that the circumstances are met at the end of the three-month period, then the lessor is required to provide the notice within 30 days of coming to know of them.

The notice must specify any of the non-resident joint lessees to whom the plant or machinery has been leased and (if the notice is given by reference to a chargeable period) all the plant or machinery (if more than one) relevant to that period. Again, penalties apply for failure to meet these conditions.

Legislation: CAA 2001, s. 110, 114–115, 119

Meaning of 'lease'

Many of the issues contained in CAA 2001, s. 110 were tested in *Delta Finance Newco v IR Commrs*, later known as *BMBF (No. 24) Ltd v IR Commrs*, where judgment was given on what was meant by 'the lease' in a case involving a series of complex transactions.

Cases: *Delta Finance Newco v IR Commrs* (2001) Sp C 316, later *BMBF (No. 24) Ltd v IR Commrs* [2004] BTC 26

BMBF (No. 24) Ltd v IR Commrs

The taxpayer claimed writing-down allowances on the purchase in 1995 for £165.8m from a company resident in the UK (CIL), of moveable plant and machinery being used in the factories of the parent of CIL in the US. CIL had acquired the equipment on the same day from its US parent. Also, on the same day, the taxpayer leased the equipment back to CIL for a term of 30 years and 19 days ('the headlease') at an escalating rent and CIL, with the taxpayer's consent, subleased it to its US parent for a term of 11 years at a fixed rent ('the sublease'). An associated company of CIL deposited £146.7m with the taxpayer's parent as security for CIL's obligations under the headlease from the taxpayer. The rent payable by CIL to the taxpayer took account of the taxpayer's capital allowances on the purchase and if there was no entitlement, would be adjusted upwards. It increased by 2.5 per cent each six months and was designed to amortise the taxpayer's investment with interest over the term.

It was held that CAA 1990, s. 42 (see now CAA 2001, s. 110) had no application where there was a lease by the owner to a non-resident if the lease was 'permitted leasing'. The section had no application to a finance lease to a UK resident if there was no onward lease to a non-resident. For the purposes of the permitted leasing condition of CAA 1990, s. 42(1), it was enough that the lease to the non-resident was 'permitted leasing'.

It did not follow, though, that in a case where there was a chain of leases 'the lease' to which reference was made in each of the five paragraphs of s. 42(3) was the sublease to the non-resident user. The question turned on the effect of s. 42(3), to which s. 42(2) was made subject and s. 42(3) was in point where each of three conditions was satisfied: If condition (i) was met, but either of conditions (ii) or (iii) were not met, then s. 42(3) was not applicable. In such a case, the provisions of s. 42(2) applied so as to reduce the amount of the writing-down allowances from 25 per cent to ten per cent. It was not acceptable to argue that the second cumulative condition in s. 42(3) (use otherwise than for a qualifying purpose) added nothing to the permitted leasing condition in s. 42(1).

In a multi-lease case the question was whether the use, in the context of the expression 'used otherwise than for a qualifying purpose', was use by the lessee under the lease from the owner (the headlease) or use by the non-resident as the person to whom the machinery and plant had been leased under a sublease. The relevant use was use by the non-resident lessee under the sublease. In such a case it was the non-resident lessee who was 'the lessee' for these purposes.

Parliament intended there to be no fiscal incentive to an owner in cases where the machinery or plant had been leased to a non-resident who did not use it exclusively for earning profits taxable in the UK.

Cases: *BMBF (No. 24) Ltd v IR Commrs* [2004] BTC 26

Joint lessees

Except as noted below, special provisions apply to assets leased to two or more persons jointly, where at least one of them is not UK-resident and does not use the assets for a trade carried on in the UK or its territorial sea. The rules do not apply to protected leasing (ie short-term leasing or the leasing of a ship, aircraft or transport container for a 'qualifying purpose' by virtue only of the extension for such assets).

The lessees may use the asset for the purposes of a qualifying activity other than leasing. In this case, it will be excluded from 'overseas leasing' if and to the extent that it appears that the profits of the qualifying activity throughout the 'qualifying period' (or, if shorter, the period of the lease) will be chargeable to income tax or corporation tax. The principal effect is that the restriction to ten per cent allowances will not apply, nor will the asset be disqualified from allowances.

The restricted allowances apply to expenditure by reference to the use of the plant or machinery, but such reference includes reference to a part of any plant or machinery (CAA 2001, s. 571(1)) so that the partial use of any assets is relevant. Where part only of

Plant and Machinery

expenditure is attributable to overseas leasing, each part is treated for the purposes of the provisions relating to lessees generally as a separate item of plant or machinery, and all necessary apportionments will be made, so that only the overseas leasing element is subject to restricted allowances or disqualification.

Legislation: CAA 2001, s. 116

Notice to HMRC

In such a case, the lessor must give written notice to HMRC specifying:

- the names and addresses of the lessees;
- the part of the expenditure which is properly attributable to each; and
- so far as the lessor knows, which lessees are 'UK-resident' (see above).

Notice must be given within three months after the end of the accounting period or period of account in which the asset is first so leased. However, if at the end of the three months the lessor does not know and could not reasonably be expected to know that an asset has been so used or leased, he must instead give notice within 30 days of becoming aware that it has been so used or leased. Penalties apply for failure to meet these conditions.

Legislation: CAA 2001, s. 120

Recovery in the case of joint lessees

Special rules apply where an asset for which normal allowances have as a result been given ceases to qualify for them during the 'designated period' (see 220-300), in circumstances where:

- no lessee uses it for a qualifying activity whose profits are chargeable to income tax or corporation tax; and
- the provisions preventing allowances altogether (see above) do not apply and have not applied at any earlier time.

In those circumstances, the clawback provisions above apply so that the allowances due must be recalculated as if the restricted allowance had always applied.

Where an asset which qualified for standard writing-down allowances under the general rules, (ie other than by virtue of the exclusion from overseas leasing of the chargeable portion of a jointly leased asset, above) begins instead to be used for overseas leasing such that, at some time in the 'designated period' (see 220-300) the above circumstances apply, the excess relief is clawed back under CAA 2001, s. 111, 112 as described above.

Legislation: CAA 2001, s. 117

Notice of recovery

Whenever it is necessary for allowances to be recovered under CAA 2001, s. 117(1) or (2), the lessor must notify HMRC within three months of the end of the chargeable period in which the conditions in CAA 2001, s. 117(1) or (2) are first met. If the lessor does not know (and cannot reasonably be expected to know) that the circumstances are met at the end of the three-month period, then the lessor is required to provide the notice within 30 days of coming to know of them.

The notice must specify any of the non-resident joint lessees to whom the plant or machinery has been leased and (if the notice is given by reference to a chargeable period) all the plant or machinery (if more than one) relevant to that period. Again, penalties apply for failure to meet these conditions.

Legislation: CAA 2001, s. 120

Recovery of excessive allowances at the end of the designated period

Where normal allowances have been given, to the extent that the jointly leased asset was used for the purposes of a non-leasing qualifying activity, and it appears, at the end of the 'designated period' (see 220-300) that these were excessive, a separate clawback charge is made. In these circumstances, the clawback applies as if a part of the expenditure corresponding to the excess were incurred on the last day of the designated period for overseas leasing which is not protected leasing. Any disposal value subsequently brought into account is apportioned by reference to the extent of such use after this adjustment.

Legislation: CAA 2001, s. 117(3)–(6)

Example

Awdry has carried on a leasing trade in the UK for many years and makes up accounts to 31 December each year. He leases an item of office equipment to Thomas and Percy jointly, the lease commencing on 23 January 1992. Thomas is UK-resident whilst Percy is not and does not intend to use the equipment for a qualifying activity carried on in the UK or its territorial sea. Awdry incurred expenditure on acquiring the asset of £200,000 on 1 January 1992. He did not use it before the commencement of the lease. Awdry has a brought-forward balance on the main pool of £21,000 and on the overseas leasing pool of £242,454. It was expected that the equipment would be used for the purposes of the qualifying activity carried on by Thomas and otherwise by Percy in the proportion of three to one. Thomas's qualifying activity does not constitute a leasing trade and the profits from it are chargeable to income tax.

At the end of the designated period (22 January 2002) it transpires that the actual use was in the proportion of one to one.

Awdry disposes of the equipment on 28 June 2004 for £33,000.

Awdry's capital allowances position in respect of the part of the expenditure used for a purpose so as to exclude it from the overseas leasing pool in so far as it is affected by that part is as follows:

	Main pool £	Overseas leasing pool £	Allowances £
Tax year 1993–94			
(12 months to 31 December 1993)			
Balance brought forward	21,000	242,454	
Capital expenditure in the period:			
Part eligible for unrestricted WDA	150,000		
Part eligible for restricted WDA		50,000	
Qualifying expenditure for period	171,000	292,454	
Disposal value	–	–	
	171,000	292,454	
Writing-down allowance at 25% or 10%	(42,750)	(29,245)	71,995
Balance carried forward	128,250	263,209	
Tax year 2002–2003	£	£	£
(12 months to 31 December 2002)			
Balancing charge on excess relief in respect of:			
Expenditure on original estimated basis of use		150,000	
Expenditure on reduced actual basis of use		(100,000)	
Expenditure on deemed item of plant or machinery		50,000	
Excess relief:			
WDA made at 25% on £50,000 for 10 years	47,185		
WDA available at 10 % on £50,000 for 10 years		32,565	
Balancing charge			(14,620)
Balance brought forward say	9,628	101,979	
Writing-down allowance at 25% or 10%	(2,407)	(10,198)	12,605
Balance carried forward	7,221	91,781	
Tax year 2003–2004	£	£	£
(12 months to 31 December 2003)			
Balance brought forward	7,221	91,781	
Deemed item of qualifying expenditure			
(£14,620 + £2,815 (see below))	–	17,435	
Qualifying expenditure	7,221	109,216	
Disposal value (£50,000 − £47,185)	(2,815)	–	
	4,406	109,216	
Writing-down allowance at 25% or 10%	(1,102)	(10,922)	12,024
Balance carried forward	3,304	98,294	
Tax year 2004–2005	£	£	
(12 months to 31 December 2004)			
Balance brought forward	3,304	98,294	
Disposal value (1:1)	(16,500)	(16,500)	
	(13,196)	81,794	
Balancing charge	13,196		(13,196)
Writing-down allowance at 10%		(8,179)	8,179
Balance carried forward		73,615	

220-300 Protected leasing, qualifying purposes and the designated period

Protected leasing is:

- 'short-term leasing' (see below); or
- where a ship, aircraft or transport container is leased and used for certain qualifying purposes by virtue only of the extension for certain such assets.

The claim for the normal allowance must be accompanied by a certificate setting out the description of such 'protected leasing', the identity of the lessee and the assets in point.

Legislation: CAA 2001, s. 105(5), 118

Qualifying purposes

Generally, the term 'qualifying purpose' is relevant only to the extended meaning of 'protected leasing' applicable to ships, aircraft and transport containers (see below). However, a fuller meaning is relevant to the rules concerning the prohibition of allowances (see above). Where an asset is used for any purpose other than a qualifying purpose (as fully defined), expenditure on that asset can fail to qualify for any capital allowances.

Plant and machinery is used for a qualifying purpose when:

- it is used by any of the persons listed below for the purposes of short-term leasing (see below) (CAA 2001, s. 122(1)); or
- it is used by any of the persons listed below for the purposes of a qualifying activity (other than that of leasing) (CAA 2001, s. 125(1)–(2)); or
- it is leased to a lessee who so uses it and who could have included it in 'qualifying expenditure' (CAA 2001, s. 125(1), (4)).

Ships, aircraft and transport containers are also used for a 'qualifying purpose' if they satisfy the conditions below.

Legislation: CAA 2001, s. 110(2)(c)

Plant and Machinery

List of persons who can use asset for short-term leasing or for the purpose of a qualifying activity without leasing it

The following persons may use the plant or machinery without making the lease not for a qualifying purpose:

(1) the person 'X' who incurred expenditure on the provision of the plant or machinery;

(2) any person connected with X;

(3) any person who has acquired the plant or machinery from X as a result of a disposal on the occasion of which, or two or more disposals on the occasion of each of which, there was a change in the persons carrying on the qualifying activity in relation to which Condition A or B was met, where:

- Condition A is that at least one person who carried on the activity immediately before or immediately after the change was within the charge to income tax in respect of that activity, and at least one person who carried on the qualifying activity before the change continued to carry it on after the change.
- Condition B is that all of the following sub-conditions are met:
  - the qualifying activity was carried on in partnership both immediately before and immediately after the change;
  - a company that was within the charge to corporation tax in respect of the activity carried it on immediately before or immediately after the change, and
  - at least one company which carried the activity on before the change continued to carry it on after the change.

(4) a lessee resident in the UK (using the asset for short-term leasing only);

(5) lessees carrying on a qualifying activity in the UK who use the plant or machinery for short-term leasing in the course of that qualifying activity.

Legislation: CAA 2001, s. 122, 125

Extension for certain ships, aircraft and transport containers

There are certain specific provisions extending the general categories above, so that certain assets may be treated as used for a qualifying purpose.

(1) It is a ship let on charter in the course of a trade which consists of or includes operating ships if:

(a) the trader is resident in the UK or carries on a trade there; and

(b) the trader is responsible (whether through an agent or not) for navigating and managing the ship and for defraying all or substantially all expenses other than those directly incidental to a particular voyage or to the employment of the ship during the period of the charter.

A person is 'responsible' for something if he is responsible as principal (or appoints another person to be responsible in his place).

A ship is not used for a qualifying purpose if the expenditure is incurred after 9 March 1982 and one of the objects of the charter was to obtain a higher writing-down allowance (or, as the case may be, a first-year allowance).

(2) It is an aircraft let on similar terms to those in relation to a ship, above.

(3) It is a transport container leased in the course of a UK trade or a trade carried on by a UK resident, and either:

(a) the trade consists of or includes the operation of ships or aircraft and the container is at other times used by that person in connection with the operation of ships or aircraft; or

(b) the container is leased under a succession of leases to different persons who, or most of whom, are not connected with each other.

Legislation: CAA 2001, s. 123, 124, Sch. 3, para. 23

Short-term leasing

There are two ways in which leasing may fall within the definition of 'short-term leasing'.

First, it will do so if both of the following conditions are met:

(1)   the number of consecutive days for which it is leased to the same person will normally be less than 30; and

(2)   the total number of days for which it is leased to the same person in any period of 12 months will normally be less than 90.

The second way in which leasing will be defined as short-term is when both of the following conditions are met:

(1)   the number of consecutive days for which the plant or machinery is leased to the same person will not normally exceed 365; and

(2)   the plant or machinery will not be leased to a non-qualifying lessee for more than half (in total) of any consecutive four-year period within the designated period (see 220-300).

For these purposes, a non-qualifying lessee is one who uses the plant or machinery for the purposes of a qualifying activity but without leasing it and who could claim plant and machinery allowances on capital expenditure incurred at that time.

Where any plant or machinery is leased as one of a number of items which form part of a pool of items of the same or a similar description and are not separately identifiable, all the items in the pool may be treated as used for short-term leasing if substantially the whole of the items in the pool are so used.

Legislation: CAA 2001, s. 121

Designated period

The 'designated period' may vary for different purposes.

As regards the restriction of allowances for expenditure on assets leased outside the UK (see 220-200) the 'designated period' is generally ten years from the date the asset is first brought into use by the person incurring the expenditure (for his own purposes or when first leased). However, if the person who incurred the expenditure ceases to own the asset before the end of that ten-year period, the designated period ends on the date when he ceases to own it.

An asset is treated as continuing to belong to a person if it belongs to either:

- a person connected with him; or
- a person who acquired it from him as a result of one or more disposals on the occasion of which, or each of which there was a change in the persons carrying on the qualifying activity in relation to which Condition A or Condition B was met.

Plant and Machinery

Condition A is that at least one person who carried on the activity immediately before or immediately after the change was within the charge to income tax in respect of that activity, and at least one person who carried on the qualifying activity before the change continued to carry it on after the change.

Condition B is that all of the following sub-conditions are met:

- the qualifying activity was carried on in partnership both immediately before and immediately after the change;
- a company that was within the charge to corporation tax in respect of the activity carried it on immediately before or immediately after the change, and
- at least one company which carried the activity on before the change continued to carry it on after the change.

Legislation: CAA 2001, s. 106, 575(1)

220-400   Special provisions relating to finance leases

The two Finance Acts of 1997 introduced a range of provisions aimed at countering situations where finance lessors could obtain tax advantages by manipulating certain reliefs and allowances.

220-410   Treatment of lump sum payments

The *Finance Act* 1997 introduced provisions aimed at leasing arrangements which provide for low initial rental payments and a compensating capital payment later on, and those which defer the rental payments to the back end of the lease. Under normal tax rules, the rent is charged to tax when receivable, so that such schemes attract low tax at the start when the rents are low, with the main liability being postponed to the end of the lease when rental payments are high. Under commercial accountancy principles, however, the rental under finance leases is spread evenly as it accrues over the term of the lease. By aligning the tax with the accountancy treatment, any fiscal advantage gained from concentrating the rent at the back end of the lease is removed.

The basis of this approach is that finance leases are in essence loans secured on the leased asset. Under a finance lease, unlike an operating lease, effective ownership of the leased asset, and the risks and rewards that this entails, passes to the lessee from the outset. The lease itself provides for a rental, or interest, element during its term, and ends with a lump sum capital payment in settlement of the outstanding 'loan'. That is how payments under finance leases are treated under SSAP 21, under which the lessor recognises the interest earned each year in accordance with the accruals principle.

The 1997 rules require a disposal value to be brought into account when a 'major lump sum' is paid. The 1997 legislation refers to a 'major lump sum' as a sum which, while not itself rent, falls for accounting purposes, in accordance with normal accountancy practice, to be treated partly as repayment of a finance lease or loan, and partly as a return on investment. When a 'major lump sum' is paid, provision is made to introduce a disposal value (or balancing charge or revenue receipt where appropriate) for capital allowances purposes. Such a payment is described by the legislation as a 'relevant occasion'.

Legislation: FA 1997, Sch. 12, para. 11

220-420   Sale and leaseback using finance leases

Overview

The *Finance (No. 2) Act* 1997 brought in provisions to counter arrangements under which unused past allowances were sold to a finance lessor. They were not intended to affect the sale of future allowances, nor to interfere with arrangements under which sale and leaseback occurred after delivery of equipment in order to remove from the lessor any risk over the provision of the equipment.

Under the provisions, where there is a sale, or a lease/purchase, and leaseback transaction involving plant or machinery under which the seller, or hirer, continues to have use and enjoyment of the asset under the terms of a finance lease, the allowances available to a lessor are restricted to the notional written-down value of the plant or machinery of the seller or hirer, rather than the cost as before. Additionally, allowances are denied where the terms of the finance lease are such that the lessor suffers no real risk of loss if payments under the lease are not made in accordance with its terms. In the commentary which follows, where the seller is referred to, the remarks made apply equally to the hirer under a lease/purchase contract, or the assignor of such a contract, where either ss. 213(1) or 241 are applicable.

Legislation: CAA 2001, s. 221–228, CAA 2001, Sch. 3, para. 45, 51

Non-trading activities

Under CAA 2001, s. 221, the restrictions imposed by CAA 2001, s. 214–218 (where, following a sale and leaseback of plant and machinery, the seller continues to use the asset for the purpose of its qualifying activity) are extended. Where the leaseback takes the form of a finance lease, the restriction applies to cases where the asset is subsequently used for non-qualifying activities.

The legislation applies if, after the transaction:

- the plant or machinery continues to be used for the purposes of a qualifying activity carried on by the seller;
- it is used for the purposes of a qualifying activity carried on by the seller or by a person (other than the buyer) who is connected with the seller, without having been used since that date for the purposes of any other qualifying activity, except that of leasing the plant or machinery; or
- it is used for the purposes of a non-qualifying activity carried on by the seller or by any person (other than the buyer) who is connected with the seller, without having been used

Plant and Machinery

199

since that date for the purposes of a qualifying activity, except that of leasing the plant or machinery.

The terms 'seller' and 'buyer' also cover hire purchase and similar transactions, with the meanings amended accordingly.

This is intended to embrace cases where the asset is used, for instance, by a public authority or other non-taxpayer for various statutory duties or other non-trading activities, which were not covered under the previous rules.

Legislation: CAA 2001, s. 213

Restriction of allowances to notional written-down value

Under the pre-existing rules, where plant or machinery was sold and leased back, the allowances available to the purchaser were restricted to the disposal value of the seller or, where no disposal value fell to be brought into account, to the lowest of three amounts: the open market value; the cost to the seller of providing the plant or machinery; and the cost to any person connected with the seller (former CAA 1990, s. 75(1), 76(2)). The combined effect of CAA 2001, s. 224 and 243 is to modify the three amounts so specified, where the leaseback takes the form of a finance lease, so that the seller's disposal value, and hence the allowances available to the purchaser, is restricted to the lowest of:

- the open market value;
- the notional written-down value of the capital expenditure incurred by the seller; and
- the notional written-down value of the capital expenditure incurred by any person connected with the seller.

The amendment was intended to stop unused past allowances being transferred to the finance lessor through a sale and leaseback at more than the notional written-down value to the seller, while still allowing the transfer of any entitlement to future allowances to the finance lessor. Notional written-down value is calculated in accordance with CAA 2001, s. 222(3) by taking the capital expenditure of the seller and deducting the maximum allowances that the seller could have claimed on that expenditure, assuming that:

- the expenditure was incurred for the purposes of a trade within the charge to tax;
- the expenditure was the only capital expenditure taken into account in respect of the trade;
- the six per cent rate for long-life assets (see 210-000) applies if, and only if, it actually applies to the expenditure.

See below ('Election for special treatment') for circumstances in which these restrictions may be lifted.

Limit on allowances available to future owner under finance lease

In the rare case where an asset sold and leased back under a finance lease subsequently changes hands, the allowances available to the new owner are restricted to the disposal value brought into account by the seller on the sale and leaseback, plus any installation costs incurred by the claimant. This ensures that the restriction imposed on the sale and leaseback is continued throughout the life of the asset, and that allowances are not given more than once in respect of any part of the cost.

Legislation: CAA 2001, s. 226

220-430   Denial of allowances where non-compliance risk removed from lessor

Where the terms surrounding the finance lease on a sale and leaseback are such that neither the lessor nor any person connected with the lessor faces any real risk of loss if payments under the lease are not made in accordance with its terms ('non-compliance risk'), the buyer is denied any allowances in respect of the expenditure. Furthermore, the rules prevent any other person from being able to claim allowances where the buyer and the lessor are not the same person (for instance, where the asset is sold on before being leased back).

This provision does not apply to arrangements involving guarantees from persons connected with the lessee, but, apart from that, is widely drawn to catch any arrangements which remove the whole or the greater part of any non-compliance risk falling directly or indirectly on the lessor or persons connected with him.

Legislation: CAA 2001, s. 225

Public authorities

Where plant or machinery is sold and leased back by way of a finance lease, and the asset has at any time been acquired by one public authority from another otherwise than by purchase (for instance, on a reorganisation), the public authority from whom the asset is acquired is treated as connected with the acquiring authority and with every person connected with the acquiring authority. 'Public authority' includes the Crown or any government or local authority.

Legislation: CAA 2001, s. 232

220-440   Other restrictions applicable to finance lessors

Two other restrictions were introduced by the *Finance (No. 2) Act* 1997 to counter perceived exploitation by finance lessors of certain pre-existing rules.

Writing-down allowances

The writing-down allowances that may be claimed by a lessor under a finance lease in the first year are restricted to a rateable proportion of the full amount for the chargeable period, reckoned from the date on which the expenditure was incurred to the end of the chargeable period. The purpose of this rule was to counter the exploitation by many finance lessors of the pre-existing rule under which writing-down allowances were given in full through the pooling mechanism, irrespective of when the expenditure was incurred.

This rule does not prevent the whole of the expenditure being brought into account if the asset is disposed of in the same chargeable period as that in which the expenditure is incurred, and any necessary assessments and adjustments must be made accordingly; nor does it prevent the rest of the expenditure from being added to the pool for a later chargeable period.

Since 1 April 2006, the rule has been restricted to companies. From the same date, the rules do not apply if the leasing company that buys the plant has the same accounting date as the principal company of the group. The term 'ICTA period of account' is used and defined for the purpose of that rule.

The rule is now also subject to the *Finance Act* 2006 legislation regarding long funding leases. From 1 April 2006, the rules apply to capital expenditure on the provision of plant or machinery for leasing under either a finance lease or a qualifying operating lease. The latter expression is defined as a lease (other than a finance lease) that is a funding lease with a term of more than four years but no more than five years.

The terms 'funding lease', 'plant or machinery lease' and 'term' are for these purposes defined as for the long funding lease rules: see, respectively 230-250, 230-300, 232-300.

Legislation: CAA 2001, s. 220, 231

Hire-purchase

Under the normal rules, where an asset is acquired on hire-purchase, the hirer is entitled to capital allowances on the full amount of its anticipated expenditure under the hire-purchase agreement at the time the asset is brought into use. This rule is replaced in cases where the hirer leases the asset out under a finance lease, so that capital allowances are given on the asset as expenditure is incurred and not before.

Legislation: CAA 2001, s. 229(3)

220-450   Meaning of 'finance lease'

A 'finance lease' is defined as any arrangements which provide for plant or machinery to be leased, or otherwise made available, by a lessor to a lessee, and which fall, in accordance with generally accepted accounting practice ('GAAP'), to be treated in the accounts of the lessor or any persons connected with the lessor as a finance lease or loan. However, the term excludes a lease which is a long funding lease for the lessor.

The test is also applied to the consolidated group accounts of any group of which the lessor or any connected person is a member. This enables the full commercial picture to be brought into account for tax in cases where the leasing arrangements are such as to spread the profit from the letting throughout the lessor group, and the true picture emerges only from a study of the consolidated accounts.

Legislation: CAA 2001, s. 219(1)

220-460   Election for special treatment

CAA 2001, s. 227–228 provide an election for special treatment for taxpayers who enter into a sale and leaseback arrangement in respect of plant or machinery. Generally, the allowances to which the lessor is entitled are restricted by the open market value of the plant or machinery. In cases where there is a sale and finance-leaseback, there is a further restriction, known as the 'notional written-down value' of the equipment. This notional figure is what the tax written-down value of the equipment would have been, had the maximum allowances been claimed by the seller (and no other capital expenditure had been taken into account).

These two restrictions will be lifted (if both parties elect) on the sale and leaseback of new equipment, provided certain conditions are met. These will generally allow the finance lessor to obtain allowances on the full cost of the plant or machinery. The conditions are that:

- there is a sale and leaseback of equipment (or an equivalent transaction);
- the buyer and seller are not connected persons;
- the arrangement is not part of an avoidance scheme;
- the seller incurred capital expenditure on the equipment;
- the seller did not acquire the equipment in cases caught by CAA 2001, s. 217, 218, 223 or 224, (ie from a connected person, under a leaseback arrangement, or as part of an avoidance scheme);
- the equipment is new when (or after) it was acquired by the seller – 'new' means unused and not second-hand;
- the sale takes place within four months of the plant or machinery being first brought into use by any person; and
- the seller has not made any claim for capital allowances in respect of the expenditure incurred on the plant or machinery.

The buyer and seller must elect for CAA 2001, s. 228 to apply and any such leaseback rules to cover hire-purchase transaction. Any election must be made within two years of the sale.

Example

Suppose Purple incurs expenditure of £300,000 on some plant. The plant is new and starts to be used by Purple on 1 September 2004. Purple sells it to Yellow Leasing Ltd on 29 November 2004 for £280,000, when the open market value is £250,000. Purple has not claimed any capital allowances in respect of the plant.

But for s. 228, Yellow Leasing Ltd would have been able to claim capital allowances in respect of only £250,000 (the open market value).

Plant and Machinery

However, provided Yellow Leasing Ltd and Purple make an election by 29 November 2006, then Yellow Leasing Ltd will be able to claim allowances in respect of the £280,000 (the actual purchase price).

Purple will not be able to claim allowances on this amount in respect of the plant if an election has been made.

If the seller has made a claim for allowances in respect of equipment, CAA 2001, s. 227(2)(e) prevents the seller from withdrawing the claim and entering into an election under that section.

Legislation: CAA 2001, s. 224, 227

220-470   Anti-avoidance provisions in CAA 2001, s. 228A–228J

Measure to counter double benefit leasing

Some businesses used loopholes in the capital allowances legislation to gain an unintended double benefit. Plant or machinery could be sold for a sum, or leased out for a premium, that was largely or wholly untaxed and thereby allowing the seller or lessor to retain capital allowances. The plant or machinery was then leased back and the lease rentals were allowed to be deducted and so there was a double benefit of retention of capital allowances with the deduction of lease rentals. The commercial effect of the transactions is that the business:

- receives a sum of money or premium which is like a loan; and
- makes lease payments which are like repayments of the amount borrowed and the cost of borrowing (viz, interest), for which all or part of the repayment and interest.

Normally, only the interest would be deductible, but here the amount borrowed is also being deducted on revenue account. A measure was introduced by FA 2004, s. 134 to remove the unintended tax benefits for lessees. The measure limits the relief for the lease rental payments and thus brings the tax treatment of these transactions more closely into line with their commercial substance.

Effects on lessees

Where S sells plant or machinery to B who, in turn by way of a finance lease, leases the plant or machinery back to S (and S, who is the lessee, accounts for the lease as a finance lease in accordance with Statement of Standard Accounting Practice 21), the amount of the lease rentals that are allowed to be deducted is restricted to:

(1)   the finance charge element of the lease rentals that is shown in the accounts; and

(2)   a further amount equivalent to a depreciation charge where the cost being depreciated is taken to be the restricted disposal value brought into account for capital allowances purposes.

With regard to (2) above, the restricted disposal value is S's disposal value as restricted by CAA 2001, s. 222. The period of depreciation is the term (life) of the finance lease which is from the beginning of the leaseback to the end of the life of the lease. Hence, the disposal proceeds brought into account for capital allowances purposes are spread over the life of the lease in proportion to the depreciation of the leased asset.

If S leases the plant or machinery to B who in turn leases the plant or machinery back to S under a finance lease (and, again, S accounts for the lease as a finance lease in accordance with Statement of Standard Accounting Practice 21) then the amount of the lease rentals to be deducted is restricted to only the finance charge element of the lease rentals that is shown in the accounts; the depreciation is disregarded as there is no disposal value for the purposes of S's capital allowances.

The measure introduced by FA 2004, s. 134 counters the retention of tax benefits where the finance lease is terminated on or after 17 March 2004 (Budget Day that year). A termination includes an assignment of the finance leaseback by a lessee (S). In relation to a period of account during which the leaseback terminates, the permitted maximum lease rental to be deducted by S is:

(1)   finance charge;

(2)   depreciation (if there is a sale and finance leaseback); and

(3)   an amount equal to 'Current Book Value × Original Consideration/Original Book Value'.

The 'Current Book Value' is the net book value of the leased plant or machinery immediately before the termination; the 'Original Consideration' is the consideration payable to S for entering into the relevant transaction (ie, as defined in CAA 2001, s. 213(1)), and the 'Original Book Value' is the net book value of the leased plant or machinery at the beginning of the leaseback.

Also, in the case of the leaseback terminating, the income or profits of the lessee (S) from the relevant qualifying activity (ie the qualifying activity for which the leased plant or machinery was being used immediately before the termination) is increased by the following amount:

Net Consideration × Current Book Value/Original Book Value.

The 'Net Consideration' is the consideration payable to S for entering into the relevant transaction (ie as defined in CAA 2001, s. 213(1)) *minus* any restricted disposal value (ie the amount of disposal value brought into account for computing S's capital allowances).

The 'Current Book Value' and 'Original Book Value' are defined as above – ie for the purposes of computing the permitted maximum, or, in other words, the allowable lease rental, to be deducted under CAA 2001, s. 228B.

In most arrangements, the lessee will account for the leaseback as a finance lease in accordance with Statement of Standard Accounting Practice 21 under generally accepted accounting practice (GAAP). However, in some cases, the lessee treats the leaseback as an operating lease while a person connected with the lessee (eg parent company of a group that

Plant and Machinery

includes the lessee) accounts for the leaseback as a finance lease (eg in the consolidated accounts). In such cases:

- the permitted maximum for deduction by the lessee (S) under CAA 2001, s. 228B; and
- the increase to the income or profits of the lessee (S) from the relevant qualifying activity (ie the qualifying activity for the purposes of which the leased plant or machinery was used immediately before the termination),

are computed by reference to the connected person's accounts (eg as per the consolidated accounts) – this is referred to in CAA 2001, s. 228G as the 'relevant calculation'.

Legislation: CAA 2001, s. 228B

Effects on lessors

Where S sells plant or machinery to B who, in turn by way of a finance lease, leases the plant or machinery back to S, basically the rule for B is that B is taxed on the lease rentals up to, and including, the total of:

(1) gross earnings; and

(2) the allowable proportion of the capital repayment – in effect, the part of the lease rentals that recovers the capital expenditure incurred by B on which capital allowances are available (CAA 2001, s. 228D(3) and (4)).

The excess of lease rentals over and above the aforementioned total is not charged to tax (CAA 2001, s. 228D(2), (3) and (4)).

With regard to (1) above, the 'gross earnings' is the amount shown in the lessor's accounts in respect of the lessor's (ie B's) gross earnings under the leaseback. Gross earnings are more specifically defined in Statement of Standard Accounting Practice 21 (SSAP 21) which forms part of Generally Accepted Accounting Practice (or GAAP). Paragraph 28 of SSAP 21 states:

'**28.** *Gross earnings* comprise the lessor's gross finance income over the lease term, representing the difference between his gross investment in the lease (as defined in paragraph 21) and the cost of the leased asset less any grants receivable towards the purchase or use of the asset.'

Paragraph 21 of SSAP 21 defines the term 'gross investment' which is used in defining 'gross earnings' in paragraph 28 above. Paragraph 21 of SSAP 21 states:

'The *gross investment* in a lease at a point in time is the total of the minimum lease payments and any unguaranteed residual value accruing to the lessor.'

In effect, 'gross earnings' are the finance charge element of the lease rentals.

With regard to (2) above, the 'allowable proportion of the capital repayment' is equal to:

Restricted Disposal Value $\times$ Investment Reduction for Period/Net Investment.

The 'Restricted Disposal Value' is the lessee's (ie S's) disposal value as restricted in accordance with CAA 2001, s. 222 (see *Restriction of allowances to notional written-down value* within 235-500).

The 'Investment Reduction for Period' is the amount shown in the lessor's (ie B's) accounts in respect of the reduction in 'Net Investment' in the leaseback. The 'Net Investment' is the amount shown in the lessor's accounts as the lessor's net investment in the leaseback at the beginning of its term (life). With respect to 'Net Investment', paragraph 22 of Statement of Standard Accounting Practice 21 (SSAP 21) states:

'The *net investment* in a lease at a point in time comprises:

(a)   the gross investment in a lease (as defined in paragraph 21), less
(b)   gross earnings allocated to future periods.'

In effect, the 'allowable proportion of the capital repayment' is that part of the lease rentals which recovers the capital expenditure on which capital allowances are available.

As we have already seen, the definitions of 'gross investment' and 'gross earnings' are in paragraphs 21 and 28 of SSAP 21 respectively.

To reiterate, with regard to the definition of 'gross earnings', paragraph 28 of SSAP 21 states:

'**28.**   *Gross earnings* comprise the lessor's gross finance income over the lease term, representing the difference between his gross investment in the lease (as defined in paragraph 21) and the cost of the leased asset less any grants receivable towards the purchase or use of the asset.'

With regard to the definition of 'gross investment', paragraph 21 of SSAP 21 states:

'The *gross investment* in a lease at a point in time is the total of the minimum lease payments and any unguaranteed residual value accruing to the lessor.'

Where S leases plant or machinery to B who, in turn by way of a finance lease, leases the plant or machinery back to S, basically the rule for B is that B is taxed only on the gross earnings. In the case of a lease and leaseback, there is no disposal value for the lessee (ie for S) and thus there is no restricted disposal value.

On the termination of a leaseback, as well as the lessee (ie S) being charged to tax under CAA 2001, s. 228C, there is a corresponding adjustment to the lessor's (ie B's) computation. This adjustment is set out in CAA 2001, s. 228E.

If:

(1)   the leaseback terminates;

(2)   the lessor (ie B) disposes of the plant or machinery that was the subject of the leaseback; and

Plant and Machinery

(3)   the disposal value brought into account by the lessor (ie B), as a result of the disposal in (2) above, is limited by CAA 2001, s. 62 (general limit on amount of disposal value),

then, for the purposes of computing the lessor's (ie, B's) income or profits for the period in which the terminations occurs, the amount deducted in respect of any amount refunded to the lessee (ie S) must not exceed the amount to which the disposal value has been limited under CAA 2001, s. 62 (CAA 2001, s. 228E).

Leasebacks and further operating leases

The provisions in CAA 2001, s. 228J apply where:

(1)   plant or machinery is the subject of either a sale and finance leaseback or a lease and finance leaseback; and

(2)   while the subject of the leaseback, some or all of the plant or machinery becomes *also* the subject of a 'operating lease' (CAA 2001, s. 228J(1)).

For the purposes of the provisions in CAA 2001, s. 228J, an 'operating lease' is defined in CAA 2001, s. 228J(8). An 'operating lease' is a lease in relation to which the following conditions are met:

(1)   the term of the lease begins on or after 18 May 2004;

(2)   the lessee under the lease is either S or a person connected with S; and

(3)   the lease is not accounted for as a finance lease in the lessee's accounts.

If only some of the plant or machinery is the subject of the operating lease (as defined in CAA 2001, s. 228J(8)) then just and reasonable apportionments are required in order to apply the rules that are for the purposes of computing the lessee's and lessor's income or profits – these rules are in the provisions from CAA 2001, s. 228J(2)–(5) inclusive.

With regard to calculating the lessee's (ie S or a person connected with S) income or profits for a period of account, the rule is that the amount deducted in respect of amounts payable under the operating lease cannot exceed the 'relevant amount' as defined in CAA 2001, s. 228J(8) (see below).

With regard to calculating the lessor's (ie B) income or profits for a period of account, the amounts receivable, in respect of the lessor's (ie B's) interest under the operating lease (as defined in CAA 2001, s. 228J(8)), that fall to be taken into account in the calculation are disregarded to the extent that they exceed the relevant amount.

The 'relevant amount' is defined in CAA 2001, s. 228J(8). It is an amount equal to the **permitted maximum** under CAA 2001, s. 228B which is applicable in relation to the leaseback (see under 'Effects on lessees', above).

220-500   General anti-avoidance rules applying to leases

Overview

Various anti-avoidance rules apply to prevent the artificial exploitation of the plant and machinery legislation. Some of these rules are addressed in their relevant context. There are also, though, some anti-avoidance sections that are of more general application.

This anti-avoidance legislation applies to 'relevant transactions' which are widely defined to include the sale of an asset, the entering into of a hire purchase contract (where the buyer shall or may become the owner of the asset on performance of the contract) and the assignment of the benefit of a hire purchase contract. HMRC seek to apply these definitions broadly:

> 'The purpose of the legislation is to prevent the acceleration or uplift in capital allowances on a sale between connected persons, a sale and leaseback or a transaction to obtain allowances. Any transfer of the benefit of a hire purchase type contract that could give rise to an acceleration or uplift in capital allowances may therefore be caught by the anti-avoidance legislation.'

Restrictions may apply where the relevant transaction is:

* between connected persons;
* for the sole or main benefit of getting plant and machinery allowances; or
* a sale and leaseback transaction (where the buyer leases the asset back to the seller or to a person connected with the seller).

Legislation: CAA 2001, s. 213–218

Other material: CA 28200

First-year allowances

Where the rules apply, no first-year allowances are given to the purchaser (and, if they have been given, are to be withdrawn).

Legislation: CAA 2001, s. 217

Annual investment allowances

Where the rules apply, no annual investment allowances are given to the purchaser (and, if they have been given, are to be withdrawn). This extension of the restriction was made in the *Finance Act* 2008.

Legislation: CAA 2001, s. 217

Plant and Machinery

209

Restriction on buyer's allowances

In cases other than that of a sale and *finance* leaseback transaction, the buyer's allowances are restricted to the lowest of the following figures if the seller does not have to bring a disposal value to account:

- the market value of the asset;
- the amount of any capital expenditure incurred by the seller on the asset; and
- if a person connected with the seller incurred capital expenditure on the asset, that person's capital expenditure.

HMRC acknowledge that: 'these restrictions do not apply if the asset is new, the seller's business includes manufacturing or supplying assets of that class and the asset is sold as part of the seller's normal business'.

HMRC illustrate this with an example of a man who runs an electrical store and who sells his sister a new computer from his stock. If his sister claims plant and machinery allowances on the computer the restrictions on allowances do not apply; she can claim allowances on the price she pays.

Legislation: CAA 2001, s. 218

Other material: CA 28300

220-550   Further anti-avoidance measures

Further measures were introduced by Schedule 32 of Finance Act 2009 concerning disclosed avoidance schemes involving the leasing of plant or machinery. According to the *Explanatory Notes* issued with the 2009 Bill, HMRC do not accept that the schemes achieve their aim. The intention of the 2009 rules is therefore to provide greater certainty on the matter. Measures countered by the rules include:

- an asset owner who has claimed allowances granting a long funding finance lease of the asset to another person who leases the asset back to the first under a long funding operating lease.
- arrangements that are commercially equivalent to a secured loan: an owner sells plant to a finance provider and leases it back when it is worth more than its original cost to the owner.

Long funding leasing

230-000   Background and overview

Extensive new legislation was introduced in the *Finance Act* 2006 to address a perceived anomaly between the tax treatment of loan finance and leasing finance. The commercial effect of the two methods of financing could be very similar (a business uses an asset which is financed by a third party) but there were often significant differences in the timing of tax relief for expenditure incurred. The view was, therefore, that commercial decisions were being distorted, and sometimes driven, by the differing tax treatments.

In essence, the rules aim to remove such distortions by transferring entitlement to capital allowances on leased plant and machinery from lessors to lessees, where the reality is that the leases are essentially financing transactions. No change was made to the tax treatment of leases which do not function as financing transactions.

The 2006 rules are complex but the core provision denies capital allowances to an entity that incurs expenditure on plant or machinery that is acquired for long funding leasing. A mechanism is then given for granting capital allowances to the lessee. Fairly complex rules apply to determine the amount of capital expenditure on which the lessee can claim tax relief, including the treatment of additional expenditure incurred, and there are also detailed rules to deal with disposals of assets that are subject to the long funding rules.

A lessee is only permitted to claim allowances under these rules if it treats the lease as a long funding lease in the accounts for the period in which the lease begins. If the lease is not so treated in those accounts, and the return has become final, the same treatment must then be followed in later periods.

If plant or machinery has been used for qualifying purposes, but then starts to be used as a long funding lease, the capital allowances rules treat the change as a disposal and a balancing event will need to be considered.

Losses computed under the CGT rules are in certain circumstances restricted where a person disposes of an asset that includes fixtures that have been used for the purpose of leasing under a long funding lease.

Legislation: TCGA 1992, s. 41A; CAA 2001, s. 34A, 70A

Other material: CA 23800ff.

230-050   Commencement and transitional provisions

The commencement and transitional provisions for long funding leases (LFL) are complex and, in themselves, occupy half a dozen pages of legislation. The normal rule, but subject to all the complexities, is that the legislation applies where:

- a lease was finalised on or after 1 April 2006;
- the commencement of the term of the lease was on or after that date; or
- the commencement of the term of the lease was before that date but the plant or machinery was not brought into use for the purposes of a qualifying activity carried on by the person concerned until after that date.

Legislation: FA 2006, Sch. 8, para. 15(1)

Plant and Machinery

230-200   Meaning of 'long funding lease'

The rules introduced in the *Finance Act* 2006 apply only to a 'long funding lease', defined as a 'funding lease' (see 230-250) which is *not* any of the following:

- a short lease (of up to five years or, subject to conditions, up to seven years);
- an excluded lease of background plant or machinery for a building (but this is subject to anti-avoidance provisions); or
- a lease that is excluded under de minimis provisions (where relatively small amounts of plant or machinery are leased with land but are not excluded under the background rules as above).

The definitions apply for both the lessor and the lessee. As explained in an HMRC Technical Note of 1 August 2006, however, 'the tests for a long funding lease are carried out independently by lessors and lessees. Therefore a lease may be a long funding lease for a lessor, and not a long funding lease for the corresponding lessee'. There are, though, rules to prevent a double claim of allowances.

Only leases of plant or machinery can be long funding leases. Where plant or machinery is leased with other assets (whether or not those other assets are also plant and machinery) then the legislation creates a fiction of different leases so that the rules can be considered separately for each deemed lease.

The exclusion from the long funding lease rules of short leases is intended to remove the great majority of leases from the scope of the rules (*Regulatory Impact Assessment for Leased Plant and Machinery (Leasing Reform)*, para. 19.7).

In certain circumstances, a lessor may elect to join the long funding lease regime in respect of leases of plant and machinery that would not otherwise be long funding leases: see 230-225.

Legislation: CAA 2001, s. 70G

Other material: CA 23830

Need for a return

A lease is not treated as a long funding lease for the tax purposes of the lessee unless a proper return is made by him to that effect.

Such a return must be made for 'the initial period' on the basis that the lessee is to be taxed in relation to the lease in accordance with ICTA 1988, Pt. XII, Ch. 5A (corporation tax) or ITTOIA 2005, Pt. 2, Ch. 10A (income tax). The 'initial period' is defined as the first accounting period, or tax year, in which the question of whether or not it is a long funding lease makes a difference in calculating the profits or losses for tax purposes. This does not apply in respect of a lease of plant or machinery ('lease A'), however, if the lessee is the lessor of a lease of any of that plant or machinery ('lease B') and lease B is a long funding lease.

If a lessee has made a return for the initial period, and if that return has become final, the tax treatment of the lease (ie whether or not to treat it as a long funding lease) cannot then be changed for that period or for any subsequent period. It is specifically provided that the 'error or mistake' provisions of the *Taxes Management Act* 1970 (or of FA 1998, Sch. 18, para. 51) cannot be invoked to reverse an earlier decision.

Legislation: CAA 2001, s. 70H

Complicating factors

In certain cases, a lessor might have an overriding right to claim allowances, in which case the lessee will not be able to do so – see 231-000).

Certain other restrictions apply in the case of tonnage tax (ship leasing).

Legislation: CAA 2001, s. 70Q; FA 2000, Sch. 22, para. 91A

Plant that starts to be used for the purposes of a qualifying activity

It may be the case that an item of plant or machinery was not – at the start of the term of the plant or machinery lease – used for the purposes of a qualifying activity but that it starts later to be used for such purposes. The lease will then be treated as a long funding lease if it would have been such a lease at its inception if the asset in question had been used at that time for the purposes of a qualifying activity carried on by the person concerned.

In considering whether it would have been a long funding lease at its inception, the requirement that a return would need to have been made at that time is obviously ignored: no return could then have been made as it was not in fact a long funding lease. Nevertheless, the usual rules about making a return apply when the change of use occurs.

Legislation: (CAA 2001, s. 70E(4)(a))

230-225   Electing to join long funding lease scheme

General principle

As a general rule, the long funding leasing regime is obligatory for those that meet the appropriate criteria. In certain circumstances, however, a lessor may elect to join the regime in respect of leases of plant and machinery that would not otherwise be long funding leases. A lessor (an 'electing lessor') may make a long funding lease election in respect of all his eligible leases and qualifying incidental leases.

Plant and Machinery

HMRC's *Business Leasing Manual* contains extensive guidance in relation to these elections, beginning at BLM 24000.

Legislation: SI 2007/304, reg. 2

Effect of election

If the election is made, the electing lessor is treated as if certain leases had been long funding leases for the purposes of the plant and machinery rules since the leases were finalised. The leases affected are all of the electing lessor's eligible and qualifying incidental leases that are finalised on or after the effective date (including any finalised in subsequent chargeable periods or years of assessment).

HMRC has explained the background to the right of election, including the following key points:

- The rules for taxing long funding leases do not normally apply to short leases.
- An election allows lessors to remove a distortion whereby lessors of short-lived assets receive relief via capital allowances at a slower rate than they depreciate.
- An election for short leases to be taxed as long funding leases has the effect that the lessor is taxed on its commercial profits over the life of the lease. In contrast, where the lessor claims capital allowances they are likely to be claimed over a period longer than the lease term.
- An election may also have the practical effect of allowing lessors to be taxed on the basis of the profits shown in the accounts, thus reducing the taxpayer's administrative burden.
- If an election is made, all eligible leases and qualifying incidental leases are treated as long funding leases in the hands of the lessor. The lease of plant or machinery that does not qualify for capital allowances (eg because the lessee is not carrying on a qualifying activity or because the equipment is used in a dwelling-house) still falls within the scope of the election (confirmed at BLM 24015).
- An election does not directly affect lessees. More specifically, as explained at BLM 24020, the election 'does not generally affect whether a lease is a long funding lease in the hands of the lessee and it has no effect on whether the leased asset is plant or machinery in the hands of the lessee'.

Legislation: SI 2007/304, reg. 2(5)

Other material: *Business Leasing Manual* BLM 24005ff

Time and method of making an election

Any election under these provisions must be made within a defined timeframe. It may be withdrawn by amending the return within the same timeframe but is otherwise irrevocable.

For income tax purposes, the election may not be made before the end of the year of assessment to which it relates. Such an election must be made by 31 January some 22 months after the end of that tax year. For the year 2008–09, for example, the election must be made between 5 April 2009 and 31 January 2011.

For corporation tax purposes, an election must be made in the period of two years from the end of the relevant chargeable period. If accounts are drawn up to 31 December 2009, for example, the election must be made between 31 December 2009 and 31 December 2011.

An election may only be made in the return for the period to which the election relates, whether in the return as originally made or in an amendment to that return. It must specify the date from which it is to take effect (the 'effective date'). The effective date can never be earlier than the start of the year of assessment or chargeable period to which the election relates (and can in any case never be earlier than 1 April 2006).

For these purposes, the relevant chargeable period means the chargeable period in which the effective date falls. The year of assessment to which an election relates means the tax year in which ends the basis period in which the effective date falls. The concept of 'chargeable period' is defined in accordance with CAA 2001, s. 6 (see 106-200).

Example

Income tax accounts are drawn up to 30 June 2008, and the effective date is chosen as 1 January 2008. The effective date falls in the basis period to 30 June 2008. That basis period ends in 2008–09, which is therefore the year of assessment to which the election relates. Time limits are calculated accordingly.

Legislation: SI 2007/304, reg. 2(2)–(6)

Eligible leases

The legislation lists numerous conditions that must all be met if a lease is to be an eligible lease for these purposes, as below:

Condition A
The lease must be one of plant or machinery.

Condition B
The lease must not otherwise be a long funding lease.

Condition C
The lease must have been finalised on or after 1 April 2006.

Condition D
The term of the lease must be at least 12 months.

Plant and Machinery

Condition E

The plant or machinery that is made available under the lease must meet one of the following conditions:

(a) it must be unused and not second-hand at the commencement of the term of the lease;
(b) if previously leased, it must last have been leased under a long funding lease (whether under the rules in the *Capital Allowances Act* 2001 or under these special rules) before the commencement of the term of the lease;
(c) it must have been the subject of a valid election under CAA 2001, s. 227 before the electing lessor made a return for the period in which the commencement of the term of the lease occurred; or
(d) it must replace (whether by one or more substitutions) plant or machinery of the same type and quantity previously made available by the electing lessor to the lessee under a lease which is an eligible lease by virtue of one of paragraphs (a) to (c) above.

Condition F

The lease must not be for the provision of a car (as defined: see 200-020).

Condition G

The lease must not provide for the leasing of any asset with a market value of more than £10 million at its commencement.

Condition H

The lease must not be one to which CAA 2001, s. 70R (excluded leases of background plant or machinery) or CAA 2001, s. 70U (plant or machinery leases with land – low percentage value) applies.

Condition I

If the original lessor's interest under the lease has been assigned, then:

(a) the assignment (or all such assignments) must have occurred within four months of the commencement of the term of the lease; and
(b) the original lessor, and any person later owning the leased assets and through whom the lessor making the long funding lease election derives title to them, must not claim, or have claimed, capital allowances at any time in respect of those assets.

Legislation: SI 2007/304, reg. 3

Qualifying incidental leases

A qualifying incidental lease is a lease of plant or machinery which is wholly incidental to an eligible lease and which would have been an eligible lease were it not for the condition requiring a lease to be of at least 12 months.

Legislation: SI 2007/304, reg. 4

230-250   Meaning of 'funding lease'

A funding lease is a lease of plant or machinery that meets at least one of the following tests at the time of its inception:

- the finance lease test (see 230-400, but broadly if the lease falls to be treated as a finance lease or loan under generally accepted accounting practice);
- the lease payments test (see 230-450); or
- the useful economic life test (where the term of the lease is more than 65 per cent of the remaining useful economic life of the leased plant or machinery).

The lease payments test requires a comparison of the present value of the minimum lease payments with the fair value of the leased plant or machinery; the test is met if, broadly, the present value is at least 80 per cent of the fair value.

Legislation: CAA 2001, s. 70J, 70P

Other material: CA 23830

Meaning of 'funding lease': exclusions

Hire purchase contracts are specifically excluded from the long funding lease provisions.

A lease of plant is not treated as a funding lease if all three of the following conditions are met:

- the lessor has leased the plant in question before the start of the term of the lease under one or more other plant or machinery leases;
- in aggregate, the terms of those other leases exceeded 65 per cent of the remaining useful economic life of the plant at the start of the term of the earliest of those other leases; and
- none of the earlier leases was a funding lease.

In applying this test, all lessors before 1 April 2006 are treated as if they were the same as the lessor at that date.

A plant or machinery lease is not a funding lease for the lessor if the plant or machinery was leased for at least 10 years before 1 April 2006, and the lessor under the lease was also the lessor of the plant or machinery on the last day before 1 April 2006 when the plant or machinery was leased.

Legislation: CAA 2001, s. 70J

230-300   Meaning of 'plant or machinery lease'

The long funding lease rules apply only to a 'plant or machinery lease'. The legislation provides three definitions of such leases.

Plant and Machinery

The first type of plant or machinery lease is any agreement or arrangement which falls to be treated as a lease under generally accepted accounting practice and under which one person grants to another person the right to use plant or machinery for a period.

The second definition applies to the extent that an agreement or arrangement falls to be treated as a lease under generally accepted accounting practice and (broadly) conveys the right to use an item of plant or machinery. As generally-accepted accounting practice does not recognise a lease before commencement, there is a provision to treat an arrangement as a lease in the period between its inception and the commencement of its term. This applies for both of the first two definitions referred to above.

There is also a plant and machinery lease where the plant in question is the subject of a sale and finance leaseback arrangement. The *Explanatory Notes* explain that this 'ensures that the new regime applies where a lease is accounted for as a loan (which it may be in a sale and finance leaseback)'.

The Treasury may, by means of secondary legislation but subject to House of Commons approval, amend the meaning of 'plant or machinery lease'.

Legislation: CAA 2001, s. 70K, 70YJ

Other material: CA 23830

230-350 Derived leases and mixed leases

The term 'mixed lease' is given to an agreement or arrangement which relates to both plant or machinery ('the relevant plant or machinery') and to other assets (which may or may not also be plant or machinery).

The term 'eligible mixed lease' is then given to any mixed lease which is treated as a lease under generally-accepted accounting practice. As generally-accepted accounting practice does not recognise a lease before commencement, there is a provision to treat an arrangement as a lease in the period between its inception and the commencement of its term.

There will also be an eligible mixed lease if the relevant plant or machinery is the subject of a 'sale and finance leaseback', as defined in CAA 2001, s. 221, and if the mixed lease is or includes the finance lease mentioned in s. 221(1)(c).

An eligible mixed lease is treated for these purposes as consisting of two separate agreements or arrangements and the term 'derived lease' is given to any such notional separate agreement or arrangement. In deciding whether the derived lease is a plant or machinery lease, and (if so) whether it is a long funding lease, the same rules apply to derived leases as to other leases. The term of the derived lease similarly follows the general rules, except that the term is limited to the remaining useful economic life of the relevant plant or machinery at the start of the term of the derived lease.

The rentals that are deemed to be payable under the derived lease are determined on the basis of what is just and reasonable in all the circumstances. Unless it is reasonable to do otherwise, it is assumed that rentals payable under the derived lease are payable in equal instalments throughout the lease term. In determining the level of deemed rental, account is taken of all of the following:

- all the provisions of the eligible mixed lease;
- the nature of the relevant plant or machinery;
- the value of the plant or machinery at the start of the term of the derived lease;
- the amount which, at the start of the term of the derived lease, is expected to be the market value of the relevant plant or machinery at the end of that term;
- the remaining useful economic life of the relevant plant or machinery at the start of the term of the derived lease; and
- the term of the derived lease.

Legislation: CAA 2001, s. 70L, 70M(3)

Other material: CA 23835

230-400   The finance lease test

As noted at 230-250, the definition of 'funding lease' requires one or more of three tests to be met, the first of which is the finance lease test. A lease meets the finance lease test in the case of any particular person if the lease is one which is or would be treated, under generally-accepted accounting practice, as a finance lease or a loan in the accounts of either:

- that person; or
- (if that person is a lessor) any person connected with him.

The Treasury may, by means of secondary legislation but subject to House of Commons approval, amend the meaning of 'finance lease'.

Legislation: CAA 2001, s. 70N, 70YJ

Definition of 'long funding finance lease' and 'long funding operating lease'

Where the test is met by virtue of the first of the two bullet points above, it is known as a 'long funding finance lease'. Any other long funding lease is a long funding operating lease. As HMRC has confirmed (see www.hmrc.gov.uk/leasing/tech-note.pdf at paragraph 3.3):

> 'Therefore if a long funding lease is accounted for by the lessor as an operating lease but by a connected party as a finance lease it is a long funding operating lease. This is so, even though it may be a funding lease because it meets the finance lease test by virtue of s. 70N(1)(b).'

For these purposes, 'accounts' include those that relate to two or more companies, as long as they are drawn up in accordance with generally-accepted accounting practice. International accounting standards are used to determine generally-accepted accounting practice where a

Plant and Machinery

non-resident is not within the charge to income or corporation tax and does not prepare accounts in accordance with either international accounting standards or UK generally-accepted accounting practice.

Legislation: CAA 2001, s. 70YI

Other material: CA 23830

230-450   The lease payments test

As noted at 230-250, the definition of 'funding lease' requires one or more of three tests to be met. The second such test is the lease payments test.

A lease is said to meet the lease payments test if the present value of the minimum lease payments (see 231-350) is at least 80 per cent of the fair value of the leased plant or machinery. The present value is calculated using the interest rate implicit in the lease.

For these purposes, the fair value is defined as the market value of the leased plant or machinery, less any grants receivable towards either the purchase or the use of that plant or machinery.

The concept of the 'interest rate implicit in the lease' is for these purposes defined as the interest rate that would apply in accordance with normal commercial criteria including, in particular, generally-accepted accounting practice. However, if it is not possible to determine the interest rate using that principle then the rate to be used is the 'temporal discount rate' as it applies for the purposes of FA 2005, s. 70 (a provision connected with certain aspects of film tax relief for companies).

Legislation: CAA 2001, s. 70O

230-500   Meaning of 'short lease'

As noted at 230-200 above, a lease is not a long funding lease if it is a 'short lease'.

Any lease with a term of five years or less is a short lease.

A lease with a term of more than five years but no more than seven years is a short lease if three conditions are met.

First, the lease must be correctly treated as a finance lease under generally-accepted accounting practice.

Secondly, the residual value of the plant or machinery, as implied in the terms of the lease, must not exceed five per cent of the market value of the plant or machinery at the commencement of the lease term.

The third condition is more complex and requires a comparison of the rentals in the second full year of the lease and the rentals in other years. To spell out the rules, the legislation uses the term 'first reference year', which is defined as the period of 12 months beginning with the day after the start of the term of the lease. Other reference years follow as would be expected but the 'final year' is the period of 12 months ending with the last day of the lease term. As such, some days may fall both into a reference year and into the final year.

A condition is then that the total rentals falling due in the first reference year must be at least 90 per cent of the rentals falling due in the second reference year. A further condition is that the total rentals falling due in any later reference year, or in the final period, must not be more than 110 per cent of the rentals falling due in the second reference year. The effect of the rule is to allow higher payments at the start but, broadly, to disallow significant increases during the term of the lease.

In considering the third of the conditions listed above (to determine whether a lease of between five and seven years is a short lease), any rental variation is ignored if it results from changes made in any 'standard published base rate for interest'.

Anti-avoidance measures (effective from 7 April 2006) sometimes prevent a lease from being treated as short. Although the *Explanatory Notes* to the Finance Bill 2006 state that 'this ensures that arrangements between connected parties cannot be used to create artificially short leases', there is in fact no condition that any of the parties should be connected. The rule applies simply where, at or around the time of the inception of the lease, arrangements are entered into for other leases to other parties, and the total term of the leases exceeds five years.

Example

A enters into a three-year lease with B and, at the same time, agrees to lease the same plant or machinery to C for a 30-month period when the first lease expires. The three parties are unconnected with each other.

The total lease period exceeds five years so the lease to B is not treated as a short lease.

Extension of term of existing lease

The term of a lease that is not a long funding lease may be extended. In such circumstances, the lease may become a long funding lease at that point.

Legislation: CAA 2001, s. 70I

Sale and finance leaseback

Further anti-avoidance provisions have applied in the case of plant or machinery that is the subject of a sale and finance leaseback (as defined in CAA 2001, s. 221), where the date of the transaction (as also defined at s. 221) is on or after 9 October 2007.

Plant and Machinery

In such a case, the finance lease referred to in CAA 2001, s. 221(1)(c) is deemed not to be a short lease (if it would otherwise be one). However, a buyer and seller may make a joint election if the conditions set out in s. 227(2) are met. The effects of that are as follows:

- the deeming provision is disapplied;
- the provisions of s. 228(2) and (3) apply in relation to the buyer (relaxed rules regarding restriction of buyer's expenditure);
- s. 225 (restriction where lessor does not bear the risk of non-compliance – see 220-430) still applies;
- the seller's allowances are restricted by virtue of s. 228(5).

Legislation: CAA 2001, s. 70I(10)–(12)

231-000   Leases excluded by right of lessor to claim capital allowances

A lease is not treated as a long funding lease for the lessee if the lessor (or any superior lessor, but see below):

- is entitled, at the start of the term of the lease, to claim a capital allowance in respect of the leased plant or machinery;
- would have been entitled to claim such an allowance were it not for the anti-avoidance rules (in CAA 2001, s. 70V) relating to international leasing;
- has previously been entitled to claim such an allowance and has not been required to bring a disposal value into account as per CAA 2001, s. 61(1)(ee); or
- would fall within any of the above three categories if it had been within the charge to income or corporation tax at the inception of the lease any at any earlier times.

It is possible that the lessor (or superior lessor) will be non-resident in the UK and not within the charge to income or corporation tax, and will not prepare accounts under generally accepted accounting practice or international accounting standards. In such a case, any questions concerning accounting standards for the purposes of the last bullet point above are determined by reference to international accounting standards.

In practice, therefore, a lessee will need to know whether or not the lessor (or any superior lessor) is able to claim allowances. It will be important for those advising the lessee to build into the arrangements a requirement that the lessor should provide the necessary assurances. If the lessee cannot prove that no other claim has been made then he will be unable to claim allowances.

For the purposes of the above, it may be that the lessor has claimed an allowance other than under the plant or machinery rules. If, for example, the asset is in a building in an Enterprise Zone then the lessor may have claimed a 100 per cent Enterprise Zone allowance (see, generally, 320-000).

Under a transitional rule, a lease is not prevented by the above rules from being a long funding lease if the inception of the lease was before 28 June 2006 and, by virtue only of

CAA 2001, s. 70J(6), the lease is not treated as a long funding lease in the case of the lessor. This applies in certain cases where the plant had been leased for a minimum of 10 years before 1 April 2006.

There is said to be a superior lessor only if the leased plant or machinery is the subject of a chain of superior leases. This would arise, for example, if the lessor has his interest in the plant or machinery by virtue of a lease from a third person, in which case that third person would be the superior lessor. It is possible that the chain will be much longer.

Legislation: CAA 2001, s. 70Q

231-050   Excluded leases of background plant or machinery

Certain leases of plant or machinery are excluded from the rules concerning long funding leases where 'background plant or machinery' is leased with the land to which it belongs. Specifically, the rules apply where:

- plant or machinery is affixed to, or installed in or on, land which includes a building;
- the plant or machinery is of such a description as 'might reasonably be expected to be installed in, or in or on the sites of, a variety of buildings of different descriptions';
- the sole or main purpose of the plant or machinery is to contribute to the functionality of the building or its site as an environment in which to carry on activities;
- the plant or machinery is leased with the land under a mixed lease (see 230-350); and
- none of the disqualifications listed below applies.

The Treasury is empowered to issue further secondary legislation to clarify which items might or might not fall within the second and third bullet points above (CAA 2001, s. 70T). Under this power, HMRC issued SI 2007/303, the *Capital Allowances (Leases of Background Plant or Machinery for a Building) Order* 2007, with the following key parts:

- examples of background plant or machinery (SI 2007/303, art. 2);
- plant or machinery deemed to be background plant or machinery (SI 2007/303, art. 3); and
- plant or machinery deemed *not* to be background plant or machinery (SI 2007/303, art. 4).

Each of these is considered below. The Order came into force from 28 February 2007 but with retrospective effect to 1 April 2006 (SI 2007/303, art. 1).

Where the rules apply, the derived lease of the plant or machinery (see 230-350) is an excluded lease of background plant or machinery for a building. The effect of this is that the lease cannot then be a long funding lease.

Legislation: CAA 2001, s. 70G(1)(b), 70Rff.

Other material: CA 23835

Disqualifications

The legislation specifies two disqualifications which disapply the excluded lease rules and which therefore have the effect that the lease may after all qualify as a long funding lease.

The first disqualification applies where the rentals payable under the mixed lease (of plant and any other asset), or under any other arrangement, vary according to the capital allowances that the lessor can claim in relation to his expenditure on the background plant or machinery.

The second disqualification applies where the purpose (or a main purpose) of entering into the mixed lease, or a transaction or series of transactions including the mixed lease, is to enable the lessor to claim capital allowances (ie by preventing the long funding lease rules from applying).

Legislation: CAA 2001, s. 70S

Examples of background plant or machinery

The following are listed as statutory examples of background plant or machinery (but subject to those items that are prescribed as not being plant and machinery under article 4 – see under 'plant or machinery deemed not to be background plant or machinery' below):

(a) heating and air conditioning installations;
(b) ceilings which are part of an air conditioning system;
(c) hot water installations;
(d) electrical installations that provide power to a building, such as high and low voltage switchgear, all sub-mains distribution systems and standby generators;
(e) mechanisms, including automatic control systems, for opening and closing doors, windows and vents;
(f) escalators and passenger lifts;
(g) window cleaning installations;
(h) fittings such as fitted cupboards, blinds, curtains and associated mechanical equipment;
(i) demountable partitions;
(j) protective installations such as lightning protection, sprinkler and other equipment for containing or fighting fires, fire alarm systems and fire escapes; and
(k) building management systems.

Legislation: SI 2007/303, art. 2

Plant or machinery deemed to be background plant or machinery

The following are listed as statutory examples of plant or machinery deemed to be background plant or machinery:

(a) lighting installations including all fixed light fittings and emergency lighting systems;

(b)   telephone, audio-visual and data installations incidental to the occupation of the building;

(c)   computer networking facilities incidental to the occupation of the building;

(d)   sanitary appliances and other bathroom fittings including hand driers, counters, partitions, mirrors, shower and locker facilities;

(e)   kitchen and catering facilities for producing and storing food and drink for the occupants of the building;

(f)   fixed seating;

(g)   signs;

(h)   public address systems; and

(i)   intruder alarm systems and other security equipment including surveillance equipment.

Legislation: SI 2007/303, art. 3

Plant or machinery deemed not *to be background plant or machinery*

Plant or machinery used for any of the following purposes is deemed not to be background plant or machinery:

(1)   storing, moving or displaying goods to be sold in the course of a trade, whether wholesale or retail;

(2)   manufacturing goods or materials;

(3)   subjecting goods or materials to a process;

(4)   storing goods or materials

(a)   which are to be used in the manufacture of other goods or materials;

(b)   which are to be subjected, in the course of a trade, to a process;

(c)   which, having been manufactured or produced or subjected in the course of a trade to a process, have not yet been delivered to any purchaser; or

(d)   on their arrival in the UK from a place outside the UK.

If there is any conflict between this list and the list in article 3, then the article 3 list takes precedence, so the item in question *is* then treated as background plant and machinery.

Legislation: SI 2007/303, art. 4

231-100   Plant or machinery leased with land

It may be that the amounts of plant or machinery leased with land are relatively small, such that it is easier to keep the arrangements outside the scope of the long funding lease régime (even though it is not 'background' plant or machinery).

A special rule therefore applies where 'relevant' plant or machinery, other than background plant or machinery, is leased with land under a mixed lease. The effect is to keep the lease outside the scope of the long funding lease rules. The 'disqualifications' outlined at 231-050 above still apply, in modified form, to such relevant plant or machinery as they apply to background plant or machinery.

To be excluded under these rules, the aggregate of the market value of that plant or machinery and of any other plant or machinery leased along with the land does not exceed both 10 per cent of the value of the background plant or machinery and five per cent of the market value of the land and buildings (including fixtures). Market value is for these purposes determined on the basis of 'a sale by an absolute owner of the land free from all leases and other encumbrances'.

Legislation: CAA 2001, s. 70U

231-150   Entitlement to allowances

Allowances are in principle available if a person who carries on a qualifying activity incurs expenditure on the provision of plant or machinery for the purposes of that activity, under a long funding lease. It does not matter whether the expenditure incurred is capital or revenue in nature.

The plant or machinery is treated for these purposes as owned by that person at any time when he is the lessee under the long funding lease. He is treated as having incurred capital expenditure accordingly, at the commencement of the term of the long funding lease. The question of whether or not the lease is treated as a long funding lease for the lessor is not relevant as far as the lessee's tax position is concerned.

The amount of expenditure that is treated as incurred depends on whether it is a long funding operating lease or a long funding finance lease.

Legislation: CAA 2001, s. 70A

231-200   Anti-avoidance: international leasing

Particular rules apply in cases of tax avoidance involving international leasing. Specifically, allowances are denied where arrangements are made to lease plant or machinery into the UK and then back out again, so as to benefit from UK allowances without any real commercial purpose.

Legislation: CAA 2001, s. 70V

Other material: CA 23845

231-250   Amount of capital expenditure: operating leases

In the case of a long funding operating lease, the amount of the capital expenditure that is deemed to be incurred by the lessee is the market value of the plant or machinery at the commencement of the lease term (or, if later, at the date on which the asset is first brought into use for the purpose of the qualifying activity.

Legislation: CAA 2001, s. 70B

231-300   Amount of capital expenditure: funding leases

Overview

The amount of the capital expenditure that is deemed to be incurred under these leases is more complex. These more complex rules apply to long funding finance leases but also to any lease which, under generally-accepted accounting practice, falls (or would fall) to be treated as a loan.

The capital expenditure consists of either one or two parts, and is in certain cases subject to an overall restriction. The first part is known as 'commencement PVMLP' (see below).

A further element is added in some cases where the person has paid rentals under the lease before the commencement of its term.

The restriction is an anti-avoidance measure that applies where there has been a deliberate attempt to obtain allowances in respect of an amount that materially exceeds the market value of the leased asset at the start of the term of the lease.

Legislation: CAA 2001, s. 70C

Commencement PVMLP

The key element of capital expenditure in the case of a long funding finance lease is known as 'commencement PVMLP'. This is defined as the amount that would fall to be recognised as the present value, at the 'appropriate date', of the 'minimum lease payments' (see 232-100) if 'appropriate accounts' were prepared.

The 'appropriate date' is the commencement of the lease or, if later, the date on which the asset is first brought into use for the purposes of the qualifying activity. 'Appropriate accounts' are accounts prepared in accordance with generally-accepted accounting practice on the date on which the amount in question is first recognised in the lessee's books or other financial records.

Legislation: CAA 2001, s. 70C(4), (5)

Additional capital expenditure where certain lease rentals paid

As noted above, a further element may be added to the capital expenditure where a person has paid rentals under the lease before the commencement of its term. The legislation uses the term 'unrelievable pre-commencement rentals' (which it abbreviates to 'UPR') for such additional amounts.

UPR will arise where the person has paid rentals under the lease before the commencement of its term and relief is not otherwise available for some or all of those rentals. If the asset in question was not used for the purposes of a qualifying activity before the commencement of the lease term, it must be the case that relief would not have been available if the asset had been so used.

The amount of UPR is the amount of the rentals for which relief is not available (and, if appropriate, would not have been available). The term 'relief'' may consist of a capital allowance, a deduction in computing profits for income or corporation tax purposes, or a deduction from total profits or total income for the purposes of either of those taxes.

Legislation: CAA 2001, s. 70C(6)–(9)

Restriction on capital expenditure

Capital expenditure treated as incurred under these rules is restricted in certain circumstances. The restriction applies in the main purpose, or one of the main purposes, of entering to the lease is to obtain allowances on an amount of capital expenditure that 'materially exceeds' the market value of the leased asset at the commencement of the lease term.

The restriction similarly applies where such is a main purpose of entering into a series of transactions of which the lease is one, or entering into any particular transaction in such a series.

In such a case, the amount of the capital expenditure (including, if appropriate, any unrelievable pre-commencement rentals (see 231-300) is restricted to the market value of the leased asset at the commencement of the lease term.

Legislation: CAA 2001, s. 70C(7)

Additional expenditure incurred by lessor

In some circumstances, a lessee under a long funding finance lease is treated as incurring additional capital expenditure on the provision of plant or machinery as a result of additional expenditure incurred by the lessor on the asset in question.

The rules apply where the lessee is treated as having incurred qualifying expenditure on the provision of plant or machinery under these rules and where the lessor incurs expenditure in relation to the asset in question, as a result of which there is an increase (known as 'the relevant increase') in the present value of the minimum lease payments.

The lessee is treated as having incurred further capital expenditure on the date on which the relevant increase is first recognised in the lessee's financial records, known as the 'date of first recognition'.

The amount of the additional expenditure is the amount that would be recognised as the amount of the relevant increase if the lessee prepared accounts in accordance with generally-accepted accounting practice on the date of first recognition.

Legislation: CAA 2001, s. 70D

231-350   Disposal events and values

Overview

The termination of a long funding lease is in certain circumstances treated as a disposal event for capital allowance purposes. This will be the case where the lessee has been regarded, under the long funding lease rules, as incurring qualifying expenditure on the provision of plant and machinery. In such a case, the lessee will be required to bring a disposal value into account if a relevant event occurs. Such a relevant event occurs if the lease terminates, if the plant begins to be used wholly or partly for other purposes, or if the qualifying activity is permanently discontinued.

The rules changed for relevant events occurring from 13 November 2008. See 231-355 for details of the rules previously applying.

If the lease termination would already have given rise to a disposal event apart from under these rules, then that other disposal event is ignored.

The amount of the disposal value is given by the formula (QE - QA) + R, where QE is the person's qualifying expenditure on the asset, QA is the qualifying amount (as defined) and R is the relevant rebate (again, as defined). The definition of the qualifying amount varies according to whether the lease is a long funding finance lease or a long funding operating lease.

Legislation: CAA 2001, s. 70E

Other material: CA 23825

Legislation: CAA 2001, s. 70E

231-355   Disposal events and values: old rules

Overview

The following rules applied instead of those outlined at 231-350 if the relevant event occurred before 13 November 2008.

The termination of a long funding lease is in certain circumstances treated as a disposal event for capital allowance purposes. This will be the case where the lessee has been regarded, under the long funding lease rules, as incurring qualifying expenditure on the provision of plant and machinery. In such a case, the lessee will be required to bring a disposal value into account for the chargeable period in which the lease was terminated.

If the lease termination would already have given rise to a disposal event apart from under these rules, then that other disposal event was ignored.

The amount of the disposal value depended on whether it was a long funding operating lease or a long funding finance lease.

Legislation: CAA 2001, s. 70E

Other material: CA 23825

Amount of disposal value: operating leases (old rules)

In the case of a long funding operating lease, the disposal value was the sum of two elements, referred to in the legislation as elements A and B.

Element A was the amount (if any) by which the market value at a given date exceeded the aggregate amount of deductions that fell to be made under ICTA 1988, s. 502K or ITTOIA 2005, s. 148I for periods of account in which the person was the lessee. The given date for these purposes was the later of the date on which the lease term began and the date on which the plant or machinery was first brought into account for the purposes of a qualifying activity.

Element B was the sum of any amounts payable to the lessee that were calculated by reference to the termination value. This would therefore apply if the lessee received an amount when the lease terminated or if he received some other sum that was calculated by reference to the termination value, typically a refund of rentals. See 232-200 for the definition of 'termination value'.

Legislation: CAA 2001, s. 70E(4)

Amount of disposal value: finance leases (old rules)

Where the lease was a long funding finance lease, the disposal value may be stated (though this was not a statutory formula) as (X plus Y) minus Z where:

- X consisted of any amounts that were payable to the lessee and calculated by reference to the termination value (see 232-200);
- Y applied if the lease terminated before the end of the term and was the present value, immediately before the termination, of the balance of the minimum lease rentals (see below), on the basis that appropriate accounts (again, see below) were prepared by the lessee, and
- Z was any amount payable by the lessee to the lessor for, or in consequence of, the termination.

The result could never be below zero.

For these purposes, the balance of the minimum lease payments was the amount by which the amount of the minimum lease payments exceeded the amount that would have been the minimum lease payments if the term of the lease had been such as to expire on the lease termination date.

Appropriate accounts for these purposes were such as were prepared in accordance with generally-accepted accounting practice immediately before the termination of the lease.

Legislation: CAA 2001, s. 70E

231-400   Transfers and assignments by lessor or lessee

Sometimes the ownership of a leased asset will be transferred from one lessor to another, a transaction which may or may not involve the creation of a new lease from the point of view of the lessee.

Particular rules apply where such a transfer does not constitute the grant of a lease by the lessor, as long as – immediately after the transfer – the new lessor is the lessor of the plant or machinery under a lease (which can be the same lease or a new one).

In such a case:

- the lessors will be treated as if the old lease terminated immediately before the transfer and a new lease was entered into immediately thereafter;
- for the new lessor, the date of transfer will be treated as the date of both the inception of the new lease and the commencement of the term of the new lease; and
- the question of whether or not the new lease is a long funding lease follows the treatment of the old lease, as long as the term of the new lease is the unexpired term of the old one, and the amounts receivable under the new one are the same as would have been receivable if the old lease had continued to have effect. Where these conditions are met, the lessee is taxed as if the old and new leases were one and the same.

For the purposes of these provisions, a transfer of plant or machinery includes any kind of disposal of a person's interest in it or any arrangements under which a person's interest in the plant or machinery is terminated and another person becomes the lessor. In the case of fixtures, it also includes a cessation of ownership under the special fixtures rules.

Plant and Machinery

Where it is the lessee who transfers the plant or machinery to a new lessee, the above rules are mirrored so that, for example, the lessor is treated as if the old and new leases were one and the same, subject to the necessary conditions being met.

Legislation: CAA 2001, s. 70W, 70X

Other material: CA 23840

Commencement provisions

The commencement provisions (see, generally, 240-225) are modified when there has been a transfer of plant or machinery in accordance with the provisions of CAA 2001, s. 70W or s. 70X.

The modification applies where the long funding lease rules would not normally have effect under the commencement provisions but where there is a transfer or plant or machinery.

The long funding lease rules do not apply to a new lessor if the old lessor was within the charge to tax immediately before the transfer and if the transfer was made in circumstances such that, if the long funding lease rules did not apply to the lease, CAA 2001, s. 70W(4)(b) would have effect in relation to the new lessor to treat the lease as not being a long funding lease.

Once more, there are mirror rules for lessees.

Legislation: FA 2006, Sch. 8, para. 15(5), (6)

231-450   Sale and leaseback transactions

Where there is a sale and leaseback of an asset, the new head lease is treated as a long funding lease. This ensures that capital allowances are denied to the new head lessor. Similar rules apply where the leaseback is made via a series of leases. The terms are widely drawn.

Legislation: CAA 2001, s. 70Y

231-500   Change in accounting treatment of long funding leases

The accounting treatment of a long funding lease may be changed, so that the status switches between finance lease or operating lease. In such a case, the lease is treated as coming to an end and a new long funding lease is treated as commencing. The relevant accounts are those of the person concerned or, in the case of a lessor, of any connected person.

Legislation: CAA 2001, s. 70YA

232-000   Extension of term of lease

Various rules operate where the term of a lease is extended.

If the term of a long funding operating lease is extended, a new lease is treated as starting at that time. The term of the new lease is taken to be the unexpired portion of the term of the old lease, as extended. The new lease is treated as a long funding operating lease.

The concept of extending the term is widely defined, to include the making of a further non-cancellable period, the granting to the lessee of an option to extend where it is reasonably certain that this option will be exercised, and the exercising by the lessee of an option to extend the term. Any other event is also covered if it has the effect that the lessee will (or is reasonably certain to) lease the plant or machinery for a further period.

These rules do not apply where there is a change in accounting treatment that falls within CAA 2001, s. 70YA as described at 231-500.

A lease that is not a long funding lease may become one if the term is extended. The concept of extending the term is widely defined, in accordance with the provisions of CAA 2001, s. 70YB(2) discussed immediately above.

The rules apply if the new lease would be a long funding lease on the assumption that the lease terminated immediately before the 'effective date' and a new lease was entered into on that date. For these purposes, the effective date is the earlier of two dates:

- the day after the end of the pre-existing term of the existing lease; or
- the date on which the variation takes place, if the rentals that are payable are varied in connection with the event that has the effect of extending the lease.

There are provisions for re-applying these rules on a subsequent term extension if they do not initially have the effect of making the lease into a long funding lease.

Legislation: CAA 2001, s. 70YB, 70YC

Other material: CA 23845

Plant and Machinery

232-050   Definition of 'market value'

The market value of any plant or machinery at any time is determined, for these purposes, on the assumption that there is a disposal by an absolute owner who is free from all leases and other encumbrances.

Legislation: CAA 2001, s. 70YI(2)

232-100   Definition of 'minimum lease payments'

There is a statutory definition of this term, to mean the minimum payments under the lease (including any initial payment) over the lease term, together with:

- in the case of the lessee, so much of any residual amount as is guaranteed by him or by a person connected with him; or
- in the case of the lessor, so much of any residual amount as is guaranteed by the lessee or by any other person who is not connected with the lessor.

For these purposes, the 'residual amount' means so much of the fair value of the plant subject to the lease as the lessor cannot reasonably expect to recover from the payments made under the lease. In applying this definition, the fair value is taken to be the market value of the leased plant or machinery, less any grants that are receivable towards the purchase or use of that asset.

An 'initial payment' means a payment by the lessee that is made at or before the time the lease is entered into and is made in respect of the plant or machinery that is the subject of the lease.

Legislation: CAA 2001, s. 70YE, 70YI(1)

Increase in guaranteed residual amount

Anti-avoidance measures prevent abuse of the rules that define a long funding lease by reference to the guaranteed residual amount (see above).

The measures apply where a person is a lessor under a lease that is not a long funding lease and where that person enters into arrangements that meet two conditions. The first condition is that the arrangements have the effect of producing an increase, after the inception of the lease, in the proportion of the residual amount that is guaranteed. The second condition is that the lease would have been a long funding lease if those arrangements had been entered into before the inception of the lease.

Where these measures apply, the lease is treated as terminated and a new lease is treated as being entered into from the date of the 'relevant transaction'. This date is the date (or latest date) on which such arrangements have been entered into.

The term of the new lease is the unexpired portion of the old one and the date of the relevant transaction is taken to be the date of inception and commencement of the new lease.

Legislation: CAA 2001, s. 70YD

232-150   Termination of a lease

The concept of the termination of a lease is defined as the coming to end of the lease, whether by effluxion of time or otherwise. It specifically includes the bringing together of a lease by any person or by the operation of law.

Legislation: CAA 2001, s. 70YI(1)

232-200   Definition of 'termination value'

In the case of plant or machinery leased under a long funding lease, the 'termination value' is the value of the plant or machinery at or about the time when the lease terminates.

A reference to a calculation that is made by reference to the termination value includes a reference to calculation by reference to any one or more of the following:

- the proceeds of any sale, after the termination of the lease, of the plant or machinery;
- insurance proceeds, compensation or similar sums received in respect of the plant or machinery;
- the estimated market value of the plant or machinery;
- determination of the value in a way, or using criteria, which might reasonably be expected to produce a broadly similar result to calculation by reference to the termination value; or
- any other form of calculation that is made, directly or indirectly, by reference to the termination value.

Legislation: CAA 2001, s. 70YH

Other material: CA 23850

232-250   Definition of 'termination amount'

The concept of 'termination amount' is defined for cases where plant or machinery is leased under a long funding lease. Care is needed to distinguish between this expression and 'termination value', which is given a separate legal definition (see 232-200).

The normal rule for establishing the termination amount applies if the lease terminates as a result of a plant or machinery disposal event (see, generally, 238-150) or if such an event occurs in connection with the termination of the lease. (The concept of the 'normal rule' in this context is not a statutory one but is used here for ease of reference.)

Where the normal rule applies, the termination amount is the disposal value that would be brought into account assuming that CAA 2001, s. 34A did not apply (so that the lessor could claim capital allowances) and assuming that the lessor had claimed all capital allowances that would then have been due. (The same assumptions are made for the purposes of deciding if there is a disposal event.)

If the normal rule does not apply, and the lease is a long funding finance lease, the termination value is the value that the plant or machinery would have had in the lessor's financial records immediately before the termination of the lease.

If the normal rule does not apply, and the lease is a long funding operating lease, the termination value is the market value of the plant or machinery immediately after the termination of the lease.

Legislation: CAA 2001, s. 70YG

Other material: CA 23850

232-300   Definition of 'lease term'

The concept of the lease term is a key one in the long funding lease rules and is defined to include two elements:

- so much of the 'post-commencement period' as is a 'non-cancellable period'; and
- any subsequent periods that meet two specified conditions.

The specified conditions are that the lessee has the option to continue to lease the asset for the period in question (with or without further payment) and that it is reasonably certain, at the inception of the lease, that the lessee will exercise that option.

The post-commencement period is simply the period beginning with the commencement of the lease.

A non-cancellable period is a period during which the lessee may terminate the lease only in the event of some remote contingency or on the payment by the lessee of an amount which is so high that he is reasonably certain to choose to continue the lease rather than paying the amount.

HMRC has provided the following example to illustrate this (www.hmrc.gov.uk/leasing/tech-note.pdf at paragraph 2.51):

> 'Fred leases a printing press for 10 years from Barsetshire Bank. The first three years of the lease cannot be cancelled for any reason. The final seven years can be cancelled on payment of £6,000 before the end of year 3. Fred would not be guaranteed any rebate if the printing press were sold by Barsetshire Bank. The present value of the rentals for the last seven years of the lease is around £6,000. Fred has to pay roughly the same amount whether he leases the press or

not. He is unlikely to pay £6,000 to cancel the lease as he would be expected to continue to pay the lease rentals and enjoy the use of the press.'

Legislation: CAA 2001, s. 70YF(1)

Other material: CA 23850

High value leases with a term of five years or less

Special rules apply if:

- the market value of the asset at the commencement of the lease exceeds £1 million;
- the estimated market value five years later is more than half of the original market value;
- the term of the lease would otherwise be five years or less;
- the lessee has an option to continue to lease the asset;
- the lease term would exceed seven years on the assumption that it is reasonably certain, at the inception of the lease, that the lessee will exercise such an option; and
- the lessee would be required to make a payment to the lessor if failing to exercise such an option.

In such a case, it is assumed for these purposes that the lessee will exercise any option to continue to lease the asset unless, at the inception of the lease, it is reasonably certain that the option will not in fact be exercised. See www.hmrc.gov.uk/leasing/tech-note.pdf at paragraph 2.53 for several examples of how HMRC intend to interpret, in practice, the concept of 'reasonably certain'.

As noted at 230-500, a lease with a term of more than five years but no more than seven years is a short lease if three conditions are met. The rules described immediately above do not apply if those three conditions are met if there are left out of account any options that would result in the term of the lease exceeding seven years.

See also 232-000 for details of circumstances in which the term of a lease may be extended (CAA 2001, s. 70YC(5) applied here by s. 70YF(8)).

Legislation: CAA 2001, s. 70YF

232-350   Commencement and inception of a lease

These terms have different meanings.

The commencement date of a lease is the date from which the lessee is entitled to exercise his right to use the complete leased asset under the lease. An asset is for these purposes regarded as complete if its construction is substantially complete.

Plant and Machinery

The inception of the lease means the date on which there is a written contract between the lessor and the lessee, any lease conditions have been met and no terms remain to be agreed.

Legislation: CAA 2001, s. 70YI(1)

232-400   Definition of 'remaining useful economic life'

This term comes up in several parts of the long funding lease legislation and has its own definition for those purposes. It is defined as the period that starts with the commencement of the lease term and ends when the asset is no longer used, and no longer likely to be used, by any person as a fixed asset of a business.

Legislation: CAA 2001, s. 70YI(1)

Ships

235-000   Background to allowances for ships

When first-year allowances were available for ships, they could effectively be taken in any period after that in which they were first available. Until such allowances were reduced from 100 per cent, and later phased out before being reintroduced in certain circumstances, there was no need for writing-down allowances. When first-year allowances were withdrawn, provisions were introduced to permit a taxpayer to obtain writing-down allowances for ships. Where first-year allowances and writing-down allowances are available thereafter the taxpayer may effectively choose which to take.

235-100   Definition of 'ship'

The word 'ship' is not defined in the legislation, though it is understood that HMRC adopts the definition used in the *Merchant Shipping Act* 1894, s. 742, which defines a ship as including 'every description of vessel used in navigation not propelled by oars'. Non-sea going craft, such as canal barges, would thus appear to be within the term.

Instructions issued to inspectors of taxes direct that 'any vessel which is capable of being manoeuvred under direct or indirect power' should be treated as a ship for capital allowances purposes, as should a vessel which the Department of Trade and Industry is prepared to register as a ship in the Register of British Shipping.

Other material: CA 25100

Jack-up drilling rigs and similar vessels

Jack-up drilling rigs and similar vessels are also within the definition of 'ships'. This is so even if the rig, has no motive power of its own. The point was established in the case of

Clark (HMIT) v Perks and related appeals, which concerned the availability of the (then) Sch. E Foreign Earnings Deduction (FED) for seafarers aboard a 'ship'.

The Revenue accepted the Court of Appeal decision in those cases that the jack-up drilling rigs were 'ships' and issued an article on the topic in HMRC Tax Bulletin Article TB01/02-2 (January 2002, Issue 57). In the article the Revenue indicated a change to their previous view that the ability of a rig to engage in 'navigation' had to be more than merely incidental in order for it to be a 'ship'. The relevant text of the article was as follows:

'In the absence of a statutory definition of the word ship, our previous view was that for the purposes of FED a ship had to satisfy three conditions. These were that it had to be:

(a) capable of navigation;
(b) used in navigation; and
(c) navigation was more than incidental to its function.

It is clear from the [Court of Appeal] judgement [in *Clark (HMIT) v Perks*] that the third of these tests is not a relevant consideration. The critical question is whether a structure is used in navigation. Provided navigation is a significant part of the function of the structure in question, the mere fact that it is incidental to some specialised function does not take it outside the definition of ship.

It is also clear that relative infrequency of navigation does not necessarily exclude a structure from the definition of ship.

The Court agreed that in most cases, the categorisation of a structure should be governed by its design and capability rather than by its actual use at any time.

In addition to jack-up rigs, there may be other floating structures in the offshore oil and gas industry that are capable of satisfying the tests advocated by the Court of Appeal. We will consider such structures on the specific facts of each case also be settled.'

The position is summarised in the HMRC manual as follows:

'Oil-rigs and platforms, accommodation barges, light and weather ships, etc, are not generally regarded as ships. They do not normally move about and are not used in navigation. Semi-submersible oil-rigs and similar vessels in the oil and gas industry may be ships, depending on the use made of them. This use-based approach was followed by the Court of Appeal in Clark v Perks (2001) (which held that a semi-submersible drilling rig could be considered as a ship). As a result, you should not automatically accept that all such vessels qualify as ships.'

Cases: *Clark (HMIT) v Perks* [2001] BTC 336

Other material: CA 25100

235-200 First-year allowances for ships

New and second-hand ships will not qualify for first-year allowances. Even before the withdrawal from April 2008 of the first-year allowances that were given only for small and medium-sized enterprises it was unusual for first-year allowances to be available for ships. If the ship was a long-life asset, it was likely to be caught under first principles, as former

CAA 2001, s. 44(2) denied first-year allowances to long-life assets owned by small or medium-sized enterprises.

The other major hurdle is 'General exclusion 3' within CAA 2001, s. 46(2), which refers to 'expenditure of the kind described in section 94 (ships)' – the section dealing with long-life asset treatment of ships. This is an unfortunate wording, as the section referred to is couched in negatives such that the meaning of the words 'the kind described' is ambiguous. HMRC's Capital Allowances Manual provides some assistance, though even this is not clearly set out.

Long-life asset treatment does *not* apply to expenditure incurred before 1 January 2011 on the provision of ships of a sea-going kind as long as:

* the ship is not an offshore installation for the purposes of the *Mineral Workings (Offshore Installations) Act* 1971, such as oil rigs or gas installations; and
* the primary use to which such types of ships are put is otherwise than for sport or recreation.

In other words, a ship of a type used mainly for sport or recreation is not specifically exempted from long-life asset treatment. Offshore installations are in a similar position. Presumably this means that the long-life asset rules – in particular, the stricture regarding a useful economic life of at least 25 years – must be applied to these assets.

Legislation: CAA 2001, s. 94, CAA 2001, s. 130–131

235-300 'Single ship trade'

Writing-down allowances are available in respect of expenditure on new and second-hand ships. However, writing-down allowances which have become due at any time can be postponed and used largely at will in the future (see below).

To achieve this, ships are excluded from the main pool of assets and from any other pool of the taxpayer. Each ship is treated as an individual asset in its own pool, referred to as a 'single ship pool'. However, the shipowner may elect otherwise (see below).

The shipowner may require the postponement of all or part of the allowances to which he is entitled for a chargeable period.

Unless the chargeable period in point is the one in which a disposal event occurs (see below), a writing-down allowance is effectively available equal to 20 per cent per cent of the available qualifying expenditure in the single ship pool, (ie the expenditure on, or tax written-down value of, the asset). This is proportionately reduced, or increased if the period is less or more than 12 months or, for unincorporated taxpayers (or companies not within the charge to corporation tax), reduced if the trade has been carried on for only part of the period.

Legislation: CAA 2001, s. 56

Disposal events and the single ship pool

The 'chargeable period' in which a disposal event occurs means, in relation to incorporated taxpayers, the accounting period in which the disposal event takes place, or, in relation to unincorporated taxpayers, etc the period of account in which the disposal event takes place. The disposal event may take place by virtue of a number of alternative events (see further below):

- the sale, scrapping, etc of the asset so as to bring its disposal value into account;
- the occasion of the asset being used for purposes other than for a qualifying purpose (CAA 2001, s. 123(1), 132(1)(b));
- the permanent discontinuance of the qualifying activity (including matters treated as equivalent to the permanent discontinuance of the trade: CAA 2001, s. 577(2));
- the use within the requisite period for a purpose other than a qualifying purpose of an asset intended to be leased out (CAA 2001, s. 132(1)(a); see below); and
- the election by the shipowner for the single ship pool to cease to apply (CAA 2001, s. 129(1)).

Connected persons, persons under common control, successions, etc

There are special provisions relating to transactions between connected persons or persons under common control, successions to trade and tax-structured transactions (sole or main benefit test).

In particular, where all or part of an allowance has been postponed, subsequent allowances are given as if no postponement had been made. However, in addition, the shipowner may claim that all or part of the amount postponed be treated as a writing-down allowance due to him in any subsequent chargeable period in which his actual trade is carried on. In the case of a ship leased out, this applies until (but not including) the period in which it becomes leased to a person who is non-resident and does not use it for a trade in the UK or its territorial sea, such that only ten per cent writing-down allowances are available. He may therefore make as many such claims as he wishes until the amount postponed is exhausted.

Loss relief and group relief

The amount postponed is then treated as a capital allowance for a subsequent period for the purposes of:

- surrendering by way of group relief capital allowances given by discharge or repayment; or
- creating or augmenting a trader's loss available for relief.

Plant and Machinery

Writing-down allowance rights unaffected

A claim for an amount to be treated as a writing-down allowance for a subsequent period (rather than a notice of postponement) does not affect any other claim for allowances or overlap with a disclaimer under other statutory provisions in respect of that period.

Legislation: CAA 2001, s. 131(6)

Disclaimers, etc

As an alternative to postponement, the taxpayer may disclaim, or in the case of an unincorporated taxpayer, not claim, or reduce, the amount of the writing-down allowance to which he is entitled, the amount remaining being the amount eligible for postponement.

Example

Onedin Line Ltd incurs capital expenditure of £4,145,800 in the accounting period of 12 months to 30 September 2009. The company is not entitled to a first-year allowance.

The company notifies the HMRC officer that it wishes to reduce its writing-down allowance for the period to £800,000. It also notifies the inspector that it wishes to postpone £600,000 of that writing-down allowance. It subsequently claims for £142,245 of the postponed amount to be treated as a writing-down allowance for the following 12 month period to 30 September 2010.

The writing-down allowances for the periods to 30 September 2009 and 2010 are as follows:

			Allowances
Period ending 30 September 2009	£	£	£
Balance brought forward		–	
Capital expenditure incurred in period		4,145,800	
Qualifying expenditure for period		4,145,800	
Disposal value to be brought into account		–	
		4,145,800	
Writing-down allowance at 20%	(829,160)		
Less: amount disclaimed	29,160		
	800,000	800,000	
Less: amount postponed	600,000		
Allowance for period			200,000
Balance carried forward		3,345,800	

Period ending 30 September 2010	£	£	Allowances £
Balance brought forward		3,345,800	
Capital expenditure incurred in period		–	
Qualifying expenditure for period		3,345,800	
Disposal value to be brought into account		–	
		3,345,800	
Writing-down allowance at 20%		(669,160)	669,160
Postponed writing-down allowance brought forward	600,000		
Claim for writing-down allowance	(142,245)		142,245
Postponed writing-down allowance c/fwd	457,755		
Allowances for period			811,405
Balance carried forward		2,676,640	

Legislation: CAA 2001, s. 131(7)

235-400   Sale, scrapping, non-qualifying activity use, discontinuance of the qualifying activity

The scrapping, sale, etc of the ship, the occasion of its being used for purposes other than those of the qualifying activity and the permanent discontinuance of the qualifying activity result in the end of the single ship pool except in relation to certain special situations.

No balancing allowance or charge is made, but the effect is, in general, that the difference between the disposal value and the written-down value is added to (or subtracted from) the shipowner's appropriate non-ship pool of assets. Any allowance that would otherwise be made is treated as qualifying expenditure for the period in point, whilst any charge is treated as a disposal value to be brought into account. However, there are circumstances in which a balancing charge could arise and may in certain circumstances be deferred.

If the ship is disposed of or otherwise ceases to be owned by the shipowner without ever having been brought into use for the purposes of the shipowner's qualifying activity, any writing-down allowances previously available in respect of the single ship pool are withdrawn, regardless of whether they have been postponed: an equivalent amount is then added to the shipowner's non-ship pool as an item of qualifying expenditure for the 'chargeable period' in which the person ceases to own the ship.

Example

Onedin Line Ltd incurs capital expenditure of £1,000,000 on 1 February 2009, in the accounting period to 31 December 2009. The company is not entitled to a first-year allowance. The ship is sold on 1 December 2009 for £900,000.

Plant and Machinery

The position is as follows:

		Allowances
Year ended 31 December 2009	£	£
Capital expenditure incurred in the period	1,000,000	
Writing-down allowance	200,000	200,000
	800,000	
Disposal value	(900,000)	
Amount to be subtracted from non-ship pool	100,000	

In addition, WDAs of £200,000 are withdrawn, and added to the non-ship pool. The net effect is that allowances of £100,000 (£200,000−£100,000) will be given through the non-ship pool.

Legislation: CAA 2001, s. 132(2), (3), 133

235-500 Roll-over relief for balancing charges

As described above, any balancing charge arising in respect of a ship is effectively used to reduce the main pool of qualifying expenditure. However, if the disposal value to be brought into account exceeds the pool of unrelieved expenditure, the excess is recoverable immediately by way of a balancing charge. If certain conditions are satisfied, claims may be made to defer balancing charges in respect of qualifying ship disposals. The deferment provisions (commonly known as 'roll-over relief for balancing charges') were announced in reply to a Parliamentary Question on 21 April 1994, when the Chancellor of the Exchequer said:

> 'We ... recognise that, competitively, tax measures available overseas put our shippers at a particular disadvantage. We have therefore decided to introduce a provision which will allow capital allowance balancing charges for ships to be rolled over for a period of up to three years [later increased to six years] from the date on which the ship is disposed of, to be set off against subsequent expenditure on ships within that period. The amount of any balancing charge which can be rolled over will be limited to the amount needed to ensure that no tax liability arises as a result of a ship's disposal. We estimate that this measure will benefit the shipping industry by up to £20 million per annum in a full year. In drawing up this provision we will be considering whether it should be restricted to ships on the UK register; and in doing so will take account of what our European Union partners do.
>
> As with any measure of this sort we have an obligation to notify the Commission of the proposal. Subject to the outcome of discussions with the Commission, we will be bringing forward the necessary legislation in next year's Finance Bill, with retrospective effect from today [21 April 1994] ....'

Extensions made to the deferment provisions in 1996 allow a balancing charge to be rolled over in circumstances where expenditure on new shipping is incurred, where the shipowner is a company, by any company which is a member of the same group of companies.

All of the following conditions must be met if deferment of a balancing charge is to be claimed.

(1)   A charge must arise for a chargeable period ('relevant period') as a result of one of the following events in respect of a 'qualifying ship' (see below):

(a)   the ship ceasing to belong to the shipowner, or ceasing to exist; or

(b)   his having lost possession of the ship, it being reasonably assumed that the loss is permanent.

(2)   The ship must have belonged to the shipowner at some time in that period.

(3)   The shipowner must have provided the ship for the purposes of his qualifying activity.

(4)   The shipowner must not have incurred a loss in respect of the qualifying activity for the chargeable period for which the balancing charge arises.

(5)   No amount must have been allocated, in respect of the old ship, to an overseas leasing pool, a single asset pool under CAA 2001, s. 206 (asset used partly for other purposes), a single asset pool under s. 211 (partial depreciation subsidy) or a pool for a qualifying activity consisting of special leasing.

The amount which may be deferred is limited to the smallest of (CAA 2001, s. 138):

(1)   The amount set out in CAA 2001, s. 139 (see below).

(2)   'Expenditure on new shipping' by a 'qualifying person' (see below) in the next six years.

(3)   the balancing charge arising on the actual qualifying activity for that period, disregarding balancing charges in respect of the following:

(a)   leased assets and inexpensive cars;

(b)   assets used partly for qualifying activity and partly for non-qualifying activity purposes; and

(c)   subsidised assets.

(4)   The amount needed to reduce the trading profit for the year to nil.

Where the claim is made, the amount deferred is added to the pool of qualifying expenditure for the chargeable period in which the balancing charge would otherwise arise, thus effectively cancelling out the balancing charge.

However, if a balancing charge is deferred in this way and no 'qualifying person' (see below) incurs expenditure on new shipping of an amount equal to or exceeding the amount of the deferred charge within the six-year period, the relief given is withdrawn, up to the amount by which the balancing charge deferred exceeds the expenditure within the six-year period.

The legislation sets out the mechanism for preventing expenditure on new shipping from qualifying for allowances where the expenditure is needed to 'frank' a deferred balancing charge. Where:

● an addition is made under CAA 2001, s. 137 above; and

● a qualifying person incurs expenditure on new shipping in the six-year period mentioned above,

Plant and Machinery

245

the shipowner may, by written notice to HMRC, attribute to the expenditure so much of the addition as equals the expenditure not previously under the present provision. Where the shipowner and the qualifying person to whose expenditure the notice relates are different persons (members of the same group), the notice must be given jointly.

An amount equal to the deferred charge is then taken out of the group member's 'qualifying expenditure' for the chargeable period. Deferment cannot be used to create or increase a trading loss.

Legislation: CAA 2001, s. 135ff.

Qualifying persons

'Qualifying persons' are:

* the shipowner; and
* where the shipowner is a company, any company which, at the time when the expenditure is (or is to be) incurred, is (or would be) a member of the same group of companies as the shipowner for group relief purposes.

Legislation: CAA 2001, s. 158

Amount of balancing charge

Where the old ship has been dealt with separately from all other assets under the 'single ship pool' rules in CAA 2001, s. 127, the charge is that which arises in the separate ship single pool.

Where the old ship has been included in the general plant or machinery pool, so that there is no identifiable balancing charge, a notional computation is made of the charge which would arise on the following assumptions:

* the ship was the only asset in the non-ship pool;
* any first-year allowance claimed was actually made to the shipowner; and
* the maximum amount of writing-down allowances available were made.

The assumptions listed above are also applied where expenditure on a ship is first included in the separate single ship pool, but the shipowner later gives notice under CAA 2001, s. 129, which transfers all or part of the expenditure to the appropriate non-ship pool.

Legislation: CAA 2001, s. 139

Re-imposition of deferred charge

The deferred charge is re-imposed in the following circumstances:

* a balancing charge has been deferred under CAA 2001, s. 135; and
* within the six-year period a 'qualifying person' (see above) incurs 'expenditure on new

shipping' (see below), the whole or part of which is expenditure on the new ship falling within CAA 2001, s. 140 (see above).

The amount of expenditure under the second point above is treated as disposal value falling to be brought into account in the chargeable period in which the 'expenditure on new shipping' (see below) is incurred.

Legislation: CAA 2001, s. 143

Expenditure on new shipping

Expenditure is 'expenditure on new shipping' for the purposes of CAA 2001, s. 140–145 insofar as it is both:

(1) capital expenditure incurred on the provision, wholly and exclusively for the purposes of a qualifying activity carried on by a person who incurs the expenditure of a ship which it appears:

    (a) will be brought into use for the purposes of that qualifying activity as a qualifying ship; and

    (b) will continue to be a qualifying ship throughout a period of at least three years after that; and

(2) expenditure which, by virtue of CAA 2001, s. 127(1), (2), falls to be taken into account for the purposes of the normal capital allowances rules in CAA 2001, Pt. 2, Ch. 5.

The circumstances under which expenditure incurred on providing a new ship does not qualify for relief are as follows:

- where the ship has previously belonged to the person who incurred the expenditure or a person connected with him (see below);
- during the three years from when the ship is brought into use, it is regarded as a non-qualifying ship; or
- the ship ceases to belong to the shipowner or a person connected with him (CAA 2001, s. 149).

In the context of a group of companies, the circumstances in which expenditure on new shipping does not qualify for relief also include situations where (CAA 2001, s. 150):

- the ship ceases to belong to a group member without having been brought into qualifying activity use;
- disposal value of the ship falls to be brought into account within three years of first use; or
- within three years of first use, the shipowner and group member cease to be members of the same group for group relief purposes.

There are, however, the following let-outs for:

- total loss of the ship; or
- damage to the ship such that it is impossible or not commercially worthwhile to restore it.

Plant and Machinery

247

Where expenditure which satisfies the conditions in CAA 2001, s. 146 above is attributed to a non-ship pool, or the ship is leased outside the UK so that CAA 2001, Pt. 2, Ch. 11 (overseas leasing) applies (see 220-200), the expenditure is treated as if it is not and never has been expenditure on new shipping.

Expenditure on the provision of a ship is not treated as expenditure on new shipping where:

- the ship had already belonged to the person who incurred the expenditure at some time in the period of six years ending with the time when it first belongs to him in consequence of his incurring the expenditure;
- the ship has at any time in that period belonged to a person who has, at 'a material time', been a person 'connected with' the person who incurred the expenditure, etc; or
- the main object, or one of the main objects, of acquiring the ship for the purposes of a qualifying activity carried on by the person who incurred the expenditure, either directly or through a series of transactions, was to secure deferment of the balancing charge under CAA 2001, s. 135(1).

'A material time' is the time when the expenditure is incurred or any earlier time in the period of six years allowed for investment in new shipping allowed by CAA 2001, s. 138(1) (see above).

A charge deferred under CAA 2001, s. 135 or 143 cannot be attributed to expenditure on new shipping where the 'qualifying person' (see above) has incurred earlier in the six-year period allowed by CAA 2001, s. 138(1) other expenditure:

- which is expenditure on new shipping; or
- would fall to be treated as such but for any notice under CAA 2001, s. 130(2) or 129(1),

unless the earlier expenditure has already been attributed to that or an earlier deferred charge (CAA 2001, s. 141).

Expenditure is treated as incurred by the shipowner where:

- a person is carrying on the qualifying activity previously carried on by the shipowner; and
- the only changes in the persons carrying on the qualifying activity since the shipowner carried it on are changes which do not involve all of the persons carrying it on before the changes permanently ceasing to carry it on, or in respect of which the qualifying activity is treated as continuing under ICTA 1988, s. 343(2) (CAA 2001, s. 155).

Legislation: CAA 2001, s. 147ff.

Connected persons

For the purposes of the rule which prevents expenditure on a ship acquired from a connected person from qualifying as new expenditure, a person is connected with another person if:

- he is connected (as defined in CAA 2001, s. 575) with that person or a person connected with that person by virtue of the following point; or
- he is carrying on a qualifying activity previously carried on by that other person where

either the only changes in the persons carrying on the qualifying activity since the other person carried it on are changes which do not involve all of the persons carrying it on before the changes permanently ceasing to carry it on, or in respect of which the qualifying activity is treated as continuing under ICTA 1988, s. 343(2).

In addition, where expenditure is incurred by someone other than the shipowner, a person connected with the shipowner is also treated as connected with the person incurring the expenditure.

Legislation: CAA 2001, s. 156

'Qualifying ships'

A 'qualifying ship' for the purposes of CAA 2001, Pt. 2, Ch. 12 is one which is of a sea-going kind and is registered on a shipping register established and maintained under the law of the UK or elsewhere as a ship with a gross tonnage of at least 100 tons.

However, in a case where the balancing event in CAA 2001, s. 135 above consists in, or results from, either:

- the total loss of the old ship; or
- damage to the old ship which puts it in a condition in which it is impossible, or not commercially worthwhile, for the repair required for restoring it to its previous use to be undertaken,

the references to a 'qualifying ship' in CAA 2001, s. 136(b) and s. 146(3)(b), s. 149(1)(a) have effect as if the 100 tons requirement in s. 151 above were omitted. As the Financial Secretary to the Treasury explained (IR press release, 17 February 1995): 'where a vessel is lost at sea it can be very difficult for the owner to purchase a new boat in time to prevent a balancing charge arising'.

A ship is not a qualifying ship if:

- the primary use to which ships of the same kind are put is for sport or recreation; or
- it is an offshore installation.

Further, a ship is not a qualifying ship if it is not registered in a 'relevant register' within three months from the start of the 'qualifying period', ie the period between the time when the ship is first brought into use for the purposes of any qualifying activity of the shipowner (or the person incurring the expenditure) or a person 'connected with' him and the earlier of:

- the third anniversary of that date; or
- the date when the ship ceases to belong to the shipowner or a person connected with him.

A 'relevant register' is any register of shipping established and maintained under the law of any part of the British Islands, (ie the UK, Channel Islands or the Isle of Man) or of any country or territory which, at the time when the ship is first registered in that register, is a

Plant and Machinery

member state, another state within the European Economic Area (as defined in the European Economic Area Act 1993) or a 'colony'.

Legislation: CAA 2001, s. 151–154

'Connected with'

The references in CAA 2001, s. 154 above to 'connected' persons are construed in accordance with CAA 2001, s. 156 above. However, in relation to the old ship there is included as 'connected' any person carrying on a qualifying activity subsequently carried on by the shipowner, or by a person connected with him, which do not involve all of the persons who were carrying it on before the changes permanently ceasing to carry it on, or in respect of which the qualifying activity is treated as continuing under ICTA 1988, s. 343(2) (CAA 2001, s. 156(2)).

Legislation: CAA 2001, s. 156(2)

Procedural provisions relating to deferred charges

For the purposes of corporation tax, a deferment claim under CAA 2001, s. 135(1) above is to be considered in accordance with FA 1998, Sch. 18, Pt. IX (claims for corporation tax allowances). For income tax purposes, a claim under s. 135(1) will not be allowed unless it is made within 12 months from the 31 January following the tax year in which 'the relevant period' ends.

The shipowner may give notice to HMRC to vary the attribution made under CAA 2001, s. 140 or 143 (see above). The notice of variation must be made within the period of time for making a claim under s. 135(1) (see above). Where the shipowner and the qualifying person to whose expenditure the notice relates are different persons (members of the same group), the notice must be given jointly.

Where a claim for deferment has been made under s. 135(1) and it is subsequently found that the shipowner was not entitled to the deferment, either in whole or in part, the shipowner must advise the inspector accordingly, specifying the circumstances, within three months after the end of the chargeable period in which they first arise.

Legislation: CAA 2001, s. 135, 142, 145

Assessments and adjustments

Assessments and adjustments can be made as necessary to give effect to the provisions of CAA 2001, Pt. 2, Ch. 12. An assessment required in consequence of CAA 2001, s. 145(1)–(3) above may, notwithstanding any time limitation for the making of assessments, be made at any time between:

- the time when those circumstances arise; and
- the time 12 months after the shipowner notifies the inspector of the circumstances.

Provision is made for notice under CAA 2001, s. 145 to be given to the inspector where there have been such changes in the persons carrying on the qualifying activity as are mentioned in CAA 2001, s. 155: the notice is to be given by the persons actually carrying on the qualifying activity at the time of the giving of the notice or, as the case may be, when the notice is required to be given.

Legislation: CAA 2001, s. 155

235-600   Leasing assets

The single ship pool does not apply to expenditure in respect of which other special pooling requirements, etc prevail, as follows:

- ships intended to be leased out but which it is intended will be used in the 'designated period' for a purpose which is not a 'qualifying purpose';
- virtually all ships leased in the 'designated period' to persons (including joint lessees) in such circumstances that any one or more of them is a non-resident (excluding certain persons involved in oil or mineral activities) unless the leasing is short-term leasing or, in general, that of specific ship chartering, ie when writing-down allowances restricted to 10 per cent; and
- ships let otherwise than in the course of a trade, ie where the shipowner's trade is not a qualifying activity.

A ship which it is intended should be leased out but which does not satisfy the requirements as to intended qualifying use (see above) forms part of the non-ship pool of assets.

The use within the 'designated period' for a purpose other than a 'qualifying purpose' of a ship intended to be leased out is the occasion of the single ship pool being treated as having discontinued. A ship which ceases to be used for a qualifying purpose in the designated period reverts to its position if it had never been intended for such use: it is effectively transferred to the appropriate non-ship pool, mentioned above. No balancing adjustment is made, but the effect is, in general, that the difference between the disposal value to be brought into account and the written-down value is added to (or subtracted from) the shipowner's non-ship pool or separate pool of assets. Any allowance which would otherwise be made is treated as qualifying expenditure for the period in point, whilst any charge is treated as a disposal value to be brought into account.

Legislation: CAA 2001, s. 127, 128, 132

235-700   Election for the single ship pool not to apply

The shipowner may elect that the provisions which provide for the 'single ship pool' shall not, or shall no longer, apply. If so, the ship is added to the shipowner's non-ship pool of expenditure for writing-down in the normal way. The election must be made in writing to

Plant and Machinery

HMRC within the normal time limits. For HMRC's discretion to extend the time limit for an election, see para. 12 and 13 of SP 6/94.

Legislation: CAA 2001, s. 129

Other material: SP 6/94

Effect of election before any allowance made

If no writing-down allowance has been given before the shipowner elects, the single ship pool provisions are wholly ignored. Allowances are treated as given when they fall to be made irrespective of any insufficiency of profits, etc against which to set them.

Legislation: CAA 2001, s. 577(3)

Effect of election after an allowance made

Where allowances have already been given, the ship is effectively transferred to the main non-ship pool at such value as ensures that no balancing charge or allowance arises. The single ship pool is treated as having been permanently discontinued in the chargeable period in point, but no balancing adjustment is made (the period in point being that to which the election relates, not in which it is made).

The effect of such an election is that a shipowner may choose at any time to wind up the 'single ship pool' with its rolled-up allowances, and transfer the written-down value to the main non-ship pool. There will clearly be circumstances in which there will be cash-flow benefits in doing so, (eg to prevent a balancing charge arising on the main non-ship pool). There is no provision permitting the ship to be 'de-pooled' again, after having been brought into the non-ship pool (but see below).

Legislation: CAA 2001, s. 129(1)

Further election by shipowner

The shipowner may also elect that any fraction of his 'qualifying expenditure' for a particular period in respect of his 'single ship pool' be attributed to his non-ship pool instead. The election must be made in writing to HMRC within the normal time limits. For HMRC's discretion to extend the time limit for an election, see para. 12 and 13 of SP 6/94.

Legislation: CAA 2001, s. 129

Other material: SP 6/94

Mining and oil activities

237-000   Expenditure connected with mineral extraction trades

With one exception, expenditure on plant or machinery is not qualifying expenditure for mineral extraction purposes. Instead, where a person carrying on a trade of mineral extraction (see the Chapter headed 'Mineral Extraction Allowances', which begins at 500-000) incurs expenditure in connection with that trade on plant or machinery for mineral exploration and access, it will be taken to be incurred on the provision of plant or machinery wholly and exclusively for the purposes of that trade.

The exception where mineral extraction allowances are given is where the plant or machinery is used for mineral exploration and access and, before commencement of trade, the plant or machinery is sold, demolished, destroyed or abandoned (CAA 2001, s. 402 – see 500-150).

Other pre-trading expenditure, not abandoned, etc is effectively treated for plant and machinery allowances as incurred on the first day of trading. The person is then treated as having incurred the expenditure on the day of commencement of trading.

Legislation: CAA 2001, s. 399(1), 160–161

237-100   Expenditure connected with re-use of offshore infrastructure

Annual reducing balance capital allowances are given in respect of the capital costs of preparing oil installations for re-use or for removing and mothballing oil installations where their future use is uncertain. For both of these categories, 100 per cent up-front relief is claimable in cases where the costs are incurred in connection with the closing down of an oil field.

Writing-down allowances for plant and machinery are given at 20 per cent, but allowances for ring fence trade expenditure are given at 25 per cent.

Legislation: CAA 2001, s. 56(1A), s. 161A to 161D

Background

Where a person carrying on a trade of oil extraction incurs decommissioning costs on plant and machinery used in that trade as offshore infrastructure, and subject to various conditions, it is allocated to that person's appropriate qualifying capital allowance pool for the chargeable period in which incurred.

Decommissioning expenditure on UK infrastructure, as defined, only qualifies under these rules where the costs incurred are substantially in compliance with an approved

253

abandonment programme or related conditions. Provided no election is made for a 100 per cent deduction (see below), annual writing-down allowances are given for qualifying decommissioning expenditure.

In this context:

- *decommissioning expenditure* relates only to plant and machinery in terms of its preservation pending re-use or demolition, its preparation for re-use, arranging its re-use or its demolition. It does not affect the application of the relief if an item of plant and machinery is both re-used and demolished or not re-used at all;
- *offshore infrastructure* relates to any part of an installation which, as provided in the *Petroleum Act* 1998, s. 44, is maintained offshore in connection with exploitation/ exploration of the seabed, storage /recovery of gas, conveyance by pipe, associated accommodation of offshore workers. Its scope extends to include installations maintained for the purposes mentioned, even if outside UK waters, and also pipelines and pipeline systems in foreign waters.

No tax relief is allowable under these provisions in any case where the costs incurred would otherwise qualify for a deduction in respect of any other income tax or corporation tax provision.

Legislation: CA 2001, s. 161A to 161D

237-200   Ring-fence trades: abandonment expenditure

The case of *RTZ Oil & Gas Ltd v Elliss (HMIT)* established that the costs of restoring or removing assets are capital expenditure and, in practice, much of the expenditure on abandonment will fall to be so regarded. Most of the expenditure will be in relation to plant and machinery. The general rule (CAA 2001, s. 26) is that where any machinery or plant, in use for the purposes of a trade, is demolished and not replaced, the qualifying expenditure for the period of demolition is treated as increased by the net cost of demolition. The costs of removing plant, less any salvage proceeds, therefore qualify for writing-down allowances. However, more generous allowances are given in relation to abandonment expenditure incurred in the UK continental shelf or UK territorial sea, as follows.

The allowances apply to demolition costs where the machinery or plant which is in use for a ring-fence trade is not replaced and which is or forms part of an offshore installation or a submarine pipeline. The expenditure must be incurred for the purposes of closing down a field or part of a field within the meaning of the *Oil Taxation Act* 1975 and the demolition must be carried out, wholly or substantially, in order to comply with an abandonment programme within the meaning of the *Petroleum Act* 1987.

A company incurring any abandonment expenditure which qualifies under the above rules may elect to have a 100 per cent allowance for the expenditure, less any related salvage proceeds, instead of adding this net expenditure to the pool. An election must be made within two years of the end of the period to which it relates and is irrevocable.

Where a company ceases to carry on a ring-fence trade and, subsequently, incurs expenditure which would have qualified under the above rules if the trade had continued, any such expenditure incurred within three years of cessation, less any salvage proceeds, may be added to the pool in the period of cessation.

The 100 per cent also applies to the wider category of decommissioning expenditure as defined in CAA 2001, s. 161B(1) (ie preservation, preparation, arrangement, demolition). This 100 per cent election is (and is deemed always to have been) available only in respect of plant and machinery that has been brought into use for the ring-fence trade.

As before, it does not affect the application of the relief if an item of plant and machinery is both re-used and demolished or not re-used at all. There is a requirement for the claimant to make an election for the 100 per cent relief in respect of qualifying expenditure, then deductible in the period in which it is incurred, and no other allowances are available. Also, the decommissioning costs claimable for this 100 per cent relief are net of any proceeds received for scrapping the plant and machinery. Any proceeds received are set off in the following order – against allowances for the period in which proceeds received, then against allowances for previous periods on a LIFO (last in first out) basis and finally against allowances for future periods on a FIFO (first in first out) basis.

Legislation: CAA 2001, s. 45F, CAA 2001, s. 163–165

Cases: *RTZ Oil & Gas Ltd v Elliss (HMIT)* [1987] BTC 359

Anti-avoidance

In relation to decommissioning costs incurred from 22 April 2009, anti-avoidance provisions ensure that companies can claim relief for such costs only for the accounting period in which the work is in fact carried out. According to the *Explanatory Notes* issued with the 2009 Finance Bill:

> 'the Government [had] become aware of arrangements that have been entered into which seek to establish a claim for tax relief for decommissioning costs several years in advance of any decommissioning work being carried out. These arrangements are an attempt to undermine the integrity of the North Sea ring fence.'

237-300   Transfer of interests in oil fields

An anti-avoidance provision applies where there is a transfer by a participator in an oil field of the whole or part of his interest in the field and, as part of the transfer, the old participator disposes of, and the new participator acquires:

- plant or machinery used, or expected to be used, in connection with the field; or
- a share in such plant or machinery.

Plant and Machinery

Any excess of the new participator's expenditure over the old participator's disposal value is to be left out of account in determining the new participator's available qualifying expenditure.

Legislation: CAA 2001, s. 166

237-400   Oil production sharing contracts

It is common for oil companies to enter into 'production sharing contracts' with overseas governments. Typically, the contract allows the company to set up oil production within the overseas country or territory and to take all the profits from the source. After a number of years, the overseas government takes control of the production and enjoys the profits thereafter. It is usual under these agreements for ownership of the oil production equipment to be transferred at some stage to the government.

The oil company is deemed to continue owning the plant or machinery until it ceases:

- to belong to the government (or a representative of the government); or
- to be used (or held for use) under the production sharing company.

This beneficial treatment will be given when:

- a person ('the contractor') enters into an agreement with the overseas government (or representative) where oil is or may be produced;
- under the agreement, plant or machinery which must have an oil-related use is transferred either immediately or subsequently to the government;
- the contractor incurs capital expenditure on this plant or machinery which is for the purposes of oil extraction;
- the amount of the contractor's capital expenditure on the plant or machinery is reasonable, considering the contractor's interest under the contract; and
- the equipment is actually transferred to the government (or representative)

Legislation: CAA 2001, s. 167–170

Definition of 'oil-related use'

An 'oil-related use' is defined as use:

- to explore for, win access to, or extract oil;
- for the initial storage or treatment of oil; or
- for other purposes ancillary to the extraction of oil.

Legislation: CAA 2001, s. 167(2)

Extension of rules when an interest in the contract passes to another party

These rules are extended to include persons who purchase an interest in the production sharing contract. These persons are known in the legislation as 'participators'. A participator will be deemed as the owner of plant or machinery, until it either:

- ceases to belong to the government (or representative); or
- ceases to be used (or held for use) under the contract.

Furthermore, if the participator passes an interest on to another participator, the rules will benefit the next participator (and so on) provided that the rules continue to be met. To qualify for this:

- the participator must acquire an interest in a production sharing contract, either from the contractor; or from another person who acquired it (directly or indirectly) from the contractor;
- the participator must incur capital expenditure on the provision of the plant or machinery to be used either for 'oil-related use' under the contract, or for the purposes of an oil extraction trade carried on by the participator;
- the capital expenditure incurred must be at a reasonable level as regards the interest in the contract; and
- the plant or machinery must actually be transferred to the government (or representative) in accordance with the contract.

Legislation: CAA 2001, s. 169

Further extension to cover cases where plant or machinery under production-sharing contract 'acquired'

These rules are extended further to deal with cases where:

- capital expenditure is incurred on the interest in a production-sharing contract;
- some of this expenditure relates to plant or machinery; and
- the plant or machinery is already deemed under these provisions to belong to the contractor or a participator, (ie true ownership has already passed to the government or representative).

In these circumstances:

- the person incurring the capital expenditure will be deemed to own the plant or machinery (until it either ceases to belong to the government, or ceases to be used under the contract or held for such use);
- the previous deemed owner, (ie the contractor or participator) will be deemed to have disposed of the plant or machinery;
- the disposal proceeds to be taken into account is the amount of the capital expenditure incurred which is attributable to the plant or machinery;
- this amount is also the deemed expenditure by the person 'acquiring' the plant or machinery; but

Plant and Machinery

- this amount is limited to the lowest disposal value taken into account by the previous participators or the contractor.

This last limit ensures that capital allowances are not claimed in respect of any amount more than the original cost of the plant or machinery, because each disposal value is subject to the general limit of the original capital expenditure incurred.

To obtain the amount which is attributable to the plant or machinery, regard should be had to 'what is just and reasonable in all the circumstances'.

This change was accompanied by two modifications to the list of disposal values to deal with cases covered by.

If the disposal event is either:

- the plant or machinery ceasing to belong to the government; or
- it ceasing to be used (or held for use) under the contract,

then the disposal value to be taken into account is the amount of any compensation received for that event (or nil, if there is no such compensation).

Example

Saturn Ltd is an oil producer. On 1 April 2000, it enters into a production sharing contract with the government of Uranus. Under the terms of the contract, Saturn Ltd will incur £1,000,000 expenditure on plant and machinery for qualifying purposes on 1 May 2000 and this equipment will transfer to the government's ownership on 1 May 2010.

On 1 May 2015, Saturn Ltd enters into a further agreement with Neptune plc in which it transfers its interest in the contract. Neptune plc pays £2,000,000 for the interest in the contract (for which it is just and reasonable to attribute £1,200,000 to the plant or machinery).

In 2020, the ownership of the equipment is transferred to another company and Neptune plc receives compensation of £500,000.

Saturn Ltd is the contractor here and can add the £1,000,000 incurred to its plant and machinery allowances pool. It can continue to claim writing-down allowances on this expenditure even after it ceases to own the equipment in 2010.

In 2015, Neptune plc acquires the plant or machinery which strictly belongs to the government of Uranus, but is deemed under CAA 2001, s. 168(2) to belong to Saturn Ltd.

Neptune plc can therefore be treated as owning the plant or machinery.

Saturn Ltd must bring in a disposal value of £1,200,000, but this would be limited to the original cost of £1,000,000. Neptune plc's expenditure qualifying for capital allowances is therefore limited to £1,000,000.

In 2020, the transfer of the plant or machinery from the government will give rise to a disposal event for Neptune plc. As compensation is received, the amount received (£500,000) must be brought in as a disposal value.

Legislation: CAA 2001, s. 62(1), 170–171

Additional VAT liabilities and rebates

238-000 First-year allowances

A person may receive a 100 per cent first-year allowance under CAA 2001, s. 52 for expenditure incurred on plant and machinery, eg a computer or an item of computer equipment. If he incurs an additional VAT liability, then that liability may be treated as capital expenditure incurred on plant and machinery, in which case it will attract a first-year allowance for the period related to incurring that liability. The rate of first-year allowance is the same as applied to the original expenditure. Additional VAT paid by the owner of an asset is qualifying expenditure provided that:

- the original expenditure was qualifying expenditure; and
- the original asset is provided for the purposes of the qualifying activity when the additional VAT liability is incurred.

This section also applied to additional VAT liabilities incurred in respect of expenditure qualifying for first-year allowances under earlier regimes (former CAA 2001, Sch. 3, para. 46(1), repealed by the *Finance Act* 2008).

No additional VAT liability can be added to qualifying expenditure if there has been a disposal event within before it is incurred, or if the asset is leased overseas (other than by protected leasing).

Legislation: CAA 2001, s. 61(2); s. 236–237; Sch. 3, para. 46(1).

Withdrawal of first-year allowances

The *Finance Act* 2008 withdrew many types of first-year allowance, including in particular the allowances given for expenditure incurred by small or medium-sized enterprises. Such allowances ceased to be available for expenditure incurred from 1 April 2008 (corporation tax) or 6 April 2008 (income tax).

Those dates do not apply, however, in the case of additional VAT liabilities and rebates. As explained in the *Explanatory Notes* to the Finance Bill (clause 72(7) but see now FA 2008, s. 75(7)):

> 'where a business incurs an additional VAT liability (under the VAT Capital Goods Scheme) then if the original expenditure was first-year qualifying expenditure then Chapter 18 of Part 2 will still apply to determine if there is an entitlement to a first-year allowance in respect of the additional VAT liability as if section 44 had not been repealed.'

A similar provision has the same effect for additional VAT liabilities and rebates related to Northern Ireland expenditure and to ICT expenditure incurred by small enterprises.

238-050 Annual investment allowances

The treatment of AIAs, introduced by the *Finance Act* 2008, is covered at 181-000ff.

Measures were introduced in the same Act to ensure that if the original expenditure qualified for an AIA, then the additional VAT liability will in principle also qualify.

The provisions apply where the original expenditure was AIA qualifying expenditure, and additional VAT liability is incurred at a time when the plant or machinery is still provided for the purposes of the qualifying activity. The additional VAT liability is then treated as AIA qualifying expenditure that has been incurred on the same plant or machinery as the original expenditure in the chargeable period in which the liability accrues. A person then may claim AIAs on all or part of the expenditure, in the normal way and subject to normal principles.

No additional VAT liability can be added to qualifying expenditure if the asset is leased overseas (other than by protected leasing).

No AIA is given for additional VAT liabilities if the transaction is caught by the anti-avoidance provisions of CAA 2001, s. 241. Those provisions apply where a person (B) enters into a transaction with another person (S) which is a 'relevant transaction' for the purposes of the anti-avoidance rules in CAA 2001, Pt. 2, Ch. 17.

Legislation: CAA 2001, s. 236ff.

238-100   Writing-down allowances

If a person who is entitled to a writing-down allowance incurs an additional VAT liability when the item is provided wholly and exclusively for qualifying activity purposes, then that liability is capital expenditure on the provision of plant or machinery wholly and exclusively for qualifying activity purposes in consequence of which it belongs to him. Thus the liability is added to the pool of expenditure in the year in which the liability arose.

Should the person receive an additional VAT rebate, that rebate increases the disposal value brought into account by CAA 2001, s. 60–63. If there is no disposal value – for example, the item is 'sold for nothing' – then that rebate is the disposal value.

The disposal value equals the additional VAT rebate. The disposal value is restricted to the expenditure on the item as reduced by any additional VAT rebates for the purpose of calculating any balancing adjustment. If the expenditure was as a result of transactions between 'connected persons', the expenditure is reduced by the amount of any rebate but no further reduction arises under CAA 2001, s. 62(2).

> ### Example
>
> Sara acquired a large computer system for £90,000 plus VAT of £15,750 during her basis period to 31 December 2005. Her initial VAT recovery was, say, one-half of £15,750, ie £7,875, and she claimed 25 per cent writing-down allowances on the reducing-balance basis. In 2006 her recovery rate rose, so using the five-year adjustment period she

received, say, a £900 additional VAT rebate, and in 2007 it fell so she incurred a £300 additional VAT liability.

Sara's capital allowances were as follows:

	£
Year to 31/12/05	
Expenditure (£90,000 + 50% x £15,750)	97,875
WDA 25% × £97,875	(24,469)
Carried forward	73,406
Year to 31/12/06	
Additional VAT rebate	(900)
Expenditure qualifying for WDAs	72,506
WDA 25% × £72,506	(18,126)
Carried forward	54,380
Year to 31/12/07	
Additional VAT liability	300
Expenditure qualifying for WDAs	54,680
WDA 25% × £54,680	(13,670)
Carried forward	41,010

Legislation: CAA 2001, s. 235–239

238-200 Short-life assets

An additional VAT liability may arise after a balancing allowance was given under CAA 2001, s. 86(1) for an asset affected by the 'short-life asset' rules (see 205-000). If that balancing allowance did not take into account such liability, then a further balancing allowance arises and equals that liability.

If the short-life asset pool period expires before the asset is disposed of, the asset transfers to the main pool of assets. Section 86 disregards any additional VAT rebate in deciding whether a balancing charge has arisen.

Legislation: CAA 2001, s. 240

238-300 Connected persons

Anti-avoidance provisions can prevent some connected persons from using the capital allowance rules to obtain 'undue' allowances. For example, the provisions can substitute market value when connected persons transfer an asset between them for an amount in excess of that value. CAA 2001, s. 217 and 218, in restricting capital allowances, take into account any additional VAT liability incurred.

Legislation: CAA 2001, s. 241–242

Plant and Machinery

238-400   Contracts where a person may become plant owner

Anti-avoidance provisions can prevent some persons obtaining capital allowances where under a contract a person will or may become the owner of plant or machinery (CAA 2001, s. 216: see 220-500). Section 216, in restricting capital allowances, takes into account any additional VAT liability incurred.

Legislation: CAA 2001, s. 241–245

238-500   No disposal value

Anti-avoidance provisions can stop persons receiving capital allowances if, for example, a person disposes of plant or machinery but continues to use the item for his qualifying activity and no disposal value is otherwise taken into account: see 220-500). If the open market value of the item for these purposes is VAT inclusive, then any additional VAT liability is disregarded. However, in determining the amount of capital expenditure incurred on the provision of plant or machinery for the purposes of s. 218(3), that expenditure includes any additional VAT liability but excludes any additional VAT rebate, to the extent that they would otherwise be disregarded.

Legislation: CAA 2001, s. 218(3), CAA 2001, s. 242(5), (6)

238-600   Time additional VAT liability incurred

As regards the time any additional VAT liability is incurred or rebate made, see 120-200.

Partnerships and successions

240-000   Overview

Special rules apply for most capital allowance purposes to partnerships, successions and transfers (CAA 2001, Pt. 12, Ch. 4) but these are specifically not applied in relation to plant and machinery claims. Instead, the plant and machinery legislation contains its own rules on the subject of partnerships and successions.

Legislation: CAA 2001, s. 263ff.

240-010   Partnerships

Most partnership changes are not treated as a cessation. For the purposes of the plant and machinery regime, this applies where:

• a qualifying activity has been set up and is carried on in partnership;

- there has been a change in the persons carrying on the qualifying activity, and
- where the activity is a trade or property business, one of the following conditions (as appropriate) is met:
  - (for income tax), a person carrying on the business immediately before the change continues to carry it on after the change;
  - (for corporation tax), a company carrying on the business in partnership immediately before the change continues to carry it on in partnership after the change.

As a general principle, partnership changes are ignored for the purposes of claiming plant and machinery allowances, as long as the change does not have the effect that all the partners permanently cease to carry on the trade or other qualifying activity. The present partners step into the shoes of their predecessors and any first-year allowance, writing-down allowance or annual investment allowance is made to the present partners. The amount of any allowance is calculated as if anything done by the former partners had in fact been done by the present ones. Any balancing charge or allowance is made to the partners at the time of the balancing event.

In the case of company reconstructions, allowances and charges are made to or on the successor as if the predecessor had continued to carry on the trade (ICTA 1988, s. 343(2)). This is subject to the provisions of ICTA 1988, s. 343(1) (at least a three quarter share of the trade to belong to the same persons, etc.) and to ICTA 1988, s. 343A (company reconstructions involving business of leasing plant or machinery).

Legislation: CAA 2001, s. 263; s. 558

240-020 Partnership using property of partners

Capital allowances are available in respect of plant or machinery owned by a partner but used in the partnership trade. Where, however, one partner owns an item of plant and lets it to the partnership, or otherwise receives a payment from the partnership that is deductible in calculating the profits of the trade, then the partner or partners owning the item in question are not treated as using it for the purposes of a trade. As such, no allowances will be due to them under the partnership rules.

Where relief is due as above, capital allowances are given to (and balancing charges made on) the partnership rather than the individual partner. Claims must be made in the partnership return, a point known to be of practical difficulty in some large professional partnerships where the partners are too busy to attend diligently to their personal tax affairs.

Tax relief is available for interest paid on a loan taken out by a partner to buy plant or machinery that would qualify for relief under the provisions outlined above. Relief would be due for the year in which the loan is taken out and for the following three years of assessment.

Special rules ensure that where ownership of an item of plant or machinery passes from one partner to another within a single partnership, no disposal value is to be brought into account. This applies whether the item is sold or given to the acquiring partner.

Legislation: CAA 2001, s. 263–264, 557(a); ITA 2007, s. 383, 388

240-100 Successions

The main capital allowances legislation dealing with sales between connected persons does not apply to capital allowances on plant or machinery.

The tax treatment of transfers between connected persons will depend on whether or not the transfer takes place as part of a 'succession' to a trade. Broadly, there is a succession where a business changes ownership as a going concern, as distinct from a transfer of ownership of a particular asset.

Where there is no succession then the actual treatment will follow normal principles, even if the parties are connected with each other.

Where there is a succession, the tax treatment will be determined under special rules. An election may in some circumstances be made to transfer the assets at their tax written-down value, ie at a value which produces no balancing adjustment either way. In this case, the actual sale or transfer figure will be ignored and the successor will calculate future capital allowances or balancing charges 'as if everything done to or by the predecessor had been done to or by the successor'. The election may be made where all of the following conditions apply:

- there is a succession to a qualifying activity; and
- where income tax is concerned, no person carrying on the trade or property business immediately before the succession continues to carry it on after the succession;
- where corporation tax is concerned, no company carrying on the trade or property business in partnership immediately before the succession continues to carry it on in partnership after the succession;
- the predecessor and successor are connected;
- both the predecessor and the successor are within the charge to UK tax on the profits of the qualifying activity;
- the successor is not a dual resident investment company (as defined in ICTA 1988, s. 404);
- an election is made by notice to a Revenue officer within two years of the date of the succession, whether or not any plant or machinery has actually been sold by the time the election is made;
- CAA 2001, s. 561 (transfer of UK trade to a company in another member state) does not apply.

The legislation (CAA 2001, s. 266(5)) contains a special definition of 'connected' for these purposes. Broadly, the parties will be connected if they are so connected within the terms of

CAA 2001, s. 575, or if there is common control or (in the case of a partnership) they share a common partner.

Where there is a succession to a trade but no election is made in accordance with the above provisions, assets transferred will normally be deemed to be sold at open market value. No first-year allowance or annual investment allowance is due to the purchaser. The rule against obtaining such allowances would include, for example, the case where a business is incorporated, which would be a succession between connected persons and therefore caught under this provision.

Where the succession is by a beneficiary of a deceased person's estate (whether under a will or under the intestacy rules) then an election can be made to take over the assets at the tax written-down value of the deceased person.

In relation to any succession occurring on or after 5 December 2005, however, there is a restriction on the effect of CAA 2001, s. 266 where the transferor and transferee are both carrying on a business of leasing plant and machinery (CAA 2001, s. 267A). The restriction applies, for corporation tax only, if:

(1) on any day ('the relevant day'), a person ('the predecessor') carries on a business of leasing plant or machinery;

(2) another person ('the successor') succeeds to the business on the relevant day; and

(3) the predecessor and the successor make an election under CAA 2001, s. 266.

In such a case, neither CAA 2001, s. 266(7) (in connection with special rate expenditure) nor s. 267 (effect of election under s. 266) has effect in relation to any plant or machinery which, in determining whether the business is a business of leasing plant or machinery on the relevant day, is qualifying plant or machinery. The definition of the term 'business of leasing plant or machinery' depends on whether or not the business is carried on in partnership.

If it is not so carried on then the term is defined in accordance with FA 2006, Sch. 10, para. 6.

If the business *is* carried on in partnership then the definition is in accordance with FA 2006, Sch. 10, para. 25.

Subject to the rules outlined above, there are also restrictions on the allowances available where the sale is between connected persons, where it is a sale and leaseback transaction, or where it appears that the sole or main benefit of the transaction is to obtain allowances. In such cases, the purchaser cannot obtain any first-year allowances and the amount on which he will be able to claim writing-down allowances is restricted to the disposal value that the vendor has to bring into account. This anti-avoidance legislation is contained in CAA 2001, Part 2, Ch. 17.

Plant and Machinery

There appears to be an overlap in the legislation between the CAA 2001, s. 266 rules described above and ICTA 1988, s. 343 (which applies to company reconstructions where, broadly, there is at least 75 per cent common ownership of the predecessor and successor company). Section 343(2) provides that the trade is not to be treated as permanently discontinued, and the successor company is entitled to claim capital allowances 'as if the successor had been carrying on the trade since the predecessor began to do so and everything done to or by the predecessor had been done to or by the successor'. No balancing allowance or charge is produced in these specific circumstances. Arguably, no election under CAA 2001, s. 266 is needed where the reconstruction falls within the terms of ICTA 1988, s. 343.

CAA 2001, s. 104E, 108 and 265 (disposal value in connection with special rate expenditure, effect of disposal to connected person on overseas leasing pool and general provisions about successions) do not apply if an election is made under this section. However, see a restriction on this provision at 267A.

Legislation: CAA 2001, s. 265–268, 567(1)

Anti-avoidance provisions

240-500   Overview

Various anti-avoidance rules apply to prevent the artificial exploitation of the plant and machinery legislation. Some of these rules are addressed in their relevant context in this commentary. There are also, though, some anti-avoidance sections that are of more general application.

The anti-avoidance provisions relating to plant and machinery are mostly contained in CAA 2001, Pt. 2, Ch. 17, and the legislation divides these provisions up as follows.

- Relevant transactions (beginning at CAA 2001, s. 213).
- Restrictions on allowances (beginning at CAA 2001, s. 214).
- Finance leases and certain operating leases (beginning at CAA 2001, s. 219).
- Sale and finance leasebacks (beginning at CAA 2001, s. 221).
- Sale and leaseback: election for special treatment (beginning at CAA 2001, s. 227).
- Finance leaseback: parties' income and profits (beginning at CAA 2001, s. 228A).
- Disposal of plant or machinery subject to lease where income retained (beginning at CAA 2001, s. 228K).
- Miscellaneous and supplementary (beginning at CAA 2001, s. 229).

All assessments and adjustments of assessments may be made as are necessary to implement these provisions (CAA 2001, s. 231).

Some of the more common avoidance issues are considered in detail below. There then follows a summary of the changes that were introduced in Finance Acts 2008 and 2009.

Connected persons

One person is treated as connected with another for the purposes of these anti-avoidance rules if they would be treated as connected under CAA 2001, s. 575. However, the definition is extended for these purposes in connection with a public authority.

Where plant or machinery is sold and leased back by way of a finance lease, and the asset has at any time been acquired by one public authority from another otherwise than by purchase (for instance, on a reorganisation), the public authority from whom the asset is acquired is treated as connected with the acquiring authority and with every person connected with the acquiring authority. 'Public authority' includes the Crown or any government or local authority.

Legislation: CAA 2001, s. 232

240-520   Relevant transactions

Intended effect of legislation

The first category of anti-avoidance provisions applies to 'relevant transactions'. The HMRC guidance (at CA 28100) summarises the intended effect of the legislation by saying that it is aimed at 'a case where the taxpayer is using the capital allowance legislation in a way that it was not intended to be used.' The following example is used to illustrate the sort of transaction that might be caught:

> 'Frank and Jesse are brothers. They are both motor dealers. Frank buys a car transporter for £120,000 and adds the expenditure to his pool of qualifying expenditure. He sells the car transporter to Jesse for £200,000. Frank brings a disposal value of £120,000 (sale proceeds £200,000 restricted to cost, £120,000) to account. Jesse claims FYA at 40% on the £200,000 he has paid Frank for the car transporter. If this scheme worked the brothers would have obtained PMAs on expenditure of £200,000 for a car transporter that cost them £120,000.'

HMRC go on to say (at CA 28200) that:

> 'The purpose of the legislation is to prevent the acceleration or uplift in capital allowances on a sale between connected persons, a sale and leaseback or a transaction to obtain allowances. Any transfer of the benefit of a hire purchase type contract that could give rise to an acceleration or uplift in capital allowances may therefore be caught by the anti-avoidance legislation.'

Definition of 'relevant transactions'

The term 'relevant transactions' is widely defined (CAA 2001, s. 213(1)) to include:

- the sale of an asset;
- the entering into of a hire purchase contract (where the buyer shall or may become the owner of the asset on performance of the contract); and
- the assignment of the benefit of a hire purchase contract.

Plant and Machinery

These various circumstances are considered in detail at 240-540. There is no general test of motive, so a sale to a connected party is caught even if it was intended to be an arm's length transaction.

HMRC is not prepared to accept a legalistic interpretation of the term 'assignment' in the third bullet point above. Their view is that such a legal argument does not hold water and that 'any transfer of the benefit of a hire purchase type contract that could give rise to an acceleration or uplift in capital allowances may therefore be caught by the anti-avoidance legislation'.

HMRC accepts that these anti-avoidance rules should not be applied if a hire purchase type contract is novated or otherwise replaced with a new contract before the asset has been brought into use by the lessee or any connected person and:

- neither the lessee nor any person connected with the lessee has claimed or will claim capital allowances in respect of the asset;
- the obtaining of an acceleration in the allowances due to the lessee, or to any person connected with the lessee or the lessor, is not a main object of the leasing arrangements'

The HMRC guidance goes on to comment on the treatment of assets built by the trader for use in the trade. According to HMRC's application of the rules:

'the anti-avoidance legislation applies unless the trade includes the manufacture or supply of assets of that class and the asset was manufactured in the ordinary course of that trade. An item which is not part of the usual stock in trade of the manufacturer or which is purpose built for use as a fixed asset of the trade is unlikely to fall within this exclusion.'

Legislation: CAA 2001, s. 230

Other material: CA 28200

Buyer's expenditure

The concept of a buyer's expenditure is given its own definition for the purposes of the anti-avoidance rules in CAA 2001, Pt. 2, Ch. 17:

(1) where there is a sale of plant or machinery from a Seller ('S') to a Buyer ('B') then B's expenditure under the relevant transaction is simply the price paid for the asset;

(2) where B enters into a contract with S providing that B shall or may become the owner of plant or machinery on the performance of the contract, then B's expenditure under the relevant transaction is B's *capital* expenditure under the contract so far as it relates to the plant or machinery. This is obviously not the same as the total expenditure as the latter would include the revenue hire cost;

(3) where S assigns to B the benefit of a contract providing that S shall or may become the owner of plant or machinery on the performance of the contract then B's expenditure under the relevant transaction is B's capital expenditure under the contract so far as it relates to the plant or machinery or is by way of consideration for the assignment. HMRC illustrate this as follows:

'George is buying a car under a 3 year hire purchase contract. The total price is £18,000 plus hire charges. After one year when he has made capital payments of £12,000 he assigns the contract to Andrew for £10,000. Andrew's capital expenditure is £16,000 (£6,000 that he will pay under the contract plus £10,000 paid for the assignment).'

Legislation: CAA 2001, s. 213(2)

Assets received as a gift

Under the provisions of CAA 2001, s. 14, a person may be treated as incurring capital expenditure on plant or machinery received as a gift (see 161-000). If B is treated under that provision as having incurred expenditure on plant or machinery, and the donor was S, then for the purposes of these anti-avoidance provisions, B is treated as having incurred capital expenditure on the provision of the plant or machinery by purchasing it from S.

The effect of this is that if the asset has appreciated since it was bought, and the giver was connected with the recipient, the recipient's qualifying expenditure is restricted to the giver's cost.

Legislation: CAA 2001, s. 213(3)

240-540   Restrictions on allowances

Circumstances in which allowances may be restricted

The concept of 'relevant transactions', together with the general aim of the anti-avoidance legislation, is considered at 240-520. Restrictions may apply where the relevant transaction is:

- between connected persons (CAA 2001, s. 214); or
- for the sole or main benefit of getting plant and machinery allowances (CAA 2001, s. 215); or
- a sale and leaseback transaction (where the buyer leases the asset back to the seller or to a person connected with the seller (CAA 2001, s. 216)).

First-year allowances and annual investment allowances

Where the rules apply, no first-year allowances or annual investment allowances are given to the purchaser (and, if they have been given, are to be withdrawn).

Legislation: CAA 2001, s. 217

Restriction on buyer's allowances

In cases other than that of a sale and *finance* leaseback transaction (see 240-580), the buyer's allowances are restricted as follows.

Plant and Machinery

If the seller has to bring in a disposal value as a result of the relevant transaction then the buyer's available qualifying expenditure is restricted to that figure.

If the seller does *not* have to bring a disposal value to account as a result of the relevant transaction then the buyer's qualifying expenditure is restricted to the lowest of:

(1)   the market value of the asset;

(2)   the amount of any capital expenditure incurred by the seller on the asset; and

(3)   if a person connected with the seller incurred capital expenditure on the asset, that person's capital expenditure.

HMRC acknowledge that:

> 'these restrictions do not apply if the asset is new, the seller's business includes manufacturing or supplying assets of that class and the asset is sold as part of the seller's normal business.'

HMRC illustrate this with an example of a man who runs an electrical store and who sells his sister a new computer from his stock. If his sister claims plant and machinery allowances on the computer the restrictions on allowances do not apply; she can claim allowances on the price she pays.

Legislation: CAA 2001, s. 218

Other material: CA 28300

240-560   Hire purchase

Under the normal rules, where an asset is acquired on hire-purchase, the hirer is entitled to capital allowances on the full amount of its anticipated expenditure under the hire-purchase agreement at the time the asset is brought into use. This rule is replaced in cases where the hirer leases the asset out under a finance lease, so that capital allowances are given on the asset as expenditure is incurred and not before.

Legislation: CAA 2001, s. 229(3)

Assignment of contract

If a person buying an asset under a hire purchase type contract assigns the benefit of the contract then the disposal value normally depends on whether or not the asset has been brought into use. If it has not been brought into use, the disposal value consists of any capital sums received as consideration, compensation, damages or insurance for the person's rights under the contract or the asset. If it has been brought into use, the disposal value also includes expenditure that the person was treated as having incurred when the asset was brought into use (but that that person has not yet actually incurred).

HMRC acknowledges that this could produce an unfair result if these anti-avoidance provisions apply. In such cases, the buyer's qualifying expenditure cannot be more than the seller's disposal value. If the asset has not been brought into use by the seller then the disposal value takes no account of the capital expenditure still to be incurred under the contract. HMRC illustrates this with the following example:

'Lowell runs a trucking company. He enters into a hire purchase contract to buy a truck for £50,000. He pays the deposit of £10,000 but then decides that he doesn't like the truck, so he does not bring it into use and assigns the contract to Jackson, a connected person, for £10,000.

Lowell's disposal value is £10,000. Jackson will incur capital expenditure of £50,000 on the truck (£10,000 paid to Lowell plus £40,000 still to be paid under the contract).

If the normal rules about assignment of a hire purchase contract applied Jackson's qualifying expenditure would be restricted to Lowell's disposal value, £10,000 even though Jackson will incur capital expenditure of £50,000 on the truck.'

The HMRC guidance goes on to explain how this is resolved (based on CAA 2001, s. 229(2)):

'So the normal rules do not apply where a person buying an asset under a hire purchase contract assigns the benefit of the contract in a transaction where the provisions of this Chapter apply. Instead the seller's disposal value is – for the purposes only of this Chapter –

- any capital sums received as consideration, compensation, damages or insurance for the persons rights under the contract or the asset, and
- any capital expenditure still to be incurred under the contract.

The seller is treated as incurring any capital expenditure still to be incurred under the contract in the chargeable period in which the contract is assigned.

In the example above, the £40,000 still to be incurred under the contract is added to Lowell's qualifying expenditure and disposal value. Lowell's disposal value becomes £50,000, and this is the limit on Jackson's qualifying expenditure.'

Other material: CA 28700

Finance leasing

If plant or machinery is acquired on hire-purchase for finance leasing then the person is not treated as incurring the balance of the capital expenditure under the contract when the plant or machinery is brought into use. However, different rules again apply if the person subsequently assigns the benefit of the contract. In that case, the disposal value is again the total of any capital sums received as consideration, compensation, damages or insurance for the person's rights under the contract and any capital expenditure still to be incurred under the contract. For the purposes of bringing that disposal value into account the person is treated as having incurred the balance of the capital expenditure under the contract.

Legislation: CAA 2001, s. 229(5)

240-580   Anti-avoidance measures introduced in the *Finance Act* 2008

Provisions were introduced in FA 2008, Sch. 20 to counter four different types of avoidance scheme involving plant and machinery allowances, each of which had been notified to HMRC under the tax avoidance disclosure rules. The nature of these provisions is fairly

Plant and Machinery

obscure but the following paragraphs reproduce comments from the *Explanatory Notes* to the 2008 Finance Bill (and the numbering of those Notes has been retained).

Sale and finance leaseback

'153. Rules were introduced in 1997 to counter tax avoidance involving the sale and finance leaseback of plant or machinery by entities that were not liable to tax. These arrangements relied on the purchaser being able to claim capital allowances on the plant or machinery it leased back to the original owner. These rules allow most of the sales proceeds to be received untaxed but restricted the capital allowances that could be claimed by the purchaser. Abuse of these rules was partially countered in 2004 but new arrangements continue to exploit the 1997 rules.

154. This measure removes the 1997 legislation that is being exploited, as well as some of the rules introduced in 2004. In order to ensure that the avoidance countered in 1997 does not return, leases in sale (or lease) and finance leaseback arrangements will be brought within the scope of the long funding lease rules.'

Long funding leases

'155. A lessor under a long funding lease is not entitled to claim capital allowances on the cost of the leased asset but, to compensate, it is only taxed on a small proportion of the lease rental income. Avoidance schemes have been developed that purport to establish an alternative deduction for the cost of the leased asset, particularly by claiming that the leased asset has been acquired on trading account. If these arrangements are effective they will generate a tax loss approximately equivalent to the cost of the leased asset, even though there is no commercial loss.

156. This measure will put beyond doubt that where a deduction is available for the cost of the leased asset the rules restricting the amount of taxable income do not apply.'

Mismatched lease chains

'157. A business may act as an intermediate lessor, leasing in plant or machinery under one lease and leasing it out under another. Such leases may be broadly similar but be designed to exploit differences in the way in which leases are taxed. The avoidance involves arrangements which allow the business, as lessee, to deduct all the lease rentals payable under the lease but, as lessor, to be taxed on only a small portion of the rentals receivable. This creates a tax loss where there is no commercial loss.

158. This measure will ensure that rentals received by intermediate lessors will be taxed on the same basis as rentals paid and that intermediate lessors are taxed on their commercial profits.'

Lease premiums etc

'159. Businesses were granting leases on plant or machinery for a premium plus a small amount of annual rentals. The premium, which is commercially broadly equivalent to the sale of the asset, escaped tax because it is not brought in as a disposal receipt for capital allowances purposes and little or no tax would be payable under the chargeable gains regime.

160. This measure will ensure that premiums and similar sums will be taxed as income of the lessor where they are not otherwise taxable as income or as a capital allowances disposal receipt.'

240-585   Anti-avoidance measures introduced in *Finance Act 2009*

Further capital allowance anti-avoidance measures were introduced in 2009. In particular, see:

- 200-520 (special rate cars), and
- 220-550 (leases).

240-620   Latent capital allowances

A further raft of anti-avoidance measures will be introduced in Finance Act 2010 but with retrospective effect to 21 July 2009.

According to a written ministerial statement issued in July 2009, the purpose of the measures will be 'to prevent tax avoidance through the transfer of an entitlement to benefit from capital allowances on plant and machinery ... where the tax written down value ... exceeds its balance sheet value ("latent capital allowances")'.

What is envisaged here is that a company (Tradingco) may disclaim substantial capital allowances, so that the tax value remains at a high level even though the commercial value of the plant has depreciated. If Tradingco is sold to another group, the trade may be brought to an end and the plant may be sold so as to give rise to a substantial balancing allowance. This will create a trading loss that may be offset by way of group relief against the profits of other companies in the group that acquired Tradingco.

According to the statement, the measures will apply in two sets of circumstances:

1   where there is a change of ownership of a company as part of arrangements, one of the main purposes of which, is to transfer to the purchasing group an entitlement to benefit from the latent capital allowances available to the company which is purchased.

2   where there is a change in ownership or profit-shares of a consortium company, or partnership involving companies, as part of arrangements where one of the main purposes is to transfer the entitlement to benefit from the latent capital allowances.

According to further HMRC guidance (see *www.hmrc.gov.uk/avoidance/ca-technote.pdf*), the effect of the legislation will be that 'the latent capital allowances only remain available to be set against the profits that they would have been able to be set against had the arrangements not been entered into. They will not be available to reduce profits of the purchaser's group or the group acquiring an interest or increased interest in a consortium company or partnership'.

The website referred to above gives examples of circumstances where HMRC would argue that there is a tax avoidance motive. It also confirms, however, that 'the proposed legislation will not apply to normal commercial arrangements, for example where a group acquires a company with a view to carrying on its trade as a going concern and the acquisition of any latent capital allowances is an incidental part of that acquisition'.

Rent factoring

241-900   Rent factoring

Rent factoring is the sale of the right to receive rents. The lump sum received for that right may be taxable as income but, if carefully structured, may instead be taxed as a capital receipt. For a business with unusable capital losses, rent factoring can transform the value of those losses.

Where the right to receive rental income from a lease of plant or machinery is sold or otherwise disposed of, the proceeds are therefore now brought into charge as taxable income.

The rules relating to leases of plant and machinery apply to individuals, trusts and companies, whereas the early rules affect only companies.

Legislation: ICTA 1988, s. 785A

Other material: CTM 36610ff.

Anti-avoidance

The rules were further tightened in relation to arrangements for transfers of rights entered into from 12 March 2008. The intention of the revised rules was to counter possible tax avoidance which might be achieved by means of transferring to another person the right to taxable rentals under a plant or machinery lease. The revised provision does not apply to the transfer of rentals receivable under a long funding finance lease. Nor will s. 785A apply in circumstances where the market value of the transferred rights is brought into account in computing income. Subject to these points, the rules as amended from 12 March 2008 apply to the value of the rights transferred at the time of the transfer, thus for example ensuring that the tax charge would still arise if the consideration is receivable after the lessor has migrated from the UK.

According to the *Explanatory Notes* to the 2008 Finance Bill, 'attempts to avoid section 785A have included arguments that, for example, where the rentals are transferred to a partnership of which the transferor is a member, the transferor remains entitled to beneficial ownership of the rentals and so there has been no transfer. This new subsection [s. 785A(5ZA)] puts it beyond doubt that such a transfer falls within the scope of section 785A'.

Fixtures

Where plant or machinery is a fixture (see the Chapter headed 'Plant and Property', which begins at 250-000) then it is potentially caught under both headings as it may be deemed to be part of the land. HMRC have given guidance on the matter, which may be summarised as follows.

A lease of land may include plant or equipment that is affixed to the associated land; HMRC give the example of a building (land) with air conditioning equipment installed (plant and equipment fixture). The HMRC guidance is that any lease that includes the land and its fixtures in this way will be a 'lease of land', though this will be subject to ICTA 1988, s. 774A to 774G.

If, on the other hand, a fixture is the subject of a lease that does not include the land, (eg an equipment lease per CAA 2001, s. 174) the transaction will be treated as a lease of plant or machinery and will be subject to ICTA 1988, s. 785A. This could arise either because the lessor explicitly excludes the land from any equipment lease or because he has no interest in the land to which the equipment has become affixed and so cannot include such rights in any lease.

With more complex arrangements, the position may be less clear cut.

HMRC have confirmed that a transfer of a trade within the meaning of ICTA 1988, s. 343, or the transfer of an asset between connected parties on a succession (CAA 2001, s. 266), will not give rise to a charge under ICTA 1988, s. 785A.

Legislation: ICTA 1988, s. 785A

Other material: CTM 36610ff.

First-year tax credits

242-000   Payable enhanced capital allowances: overview

Overview

Loss-making companies that incur expenditure on certain 'green' technology from 1 April 2008 are able to claim a cash payment if they are otherwise unable to use their losses against their own profits or those of a group member. The rules are directly linked to the first-year allowances that are given for expenditure on 'energy-saving' plant and machinery (see 185-330) or 'environmentally beneficial' plant and machinery (see 185-550). In this way, companies may gain an immediate cash payment rather than carrying losses forward indefinitely in the hope of obtaining relief when profits start to be realised in the future.

The main features of the relief are as follows:

Plant and Machinery

- relief may be given for expenditure incurred on technology currently qualifying for 100 per cent FYAs under either CAA 2001, s. 45A or s. 45H (respectively covering 'energy-saving' plant and 'environmentally beneficial' plant);
- the scheme is available to companies (small, medium or large) but not to excluded companies, or to any sole traders, partnerships or other entities;
- companies may surrender losses, to the extent that they are attributable to qualifying expenditure, so as to receive a percentage of the surrendered loss as a tax-free cash payment from HMRC;
- a payment in respect of a first-year tax credit is not treated as income of the company for any tax purpose.

Legislation: CAA 2001, s. 262A, Sch. A1, para. 23

Excluded companies

A company is excluded from these rules if, at any time during the chargeable period in question, it is able to make a claim under any of the following provisions of the *Income and Corporation Taxes Act* 1988:

- s. 488: rent, etc of co-operative housing associations disregarded for tax purposes;
- s. 489: rent, etc of self-build societies disregarded for tax purposes;
- s. 505: exemption from tax for charitable companies; or
- s. 508: exemption from tax for scientific research organisations.

Anti-avoidance

A restriction is applied to the extent that a transaction is 'attributable to arrangements entered into wholly or mainly for a disqualifying purpose'. Arrangements are said to be entered into for a disqualifying purpose if their main object, or one of their main objects, is to enable a person to obtain a first-year tax credit to which the person would not otherwise be entitled, or a tax credit that is greater than would otherwise be the case.

The term 'arrangements' is defined to include 'any scheme, agreement or understanding, whether or not legally enforceable'.

Legislation: CAA 2001, Sch. A1, para. 28

Relevant first-year expenditure

A company's 'relevant first-year expenditure' means expenditure incurred from 1 April 2008 that is first-year qualifying expenditure under CAA 2001, s. 45A or s. 45H. In determining the date on which the expenditure was incurred for these purposes, the special rules relating to pre-trading expenditure are ignored. Expenditure treated as first-year qualifying expenditure by virtue of CAA 2001, s. 236 (additional VAT liability) is not 'relevant first-year expenditure'.

The concept of 'relevant first-year expenditure' does not include expenditure incurred after 31 March 2013, but the Treasury may by order substitute a later date.

Legislation: CAA 2001, Sch. A1, para. 3

Surrenderable loss

A company is said to have a 'surrenderable loss' in a given chargeable period if, in that period:

- the company is entitled to a first-year allowance under CAA 2001, s. 45A or s. 45H;
- the expenditure is incurred on or after 1 April 2008;
- it is incurred for the purposes of a qualifying activity of which the profits are chargeable to corporation tax; and
- the company incurs a loss in that qualifying activity (see 242-080).

The amount of the surrenderable loss is the lower of the following figures:

- so much of the loss incurred in carrying on the qualifying activity as is unrelieved; or
- the amount of the FYA claimed in respect of the relevant first-year expenditure in the chargeable period in question.

Legislation: CAA 2001, Sch. A1, para. 1

Terminology

The draft legislation uses the term 'first-year tax credits' to describe the tax relief. The guidance issued by HMRC in December 2007, on the other hand, opted for 'payable enhanced capital allowances'.

242-020   First-year tax credits: companies only

The scheme of payable tax credits for enhanced capital allowances is available only for companies.

HMRC (in their technical document issued in December 2007) gave two reasons for this approach:

(1)   firstly, HMRC argue that

> 'the compliance and Exchequer risks involved in extending the scheme to self-employed individuals and partnerships would require complex additional rules, which would make the system too cumbersome, and undermine the scheme;'

(2)   secondly, the justification is given that the availability of early trade losses relief (under ITA 2007, s. 72) – a benefit not available to companies – makes it 'appropriate . . . to offer payable ECAs to incorporated businesses only'.

Plant and Machinery

277

Overseas companies

Companies incorporated outside the UK, but paying CT here because they are trading here through a permanent UK establishment, are entitled to claim the relief. Companies may claim relief for expenditure incurred in any of their qualifying activities, thus including not only trades but also property businesses and investment management activities of companies with investment businesses.

242-040   First-year tax credits: calculating the credit

Companies receive a percentage of the surrenderable loss as a cash payment. That percentage figure is set at 19 per cent (whatever the size and corporation tax rate of the company), though the Treasury has the power to substitute a higher or lower figure. According to HMRC, 'the rate at which ECA tax credits are paid is linked to the small companies rate of corporation tax, which will be 21% from April 2008'. The guidance goes on to say that 'the Government considers that the proposed payment rate will be attractive to companies that are loss making, particularly in start-up situations where the losses may not be utilised for two or more years'.

That percentage figure is applied to the amount of the 'surrenderable loss' (see 242-000).

> ### Example 1
>
> A company makes a profit of £50,000, before deduction of £90,000 of qualifying first-year allowances. The company thus has a loss of £40,000 which can be surrendered. The company will then receive a cash payment of £7,600 (£40,000 at 19 per cent).

> ### Example 2
>
> A second company makes a loss of £50,000, before deduction of £90,000 of qualifying first-year allowances. The company thus has an overall loss of £140,000 and its surrenderable loss is £90,000. The company can therefore surrender that £90,000 in return for a cash payment of £17,100 (£90,000 at 19 per cent).

A company may claim either the whole or part of the tax credit.

Legislation: CAA 2001, Sch. A1, para. 2

Upper limit on the tax credit

A cap is set on the amount of the payment that can be claimed (not the amount of loss that can be surrendered). This cap is set, for each chargeable period, at the *higher* of:

- the level of the company's PAYE and NIC liabilities for payment periods ending in the chargeable period for which the claim has been made (see below); and

- £250,000.

Legislation: CAA 2001, Sch. A1, para. 2

Total amount of PAYE and NIC liabilities

The link to PAYE liabilities is on the grounds that the relief should in principle be restricted to those companies that have 'an active commercial presence in the UK'. Nevertheless, the alternative cap of £250,000 reflects the intention that the potential payments should still be attractive for companies that have relatively low payroll costs but that still wish to invest in new technology. With a 19 per cent rate, the £250,000 figure means that even a company with minimal PAYE and NIC liabilities will be able to surrender losses of up to £1,315,789.

The total amount of PAYE and NIC liabilities includes the following for any given payment period:

(1)   the amount of income tax for which the company is required to account to HMRC for that period under the PAYE regulations, disregarding any deduction the company is authorised to make in respect of child tax credit or working tax credit; and

(2)   the Class 1 National Insurance Contributions for which the company is required to account to HMRC for that period, disregarding any deduction the company is authorised to make in respect of payments of statutory sick pay, statutory maternity pay, child tax credit or working tax credit.

For these purposes, a payment period is defined to mean a period ending on the fifth day of a month for which the company is liable to account to HMRC for income tax and NIC.

Legislation: CAA 2001, Sch. A1, para. 17

242-060   First-year tax credits: setting the credit against other liabilities

HMRC must pay to the company the amount specified in a claim. However, such an amount (and any interest thereon) may be applied first in discharging any corporation tax liability of the company.

If the company has any outstanding PAYE or Class 1 NIC liabilities for the chargeable period to which the claim relates then HMRC may withhold payment of the credit until those liabilities have been met.

If an enquiry is under way, HMRC has the discretion to make provisional payments while the return is still under enquiry, as they deem appropriate. Subject to that discretion, no payment of the credit needs to be made until the enquiries are completed.

Legislation: CAA 2001, Sch. A1, para. 18

Plant and Machinery

242-080   First-year tax credits: incurring a loss in a qualifying activity

The concept of 'incurring a loss' is specifically defined for these purposes, in relation to certain types of qualifying activity. Although the rules were only introduced in 2008, the terminology was amended in 2009 as a result of the enactment of the Corporation Tax Act 2009.

UK property business

This definition applies where the qualifying activity is a UK property business but is *not* a furnished holiday lettings business and the company is *not* an insurance company.

In this case, references to a loss incurred in carrying on the qualifying activity are interpreted for these purposes as referring to a loss incurred in carrying on that part of the business (if any) to which ICTA 1988, s. 392A (UK property business losses) applies.

Legislation: CAA 2001, Sch. A1, para. 5

Overseas property business

This definition applies where the qualifying activity is an overseas property business but is *not* an insurance company.

In this case, references to a loss incurred in carrying on the qualifying activity are interpreted for these purposes as referring to a loss incurred in carrying on that part of the business (if any) to which ICTA 1988, s. 392B (losses from overseas property business) applies.

Legislation: CAA 2001, Sch. A1, para. 6

Insurance companies

This definition applies where the qualifying activity is a UK property business or an overseas property business and the company is an insurance company.

In this case, references to a loss incurred in carrying on the qualifying activity are interpreted for these purposes as referring to a loss that is treated under ICTA 1988, s. 432AB(3) (for the purposes of ICTA 1988, s. 76) as expenses payable that are to be brought into account at Step 3 of ICTA 1988, s. 76(7).

A special rule applies if the insurance company is treated under ICTA 1988, s. 432AA as carrying on more than one UK or overseas property business. In that case, references to a loss incurred in carrying on the qualifying activity are to be construed in accordance with ICTA 1988, s. 432AB(4) (aggregation of losses).

Legislation: CAA 2001, Sch. A1, para. 7

Managing investments

This definition applies where the qualifying activity is that of managing the investments of a company with investment business.

In this case, a company is said for these purposes to incur a loss in carrying on that activity in a given chargeable period if, in that period, the sum of the expenses and charges mentioned in CTA 2009, s. 1223(2) exceeds the amount of the profits from which those expenses and charges are deductible. The amount of the loss is then the amount of that excess.

Legislation: CAA 2001, Sch. A1, para. 8

Life assurance business

This definition applies where the qualifying activity is life assurance business and the profits of that business are charged to tax under the I minus E basis.

In this case, a company is said for these purposes to incur a loss in carrying on that activity in a given chargeable period if, in that period, an amount is to be carried forward to a succeeding chargeable period under ICTA 1988, s. 76(12). The amount of the loss is then the amount that falls to be carried forward in that way.

Legislation: CAA 2001, Sch. A1, para. 9

242-100   Unrelieved losses

The concept of an 'unrelieved loss' is specifically defined for these purposes, in relation to certain types of qualifying activity, as follows.

Trades and holiday letting businesses

The rules described in this paragraph determine the amount of unrelieved losses for trading and furnished holiday businesses, other than for certain insurance and life assurance companies, regarding which, see CAA 2001, Sch. A1, para. 14 and 16 respectively.

The unrelieved loss is the loss after deduction of any of the following:

(1)   any amount for which the company could claim relief (whether or not it in fact does so) under ICTA 1988, s. 393A(1)(a) (loss relief against profits of the same chargeable period);

(2)   any other relief actually obtained by the company making a claim under ICTA 1988, s. 393A(1)(b) or s. 393B(3) (losses set against profits of an earlier chargeable period);

(3)   any loss that the company could surrender (whether or not it in fact does so) under ICTA 1988, s. 403(1) (surrender of relief to group or consortium members);

(4)   any loss surrendered under a relevant tax credit provision (see below), and

Plant and Machinery

(5) any amount set off against the loss under ICTA 1988, s. 400 (write-off of government investment).

For these purposes, no account is taken of any losses brought forward (under ICTA 1988, s. 393(1)) or carried back (under ICTA 1988, s. 393A(1)(b) or s. 393B(3)). Certain losses incurred on leasing contracts (within the meaning of ICTA 1988, s. 395) are also ignored.

Relevant tax credit provision

The following are relevant tax credit provisions:

- CTA 2009, Pt. 13, Ch 2 or 7 (tax credits for expenditure on research and development or vaccine research etc);
- CTA 2009, Pt. 14, Ch 3 (tax credits for remediation of contaminated land), and
- CTA 2009, Pt. 15, Ch 3 (film tax credits).

Legislation: CAA 2001, Sch. A1, para. 11

UK property businesses

The rules described in this paragraph determine the amount of unrelieved losses for UK property businesses that are not trading or furnished holiday businesses, and are not within Sch. A1, para. 14 (certain insurance company businesses).

The unrelieved loss is the loss after deduction of any of the following:

(1) any amount for which the company could claim relief (whether or not it in fact does so) under ICTA 1988, s. 393A(1)(a) (loss relief against profits of the same chargeable period);

(2) any loss that the company could surrender (whether or not it in fact does so) under ICTA 1988, s. 403(1) (surrender of relief to group or consortium members);

(3) any loss surrendered under CTA 2009, Pt. 14, Ch 3 (remediation of contaminated land), and

(4) any amount set off against the loss under ICTA 1988, s. 400 (write-off of government investment).

For these purposes, no account is taken of any losses brought forward under ICTA 1988, s. 392A(2).

Legislation: CAA 2001, Sch. A1, para. 12

Overseas property business

The rules described in this paragraph determine the amount of unrelieved losses for overseas property businesses that are not within CAA 2001, Sch. A1, para. 14 (certain insurance company businesses).

The unrelieved loss is the loss after deduction of any amount set off against the loss under ICTA 1988, s. 400 (write-off of government investment).

For these purposes, no account is taken of any losses brought forward under ICTA 1988, s. 392B(1).

Legislation: CAA 2001, Sch. A1, para. 13

Insurance companies

The rules described in this paragraph determine the amount of unrelieved losses for insurance companies whose qualifying activity is a UK property business or an overseas property business. The amount of the unrelieved loss depends on whether or not there is an amount that falls to be carried forward to a succeeding chargeable period under ICTA 1988, s. 76(12) (carrying forward unrelieved expenses: see below).

If no amount falls to be carried forward to a succeeding chargeable period under that section then no amount of the loss is unrelieved.

If such an amount does fall to be carried forward to a succeeding chargeable period under that section then the amount of the unrelieved loss cannot exceed the total amount which so falls to be carried forward. Subject to that, the unrelieved loss is calculated as the amount of the loss, reduced by:

- the amount of any loss surrendered under CTA 2009, Pt. 14, Ch 3 (tax credits for remediation of contaminated land); and
- any amount set off against the loss under ICTA 1988, s. 400 (write-off of government investment).

Legislation: CAA 2001, Sch. A1, para. 14

ICTA 1988, s. 76(12)

In determining whether there is an amount which falls to be carried forward under ICTA 1988, s. 76(12), it is necessary to disregard any amounts brought forward from an earlier chargeable period and treated for the purposes of s. 76 as expenses payable which fall to be brought into account:

(1) in accordance with Step 7 in s. 76(7), by virtue of a previous application of s. 76(12) or (13); or

(2) in accordance with Step 3 in s. 76(7), by virtue of the provisions of CTA 2009, s. 391(3)(b) (loan relationships deficit carried forward and so brought into account).

Managing investments

The rules described in this paragraph determine the amount of unrelieved losses for companies whose qualifying activity is that of managing the investments of a company with investment business.

The amount of the loss that is unrelieved is the amount of the loss, reduced by:

Plant and Machinery

283

(1)   any loss that the company could surrender (whether or not it in fact does so) under ICTA 1988, s. 403(1) (surrender of relief to group or consortium members); and

(2)   any amount set off against the loss under ICTA 1988, s. 400 (write-off of government investment).

No account is taken of any amount brought forward from an earlier chargeable period under CTA 2009, s. 1223.

Legislation: CAA 2001, Sch. A1, para. 15

Life assurance businesses

The rules described in this paragraph determine the amount of unrelieved losses for companies whose qualifying activity is life assurance business and where the profits of that business are charged to tax under the 'I minus E' basis.

The amount of the loss that is unrelieved is the amount of the loss (see 242-080), reduced by:

(1)   any loss that the company surrenders under CTA 2009, Pt. 14, Ch 4 (tax credits for remediation of contaminated land); and

(2)   any amount set off against the loss under ICTA 1988, s. 400 (write-off of government investment).

Legislation: CAA 2001, Sch. A1, para. 16

ICTA 1988, s. 76(12)

For these purposes, it is necessary to disregard any amounts brought forward from an earlier chargeable period and treated for the purposes of s. 76 as expenses payable which fall to be brought into account:

(1)   in accordance with Step 7 in s. 76(7), by virtue of a previous application of s. 76(12) or (13); or

(2)   in accordance with Step 3 in s. 76(7), by virtue of the provisions of CTA 2009, s. 391(3)(b) (loan relationships deficit carried forward and so brought into account).

242-150   Restriction on losses carried forward

To avoid double relief of the same loss, a loss that is surrendered to receive a tax credit is treated as used up or reduced accordingly for the purposes of other provisions that might have given tax relief for the loss.

The amount of the loss for which relief is restricted in this way is normally the whole of the surrenderable loss. However, where less than that amount is claimed (eg because it would otherwise exceed the upper limit: see 242-040) then the amount of the loss surrendered is a corresponding proportion of the surrenderable loss.

The provisions for which loss relief is restricted in this way are listed as follows:

(1)   For trading and furnished holiday businesses, where CAA 2001, Sch. A1, para. 21 or 22 (see (5) and (6) below) do not apply: ICTA 1988, s. 393 (relief of trading losses against future profits).

(2)   For companies whose qualifying activity is that of managing the investments of a company with investment business: CTA 2009, s. 1223 (relief of expenses and charges against future profits).

(3)   For companies whose qualifying activity is a UK property business other than a furnished holiday business, and where para. 21 (see (5) below) does not apply: ICTA 1988, s. 392A(2) (relief of UK property business losses against future profits).

(4)   For companies whose qualifying activity is an overseas property business, and where para. 21 (see (5) below) does not apply: ICTA 1988, s. 392B (relief of overseas property losses against future profits).

(5)   For companies whose qualifying activity is a UK property business or an overseas property business and, in any given chargeable period, all of the following conditions are met (Sch. A1, para. 21):

(a)   the company's loss in carrying on that activity is one that is treated under ICTA 1988, s. 432AB(3) (for the purposes of ICTA 1988, s. 76) as expenses payable that are to be brought into account at Step 3 of ICTA 1988, s. 76(7);

(b)   an amount falls to be carried forward to a succeeding chargeable period under ICTA 1988, s. 76(12) (carrying forward unrelieved expenses on income); and

(c)   the company claims a first-year tax credit for the chargeable period.

(6)   A special rule applies where the qualifying activity is life assurance business and the profits of that business are charged to tax under the I minus E basis. In that case, the following are both reduced by the amount of the loss surrendered (Sch. A1, para. 22):

(a)   the amount that may be carried forward under ICTA 1988, s. 76(12) from a chargeable period in which the company claims a first-year tax credit; and

(b)   the amount that may be brought into account for the next chargeable period in accordance with Step 7 in ICTA 1988, s. 76(7).

Legislation: CAA 2001, Sch. A1, para. 19–22

242-200   Clawback of first-year tax credits

Overview

Loss-making companies that incur expenditure on certain 'green' technology are in certain circumstances able to claim a cash payment in return for surrendering those losses: see 242-000. Special provisions ensure that the cash payment can be clawed back if a company buys an asset, claims first-year allowances, claims a cash payment and then sells the asset.

Legislation: Sch. A1, para. 24, 25

Computation of clawback

The appropriate part of the loss is treated as if it were not a surrenderable loss and 'the amount of first-year tax credit paid to the company in respect of the restored loss is to be treated as if it ought never to have been paid'. This amount, known as the 'restored loss', is calculated using the following formula:

$$(LS - OERPM) - (OE - DV) - ARL$$

where:

LS	is the amount of loss surrendered under this Schedule in the chargeable period for which the first-year tax credit was paid;
OERPM	is the amount (or the aggregate of the amounts) of the original expenditure on the retained tax-relieved plant and machinery after the item is disposed of;
OE	is the aggregate of the amount of the original expenditure on the item disposed of, and the amounts of the original expenditure on any items of tax-relieved plant and machinery which the company has previously disposed of;
DV	is the aggregate of the disposal value of the item disposed of, and the disposal values of any items of tax-relieved plant and machinery which the company has previously disposed of; and
ARL	is the amount of the restored loss (or the aggregate of the amounts of the restored loss) on any previous application of this paragraph.

The effect is to claw back fully if the assets are sold at cost or above, but to allow relief to the extent that the assets are sold at a loss. In HMRC's words (from the *Explanatory Notes* to Finance Bill 2008):

> 'Broadly, the loss restored is the amount of the loss surrendered less the amount of tax-relieved plant and machinery that the company still owns. From this is deducted any loss that the company has made on the disposal of the asset (this is a cumulative figure of losses on tax-relieved plant and machinery disposals). Finally, any losses already restored are taken into account. Where the formula gives a negative figure then the amount of the restored loss is nil.'

Example

A company incurs a loss of £350,000, calculated as a loss before capital allowances of £50,000, and first-year allowances of £300,000. The company has a surrenderable loss of £300,000. 19 per cent of the latter figure gives £57,000 and this amount is duly claimed.

Supposing that the company then sells an asset that was part of the £300,000 but that cost £75,000, and receives £20,000 for the asset. Using the terminology as above, the following figures apply:

LS = £300,000
OERPM = £225,000
OE = £75,000
DV = £20,000
ARL = £nil

> This gives a net figure of £20,000 ((£300,000 − £225,000) − (£75,000 − £20,000) − £nil)). The result is that £3,800 of the tax credit is repayable, and HMRC is empowered to make all such assessments and adjustments of assessments as are necessary to recover the amount.

The clawback provisions only apply if a company sells, within the clawback period, an item on which first-year allowances have been claimed. That period begins when the relevant expenditure is incurred and ends four years after the end of the chargeable period for which the tax credit was paid. A clawback is only made if the original expenditure on the company's tax-relieved plant and machinery remaining after the disposal is less than the amount of the loss that was surrendered for a first-year tax credit.

This may seem to produce a surprising result if the original claim for FYAs converted a profit to a loss.

Example

A company incurs a loss of £350,000, calculated as a profit of £50,000 less first-year allowances of £400,000. The company has a surrenderable loss of £350,000. 19 per cent of the latter figure gives £66,500 and this amount is duly claimed.

Supposing that the company then sells an asset that was part of the £400,000 but that cost £40,000. The amount of the original expenditure on the retained tax-relieved plant is £360,000. As this is still more than the loss surrendered of £350,000, this does not trigger the clawback provisions (whatever the disposal proceeds) – a possibly surprising result.

The author has spoken with HMRC about this matter, however, and it has been confirmed that this principle is correct: it errs in favour of the company but has the advantage of allowing the one formula (see above) to cover all situations without further complicating the matter.

Legislation: Sch. A1, para. 26, 27

Concept of tax credit being 'paid'

The clawback provisions apply to an as yet unpaid amount of first-year tax credit (but which is payable for a chargeable period) as they do to an amount of first-year tax credit which has been paid. References to a credit being paid include any case where the amount is applied in discharging any corporation tax liability of the company.

Legislation: Sch. A1, para. 24(7), 25(2)

Disposals

A disposal of an asset includes any event listed in CAA 2001, s. 61(1) (see 190-750). A company is also treated as disposing of an asset for these purposes if there is a change in the ownership of the item in relation to which a 'continuity of business provision' applies. This

Plant and Machinery

concept is defined to mean 'an enactment under which anything done to or by the company which ceases to be the owner of the item is treated, for the purpose of making allowances and charges under [CAA 2001], as having been done to or by the person who becomes the owner of the item'. The *Explanatory Notes* to the 2008 Finance Bill explain that:

> 'Broadly, this is one where there has been a transfer of a business and, for the purposes of making allowances and charges under CAA, anything done to or by the transferor is treated as having been done to or by the transferee.'

The general rule is that the disposal value of the item is the value that is required to be brought into account by the company in respect of the item. However, market value is used for these purposes (whether or not it would otherwise have to be used) if the company disposes of the item to a connected person for less than market value. Similarly, market value is substituted if there is a change in the ownership of the item in relation to which a continuity of business provision applies.

Legislation: Sch. A1, para. 25

Amendments

As noted above, HMRC is empowered to make all such assessments (and adjustments of assessments) as are necessary to claw back any tax relief in accordance with these provisions.

If the company has made a tax return and then becomes aware that it has become incorrect as a result of these clawback provisions, it must notify HMRC accordingly within three months of so becoming aware.

Fixtures

245-000   Fixtures: background

A fundamental condition for obtaining plant and machinery allowances is that, as a result of the expenditure incurred, the asset must belong to the person incurring the expenditure.

This requirement appears in CAA 2001, s. 11 headed 'General conditions as to availability of plant and machinery allowances'. Subsection (4)(b) imposes the condition on the person incurring the expenditure that he should own the plant or machinery as a result of incurring that expenditure.

In most cases, it will be obvious, when a person incurs capital expenditure on an asset, that the asset will then belong to him. However, there is one specific set of circumstances – concerning fixtures in leased property – where a complication arises. The tenant may incur costs on assets that become affixed to the building and that thereby become the legal property of the landlord: the tenant does not own the assets and the landlord has not incurred the expenditure, so on the face of it neither party can claim allowances.

The importance of the concept of belonging was brought out in the case of *Stokes v Costain Property Investments Ltd*. That case decided that the terms 'belong' and 'belonging' were ordinary English words to be interpreted in an ordinary sense. If somebody merely had the right to use an asset for a limited period then it could not be said that the asset belonged to him. It was not an apt use of language to say that landlords' fixtures belonged to a leaseholder: 'he cannot remove them from the building, he cannot dispose of them except as part of the hereditament and subject to the provisions of the lease and for the term of the lease'.

A distinction was made between such landlords' fixtures on the one hand and a tenant's fixture on the other. An example given was of a machine tool which might be fixed down for the better use of the tool rather than as an improvement to the premises. Such a tool could be removed by the tenant when the lease expired and could thus be said to belong to the tenant. The case had been primarily concerned, however, with the installation in leasehold buildings of major items of plant including lifts and central heating equipment amounting to nearly £500,000 out of a total construction cost of nearly £3,000,000.

It became clear from that case that the law was unsatisfactory. Firstly, there had been a perception that this was not an issue the Revenue had taken in practice. Secondly, a substantial amount of expenditure had been incurred and yet nobody would obtain any tax relief for that expenditure. As Fox LJ said in the Court of Appeal dismissing the company's case:

> 'I cannot, however, regard the state of the law as satisfactory. The purpose of the statutory provisions must be to encourage investment in machinery and plant. In this case very large sums were expended on such investment but, under the enactment as it stands, nobody will receive the tax allowance in respect of it. The freeholder will not, because the freeholder did not incur the expenditure and is not carrying on the trade and the taxpayer will not because the items did not belong to the taxpayer. The Revenue are unable to suggest any policy reason why a person in the position of the taxpayer should be refused relief. It is to be hoped that the ambit of the legislation will be reconsidered.'

The legislation was indeed reconsidered with new rules introduced in 1985 which are now contained, as subsequently amended, in Chapter 14 of CAA 2001, s. 172–204 of which come under the heading of 'fixtures'. The rules apply 'to determine entitlement to allowances under this Part in respect of expenditure on plant or machinery that is, or becomes, a fixture'. The legislation contains special rules to determine when a person is treated for tax purposes as owning a fixture or as ceasing to own one.

Legislation: CAA 2001, s. 172–204

Cases: *Stokes v Costain Property Investments Ltd* [1984] BTC 92

Other material: CA 26000ff.

Integral features

Allowances for certain 'integral features' (see 247-000ff) are given at a slower rate of 10 per cent per year rather than the standard 20 per cent. In brief, the amended fixtures rules apply to expenditure incurred from 1 or 6 April 2008 (for corporation tax and income tax respectively). Integral features are not eligible for short life asset treatment but *do* qualify for annual investment allowances, meaning that full up-front relief may be given for expenditure of up to £50,000 in the year.

The reduced rate of allowances for fixtures needs to be seen alongside the abolition of industrial (and agricultural) buildings allowances, however. Many types of buildings (such as hotels) that have hitherto been the subject of IBA claims may in future need a different approach, with a greater emphasis on claiming allowances on fixtures. In the past, the choice between an IBA claim and a fixtures claim, in relation to certain expenditure, may have been partly simply a question of timing of tax relief. Once IBAs have been completely withdrawn, the choice will be between tax relief or no tax relief at all.

245-100   Fixtures: definitions

Fixtures

For these purposes, a fixture is defined as 'plant or machinery that is so installed or otherwise fixed in or to a building or other description of land as to become, in law, part of that building or other land'. The legislation also specifically provides that a fixture includes 'any boiler or water-filled radiator installed in a building as part of a space or water heating system'.

The following terms are also defined for the purposes of the fixtures legislation:

- relevant land;
- equipment lease;
- equipment lessor;
- equipment lessee;
- lease; and
- interest in land.

Each of the above terms is considered below.

Legislation: CAA 2001, s. 173(1)

Relevant land

This is defined as a building or other description of land of which the fixture becomes part. As far as boilers and water-filled radiators are concerned, the relevant land is the building in which that item is installed as part of a space or water heating system.

Legislation: CAA 2001, s. 173(2)

Other material: CA 26100

Equipment lease

There will be an 'equipment lease' where:

* a person incurs capital expenditure on plant or machinery for leasing;
* an agreement is entered into for the lease of that asset to another person, whether directly or indirectly from the person incurring the expenditure;
* the asset in question becomes a fixture; and
* the agreement does not provide for the asset to be leased as part of the relevant land.

Where a lease is entered into 'under or as a result of' such an agreement then this too will be treated as an equipment lease.

Legislation: CAA 2001, s. 174(1), (2)

Other material: CA 26200

Equipment lessor

This is defined as the person from whom the plant or machinery will be leased (whether directly or indirectly) under the terms of the equipment lease.

Legislation: CAA 2001, s. 174(3)

Other material: CA 26200

Equipment lessee

This is the person to whom the plant or machinery is leased under the terms of the equipment lease.

Legislation: CAA 2001, s. 174(3)

Other material: CA 26200

Plant and Machinery

Lease

This subsection gives a definition of lease other than in the context of leasing plant or machinery. For the purposes of the fixtures legislation, a lease includes either of the following:

- a leasehold estate in land (or, in Scotland, a lease of land), whether a head-lease, a sub-lease or an under-lease; or
- an agreement to acquire such an estate (or, as the case may be in Scotland, such a lease).

Legislation: CAA 2001, s. 174(4)

Other material: CA 26100

Interest in land

For the purposes of the fixtures legislation, an 'interest in land' is defined to mean any of the following:

- the fee simple estate in the land or an agreement to acquire such an estate;
- in relation to Scotland, the interest of the owner or an agreement to acquire such an interest;
- a lease;
- an easement or servitude or an agreement to acquire an easement or servitude; or
- a licence to occupy land (but see below).

Where an interest in land is conveyed or assigned by way of security, but is subject to a right of redemption, then the person with that right (rather than the creditor) is treated as having the interest in land.

The HMRC manuals put the first two bullets above into simpler terms in saying that they include 'the freehold interest, or an agreement to acquire the freehold interest, or the Scottish equivalent of either of the above'.

Although the legislation referred to above states that the term 'interest in land' includes 'a licence to occupy land', this is qualified in the HMRC manuals so that it applies only to an exclusive licence. This is justified in the following terms:

'A licence to occupy is a permission to enter and remain on land for such a purpose as enables the licensee to exert control over the land. It is this level of control that suggests that a licence to occupy must be an exclusive licence. The idea of exclusive occupancy is also supported in part by ratings law that says that there can only be one occupier of land. It follows that where a person can enter onto land for a subordinate purpose, such a licence of entry would be something less than a licence to occupy.'

The conveying or assigning by way of security of an interest in land will not normally cause a loss of the interest in land for these purposes, as long as the transaction is subject to a right of redemption. For example, if a mortgage is secured on a property it is possible that the freehold interest will be held in law by the person who grants the mortgage. The borrower will remain the owner for the purposes of this legislation.

Legislation: CAA 2001, s. 175

Other material: CA 26100

245-200   Persons treated as owning fixtures

For the reasons outlined at 245-100 above, the legislation has to create a pretence of legal ownership so that capital allowances can be given for fixtures in an appropriate manner.

The legislation recognises various categories of person who may be deemed to own fixtures. The relevant headings of the legislation are as follows and each is then considered in detail below:

- persons with an interest in relevant land having fixtures for the purposes of a qualifying activity (CAA 2001, s. 176);
- equipment lessors (CAA 2001, s. 177–180);
- energy services providers (CAA 2001, s. 180A);
- purchasers of land with fixtures (CAA 2001, s. 181, 182 and 182A);
- incoming lessees (CAA 2001, s. 183 and 184).

245-210   Persons with interest in relevant land

CAA 2001, s. 176 deals with the fundamental issue of fixtures. Under the section, a person is treated as owning a fixture as a result of expenditure he has incurred if the following conditions are met:

- he incurs capital expenditure on plant or machinery;
- the asset is for the purposes of a qualifying activity that he is carrying on;
- the plant or machinery in question becomes a fixture; and
- the person incurring the expenditure has an interest in the relevant land at the date on which the asset becomes a fixture.

This will typically apply where the tenant pays for the installation of a heating or air conditioning system in the property. These rules do not apply, however, where an equipment lessor and an equipment lessee jointly elect for different treatment, as discussed below.

It is possible for two or more people with different interests in the land to be treated under the above rules as owning the same fixture. In this case, only one interest in land is to be taken into account. The legislation therefore provides a pecking order, as follows:

- if one of the interests is an easement or servitude, or an agreement to acquire an easement or servitude, then that is the interest to be taken into account;
- failing that, if one of the interests is a licence to occupy land then that is the interest to be taken into account;

- in any other case, different rules apply for Scotland and elsewhere. In this case, the legislation reads as follows:

  '(a) except in Scotland, the interest to be taken into account is the interest which is not in reversion (at law or in equity and whether directly or indirectly) on any other interest in the relevant land which is held by any of the persons referred to in subsection (2); and

  (b) in Scotland, the interest to be taken into account is the interest of whichever of the persons referred to in subsection (2) has, or last had, the right of use of the relevant land.'

The above can be summarised by saying that it is the person with the lowest interest, eg the leaseholder rather than the freeholder – who is treated as owning the fixture.

If two or more people share the same (lowest) interest in the relevant land, and they both or all incur expenditure on the same fixture, each can claim allowances on the part of the expenditure that they incur. This would apply, for example, if two tenants share the cost of a lift installation or of air conditioning.

Legislation: CAA 2001, s. 176

Other material: CA 26150

245-220 Equipment lessors

There can be problems with the allowances available to equipment lessors where the plant or machinery in question becomes a fixture. In accordance with the principles outlined above, it might be the case that no allowances would be due without special legislation. The expenditure may have been incurred by the equipment lessor but he does not own the plant or machinery because, in law, it has become a fixture in a property in which the lessor has no interest. The lessee will not be able to claim capital allowances because he has not incurred the expenditure.

To resolve this, an election may be made whereby the equipment lessor may be treated as owning a fixture as a result of incurring capital expenditure on plant or machinery that is subject to an equipment lease (in which case the equipment lessee will be treated as not owning it). This rule will only apply if both the equipment lessor and the equipment lessee so elect. An election is not possible if those two persons are connected. An election has effect from the time the equipment lessor incurs the expenditure, unless the special rules apply only by virtue of CAA 2001, s. 178 (see below) in which case the equipment lessor will be treated as incurring the expenditure when the equipment lessee begins to carry on the qualifying activity.

For corporation tax purposes, the time limit for making an election is two years from the end of the relevant chargeable period. For income tax, an election must be made within the normal time limit for amending a tax return for the year of assessment in which the relevant chargeable period ends.

For the election to be available, one of the following conditions (with all of its sub-conditions) must be met:

(1) The equipment lessee is leasing the plant or machinery (which is not for use in a dwelling house) for the purposes of a qualifying activity to be carried on by him (CAA 2001, s. 178);

   (a) a sub-condition is that the equipment lessee, had he incurred the expenditure, would have been entitled to allowances under the general rule described above.

(2) The equipment lessor has a right to sever the fixture that is not part of a building (ie it is fixed to land rather than to a building or part of a building); in this case, the following sub-conditions need to be met:

   (a) the equipment lessee must have an interest in the land when taking possession of the plant or machinery under the equipment lease;
   (b) the terms of the lease must specify the right to sever the fixture, and thereby take ownership of it, at the end of the lease period;
   (c) the nature of the fixture, and the way that it is fixed, must not 'to a material extent' prevent it from being used in the same way in other premises;
   (d) the equipment lease must be such as would fall, under generally accepted accounting practice, to be treated as an operating lease; and
   (e) the equipment lease must not be for the lease of the plant or machinery for use in a dwelling house.

(3) The equipment lease is part of an 'affordable warmth programme', and expenditure was incurred by 31 December 2007;

   (a) to qualify under this heading, the plant or machinery had to consist of boilers, radiators, heat exchangers or heating controls which must have been installed as part of an overall central heating or hot water system. The agreement for the lease had to obtain formal approval under the affordable warmth programme (and the approval must not have been withdrawn).

Legislation: CAA 2001, s. 177–178

Other material: CA 26200

245-230   Energy services providers

Overview

In certain circumstances, a provider of energy services will be treated as the owner of a fixture as a result of capital expenditure he has incurred on the provision of plant or machinery that has become a fixture. This will apply where there is a formal energy services agreement and where both the provider of the energy services and the client (who must not be connected persons) elect that this treatment should apply.

Legislation: CAA 2001, s. 180A

Plant and Machinery

Energy services agreement

An energy services agreement is defined as an agreement entered into by an 'energy services provider' and another person ('the client'). To be an energy services provider, a person must be carrying on a qualifying trade consisting wholly or mainly of the provision of energy management services. This latter concept (energy management services) is not defined by statute and it will therefore be for the courts to discern its actual meaning.

The agreement must make provision for all of the following with a view to either saving energy or increasing energy efficiency:

- the design of plant or machinery or one or more systems incorporating plant or machinery;
- the obtaining or installing of the plant or machinery;
- the operation of the plant or machinery;
- the maintenance of the plant or machinery; and
- a link between the payments in respect of the operation of the plant or machinery and the energy savings or increased efficiency resulting from the plant or machinery.

It is therefore envisaged that the plant or machinery may belong to the energy services provider but be used by the client. If the plant or machinery does not become a fixture, then the energy services provider will qualify for plant and machinery, provided that the normal rules are met. The special rules are needed to deal with the case where the plant or machinery becomes a fixture.

Legislation: CAA 2001, s. 175A

Conditions for special treatment

The conditions that must be met if an energy services provider is to be treated as the owner of a fixture are as follows:

- there must be a formal energy services agreement;
- the energy service provider must incur capital expenditure on the provision of plant or machinery;
- that expenditure must be incurred under the energy services agreement;
- the plant or machinery must become a fixture;
- when the plant or machinery becomes a fixture, the client must have an interest in the relevant land (as defined at CAA 2001, s. 173(2), ie the land to which the fixture becomes part) so that the client could in different circumstances be treated as the owner of the fixture;
- when the plant or machinery becomes a fixture, the energy services provider must not have an interest in the relevant land – so that without this legislation, the energy services provider could not be treated as the owner of the fixture;
- the plant or machinery must not be provided for leasing;
- the plant or machinery must not be provided for use in domestic property;
- the plant or machinery must be operated wholly or substantially by either the energy services provider or a connected person. Although 'substantially' is not specifically

defined, HMRC's view is that the rules are designed only to apply to providers who actively manage the equipment on a day-to-day basis as part of a comprehensive energy management service. This is to be distinguished from normal commercial leasing arrangements;

- the energy services provider and the client must not be connected (see CAA 2001, s. 575(1));
- the energy services provider and the client must elect for the deemed ownership to be given to the energy services provider. (Such an election is necessary to ensure that a unilateral claim by the energy services provider does not disentitle the client to any allowances in respect of the fixture.); and
- it must be the case that the client would have been entitled to an allowance under CAA 2001, s. 176 if he (rather than the energy services provider) had incurred the capital expenditure.

At first sight, this seems an unnecessary provision, as the conditions for allowances under CAA 2001, s. 176 are already embedded in the conditions in CAA 2001, s. 180A. However, s. 176 contains rules to determine which of two (or more) potential claimants, both with an interest in the relevant land, is entitled to be treated as the owner of a fixture. Section 180A therefore ensures that the client would have been the person treated as the owner under these rules.

Further, the tie-breaker rules in s. 176(2) and (3) will not apply for plant and machinery which fall into the technology class 'combined heat and power'.

Provided that the above conditions are met, the energy services provider is treated as the owner of the fixture from the time that he incurs the capital expenditure. Such deemed ownership is, however, subject to the provisions in CAA 2001, Pt. 2, Ch. 14 that deem a person to be ceasing to own the fixture.

If an energy services provider is claiming allowances for a fixture (and is therefore treated as the owner of the fixture) no person with an interest in the land can be treated as the owner of the fixture (and thereby claim capital allowances).

Legislation: CAA 2001, s. 172(3), 176, 180A(4); SI 2001/2541, reg. 6

Election

Any election made under the new rules is subject to the normal time limits – presumably in relation to the energy services provider – so that claims must be made:

- in the case of corporation tax, within two years of the end of the chargeable period in which the capital expenditure on the plant or machinery was incurred (or deemed to be incurred); and
- in the case of income tax, by 31 January some 22 months after the end of the tax year in which ends the chargeable period in which the expenditure on the plant or machinery was incurred.

Legislation: CAA 2001, s. 180A(5)

Plant and Machinery

Related provisions

CAA 2001, s. 192A, mirroring the rule for equipment leases in s. 192 provides for the cessation of an energy service provider's deemed ownership of a fixture. This will occur if the energy service provider assigns its rights under the energy services agreement or if a person discharges the client's financial obligations under the energy services agreement. If both occurrences arise, then it is the earlier which counts. References to 'client' include any person to whom the original client may have assigned its obligations so that the rules can apply with respect to the effective client and not just the original contracting party.

CAA 2001, s. 195A and 195B similarly mirror the rules for equipment leases in CAA 2001, s. 194 and 195. CAA 2001, s. 195A provides that if s. 192A(2)(a) applies (energy services provider assigns its rights under the agreement), then the assignee will be treated as incurring expenditure on the fixture and as the owner of the fixture. This paves the way for the assignee to qualify for capital allowances subject to the other conditions in the Chapter being met. Further, the assignee will be treated as an energy services provider so as to allow subsequent assignees (for example) to be covered by this rule.

CAA 2001, s. 195B provides that if s. 192A(2)(b) applies (discharge of client's financial obligations) because it is the client that pays the capital sum, then the client may be treated as the owner of the fixture from the time that the capital sum is paid. (The term 'client' includes assignees of the original client.)

Items 8A and 8B in the table of disposal events and corresponding disposal values (CAA 2001, s. 196(1)), deal with the deemed cessations of ownership provided by CAA 2001, s. 192A(2).

If the energy services provider ceases to be treated as the owner because it assigns its rights then the energy services provider must bring into account the consideration for the assignment as the disposal value.

If the energy services provider ceases to be treated as the owner because the client's financial obligations are discharged and the discharge is by payment of a capital sum, then the energy services provider must bring into account the capital sum as the disposal value. (If the discharge is not by a capital sum, it is assumed that a fair market value would be used as a disposal value in accordance with CAA 2001, s. 61(2), Table, item 7.)

The word 'client' in item 8B also applies to the assignee of a client (CAA 2001, s. 196(4A)).

Such disposal values are subject to the normal rules (CAA 2001, s. 62(1)) limiting disposal values to the original qualifying expenditure.

A person who becomes aware that a tax return has become incorrect as a result of CAA 2001, s. 182A(2) has three months to notify HMRC of the amendment that needs to be made (CAA 2001, s. 203(2)(b)). Any failure to give this notice would make the person liable to a penalty under TMA 1970, s. 98.

Legislation: s. 192A(2)

245-240   Purchasers of land with fixtures

A purchaser of an interest in relevant land is in certain circumstances treated as the owner of fixtures on that land. The basic conditions are that:

- plant or machinery has become a fixture;
- a person acquires an interest in the relevant land; and
- that interest in the land was in existence before the purchaser acquired it.

These rules may apply:

- where the purchaser of the land pays consideration for the interest in the land that is to be treated as whole or in part as expenditure on a fixture (CAA 2001, s. 181); or
- where the purchaser of the land discharges certain obligations of the equipment lessee (CAA 2001, s. 182); or
- where the purchaser pays to discharge certain obligations under an energy services agreement (CAA 2001, s. 182A).

The rules will not apply if any person has, immediately after the time of the acquisition, a prior right in relation to the fixture. A person will have such a prior right if he:

- is treated as the owner of the fixture immediately before the acquisition as a result of incurring expenditure on the provision of the fixture;
- is not so treated as a result of CAA 2001, s. 538 (contribution allowances for plant and machinery);
- is entitled to an allowance in respect of that expenditure; and
- does make or has made a claim in respect of that expenditure.

The point is well illustrated by the following example as reproduced from the HMRC manual (HMRC using 'PMAs' as shorthand for plant and machinery allowances):

'Xanadu Properties Plc owns the freehold of Kane House, an office block, which it leases to its tenant, Budokan Computers. Xanadu Properties Plc installs central heating before it leases Kane House to Budokan computers and claims PMAs on the central heating. Budokan Computers installs air conditioning on which it claims PMAs. After the air conditioning has been installed in Kane House, Budokan assigns its lease to Shangri-la Software for a capital sum.

After the assignment of the lease Shangri-la Software can claim PMAs on the air conditioning but not on the central heating. Xanadu Properties Plc has the freehold interest in the relevant land (Kane House) and a prior right in relation to the central heating. The air conditioning is different. Budokan computers had a leasehold interest in the relevant land for the air conditioning when they installed it and they no longer have it after the assignment of the lease. Shangri-la Software has acquired that interest.'

Plant and Machinery

It may be necessary to apportion the overall capital sum between part relating to the fixture and part to the rest of the land. The parties can determine the matter by making an election under CAA 2001, s. 198 (see 245-700). Failing this, a 'just and reasonable apportionment' will be made under CAA 2001, s. 562, irrespective of the wording of any documents relating to the purchase and sale. From April 2008, it will also be necessary to consider (for either an election or an apportionment) which of the assets constitutes integral features.

Legislation: CAA 2001, s. 181ff.

Other material: CA 26250

Purchaser of land discharging obligations of equipment lessee

The CAA 2001, s. 181 rules are extended to include cases where a purchaser acquires an interest in land after an item of plant or machinery becomes a fixture. The purchaser will be treated as incurring expenditure on that fixture if:

- that interest in land was in existence before the purchaser acquired it;
- before the acquisition, the plant or machinery was let under an equipment lease; and
- the purchaser pays a capital sum, in connection with the acquisition, to discharge the obligations of the equipment lessee under the equipment lease.

The same condition regarding no prior rights applies here as described above.

Legislation: CAA 2001, s. 182

Purchaser of land discharging obligations of client under energy services agreement

The CAA 2001, s. 181 rules are also extended to include cases where a purchaser acquires an interest in land after an item of plant or machinery becomes a fixture in cases where the plant or machinery was – before the transaction – provided under an energy services agreement (see 185-350). The purchaser will be treated as incurring expenditure on that fixture if:

- that interest in land was in existence before the purchaser acquired it;
- before the acquisition, the plant or machinery was provided under an energy services agreement; and
- the purchaser pays a capital sum, in connection with the acquisition, to discharge the obligations of the client under an energy services agreement.

The same condition regarding no prior rights applies here as described above.

Legislation: CAA 2001, s. 182A

245-250   Incoming lessees

In certain circumstances, where a lease is granted after plant or machinery has become a fixture, the lessee will be treated as if he were the owner of the fixture as a result of incurring expenditure.

The rules for this treatment to apply depend on whether or not the lessor is entitled to an allowance in respect of the fixture for the chargeable period in which the lease is granted (or would be entitled to such an allowance if he were within the charge to tax).

Where the lessor is or would be entitled to allowances, the rules in CAA 2001, s. 183 apply. In this case, the lessor and lessee (as long as they are not connected) can make an election to transfer deemed ownership, and therefore capital allowances, from lessor to lessee. The fixture is treated as being acquired by the incoming lessee for so much of the premium as relates to the fixture. The election must be signed by both lessor and lessee and must be submitted within two years of the date on which the lease takes effect. The conditions for an election in these circumstances are as follows:

- a person ('the lessor') with an interest in the relevant land grants a lease after plant or machinery has become a fixture;
- the lessor is entitled to an allowance in respect of the fixture for the chargeable period in which the lease is granted, or would be if he were within the charge to tax;
- the consideration given by the lessee for the lease includes a capital sum that (in whole or in part) is treated as expenditure on the provision of the fixture; and
- the lessor and the lessee are not connected persons.

Ownership of the fixture is then deemed to pass to the lessee from the time when the lease is granted.

Where the lessor is not (or would not be) entitled to allowances, the rules of CAA 2001, s. 184 apply. In this case, the lessee is automatically treated as owning the fixture as long as the fixture has not previously been used for the purposes of a qualifying activity by the lessor or by any person connected with him. The HMRC manuals explain that 'the sort of case where this can happen is where the interest held by the lessor is held on trading account'.

The lessee is not entitled to allowances in these circumstances if, when the interest is acquired, any person has a prior right in relation to the fixture.

Legislation: CAA 2001, s. 183–184

Other material: CA 26350

Plant and Machinery

245-300   Restrictions on qualifying expenditure

Qualifying expenditure on fixtures is restricted if a claim has already been made under the plant and machinery rules, the IBA rules or the research and development rules. A different statutory formula is used in each case.

Prior plant and machinery claim

In the case of fixtures on which plant and machinery allowances have been claimed, the broad effect of the legislation is to restrict the allowances available on a fixture to the original cost of that fixture plus any allowable installation costs. The HMRC view is that 'it is the responsibility of the taxpayer to obtain and provide details of the past owner and the disposal value'. If necessary, HMRC will deny all allowances where it seems likely to the inspector that this restriction will apply.

More specifically, the restriction operates where the following conditions apply:

- a person ('the current owner') is treated as the owner of a fixture as a result of incurring new expenditure on its provision;
- the fixture is treated as having been owned at a 'relevant earlier time' (see below) by a past owner (who may in fact be the same as the current owner) as a result of incurring other expenditure (and not just by way of a contribution allowance – see 115-200);
- a capital allowances claim has been made in respect of that other expenditure, as a result of which the past owner has been required to bring a disposal value into account.

Expenditure must be left out of account in determining the current owner's qualifying expenditure, to the extent that it exceeds the 'maximum allowable amount' which is defined as $D + I$, where:

D   is the disposal value of the plant or machinery brought (or to be brought) into account by the past owner; and
I   is any of the new expenditure that is treated under CAA 2001, s. 25 (building alterations in connection with installation – see 160-000) as expenditure on the provision of plant or machinery.

If there has been more than one such disposal event then account is to be taken only of the most recent such event.

The expression 'relevant earlier time' normally means any time before the current owner is treated as owning the plant or machinery as a result of incurring the new expenditure. But the relevant earlier time does not include any time before the seller ceased to own the plant or machinery if (before the earliest time when the current owner is treated as owning the plant or machinery):

- a person has ceased to own the plant or machinery as a result of a sale;
- the sale was not a sale of the plant or machinery as a fixture; and

- the buyer and seller were not connected persons at the time of the sale.

Legislation: CAA 2001, s. 185(6), (7)

Other material: CA 26400

Prior IBA claim

The restriction in relation to an earlier IBA claim applies where:

- a past owner has claimed an allowance under the IBA code (see the Chapter headed 'Industrial Buildings Allowances', which begins at 300-000) in respect of expenditure which included expenditure on the provision of plant or machinery;
- the past owner has, in terms of the IBA legislation, transferred the relevant interest; and
- the current owner makes a claim in respect of new expenditure on the provision of the plant or machinery at a time when it is a fixture in the building.

Expenditure must be left out of account in determining the current owner's qualifying expenditure to the extent that it exceeds the 'maximum allowable amount', which is in this case defined as $(F/T) \times R$, where:

F   is the part of the consideration for the transfer by the past owner that is attributable to the fixture;
T   is the total consideration for that transfer; and
R   is the residue of qualifying expenditure attributable to the relevant interest immediately after that transfer, calculated on the assumption that the transfer was a sale of the relevant interest.

The *Finance Act* 2008 (at Sch. 27, para. 5) adapts the provisions to take account of the abolition from April 2011 of the IBA rules. It also provides that if the rules of CAA 2001, s. 186(3) do not apply then (from April 2011) the maximum allowable amount will be that part of the consideration (for the transfer by the former owner) that is attributable to the fixture.

Legislation: CAA 2001, s. 186

Prior R & D claim

The restriction in relation to an earlier claim under the code for research and development (formerly scientific research) allowances applies where:

- a past owner has claimed an allowance under the R & D code (see the Chapter headed 'Research and Development Allowances', which begins at 525-000) in respect of qualifying expenditure under that code which included expenditure on the provision of plant or machinery;
- the past owner has ceased to own an asset representing all or part of that qualifying expenditure; and
- the current owner makes a plant and machinery claim in respect of new expenditure on the provision of the plant or machinery at a time when it is a fixture in the building.

Expenditure must be left out of account in determining the current owner's qualifying expenditure to the extent that it exceeds the 'maximum allowable amount', which is in this case defined as (F/T) $\times$ A, where:

F   is the part of the consideration for the disposal of the asset by the past owner that is attributable to the fixture;

T   is the total consideration for that disposal; and

A   is the smaller of:

(1)   the disposal value of that asset when the past owner ceased to own it; and

(2)   so much of the qualifying R & D expenditure as related to the provision of that asset.

The current owner is for these purposes the person who acquired the asset from the past owner, or any person who is subsequently treated as the owner of the plant or machinery.

Legislation: CAA 2001, s. 187

245-400   Ceasing to own fixtures

Main principle

A disposal value must be brought into account by a person who has been eligible for allowances in respect of it if the fixture is sold or otherwise disposed of, is permanently lost, ceases to exist, becomes used for non-trade purposes, or if the person's trade is permanently discontinued.

Legislation: CAA 2001, s. 196(5)

End of qualifying interest

In addition, a person who ceases to have 'the qualifying interest' in a fixture will be treated as disposing of it. 'The qualifying interest' is, generally, the interest of the person treated as the person to whom it belongs, ie the lessee, tenant, etc. Specifically, the fixtures legislation treats a person as disposing of fixtures as follows:

- if the person ceases to have a qualifying interest in the relevant land;
- if a lessee ceases to have the lease (per CAA 2001, s. 183 or 184);
- a lessor will be treated as disposing of a fixture where the lessee is treated as becoming the owner of the fixture under CAA 2001, s. 183 (see 245-200);
- where a person has been treated as the owner of the fixture under the special fixtures legislation but where that fixture is then permanently severed from the relevant land, (ie it is no longer a fixture). In these circumstances, the person will be treated as ceasing to own the fixture unless, once it is severed, he actually owns it (ie rather than is merely deemed to own it);
- if an equipment lessor is treated under CAA 2001, s. 177 (see 245-200) as owning a fixture, he will be treated as ceasing to own it if he assigns his right under the equipment

lease or if the financial obligations of the equipment lease are discharged (whether by payment of the capital sum or otherwise);

- if an energy services provider assigns his rights under the agreement or if the financial obligations of the client under the agreement are discharged, whether or not this is by payment of a capital sum; in this case, if the financial obligations of the client have by whatever means become vested in another person, the reference to the client is to be taken as a reference to that other person.

Legislation: CAA 2001, s. 188–192A

No disposal in certain circumstances

No deemed disposal arises if:

- the qualifying interest is merged with another interest acquired by the same person;
- on the expiry of a lease, a new lease is granted to the lessee;
- an agreement to acquire an interest results in the acquisition of that interest;
- on the expiry of a licence to occupy, a new licence is granted to the licensee; or
- on the expiry of a lease, the lessee remains in occupation with the consent of the lessor.

In each such case the qualifying interest is thereafter to take into account the change in circumstance.

Legislation: CAA 2001, s. 188(3)–(4), 189

245-500   Acquisition of ownership of fixture when another ceases to own it

Where, under the rules described immediately above, a person is treated as ceasing to own a fixture, somebody else may be treated as acquiring the fixture at that time.

Termination of lease or licence

The first circumstance given in the legislation is where an outgoing lessee or licensee is treated under CAA 2001, s. 188 as ceasing to be the owner of a fixture on the termination of a lease or licence. In such a case, the lessor or the licensor is to be treated as the owner of the fixture from the time that the lease or licence is terminated.

Legislation: CAA 2001, s. 193

Assignment of equipment lease

Where an equipment lessor assigns his rights under an equipment lease then the assignee is treated as being the owner of the fixture at that time. Furthermore, the assignee is treated as having incurred expenditure on the provision of the fixture, the amount of the expenditure being the consideration given by him for the assignment. The assignee is then treated as the

Plant and Machinery

equipment lessor for the purposes of a future application of CAA 2001, s. 192, ie a deemed disposal by him of the fixture in the future.

Legislation: CAA 2001, s. 194

Acquisition by equipment lessee

Where an equipment lessee pays a capital sum to discharge his obligations under an equipment lease then he is treated as incurring expenditure, consisting of the capital sum, on the provision of the fixture. He will then be treated as the owner of the fixture from that time.

Legislation: CAA 2001, s. 195

Acquisition by assignee of energy services provider

Where CAA 2001, s. 192A(2)(a) (cessation of ownership of energy services provider as a result of assignment) applies (see 245-200), the assignee is treated, from the time of the assignment, as being the owner of the fixture as a result of having incurred expenditure, (ie the consideration given by him for the assignment) on the provision of the fixture.

For these purposes the assignee is to be treated as being an energy services provider who owns the fixture under CAA 2001, s. 180A (see 245-200).

Legislation: CAA 2001, s. 195A

Acquisition of ownership by client

Where CAA 2001, s. 192A(2)(b) (discharge of obligations of client) applies because the client has paid a capital sum, the client is to be treated as being the owner of the fixture from the time of the payment as a result of having incurred expenditure (the capital sum) on the provision of the fixture.

Legislation: CAA 2001, s. 195B

245-600 Disposal values of fixtures

Normal rules

The disposal value that has to be brought into account in respect of a fixture will depend on the nature of the event giving rise to the disposal. The legislation (at CAA 2001, s. 196) contains a table listing the different types of disposal event and, in each case, describing how the disposal value is calculated. This table, and the notes that follow it are as follows:

'Disposal values: fixtures

1. Disposal event	*2. Disposal value*
1. Cessation of ownership of the fixture under section 188 because of a sale of the qualifying interest except where item 2 applies.	The part of the sale price that– (a) falls to be treated for the purposes of this Part as expenditure incurred by the purchaser on the provision of the fixture; or (b) would fall to be so treated if the purchaser were entitled to an allowance.
2. Cessation of ownership of the fixture under section 188 because of a sale of the qualifying interest where– (a) the sale is at less than market value; and (b) the condition in subsection (2) is met by the purchaser.	The part of the price that would be treated for the purposes of this Part as expenditure by the purchaser on the provision of the fixture if– (a) the qualifying interest were sold at market value; (b) that sale took place immediately before the event which causes the former owner to be treated as ceasing to be the owner of the fixture, and (c) that event were disregarded in determining that market value.
3. Cessation of ownership of the fixture under section 188 where– (a) neither item 1 nor 2 applies; but (b) the qualifying interest continues in existence after that time or would so continue but for its becoming merged in another interest.	The disposal value given for item 2.
4. Cessation of ownership of the fixture under section 188 because of the expiry of the qualifying interest.	If the person receives a capital sum, by way of compensation or otherwise, by reference to the fixture, the amount of the capital sum. In any other case, nil.
5. Cessation of ownership of the fixture under section 190 because the lessee has become the owner under section 183.	The part of the capital sum given by the lessee for the lease referred to in section 183 that falls to be treated for the purposes of this Part as the lessee's expenditure on the provision of the fixture.

Plant and Machinery

307

6. Cessation of ownership of the fixture under section 191 (severance).	The market value of the fixture at the time of the severance.
7. Cessation of ownership of the fixture because section 192(2)(a) (assignment of rights) applies.	The consideration given by the assignee for the assignment.
8. Cessation of ownership of the fixture because section 192(2)(b) (discharge of equipment lessee's obligations) applies on the payment of a capital sum.	The capital sum paid to discharge the financial obligations of the equipment lessee.
8A. Cessation of ownership of the fixture because section 192A(2)(a) (assignment of rights) applies.	The consideration given by the assignee for the assignment.
8B. Cessation of ownership of the fixture because section 192A(2)(b) (discharge of client's obligations) applies on the payment of a capital sum.	The capital sum paid to discharge the financial obligations of the client.
9. Permanent discontinuance of the qualifying activity followed by the sale of the qualifying interest.	The part of the sale price that– (a) falls to be treated as expenditure incurred by the purchaser on the provision of the fixture; or (b) would fall to be so treated if the purchaser were entitled to an allowance.
10. Permanent discontinuance of the qualifying activity followed by the demolition or destruction of the fixture.	The net amount received for the remains of the fixture, together with – (a) any insurance money received in respect of the demolition or destruction, and (b) any other compensation of any description so received, so far as it consists of capital sums.
11. Permanent discontinuance of the qualifying activity followed by the permanent loss of the fixture otherwise than as a result of its demolition or destruction.	Any insurance money received in respect of the loss and, so far as it consists of capital sums, any other compensation of any description so received.
12. The fixture begins to be used wholly or partly for purposes other than those of the qualifying activity.	The part of the price that would fall to be treated for the purposes of this Part as expenditure incurred by the purchaser on the provision of the fixture if the qualifying interest were sold at market value.'

2. The condition referred to in item 2 of the Table is met by the purchaser if–

(a) the purchaser's expenditure on the provision of the fixture cannot be qualifying expenditure under this Part or Part 6 (research and development allowances); or

(b) the purchaser is a dual resident investing company which is connected with the former owner.

3. Items 1 and 5 of the Table are subject to sections 198 and 199 (election to fix apportionment on sale of qualifying interest or grant of lease).

4. Section 192(3) (assignee of equipment lessee) applies in relation to item 8 of the Table.

4A. Section 192A(3) (assignee of client) applies in relation to item 8B of the Table.

5. Nothing in sections 188 to 192A or this section prevents a disposal value having to be brought into account under Chapter 5 because of a disposal event not dealt with in these sections.

6. This section is subject to section 197.'

Legislation: CAA 2001, s. 196

Disposal values – avoidance cases

A higher disposal value will need to be brought into account where a disposal event 'is part of, or occurs as a result of, a scheme or arrangement the main purpose or one of the main purposes of which is the obtaining by the taxpayer of a tax advantage' under the plant and machinery rules.

The anti-avoidance rules will apply where the disposal value to be brought into account would otherwise be less than what is termed the notional written-down value. In this case, the person concerned must bring into account the notional written-down value of the asset in question.

The notional written-down value is defined as being QE minus A where:

QE is the taxpayer's qualifying expenditure on the plant or machinery; and

A is the total amount of allowances that could have been made to the taxpayer in respect of that expenditure if:

'(a) that expenditure had been the only expenditure that had ever been taken into account in determining his available qualifying expenditure, and

(b) all allowances had been made in full.'

Legislation: CAA 2001, s. 197

245-700   Elections to fix apportionments re fixtures

An important aspect of the fixtures election is the opportunity, in certain circumstances, to choose how the overall value of a purchase and sale should be allocated between different elements. The following paragraphs give the technical background and the practical implications are considered in depth at 250-000ff.

Plant and Machinery

309

The legislation provides for a possible apportionment of the sale price when the qualifying interest is sold (CAA 2001, s. 198) and an apportionment of a capital sum given by a lessee on the grant of a lease (CAA 2001, s. 199). It then provides supplementary rules and procedural rules.

An apportionment made by an election under these sections takes precedence over any apportionment that would otherwise be made under CAA 2001, s. 562, 563 or 564(1) (apportionment and procedure for determining apportionment).

Elections made under CAA 2001, s. 198 or 199 are irrevocable; but if, as a result of circumstances arising after the making of an election, the maximum amount which could be fixed by the election proves to be less than the amount that has been specified, the election is treated as if it had specified the maximum allowable amount.

Legislation: CAA 2001, s. 198–201

Election to apportion sale price on sale of qualifying interest

An opportunity to elect for a particular apportionment of the transaction value arises where the disposal value of a fixture has to be brought into account in accordance with item 1 of the table in CAA 2001, s. 196 (sale of qualifying interest at not less than market value, etc – see 245-600).

The requirement to bring in a disposal value should not be overlooked. No election is possible, for example, if the vendor is a property developer for whom the property represents trading stock - the vendor will not have claimed any capital allowances on the building and does not therefore bring a disposal value into account. Another effect of the requirement is that no election may be made for any asset on which no capital allowances claim has been made. In practice, many vendors have claimed allowances on certain fixtures but not others and it follows that an election that purports to cover all fixtures, including those on which no claim has been made, is flawed and potentially invalid.

The seller and the purchaser may jointly elect to fix the amount (being part of the overall proceeds of the transaction) that is to be treated as the expenditure incurred by the purchaser on the provision of the fixture. The amount fixed by the election must not exceed either the overall sale price or the amount of the vendor's capital expenditure on the provision of the fixture.

Example

A property containing fixtures is sold for £1 million. The cost of the plant within the building had historically amounted to £160,000. The value of the plant is currently £20,000. The vendor company has large trading losses brought forward.

The vendor and purchaser may agree to allocate £160,000 to the fixtures. The vendor will incur balancing charges but these may be covered by the trading losses brought forward. The purchaser can claim capital allowances on the £160,000.

If such an election is made then the remaining amount (if any) of the sale price is allocated to other property which is not the fixture but which formed part of the overall transaction.

This section is subject to CAA 2001, s. 186 (fixtures on which industrial buildings allowances have been claimed – see 245-300); s. 187 (fixtures on which research and development allowances have been claimed – see 245-300); s. 197 (disposal values in avoidance cases – see 245-600); and s. 200 and 201 (further provisions about elections).

Election to apportion capital sum given by lessee on grant of lease

An election may also be made if the disposal value of a fixture has to be brought into account in accordance with item 5 of the Table in CAA 2001, s. 196 (on acquisition of ownership by incoming lessee under CAA 2001, s. 183 – see 245-200).

The lessor and lessee may jointly elect to fix the amount to be treated as expenditure incurred by the lessee on the provision of the fixture. The amount fixed by the election must not exceed either the actual capital sum or the amount of the lessor's capital expenditure on the provision of the fixture.

If such an election is made then the remaining amount (if any) of the capital sum is allocated to the acquisition of other property which is not the fixture but which formed part of the overall transaction.

Once more, this section is subject to CAA 2001, s. 186, 187, 197, 200 and 201 (further provisions about elections).

Procedures

Any election under these sections must be made within two years from the date on which the purchaser acquires the qualifying interest (election under CAA 2001, s. 198) or on which the lessee is granted the lease (election under CAA 2001, s. 199).

The notice must include:

- the amount fixed by the election;
- the name of each of the persons making the election;
- information sufficient to identify both the plant or machinery and the relevant land;
- particulars of the interest acquired by the purchaser (election under CAA 2001, s. 198) or of the lease granted to the lessee (election under CAA 2001, s. 199); and
- the tax district references of both parties making the election (see below).

Once a person has made such an election, he must include a copy of the notice containing the election when submitting his tax return for the first period for which the election has an effect for tax purposes in his case. These rules override the normal rules in the *Taxes Management Act* 1970 and the *Finance Act* 1998 relating to claims and elections for income tax and corporation tax purposes respectively. For partnerships, the relevant return is that required under TMA 1970, s. 12AA (partnership returns).

Plant and Machinery

Overseas buyers

The requirement to provide details of tax district references has in the past been used by HMRC as justification for denying the right to make an election where the purchaser is not resident in the UK, as in the following quotation formerly at CA 26850:

> 'Do not accept an election if the buyer is non resident and outside the UK tax net. The election must give the tax district and reference of each person making the election. If the buyer is outside the UK tax net the buyer will not have a tax district and reference. This means that an election cannot be made because the tax district and reference of the buyer cannot be given.'

That wording was removed from the guidance around October 2007, though the motivation for that change is unclear. This raises an interesting technical issue as to whether or not an election can be entered into by someone who is not a taxpayer. It is clear from the wording of CAA 2001, s. 198(1) that the vendor must be paying tax, but what about the purchaser? It is arguable that s. 198(2) imposes a requirement for the purchaser to be subject to UK tax, but the matter is open to some discussion. Failing that, the only statutory requirement is that in s. 201(3), namely the need to state the tax district references of both parties, as referred to above. Again, though, it does seem at least possible that the requirement to provide details of tax district references should be read as the requirement to provide them if they exist.

Other material: CA 26850

245-800   Administration

The final sections under the Chapter dealing with fixtures contain various administrative provisions. These deal with the allocation of expenditure on a fixture to a pool, the procedure for amending a return where subsequent events make that return incorrect, and procedures relating to appeals.

Notification must be made to HMRC within three months of the taxpayer becoming aware that something in a tax return has become incorrect.

If a dispute arises as to whether an item of machinery has become, in law, a fixture, and that question is material to the tax liability of two or more persons, then the question is settled by the tribunal in the same manner as if it were an ordinary appeal.

Legislation: CAA 2001, s. 202–204

Integral features

247-000   Overview

With effect from April 2008, expenditure on so-called 'integral features' is treated separately from other capital expenditure for the purposes of claiming plant and machinery allowances. Expenditure on these integral features is excluded from the main capital allowances pool and writing-down allowances are given at a rate of 10 per cent (rather than the new standard 20 per cent rate) on the reducing balance of the pool.

Key features of the treatment of integral features are as follows:

- Integral features are specifically included in the list of assets that are unaffected by the restrictions in CAA 2001, s. 21 and 22 (buildings, structures, etc) (s. 23(2)).
- Integral features qualify for plant and machinery allowances in their own right, without regard to case law precedents as to what constitutes plant and machinery. So, for example, a general cold water system for an office or factory will now always qualify for allowances.
- Certain items that were previously protected from the effects of CAA 2001, s. 21 and 22, by virtue of being included in List C (see 10-200) in s. 23(4), are no longer so protected. The effect of this is that the assets in question (eg specialised electrical systems) can only qualify for plant and machinery allowances under the rules relating to integral features. As a result, such assets now unambiguously qualify for plant and machinery allowances but only do so at the lower rate of tax relief.
- A list of integral features is specified in the legislation (CAA 2001, s. 33A(5)), but it is open to the Treasury to add to that list any other feature of a building or structure that would not otherwise qualify as expenditure on plant or machinery.
- Expenditure on integral features is classified (together with expenditure on thermal insulation, on long-life assets and on higher emissions cars) as 'special rate expenditure' (CAA 2001, s. 104A), which is allocated to its own 'special rate pool' (s. 104C) and which attracts allowances at a rate of 10 per cent on a reducing balance basis (s. 104D).
- Integral features may, however, qualify for 100 per cent relief by way of the annual investment allowance (see, generally, 181-000ff.), subject to the rules applying for the purposes of that allowance.

The integral features rules apply when 'a person carrying on a qualifying activity incurs expenditure on the provision or replacement of an integral feature of a building or structure used by the person for the purposes of the qualifying activity' (CAA 2001, s. 33A(1)).

The mechanics of the legislation are that capital allowances are given *as if* expenditure on integral features were capital expenditure on plant and machinery, incurred for the purposes of the qualifying activity. The person incurring the expenditure is then treated as owning the item in question (CAA 2001, s. 33A(2)).

The rules giving allowances for integral features apply to expenditure incurred on or after the 'relevant date'. This is 1 April 2008 for corporation tax purposes and 6 April 2008 for income tax purposes (FA 2008, Sch. 26, para. 14).

Legislation: CAA 2001, s. 33A

247-050   Definition of 'integral features'

The following assets are integral features:

(1)   an electrical system (including a lighting system);

(2)   a cold water system;

(3)   a space or water heating system, a powered system of ventilation, air cooling or air purification, and any floor or ceiling comprised in such a system;

(4)   a lift, an escalator or a moving walkway; and

(5)   external solar shading.

Legislation: CAA 2001, s. 33A

Exclusions

An asset does not qualify as an integral feature if it is one 'whose principal purpose is to insulate or enclose the interior of a building or to provide an interior wall, floor or ceiling which (in each case) is intended to remain permanently in place'. This provision precisely mirrors that of CAA 2001, s. 23(4). This would apply, for example, to deny allowances on the cost of a wall that happens to form the fourth side of a ventilation pipe.

Expanding the list of qualifying items

The Treasury has power to add to the list of items qualifying as integral features but only if such items would not otherwise qualify for plant and machinery allowances. Thus it is not possible for the Treasury to reclassify as integral features any assets that would already qualify for the higher rate of writing-down allowance, but new assets that would not otherwise qualify at all (such as some features providing environmental benefits) may be added so as to qualify for the lower rate of relief rather than for no relief at all.

Legislation: CAA 2001, s. 33A(7)

247-100   Overlap with other capital allowance rules

Rules address the overlap between integral features and other items of plant or machinery.

CAA 2001, s. 33A(3), for example, ensures that no revenue deduction may be given in calculating the income of the qualifying activity. This is particularly relevant for the treatment of replacement assets. It is needed, fundamentally, because of the deeming provision in s. 33A(2), which applies the plant and machinery rules 'as if ... the expenditure were capital expenditure'. If, however, an item falls within the statutory definition of 'integral feature', but is not qualifying expenditure (eg because it is in a dwelling-house) then the capital allowances rules are ignored when determining whether or not a revenue deduction may be claimed (s. 33A(4)).

A more general issue arises with regard to items that are integral features but that still fall within one of the categories of expenditure in List C at CAA 2001, s. 23. Lifts, for example, are no longer included in List C, but the first item still refers to machinery.

The definition of 'integral features' at CAA 2001, s. 33(5) includes 'a lift, an escalator or a moving walkway'. In other words, a distinction is drawn between the lift shaft (which will not normally qualify, but see below) and the lift itself, with parallel rules for escalators, etc (which will qualify as integral features).

But is the position as simple as that? Ignore, for a moment, the rules relating to integral features. List C at CAA 2001, s. 23 contains numerous items that are protected from the restrictive effects of CAA 2001, s. 21. Before April 2008, the position could therefore be summarised as follows:

- a lift is incorporated into a building and allowances are therefore denied, initially, by s. 21(3)(a);
- the treatment of a lift was previously rescued by item 6 in List C at s. 23;
- it was therefore necessary to consider whether, on ordinary case law principles, a lift was plant or machinery;
- case law principles would lead clearly to the conclusion that a lift would indeed qualify as such.

At first glance, the position has changed now that the wording of item 6 at List C has been amended. In its revised format, that item refers only to hoists. The apparent intention of the legislation is therefore that lifts should qualify only as integral features. However, this does not take account of item 1 at List C which refers to 'machinery'.

HMRC's *Capital Allowances* manual states uncontroversially that 'lifts and escalators are machinery'. It seems to the author that either route can be justified, and there does not seem to be a statutory principle that gives priority for one set of rules over the other. However, the author has now heard from the HMRC specialists that they do not accept this view. In an e-mail exchange, the HMRC view was expressed as follows:

> 'I don't think we would argue with you that a lift is machinery. However we take the view that the legislation is clear that lifts are integral features and expenditure on integral features has to be allocated to the special rate pool.
>
> So in our view the person making the claim does not have a choice, it may be qualifying expenditure on machinery but more specifically it is qualifying expenditure on a lift which is an integral feature and that qualifying expenditure has to be allocated to the special rate pool.'

The dispute relates only to the heading under which allowances can be claimed for lifts – it is absolutely clear that they qualify one way or the other. But the point is not merely academic, as the route followed will determine whether or not any writing-down allowances need to be restricted to the lower rate. Possibly it will one day be tested in front of a tax tribunal.

Other material: CA 21190

247-150 Allowances for special rate expenditure

Allowances and charges are not given for integral features in isolation: rather, there are rules for 'special rate expenditure', covering not only integral features but also certain long-life asset expenditure and expenditure on thermal insulation. More specifically, the term 'special rate expenditure' is defined to include the following:

- expenditure incurred from 1 or 6 April 2008 (for corporation tax and income tax respectively) to which CAA 2001, s. 28 (thermal insulation) applies;
- expenditure incurred from those dates to which CAA 2001, s. 33A (integral features) applies;
- expenditure from 1 or 6 April 2009 (*not* 2008) on the provision of a car that is not a 'main rate car' (as defined at CAA 2001, s. 104AA).
- expenditure incurred from 1 or 6 April 2008 (for corporation tax and income tax respectively) on long-life asset expenditure (within the meaning of CAA 2001, Pt. 2, Ch. 10);
- expenditure incurred *before* those 2008 dates on long-life asset expenditure (again within the meaning of CAA 2001, Pt. 2, Ch. 10), where the expenditure was only allocated to a pool in a chargeable period beginning on or after those dates.

The last category may seem puzzling, but the following explanation was given in the *Explanatory Notes* to the Finance Bill 2008:

'This rule ensures that if, exceptionally, a business failed to realise that expenditure incurred in a chargeable period ending before the relevant date was qualifying long-life asset expenditure, it is not prevented from allocating the expenditure to the special rate pool in a later chargeable period.'

Legislation: CAA 2001, s. 104A

Annual investment allowance

There is nothing to stop a person claiming the annual investment allowance (see 181-000ff.) for special rate expenditure incurred on integral features, long-life assets, etc. The point was confirmed in HMRC's guidance notes, issued in December 2007. Paragraph 3.9 of those notes states the following:

'Businesses will be free to allocate their AIA to qualifying expenditure in any way they wish; there will be no rules to restrict their freedom of choice. They will therefore be able to set their allowance against expenditure qualifying for a lower rate of allowances (such as expenditure on "long-life assets" or "integral features") before using any balance against their general plant and machinery expenditure. In this way, the AIA may be seen as a sort of de minimis provision, allowing modest amounts of annual expenditure on the new category of "integral features" or on "long-life assets" to be completely covered by the new 100 per cent allowance. This may be of particular assistance to smaller businesses.'

The most basic form of tax planning will therefore be to ensure, each year, that the annual investment allowance is allocated first to absorb any expenditure that would otherwise qualify only for a lower rate of tax relief.

Writing-down allowances

Writing-down allowances are given at a lower rate for expenditure on integral features and other special rate expenditure. The mechanics of achieving this are to exclude such expenditure from the main capital allowances pool and to allocate it instead to a 'special rate' pool. Expenditure on integral features is pooled with expenditure on certain long-life assets, and with expenditure qualifying under CAA 2001, s. 28 (thermal insulation). Where only part of the expenditure is to be categorised as on such assets (for example, part of the expenditure is on integral features and part on ordinary plant and machinery) then the two parts of the expenditure are treated separately and an apportionment is made to determine how much falls within each part. See below for cases in which the whole of the expenditure is on integral features but the use of the asset is mixed.

Allowances are given in accordance with normal principles, but with a 10 per cent rate rather than the standard 20 per cent rate that otherwise applies. Allowances are increased or decreased proportionately where the chargeable period is greater or shorter than one year and the normal restrictions apply where the qualifying activity was carried on for only part of the chargeable period (CAA 2001, s. 56 applied by s. 104D(4)). Once the value of the pool has fallen below £1,000, the small pool provisions apply to it as they do to the main pool. See 190-250.

The transitional rules, including the interaction with any existing long-life asset pool, are explained and illustrated at 210-050.

Legislation: CAA 2001, s. 104A–104D

Exclusions from the special rate pool

There are two circumstances in which expenditure is excluded from the special rate pool.

Wholly and exclusively
Expenditure is only allocated to the special rate pool if it is incurred wholly and exclusively for the purposes of the qualifying activity. This is slightly more complex than it may first seem.

As a general principle, the 'wholly and exclusively' condition does not apply for the purposes of claiming plant and machinery allowances. Thus the general condition is that a person must incur 'capital expenditure on the provision of plant or machinery wholly or partly for the purposes of the qualifying activity' (CAA 2001, s. 11(4)). Nevertheless, expenditure incurred for mixed purposes is kept out of the main capital allowances pool and allocated instead to a single asset pool (CAA 2001, s. 206(2)), and allowances are given only on a proportionate basis.

The interaction of the special rate expenditure rules and those relating to the single asset pool may be summarised as follows:

- expenditure on integral features or other special rate assets is invariably 'special rate expenditure';
- as a general principle, such expenditure is allocated to the 'special rate pool';
- it is instead allocated to a single asset pool if it is incurred partly for other purposes;

Plant and Machinery

- nevertheless, allowances are given at the restricted rate of 10 per cent for such expenditure.

This last point is made explicit in CAA 2001, s. 104D(2).

Legislation: CAA 2001, s. 104C

Other assets allocated to single pool

The same principles as described immediately above (under 'wholly and exclusively') apply to any other expenditure on integral features that is required to be allocated to a single asset pool. This would be the case, for example, where a person receives a partial depreciation subsidy.

Legislation: CAA 2001, s. 211

Disposal value: anti-avoidance rules

Special rules apply if a disposal event 'is part of, or occurs as a result of, a scheme or arrangement the main purpose or one of the main purposes of which is the obtaining by the taxpayer of a tax advantage' under the plant and machinery legislation.

Where these rules apply, the disposal value of an asset that has attracted allowances under the 'special rate expenditure' rules of CAA 2001, s. 104D may be increased. Specifically, the disposal value to be brought into account will be the notional written-down value of the asset if this is higher than the actual disposal value.

The notional written-down value is defined as 'QE minus A' where:

QE is the taxpayer's qualifying expenditure on the asset in question; and
A   is the total of all allowances that could have been made to the taxpayer in respect of that expenditure if:

- that expenditure had been the only expenditure that had ever been taken into account in determining his available qualifying expenditure;
- that expenditure had not been prevented by the application of a monetary limit from being long-life asset expenditure; and
- all allowances had been made in full.

The fact that the notional written-down value is used for the computations of the vendor does not affect the position of the purchaser, whose allowance claim is still to be restricted to the actual sale price. This is made clear in the HMRC manuals in relation to long-life asset expenditure and there seems to be no reason of principle for any different treatment in this case.

Legislation: CAA 2001, s. 104E

Other material: CA 23770

247-200   Replacement of integral features

When the whole or the majority of an 'integral feature' is replaced, that expenditure is also treated as capital expenditure on the integral feature, rather than attracting a revenue deduction in the accounts.

If the expenditure on the feature in question is a one-off cost then the rule applies if the amount spent on the feature is more than half of the cost that would be incurred if, at that time, the integral feature were to be replaced.

A further rule applies, however, if the amount incurred is initially less than half the replacement cost but if further expenditure is incurred on the same integral feature in the period of 12 months beginning with that initial expenditure. If the aggregate of the initial expenditure and any further expenditure amounts to more than half of the cost of replacing the asset then both the initial and the later expenditure are treated as capital expenditure on the integral feature. Note that the term 'initial expenditure' refers not to the original cost of the asset but to the first amount of additional expenditure incurred on that asset. The test is determined by reference to the replacement cost of the asset at the time that initial expenditure is incurred (CAA 2001, s. 33B).

The effect of this is that it may be necessary to re-open accounts and computations that have already been submitted. The legislation specifically allows for the making of all such assessments (and adjustments to assessments) as may be necessary to give effect to the rule.

Example

A company incurs expenditure of £40,000 on a central heating system in June 2008. In drawing up its accounts to 31 December 2008, it claims annual investment allowances of £37,500, and the balance of £2,500 goes into the special rate expenditure pool, attracting writing-down allowances at 10 per cent.

A major flaw is discovered with the type of pipes that have been used and the business that installed the system goes bust. The company that paid for the heating system therefore has to bear the costs of replacing many of the pipes. Costs of £17,000 are incurred in October and November 2010. It is calculated at this point that to replace the entire system would now cost £43,000, so the £17,000 is less than half of the replacement cost. These costs are therefore treated as repairs and are written off in the accounts to 31 December 2010, submitted in June 2011.

Further problems arise when some other pipes start to leak in July, and additional costs of £5,000 are incurred in August 2011. The company is advised that the overall costs of this type of system have now increased further and that the whole system would now cost £50,000.

The total costs incurred in the 12-month period are £22,000. This figure has to be compared not with the £50,000 but with the £43,000 ('the cost of replacing the integral feature at the time the initial expenditure was incurred'). As the £22,000 is more than half of that cost, the special rules relating to replacement of integral features are applied. The £5,000 has to be treated as expenditure on integral features. Furthermore, it is now

> necessary to go back and re-open the accounts to 31 December 2010, adding back the repairs of £17,000 and instead claiming capital allowances on the cost.

Legislation: CAA 2001, s. 33B

Expenditure incurred before April 2008

What if the central heating system, in the above example, was installed before the rules relating to integral features were introduced in April 2008? It does appear that these rules then apply anyway, as long as the *further* expenditure is incurred after 1 or 6 April 2008. If, however, the original expenditure was incurred in, say, 2005, the initial expenditure was incurred in February 2008 and then further expenditure was incurred in August 2008, then the February expenditure would, it seems, be ignored in determining whether or not the August expenditure represented more than half of the replacement cost. It would therefore be necessary to compare the August 2008 expenditure with the amount that it would cost, at that time, to replace the whole system.

This appears to be the correct reading of FA 2008, s. 73(6)), which states that the rules have effect in relation to expenditure incurred on or after 1 or 6 April 2008 (for corporation tax and income tax respectively).

Annual investment allowances

Annual investment allowances (AIAs) (see, generally, 181-000ff.) are in principle available for expenditure on integral features. This applies both to original and replacement expenditure. The point is clear from the legislation and was explicitly confirmed in the *Explanatory Notes* to Finance Bill 2008 (para. 165) as follows:

> 'The rules provide businesses with almost complete freedom to allocate the AIA between different types of expenditure. For example, they may allocate it first against any expenditure on "integral features", qualifying for the lower ten per cent "special rate" of WDA. As well as being financially beneficial, this should operate as a proxy for a de minimis provision in respect of "integral features" for smaller businesses – in other words, they may be able to dispense altogether with a ten per cent "special rate pool" if the amounts of "integral features" expenditure do not exceed £50,000 a year.'

AIAs are given for the chargeable period in which expenditure is incurred, so in the above example there is no reason why the £17,000 that has to be added back in the tax computation cannot be fully allowed by way of 100 per cent AIAs in the earlier year. But what if AIAs have already been claimed in that earlier year against expenditure that would have attracted writing-down allowances at the full 20 per cent rate? It appears to be the case that, in re-opening that earlier year, the person carrying on the qualifying activity has the right to re-work the capital allowances computation so as to set the AIA against the expenditure on integral features that has been re-classified as capital expenditure because of further expenses incurred in the following year (as illustrated in the example above). In many cases, the issue will in any case be identified in time to re-open the earlier year's computations on ordinary self-assessment principles.

247-250   Sales between connected persons

Background

The rules relating to integral features sometimes offer a tax advantage but in other circumstances represent a tax cost. The first is illustrated by expenditure on cold water systems (now qualifying for relief at 10 per cent but previously qualifying for no allowances at all in many cases). The opposite effect can be illustrated by reference to an air conditioning system, which previously qualified for full allowances but where the expenditure would now qualify only at the lower 10 per cent rate.

The need for anti-avoidance provisions

Without special anti-avoidance legislation, the rules could be manipulated by selling to a related party an asset that did not previously qualify for relief. For example, Company A might have incurred expenditure on a cold water system in the year 2007, claiming no tax relief on that expenditure. By selling the building in August 2008 to related Company B, the latter company would be able to claim tax relief, under the integral feature provisions, on the element relating to the cold water system. This opportunity is blocked in certain circumstances.

Legislation: *Finance Act* 2008, Sch. 26, para. 15

When the provisions apply

The anti-avoidance rules apply where there is a sale between connected parties of an integral feature bought by the seller before the commencement date (1 or 6 April 2008 for corporation tax and income tax respectively). The rule is also extended to cover situations where there is a succession of connected party transfers (A sells to B who sells to C) with at least one of those transfers taking place before the April 2008 date.

For these purposes, the concept of 'connected persons' is defined in accordance with CAA 2001, s. 575.

Effect of the anti-avoidance provisions

The rules do not seek to deny relief merely because the transaction is between connected parties. However, the expenditure will not qualify for relief unless the original expenditure was qualifying expenditure (or the buyer's expenditure would have been qualifying expenditure if it had been incurred at the time the original expenditure was incurred).

HMRC has summarised the effect of the rules as follows (in the *Explanatory Notes* to Finance Bill 2008):

> 'These rules ensure that in a connected party transaction the buyer is not denied relief for any asset where plant and machinery allowances were available prior to 1 or 6 April 2008 in respect

Plant and Machinery

of the integral feature but ensure that historic non qualifying expenditure is not relieved after the changes made by this legislation.'

Legislation: *Finance Act* 2008, Sch. 26, para. 15

247-300   Intra-group transfers

Background

The legislation recognises that – as a result of the rules relating to integral features – normal movements of assets between group companies could have a detrimental effect on the tax relief available. For example, Company A might have incurred substantial expenditure on a number of escalators in a large shop in 2007. Such expenditure would have qualified for unrestricted capital allowances. In principle, if the shop is now sold to a third party, the buyer would only be able to claim allowances at 10 per cent on the expenditure relating to the escalators because they are now classified as integral features.

Relaxation of integral feature restriction

In certain circumstances, the purchaser will still be able to claim allowances without restriction to the 10 per cent rate. The relaxation applies only where the buyer and seller elect for it to do so and where both are companies and are members of the same group, using the definition at TCGA 1992, s. 170(3)–(6).

The transaction must involve a 'pre-commencement integral feature', which is normally simply an asset that was bought before 1 (or conceivably 6) April 2008 and allocated to the seller's main pool. However, the rules also allow for a succession of intra-group transfers (A sells to B who sells to C) with at least one of those transfers taking place before the April 2008 date as long as each stage has been protected by this particular rule and by the making of a valid election.

Legislation: *Finance Act* 2008, Sch. 26, para. 16

Election: mechanics and effect

The relaxation described above only applies if the buyer and seller jointly elect that it should do so. The election must be made by notice to an officer of HMRC within two years from the date of the transaction. All such assessments and adjustments are then to be made as are necessary to give effect to the election. The election is for FA 2008, Sch. 26, para. 17 to apply.

The effect of the election is that the integral feature is treated as sold at a price that gives rise to no balancing adjustment. The buyer's expenditure is treated as qualifying expenditure that is not special rate expenditure. If it is to be allocated to a pool, it is therefore allocated to the buyer's main pool. HMRC has explained the effect of this as follows (in the *Explanatory Notes* to Finance Bill 2008):

'In effect this means the seller treats the asset as if it was in a pool of its own to establish the tax-written down value of the integral feature at the date of sale and the asset is transferred for that value'

Allowances and charges are then given to or made on the buyer as if everything done to or by the seller had been done to or by the buyer. Once more, HMRC has explained the effect of this as follows (in the *Explanatory Notes* to Finance Bill 2008):

'[This rule] ensures that when or if the buyer subsequently sells the integral feature then the correct amount of the disposal proceeds is taken into account in the main pool. For example, if two companies in the same group: Company A & Company B, elect on or after 1 April 2008, for a lift in a building which was installed by company A prior to 1 April 2008 for a cost of £80,000 to be sold to company B at its tax-written down values of (say) £16,000, then when company B sells the lift (as part of the sale of the building) when the value of the lift is (say) £30,000, the part of the sales proceeds that relates to the lift is not capped at £16,000 and company B must bring in the full amount of £30,000.'

Plant and machinery: property transactions

Introduction

250-000   Opportunities

The interaction between plant and property is one of the more difficult capital allowance topics but is also where most of the tax planning opportunities arise. It is still the case that the rules relating to capital allowances on the purchase and sale of a property are poorly understood.

The technical rules relating to fixtures have been covered at 245-000ff above, explaining why special legislation is needed and how it achieves its end. The purpose of this part of the book is to examine the very practical considerations that arise in relation to fixtures, especially in the context of buying and selling property, but also in relation to property refurbishments.

The fixtures rules are now subject to the legislation relating to long funding assets (see 240-220ff.). Specifically, the fixtures rules do not apply where fixtures are the subject of a long funding lease (including certain cases involving further leases) (CAA 2001, s. 172A).

250-020   Common misconceptions

One of the areas that can create surprises for businesses and their tax advisers concerns the tax effect of wording in a contract for the purchase and sale of a property. It is often thought that as long as the vendor and purchaser write agreed figures into a sales contract, this will be effective for tax purposes. In fact, the inspector has a statutory obligation to impose a 'just and reasonable apportionment' where different types of property are sold together, even where separate prices are agreed for separate parts of the overall transaction. Signing a joint election can, however, override this power.

A second misconception is that the allocation of the proceeds/purchase price can be sorted out at the time the relevant tax computations are prepared. In fact, it may be very advantageous for either purchaser or vendor to consider the position before the transaction is completed, not least because the tax effect may well have a legitimate bearing on the value of the property sold and acquired. This is considered in more depth below.

Finally, it is often thought that the interaction of the capital allowances and capital gains tax rules will mean that what is lost on the one side can be gained on the other. This is rarely the case, for the reasons discussed at 251-020.

Legislation: CAA 2001, s. 562

250-040   Fixtures elections

First principles

The statutory rules relating to the making of a fixtures election are considered at 245-700.

Where there is an arm's length sale of a building, the seller and the purchaser may jointly elect to fix the amount (being part of the overall proceeds of the transaction) that is to be treated as the expenditure incurred by the purchaser on the provision of the fixture. The amount fixed by the election must not exceed either the overall sale price or the amount of the vendor's capital expenditure on the fixture. Subject to that, there is no question of the figures in the election having to be 'reasonable' or 'realistic'.

Legislation: CAA 2001, s. 198ff

Further claim

It should be borne in mind that a fixtures election is not necessarily the end of the matter from the purchaser's point of view. Legally, the election can only relate to expenditure in respect of which a disposal value has to be brought into account, and therefore only expenditure in respect of which an earlier claim has been made.

It is quite possible that the vendor will have made an inadequate claim, perhaps covering the cost of air conditioning in a building but not the cost of the sanitaryware. The election can in such a case only cover the expenditure in respect of which the claim had been made (the air conditioning, in this instance) so the purchaser is in principle free to make a subsequent claim in relation to other fixtures. It is possible, however, that in seeking to obtain the information needed to submit the claim the purchaser will alert the vendor to the need to make a final claim which may then restrict the opportunities available to the purchaser. For all these reasons, the issues should be wrapped up in the legal documentation.

250-060   Elections and integral features

The wording of the legislation governing fixtures elections was not changed to reflect the concept of integral features, introduced from April 2008. Nevertheless, that new concept cannot be ignored.

Subsections (1) and (2) of s. 198 refer respectively to 'a fixture' and to 'the fixture' - in each case in the singular. Strictly, therefore, an election is to be made separately for every fixture. This would be absurd in practice, as a property may have many thousands of fixtures in it, so HMRC have long adopted a pragmatic approach whereby an election may be accepted by reference to groups of assets (though a single election may never be made for more than one property). The HMRC guidance states that their staff 'may accept a degree of amalgamation of assets where this will not distort the tax computation'.

An election that does not distinguish between integral features and other fixtures will inevitably distort the computations of the purchaser. It follows that all elections should make an absolutely clear distinction between these two categories of fixture. Pending any HMRC statement of advice to the contrary, it is probably reasonable to continue to use a single election, but there should be discrete schedules that identify separately the integral features and the other assets.

250-080 Buying and selling fixtures: the need for apportionment

Plant or machinery will often be sold in a single transaction which also involves other assets, such as land or buildings. In the absence of an election, an apportionment has to be made of the overall sale even if 'separate prices are, or purport to be, agreed for' a variety of assets, as long as the various items are sold 'as a result of one bargain'. Specifically:

- the net proceeds of the sale of any given item are to be treated as being so much of the net proceeds of sale of all the property as, on a just and reasonable apportionment, is attributable to that item, and
- the expenditure incurred on the provision or purchase of that item is to be treated as being so much of the consideration given for all the property as, on a just and reasonable apportionment, is attributable to that item.

The apportionment rules apply not only to an ordinary sale but also to any consideration for the exchange or surrender of an asset.

The HMRC officer may insist on 'a just and reasonable apportionment' but, if he increases or reduces the amount allocated to the plant or machinery, he will need to adjust the figures for other assets accordingly and indeed must justify the value he attributes to those other assets. See, in this respect, the cases of *Fitton v Gilders and Heaton* and *Wood (t/a A Wood & Co) v Provan*.

In practice, the amount to be apportioned between different assets often features in the negotiations for the sale of a business, etc. In most cases, what suits the vendor does not suit the purchaser, as the latter will often wish to attribute as much as possible to plant and machinery which will produce a balancing charge for the vendor. Each case is different, however, and it may be relevant to take account of many different factors including (for example) the availability of trading losses or the different tax rates of purchaser and vendor. The valuation of plant is not an exact science and so there is usually some scope for obtaining a result that is favourable from the tax point of view if both parties can agree.

However, it should be borne in mind that unless a joint election is signed in respect of fixtures (see 245-700) the HMRC officer can impose his own figures 'even though separate prices are, or purport to be, agreed for separate items'. Indeed, there is a statutory obligation to do this if the apportioned figures would not otherwise be just and reasonable.

Plant and Machinery

If no election is made, the question therefore arises of what is 'just and reasonable'.

Legislation: CAA 2001, s. 562, 572

Cases: *Fitton v Gilders and Heaton* (1955) 36 TC 233 and *Wood (t/a A Wood & Co) v Provan* (1968) 44 TC 701

Method of apportionment

Where necessary, HMRC will involve the Valuation Office for the purposes of reaching a proper apportionment between plant and other items. The Valuation Office Agency manuals are of interest in this respect (see *www.voa.gov.uk/instructions/Index.htm*). The relevant parts of the manuals are in the 'Capital gains and other taxes' manual, section 3 of which deals specifically with capital allowances. Within this, part three is entitled 'Approach to apportionments'.

The manuals make it clear that, when apportioning a purchase price between plant and other non-qualifying elements, the approach taken will 'usually' be to use the formula whereby the value of plant and machinery is calculated as:

$$\text{Purchase price} \times \frac{A}{A + B + C}$$

where:

A   is the replacement cost of qualifying items of plant;
B   is the replacement cost of the rest of the building, (ie excluding plant); and
C   is the value of the bare land.

Example

Those manuals go on to give an example involving the purchase of a 20-year old building for £5 million. They suggest that if the total replacement cost of the building were £6 million, including £1.5 million representing the replacement cost of qualifying plant, and if the land value were £2 million, then the apportionment would be as follows:

$$\text{Value of plant} = £5 \text{ million} \times \frac{£1.5 \text{ million}}{£8 \text{ million}} = £937,500$$

The resulting value is likely to lie somewhere between the original cost of the plant and its replacement value, depending on the average age of the plant. Interestingly, the formula has the effect of depreciating the values of all elements of the purchase price, including the land. The manuals go on to explain that 'although land does not of course depreciate in value with age, the bare site in this case is encumbered by an ageing building'. The point is that whatever the actual bare site value, it will not be possible to realise this value as long as there is a building on the site that is not ready for demolition.

A further HMRC example demonstrates that the apportioned value of the plant and machinery may exceed the replacement cost of those assets. This is explained as being because the element of the developer's profit will be apportioned on a pro rata basis and part of it will therefore increase the value of the plant and machinery.

Example

The example illustrating this involves a new property costing £10 million. If the replacement cost of the building excluding plant and machinery is £4.5 million with £1.5 million allocated as the replacement cost of the plant and £2 million as the bare site value, then the apportioned value of the plant and machinery will be calculated as follows:

$$\text{Purchase price} \times \frac{A}{A + B + C}$$

$$£10 \text{ million} \times \frac{£1.5 \text{ million}}{£1.5 \text{ million} + £3.5 \text{ million} + £2 \text{ million}} = £1.875 \text{ million}$$

Where agreement cannot be reached, there is legislation enabling a determination to be made by the tax tribunal. Where (before April 2009) the general or special commissioners considered an apportionment for capital allowances purposes then HMRC staff were instructed to accept their decision as it would be a question of fact rather than of law. There is no reason of principle why that approach should have changed with the introduction of the new tax tribunal system.

HMRC issued further guidance, early in 2009, in the form of a 'practice note' entitled 'Apportioning the Price Paid for a Business Transferred as a Going Concern' (available at *www.hmrc.gov.uk/svd/practice-note.pdf*). It is not primarily concerned with capital allowance issues, but may have some relevance where it is necessary to apportion between (for example) buildings and goodwill.

Example

A further example might be a sale and purchase agreement which allocates the proceeds of a business sale as follows:

- Freehold property £990,000
- Goodwill £250,000
- Fixtures and fittings £10,000

The £10,000 may have been chosen by the vendor's accountants on the basis that this is the tax written down value of the fixtures in question, which are in any case old and in need of replacement. The thinking may therefore be that this will avoid any balancing charge on the disposal. In the absence of an election, however, there is no guarantee that this will be the result.

Although the fixtures are old, their *replacement* cost will be much higher than £10,000. Suppose that the Valuation Office Agency were to come out with a figure of £150,000 as the replacement cost of the fixtures, £350,000 as the value of the land and £650,000 as

---

Plant and Machinery

> the replacement cost of the building excluding plant. The figure to be allocated to the plant will therefore be calculated as £130,435. This would then produce a large balancing charge for the vendor.

Falling land values

One aspect of the above formula is particularly noteworthy in difficult economic times. If land values are depressed, this has the effect of increasing the value of the fixtures. In the last example above, suppose that the land value has dropped from £350,000 to £250,000 but that the other figures remain constant. If the purchase price of the business remains unchanged, the result of applying the formula will now be to produce a higher fixtures figure of £142,857.

Legislation: CAA 2001, s. 563

Other material: CA 12500; www.voa.gov.uk/instructions/Index.htm

250-100   HMRC approach to apportionments in practice

Would HMRC insist on a correct apportionment in practice? If the tax position is neutral then they may not bother - from their perspective, what is gained by the vendor from a low figure is lost by the purchaser. However, the purchaser could insist on applying the letter of the tax law, thereby gaining much higher capital allowances than would otherwise be the case. (The purchaser would argue, presumably, that the wording of the purchase and sale agreement was simply to agree the price and that it merely reflected the current value of the fixtures; however, the vendor might take the very different view that such a claim would represent a breach of contract.)

It is also possible, for example, that the purchaser could be a non-taxpayer for one reason or another: a local authority, a charity, a company in a group where there are sufficient losses to offset any profits generated and so on. In this case, HMRC will raise more tax sooner if they insist on the correct treatment. The final word goes with the legislation; apportionment is not an optional extra or in any way at the discretion of the HMRC officer. Rather, the wording is that the net proceeds of sale of a given item are to be treated as so much of the overall proceeds as is attributable to the item on a just and reasonable apportionment. The method of apportionment is not laid down by statute but the principle is there.

The most significant point for any adviser is that the position is uncertain: in this scenario, the vendor may avoid a balancing charge but there is a real risk of a different outcome. It obviously makes sense for any adviser to eliminate that risk if possible. This is where the concept of an election comes in, as discussed at 250-040.

Looking at the other side of the coin, it is common for property owners to seek to make retrospective claims, often several years after the acquisition of the building. In statutory terms, it seems quite clear that they have a right to do so if no election was signed and if the apportionment was clearly not 'just and reasonable'. However, HMRC will be unwilling to accept additional allowances for the purchaser unless they can also amend those of the vendor. HMRC have been known to use a variety of spurious arguments to resist this approach by a property owner, and it seems likely that the point will be tested in the courts in the foreseeable future, or that there will be a change to the legislation. (If the latter course is chosen, it will no doubt be labelled as a tax avoidance measure even though, in reality, it is in fact the correct application of the statutory principles.)

250-120   Typical apportionment figures

If no election is made, the question therefore arises of what is 'just and reasonable'. Early indications are that the valuation of integral features will tend to be higher than that of the other fixtures in a property.

Each case will depend on its own facts but the following may be considered as a guideline for the approximate percentage of the *overall* acquisition price of the property (ie including the land) that will qualify as fixed plant when purchasing an existing building:

	Integral features (%)	Other fixtures (%)	Total (%)
Basic office	10	5–10	15–20
Prestigious office	15	5–15	20–30
Hospitals and nursing homes	15	5–20	20–35
Hotels	15	5–20	20–35
Shopping centres	10	5–20	15–30
Industrial units	4	1–11	5–15
Sports centres	10	5–15	15–25

For example, the purchaser of a nursing home might spend £1 million on the property, a figure which will obviously include the cost of the underlying land. Of that amount, perhaps £300,000 will be qualifying expenditure on fixtures. The plant and machinery claim will include both the £300,000 and an appropriate value for all of the moveable furniture (beds, tables, chairs, etc).

These figures are very broad and should be used only to assess the approximate potential value of a claim; they do not represent a minimum or maximum but only a typical range. A figure based on such a simplistic table is very unlikely to be the best one to include in any capital allowances claim. Given the amounts of tax at stake it is rarely advantageous for the client if corners are cut; a professional valuation, undertaken by a capital allowances specialist, will greatly increase the chances of an optimum claim. Automatic acceptance by HMRC is often a sign that a claim has been understated. If, on the other hand, the claim is pitched too high then prolonged and ultimately unfruitful discussions are likely to ensue.

250-140   Residential property

The cost of plant or machinery bought for use in a dwelling house is not normally allowable. Specifically, such expenditure is not qualifying expenditure for an ordinary property

Plant and Machinery

business or an overseas property business. The main exception is in relation to furnished holiday lettings: the exclusion of relief for plant and machinery in a dwelling-house does not apply to property used for these lettings, so allowances may be claimed for fixtures and other plant and machinery in such property. See, generally, 165-200.

Newly built property

250-200   Principles

Where a new property is constructed, the operation of the tax rules should be relatively straightforward. Nevertheless, it is still the case that the claiming of valuable allowances is often overlooked.

No allowances are due for the cost of land but a substantial part of the expenditure on the construction of the building itself will qualify for plant and machinery allowances. This is nothing to do with allowances for moveable furniture and so on (though allowances will also be claimed for such items); allowances are due for substantial systems within the building.

On a practical level, those preparing tax computations must be aware that it is completely inadequate to claim allowances only for items listed in the accounts as 'fixtures and fittings'. The general electrical wiring, lighting and so on will - for example - undoubtedly qualify now as integral features within the property, even though they will correctly be shown as part of the overall cost of the building in the accounts. The same applies to sanitaryware, lifts or escalators, fitted furniture, heating and air conditioning: all will qualify as fixtures for the purposes of claiming plant and machinery allowances (whether or not as integral features) even though all simultaneously form part of the building itself.

Capital gains tax

When the property is subsequently sold, these items will qualify as part of the base cost of the building for the purposes of calculating any capital gain, even though capital allowances have been claimed on them. Only if the disposal of the property is at a loss will there be any restriction as a result of the capital allowance claim.

This principle applies both for capital gains tax as such and for the purposes of calculating any gains chargeable to corporation tax. It applies irrespective of the disposal proceeds (if any) allocated to the fixtures for capital allowance purposes at the time of sale.

Example

A company buys land for £300,000 and spends £850,000 building a new property. Of the £850,000, a total of £275,000 is identified as representing qualifying fixtures for capital allowance purposes (including integral features of £150,000). Items covered by the £275,000 include water and electrical systems, sanitaryware, alarms etc. A plant and machinery claim is therefore made for the £275,000 (in addition to any amounts spent on moveable items of plant and machinery).

> Five years later, the building is sold for £1.5 million. The base cost when calculating the capital gain is £1,150,000 (ie the cost of the land and the building). The claiming of the capital allowances has no bearing on the cost.

Legislation: TCGA 1992, s. 41(1)

250-220   Worked example

A company acquires land for £350,000 and pays £1 million (including professional costs) on the construction of a warehouse and office complex. This includes £400,000 paid ('phase one expenditure') to the builders for the initial shell of the building including floor, walls, roof, ground floor windows. The £400,000 also covers the cost of electrically operated loading bay doors, including wiring and a mechanical override system, and a value of £18,000 is placed on these items. The overall construction costs are analysed as follows:

Expenditure	£
Bay doors and associated wiring	18,000
Other phase one expenditure	382,000
Computer wiring	20,000
Phone and alarm system	20,000
Heating, ventilation, air conditioning	50,000
Other general electrical work	75,000
Hot and cold water system	30,000
Sanitaryware	20,000
Storage and fitted furniture	30,000
Other fixtures	40,000
Professional costs	80,000
General 'building works in connection' ('BWIC')	50,000
Non-qualifying building costs	185,000
Total building costs	1,000,000

The company also spends £82,000 fitting out the building with chairs, desks, computers, moveable partitions, etc. These are shown in the accounts as 'fixtures and fittings' whereas the whole of the £1 million is shown as 'additions to property'.

Despite the wording in the accounts, the items costing £82,000 are not fixtures for tax purposes as they do not legally form part of the building. Conversely, a large part of the £1 million has been expended on fixtures, even though the wording in the accounts may be thought to imply otherwise. A plant and machinery claim will be made for the £82,000 but these items are ignored for present purposes.

The first stage in claiming allowances for the building costs is to analyse the expenditure into three categories: items that do not qualify at all, items that qualify as integral features, and items that qualify as fixtures that are not integral features. The professional and overhead costs should be left out at this stage. The analysis may be on the following lines, though for present purposes a broad-brush approach has been used whereas in reality it may be appropriate to break the expenditure down further before carrying out the analysis. Sight

Plant and Machinery

of the detailed invoices (probably an initial detailed schedule of works, together with a schedule reconciling the costings to the actual expenditure) will be essential. In this case, the analysis may be on the following lines:

Bay doors and associated wiring

Although doors do not generally qualify for allowances (see item 1 of List A at s. 21(3)), it is possible to argue quite convincingly that the restriction should not apply here. If the door can be described as machinery, it is rescued from that restriction by virtue of item 1 at List C in s. 23(4). There is quite a strong argument that this is a reasonable interpretation; for capital gains tax purposes, HMRC have stated that machinery includes 'any apparatus that applies mechanical power'; in the absence of any statutory definition, it is acceptable to transpose that definition into the capital allowances rules. In a letter to the Football League back in 1991, the Revenue accepted that automatic exit doors at a football ground qualified as plant and machinery.

Failing that, it certainly seems reasonable to consider it part of an electrical system that would therefore qualify as integral features.

Assume for now that it qualifies as general fixtures.

Other phase one expenditure

On the face of it, this does not qualify. More detailed analysis may reveal that the cost includes expenditure on integral features (electric wiring or cold water systems, for example), in which case the claim should be adjusted accordingly.

Assume for now, however, that no part of this cost qualifies.

Integral features

Water systems will all be classed as integral features.

Although the computer wiring is obviously an electrical system, it also clearly falls within item 8 of List C at s. 23 ('computer, telecommunication and surveillance systems (including their wiring or other links)'). See the related argument regarding lifts at 247-100.

It seems to be justifiable to claim this cost as on fixtures that are not integral features.

Other expenditure

The phone and alarm system will qualify as standard fixtures, as will the sanitaryware, furniture and other fixtures. The general costs of £185,000 will not qualify.

Summary

The overall position may therefore be summarised as follows:

	£
General fixtures	148,000
Integral features	155,000
Non-qualifying expenditure	567,000
Total (before professional and BWIC)	870,000

At this stage, therefore, the total fixtures claim is worth around 35 per cent of the construction costs, split 17 per cent to general fixtures and 18 per cent to integral features.

The next stage is to allocate the BWIC figure of £50,000 and the professional costs of £80,000. In the absence of any particular indications, it is reasonable to allocate these costs pro-rata, so £8,500 to general fixtures, £9,000 to integral features and £32,500 to non-qualifying costs.

A little more care is needed with the professional costs and, at the least, these costs should be split between the various professionals involved. The costs of an electrical engineer should be allocated either entirely to integral features, or perhaps mainly to those but partly to other general fixtures. Similar considerations would apply to the professional costs of mechanical or service engineers. The costs of a lawyer involved with the purchase of the land, on the other hand, would be disallowed in full. Falling somewhere between those two extremes will be the costs of a quantity surveyor, an architect or a structural engineer. Say, to complete the example, that the split comes out at £35,000 for integral features, £12,000 for other fixtures, and £33,000 as relating to non-qualifying expenditure.

These various amounts will then be added to the other costs and the overall claim will be as follows:

	£
General fixtures	168,500
Integral features	199,000
Non-qualifying expenditure	632,500
Total	1,000,000

Refurbishing a property

250-300 Principles

Where an existing building is renovated, there will be no new land cost so any plant and machinery claim will simply be a question of analysing the expenditure between assets ('fixtures' in the tax sense) that qualify and those that do not. The former will then need to be sub-divided between integral features and other qualifying expenditure. Such an exercise should be relatively straightforward, but it still happens quite often that the claim for plant and machinery allowances is overlooked, or that an inadequate claim is made.

Plant and Machinery

As always in relation to claims for allowances on fixtures, the differences between the accounting and taxation terminology need to be appreciated. It may well be that the whole cost of the fit-out is properly shown in the accounts as 'additions to property' but the reality is that a substantial part of the cost will qualify as fixtures on which plant and machinery allowances may be claimed. There may also be a claim for other plant and machinery, bought as part of the overall expenditure but not constituting fixtures.

250-320   Worked example

A retailer owns the freehold of a building with a historic cost of £500,000. Bucking the general economic trend, the shop is doing well in 2009 and the owner decides to spend money refurbishing the site at an overall cost of £300,000. This includes the knocking down of an internal wall, a complete re-wire of the premises, new and improved lighting throughout and an extension to provide additional storage and better toilet facilities for staff. The cost also includes some new free-standing filing cabinets and some new computers.

To make a capital allowances claim, it will be necessary to identify those parts of the overall expenditure that qualify as fixtures. Of the overall cost of £300,000, the great majority will be classified as additions to property. Perhaps £280,000 of the total will go to that heading, with £20,000 allocated to other classes of fixed assets in the accounts.

Plant and machinery allowances can certainly be claimed on all or most of the £20,000 (cabinets, computers, etc) but these are not fixtures for tax purposes as they do not legally become part of the property. The £280,000 also contains substantial amounts of expenditure qualifying for capital allowances, however. The knocking down of the wall and the basic cost of the extension will not qualify, but relief will certainly be due for the whole cost of the re-wire (by way of capital allowances rather than as revenue expenditure if it is deemed to be part of an overall project of capital expenditure, though the point may be debatable). The new lighting, and the storage and toilet facilities will probably qualify in full for plant and machinery allowances, though it will be necessary to separate the cost of integral features from the cost of other items of expenditure.

There is no substitute here for an in-depth analysis of the expenditure, including the professional and general overhead costs. The end result may be that plant and machinery allowances can be claimed on a total of (for example) £175,000 of the £300,000. The £175,000 will include the £20,000 and may be split (say) £80,000 to general plant and machinery (including the £20,000) and £95,000 to integral features.

If the property one day comes to be sold at a gain, the base cost for calculating any capital gain (whether for capital gains tax or corporation tax purposes) is unaffected by the capital allowances claim. As such, the base cost will in principle be £780,000 (ie to include the whole of the new expenditure except for the £20,000 on items that were not fixtures). This is subject to the general principle that enhancement expenditure is only deductible for the purposes of calculating a capital gain if the expenditure is still reflected in the nature of the asset at the time when it comes to be sold. If, therefore, the property is retained for a further 20 years before being sold, and if the toilet facilities have again been replaced in that time, that part of the costs incurred now will not be deductible in the event of a sale at that later time.

Legislation: TCGA 1992, s. 38(1)(b), s. 41(1)

250-340   Incidental expenditure

Where a person incurs capital expenditure altering an existing building, and the alteration is incidental to the installation of plant or machinery for the purposes of the trade, the expenditure may be treated as part of the cost of that plant or machinery.

For example, a lift will invariably qualify as plant, whether under first principles or as an integral feature. A lift shaft does not qualify in its own right but, in an existing building, the expense may qualify as being incidental to the cost of installing a lift. Thus, the cost of the lift shaft will generally be allowed in an existing building but not in a newly constructed one.

Legislation: CAA 2001, s. 25

Other material: CA 21190

Buying a property

250-400   Principles

Overview

The purchase of any commercial property raises important capital allowance issues, all the more so since the introduction of the concept of integral features in April 2008. Any person who has bought a commercial property in recent years, and has not made a substantial capital allowances claim, is free to review the position and make a claim for any later year in which the property is still owned - there are no time limits for this and it is one way of generating significant tax savings to protect cash flow in difficult economic times.

In simple terms, a person buying a building is by definition buying the fixtures in that building. A straightforward example is the cold water system, which is part of the building but which qualifies for plant and machinery allowances.

The capital allowances available to a purchaser of a property will depend in part on the history of any allowances claimed by the vendor. It is therefore essential to establish the relevant facts before a purchase transaction is completed.

Plant and Machinery

New rules applied from 24 July 1996 and that date continues to be relevant for new claims made today. It is important to establish whether or not the vendor (or any previous person who has owned the property since 24 July 1996) has claimed allowances.

If such a claim has been made then any claim by the purchaser will be restricted to the lower of his purchase price and the expenditure incurred by the vendor or earlier owner. Subject to this cap, it is likely to be beneficial for the purchaser to sign a fixtures election under CAA 2001, s. 198(2).

If the vendor (or earlier owner since 24 July 1996) has not claimed allowances then the purchaser's allowances will be based on a 'just and reasonable' apportionment of the overall purchase cost.

Example

Company A buys a property in 1980 for £1 million and sells it to Company B for £5 million in 2002.

It is agreed that at all times a proportion of 25 per cent is appropriate as relating to the fixtures.

If Company A claimed plant and machinery allowances at 25 per cent then the disposal value to be brought into account for fixtures will be restricted to the £250,000 claimed on the original purchase. This will in turn provide the ceiling figure for any claim by Company B.

If Company A did not make any claim, and assuming that no other complications arise in respect of other claims by third parties, then the purchase price will be apportioned on the 'just and reasonable' basis. In this case, B may well be able to claim allowances on £1.25 million.

Key principles

The principles underlying this are discussed earlier in this book but a few key planning points arise:

- a purchaser needs to determine the history of claims in respect of the building, in relation to any sales that have taken place since 24 July 1996. These details cannot be vague and therefore need to be legally underpinned;
- the question of a fixtures election should be considered by both vendor and purchaser. They will have different perspectives on this but this is all the more reason why agreement should be reached as part of the negotiations;
- the sale and purchase agreement should create a legally binding commitment on the vendor to sign a fixtures election (usually under s. 198) where appropriate, and at an agreed figure;
- clarity is needed in any legal documentation to distinguish between fixtures on the one hand and loose plant and machinery on the other; and
- as a general principle, attention should be given to the effective tax rates of purchaser and vendor of a property. If, for example, a 40 per cent tax rate partnership is buying a

property from a company paying tax at a lower rate then this may create opportunities for reaching an agreement that is more tax effective overall. Issues such as the availability of trading losses or group relief also merit attention.

The following flow chart gives a simplified summary of how the rules apply on the purchase of a property:

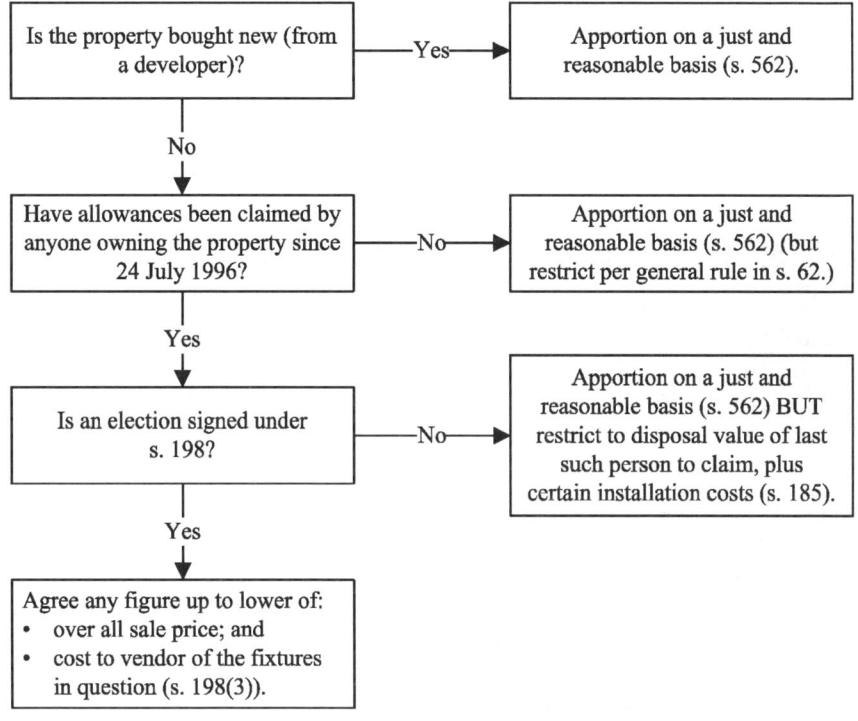

24 July 1996

The change relating to the date of 24 July 1996 is a subtle but vital one. Before that change it would be possible, for example, for Company A to sell a property to Pension Fund B which in turn sold to Company C. As the pension fund did not claim allowances, it had no disposal value and Company C could claim allowances by making an apportionment based on the values at the time it acquired the property, which might considerably exceed the original construction costs.

Under the rules as they now stand, Company C's claim is restricted by reference to Company A's disposal value, if Company A owned the property at any time since 24 July 1996. The cost of building alterations incurred by Company C in connection with the installation is also allowable.

Suppose, instead, that Company A sold not to a pension fund but to Company B which in turn sold to Company C, all transactions occurring after 24 July 1996. Ignoring any additional expenditure incurred by Company B, it must follow that Company B's disposal value will be the same as, or lower than, Company A's disposal value: the cost to Company B is restricted to Company A's disposal value, and Company B's disposal value cannot exceed the cost incurred by it.

Legislation: CAA 2001, s. 198, Sch. 3, para. 38

Significance of earlier claim

It is easy to underestimate the effect of a claim by a previous owner of the property.

> ### *Example*
>
> Macbeth buys a property in 1997 for £2 million and sells the property to Macduff in 2007 for £7 million. It is agreed, based on the nature of the property, that a fair value of the fixtures would be 25 per cent of the overall property value, so £500,000 in 1997 and £1,750,000 in 2007.
>
> If Macbeth made a claim for allowances on £500,000 then its disposal proceeds will be capped at that figure. This will in turn cap Macduff's expenditure at the same level. However, if Macbeth did not make a claim, Macduff's fixtures claim can be of £1,750,000.

This simple example shows why it is so important to establish the capital allowances history of the property in question: how can the sale price be agreed without any idea of the tax relief due to the purchaser? The example also shows that the vendor needs to understand that making a last minute claim may be the worst thing to do – in this case, it would probably be much better to make no claim but to negotiate a higher price based on the tax relief due to the purchaser. On the other hand, it is possible that the purchaser may be a non-taxpayer, (eg a local authority or, in some circumstances, a charity). In this case, the vendor might indeed wish to make a last minute claim and then agree with the purchaser that an election should be signed setting the fixtures value at zero, so as to retain the allowances in full. Vendors, purchasers, lawyers and tax advisers all need to be clear about what they are doing!

Further claim

Another point to bear in mind is that an election under CAA 2001, s. 198 is not necessarily the end of the matter. Legally, the election can only relate to expenditure in respect of which a disposal value has to be brought into account, and therefore only expenditure in respect of which an earlier claim has been made.

It is quite possible that the vendor will have made an inadequate claim, perhaps covering the cost of air conditioning but not the cost of the lift. The election can in such a case only cover the expenditure in respect of which the claim had been made (the air conditioning, in this instance) so the purchaser is in principle free to make a subsequent claim in relation to other fixtures. It is possible, however, that in seeking to obtain the information needed to submit the claim the purchaser will alert the vendor to the need to make a final claim which may then restrict the opportunities available to the purchaser. For all these reasons, the issues should be wrapped up in the legal documentation.

Legal documentation

For the various reasons alluded to above, the legal documentation in relation to the purchase and sale of any commercial property is critical. The blunt reality is that some lawyers know what they are doing in this area but many others do not. When combined with the fact that capital allowances on property are poorly understood by many other professionals too, opportunities to maximise tax relief in this area are frequently overlooked.

As a minimum, the purchaser of a property should gain legal certainty in relation to the following points:

(1) Is the property in question held as a fixed asset or as trading stock?

(2) What capital allowances have been claimed by the present owner in relation to fixtures? (Establish the quantum of the claim and the precise assets in relation to which the claim was made.)

(3) Is the vendor required to bring in a disposal value as a result of the purchase and sale?

(4) Has the current vendor owned the property since at least 24 July 1996? (If not, obtain full details of the previous owner(s) back to that date and, if possible, of any claims made by those previous owners.)

(5) Did the current vendor claim any allowances in relation to fixtures when acquiring the property?

(6) Will the vendor give a legal commitment to make no further claims in relation to fixtures in the property?

(7) Will the vendor give a legal commitment to sign an election under s. 198 if so requested by the purchaser? The legal agreement should also commit the vendor to including a particular figure for fixtures in that election. (This will be subject to negotiation but the agreement to sign the election is otherwise of little or no value.)

(8) What other capital allowance claims (eg regarding IBAs) have been made by the current vendor or by previous owners?

250-420 Elections in practice: the buyer's perspective

The theory behind the making of a fixtures election under CAA 2001, s. 198 is considered at 245-700. An important aspect of the fixtures rules is the opportunity, in certain circumstances, to choose how the overall value of a purchase and sale should be allocated between different elements. A valid election takes precedence over any apportionment that would otherwise be made.

Where there is an arm's length sale of a building, the seller and the purchaser may jointly elect to fix the amount (being part of the overall proceeds of the transaction) that is to be treated as the expenditure incurred by the purchaser on the provision of the fixture. The amount fixed by the election must not exceed either the overall sale price or the amount of the vendor's capital expenditure on the provision of the fixture. Subject to that, there is no question of the figures in the election having to be 'reasonable' or 'realistic'.

Example

A property containing fixtures is sold for £1 million. The cost of the plant within the building had historically amounted to £160,000. The value of the plant is currently £20,000. The vendor company has large trading losses brought forward.

The vendor and purchaser may agree to allocate £160,000 to the fixtures. The vendor will incur balancing charges but these may be covered by the trading losses brought forward. The purchaser can claim capital allowances on the £160,000.

If such an election is made then the remaining part of the sale price is allocated to other property which is not the fixture but which formed part of the overall transaction.

The above example demonstrates how the election can offer the buyer a significant tax saving. If no election had been made, and if the inspector had insisted on a just and reasonable apportionment, it is likely that a much lower figure would have been agreed (though this should *not* be the market value of the assets at the time of sale: see, instead, the formula explained at 250-200). Furthermore, the election removes most of the uncertainties (and costs) that can arise if an apportionment is needed.

The buyer should always ask the vendor, however, for a complete list of assets that are covered by the election, together with confirmation that the elected figure does not exceed the historic cost of those assets, and also confirmation that the vendor has not made capital allowance claims in relation to any other fixtures. It is quite common, for example, to see cases where the vendor has claimed for some assets but not others: for example, a hotel vendor may list numerous assets within the building that have been the subject of a fixtures claim but may make no mention of the hotel swimming pool. Armed with the list of items on which the claim has been made, and with confirmation that no other claims have been made, the purchaser can make an apportioned claim on the swimming pool. As the vendor has not claimed any part of that cost, his or her tax computation is not affected by the purchaser's claim and the value of the new claim will be related to replacement rather than historic cost.

250-440   Worked example (no previous claim)

This worked example concerns the purchase of a care home from a local authority which has owned the property since 1995. This is a straightforward case because:

- the local authority will not be a taxpayer, and so will not have claimed any capital allowances; and

- as it has owned the property since before 24 July 1996, there is no requirement to consider the position of any earlier owner.

Assume that the purchaser is a company which bought the care home as a going concern in May 2009. The cost of the property is £2 million and a separate payment of £40,000 is made for the 'fixtures and fittings' which are listed in an inventory and consist of tables, beds, chairs, mirrors and a few other items of moveable furniture.

It is assumed (surprisingly often) that the capital allowances claim should be for just £40,000, and it often happens that the claim is restricted to that figure. In reality, none of that figure relates to 'fixtures' in the tax sense as the items are all moveable and do not therefore come within the statutory definition, which covers 'plant or machinery that is so installed or otherwise fixed in or to a building ... as to become, in law, part of that building ...'.

Even if it is accepted that a separate claim is to be made for the fixtures, it may be argued that the value of those fixtures is minimal - the care home is perhaps in a fairly shabby state of repair and nobody would pay anything for the fixtures if they were stripped out for sale. Fortunately, this is completely irrelevant.

The £2 million has to be apportioned between the fixtures and the rest of the property, using the formula discussed at 250-080. This requires the claimant to establish the replacement cost of the fixtures. As the property has been acquired since April 2008, the fixtures in question will include the whole lighting and general electrical system, and all hot and cold water facilities as well as the sanitaryware, perhaps a lift and a wide range of other fitted equipment, etc.

Valuation expertise is required to establish the three key elements to be used in the formula, namely the replacement cost of the fixtures, the replacement cost of the rest of the building and the value of the bare land. Many claims break down at this point as accountants may be reluctant to involve other professionals, perhaps fearing that costs will be incurred that cannot be recovered or that this is something that can be done easily enough in-house. However, HMRC instructions to their own staff are to involve the Valuation Office Agency in all cases and it is unlikely that anyone without valuation expertise will pitch the claim at the level that gains the best outcome for the client whilst being defendable against a probe by the District Valuer or Regional Building Surveyor. The amounts of money at stake are such that professional valuation costs should be readily justifiable.

Suppose, in this case, that the replacement cost of the fixtures is valued at £700,000, the replacement value of the rest of the building at £1,200,000 and the value of the bare land at £500,000. This would then mean that the fixtures valuation for capital allowances purposes would be calculated as £2 million $\times$ 700,000/(700,000 + 1,200,000 + £500,000). This would produce a figure of £583,333 for the fixtures and a plant and machinery claim can be made for that amount (in addition to the £40,000 already claimed). The surveyor carrying out the valuation will need to split this amount between integral features and other fixtures.

250-460 Worked example (election)

This example considers a scenario where Company A is buying an office from Company B and where Company B has claimed allowances.

Assume once more that the transaction takes place in May 2009, that the consideration for the purchase of the office is agreed at £800,000 but that the vendor is asking for an additional £30,000 for moveable fixtures and fittings. It has been agreed in principle that an election will be signed (under s. 198) to establish for capital allowances purposes the value of the fixtures on the transfer.

Where the purchaser knows that the vendor has claimed plant and machinery allowances, it is very important for the purchaser to establish in detail the history of any claims made. Whilst this enquiry process sometimes has to take place after the event (sometimes many years later) it is far better for the purchaser to gain certainty on past claims as part of the negotiation for the purchase.

The details to be obtained should be a complete list of assets forming part of the sale agreement on which capital allowances have been claimed. At this stage, the purchaser must insist on absolute clarity between those assets that constitute fixtures as defined for tax purposes and those that are plant and machinery but not fixtures. This distinction is often not clearly understood but the statutory rules are different in many significant respects.

The vendor may produce a schedule on the following lines, listing all the fixtures (in the tax sense) on which plant and machinery allowances have been claimed:

Item	Current valuation £
Alarms	500
Central heating system	5,000
Lift	10,000
Reception desk (fitted)	500
Sanitaryware	2,500
Switchboard and telephone system	3,000
Total	21,500

Quite possibly, the vendor will wish to sign an election under s. 198 and will suggest that the figure to go into the election will be £21,500 as above. In practice, vendors are often unwilling to sign an election with any figure that will produce a balancing charge for them. This then raises many considerations for the purchaser, as per the headings below.

Assets on which allowances have been claimed

The first consideration is that of whether or not the purchaser wishes to agree to sign an election in relation to the assets listed above. Signing an election has many practical advantages as it creates certainty for both parties and removes the need for any valuation of the assets concerned.

Against this, however, is that to value the assets according to their current market value is quite wrong in principle. What is being sought here is not an additional sum of money to be paid in addition to the cost of the building. Rather, the fixtures form a part of that building and established valuation principles would give a very much higher figure (based on replacement cost) than simply the current used asset value. That figure will, however, be capped at the historic cost of the assets concerned.

If an apportionment is made rather than an election being signed, the value to be attributed to these assets is likely to be many times higher than the £21,500 suggested by the vendor. Thus the certainty gained by the election comes at a very high tax cost to the purchaser. At the very least, the purchaser should use this as a negotiating tool to obtain a much higher figure than £21,500 to go into the election.

Other assets

The next point is for the purchaser to ensure that the list of fixtures on which allowances have been claimed is watertight and therefore built in to the legal paperwork. There are two reasons for this. Firstly, the vendor should enter into a legally binding agreement to make no further capital allowance claims in relation to the fixtures in the property. If the vendor draws accounts up to 31 December 2009, for example, a further claim could in theory be made at any time up to 31 December 2011. This would considerably reduce the scope for the purchaser to claim on other fixtures and the legal agreement should therefore contain a binding agreement that the vendor will make no further claim.

The second and related point is that if there are assets on which no claim has been made then the purchaser can claim separately on those items, in addition to whatever figure is agreed for the fixtures election. This separate part of the purchaser's capital allowance claim (relating only to the assets on which no claim has previously been made) will be based on the replacement cost of the fixtures in question and will be in accordance with the worked example at 250-440. This part of the purchaser's claim will not have any impact on the vendor's tax position - the vendor has not claimed allowances on the additional items and therefore does not have any disposal proceeds to bring into account.

If the vendor has owned the property since before April 2008, then no claim will have been made for those integral features (such as general electrical and lighting systems and cold water systems) that did not previously qualify for plant and machinery allowances. In addition, however, it is likely that there will be many other fixtures on which a claim may be made. In an office, these may include (for example) air conditioning, blinds, canteen and kitchen equipment, carpets, built-in display units, hand driers, moveable partitions, shelving. As in the example at 250-440, a claim can be made based on the replacement cost of these items (in accordance with the formula 250-080).

Summary

The claim to be made by the purchaser will therefore consist of three elements. The first is £30,000 for the moveable items of furniture. The second is the figure for those fixtures on which a claim has been made by the vendor. If an election is signed, the figure will lie

Plant and Machinery

somewhere between zero and the historic cost to the vendor of the identified assets, but in principle it should be considerably higher than the current market valuation of £21,500. The third element will be the apportioned value of those assets, often including all integral features, on which no previous plant and machinery claim has been made.

250-480 Worked example (no election, advising three years later)

This example addresses the issue of a retrospective claim on a property - a restaurant - that was bought several years earlier, say in 2006. No fixtures election was signed. The sale and purchase agreement showed an analysis of expenditure as follows:

	£
Freehold property	800,000
Goodwill	120,000
Plant and equipment	14,000
Total purchase price	934,000

Nothing further was said in the legal documentation about capital allowances, which were duly claimed on £14,000. However, the agreement did relate the £14,000 to a list of certain items that were to be left behind by the vendor (cutlery, crockery, glassware, various items of moveable kitchen equipment, tables, chairs).

The current owner ('the Client') has heard that it may be possible to make a further claim. The restaurant is profitable and the allowances can be used if available.

This scenario arises frequently in practice and it raises some important practical questions. The technical issues become quite complex and it is therefore important to ensure that the statutory path to any further claim is clearly thought through.

The Client has bought an interest in a property and can therefore claim plant and machinery allowances on fixtures in that property. There is clear evidence here that the £14,000 relates to moveable items of plant and equipment (which are therefore not fixtures in the tax sense). It follows that the £800,000 paid for the property must also represent payment for any fixtures in the property. This is entirely normal as, by definition, those fixtures form part of the property and it is therefore a false dichotomy to say that there are two separate assets, the property and the fixtures.

Apportionment

As discussed at 250-080, the legislation requires that where an item of property is sold with other property then a 'just and reasonable apportionment' must be made to allocate the payment between the various types of property (i.e. in this context, to allocate the overall capital expenditure between the fixtures on the one hand and the other parts of the property on the other). There is a further requirement about restricting the claim to the vendor's disposal proceeds, and this is considered below, but first it is worth going into more depth on the apportionment issue.

The requirement to make an apportionment is set out at CAA 2001, s. 562. Key parts of that section read as follows, with emphasis added in relation to wording discussed below:

- s. 562(2) states that 'all property sold as a result of one bargain *is to be treated* as sold together even though ... separate prices are ... agreed for separate items of that property';
- s. 562(3)(a) covers the scenario where one item is sold with other assets and states that 'the net proceeds of the sale of that item *are to be treated* as being so much of the net proceeds of sale of all the property as, on a just and reasonable apportionment, is attributable to that item';
- s. 562(3)(b) then states that 'the expenditure incurred on the provision or purchase of that item *is to be treated* as being so much of the consideration given for all the property as, on a just and reasonable apportionment, is attributable to that item'.

The words in italics make it clear that this is not just one possible way of determining the amount to be allocated to different items that are bought or sold - it is the only correct statutory path. This section of legislation imposes a duty on the vendor, on the purchaser and on HMRC to ensure that the computations on sale are dealt with by way of a just and reasonable apportionment (unless the provisions are overridden by an election under s. 198).

It is also worth noting at this point that s. 562(3) gives the context, which is that these provisions apply *if an item of property is sold*, so the statutory requirement is applied on an item by item basis - it is necessary to find the just and reasonable apportionment for each item that is sold.

HMRC instructions recognise these principles and state the following at CA 12300:

> 'An interest in land to which an asset that qualifies for capital allowances is attached may be sold. The asset may be a building, structure or fixture. If so you need to apportion the sale price to find out how much of the sale price is attributable to the asset. The normal apportionment provisions in CAA 2001, s. 562(1)-(3) apply and you should make a just apportionment.'

Instructions to tax officers who open an enquiry into these matters are that they **must** [HMRC's emphasis] refer all such apportionments to the District Valuer, that they **must** use the DV's figures and that they **must** not settle cases by negotiating figures themselves.

So this raises the issue of what is a 'just and reasonable apportionment' in relation to the fixtures acquired with the property acquired by the Client in this example. There is no statutory guidance as to the meaning of this phrase, but there are long established principles about how it is to be interpreted. These principles are as laid out at 250-080 and are based on a formula that looks at the replacement cost of the items concerned, so the current market value is not in point. In the majority of cases, the apportionment figure will produce a valuation in excess of historic cost.

In the example, the Client has paid £800,000 for the property. That property will certainly have included substantial amounts of fixtures (central heating, ventilation, sanitaryware,

Plant and Machinery

fitted kitchen equipment, etc.) but no value has been attributed to these items (as the £14,000 related only to moveable items of equipment, which are by definition not fixtures). The property was bought before the rules relating to integral features increased the overall value of the fixtures qualifying for plant and machinery allowances. The actual value of qualifying expenditure will depend very much on the nature of the restaurant but it may well be in six figures. Using £100,000 as a sample figure, the scenario is therefore that assets have been treated as being transferred at a value of nil when the correct value should have been £100,000 (but still subject to historic cost, to be discussed below).

If the Client's advisers put it to HMRC that the figures used in the computation relating to the transaction were incorrect, it is likely that this will provoke a rash of arguments in response. The instinctive reaction is understandable, as HMRC are faced with a purchaser who is asking for a radically different application of the tax rules (ie one that is now based on correct interpretation of those rules) at a time when the vendor has probably disappeared into the sunset and is not the slightest bit interested in re-working the tax computations of a few years earlier, quite possibly in a way that will prove extremely expensive.

Regrettably, many of the HMRC arguments will be incorrect as the unfortunate reality is that many Inspectors do not understand the capital allowance rules in relation to property transactions. The only solution in these cases is to insist that the Inspector brings the case back to the statutory wording and to ensure that the claims are correctly calculated on that basis. Two particular arguments are worth considering.

First, the issue of the vendor's tax liabilities is of no direct interest to the purchaser Client - that is simply a matter for HMRC to sort out with the vendor. The Client as purchaser has every right to insist on a correct application of the rules to his own tax position. (In practice, a purchaser will obviously wish to ensure that he has not signed any indemnity provisions or warranties or otherwise given any relevant contractual promise to the vendor (eg to claim no further capital allowances). In practice, however, this is rarely the case.)

Second, HMRC may possibly argue that anything agreed between the parties at arm's length must be de facto a just and reasonable apportionment. There are, however, several problems with this, including in particular the following:

- there is the fundamental question of whether a zero value can conceivably be a just and reasonable valuation for a wide range of assets that clearly have value on any possible approach;
- the legislation is quite specific and explicit in requiring an apportionment that overrides anything that may have been agreed between the parties;
- the Valuation Office Agency formulas have been in the public domain for many years (following, it is understood, some lengthy and detailed discussions between professional valuers outside and inside the Revenue) and have been applied consistently and regularly over that period;
- those formulas would never come out with a zero figure in a case such as this and, as mentioned above, might well come out with a figure in the region of £100,000; and
- there is no evidence that the specific issue of how to value the fixtures has in fact been considered at all. It is much more likely in reality that the list of plant and equipment

was produced simply to ensure that the purchaser did not find that certain essential items had been sold off; certainly it has nothing to do with fixtures in their tax sense.

There is, however, one HMRC argument that is based on sound principles and that needs to be seriously addressed. This is the question of the restriction of any claim to cost where the vendor had already claimed allowances. This is now considered.

Restriction to cost
If the vendor of the property had already claimed capital allowances on any particular fixture then the value to be attributed to the fixture is capped at the vendor's sales proceeds figure for that particular asset (s. 185(2)). That disposal figure is in turn capped at the historic cost figure of the asset in question (s. 62(1)). If the vendor had in turn bought the property since 24 July 1996 then it will be necessary to restrict allowances to expenditure incurred by that owner (s. 185(4) and Sch. 3, para. 38).

These provisions raise many practical issues, the most obvious one being that the purchaser is unlikely to know which assets had been the subject of an earlier capital allowances claim. The Client, of course, has no power at this stage to force the vendor to co-operate in any way.

The restrictions only apply (on an asset by asset basis) where the vendor or previous owner had claimed allowances. It is quite possible, for example, that allowances were claimed on an air conditioning unit but were never claimed on the cost of the toilets and urinals. In that case, the claim by the Client now would need to be restricted to the historic cost for the air conditioning but no such restriction would apply to the toilets. Indeed, it is worth noting that the claim by the Client in relation to the toilets and urinals will have no bearing on the vendor's tax position as no claim was ever made for those items.

Even where a claim was made (or may have been made) in relation to a particular fixture, it is unlikely that the Client will have details of the historic cost of that item. So what is to be done in practice? HMRC guidance at CA 26400 states as follows:

> 'It is the responsibility of the taxpayer to obtain and provide details of the past owner and the disposal value. Where it seems likely that Section 185 will apply but the taxpayer does not provide details of the previous disposal value, no allowances should be given as the previous disposal value may be nil or negligible.'

This is the crunch issue, but it is strongly suggested that the HMRC guidance is at best misleading and is in reality simply wrong. Once more, it is necessary to go back to statutory principles and to ask whether it is justifiable for HMRC to claim that 'the previous disposal value may be nil or negligible'.

The apportionment rules at s. 562(3)(a) (as quoted above) state that where one item is sold with other assets 'the net proceeds of the sale of that item are to be treated as being so much of the net proceeds of sale of all the property as, on a just and reasonable apportionment, is attributable to that item'. In other words, the obligation to make a just and reasonable apportionment applies as much to the vendor as to the purchaser, and is (as argued above) unambiguously a statutory provision that must be applied.

Plant and Machinery

As also explained above, it is likely in practice that the just and reasonable apportionment figure will be higher than the historic cost. But even if this is not accepted as a working principle, there are only two possible outcomes:

(1)   The just and reasonable apportionment figure comes out higher than the historic cost, in which case the value to be used for capital allowance purposes must be the historic cost. That cost, self-evidently, can never be nil and there is no justification whatsoever for saying that the value should be negligible.

(2)   The just and reasonable apportionment figure comes out at or below the historic cost, in which case the concept of restricting to cost simply goes away.

This still leaves the question of how to establish the historic cost if the vendor is not willing to co-operate. Fortunately, professional valuers are able to make a fairly accurate estimate of costs, using their expertise to assess the age of the fixtures in question and then applying published tables of values to reach a cost figure.

There is only one circumstance in which there can be a justification for a 'nil or negligible' value. That is the scenario in which the vendor had in turn bought the property and signed an election to agree a low value for the fixtures in question. It is in practice unlikely that the vendor will have signed an election when buying the property but completely ignored the issue of fixtures when selling it. It may also be possible, from planning records or again from the professional expertise of the valuers, to demonstrate that particular fixtures had clearly been installed in the property since the (verifiable) date on which the vendor had acquired the property. Furthermore, of course, any election signed by the vendor when acquiring the property should still be on that vendor's tax file and it is open to HMRC to go and have a look. In the end, the point is that the computations on the transaction between the vendor and the Client did not contain an election and it is quite clear that all parties, including HMRC, failed to ask the correct technical questions at the time.

Selling a property

250-600   Principles

A person contemplating the sale of a commercial property should never ignore capital allowances as they can be a very significant part of the overall financial deal.

In principle, a potential vendor should ask two questions:

(1)   have all available allowances been claimed?

(2)   to what extent can the value of those allowances be retained in the context of a sale?

It is possible, of course, that the vendor will not need the allowances (if, for example, it has incurred trading losses) or that it will wish to give up the value of those allowances in return for a better commercial price for the property itself. That is not the same, however, as simply overlooking the potential value. It is surprising how often the price of a property is agreed before any decision has been made as to who will benefit from the substantial value of the allowances.

There are occasions where it makes good sense for the vendor to give up the chance of claiming allowances on certain fixtures, so that a greater benefit may pass to the purchaser, as illustrated in the example at 250-640.

If a vendor has claimed allowances in full, it will almost certainly be in his interests to sign a fixtures election with the purchaser (see, generally, 250-040). If no election is signed, the apportioned value to be attributed to the fixtures (see 250-080) is likely to be higher than their historic cost, in which case the full amount of allowances received will be given back by way of a balancing charge. If the purchaser is not particularly alert to the capital allowance issues, or is simply keen to secure the property, he may agree to sign a fixtures election that assigns a low value to the fixtures on which claims have been made. It is quite common for this to be a figure that equates either to current market value or to the value that will ensure that the vendor suffers no balancing charge. This is illustrated at 250-660.

250-620   Elections in practice: the seller's perspective

The theory behind the making of a fixtures election under CAA 2001, s. 198 is considered at 245-700 and the buyer's perspective is commented on at 250-420. An important aspect of the fixtures rules is the opportunity, in certain circumstances, to choose how the overall value of a purchase and sale should be allocated between different elements. A valid election takes precedence over any apportionment that would otherwise be made.

For the seller, an election removes uncertainty (allowing an earlier and cheaper resolution of the final capital allowances computation) and provides an opportunity to retain earlier allowances or even to claim new allowances (if, in either case, they can be used) or the chance to reflect the value of the potential allowances (if they cannot).

Suppose, for example, that the vendor company has been well advised and has claimed significant levels of allowances in relation to fixtures in a modern office that is being sold for £3 million. Perhaps the total cost of the fixtures was £500,000 and the written down value is £100,000. Assume that the market value of those fixtures is taken to be £50,000. The vendor company has various options:

(1)   If it can use all available allowances, the vendor could insist on writing into the agreement for the sale that the fixtures will be the subject of an election in the figure of £1. In this way, the company will bring a disposal value of just £1 into the tax computations and will obtain further allowances to the value of £99,999.

(2)   If the purchaser is on the ball, he will at least seek to negotiate on that figure. Suppose that he is willing to sign an election, but only if it is made at market value. The vendor may accept this, in which case the vendor will still be able to claim additional allowances, based on a disposal figure of £50,000. Those allowances may be given either by ongoing writing-down allowances, or as a balancing allowance, depending on all the circumstances.

Plant and Machinery

(3) The purchaser may negotiate harder, and insist that the assets should be transferred at the tax written down value of £100,000. The vendor's tax position will then be neutral, in that the disposal value will wipe out the value brought forward. The vendor still gains certainty on the issue, is still sure of retaining all allowances already received and, if giving a level of allowances in excess of market value, can legitimately highlight that fact in negotiating about the value of the building being sold.

(4) Finally, it is open to the parties to agree that the fixtures should be sold for a higher figure of up to the historic cost of the fixtures (£500,000). The vendor can, of course, refuse to sign an election in such a figure. On the other hand, it may be (for example) that the vendor company has unused losses that can cover any balancing charge (or make it unimportant if there are reduced writing-down allowances) in which case the vendor may be willing to allow a higher figure to go into the election in return for a higher overall disposal value for the building.

The point in all cases is that the well-advised purchaser or seller will be considering the true value of the allowances and will be negotiating accordingly. It remains the case that many businesses, and their advisers, fail to grasp the issues and a party to the transaction who *is* properly advised may therefore still be able to achieve a surprisingly good result.

250-620   Worked example (vendor has unclaimed allowances)

Nora has owned a cafe since the late 1980s and is about to sell it. It is established during the sale process that no capital allowances have been claimed for certain refurbishment works that were carried out in 1994. These included new toilet facilities and a new bar area, both of which are still in place today.

The cost of the 1994 work was thought to be about £30,000 and Nora thinks she may have the paperwork somewhere to back up a claim at this late stage. As a basic rate taxpayer, the allowances are potentially worth in the region of £6,000, if she claims now and retains the full benefit. She will not be able to claim either first-year allowances or annual investment allowances as these are only available for the year in which the expenditure is incurred. However, as she still owns the assets she can claim writing-down allowances for any year that is not yet finalised under self-assessment principles (so by 31 January 2011, for example, in relation to a claim for 2008-09). In practice, if the business is coming to an end, any relief will be by way of a balancing allowance.

A draft apportionment exercise (see 250-080) reveals that the value to be attributed to the refurbishment works now would be £70,000. The purchaser is a company paying tax at 28 per cent, so the potential value of the allowances is nearly £20,000. However, if Nora claims allowances then the £70,000 would be restricted to the historic cost of £30,000.

It therefore makes sense for Nora to give a legally binding commitment not to claim allowances on those works, and for the purchase price to be increased by an amount that leaves both parties better off in overall terms.

On the other hand, if the price has already been fixed and Nora has not given any commitment to the contrary, then she may as well make the claim and gain the tax advantage. Ideally, she would then sign a fixtures election allocating a minimal value to the assets in question.

250-640   Worked example (vendor has claimed full allowances)

Ann and Arthur, a married couple trading as a partnership, have run a successful restaurant and are now planning to sell it as a going concern. They have been well advised on capital allowance issues and have claimed significant levels of allowances in relation to the fixtures within the property. The expected sale price of the business is £700,000, to include goodwill, property and fixtures and fittings. The purchasers' solicitors have asked for an inventory of furniture and equipment that will be left behind and have asked for a suggested allocation of the overall figure between the different assets.

Ann and Arthur list out the moveable items that they will be leaving behind (excluding trading stock). The main assets are pieces of free-standing kitchen equipment and machinery, tablecloths, napkins, chairs, glasses, crockery, cutlery. They make a schedule of these items, confirm that all fixtures will also be left and suggest that the proceeds should be allocated £4,998 to the items in the schedule, a nominal £2 to fixtures, £50,000 to goodwill and £645,000 to the property. They suggest that a fixtures election should be signed under s. 198 of CAA 2001 in relation to all fixtures in the property, with £1 each allocated to integral features and to other fixtures. Ann and Arthur make it clear that the £2 is in addition to the £4,998 for the items in the schedule.

If the purchasers accept this arrangement, this is the best possible outcome for Ann and Arthur in relation to the sale of the fixtures. They gain certainty on the tax treatment and their disposal value - at just £2 - is as good as it can be.

If the purchasers are well advised, however, and as long as they are in a reasonably strong negotiating position, they may well wish to insist on a more favourable outcome for themselves. Signing an election does give them the benefit of certainty, but to do so at a figure of just £1 each for integral features and other fixtures is not in their best interests.

Capital gains tax issues

251-000   Capital gains tax implications

Basic principle

Where a property is sold, and the property contains plant and machinery that is sold as part of a single transaction, an issue may arise as to how any capital allowances will affect either the base cost or the disposal proceeds of the property for capital gains tax purposes.

There is specific legislation within the *Taxation of Chargeable Gains Act* 1992 ('TCGA 1992') to address this issue. Section 37(2) of that Act makes it clear that the full consideration still needs to be brought into account in the capital gains computation even where it partly represents disposal proceeds for capital allowances purposes. Section 41, on the other hand, makes it clear that allowable expenditure for the purposes of the capital gains computation does not have to be restricted by reference to any capital allowances claimed. This is subject to special rules where the capital gains tax computation produces a loss.

The following examples illustrate the above principles. For simplicity, they ignore indexation allowance. It should be borne in mind that indexation is not now able to create or augment a capital gains tax loss.

Example

In the ordinary way, where no capital allowances are involved, a small property may be bought for £100,000 and sold for £150,000. This will produce a capital gain of £50,000.

Suppose that when the property is bought for £100,000, a claim is made in respect of £20,000 of that £100,000 as representing fixtures that qualify as plant. Suppose that the property is still sold for £150,000 but at that stage no value is allocated to plant or machinery. In this case, the capital gain is still calculated as £50,000 since the legislation 'shall not require the exclusion from the sums allowable as a deduction in the computation of the gain of any expenditure as being expenditure in respect of which a capital allowance or renewals allowance is made' (TCGA 1992, s. 41(1)). The net result is therefore that there is still a capital gain of £50,000 but allowances totalling £20,000 will be available (made up of any combination of first-year, writing-down and balancing allowances).

Suppose that, instead, the property is bought for £100,000 and sold for £150,000 and that at the time of both the purchase and the sale an amount of £20,000 is allocated to plant (bearing in mind that the amount allocated as proceeds of plant cannot for capital allowance purposes exceed the cost.) In this case, there will still be a gain of £50,000. However, in these circumstances no allowances will have been given overall since any first-year or writing-down allowances will have been recaptured, normally through a balancing charge but possibly by way of a reduction in the pool value, at the time of the sale.

The above examples make it clear first that there is every benefit in claiming capital allowances even where the property containing the fixtures will be sold, and second that a crucial part of a sales process is to consider how much should be allocated to plant and machinery.

In the above examples, the trader has gained tax relief on £20,000 more in the earlier example than in the latter one. If this appears to create an imbalance as far as the Public Revenue is concerned, that imbalance will be removed when the new purchaser comes in turn to sell the assets. Suppose that he in due course sells with nothing allocated to plant or machinery. In the earlier example he is deemed to have paid nothing for the plant and so will obtain no balancing allowance. In the second example he is deemed to have paid £20,000 and so will have allowances on that amount.

Legislation: TCGA 1992, s. 37(2), 41(1)

Modification of normal rule where disposal produces CGT loss

The above rules are modified where under the capital gains tax rules a loss is made. In this case, the legislation requires that 'the amount of any losses accruing on the disposal of an asset shall be restricted by reference to capital allowances and renewal allowances'. The effect of this legislation is that the allowable expenditure must be reduced by the amount of allowances actually given. For these purposes, it is necessary to establish the amount of allowances net of any balancing charge.

Example

Suppose, for example, that a property was bought for £170,000 and sold for £140,000. Suppose that £20,000 was allocated to plant at the time of purchase but nothing was allocated to plant at the time of sale. Without any special rules, there would simply be a capital loss of £30,000. However, the £170,000 needs to be adjusted for the net allowances given of £20,000, thereby reducing the deemed cost of the property to £150,000. As such, the loss arising will be £10,000. Thus the £30,000 'real' loss is relieved as to £20,000 through the capital allowances system and as to £10,000 through the capital gains tax system.

Finally, suppose that of the sale proceeds of £140,000, £6,000 was allocated to plant. In this case, the capital gains computation would show disposal proceeds of £140,000 and an allowable cost of £156,000 (£170,000 less net allowances given of £14,000). In this case, the real loss of £30,000 is relieved as to £14,000 through the capital allowances system and as to £16,000 through the capital gains tax rules.

Legislation: TCGA 1992, s. 41(1)

Further modification where asset acquired at written-down value

In certain circumstances, the adjustment of the loss (as discussed above) will need to take account of capital allowances enjoyed not only by the vendor but also by previous owners of the asset. This will apply when the vendor had acquired the asset at its tax written-down value where either:

- an election was made under CAA 2001, s. 569 (sales without change of control or between connected persons); or
- the transfer was one to which CAA 2001, s. 268 applied (succession to trade on death).

In these circumstances, it will be necessary to look at capital allowances given both to the actual vendor and to previous owners who had then transferred the asset to the current vendor at the written-down value for capital allowance purposes.

Legislation: TCGA 1992, s. 41(3)

Plant and Machinery

Particular types of property

252-000 Introduction

The capital allowances legislation, as it applies in relation to plant and machinery, does not generally distinguish between different types of buildings: there are no special rules relating only to offices or to retail premises, for example. Nevertheless, different types of property do in practice tend to generate particular issues, not least in terms of the parts of the building likely to qualify for plant and machinery allowances. The purpose of this short chapter is therefore to provide a few pointers to practical matters relating to some common types of property.

252-050 Offices

General comments

The question of whether an office qualifies for industrial buildings allowances is worth considering for as long as those allowances are available. Almost invariably, the answer is that they do not, but it is worth bearing in mind that the definition of 'office' for IBA purposes has certain nuances. These are considered in depth at 302-825.

Plant and machinery

Any office should contain a substantial number of items qualifying as plant and machinery.

Moveable items do not generally present any difficulties. Allowances will be due without problem for office furniture (chairs, desks, tables, computers, printers, telephones and fax machines, bookcases, clocks, filing cabinets, all other office machinery, all moveable furniture). Books should also be claimed as plant if they are not properly written off as a revenue expense.

As always, it is the fixtures in the office that may be more easily overlooked. Items that will typically qualify as office fixtures will include the following. (These items should normally be classified as improvements to property (and should therefore be counted when computing any capital gain on a future disposal of the office) but should also be the subject of a plant and machinery claim for fixtures.) The list is intended to be indicative rather than exhaustive and reference should be made to the A to Z section beginning at 260-000 for any cases where the tax treatment is in doubt:

- aerials;
- alarms (burglar, fire, etc);
- air conditioning units, fans, etc (now as integral features);
- blinds;
- boilers;
- cameras;
- canteen fittings and equipment;

- car park bollards, automatic barriers, etc;
- carpets;
- central heating systems (as integral features);
- closed circuit TV systems;
- cold water systems (as integral features);
- computer servers and related items;
- conduits for computer or other specialist wiring;
- counters and checkouts;
- curtains;
- display equipment;
- door entry systems;
- drink machines;
- electrical installations (as integral features);
- electrically operated doors, etc;
- electricity generators;
- emergency lighting;
- escalators, conveyors etc (as integral features);
- external solar shading (as integral features);
- fire alarm systems (but see 160-500);
- fitted furniture;
- floodlighting;
- flooring materials;
- fridges and freezers;
- furniture and furnishings;
- gas systems for hot water, central heating, etc (as integral features if part of a space or water heating system);
- hand driers;
- hot water supplies (as integral features);
- humidity control systems;
- kitchen equipment and fittings;
- letter boxes;
- lifts (and, in some circumstances, lift shafts) (as integral features);
- lighting systems (as integral features);
- machinery;
- mezzanine floors (in some circumstances only – see 260-780);
- mirrors;
- moveable partitions if there is a real intention that they should be moved;
- public address systems;
- radiators;
- safes;
- sanitaryware (basins, showers, baths, WCs, etc);
- screens;
- security systems;
- shelving;
- shutters;
- signs;

Plant and Machinery

- smoke detectors and sprinklers;
- suspended ceilings if forming part of an air conditioning system;
- switchboards;
- telephone, paging and intercom systems;
- ventilation equipment; and
- window cleaning equipment (cradles, anchor points, etc).

252-100   Residential and nursing homes

These buildings contain a high percentage of items qualifying for plant and machinery allowances.

Moveable items qualifying for plant will include furniture (beds, chairs, desks, tables, telephones, bookcases, clocks, filing cabinets, office machinery, moveable furniture). Books should also be claimed as plant if they are bought as a library to be kept for the longer term.

Items that will typically qualify as fixtures in a nursing or residential home will include the following. (These items should normally be classified as improvements to property (and should therefore be counted when computing any capital gain on a future disposal of the office) but should also be the subject of a plant and machinery claim for fixtures.) Once more, the list is intended to be indicative rather than exhaustive and reference should be made to the A to Z section beginning at 260-000 for any cases where the tax treatment is in doubt. Again, some of these items will now be classified as integral features:

- aerials;
- alarms (burglar, fire, nurse-call, etc);
- air conditioning units, fans, etc;
- blinds;
- boilers;
- cameras;
- carpets;
- central heating systems;
- curtains;
- display equipment;
- door entry systems;
- drink machines;
- electrical installations (but see 260-600);
- electrically operated doors, etc;
- electricity generators;
- emergency lighting;
- fire safety equipment, hoses, etc (but see 160-500);
- fitted furniture;
- floodlighting;
- flooring materials;
- fridges and freezers;
- furniture and furnishings;

- gas systems for hot water, central heating, etc;
- heated towel rails;
- hot water cylinders;
- kitchen equipment and fittings;
- letter boxes;
- lifts and (in some circumstances) lift shafts;
- lighting systems (probably in part – see 261-330);
- machinery;
- mirrors;
- music systems;
- office equipment;
- pictures and other decorative assets;
- radiators;
- safes;
- sanitaryware (basins, showers, baths, WCs, etc);
- screens;
- security systems;
- shaver points;
- shelving;
- shutters;
- signs;
- smoke detectors and sprinklers;
- stair lifts;
- suspended ceilings if forming part of an air conditioning system;
- switchboards;
- telephone and intercom systems;
- trouser presses;
- ventilation equipment, extractor fans, etc; and
- washing machines, dishwashers.

252-150   Hotels and sports centres

Hotels typically qualify for industrial buildings allowances (see ¶315-000). Even before the announcement that IBAs are to be phased out, however, it has been essential to identify items that qualify for plant and machinery allowances, not least because tax relief for such items is given at a much faster rate.

Hotels may well have any of the fixtures listed either at 252-050 (offices) or 252-100 (residential and nursing homes). Reference should therefore be made first to those lists. *Additional* items of plant and machinery that are typically found in hotels will include the following fixtures. Many of these will also be found in sports centres:

- bars, cafes, restaurants: all associated equipment;
- cold rooms;
- conference facilities, including projectors, sound systems, etc;
- decorative features;

Plant and Machinery

- electronic door locks;
- revolving doors, turnstiles, etc;
- room safes;
- swimming pools, jacuzzis, etc;
- trouser presses; and
- urinals.

252-200 Retail premises

Retail premises do not generally qualify for industrial buildings allowances (see 302-700). Furthermore, the definition of retail premises for those purposes is widely drawn, and includes premises that are ancillary to those of a retail shop.

Retail premises can of course vary from a small local shop to a huge shopping centre, and it is more difficult to identify a standard list of items likely to qualify as plant. In general terms, however, the following categories are likely to contain items qualifying as plant, some now in the category of integral features:

- air conditioning and heating systems;
- alarms (fire, smoke, burglar, etc);
- carpets, floor tiles, specialist flooring (non-slip, heavy duty, etc);
- car park barriers, ticket machines, security cameras, bollards, floodlighting;
- display and other specialist lighting (see 261-330);
- electric or revolving doors, and associated pressure mats, visual sensors, etc;
- fire safety equipment, sprinklers, etc;
- lifts, escalators, moving walkways;
- moveable partitions if there is a real intention that they should be moved;
- security equipment and systems, including electric shutters, security mirrors, etc;
- shelves, display equipment, signs; and
- toilets, basins, driers, hot water systems.

PLANT AND MACHINERY: A TO Z OF EXPENDITURE

260-000   A to Z of expenditure: how to use this chapter

The question of what constitutes plant is, in a sense, one of the most difficult areas of tax law. The difficulty does not arise from the complexity of the legislation – many parts of the statutes are far more obscure – but because scores of cases going to the courts over many decades have failed to provide a set of guidelines that can lead with confidence to a decision on any specific item.

If it is necessary to engage in detailed correspondence with HMRC over the tax treatment of a particular item, readers should refer to the Chapter headed 'Meaning of Plant', which begins at 180-000. Since April 2008, it has also been necessary to consider whether an asset may qualify for plant and machinery allowances by virtue of the special rules relating to 'integral features', whereby certain items are treated as if they were plant and machinery even if they would fail to qualify as such under traditional case law principles. The concept of 'integral features' is discussed at 247-000ff. and a list of the items qualifying as such is at 247-050.

In many cases, though, what is needed at first is an initial view of the likely treatment of a particular item, together with signposts to indicate where further research should be made. This Chapter aims to meet that need.

Each of the headings in the following A to Z Chapters is divided into five parts, as follows:

Legislation

First, many items are specifically referred to in the legislation. The bulk of these – in relation to buildings and structures – are in Lists A, B and (mainly) C of CAA 2001, s. 23. The starting point for any tax issue should be in the legislation.

Key case law

This next section lists some of the key case law relating to the particular heading. There is a degree of subjectivity in this. The intention has been to list those cases that are most directly relevant to the particular item, either because they specifically refer to that item or because they contain a discussion of the general principles that are likely to be relevant. The case of *Yarmouth v France*, heard by the Court of Appeal in 1887, has not normally been listed under the heading of 'Key case law'. The case, concerning a horse, will not be of direct relevance to many issues today. However, the principles of that case are fundamental to an understanding of what constitutes plant for tax purposes.

HMRC material

Each section makes a reference to 'HMRC material'. This generally means references to the published Revenue manuals, in most cases to the manual on capital allowances. There are other references under this section, however, both to other manuals and to a variety of other HMRC material.

Commentary

The main section under each heading is the commentary on the treatment of each item. The commentary does not normally quote extensively from the relevant tax cases but rather aims to bring together the principles arising from the legislation and from established case law. The commentary also brings out key elements of the HMRC perspective as indicated in the manuals or press releases, etc. Where the writer has considered it appropriate, the HMRC view has been explored and, if necessary, questioned.

Cross-references

Finally, each section contains a heading for cross-references. Again, this is necessarily subjective but the aim has been to picture a reader looking at one particular section and then to consider which other sections are likely to be of relevance to that reader if further research is needed.

260-010 Advertising hoardings

Legislation: CAA 2001, s. 23 (List C, item 15)

Cases: *Dixon v Fitch's Garage Ltd* (1975) 50 TC 509

HMRC material: CA 21230, CA 22030, CA 22110

Commentary

Advertising hoardings are deemed to be part of a building but are not disqualified from being plant (CAA 2001, s. 23, List C, item 15). Whilst it does not follow from this that all advertising hoardings will necessarily qualify as plant, it does mean that there is a good chance that will be the case.

In a letter sent by the (then) Inland Revenue to the Football League in January 1991 (reproduced at 180-400), advertising hoardings were included as expenditure 'likely to qualify' as plant (CA 21230). Only where the circumstances are exceptional, therefore, should there be any problem in persuading an inspector to accept such an item as plant. Advertisers will sometimes erect bus shelters for the purposes of displaying their advertisements. These shelters may then be leased to bus companies, local authorities, etc. In such circumstances, HMRC will accept that these shelters qualify as plant or machinery (CA 22110).

One word of warning is needed. If an asset is fundamentally a structure then the mere fact that it carries some advertising material is unlikely to turn it into plant. In the *Fitch's Garage* case, a canopy had been erected to provide protection from the elements for drivers filling their cars with petrol. The fascia of the canopy was designed to carry advertisements (although it in fact only advertised the name of the establishment itself, together with the fact that trading stamps were issued). This was not enough to persuade the courts that the canopy should be treated as plant. The canopy was not part of the means by which petrol was supplied. Rather, it was considered merely part of the setting where the petrol was supplied. In the circumstances, it did not qualify as plant.

Cross-references

The following headings from this A to Z Chapter may be relevant in particular cases where this type of expenditure is being considered. See also the Chapter headed 'Meaning of Plant', which begins at 180-000.

- Alterations to buildings (260-040)
- Buildings (260-150)
- Bus shelters (260-170)
- Ceilings and canopies (260-280)
- Demolition costs (260-510)
- Display equipment (260-530)
- Fencing (260-700)
- Finance costs (260-720)
- Professional fees and preliminary costs (262-240)
- Screens (262-430)
- Shop fronts (262-490)
- Structures (262-590)

260-020   Aerials

Legislation: CAA 2001, s. 21(1)–(3), 23 (List C, item 8)

Cases: none dealing specifically with this category of expenditure

HMRC material: CA 32217

Commentary

There is little specific guidance as to whether television aerials qualify as plant.

The HMRC manuals (CA 32217) specify that 'transmission aerials qualify for plant and machinery allowances'. This, however, is from the point of view of a television company.

As to whether a receiving aerial qualifies as plant, it will of course be necessary to show firstly that it is for trade purposes. Secondly, it needs to be shown that the aerial is neither 'incorporated into the building' nor 'of a kind normally incorporated into buildings'. It is the author's view that most television aerials could not be said to be incorporated into the building as they can be removed relatively easily without in any way damaging the fabric of the building.

Plant and Machinery: A to Z

It seems probable in any case that receiving aerials are exempt from the provisions of CAA 2001, s. 21 by virtue of List C, item 8 'computer, telecommunication and surveillance systems (including their wiring or other links)'.

Cross-references

The following headings from this A to Z Chapter may be relevant in particular cases where this type of expenditure is being considered. See also the Chapter headed 'Meaning of Plant', which begins at 180-000.

- Alterations to buildings (260-040)
- Buildings (260-150)
- Electrical installations and equipment (260-600)
- Fixtures (260-760)
- Professional fees and preliminary costs (262-240)
- Public address systems (262-250)
- Removal costs (262-300)
- Structures (262-590)
- Telecommunication systems (262-710)
- Telephones and fax machines (262-720)
- Televisions and videos (262-730)

260-030   Air conditioning systems

Legislation: CAA 2001, s. 23 (List C, item 3 (formerly) and 9), s. 33A

Cases: *Jarrold v John Good & Sons Ltd* (1963) 40 TC 681; *Cooke v Beach Station Caravans Ltd* (1974) 49 TC 514; *Wimpy International Ltd v Warland* [1989] BTC 58*Melluish v BMI (No. 3) Ltd* [1995] BTC 381

HMRC material: CA 21200, CA 21230

Commentary

Air conditioning is now treated as an 'integral feature' (see 247-000ff.). Specifically, a 'powered system of ventilation, air cooling or air purification' is listed as one of the categories of integral feature.

For expenditure incurred before April 2008, HMRC accepted as plant all of the following (per CA 21200):

- central heating systems;
- hot-water systems;
- air conditioning systems;
- alarm and sprinkler systems;
- ventilation systems; and
- baths, basins, toilet suites.

There is case law authority for this treatment. For example, in the *Jarrold v Good* case, the judge commented:

'The heating installation of a building may be passive in the sense that it involves no moving machinery, but few would deny it the name of "plant". The same thing could no doubt be said of many air conditioning and water softening installations. All that the Income Tax Acts require in this context is that the plant shall have been provided "for the purpose of the trade" – an expression wide enough to cover assets which play a passive as well as an active role in the accomplishment of that purpose.'

Where a suspended ceiling or plenum floor forms an integral part of a heating or ventilation system (for example, the fourth side of a duct for the air), then HMRC accept that this cost should be treated as on plant or machinery (CA 22070). By contrast, a floor that merely *covers* a heating or ventilation system will not qualify.

An asset does not qualify – either as an integral feature or under general principles – if it is one 'whose principal purpose is to insulate or enclose the interior of a building or to provide an interior wall, floor or ceiling which (in each case) is intended to remain permanently in place'. This would apply, for example, to deny allowances on the cost of a wall that happens to form the fourth side of a ventilation pipe.

Cross-references

The following headings, mostly from this A to Z Chapter, may be relevant in particular cases where this type of expenditure is being considered. See also the Chapter headed 'Meaning of Plant', which begins at 180-000 and the commentary on 'integral features' beginning at 247-000ff.

- Alterations to buildings (260-040)
- Cold rooms (260-310)
- Central heating systems (260-290)
- Electrical installations and equipment (260-600)
- Fire safety (see 160-500)
- Fixtures (260-760)
- Insulation (see 160-400)
- Machinery (262-000)
- Plant rooms (262-210)
- Professional fees and preliminary costs (262-240)
- Temporary buildings (262-740)
- Water supplies and water tanks (262-920)

260-040 Alterations to buildings

Legislation: CAA 2001, s. 25

Cases: *IR Commrs v Barclay, Curle and Co Ltd* (1969) 45 TC 221; *Wimpy International Ltd v Warland* [1989] BTC 57; *Melluish v BMI (No. 3) Ltd* [1995] BTC 381; *J D Wetherspoon plc v R & C Commrs* (2007) Sp C 657

HMRC material: CA 21190, CA 22020–22030, CA 22230

Commentary

There is a specific provision to give relief where a trader incurs capital expenditure altering an existing building, if that alteration is incidental to the installation of plant or machinery for the purposes of the trade. Such expenditure is treated as part of the cost of that plant or machinery.

There are a few points to watch to ensure that the relief will be available.

Existing building

The relief only applies to alterations to an *existing* building. There is no definition of this word. Clearly, where a new building is being constructed, CAA 2001, s. 25 cannot be relied on to provide any relief. Conversely, a building which is clearly in use will be able to benefit from the relief. There could be an argument if, for example, a trader buys a brand new building and carries out some alterations prior to moving in. HMRC may try to argue that this does not constitute an existing building. A more reasonable argument may be that CAA 2001, s. 25 should apply to anything done to the building after it is substantially complete. However, there could be room for debate.

Link with installation of plant

Relief is only due under this provision if the alterations are 'incidental to the installation of plant or machinery'.

The HMRC manuals (at CA 21190) state that there must be 'a direct link between the incurring of expenditure on alterations and the plant or machinery said to have given rise to that expenditure'. The following paragraph goes on to say that 'the main purpose of the alterations must be the installation of plant or machinery. Work done for some other purpose such as the better operation of the asset does not qualify'. It is the author's view that this interpretation would be open to challenge. The words 'main purpose' seem to pose a more stringent test than that in the legislation itself, which says merely that alterations must be 'incidental' to the installation of plant or machinery. It is conceivable that the case of *Robson v Dixon* (1972) 48 TC 527 could be relevant in interpreting the word 'incidental'. It should be noted, however, that what was being considered in that case was whether certain duties carried out in the UK were incidental to the performance of duties outside the UK.

In the more directly relevant case of *J D Wetherspoon plc v R & C Commrs*, the commissioners drew a distinction between alterations *incidental to* the installation of plant and alterations *consequential on* such installation. The company had claimed the cost of constructing new walls, on the grounds that the exigencies of the taxpayer's trade, including statutory or regulatory requirements, required the kitchen walls to be constructed to enable the cooker to serve its proper purpose. However, the commissioners rejected this claim, as the construction of the kitchen walls was not incidental to the installation of the cookers but part of the creation of a kitchen, in which the cookers and other kitchen equipment could function properly. The cost of the walls did not have sufficient nexus to the installation of the cookers.

By contrast, it was also held in that case that timber partitions and doors to individual toilets were properly treated as incidental to the installation of plant as the toilets could not be properly used without partitions or cubicles. The drainage items in both premises also qualified as a trade specific sewerage system or as incidental alterations.

The provision of CAA 2001, s. 25 needs to be contrasted with that of CAA 2001, s. 273, 'preparation of sites for plant and machinery'. CAA 2001, s. 273 gives relief as an industrial buildings allowance for capital expenditure incurred on 'preparing, cutting, tunnelling or levelling land for the purposes of preparing the land as a site for the installation of plant or machinery'. Treatment as an industrial building is available only where the expenditure does not otherwise qualify for plant or machinery allowances. However, the HMRC view – as previously expressed at old CA 1455 – was that it is unlikely so to qualify 'because it is not expenditure on the provision of plant or machinery'.

The *Wimpy* case provides an example of where expenditure was allowed under CAA 2001, s. 211. The existing roof structure had to be adapted as part of the process of installing plant or machinery. This expenditure was therefore allowed. By contrast, the cost of a brick plant room was not allowed as it did not amount to an alteration to the existing building.

Cross-references

Depending on the nature and purpose of the alterations, many of the headings in this A to Z Chapter may apply. In particular, see the following.

- Air conditioning (260-030)
- Buildings (260-150)
- Central heating, etc systems (260-290)
- Demolition costs (260-510)
- Electrical installations and equipment (260-600)
- Removal costs (262-300)
- Temporary buildings (262-740)

See also the Chapter headed 'Meaning of Plant', which begins at 180-000.

260-050 Amusement parks

Legislation: CAA 2001, s. 23 (List C, item 32)

Cases: *Cooke v Beach Station Caravans Ltd* (1974) 49 TC 514

HMRC material: CA 22030

Plant and Machinery: A to Z

Commentary

Amusement parks as a whole will rarely, if ever, qualify for plant as a single item. However, an amusement park is likely to contain many items that will qualify as either plant or machinery.

Item 32 provides a specific exemption from the 'structure' restriction, stating that expenditure on 'the provision of structures and other assets for providing the setting for any ride at an amusement park or exhibition' should not be disqualified as a building or structure. It does not follow that such items necessarily qualify as plant but it does mean that they stand a chance of so qualifying based on case law principles. To the extent that any expenditure is on machinery it will qualify anyway – see 262-000.

The *Beach Station Caravans* case provides a precedent for treating a swimming pool as plant. It may be possible to extend the reasoning of that case to cover some other attractions to be found in amusement parks.

Cross-references

The following headings, mostly from this A to Z Chapter, may be relevant in particular cases where this type of expenditure is being considered. See also the Chapter headed 'Meaning of Plant', which begins at 180-000.

- Animals (260-060)
- Buildings (260-150)
- Canals (260-210)
- Caravans and caravan sites (260-230)
- Car parks (260-250)
- Display equipment (260-530)
- Electrical installations and equipment (260-600)
- Entertaining-related expenditure (260-630)
- Finance costs (260-720)
- Fire safety (see 160-500)
- Fish tanks and ponds (260-740)
- Floodlighting (260-770)
- Land (261-300)
- Professional fees and preliminary costs (262-240)
- Public address systems (262-250)
- Roads, etc (262-320)
- Sanitary ware (262-420)
- Sports grounds (safety) (262-550)
- Zoo cages (263-000)

260-060   Animals

Legislation: none

Cases: *Yarmouth v France* [1887] 4 TRL 1 (horse); *Derby (Earl) v Aylmer* (1915) 6 TC 665 (stallion); *Abbott v Albion Greyhounds (Salford) Ltd* (1945) 26 TC 390; *Norman v Golder* (1945) 26 TC 293; *Cole Brothers Ltd v Phillips* [1982] BTC 208

HMRC material: CA 21220

Commentary

The legislation is silent on whether or not animals can qualify as plant. However, there is plenty of case law making it clear that they can. The HMRC manuals confirm the position.

The primary case on which all capital allowance law has been developed, *Yarmouth v France*, concerned a horse and the judge was quite specific in his comments: 'Plant includes whatever apparatus is used by a business man for carrying on his business – not his stock-in-trade which he buys or makes for sale; but all goods and chattels, fixed or moveable, live or dead, which he keeps for permanent employment in his business'. In that case, the cart-horse was therefore agreed to be plant.

HMRC may quote the case of the *Earl of Derby v Aylmer* against this argument. However, in that case the commissioners were specifically required to consider 'the diminished value by reason of wear and tear during the year' of any plant or machinery. The judge held that a stallion could not be said to have had a diminished value by reason of wear and tear. However, that exact test is no longer applicable. The judge was quite specific on this, saying that: 'I am not deciding that horses kept for traction in a business are or are not plant. I do not express an opinion either way'.

The Revenue expressed their view on this point as follows (*Farm Tax and Finance*, Vol. 2, No. 1, 14 January 1984, at p. 6):

> "In order to qualify for capital allowances a trader needs to show that he has incurred capital expenditure on the provision of plant .... Where there has been expenditure on a work horse and the practice has not been to write the cost off in computing profits such expenditure may be treated as capital expenditure on plant for these purposes and a capital allowance claimed. Expenditure on horses kept or bred for sale would not however qualify for a capital allowance.'

The HMRC manuals now instruct inspectors that they should accept a plant claim on an animal if it functions as apparatus with which the trade is carried on and it has an expected life of two years or more (CA 21220). Examples are given of 'a horse used in a riding school or show jumping business, a guard dog or a circus animal'.

Farm animals that are trading stock or are subject to the herd basis treatment will not qualify as plant, though a sheepdog, for example, might qualify.

It is true that in the *Albion Greyhounds* case, the judge ruled that 'this kennel of greyhounds is not plant or machinery'. However, there was no explanation of the reasoning. It could well have been because, as found in the facts of the case, 'the average racing life of these dogs was less than two years'. As such, they may have failed to qualify as plant simply

Plant and Machinery: A to Z

because they did not survive long enough to do so, the animals not meeting the 'permanent employment' test referred to above.

The suggestion has sometimes been made that no living thing can qualify as plant. However, this view was clearly rejected in the *Yarmouth v France* case, in which the judge said:

> 'It is suggested that nothing that is animate can be plant; that is, that living creatures can in no sense be considered plant. Why not? In many businesses horses and carts, wagons, or drays, seem to me to form the most material part of the plant: they are the materials or instruments which the employer must use for the purpose of carrying on his business, and without which he could not carry it on at all.'

This view was confirmed, albeit in an informal manner, by Stephenson LJ in the *Cole Brothers* case when he made the following observation:

> 'The philosopher/statesman Balfour, is reported to have said it was unnecessary to define a great power because, like an elephant, you recognised it when you met it. Unhappily plant in taxing and other statutes is no elephant (though I suppose an elephant might be plant).'

Overall, it is considered that there is an overwhelming case for treating animals as plant where they do not form part of the trading stock of a business. In particular, it should be remembered that the *Yarmouth v France* case has been approved in virtually every single case concerned with the meaning of plant and machinery and the decision has stood the test of time by lasting for more than 110 years.

Finally, and by way of contrast, it should be noted that the human body does not qualify as plant – see 261-020.

Cross-references

The following headings from this A to Z Chapter may be relevant in particular cases where this type of expenditure is being considered. See also the Chapter headed 'Meaning of Plant', which begins at 180-000.

- Fish tanks and ponds (260-740)
- Human body (261-020)
- Poultry houses (262-230)
- Zoo cages (263-000)

260-100 Bicycles and bicycle holders

Legislation: none

Cases: none

HMRC material: CA 21230

Commentary

Bicycles themselves will in all normal circumstances qualify as plant, as will exercise bicycles.

The treatment of bicycle holders may depend on the precise way in which they are constructed. It is possible that if they are very much part of a building then they may fail to qualify. Normally, however, there should be no problem obtaining HMRC agreement that they do so qualify.

Bicycle holders were included in the list of items 'which would normally qualify as plant or machinery' in a letter sent by the Revenue to the Football League in January 1991 (see 180-400). It will now be necessary, however, to show that they are not a 'structure', so that they are not caught by CAA 2001, s. 22.

Cross-references

The following heading from this A to Z Chapter may be relevant in particular cases where this type of expenditure is being considered. See also the Chapter headed 'Meaning of Plant', which begins at 180-000.

● Structures (262-590)

260-110 Books

Legislation: none

Cases: *Daphne v Shaw* (1926) 11 TC 256; *McVeigh v Arthur Sanderson & Sons Limited* (1969) 45 TC 273; *Munby v Furlong* (1977) 50 TC 491

HMRC material: BIM 46970; EIM 36710

Commentary

Books will, in principle, qualify as plant unless they have such a short shelf-life that they are an ordinary trading expense. Authority was previously found for this in the Revenue manuals at old CA 1565: 'Books are plant if they satisfy the two-year test'. The current capital allowances manual is silent on the matter.

In practice, HMRC allow a deduction for new additions of and supplements to technical books already owned, for replacements of versions that have become obsolete, for technical periodicals, etc and periodical parts of law reports, etc as well as for the cost of binding supplements, periodicals, etc (BIM 46970). Thus, it is normally just the initial cost of setting up the library in the first place that will be claimed as plant. Even in these cases, though, HMRC will only insist that the cost of the books should be capitalised where the amount of expenditure involved is considerable. In relation to employees, Revenue instructions to

Plant and Machinery: A to Z

inspectors are that they 'only spend time in establishing whether an allowance is due as an expenses deduction or as a capital allowance in worthwhile cases' (EIM 36710).

It was not always the case that books could qualify as plant. In the case of *Daphne v Shaw*, the normally excellent Judge Rowlatt appears to have reached the wrong conclusion. Certainly, his view has not stood the test of time. He ruled:

> 'I cannot bring myself to say that the books of a lawyer, whether a barrister or a solicitor or, I am sorry to say, a Judge … are "plant". It is impossible to define what is meant by "plant and machinery". It conjures up before the mind something clear in the outline, at any rate; it means apparatus, alive or dead, stationary or movable, to achieve the operations which a person wants to achieve in his vocation. But the books which he consults, on his shelves, and which he does not use as "implements", really, in the direct sense of the word, at all, I cannot believe are included in it.'

This judgment was questioned but not overruled in the *Arthur Sanderson* case, in which Cross J felt himself constrained by the Rowlatt precedent. Cross clearly had difficulty with Rowlatt's conclusion:

> 'If a barrister has to buy a new edition of a textbook in order to help him to write his opinions, I cannot see as a matter of principle why the book should not be regarded as a tool of his trade just as much as the typewriter on which his opinions are typed.'

It was not until *Munby v Furlong*, however, that the issue of whether books are plant was comprehensively reviewed and the earlier judgment overturned. As Lord Denning said:

> 'I do not think "plant" should be confined to things which are used physically. It seems to me that on principle it extends to the intellectual storehouse which a barrister or a solicitor or any other professional man has in the course of carrying on his profession. The difficulty has arisen because the Legislature, when it extended this provision to professions, did not make clear the scope of the word "plant" in that context. It seems to me, in the context of a profession, the provision of "plant" should be so interpreted that a lawyer's books – his set of law reports and his textbooks – are "plant".'

In the same case, Sir John Pennycuick agreed with him:

> '[Plant] seems to me quite plainly to cover books purchased by a barrister for the purpose of his profession. Those books do indeed represent apparatus used by him for carrying on his profession, and that to my mind is the end of the case.'

Thus, the *Munby v Furlong* case overturned 50 years of precedent and established once and for all that books, and potentially other assets used in a less physical way, can indeed qualify as plant.

Cross-references

The following headings from this A to Z Chapter may be relevant in particular cases where this type of expenditure is being considered. See also the Chapter headed 'Meaning of Plant', which begins at 180-000.

- Designs and patterns (260-520)

- Software (260-330)
- Wallpaper designs and pattern books (262-900)

260-130   Bridges, etc

Legislation: CAA 2001, s. 21 (List B, item 1), see also s. 271 (IBAs)

Cases: none

HMRC material: none (except re IBAs)

Commentary

Bridges are specifically disqualified from being plant by CAA 2001, s. 21, List B, item 1. In the same way, tunnels, viaducts, aqueducts, embankments and cuttings are not eligible to be treated as plant.

As regards a building or structure in use for the purposes of a bridge or tunnel undertaking, see items 7 and 8 of Table B in CAA 2001, s. 274 (Industrial buildings and structures), and commentary in the Chapter headed 'Industrial Buildings Allowances', which begins at 300-000.

Cross-references

The following heading from this A to Z Chapter may be relevant in particular cases where this type of expenditure is being considered. See also the Chapter headed 'Meaning of Plant', which begins at 180-000.

- Structures (262-590)

260-140   Briefcases

Legislation: none

Cases: none

HMRC material: EIM 36720

Commentary

The cost of a briefcase will, in most cases, be strictly treated as capital rather than as a revenue deduction. HMRC accept that 'a briefcase is likely to fall within the definition of "plant"' (EIM 36720).

For a business there should normally be no problem in satisfying the 'wholly and exclusively' requirement. However, HMRC's view is that an employee will rarely satisfy

Plant and Machinery: A to Z

the stricter requirement which is that the briefcase should have been provided 'necessarily' and for use 'in the performance of the duties'. The reasoning for this is given as follows (again at EIM 36720):

> 'Where it forms part of the employee's duties to transport documents or materials securely the employer will usually make some suitable receptacle available. If the employer does not consider this necessary, the duties themselves must be considered to establish whether the employee uses his own case simply as a matter of convenience or choice. When transporting papers between home and work the case is not being used in the performance of the duties unless the employee's home is itself a genuine place of work.'

Cross-references

The following headings from this A to Z Chapter may be relevant in particular cases where this type of expenditure is being considered. See also the Chapter headed 'Meaning of Plant', which begins at 180-000.

- Books (260-110)
- Containers (260-350)

260-150   Buildings

Legislation: CAA 2001, s. 21–25, s. 33A; see also s. 271 (IBAs)

Cases: *Yarmouth v France* [1887] 4 TRL 1; *J. Lyons & Co Ltd v Attorney General* [1944] 170 LT 348; *Jarrold v John Good & Sons Ltd* (1963) 40 TC 681; *Leeds Permanent Building Society v Proctor* [1982] BTC 347; *Wimpy International Ltd v Warland* [1989] BTC 58; *Carr v Sayer* [1992] BTC 286

HMRC material: numerous, but see especially: CA 21140, CA 22010ff.

Commentary

The question of whether a building, or part of a building, qualifies as plant is now determined by CAA 2001, s. 21ff. This legislation was introduced (in its earlier form) in the early 1990s.

Background

It appears that the Revenue felt that the courts were 'eroding' the distinction between plant on the one hand and structures on the other. They had, in the Revenue's words, 'increasingly reclassified expenditure on buildings and structures as being expenditure on plant' (letter to *Taxation Practitioner*, August 1994).

The stated intention of the legislation was therefore 'to strengthen the current [1993] boundary, and to ensure that no further erosion takes place'. Whilst it was not expected that the legislation would perfectly replicate the whole of case law that had gone before it, the Revenue stated that 'the broad aim is to provide exclusions for assets currently regarded as plant as a result of court decisions, so as to leave the current position unchanged'.

It is worth bearing in mind, however, that when the new clauses were being debated in Parliament, the Government spokesman (Mr Stephen Dorrell) repeatedly stated that there was no intention to change previous decisions on what constituted plant. Thus, he stated 'the purpose of the clause is to prevent further changes in the law on entitlement to capital allowances ... in order to introduce a degree of stability into the law and to prevent further development of case law'. He went on to say 'we are not seeking to revisit the law established by the courts' and then again 'it is not our intention to change the capital treatment of any class of asset under the clause'. Yet again he went on to say that 'nothing in the clause is intended to change existing practice of how cases are treated for capital allowance purposes'.

Given the number of times that this statement was reiterated, there are very strong grounds for arguing that any items established as qualifying as plant before the 1994 legislation was introduced should continue so to qualify if there is any ambiguity at all in what is or is not covered by the Schedule. Care should be taken over special commissioner decisions, however. Mr Dorrell made it clear that the purpose of the Schedule was to draw a line in the sand 'in terms of the one-way development of case law' but went on to clarify that special commissioner decisions did not establish legal precedents and therefore may have been reversed in the new legislation.

The old CAA 1990, Sch. AA1, now broadly re-enacted in CAA 2001, s. 21 onwards, is a peculiar piece of legislation. Not only is the background bizarre (a notion that somehow the courts were starting to err too much against the proper Revenue view), but also there are strange features of the way the legislation tries to achieve its goals.

Effect of rules: exclusions from plant

CAA 2001, s. 21 opens clearly enough by declaring that 'expenditure on the provision of plant or machinery does not include expenditure on the provision of a building'. Provision is for these purposes defined to include either construction or acquisition.

The term 'building' is then specifically stated to include the following:

(1)   Any asset which is incorporated into the building. There is no statutory guidance as to how this expression should be interpreted.

(2)   An asset which is 'of a kind normally incorporated in a building' but which is not in fact so incorporated, whether 'because the asset is moveable or for any other reason'. In a letter to *Taxation Practitioner* written in August 1994, the Revenue gave the following assistance in interpreting this last expression:

> 'the words "moveable or otherwise" [this was the wording in CAA 1990] are not intended to describe a category of assets. They are simply saying that it does not matter whether, as a matter of fact, the asset in question can be moved. The words are aimed at modern building techniques which, for example, permit an entire room (such as a toilet) to be placed in a building as a complete module.'

(3)   Any asset which is in, or connected with, the building and is in List A.

List A, still within CAA 2001, s. 21, contains the following items:

Plant and Machinery: A to Z

375

(1) walls, floors, ceilings, doors, gates, shutters, windows and stairs;

(2) mains services and systems for water, electricity and gas;

(3) waste disposal systems;

(4) sewerage and drainage systems;

(5) shafts or other structures in which lifts, hoists, escalators and moving walkways are installed; and

(6) fire safety systems.

Between them, the items in the above list give an indication of the broad range of assets which are deemed by HMRC to be part of a building.

The concept 'incorporated into the building' may be approximately synonymous with having become 'part of the premises' and in this respect the following HMRC commentary (from CA 21140) is of interest:

> 'Hoffman J [in the Wimpy case] was not using "part of the premises" here to mean the same as whether the item has become part of the realty for the purposes of the law of real property or a fixture for the purposes of the law of landlord and tenant. He suggested four general factors to be considered in deciding whether an item is part of the premises:
>
> (i)   does the item appear visually to retain a separate identity.
> (ii)   with what degree of permanence has it been attached to the building.
> (iii) to what extent is the structure complete without it.
> (iv)   to what extent is it intended to be permanent or alternatively is it likely to be replaced within a short period.
>
> These are questions of fact and degree. They are not absolute hurdles each of which must be surmounted.'

List B, at CAA 2001, s. 22, then lists various 'excluded structures and other assets', many relating to marine or river assets (dams, docks, dikes, etc). Once more, these are excluded from the definition of plant or machinery, but subject to the relaxations at CAA 2001, s. 23, discussed below.

Exceptions to the exclusions: overview

As noted above, CAA 2001, s. 21 and 22 establish a general principle that buildings and structures, and assets incorporated into buildings, do not qualify as plant or machinery. Those sections reinforce that general principle by listing numerous specific types of asset that do not so qualify.

The legislation then goes on, however, to specify various exceptions that are unaffected by CAA 2001, s. 21 and 22. These exceptions fall into two categories: first, a list of statutory provisions relating to particular categories of expenditure, each of which is subject to its own rules; and secondly, a list of specific assets (List C at s. 23).

Exceptions to the exclusions: statutory provisions

The restrictions in CAA 2001, s. 21 and 22, described above, do not apply to expenditure for which the tax treatment is determined under any of the following provisions (as amended by the *Finance Act* 2008):

- CAA 2001, s. 28: thermal insulation of buildings (see 160-400);
- CAA 2001, s. 30–32: various categories of expenditure on safety at sports grounds (see 160-600);
- CAA 2001, s. 33: expenditure on personal security (see 160-700);
- CAA 2001, s. 33A: expenditure on integral features (see 247-000).

(The list also includes certain software and film costs, unlikely to be of relevance in the context of expenditure on buildings. The category relating to fire safety expenditure was removed by the *Finance Act* 2008.)

Exceptions to the exclusions: List C

As noted above, an item within List C at CAA 2001, s. 23 has to be considered on general case law principles, ignoring the restrictive provisions in s. 21. However, this relaxation does not apply to any of items 1–16 of List C if the principal purpose of the asset is to insulate or enclose the interior of a building or to provide an interior wall, floor or ceiling which (in each case) is intended to remain permanently in place. Thus an ordinary wall that happens to form one side of a heating or ventilation duct will not qualify for plant and machinery allowances. (See, however, 160-400 as far as sound insulation is concerned.)

For the general principles of case law, see the Chapter headed 'Meaning of Plant', which begins at 180-000. As regards the specific items listed above, see the relevant heading in these A to Z Chapters.

There are no UK cases where a building was held to be plant. There have, however, been cases where large structures have been so held. For details of these, see under 'Structures' at 262-590.

Integral features

Many of the most common types of expenditure on a building, including cold water and general electrical systems, are now classified as 'integral features' and are subject to their own particular rules. Those rules are considered in depth at 247-000ff.

Cross-references

Many of the categories listed in this A to Z Chapter may need to be individually considered. See also the Chapter headed 'Meaning of Plant', which begins at 180-000. See 262-740, however, for the treatment of temporary buildings.

260-170   Bus shelters

Legislation: CAA 2001, s. 23 (List C, item 15)

Cases: *JC Decaux (UK) Ltd v Francis* (1996) Sp C 84

HMRC material: CA 22110, CA 26200

Commentary

The HMRC manuals (CA 22110) allow as plant bus and similar shelters which are erected by advertisers for the purposes of displaying advertisements and then leased to bus companies or local authorities.

The special commissioners' case of *JC Decaux (UK) Ltd v Francis* (1996) Sp C 84 confirms that bus shelters used in such circumstances are indeed plant but the case was primarily dealing with the question of whether they became fixtures. The special commissioner concluded that they did.

Cross-references

The following heading from this A to Z Chapter may be relevant in particular cases where this type of expenditure is being considered. See also the Chapter headed 'Meaning of Plant', which begins at 180-000.

- Advertising hoardings (260-010)

260-200   Cameras

Legislation: CAA 2001, s. 23 (List C, item 8)

Cases: none

HMRC material: CA 21230

Commentary

A portable camera would normally qualify as plant. This is based on ordinary principles as there is little specific authority on the issue.

Cameras have been listed by HMRC as one of the types of assets 'used by a football club in its trade which would normally qualify as plant or machinery'. This was in a letter from the Revenue to the Football League in January 1991, reproduced at 180-400. As always, care is needed in applying to one trade a set of rules about what qualifies as plant in another.

Where the camera is attached to a building, for example as part of security arrangements, it will be necessary to consider whether CAA 2001, s. 21 or 22 produce a problem. The camera will not qualify if it is 'incorporated into the building'. In the author's opinion, though HMRC could take a different view, a camera would not be 'of a kind normally incorporated into buildings'.

The question of whether the camera is in fact incorporated into the building will be one of fact and degree.

Normally, it will be possible to show that a camera is outside the restrictions imposed by CAA 2001, s. 21 and 22, on the grounds that it is within the category of 'computer, telecommunication and surveillance systems (including their wiring or other links)' (item 8 of List C). As a last resort, it may be part of an electrical system (former item 2, but now to be considered under the integral feature rules). A camera will also be outside the restrictions if it is part of a security system qualifying under CAA 2001, s. 27–33.

Cross-references

The following headings, mostly from this A to Z Chapter, may be relevant in particular cases where this type of expenditure is being considered. See also the Chapter headed 'Meaning of Plant', which begins at 180-000 and the commentary on 'Integral features' beginning at 247-000ff.

- Electrical installations and equipment (260-600)
- Football grounds (260-790)
- Security systems (262-450)
- Sports grounds (safety) (262-550)
- Televisions and videos (262-730)

260-210   Canals

Legislation: CAA 2001, s. 22 (List B, item 3)

Cases: none

HMRC material: CA 20010

Commentary

A canal does not qualify as plant. This is clear from CAA 2001, s. 22, List B, item 3.

In a few exceptional circumstances it might be possible to demonstrate that a canal formed part of a water reservoir or alternatively of an amusement park, in which case exemption might be provided by items 27 or 32 of List C respectively. In such an exceptional case, it would still be necessary to consider whether a canal would qualify as plant on ordinary principles. It is by no means certain that it would so qualify.

Cross-references

The following headings from this A to Z Chapter may be relevant in particular cases where this type of expenditure is being considered. See also the Chapter headed 'Meaning of Plant', which begins at 180-000.

- Dykes, etc (260-580)

Plant and Machinery: A to Z

- Reservoirs, etc (262-310)
- Sewerage (262-460)
- Structures (262-590)
- Water supplies and water tanks (262-920)

260-230   Caravans and caravan sites

Legislation: CAA 2001, s. 23, List B, item 19

Cases: none

HMRC material: CA 22030, CA 22100; ESC B50

Commentary

The HMRC practice in treating caravans and caravan sites as plant is odd, containing inconsistencies and secretive elements. Furthermore, even the legislation seems odd in the way it treats this topic.

Caravans

Caravans are referred to at CAA 2001, s. 23, List C, item 19, which provides that a caravan provided mainly for holiday lettings is not to be prevented, on the grounds that it is a building, etc from qualifying as plant.

Turning now from the legislation to Revenue practice (including ESC B50), the following principles emerge:

- HMRC will accept that a caravan is plant 'if it does not occupy a fixed site and is regularly moved as part of normal trade usage, even if it is only moved from its summer site to winter quarters'.
- A caravan provided mainly for holiday lettings on a holiday caravan site will qualify as plant whether it is moved or not. HMRC will only apply this treatment to sites licensed by the local authority under the *Caravan Sites and Control of Development Act* 1960 as a holiday caravan site. This will not include holiday camps, leisure parks, hotels, conference centres, etc
- A caravan which occupies a residential site will not qualify as plant. Exceptionally, however, HMRC say that they will accept as plant a caravan provided by a farmer to house a farm employee. This will be the case even if the caravan occupies a fixed site and is used only for residential purposes. HMRC instructions (at CA 22100) state specifically that this treatment 'applies only to farmers. It does not apply to any other cases.' It is not at all clear on what basis this distinction is made. A person carrying on an activity other than that of farming might see fit to challenge HMRC on this point.

Caravan sites

As regards the cost of the caravan sites themselves, HMRC still operate the terms of an agreement made with the National Caravan Council in the 1950s. However, inspectors are instructed that they 'should only apply the agreement if the taxpayer asks for it to be applied'. The agreement is an all or nothing one, so that the taxpayer cannot choose to apply only those parts of the agreement which are convenient. If the agreement is applied then HMRC will accept as plant all of the following:

- mains water supplies;
- apparatus used to convey water to or around the sites;
- hot-water systems;
- electricity supplies, including heavy cables, distributive wiring and general electrical apparatus;
- diesel generating apparatus; and
- sanitary fittings, baths and wash basins.

On the other hand, no allowances will be due for the cost of roads, sites for individual caravans, any buildings erected as sanitary blocks or sewerage and drainage pipes which are installed under public health requirements.

Cross-references

The following headings from this A to Z Chapter may be relevant in particular cases where this type of expenditure is being considered. See also the Chapter headed 'Meaning of Plant', which begins at 180-000.

- Amusement parks (260-050)
- Temporary buildings (262-740)

260-240 Cars

Legislation: CAA 2001, s. 104AA, 268A

Cases: Cases involving cars are not primarily concerned with issues of whether they are plant. See, however, *Bourne v Auto School of Motoring (Norwich) Limited* (1964) 42 TC 217.

HMRC material: CA 20015, CA 23510

Commentary

Motor cars qualify as plant. Indeed, a car would qualify both as plant and as machinery so there is no doubt that it qualifies in principle for capital allowances. CAA 2001, Pt. 2, Ch. 8 used to deal specifically with capital allowances on cars but this legislation was broadly repealed from April 2009. The revised structure removes most of the special rules for cars so that the remaining statutory provisions relate to the definition of 'car', to the distinction between cars that can go into the main plant and machinery pool and those that must be allocated to the special rate pool, and to various anti-avoidance and transitional matters.

A motor car is specifically defined for capital allowance purposes (see 200-020). The definition changed from April 2009.

The rules relating to cars are considered in depth at 200-000ff.

For employees and directors using privately-owned vehicles for work purposes, no capital allowances are available.

Cross-references

The following headings from this A to Z Chapter may be relevant in particular cases where this type of expenditure is being considered. See also the Chapter headed 'Meaning of Plant', which begins at 180-000.

* Machinery (262-000)
* Number plates (262-100)
* Ships (262-480)

260-250   Car parks

Legislation: CAA 2001, s. 22 (List B, item 2)

Cases: *Attwood v Anduff Car Wash Ltd* [1997] BTC 454

HMRC material: CA 31120 (IBAs), CA 32402 (hotels only), CA 35200

Commentary

Car parks do not qualify as plant. They are specifically excluded by virtue of item 2 of List B ('a park for vehicles or containers').

In the *Anduff Car Wash* case, the judge in the Court of Appeal said that 'it is impossible to say that the bays where the cars are parked whilst the vacuum cleaning is done have any function other than as premises. The fact that the site is purpose-designed as a whole cannot turn a site which functions as premises into plant'.

Car parks may well qualify for industrial buildings allowances (see 300-600 and CA 31120) and may qualify as part of the cost of a hotel, again for IBA purposes (see 315-000 and CA 32402).

Cross-references

The following headings from this A to Z Chapter may be relevant in particular cases where this type of expenditure is being considered. See also the Chapter headed 'Meaning of Plant', which begins at 180-000.

* Car wash apparatus (260-260)
* Land (261-300)
* Roads, etc (262-320)

260-260   Car wash apparatus

Legislation: none

Cases: *Attwood v Anduff Car Wash Ltd* [1997] BTC 454

HMRC material: none

Commentary

The only guidance on this topic comes from the case of *Attwood v Anduff Car Wash*. There are no specific references in the legislation to car washes and the HMRC manuals contain no useful commentary on the topic.

HMRC accept that a car wash system will contain items that will certainly qualify as plant or machinery. The point of the *Anduff* case, however, was that the company was seeking to claim that the entire car wash site should qualify as plant.

The company was successful in front of the special commissioners in May 1993 but the decision was overturned in the Chancery Division, and the Revenue successfully gained confirmation of their view in the Court of Appeal in July 1997.

In reaching their decision that the entire 'wash hall' should qualify as plant, the commissioners had regarded it 'not as a building but as a structure akin to a machine which takes into its large maw motor cars at up to four at a time, washes them thoroughly, dries them and ejects them'. They decided that any protection from the elements provided by the hall was merely incidental. The commissioners also noted the various special features of the structure including its unusually shaped roof designed to collect rainwater.

The courts, however, would have none of it. In the Chancery Division, the judge decided that the commissioners had failed to apply the 'premises' test. The site on which the car wash business was operated, as well as the building in which the various items of machinery were housed, all constituted the premises within which the trade was carried on rather than the apparatus. The Court of Appeal agreed with the judge in the Chancery Division. In the Court of Appeal judgment, it was pointed out that only 130 square metres out of the total of 1,150 square metres were actually occupied by the wash hall.

The judge rejected outright the view of the commissioners that most of the site was designed and operated as a conveyor belt. He concluded that it was impossible to describe the whole site as a single unit of plant.

The judge went on to consider whether the wash hall alone could be treated as one composite unit of plant. Even there, however, he concluded that such a view was untenable. The wash hall contained a lobby and WC, a pump room, an inspection area and a store. As such, the judge concluded that 'quite plainly the building functions as premises, housing the

Plant and Machinery: A to Z

machinery'. He found it 'impossible to say that the wash hall as a whole [was] apparatus functioning as plant'.

As a result of this case, HMRC have a strengthened hand. Furthermore, the legislation introduced from the end of 1993 and now contained in CAA 2001, Pt. 2, Ch. 3 produces a further barrier to treatment of such items as plant in the future.

Cross-references

The following headings from this A to Z Chapter may be relevant in particular cases where this type of expenditure is being considered. See also the Chapter headed 'Meaning of Plant', which begins at 180-000.

- Car parks (260-250)
- Machinery (262-000)
- Structures (262-590)

260-270   Cash dispensers

Legislation: none

Cases: none

HMRC material: none

Commentary

There appears to be no specific reference to the treatment of cash dispensing machines anywhere in case law, in the legislation or in HMRC material.

However, as a machine, such an item will qualify for capital allowances in its own right, whether or not it can be said to be plant. Similarly, it should be noted that machinery is not affected by the restrictions imposed by table 1 in CAA 2001, s. 21–22 (buildings and structures, etc). This is because List C item 1 specifically exempts 'machinery'.

Cross-references

The following heading from this A to Z Chapter may be relevant in particular cases where this type of expenditure is being considered. See also the Chapter headed 'Meaning of Plant', which begins at 180-000.

   Machinery (262-000)

260-280   Ceilings and canopies

Legislation: CAA 2001, s. 21 (List A, item 1), 23 (List C, items 3 (formerly), 7, and note 4)

Cases: *Dixon v Fitch's Garage Ltd* (1975) 50 TC 509; *Hampton v Fortes Autogrill Ltd* (1979) 53 TC 691; *Cole Brothers Ltd v Phillips* [1982] BTC 208; *Thomas v Reynolds* [1987] BTC 147; *Wimpy International Ltd v Warland* [1989] BTC 58; *Associated Restaurants Ltd v Warland* [1989] BTC 58

HMRC material: CA 22010 to 22070

Commentary

On the whole, ceilings have not fared well in claims that they should be treated as plant. See, for example, the mixed reactions in the *Wimpy* and *Associated Restaurants* cases.

Case law on this topic is now largely superseded by CAA 2001, Pt. 2, Ch. 3. CAA 2001, s. 21, List A specifically includes ceilings in the term 'building' so that they cannot qualify as plant. The only exception would be if they fall within any of the headings of List C at CAA 2001, s. 23. The possible headings under which such an exemption might be granted are items 3 (formerly), 7, 10 (possibly) and 14. These deal respectively with air and ventilation systems (now to be considered under the integral feature rules at s. 33A), sound insulation, fire equipment and decorative assets provided for hotel and similar trades.

The above exemptions cannot apply if the principal purpose of the asset is 'to insulate or enclose the interior of a building or provide an interior wall, floor or ceiling which (in each case) is intended to remain permanently in place' (CAA 2001, s. 23(4)).

Additional guidance can be found in the HMRC manuals. Inspectors are instructed to accept as plant a suspended ceiling which forms an integral part of a heating or ventilation system. What is envisaged here is that the ceiling is the fourth side of 'a duct or channel through which stale air is extracted for treatment' (CA 22070).

If it is claimed that the principal purpose of the ceiling is to provide sound insulation then it appears that it can be exempted under List C, item 7 and yet it is difficult to see how it can avoid being caught by the note following the table. This note will not allow it to qualify as plant if 'its principal purpose is to insulate or enclose the interior of a building'.

For those in the hotel, restaurant or similar trades it may be possible to argue that the ceiling is primarily a decorative asset provided for the enjoyment of the public. HMRC will certainly quote against this argument the case of *Fortes Autogrill Limited* which specifically concerned false ceilings in a restaurant. In the *Wimpy* case, on the other hand, some ceilings were held to be simply part of the premises but another was held to qualify as plant because it was 'an embellishment of the premises designed to create atmosphere' and was 'properly to be regarded as apparatus used in the trade'.

The question of canopies is a different one. In the *Fitch's Garage* case there was a canopy which covered a petrol filling station. It was decided that its only function was to provide protection from the weather. As it played no direct part in the trading activities it did not qualify as plant. However, if HMRC rely too closely on the *Fitch's Garage* case then their argument will be weak. In the case of *IR Commrs v Scottish & Newcastle Breweries Ltd*

Plant and Machinery: A to Z

[1982] BTC 187, for example, Lord Lowrie commented that the *Fitch's Garage* case was 'capable of decision either way'. Similarly, in the *Cole Brothers* case, the Lord Chancellor commented that it was doubtful that the *Fitch's Garage* decision could stand in the light of the decision in the *Scottish & Newcastle Breweries* case. As such, there may well be ammunition for arguing that a petrol station canopy could qualify on case law principles, particularly where (as is generally the case) the canopy plays an important advertising role.

In the Readers' Forum of *Taxation Magazine* (6 January 2000, p. 295) an 'editorial note' suggested that a major supermarket has successfully argued in front of the special commissioners for treatment of a canopy as plant.

Finally, though, it will be necessary to show that a canopy is not disqualified by virtue of being a structure and thus caught under CAA 2001, s. 22, List B, item 7.

Cross-references

The following headings from this A to Z Chapter may be relevant in particular cases where this type of expenditure is being considered. See also the Chapter headed 'Meaning of Plant', which begins at 180-000.

- Buildings (260-150)
- Bus shelters (260-170)
- Décor (260-500)
- Demolition costs (260-510)
- Floors and flooring materials (260-780)
- Professional fees and preliminary costs (262-240)
- Shelves (262-470)
- Storage equipment (262-570)

260-290   Central heating, etc systems

Legislation: CAA 2001, s. 23 (List C, item 9), s. 33A(5)(c)

Cases: *Jarrold v John Good & Sons Ltd* (1963) 40 TC 681; *Cooke v Beach Station Caravans Ltd* (1974) 49 TC 514; *Wimpy International Ltd v Warland* [1989] BTC 58; *Melluish v BMI (No. 3) Ltd* [1995] BTC 381

HMRC material: CA 20020, CA 21200, CA 21230

(See also the examples at CA 26025 to CA 26600 and accompanying text.)

Commentary

HMRC have long accepted as plant all of the following (per CA 21200):

- central heating systems;
- hot-water systems;

- air conditioning systems;
- alarm and sprinkler systems;
- ventilation systems; and
- baths, basins, toilet suites.

There is case law authority for this Revenue treatment. For example, in the *Jarrold v Good* case, the judge commented:

> 'The heating installation of a building may be passive in the sense that it involves no moving machinery, but few would deny it the name of "plant". The same thing could no doubt be said of many air conditioning and water softening installations. All that the Income Tax Acts require in this context is that the plant shall have been provided "for the purpose of the trade" – an expression wide enough to cover assets which play a passive as well as an active role in the accomplishment of that purpose.'

Where a suspended ceiling or plenum floor forms an integral part of a heating or ventilation system (for example, the fourth side of a duct for the air), then HMRC accept that this cost should be treated as on plant or machinery (CA 22070). By contrast, a floor that merely *covers* a heating or ventilation system will not qualify.

The *Wimpy* case is a reminder that something may become a fixture but remain plant, and central heating apparatus is given as an example.

Integral features

For expenditure incurred from 1 or 6 April 2008 (for corporation tax and income tax respectively), the rules have been tightened in relation to such expenditure. Costs incurred on central heating systems will continue to qualify but only as integral features, and therefore subject to the 'special rate' of just 10 per cent (though they can still be covered by the annual investment allowance if not used elsewhere: see 181-000). See 247-000 for detailed discussion of the rules relating to integral features.

Specifically, the following items – related to heating and ventilation – will qualify as integral features (CAA 2001, s. 33A(5)(c)): 'a space or water heating system, a powered system of ventilation, air cooling or air purification, and any floor or ceiling comprised in such a system'. Before April 2008, this same category was included as item 3 at List C at CAA 2001, s. 23, but that item was removed by the *Finance Act* 2008. In each case, it is subject to the proviso that no allowances are due where the principal purpose of the asset is to insulate or enclose the interior of a building, or to provide a wall, floor or ceiling that is intended to remain permanently in place. For example, no relief would be due for the cost of an external wall just because that wall happens to form one side of a heating system.

Cross-references

The following headings, mostly from this A to Z Chapter, may be relevant in particular cases where this type of expenditure is being considered. See also the Chapter headed 'Meaning of Plant', which begins at 180-000 and the commentary on 'integral features' beginning at 247-000ff.

Plant and Machinery: A to Z

- Alterations to buildings (260-040)
- Cold rooms (260-310)
- Electrical installations and equipment (260-600)
- Fire safety (see 160-500)
- Fixtures (260-760)
- Greenhouses (260-950)
- Insulation (see 160-400)
- Machinery (262-000)
- Plant rooms (262-210)
- Professional fees and preliminary costs (262-240)
- Sanitary ware (262-420)
- Temporary buildings (262-740)
- Water supplies and water tanks (262-920)

260-300   Clocks

Legislation: none

Cases: *Cole Brothers Ltd v Phillips* [1982] BTC 208

HMRC material: CG 76904

Commentary

A clock used for the purposes of the trade will qualify as plant.

In the *Cole Brothers* case the cost of wiring to clocks was an item specifically accepted by the Revenue as qualifying as plant. This was a clear implication that the clocks themselves qualified as plant.

In the *Capital Gains* Manual at CG 76904, HMRC accept that 'antique clocks and watches such as "Tompion" clocks are regarded as machinery for Capital Gains Tax purposes'. There seems no reason, however, why more ordinary clocks should be excluded from the definition of 'plant'. Certainly, there are no grounds for saying that clocks that qualify as machinery for CGT purposes would not do so for the purposes of claiming plant and machinery allowances.

Cross-references

The following headings from this A to Z Chapter may be relevant in particular cases where this type of expenditure is being considered. See also the Chapter headed 'Meaning of Plant', which begins at 180-000.

- Electrical installations and equipment (260-600)
- Machinery (262-000)

260-310   Cold rooms

Legislation: CAA 2001, s. 23 (List C, item 4, 18)

Cases: None (but regarding IBAs, see 301-550 and *Ellerker v Union Cold Storage Co Ltd* (1938) 22 TC 195 and *Bestway (Holdings) Ltd v David Alexander Luff* [1998] BTC 69)

HMRC material: CA 22030, CA 22120

Commentary

Cold rooms and cold stores each receive a separate mention in CAA 2001, s. 23. List C provides specifically that a cold room and a cold store are unaffected by the provisions of CAA 2001, s. 21 and 22. As such, they are to be considered on ordinary case law principles. It follows from the above that there is nothing in the legislation to prevent cold rooms or cold stores from qualifying as plant.

Case law specifically establishes that the operation of a cold store is a qualifying trade for IBA purposes (*Ellerker v Union Cold Storage Co Ltd*).

The fact that a cold store may qualify for industrial buildings allowances does not mean that it cannot qualify for plant and machinery allowances. This is not to say that the same building can ever qualify for a double rate of allowance. What it does mean, however, is that in some circumstances the taxpayer will be able to choose between an IBA claim or a claim for allowances as plant or machinery.

To decide whether it is possible to make a valid claim for treatment as plant, HMRC give the test as being whether the cold store is capable of independent existence as a building. If it is made up of a refrigeration unit plus a framework, such that the framework is incapable of a separate existence, then 'the whole is effectively a large fridge which qualifies as plant' (CA 22120). This is to be contrasted with the case 'where the building houses an insulated "box" which provides the insulation, and the building is capable of an independent existence'. In this latter case, the 'insulated box' will qualify as plant, but the building itself will qualify only for IBAs and not for allowances as plant and machinery.

Following the introduction of the 'long-life asset' rules (see 210-000) care is needed where expenditure is incurred after 25 November 1996. Suppose that £1 million is spent on a new cold store, of which £300,000 is on identifiable mechanical plant. If the plant claim is limited to the £300,000 then first-year or writing-down allowances may be due on this and an IBA claim at four per cent may be made on the balance. If, on the other hand, the whole unit is claimed as plant, but the inspector successfully argues that the whole constitutes a long-life asset, then allowances will be restricted to 6 per cent each year of the reducing balance. (It is unlikely that the inspector would be able to sustain a long-life asset argument in respect of the mechanical plant in isolation.)

For an illustration of the above principles, see the example at 210-300.

Plant and Machinery: A to Z

Cross-references

The following headings from this A to Z Chapter may be relevant in particular cases where this type of expenditure is being considered. See also the Chapter headed 'Meaning of Plant', which begins at 180-000.

- Buildings (260-150)
- Electrical installations and equipment (260-600)
- Fridges and freezers (260-800)
- Structures (262-590)

260-320   Computers

Legislation: CAA 2001, s. 23 (List C, item 8)

Cases: *Munby v Furlong* (1977) 50 TC 491

HMRC material: CA 21010, CA 21230; EIM 36730

Commentary

Computers come squarely within the definition of 'plant and machinery'. They are specifically unaffected by CAA 2001, s. 21 and s. 22 (List C, item 8).

The HMRC manuals refer to computers as machinery (CA 21010). In a letter from the Revenue to the Football League sent on 25 January 1991 computers were listed as an example of the sort of asset 'which would normally qualify as plant or machinery' (see CA 21230). If further justification were needed, reference could be made to the case of *Munby v Furlong*, in which the commissioners by implication accepted that a computer would qualify as plant.

It is only in exceptional circumstances that HMRC will accept that an employee can have a genuine claim for capital allowances on a computer. This is on the grounds that the employer will normally supply what is needed. For a fuller discussion of the issue, see the HMRC manuals at EIM 36730.

Computers are a good example of items where an election for treatment as a short-life asset (see 205-000) may be beneficial.

As to the treatment of computer software, see 260-330.

Cross-references

The following headings from this A to Z Chapter may be relevant in particular cases where this type of expenditure is being considered. See also the Chapter headed 'Meaning of Plant', which begins at 180-000.

- Buildings (260-150)

- Computer software (260-330)
- Electrical installations and equipment (260-600)
- Machinery (262-000)
- Telecommunication systems (262-710)
- Telephones and fax machines (262-720)

260-330   Computer software

Legislation: CAA 2001, s. 23(2), 71

Cases: none

HMRC material: CA 21010, CA 22280; BIM 35855

Commentary

Special rules treat the cost of computer software as expenditure on plant and machinery. CAA 2001, s. 71 deals specifically with the person who 'incurs capital expenditure in acquiring, for the purposes of the qualifying activity, a right to use or otherwise deal with computer software' and says that the right and the software are to be treated as plant or machinery belonging to the individual for as long as he is entitled to that right.

The fact that there is no physical asset (for example, because the software is transferred electronically) does not create any problem (CA 22280). Furthermore, a person incurring capital expenditure in acquiring a right to use or otherwise deal with computer software will be treated as acquiring plant, as long as the acquisition is for the purposes of a qualifying activity. The person in question will also be deemed to own the plant as a result of incurring the capital expenditure.

Abortive capital expenditure on computer software will qualify for plant and machinery allowances, just as if the purchase had been successful. This is the effect of CAA 2001, s. 67(2) and s. 71 and is confirmed in the Business Income manual at BIM 35855. The manual goes on to say that 'for all practical purposes there is no scope for arguing that abortive expenditure on software is neither revenue nor qualifies for capital allowances'. As for the question of whether the expenditure is capital, see below.

There is no definition in the legislation of the term 'computer software'. Inspectors are instructed that they should 'treat computer programs and data of any kind as computer software'.

A wider issue sometimes arises as to the general treatment of computer software, including the issue of whether or not it is capital in nature. Guidance on this is given at BIM 35800ff. Key principles are as follows:

(1)   Regular payments akin to a rental are revenue. The timing of deductions is governed

by correct accounting practice (which normally requires the rentals to be spread over the useful life of the software).

(2) Where software is paid for with a lump sum and is expected to have a useful economic life of less than two years, inspectors will accept that the expenditure is revenue.

(3) However, HMRC will not accept that a particular piece of software has such a limited life solely because updates appear at frequent intervals. Rather, HMRC will consider whether the business concerned in fact trades up to the new versions at intervals short enough to give a particular version only a transitory value to that business.

(4) Where software functions as a capital asset of the trade capital allowances on plant and machinery will be due under CAA 2001, s. 71, whether the software is acquired as a bundle with the hardware or on a separate CD, etc.

(5) Where a single payment is made to purchase computer hardware plus a licence to use the accompanying software, the HMRC view is that the expenditure should be apportioned except where that exercise will not have significant tax consequences.

(6) However, there is no need to apportion the expenditure if both the hardware and software are acquired on capital account and the expenditure all goes into the general machinery and plant pool.

(7) Some, particularly larger, concerns may develop their own software. The same principles apply and the question of whether the expenditure concerned is capital or revenue again depends on the economic function of the software in the trade in question.

(8) The same treatment should in principle apply to salaries of in-house computer professionals as to external costs. However, HMRC take the view that 'expenditure on salaries etc of staff engaged on making changes to computer systems, which can at most be viewed as piecemeal improvements, is unlikely to be capital'.

The guidance at BIM 35800ff. is extensive and reference should be made to it in cases of doubt or where substantial amounts are at stake.

It should be noted that the provisions of CAA 2001, s. 21 and 22 do not apply to computer software (CAA 2001, s. 23(1) and (2)).

Disposals

The granting of a right to use software will mean that the person granting the right will need to bring a disposal value into account in certain circumstances (CAA 2001, s. 72). This will apply where the consideration consists of a capital sum (or would do if the consideration were in money). An exception is made if there has already been a 'disposal event' as a result of the plant starting to be used for purposes other than those of the qualifying activity or because the qualifying activity is permanently discontinued.

To determine the amount of disposal value to be brought into account, the legislation recognises three circumstances, as follows:

(1) where the grant is for a consideration that does not consist entirely of money;

(2) where the grant is made:

   (a) either for no consideration or at less than market value;

   (b) such that no charge is produced for the employee; and

   (c) where the grantee is either a dual resident investing company connected with the grantor or is incurring expenditure that cannot qualify either for plant or machinery allowances or for research and development allowances;

(3) where the grant is made in any other circumstances.

In the case of circumstances (1) and (2), the disposal value is the market value (at the time of the grant) of the right granted.

Where the grant is made under circumstance (3) above, then the disposal value consists of the sum of the following:

(1) the net consideration in money received in respect of the grant; plus

(2) any insurance money, or other compensation that is capital in nature, that has been received because of some event that has affected the consideration obtainable on the grant.

Capping the disposal value

There is a general rule for plant and machinery that the amount of any disposal value is limited to the qualifying expenditure incurred (CAA 2001, s. 73). Where a disposal value has to be calculated in respect of computer software or the rights to use computer software, then to ensure that the overall cap is not being breached the disposal value must be increased by any other disposal values previously taken into account, when software rights have been granted as described above.

Cross-references

The following headings from this A to Z Chapter may be relevant in particular cases where this type of expenditure is being considered. See also the Chapter headed 'Meaning of Plant', which begins at 180-000.

- Computers (260-320)
- Finance costs (260-720)

260-340 Consumables

Legislation: none

Cases: none

HMRC material: none

Plant and Machinery: A to Z

Commentary

The Revenue used to state the view, quite simply, that 'consumable stores are not plant. They fail the two-year test' (old CA 1567). There is no reason of principle why this should have changed. Possibly the view was taken that the point is self-evident on ordinary principles and that it therefore did not need stating.

In practice, such items will simply qualify as an ordinary trading expense as long as the cost has been incurred wholly and exclusively for the purposes of the trade.

Cross-references

The following headings from this A to Z Chapter may be relevant in particular cases where this type of expenditure is being considered. See also the Chapter headed 'Meaning of Plant', which begins at 180-000.

- Containers (260-350)
- Loose tools (261-370)

260-350   Containers

Legislation: none

Cases: *Hinton v Maden & Ireland Ltd* (1959) 38 TC 391

HMRC material: none

Commentary

Many businesses sell their produce in containers which remain the property of the trader. As such, the containers are returnable. The Revenue used to accept explicitly that they will qualify as plant as long as they satisfy the two-year test (old CA 1568). There is no reason why they should not continue to qualify as such.

If they do not satisfy the two-year test, the cost of such containers will normally be treated as an ordinary trading expense, the costs of which will be shown in the profit and loss account and will be allowable on ordinary principles. It will be necessary to demonstrate that expenditure on the containers was incurred wholly and exclusively for the purposes of the trade.

Cross-references

The following heading from this A to Z Chapter may be relevant in particular cases where this type of expenditure is being considered. See also the Chapter headed 'Meaning of Plant', which begins at 180-000.

- Consumables (260-340)

260-360   Counters and checkouts

Legislation: CAA 2001, s. 23 (List C, item 4)

Cases: none

HMRC material: none

Commentary

There is very little guidance as to the treatment of these items.

They receive a mention in List C, item 4. The effect of this is that they are not excluded from qualifying as plant by virtue of CAA 2001, s. 21 and 22. The implication is that they do indeed qualify in some circumstances at least, but this effect is not specifically achieved by the legislation.

Such items will normally qualify as plant if they are provided for the specific purposes of the trade and if the building in which they are housed would remain complete even if the counters and checkouts were removed.

Cross-references

The following headings from this A to Z Chapter may be relevant in particular cases where this type of expenditure is being considered. See also the Chapter headed 'Meaning of Plant', which begins at 180-000.

- Fixtures (260-760)
- Furniture and furnishings (260-820)
- Screens (262-430)
- Storage equipment (262-570)

260-370   Curtains

Legislation: none

Cases: *Jarrold v John Good & Sons Ltd* (1963) 40 TC 681; *IR Commrs v Scottish & Newcastle Breweries Ltd* [1982] BTC 187

HMRC material: CA 21200

Commentary

Curtains will almost invariably qualify as plant. Inspectors are instructed to treat them as such 'if they are of a permanent and durable nature, that is if they satisfy the two-year test' (CA 21200).

In the *Scottish & Newcastle* case, the Revenue accepted without argument that curtains would qualify as plant, even though they also played 'an important and intended decorative function in creating the desired atmosphere or setting'.

The *John Good* case provides specific support for treating theatrical stage curtains as plant.

Cross-references

The following headings from this A to Z Chapter may be relevant in particular cases where this type of expenditure is being considered. See also the Chapter headed 'Meaning of Plant', which begins at 180-000.

● Fixtures (260-760)
● Windows (262-960)

260-500   Décor

Legislation: CAA 2001, s. 23 (List C, item 14)

Cases: *IR Commrs v Scottish & Newcastle Breweries Ltd* [1982] BTC 187; *Leeds Permanent Building Society v Proctor* [1982] BTC 347; *Wimpy International Ltd v Warland* [1989] BTC 58 (items 1, 12)

HMRC material: CA 21130, CA 21200

Commentary

HMRC accept that pictures and removable wall decorations will qualify as plant 'if the taxpayer's trade involves the creation of an attractive setting or atmosphere and the sale of that setting or atmosphere to their customers', as long as the items in question were specially chosen to help create the setting or atmosphere (CA 21200). In other circumstances, HMRC argue that pictures, etc do not qualify as plant as they are not apparatus with which the taxpayer carries on his trade.

HMRC give, as an example of an occasion where such items will not qualify as plant, a painting on the wall of an accountant's office. In HMRC view, such a painting 'is not plant because selling atmosphere is not part of the accountant's business'.

It seems to the author of this book that this is an incorrect interpretation by HMRC of the tax position. In the *Scottish & Newcastle Breweries* case, the commissioners decided that certain decorative items satisfied the function test required of plant *even though they formed part of the setting within which the trade was carried on*. This, surely, is the point. If an item is part of the building then it will not normally qualify as plant; the only exception will be if it can meet the special condition of providing atmosphere for the customers of the trade. If, however, there is an item which is clearly not part of the building itself then it can qualify as plant without having to pass this special test. To an extent, this interpretation is confirmed by List C, item 14 which provides that 'decorative assets provided for the enjoyment of the public in the hotel, restaurant or similar trades' are to be unaffected by CAA 2001, s. 21 and 22, ie are not deemed to be part of the building.

The *Scottish & Newcastle Breweries* case appears to contradict the strict Revenue interpretation. In the closing words of his judgment, Lord Lowry commented that 'it would ... be strange indeed if articles used in a building "for the purposes of the trade" could not also be plant within the meaning of [the Capital Allowances Act 2001]'. Lord Lowry reminded the court of the well-established definition of plant which required only that an item should come in the category of 'goods or chattels, fixed or moveable ... kept for permanent employment in the business'. Earlier in his judgment, Lord Lowry commented that 'it is fallacious to say that articles used to adorn the setting thereby ceased to be apparatus used by the taxpayers for carrying on their business'.

To summarise, the *Scottish & Newcastle Breweries* case provides a clear precedent for treating as plant any items of décor used for the purposes of a trade where the provision of atmosphere is part of what is being sold. It does appear, however, that HMRC may be extending this principle too far in saying that no item which has merely a decorative function can qualify as plant in any other business.

Cross-references

The following headings, mostly from this A to Z Chapter, may be relevant in particular cases where this type of expenditure is being considered. See also the Chapter headed 'Meaning of Plant', which begins at 180-000 and the commentary on 'integral features' beginning at 247-000ff.

- Buildings (260-150)
- Ceilings and canopies (260-280)
- Curtains (260-370)
- Fish tanks and ponds (260-740)
- Fixtures (260-760)
- Furniture and furnishings (260-820)
- Screens (262-430)

260-510   Demolition costs

Legislation: CAA 2001, s. 26, 163–165

Cases: none

HMRC material: CA 20070, CA 22210

Commentary

Where costs are incurred in demolishing plant or machinery, the tax treatment will depend on whether or not the old plant is replaced. First, however, it is necessary to calculate the net costs of the demolition. The net cost is defined as being the excess of any of the cost of the

Plant and Machinery: A to Z

demolition over any money received for the remains of the old plant or machinery (CAA 2001, s. 26(4)).

Where there are net demolition costs, then these are added to the cost of the new plant if the plant is replaced. If there is no replacement of the plant that is demolished then the net costs are added to the qualifying expenditure for the period in which the demolition is undertaken. If the costs are incurred when a trade ceases then they are added to the qualifying expenditure for the last chargeable period of the trade (CA 22210).

Obviously, it is possible that the disposal proceeds for old plant will exceed the cost of demolition. In that case, the net receipt (including any sale proceeds, insurance receipts or other capital compensation) will be brought in as a disposal value in the ordinary way.

There are special rules applying to demolition costs related to offshore plant or machinery.

Cross-references

The following headings, mostly from this A to Z Chapter, may be relevant in particular cases where this type of expenditure is being considered. See also the Chapter headed 'Meaning of Plant', which begins at 180-000 and the commentary on 'integral features' beginning at 247-000ff.

- Buildings (260-150)
- Professional fees and preliminary costs (262-240)
- Removal costs (262-300)
- Structures (262-590)

260-520   Designs and patterns

Legislation: none

Cases: *McVeigh v Arthur Sanderson & Sons Limited* (1969) 45 TC 273

HMRC material: none

Commentary

The Revenue used to accept explicitly as plant 'the cost of buying designs and patterns incorporated in machinery or tools which qualify for capital allowances as plant' (old CA 1569). The current manuals are silent on the matter though there is no reason of principle why the policy should have changed.

The *Arthur Sanderson* case concerned a manufacturer of wallpaper and fabrics. For the purpose of the manufacture, the company used blocks, rollers and screens with the appropriate design on them. The court held that the blocks were plant and therefore qualified for capital allowances.

It was held in that case that the designs themselves were not plant. However, this was based on the reasoning of Rowlatt J in *Daphne v Shaw* (1926) 11 TC 256. Rowlatt's decision in that case was overturned subsequently in the case of *Munby v Furlong* (1977) 50 TC 491. For further discussion of this issue see under 'books' at 260-110. As such, HMRC do not have a sound argument for saying that designs cannot qualify as plant. Indeed, the judge in the *Arthur Sanderson* case made it fairly clear that he would have concluded that the designs did qualify as plant if he had not felt himself bound by the earlier (incorrect) decision.

Cross-references

The following headings from this A to Z Chapter may be relevant in particular cases where this type of expenditure is being considered. See also the Chapter headed 'Meaning of Plant', which begins at 180-000.

- Books (260-110)
- Software (260-330)
- Wallpaper designs and pattern books (262-900)

260-525   Disability Discrimination Act

Legislation: none

Key case law: none

HMRC material: Guidance at www.hmrc.gov.uk/specialist/disability-act-guidance.htm

Commentary

Since October 2004, businesses providing services to the public have had certain statutory obligations under the *Disability Discrimination Acts* of 1995 and 2005, to improve access to their premises for disabled people. Broadly, the law requires service providers to make 'reasonable adjustments' to their premises to remove obstacles that would prevent disabled people from using their services.

The cost of such adjustments will, in some cases be treated for tax purposes as revenue expenditure, to be written off in full as it is incurred. HMRC give, as examples of such expenditure, the cost of printing large documents or of training staff on disability issues.

Other expenditure, however, will be capital in nature, in which case it will be necessary to consider whether or not it qualifies for plant and machinery allowances. The capital allowances legislation does not make special provision for such costs, so it is a question of applying general principles to the expenditure. However, HMRC have provided guidelines on the likely treatment of these costs and, in August 2008, updated those guidelines to take account of the changes introduced in FA 2008 (eg in relation to integral features). That guidance includes various examples of likely expenditure and the details of those examples are reproduced in full below, with the author's comments added in square brackets:

Plant and Machinery: A to Z

Ramps

'Expenditure on building or installing a permanent ramp to facilitate access by members of the public qualifies only if the work is carried out to an industrial or agricultural building or 'qualifying hotel'. Relief is given for the expenditure under the IBA code or agricultural buildings allowance ABA code.

Businesses that buy moveable ramps that are not permanently fixed to the building are able to claim PMAs on the cost of the ramp.'

Toilets and washing facilities

'Minor adjustments, such as changing doors on cubicles from opening inwards to opening outwards, would normally be wholly deductible for tax purposes as revenue expenditure.

The costs of making building alterations to toilets (for example, to widen a doorway to facilitate wheelchair access) are not allowable for tax purposes [but see 260-040], unless the building is an industrial or agricultural building or qualifying hotel. In those circumstances, the alteration costs qualify for IBA or ABA capital allowances.

The cost of new sanitary ware installed to comply with DDA requirements qualifies for PMAs. So do the costs of installing the sanitary ware.'

Signs

'The costs of permanent signage qualify for PMAs.

Expenditure on, say, affixing warning transparencies on glass doors or similar surfaces qualifies for relief as a revenue expense. The use of coloured paint to make things easier to see (by, for instance, painting doors, step edges, or passages in contrasting colours) is allowable in full for tax purposes.'

Handrails

'Where businesses replace existing handrails with special handrails to ease access for disabled people, the expenditure would normally be accepted as a repair and would be deductible in full.

Where new handrails are installed for the specific purpose of helping customers with mobility impairments, the cost would constitute capital expenditure but would qualify for PMAs.'

Lighting and electrical systems

'From 1 April 2008, new expenditure on lighting and electrical systems qualifies for a 10 per cent writing down allowance per annum as integral features. Electrical systems do not include computer, telecommunication, and surveillance systems (including their wiring), nor fire alarm or burglar alarm systems [but these will almost certainly qualify in their own right - see the various headings in this A to Z section].

If the lighting appears on the Energy Technology Criteria List 100 per cent first-year allowances can be claimed. More guidance can be found in the Capital allowances manual [and see 185-350].'

Internal and external doors

'Usually, doors are considered to be part of the premises and do not qualify for capital allowances. As such, no allowances are due on installing new doors. [See, generally, 260-550.]

But where a door is no longer fit for use, it is likely that the cost of replacing it would qualify for relief as a repair, and so is wholly deductible as a revenue expense.

Quite often simply replacing a traditional door handle with a D-shaped or similar handle enables service providers to provide improved access.

A door handle would normally be an integral part of the door to which it is affixed, with the result that it would not qualify for PMAs. Any replacement of the door handle, however, counts as a repair, and so is allowable as a revenue expense. Some mechanical door handles may not qualify as a repair, where they are actually an improvement over the previous handle, but they could qualify for PMAs as machinery.'

Lifts

'Where expenditure is incurred on constructing a new commercial building the cost of constructing the lift shaft is not allowable.

However, the cost of installing a lift or replacing an existing lift with a modern lift is considered to be expenditure on an integral feature and qualifies for a 10 per cent writing down allowance per annum [but see 247-100 for a possible argument that such expenditure qualifies for 20 per cent allowances]. In addition, if incidental to the cost of installing the lift machinery, the costs of installing the lift shaft will also qualify for PMAs [see 260-040]. More guidance can be found in the capital allowances manual.'

Steps and stairs

'Expenditure on knocking down steps and replacing them with ramps is not allowable. However, expenditure on adding fluorescent and coloured strips to the edges of steps, approaching and within business premises, to assist access by visually impaired people, is allowed as revenue expenditure on repairs and maintenance.'

[As regards the treatment of stairs generally, see 262-560.]

Alterations to walls and floors

'Alterations to the fabric of a building are not normally allowable for tax purposes, unless the building is an industrial or agricultural building or qualifying hotel [in which case the allowances would be given under the code for IBAs (see 300-000ff.) or ABAs (see 425-000ff. or under the special IBA rules relating to qualifying hotels (see 248-500)], or unless the alterations are incidental to the installation of plant or machinery [see 260-040]. So any expenditure on making new doorways or widening existing doorways would not normally qualify for relief.

However, repairs to floors, for example, to level out uneven surfacing due to wear and tear over time, is allowable as a revenue expense.

Also, HM Revenue & Customs (HMRC) accept that painting walls or floors in bright contrasting colours, to assist access by visually impaired people, is allowable as revenue expenditure on repairs and maintenance. '

Plant and Machinery: A to Z

Car parks

'HMRC accept that expenditure on, for example, redefining parking areas by repainting parking bays to provide wider, designated bays for disabled parking, is a revenue expense, which is allowable in full for tax purposes.

Where the work is more substantial, for example, to include car park resurfacing, then as long as there is no improvement element, the expenditure is allowable as normal revenue expenditure on repairs.

[But the cost of a new car park does not qualify: see 260-250.]'

Paths

'Normally expenditure on paths or land does not qualify for capital allowances. However there is a distinction between improving and repairing property. While expenditure on improvements generally counts as capital expenditure (which does not normally qualify for allowances) expenditure on repairs is a revenue expense, which is allowable in full for tax purposes.

Thus, where a business incurs expenditure on its paths in order to remove obstacles that could present a danger to the disabled, for example on:

- replacing cracked or uneven paving slabs
- cutting back protruding or overhanging objects, grass or other vegetation,

the expenditure is revenue expenditure and is allowable in full.'

Cross-references

The following headings from this A to Z Chapter (in addition to those referred to in square brackets above) may be relevant in particular cases where this type of expenditure is being considered. See also the Chapter headed 'Meaning of Plant', which begins at 188-000.

- Buildings (260-150)
- Professional fees and preliminary costs (262-240)
- Removal costs (262-300)

260-530 Display equipment

Legislation: CAA 2001, s. 23 (List C, item 4)

Cases: none

HMRC material: CA 21180, CA 22110, CA 23140

Commentary

Display equipment is outside the extended scope of 'building' as it is included in List C in CAA 2001, s. 23.

Such equipment will normally qualify as plant without any problem. Lighting is accepted by HMRC as qualifying as plant 'if it is specifically designed to encourage the sale of goods on display' (CA 21180).

On a different note, the HMRC manuals also instruct inspectors to allow as plant bus shelters, etc which are leased by advertisers for displaying advertisements. Such shelters should be treated as plant (CA 22110).

Certain refrigeration equipment, including display cabinets and compressors, may qualify as energy-saving plant (see 185-350) (CA 23140).

Revenue instructions to Inspectors (at CA 22110) are to 'treat show cases associated with a shop front which are distinct from the structure as fixtures and fittings', ie to disallow capital allowances for the shop front itself but to allow them for a separate show case.

Cross-references

The following headings from this A to Z Chapter may be relevant in particular cases where this type of expenditure is being considered. See also the Chapter headed 'Meaning of Plant', which begins at 180-000.

- Advertising hoardings (260-010)
- Buildings (260-150)
- Décor (260-500)
- Electrical installations and equipment (260-600)
- Fixtures (260-760)
- Furniture and furnishings (260-820)
- Shop fronts (262-490)
- Storage equipment (262-570)

260-540   Docks (including dry docks)

Legislation: CAA 2001, s. 22 (List B, item 5), 23 (List C, item 23, 24)

Cases: *IR Commrs v Barclay, Curle and Co Ltd* (1969) 45 TC 221; *Attwood v Anduff Car Wash Ltd* [1997] BTC 454

HMRC material: CA 21130, CA 22050

Commentary

The starting point is that docks do not qualify as plant. This is by virtue of CAA 2001, s. 22, List B, item 11. Item 5 catches not only a dock as such but also any harbour, wharf, pier, marina, jetty or 'any other structure in or at which vessels may be kept or merchandise or passengers may be shipped or unshipped'.

Plant and Machinery: A to Z

403

List C of CAA 2001, s. 23 (item 23) provides that dry docks are not caught by the provisions of the table. Similarly, a jetty or similar structure provided mainly to carry plant or machinery is not caught by the provisions of CAA 2001, s. 21 and 22 – see List C, item 24.

It follows from the above that dry docks and jetties, etc provided for carrying plant or machinery must be considered on ordinary case law principles. It will therefore be necessary to show that the structure functions as plant within the business rather than merely acting as the premises at or on which the business is carried on.

In the *Barclay, Curle* case, the company successfully argued that the dry dock was an item of plant. As Lord Donovan put it in the House of Lords:

> 'In the present case this dry dock, looked upon as a unit, accommodates ships, separates them from their element and thus exposes them for repair; holds them in position while repairs are effected, and when this is done, returns them to the water. Thus the dry dock is, despite its size, in the nature of a tool of the Respondents' trade, and therefore, in my view, "plant".'

A House of Lords decision, even though it was only by a three to two majority, will carry weight for any future appeals on the same subject matter. It is likely, however, that HMRC would scrutinise closely the facts of any future case based on the *Barclay, Curle* decision. In the case of *Attwood v Anduff Car Wash Ltd*, where on the face of it similar principles applied, the Revenue successfully countered the arguments of the company.

Cross-references

The following headings from this A to Z Chapter may be relevant in particular cases where this type of expenditure is being considered. See also the Chapter headed 'Meaning of Plant', which begins at 180-000.

- Bridges, etc (260-130)
- Dykes, etc (260-580)
- Reservoirs, etc (262-310)
- Structures (262-590)

260-550   Doors and door handles

Legislation: CAA 2001, s. 21 (List A, item 1), 22 (List B, item 4 (regarding gates on a dam or reservoir))

Cases: *Wimpy International Ltd v Warland* [1989] BTC 58

HMRC material: CA 21010, CA 21200, CA 21230, CA 22270

Commentary

Usually, a door will fail to qualify as plant. Doors are specifically within the statutory definition of 'building' and are thus excluded from qualifying as plant (CAA 2001, s. 21, List A, item 1).

In the *Wimpy* case it was argued that the doors had a function 'to attract custom'. However, this argument was rejected both by the commissioners and in the courts. It was held that they were 'in the English climate a necessary part of the premises'.

To demonstrate that a door qualifies as plant it would therefore normally be necessary to show that it has some special feature. It may qualify as an integral feature if it can be shown to be part of an electrical system. In a letter from the Inland Revenue to the Football League in January 1991, automatic exit doors and gates (at a football ground) were listed among 'the sort of assets used by a football club in its trade which would normally qualify as plant or machinery' (CA 21230).

It is possible that, in fairly extreme circumstances, a reinforced door may qualify as a security asset. In this respect, see 262-450.

As regards fire doors, etc, see 160-500.

It is also possible that there will be doors that are not incorporated into a building. A door which was merely a part of a child's play equipment would not be caught by the provisions.

There seems to be no reason why a door closer cannot qualify as plant as long as it can be identified as a separate asset. Door handles with moving parts are specifically accepted by HMRC as machinery (CA 21010), though elsewhere (CA 21200) the position is stated less clearly: 'A door handle would normally be an integral part of the door to which it is affixed, with the result that it would not qualify for [capital allowances as plant or machinery] ... Some mechanical handles can in any event constitute machines in their own right.' Nevertheless, HMRC staff are instructed that they 'should not in practice refuse a PMA [plant and machinery allowance] claim where this is the treatment adopted in the computations'.

Cross-references

The following headings, mostly from this A to Z Chapter, may be relevant in particular cases where this type of expenditure is being considered. See also the Chapter headed 'Meaning of Plant', which begins at 180-000.

- Buildings (260-150)
- Fire safety (see 160-500)
- Gates (260-920)
- Letter boxes (261-310)
- Shop fronts (262-490)
- Walls (262-910)
- Windows (262-960)

260-570   Dyehouses

Legislation: CAA 2001, s. 21, 22

Cases: *Wangaratta Woollen Mills v Commissioner of Taxation of the Commonwealth of Australia* [1969] 43 ALJR 324

HMRC material: CA 22050

Commentary

In the Australian case concerning the *Wangaratta Woollen Mills* company, a dyehouse was held to be plant. However, the external walls and roof were excluded and so it is not the case that the building as a whole was held to be plant.

The point of the case is that the dyehouse itself (excluding the walls and roof) was deemed to be a complex whole which could not properly be subdivided for these purposes. There is perhaps an analogy with HMRC treatment of greenhouses (see 260-950), which are accepted as plant when there is a sophisticated system for controlling the various elements of the required environment.

The position now would in any case be that a dyehouse would be precluded from qualifying as plant by virtue of CAA 2001, s. 21 or 22, as being either a building or a structure. There is nothing in List C of CAA 2001, s. 23 that could enable a dyehouse to qualify. Elements of the overall cost may qualify, however, for example specialist sewerage arrangements specific to the trade in question.

Cross-references

The following headings from this A to Z Chapter may be relevant in particular cases where this type of expenditure is being considered. See also the Chapter headed 'Meaning of Plant', which begins at 180-000.

- Buildings (260-150)
- Sewerage (262-460)
- Structures (262-590)

260-580   Dykes, etc

Legislation: CAA 2001, s. 22 (List B, item 6)

Cases: none

HMRC material: CA 31110

Commentary

Dykes do not qualify as plant. Along with sea walls, weirs and drainage ditches, they are prevented from so qualifying by CAA 2001, s. 22, List B, item 6. The only exception would be if the structure fell within the very specific items listed in List C at CAA 2001, s. 23 but there is nothing in that column which will obviously exempt any of these items.

Cross-references

The following headings from this A to Z Chapter may be relevant in particular cases where this type of expenditure is being considered. See also the Chapter headed 'Meaning of Plant', which begins at 180-000.

- Structures (262-590)
- Water supplies and water tanks (262-920)

260-600   Electrical installations and equipment

Legislation: CAA 2001, s. 21 (List A, item 2), 23 (List C, various, including in particular items 1 to 11, 25 and 26), 33A

Cases: *J Lyons & Co Ltd v Attorney General* (1944) 170 LT 348; *Lancashire Electric Power Company v Wilkinson* (1947) 28 TC 427; *IR Commrs v Scottish & Newcastle Breweries Ltd* [1982] BTC 187; *Cole Brothers Ltd v Phillips* [1982] BTC 208; *Wimpy International Ltd v Warland* [1989] BTC 58 (item 3); *Hunt v Henry Quick Ltd* [1992] BTC 440; *King v Bridisco Ltd* [1992] BTC 440

HMRC material: CA 21160–21180, CA 21230, CA 22030, CA 22100 (caravans), CA 23130 (computers)

Commentary

This is a vital category of expenditure which comes up over and over again in practice. The rules were radically changed from April 2008, with the introduction of the concept of 'integral features', discussed in depth at 247-000.

The starting point for the treatment of electrical items is in CAA 2001, s. 21. List A, item 2, says that 'mains services, and systems, for water, electricity and gas' are to be included in the term 'building' and that such items therefore fail to qualify as plant unless they are within the specific exemptions in List C (or, now, within the general exemption at s. 23(2) for integral features). More generally, the same principle applies – but subject to the same exceptions – for any asset that is incorporated into a building.

The approach to expenditure on electrical items may now be seen as involving three steps:

Step 1: is it part of the building?
First, it is necessary to see whether the item forms part of the building in the first place. If it does not, then:

- the expenditure is not caught by CAA 2001, s. 21 as part of the building; and
- the item will not be an 'integral feature of a building or structure' within s. 33A.

Such an item will therefore attract writing-down allowances at the full 20 per cent rate (or will be covered by the annual investment allowance).

> **Example**
>
> A business buys a laptop computer. This is an electrical item that is clearly not part of the building. It is not affected by CAA 2001, s. 21ff. or by the rules relating to integral features.

Step 2: other expenditure on electrical items

If an electrical item is integrated into a building, but is still within List C at CAA 2001, s. 23, unrestricted capital allowances will be due. The wording of List C (as amended by the *Finance Act* 2008), and the wording of the rules relating to integral features, are probably intended to be mutually exclusive (so that an item normally falls within one or the other but not both). Specifically, for example, List C no longer gives an exemption for electrical systems provided to meet the particular requirements of the trade.

But it is not always the case that there is no overlap. Computer wiring, for example, could properly be described as an electrical system (and therefore an integral feature) but is also given as item 8 in List C. It is important to know which section takes priority, as this will determine whether writing-down allowances are due at 10 or 20 per cent.

It seems reasonably clear that List C treatment should take priority (so that writing-down allowances are given at 20 rather than 10 per cent) as this is the only logical reason for the continuing inclusion of the specific items in List C. The technical summary for this would therefore be as follows:

- computer wiring (for example) is initially caught by CAA 2001, s. 21 as the wiring is incorporated in the building;
- it is removed from that restriction both by s. 23(2) (integral features) and s. 23(3) (items in List C);
- it follows that the tax treatment must be established without the influence of CAA 2001, s. 21ff.;
- if, without that influence, the item qualifies as plant or machinery on normal case law principles (as will be the case with computer wiring) then allowances are given without reference to the integral feature rules; but
- if an item would fail to qualify on case law principles – as in the case of general lighting costs – it is then possible to look to the rules on integral features, which will ensure that relief is due but at the reduced rate of 10 per cent (though a 100 per cent annual investment allowance may still be given).

There are, in fact, numerous such exemptions relating to electrical installations and reference should be made to the contents of List C in CAA 2001, s. 23. The relevant items in relation to electrical equipment are the following:

- any machinery;
- burglar alarm systems;
- ceilings comprised in space or water-heating systems or in ventilation, etc systems;
- computer, telecommunication and surveillance systems (including their wiring or other links);

- cookers;
- fire alarm systems;
- hoists (previously, 'lifts, hoists, escalators and moving walkways', but see the comments below re integral features);
- manufacturing or processing equipment;
- refrigerators and similar equipment;
- refrigeration or cooling equipment (listed separately, though it is assumed that this is in fact an error in the legislation);
- sprinkler and other fire extinguishing equipment; and
- washing machines and dishwashers.

An asset is excluded from the above list 'if its principal purpose is to insulate or enclose the interior of the building or provide an interior wall, floor or ceiling which (in each case) is intended to remain permanently in place'.

Until April 2008, the above list included a general category of 'electrical systems (including lighting systems) provided mainly to meet the particular requirements of the trade, or to serve particular plant or machinery used for the purposes of the trade'. Similarly, there was an entry for 'space or water-heater systems, ventilation, air cooling or air purification systems'. Both of these categories have been removed as part of the introduction (in the *Finance Act* 2008) of the rules on integral features.

Step 3: integral features

The third step relates to expenditure on electrical items that are part of the building, or incorporated into it. In the context of electrical expenditure, this will specifically include mains services and systems, waste disposal systems, certain liftshafts and similar items, and fire safety systems (CAA 2001, s. 21).

If such items fall within the definition of 'integral features' then the rules of CAA 2001, s. 21 are disapplied by s. 23(2). Specifically, the rules relating to integral features will apply to the following categories of electrical expenditure:

- an electrical system, including a lighting system;
- a space or water heating system, a powered system of ventilation, air cooling or air purification, and any floor or ceiling comprised in such a system;
- a lift, an escalator or a moving walkway.

The effect of this is that such items do not normally qualify as plant under the ordinary rules (though see under Step 2 above). However, capital allowances are given 'as if ... the expenditure were capital expenditure on the provision of plant or machinery' (CAA 2001, s. 33A(2)). This simple deeming provision then overrides many decades of case law precedent: it is no longer necessary to determine whether such items are really plant, as they are now deemed to be such.

If not used for other expenditure, the annual investment allowance (see 181-000) may still provide immediate tax relief for integral features. If, however, the AIA is unavailable then the expenditure will form part of the 'special rate expenditure' pool and will attract writing-down allowances at just 10 per cent (reducing balance basis).

Plant and Machinery: A to Z

Example

A business builds a new office block and spends £40,000 on mains wiring and general lighting. Before 2008, such expenditure would not have attracted plant and machinery allowances. The expenditure is now classified as on integral features, however, and relief is due. If the AIA has not been used elsewhere, the whole of the cost can attract plant and machinery allowances at the outset, as it is less than the £50,000 (but see 181-050 for circumstances in which a lower figure is available).

If the AIA is already used up by other expenditure, then the £40,000 cost goes into the special rate expenditure pool and attracts relief at just 10 per cent per year.

This is not to say that the integral feature rules are only ever beneficial. Air conditioning costs, for example, would before April 2008 have qualified as plant or machinery in their own right, and unrestricted capital allowances would have been available. Under the rules applying since the start date in April 2008, however, the treatment of such items can now be illustrated as follows:

- air conditioning is initially caught by CAA 2001, s. 21 as an asset that is incorporated in the building;
- now that item 3 of List C has been removed (which formerly gave protection for air conditioning) no allowances would be due for such costs if it were not for the integral feature rules; but
- the rules on integral features will ensure that relief is due for such expenditure, incurred from 1 or 6 April 2008, but at the reduced rate of 10 per cent (though a 100 per cent annual investment allowance may still be given).

Entity or piecemeal test

An issue that has often arisen in practice is the question of whether an electrical installation is to be considered as one single item of plant or whether the expenditure is to be broken down and each component part considered on its own merits. In the leading case on this topic, that of *Cole Brothers Ltd v Phillips* (above) the company failed in its attempt to persuade the courts to consider the whole of the expenditure as being on a single item of plant or machinery.

Before the introduction of the rules relating to integral features, HMRC would accept that an electrical installation should be treated as a single item of plant only if all of the following conditions are satisfied (per CA 21180):

(1) it is specifically designed and built as a whole as 'a fully integrated entity';

(2) the design and adaptation of the plant are to meet the particular requirements of the trade;

(3) the electrical installation is essential for the functioning of the business; and

(4) what HMRC describe as the 'end-user items' of the installation function as apparatus in the business concerned.

If any of these conditions have not been met then HMRC insist on a piecemeal approach whereby they consider each item in turn. It is doubtful whether, on the basis of case law, HMRC is justified in taking such a tough line. It is quite clear from the House of Lords' judgments in the *Cole Brothers* case that the Lords felt obliged to accept the decision of the commissioners only because they viewed it as a matter of fact and not one of law. In such circumstances, it is not possible for the judges to overrule the decision of the commissioners (per *Edwards v Bairstow and Harrison* [1955] 36 TC 207).

The Lord Chancellor in *Cole Brothers* sided with the Revenue 'not without some wavering from time to time'. Lord Edmund-Davies commented that: 'I too doubt that I should have decided this case in the same way in all respects as that which commended itself to the Commissioners'. Lord Russell of Killowen stated: 'I incline to the view that had I been the Special Commissioners I might well have come to the conclusion that electrical equipment remaining in this case in dispute was relevantly plant'.

Assuming that the piecemeal approach does have to be adopted, inspectors have hitherto been instructed to accept the following items as plant (CA 21180):

(1)   the main switchboard, the transformer and any associated switchgear as long as 'a substantial part of the electrical installation – both the equipment and the wiring ancillary to it – qualifies as plant';

(2)   a standby generator, together with any emergency lighting and power circuits;

(3)   any lighting in sales areas, including the public areas of businesses like banks and building societies, as long as the lighting is specifically designed to encourage the sale of goods on display, and whether or not there is other lighting (see 261-330 for a fuller discussion of this aspect);

(4)   any wiring, control panels or other equipment which has been installed specifically to supply plant or machinery.

To the list of qualifying items must be added any machinery (which qualifies in its own right irrespective of the definition of 'plant'). The case of *Lancashire Electric Power Company v Wilkinson* established that transformers are machinery.

The significance of this concept in the light of the *Finance Act* 2008 rules re integral features remains uncertain as yet. It seems possible, though, that the arguments will now be turned on their head. If HMRC can argue that the costs are on a single electrical system then allowances will be given only at 10 per cent. If, by contrast, a taxpayer can argue that the piecemeal approach is appropriate, then it is possible that unrestricted allowances could be claimed on any items that are included in List C at CAA 2001, s. 23, with everything else being treated as part of the electrical system.

In the *Cole Brothers* case, the following types of expenditure were listed in the case stated by the commissioners as being 'not in dispute'. This list was very useful in demonstrating the items accepted by HMRC in that case as clearly qualifying as plant. It is only necessary to sound the note of caution that the case predated the *Finance Act* 1994 legislation (now at CAA 2001, s. 21ff.), so it may be that there would be some differences. More importantly,

Plant and Machinery: A to Z

there will certainly be differences as far as expenditure incurred from April 2008 is concerned.

The list of items accepted in that case as plant was as follows, but it will be noticed that most of these would have qualified since 1994 only on the grounds that they were 'electrical systems ... provided mainly ... to serve particular plant or machinery', according to item 2 at List C at CAA 2001, s. 23. That item has now been repealed (by the *Finance Act* 2008):

- wiring, etc to heating and ventilation equipment;
- wiring, etc to fire alarms;
- wiring, etc to clocks;
- public address system and staff location;
- wiring, etc to TV workshops and cash registers;
- trunking for telephone system;
- wiring, etc to lifts;
- wiring, etc to escalators;
- wiring, etc to burglar alarms;
- wiring, etc to smoke detectors;
- 'wiring, etc to E.A.M. [this signifies the Electrical Appliance Department], compactor room, etc';
- emergency lighting systems; and
- stand-by supply systems.

All of the above would now qualify under the integral features rules but a few items (eg the telephone system trunking) might still qualify for unrestricted allowances.

Cross-references

The following headings, mostly from this A to Z Chapter, may be relevant in particular cases where this type of expenditure is being considered. See also 180-250 (which deals specifically with the treatment of lighting in the case of *J Lyons & Co Ltd v Attorney General*) and the commentary on 'integral features' beginning at 247-000ff.

- Aerials (260-020)
- Buildings (260-150)
- Cameras (260-200)
- Car wash apparatus (260-260)
- Cash dispensers (260-270)
- Central heating, etc systems (260-290)
- Clocks (260-300)
- Cold rooms (260-310)
- Computers (260-320)
- Electricity substations (260-610)
- Fire safety (see 160-500)
- Floodlighting (260-770)
- Fridges and freezers (260-800)
- Gas systems (260-900)
- Lifts, escalators and walkways (261-320)

- Machinery (262-000)
- Plant rooms (262-210)
- Professional fees and preliminary costs (262-240)
- Public address systems (262-250)
- Security systems (262-450)
- Telecommunication systems (262-710)
- Telephones and fax machines (262-720)
- Televisions and videos (262-730)

260-610   Electricity substations

Legislation: CAA 2001, s. 22 (List B, item 7)

Cases: *Bradley v London Electricity plc* [1996] BTC 95

HMRC material: none

Commentary

London Electricity plc took a case to the Chancery Division in July 1996. The case was based on legislation before enactment of what is now CAA 2001, s. 21.

The special commissioner had found for the company, allowing that the whole structure of the substation was an item of plant. However, the judge in the Chancery Division overruled the special commissioner, finding that 'the true and only reasonable conclusion he could have come to was that the structure functioned as the premises in which London Electricity's trading activity is carried on rather than the apparatus with which it was carried on'.

The special commissioner had not identified any plant-like function for this structure as a whole. The fact that features of the substation had been carefully designed to accommodate the equipment did not convert premises into plant or apparatus. In the judge's view, the substation did not qualify as plant any more than the kennels, the planteria or the car wash halls had done in, respectively, *Carr v Sayer* [1992] BTC 286, *Gray v Seymours Garden Centre Horticulture* [1993] BTC 213 or *Attwood v Anduff Car Wash Ltd* [1997] BTC 454.

Even if the claim had been successful, it is difficult to see how an electricity substation could now withstand the effect of CAA 2001, s. 22, List B, item 7, which captures all structures and, unless there is a specific exemption, says that they are not to qualify as plant.

Cross-references

The following headings from this A to Z Chapter may be relevant in particular cases where this type of expenditure is being considered. See also the Chapter headed 'Meaning of Plant', which begins at 180-000.

- Buildings (260-150)

Plant and Machinery: A to Z

- Electrical installations and equipment (260-600)
- Structures (262-590)

260-620 Energy-saving investments

Legislation: CAA 2001, s. 45A–C

Cases: none

HMRC material: CA 23110–23150

See also the website for the enhanced capital allowance scheme, www.eca.gov.uk.

Commentary

An extension to the capital allowances scheme was introduced in the *Finance Act* 2001 to encourage businesses to invest in energy-saving plant and machinery.

The rules allow for a 100 per cent first-year allowance for investments made from 1 April 2001. See 185-350 for a more detailed commentary. Key points to note are as follows:

(1) the expenditure must be on new plant or machinery bought unused;

(2) relevant conditions must be met when the expenditure is incurred or when the contract for the purchase of the plant is entered into;

(3) the plant or machinery must be of a description specified by Treasury order and meet specified energy-saving criteria.

The claims to enhanced allowances must be based on costs incurred. Complications can arise where an item is purchased that qualifies in its own right but is installed as a component in a larger item of plant and machinery. In this case, an apportionment must be made. The proportion of the cost relating to the qualifying component will attract the enhanced allowances but the remainder of the equipment will attract capital allowances at the normal rate.

Anybody seeking to claim allowances would do well to refer to the website mentioned at the start of this section. The website is jointly produced by HMRC and the Department for Environment, Food and Rural Affairs. In particular, reference should be made to that website to determine whether any particular product will qualify.

260-630 Entertaining-related expenditure

Legislation: CAA 2001, s. 269

Cases: *Fleming v Associated Newspapers Ltd* (1972) 48 TC 382; *Cole Brothers Ltd v Phillips* [1982] BTC 208

HMRC material: CA 27200

Commentary

Assets used for business entertaining do not qualify for capital allowances as plant. CAA 2001, s. 269 provides that the use of plant or machinery for providing business entertainment is to be treated as non-business use. As such, even where an item qualifies as plant, no capital allowances can be due as it fails to meet one of the other basic requirements of the capital allowances legislation.

Entertaining includes any kind of hospitality but does not include anything provided for employees, unless the employee element is merely incidental to the provision of entertainment to others (CAA 2001, s. 269(3)).

The disallowance of entertaining expenditure does not apply where it is a person's trade to provide the asset for the entertainment of others. Capital allowances will be due in such a case as long as the asset in question is provided to the public in the ordinary course of that trade, whether for payment or free of charge for advertising purposes (CAA 2001, s. 269(4)).

Cross-references

The following headings from this A to Z Chapter may be relevant in particular cases where this type of expenditure is being considered. See also the Chapter headed 'Meaning of Plant', which begins at 180-000.

- Advertising hoardings (260-010)
- Décor (260-500)

260-700   Fencing

Legislation: CAA 2001, s. 361(1)(a), Pt. 4 (agricultural buildings allowances)

Cases: *Abbott Laboratories Ltd v Carmody* (1968) 44 TC 569; *Attwood v Anduff Car Wash Ltd* [1997] BTC 454

HMRC material: CA 21230, CA 22270 (fencing as a security asset)

Commentary

Fencing is not considered by HMRC to qualify as plant or machinery. HMRC specifically stated this in its letter to the Football League written in January 1991. Even advertising hoardings and perimeter boards will not qualify as plant if they are 'simply part of a perimeter fence'.

It is possible that perimeter fences (and walls) may qualify as security assets to improve personal security (CAA 2001, s. 33).

Fences are specifically included within the definition of agricultural buildings for the purposes of ABAs (CAA 2001, s. 361(1)(a)) (see 425-500).

That fencing does not qualify as plant is confirmed (if confirmation were needed) in the *Abbott Laboratories* case, where the costs of a factory, roadways and fence on the one hand are contrasted with the cost of the land and plant and machinery on the other. Similarly, in the *Anduff Car Wash* case, the cost of the boundary fencing was not claimed as plant even though such a claim was made for almost the entire site.

There is no guidance in either UK case law or from HMRC as to the treatment of electric fences. It would appear, however, that these would stand a better chance of qualifying as plant. Certainly, if the HMRC argument against accepting a fence as plant is that it is a structure (and therefore now caught by list B, item 7 at CAA 2001, s. 22) then this can be countered if the fence can be described as part of an electrical system (formerly CAA 2001, s. 23, List C, item 2; now under the integral feature rules at s. 33A).

Cross-references

The following headings from this A to Z Chapter may be relevant in particular cases where this type of expenditure is being considered. See also the Chapter headed 'Meaning of Plant', which begins at 180-000.

- Advertising hoardings (260-010)
- Doors (260-550)
- Football grounds (260-790)
- Gates (260-920)
- Security systems (262-450)
- Shutters (262-500)
- Sports grounds (safety) (262-550)
- Structures (262-590)
- Zoo cages (263-000)

260-710   Films, tapes and discs

Legislation: FA 2006, s. 37 and Sch. 4

Cases: *Ensign Tankers (Leasing) Ltd v Stokes* [1989] BTC 110

HMRC material: www.hmrc.gov.uk/films/guidance/taxation.pdf

Commentary

The tax treatment of film production was changed for films that commence principal photography from 1 January 2007. One effect of the special rules for films is that expenditure on creating a film is generally classed as revenue expenditure, if it would otherwise be treated as expenditure on the creation of an asset (ie the film).

This treatment does not extend to the cost of capital items such as lighting equipment and cameras. Such items continue to attract capital allowances in the ordinary way.

Cross-references

The following headings from this A to Z Chapter may be relevant in particular cases where this type of expenditure is being considered. See also the Chapter headed 'Meaning of Plant', which begins at 180-000.

- Designs and patterns (260-520)
- Software (260-330)

260-720   Finance costs

Legislation: none

Cases: *Ben-Odeco Limited v Powlson* (1978) 52 TC 459

HMRC material: CA 20060

Commentary

The *Ben-Odeco* case established that finance costs cannot be treated as incurred 'on the provision of plant or machinery'. The company had paid nearly £500,000 in bank charges and interest as part of the financing of the construction of an oil rig. Although the expenditure had been properly capitalised for accounting purposes it did not qualify as expenditure on plant or machinery.

Lord Hailsham was amongst those who reached this conclusion, even though he agreed that, had the company been successful, 'what would emerge would be a coherent and superficially elegant system of taxation'.

Lord Russell gave the most precise reasoning for rejecting the company's case when he said that 'the effect of the expenditure was the provision of finance and not the provision of plant'.

The company lost the case in the House of Lords by a majority of four to one (Lord Salmon dissenting).

Cross-references

The following heading from this A to Z Chapter may be relevant in particular cases where this type of expenditure is being considered. See also the Chapter headed 'Meaning of Plant', which begins at 180-000.

Professional fees and preliminary costs (262-240)

Plant and Machinery: A to Z

260-740   Fish tanks and ponds

Legislation: CAA 2001, s. 23 (List C, item 30)

Cases: none

HMRC material: none

Commentary

Fish tanks and ponds are specifically outside the scope of the CAA 2001, s. 21 restrictions on what can qualify as plant. They are therefore to be considered on ordinary case law principles. Given that swimming pools have been held to qualify as plant (since they provide 'safe and pleasurable buoyancy'), there would seem to be an analogy for allowing fish ponds also to qualify. Furthermore, they can often be shown to have a functional purpose in providing atmosphere in a trade where the provision of atmosphere is part of what is being bought by the customer.

Fish tanks may, of course, be used for commercial purposes. Where this is the case, it is likely that they will indeed qualify as plant. It would be worth checking the facts against those in the case of *Carr v Sayer* [1992] BTC 286. This case is discussed at paragraph 261-200 (kennels). The taxpayer lost the case as the kennels in question were held to be permanent buildings or structures. Even where there is a question over the treatment of the fish tanks themselves, there will always (in a commercial setting) be associated equipment and this should qualify as plant in its own right.

Cross-references

The following headings from this A to Z Chapter may be relevant in particular cases where this type of expenditure is being considered. See also the Chapter headed 'Meaning of Plant', which begins at 180-000.

- Décor (260-500)
- Swimming pools (262-600)

260-760   Fixtures

Legislation: CAA 2001, s. 21–24, 33A, 172–204

Cases: *Stokes v Costain Property Investments Ltd* [1984] BTC 92; *Melluish v BMI (No. 3) Ltd* [1995] BTC 381; *West Somerset Railways plc v Chivers* (1995) Sp C 1

HMRC material: CA 21200, CA 23320ff., CA 26025

Commentary

The HMRC manuals (CA 21200) are surprisingly straightforward on the issue of whether fixtures and fittings qualify as plant. The HMRC view is simply that they do 'if they are of a permanent and durable nature . . . and they were bought for the purposes of the trade'. The same approach is applied to furniture, including carpets, curtains and linoleum.

It is suggested, however, that certain care is needed. The capital allowance treatment of fixtures is complex and is discussed in detail at the Chapter headed 'Plant and Property', which begins at 250-000. For those purposes, however, a fixture is defined to mean 'plant or machinery that is so installed or otherwise fixed in or to a building or other description of land as to become, in law, part of that building or other land' (CAA 2001, s. 173). It follows (from the opening words of the definition just quoted) that the special legislation concerning fixtures only applies if it can first be demonstrated that an item qualifies as plant or machinery.

In accordance with CAA 2001, s. 21, if an item is to qualify as plant then it must be shown that it does not represent expenditure on the provision of a building, or of any asset incorporated into the building. The starting point, therefore, has to be to demonstrate that even though an item is 'fixed', it is not 'incorporated into the building'. .

If the matter ended there, then almost by definition no plant and machinery allowances could be given for fixtures. Fortunately, however, the legislation goes on to list numerous categories of expenditure that are exempted from the general rule. Furniture and furnishings, for example, are unaffected by the general rule (CAA 2001, s. 23, List C, item 5), and can thus be considered on general principles. Whilst there is no similar general exemption for fixtures, many of the other items in List C are also likely to be fixtures, and can again be considered on the basis of the general meaning of plant, without regard to the excluding provisions of CAA 2001, s. 21.

For expenditure incurred since 1 or 6 April 2008 (for corporation tax and income tax respectively) there is a new complication in the form of the legislation relating to 'integral features'. A range of commonly found assets (including general electrical expenditure, cold water systems, central heating) are all treated as if they were plant and machinery, even if they would not qualify as such on general principles. The concept of integral features is covered in depth at 247-000ff.

In practice, it will be necessary to consider items on an individual basis, in accordance with the principles outlined in this book, to decide whether the fixing of the item in question causes it to be incorporated into the building.

Cross-references

The following headings from this A to Z Chapter may be relevant in particular cases where this type of expenditure is being considered. See also the Chapters headed 'Plant and Property' and 'Meaning of Plant' at 250-000 and 180-000 respectively. For the treatment of

Plant and Machinery: A to Z

expenditure from April 2008, see in particular the commentary on 'integral features' beginning at 247-000ff.

- Advertising hoardings (260-010)
- Alterations to buildings (260-040)
- Buildings (260-150)
- Cameras (260-200)
- Central heating, etc systems (260-290)
- Counters and checkouts (260-360)
- Décor (260-500)
- Electrical installations and equipment (260-600)
- Furniture and furnishings (260-820)
- Sanitary ware (262-420)
- Shelves (262-470)

260-770   Floodlighting

Legislation: CAA 2001, s. 23 (List C, item 26)

Cases: *IR Commrs v Scottish & Newcastle Breweries Ltd* [1982] BTC 187; *Thomas v Reynolds* [1987] BTC 147

HMRC material: CA 21230

Commentary

Floodlighting was listed as one of the items 'which would normally qualify as plant or machinery' in a letter sent by the Revenue to the Football League in January 1991 (CA 21230) (see 180-400). From April 2008, floodlighting would qualify under the rules relating to integral features (see 247-000ff.) as long as it constitutes a 'lighting system' (or part of an 'electrical system').

Expenditure on the provision of towers provided to support floodlights is within item 26 of List C. As such, expenditure on such towers is not precluded from qualifying as plant. Such expenditure will need to be considered on ordinary case law principles; it is likely that it will often qualify as plant. From April 2008, floodlighting would qualify under the rules relating to integral features as long as it constitutes a 'lighting system' (or part of an 'electrical system').

Before the introduction of the rules relating to integral features, it could not be assumed that HMRC would necessarily accept that floodlighting would qualify as plant. In the *Scottish & Newcastle Breweries* case, a number of different forms of lighting had been claimed as plant, including general lamp fittings, spotlights, table and bedside lamps, floodlights and some drums which had been converted to form light fittings. The inspector conceded only that the spotlights were plant. However, the commissioners decided that the light fittings more generally should be treated as plant and this view was upheld in the courts: 'All the light fittings ... are of such a design and are so laid out as to be properly regarded as apparatus serving a functional purpose in the Company's trade.'

Cross-references

The following headings, mostly from this A to Z Chapter, may be relevant in particular cases where this type of expenditure is being considered. See also the Chapter headed 'Meaning of Plant', which begins at 180-000 and the commentary on 'integral features' beginning at 247-000ff.

- Alterations to buildings (260-040)
- Décor (260-500)
- Display equipment (260-530)
- Electrical installations and equipment (260-600)
- Football grounds (260-790)
- Security systems (262-450)
- Sports grounds (safety) (262-550)

260-780 Floors and flooring materials

Legislation: CAA 2001, s. 21 (List A, item 1), 22 (List B, item 7) and 23 (List C, item 3 (formerly, but see now the integral feature rules at s. 33A) item 4, 7)

Cases: *IR Commrs v Scottish & Newcastle Breweries Ltd* [1982] BTC 187; *Wimpy International Ltd v Warland* [1989] BTC 58 (items 2, 4, 7, 8, 9); *Associated Restaurants Ltd v Warland* [1989] BTC 58; *Hunt v Henry Quick Ltd* [1992] BTC 440; *King v Bridisco Ltd* [1992] BTC 440

HMRC material: CA 21140, CA 21200, CA 21230, CA 22070

Commentary

The extent to which flooring can qualify as plant is a significant issue for many businesses. Undoubtedly, there are grey areas here but the amount of money involved can mean that expenditure on flooring merits serious consideration.

The starting point is that floors do not as a general rule qualify as plant. This is by virtue of List A, item 2, in CAA 2001, s. 21. This is reinforced by CAA 2001, s. 23(4) which says that there can be no exceptions if the principal purpose of the asset is to provide a floor which is intended to remain permanently in place. Subject to that, however, it may sometimes be possible to show that an asset that on the one hand could be described as a floor could on the other hand be viewed as (for example) part of a ventilation or heating system, as an item of storage equipment or, possibly, as a method of sound insulation. In such cases, it is possible that a successful claim could be made for treatment as plant, by virtue of List C in CAA 2001, s. 23, items 3 (formerly), 4 or 7 respectively.

Plant and Machinery: A to Z

To consider the issue of flooring in more detail, it is helpful to break down the subject matter into various categories. The following paragraphs therefore deal with the issue under the following headings:

- floors generally;
- portable floors;
- mezzanine floors;
- plenum floors; and
- carpets and other floor coverings.

Floors generally

As mentioned above, the starting point is that floors do not qualify as plant (List A, item 1); they are part of the premises and so they fail the premises test. HMRC takes the view that this will apply even if the floors are demountable. It is the author's view that demountable floors stand a better chance of qualifying as plant. However, such treatment would still be exceptional and it would be necessary to show that the floors served some purpose specific to the trade.

The mere fact that a floor may be raised does not carry any weight in trying to treat it as plant. In the *Wimpy* case, a claim for allowances on raised floors was refused on the grounds that they were still part of the premises. In the *Associated Restaurants* case, too, the commissioners described the raised floors as 'alterations to the premises' and therefore not plant. This view was confirmed in the courts.

Portable floors

HMRC makes a distinction between demountable floors (not normally plant) and 'portable floors of the type used in theatres and large buildings which are occasionally used for dancing'. This latter category is accepted by HMRC as being plant (CA 22070). It is not entirely clear where the boundary lies between a demountable floor and a portable floor, however; this will be a question of fact and degree. A floor that is regularly taken down and re-erected elsewhere stands a much better chance of qualifying as plant.

Mezzanine floors

HMRC used to take the view that 'most mezzanine floors are not plant. They are part of the premises'. For a mezzanine floor to qualify as plant, the HMRC view was that it must pass the 'business use test' and must not have become part of the premises. This was broadly a fair summary of the case law position. In the *Wimpy* case, the Revenue had been successful in arguing that mezzanine floors were not plant. In two other cases heard slightly later, however, the companies concerned (*Henry Quick* and *Bridisco*, both wholesalers) successfully claimed that mezzanine floors should be treated as plant. The *Henry Quick* case was decidedly borderline. However, the judge felt that 'it was amply within the powers of the Commissioners in the *Bridisco* case to conclude that the platforms there in question were plant'. The judge listed a number of features that helped him to reach this conclusion:

(1) there were four separate mezzanine floors;

(2) they had been installed at different times;

(3)   they covered only 60 per cent of the floor area;

(4)   one of the floors and part of another one had been removed and reinstalled in another warehouse;

(5)   fork-lift trucks which were used on the ground floor could not be used on the mezzanine floors;

(6)   hand-operated trolleys were used on the mezzanine to take pallets to a convenient point where the fork-lift trucks could reach them;

(7)   the offices were on the ground floor alone;

(8)   staff were only allowed to use the mezzanine platforms for storage and retrieval of goods.

It should be borne in mind that all three of the cases referred to above concerning mezzanine floors predate the 1994 legislation. However, the argument in favour of treatment as plant would be that such floors constitute storage equipment and are therefore exempted from automatic exclusion by virtue of List C, item 4. On this basis, the floors can be considered on principles of case law. The HMRC stance on this has hardened, however, and the guidance at CA 22070 was changed in August 2008. The wording now, in contrast to that quoted above, is that HMRC officers should 'refuse a claim for allowances on raised and mezzanine floors. The legislation applies to them like any other floor'.

An obvious but important practical issue is the label given to the mezzanine element of a building. If it can legitimately be described as shelving or as a platform (for example) then the term 'flooring' should be avoided. Architects, builders and others involved with the construction should be made aware of the possible importance of using correct terminology. The HMRC view, again expressed at CA 22070, is that 'an asset is either a floor or a large shelf (storage equipment) and will rarely, if ever, be both and so the claim either fails or it succeeds in full'.

Plenum floors

HMRC accepts that a plenum floor should be treated as plant (CA 22070). They define a plenum floor as one which 'forms part of the reticulation system of a heating or air conditioning system. For example, it may form the fourth side of a duct [or] channel through which stale air is extracted for treatment'. Although the legislation does not use the term 'plenum' it is clear that this wording is based on List C, former item 3 (and see now the integral feature rules at CAA 2001, s. 33A).

Carpets and floor coverings

Carpets and linoleum are to be treated as plant if they are of a permanent and durable nature and were bought for the purposes of the trade (CA 21200). In a letter sent to the Football League in January 1991 (reproduced at 180-400), the Revenue expressed the view that carpets would normally qualify as plant, 'but not tiles which are stuck down'. It is not clear that carpet tiles that are stuck down do not in fact qualify as plant. The treatment of floor tiles in the *Wimpy* case went in favour of the Revenue. However, the commissioners' conclusion was accepted without any great enthusiasm. For example, Lord Justice Fox concluded only that 'the Commissioners did not materially misdirect themselves and were entitled to conclude as they did', though Lord Justice Lloyd agreed more strongly with the decision of the commissioners. A question to be considered is whether, without the carpet tiles, floor tiles or whatever, the premises were unusable. In other words, do they become part of the premises or merely embellish them?

Cross-references

The following headings, mostly from this A to Z Chapter, may be relevant in particular cases where this type of expenditure is being considered. See also the Chapter headed 'Meaning of Plant', which begins at 180-000.

- Bridges, etc (260-130)
- Buildings (260-150)
- Insulation (see 160-400)

260-790   Football grounds

Legislation: none

Cases: *Brown v Burnley Football and Athletic Co Limited* (1980) 53 TC 357; *Anchor International Ltd v IR Commrs* [2005] BTC 97; *Shove (HMIT) v Lingfield Park* [2003] BTC 422

HMRC material: CA 21230

Commentary

The football world is fortunate in having received detailed guidance from the Revenue on those items which are 'likely to qualify' as plant or machinery. This guidance was given in a letter from the Revenue to the Football League in January 1991. The letter contained an appendix listing the types of assets used by football clubs which would normally be considered to qualify as plant or machinery. The list, which is given at CA 21230, is reproduced at 180-400.

The list does not have statutory force and it should be borne in mind that the letter was written before new rules were introduced by FA 1994, as now largely contained in CAA 2001, s. 2–23, though the declared intention of the 1994 legislation was to consolidate, rather than to tighten, the definition of plant.

The *Burnley Football and Athletic* case established that a football stand is not plant. As the special commissioners said: 'The stand is not plant functioning, whether passively or actively, in the actual processes which constitute the trade. The football matches take place and the spectators come to watch within, rather than by means of, the stadium.'

These words were approved in the High Court.

The waters were somewhat muddied, however, by the special commissioner decision (upheld in the Court of Session) of *Anchor International Ltd v IRC*, in which it was held that the cost of a five-a-side football pitch could qualify as plant. The expenditure included a synthetic grass 'carpet' (with 22 tons of sand on it) as well as capital expenditure on excavating, infilling and draining the site.

The commissioner decided that the carpet itself was clearly not a structure; notwithstanding the weight of sand, it was not fixed in place. The pitch and the carpet could each be seen as either plant or setting. The commissioner referred to the decisions in *Barclay Curle* (see 260-540), *Beach Station Caravans* (262-600) and *Scottish & Newcastle Breweries* (numerous references, including 260-770). In this case, the carpet was the means by which the taxpayer generated profits rather than merely the setting and was accordingly plant.

Although reference was made to the *Family Golf Centres Ltd* case (see 260-930), no distinction was drawn between the two cases. In the Court of Session, where the special commissioner decision was upheld, it was agreed that the relevant item of plant was the carpet, and that the works underneath constituted the alteration of land for the purpose of installing the plant.

As if this was not already complex enough, the July 2003 decision in *Shove (HMIT) v Lingfield Park* added a further contradiction. In that case, the company had incurred £2.9m on an artificial all weather race track. The track carried a five-year guarantee, though required daily maintenance and periodical re-grading of the uppermost layer.

The commissioners had found that the track had retained a separate identity from the grass race track, that it functioned as plant and not as part of the premises, and therefore that it qualified as plant. This view was overturned in the Chancery Division, however. It was true that the track was separately identifiable, both visually and from the way it had been constructed. However, that did not mean that it lost its character as part of the premises. In accordance with the *Wimpy* decision (see the Chapter headed 'Meaning of Plant', which begins at 180-000), an item used in carrying on the business was excluded from being plant if such use was as the premises or place upon which the business was conducted.

As regards safety at sports grounds, see 262-550.

Cross-references

The following headings, mostly from this A to Z Chapter, may be relevant in particular cases where this type of expenditure is being considered. See also the Chapter headed 'Meaning of Plant', which begins at 180-000.

- Advertising hoardings (260-010)
- Cameras (260-200)
- Car parks (260-250)
- Electrical installations and equipment (260-600)
- Fire safety (see 160-500)
- Floodlighting (260-770)

- Golf courses (260-930)
- Seats (262-440)
- Sports grounds (safety) (262-550)
- Temporary buildings (262-740)

260-800   Fridges and freezers

Legislation: CAA 2001, s. 23 (List C, item 5, 9)

Cases: none

HMRC material: CA 21230

Revenue booklet IR150, para. 347, 353 and 363

Commentary

Such items will qualify as plant.

They are specifically not affected by CAA 2001, s. 21 (buildings). List C in CAA 2001, s. 23 contains a specific exemption for 'refrigerators and similar equipment' (item 5) and 'refrigeration or cooling equipment' (item 9).

Those references do not in themselves mean that fridges and freezers qualify as plant, merely that they are not excluded by the legislation from so qualifying. However, they will qualify on first principles. In addition, they were included in a list sent by the Revenue to the Football League in January 1991 of assets 'which would normally qualify as plant or machinery'. Furthermore, fridges are specifically included in the types of plant referred to in HMRC booklet IR150 concerned with the taxation of rents (see, for example, paragraphs 347, 353 and 363).

It is not thought that fridges and freezers would normally constitute 'an electrical system' to be brought within the integral features rules.

Cross-references

The following headings from this A to Z Chapter may be relevant in particular cases where this type of expenditure is being considered. See also the Chapter headed 'Meaning of Plant', which begins at 180-000.

- Central heating, etc systems (260-290)
- Cold rooms (260-310)
- Electrical installations and equipment (260-600)
- Machinery (262-000)
- Sanitary ware (262-420)
- Structures (262-590)

260-820   Furniture and furnishings

Legislation: CAA 2001, s. 23 (List C, item 5)

Cases: *Mason v Tyson* (1980) 53 TC 333; *IR Commrs v Scottish & Newcastle Breweries Ltd* [1982] BTC 187

HMRC material: CA 21230, CA 22030, CA 27100

Commentary

Furniture and furnishings are outside the scope of CAA 2001, s. 21 (exclusions from expenditure on plant or machinery because of being part of a building) (CAA 2001, s. 23, List C, item 5).

In general, furniture and furnishings will qualify as plant without any problem. The HMRC view is that furniture (including carpets, curtains and linoleum) will qualify as plant as long as it is of a permanent and durable nature and was bought for the purposes of the trade. Items that will normally qualify without question, subject to their use within the trade, will also include canteen fittings and equipment, checkouts in supermarkets, etc dumbwaiters, fitted desks and tables, etc kitchen equipment, lockers, loudspeakers, mirrors, racking and shelving and storage equipment generally. Obviously, this list is far from exhaustive but it is intended to cover many of the items that will arise in practice from day to day.

The issue of 'for the purposes of the trade' should not be overlooked. HMRC warn that 'assets such as paintings and furniture provided for the director's home are unlikely to be plant. They will not be apparatus with which the company's trade is carried on' (CA 27100). Care is therefore needed on this issue. It may be possible to show that the cost of such expenditure is incurred wholly and exclusively for the purposes of the employer's trade (by virtue of being part of the remuneration package of the director). Nevertheless, based on the *Yarmouth v France* definition of plant (see the Chapter headed 'Meaning of Plant', which begins at 180-000), HMRC may indeed be able to deny allowances in such circumstances.

As regards the issue of fixtures, see the Chapter headed 'Plant and Property', which begins at 250-000, and 260-740.

Cross-references

The following headings from this A to Z Chapter may be relevant in particular cases where this type of expenditure is being considered. See also the Chapter headed 'Meaning of Plant', which begins at 180-000.

- Buildings (260-150)
- Clocks (260-300)
- Computers (260-320)
- Curtains (260-370)
- Décor (260-500)

Plant and Machinery: A to Z

- Display equipment (260-530)
- Fixtures (260-760)
- Sanitary ware (262-420)
- Seats (262-440)
- Storage equipment (262-570)

260-900   Gas systems

Legislation: CAA 2001, s. 21 (List A, item 2), 23 (List C, item 2)

Cases: *Cooke v Beach Station Caravans Ltd* (1974) 49 TC 514; *St John's School v Ward* (1974) 49 TC 524

HMRC material: CA 21170–21180, CA 22010

Commentary

The treatment of gas systems has in the past closely mirrored that of electrical systems, regarding which see 260-600. However, the introduction of the rules relating to integral features (see, generally, 247-000ff.) has created a new distinction.

Gas systems will normally be treated as part of the building, and will therefore initially be denied allowances by virtue of CAA 2001, s. 21. However, List C at s. 23 still contains an exclusion from the effect of s. 21 for gas systems that are provided mainly 'to meet the particular requirements of the qualifying activity' or 'to serve particular plant or machinery used for the purposes of the qualifying activity'. (A similar exclusion for electrical, lighting and cold water systems was removed by the *Finance Act* 2008.)

Caution is always needed with the items in List C – the effect of that List is never to state that an item specifically qualifies as plant but is rather to remove any statutory bar on its ability so to qualify. In practice, items in List C do generally qualify as plant in appropriate circumstances. As such, a gas supply to a company with large furnaces would be expected to qualify under the 'particular requirements' provision and a supply of gas to a school for the Bunsen burners in its chemistry laboratory would normally meet the condition of serving plant used for the purposes of the activity (notwithstanding the *St John's School* decision referred to below).

On the whole, HMRC will be unwilling to look at a gas system as a single entity (CA 21180). If this principle is accepted, each item of the whole system should be separately considered to decide whether it qualifies as plant in its own right. Again, see under the electrical installations and equipment section at 260-600 for discussion of the single entity principle.

Having said the above, HMRC does accept that, on occasions, a gas system may qualify as a whole for capital allowances as an item of plant. Based on the principles enunciated by Oliver LJ in *Cole Brothers Ltd v Phillips* [1982] BTC 208, there may be a stronger case for treatment of the whole system as plant if the system has been specially designed and installed for the particular purposes of the trade in question.

In the *St John's School* case, concerning temporary buildings, the commissioners reached the view that the prefabricated buildings were not plant. Similarly, the gas and other installations were held to be an integral part of those buildings and did not themselves qualify as plant.

Cross-references

The following headings, mostly from this A to Z Chapter, may be relevant in particular cases where this type of expenditure is being considered. See also the Chapter headed 'Meaning of Plant', which begins at 180-000.

- Buildings (260-150)
- Ceilings and canopies (260-280)
- Central heating, etc systems (260-290)
- Electrical installations and equipment (260-600)
- Fire safety (see 160-500)
- Machinery (262-000)
- Sanitary ware (262-420)
- Sewerage (262-460)
- Water supplies and water tanks (262-920)

260-920   Gates

Legislation: CAA 2001, s. 21 (List A, item 1), 22 (List B, item 4), 23 (List C, item 23)

Cases: *IR Commrs v Barclay, Curle and Co Ltd* (1969) 45 TC 221

HMRC material: CA 21230, CA 22010–22020

Commentary

Gates feature in both List A and List B so there is a presumption that they will not qualify as plant. However, there may be exceptions. The CAA 2001, s. 21 prevention of allowances only applies to an asset which is 'in or connected with' a building (subs. (3)). Thus, a gate that is not forming part of a building, and which is not in connection with the building, will be outside the prohibition.

List B prevents allowances from being given on any 'dam, reservoir or barrage, including any sluices, gates, generators and other equipment associated with the dam, reservoir or barrage'. However, expenditure on dry docks is specifically outside the prohibition (List C, item 23), thus retaining the implications of the decision in the *Barclay, Curle* case.

Plant and Machinery: A to Z

On the positive side, the HMRC manuals at CA 21230 list automatic exit doors and gates amongst 'the sort of assets used by a football club in its trade which would normally qualify as plant or machinery'.

In summary, it seems that gates will often be able to qualify but not when they are effectively part of a building or part of a dam, etc.

Cross-references

The following headings, mostly from this A to Z Chapter, may be relevant in particular cases where this type of expenditure is being considered. See also the Chapter headed 'Meaning of Plant', which begins at 180-000.

- Alterations to buildings (260-040)
- Bridges, etc (260-130)
- Buildings (260-150)
- Caravans and caravan sites (260-230)
- Car parks (260-250)
- Counters and checkouts (260-360)
- Demolition costs (260-510)
- Doors (260-550)
- Fencing (260-700)
- Fire safety (see 160-500)
- Football grounds (260-790)
- Insulation (see 160-400)
- Professional fees and preliminary costs (262-240)
- Roads, etc (262-320)
- Screens (262-430)
- Security systems (262-450)
- Shutters (262-500)

260-930   Golf courses

Legislation: CAA 2001, s. 271 (IBAs)

Cases: *Family Golf Centres Ltd v Thorne* (1998) Sp C 150; *Anchor International Ltd v IR Commrs* [2005] BTC 97

HMRC material: CA 31110

Commentary

It appears that no capital allowances of any sort are due on the cost of a golf course in its entirety. The HMRC view is that a golf course is not a structure and it cannot therefore qualify for IBAs: 'Land which essentially retains its character as land is not a structure, even if the land is cultivated or modified in some way. For example, grass football pitches, grass tennis courts, golf courses and grass bowling greens are not structures' (CA 31110).

The 1998 special commissioner case of *Family Golf Centres Ltd v Thorne* considered whether a newly constructed putting green on a golf course could qualify as plant. It was accepted by the Revenue that the greens had been specially constructed for the purposes of the company's trade. However, the commissioner concluded that the greens were part of the premises and did not therefore qualify as plant.

The commissioner decided that the greens were part of the place at which the company's trade was carried on. It is conceivable, though, that this decision could be challenged, probably including reference to *Anchor International Ltd v IR Commrs* – see 260-790).

A claim for plant allowances may well be appropriate for 'crazy golf' courses. Certainly, water features, obstacles, etc would seem to qualify but it may be possible to justify an argument that the whole course constitutes an entity that acts as apparatus with which the game is played.

Cross-references

The following headings from this A to Z Chapter may be relevant in particular cases where this type of expenditure is being considered. See also the Chapter headed 'Meaning of Plant', which begins at 180-000.

- Football grounds (260-790)
- Land (261-300)
- Structures (262-590)

260-940   Grain silos

Legislation: CAA 2001, s. 22 (List B, item 7), 23 (List C, item 28)

Cases: *Schofield v R & H Hall Ltd* (1975) 49 TC 538

HMRC material: CA 21130, CA 22050

Commentary

This is an item where care is needed. The only directly relevant case law (*Schofield v Hall*) found for the taxpayer, but it may well be that a future case could go in HMRC's favour.

Inspectors are instructed that they should 'treat a grain silo as plant where, together with its attendant machinery, it performs a function in distributing the grain and is essentially a transit silo rather than a warehouse'. This is considered to be an entirely valid distinction; there is no reason why a building which merely holds grain should qualify as plant.

The HMRC instruction is based very closely on the wording of the case itself: 'The silos are essentially transit silos, and the description illuminates their function of reception and distribution, cooling and turning over, and, if necessary, fumigation, in connection with the

Company's trade of grain importing, in which, as the commissioners have found, "storage played only a trifling part".'

As such, the buildings were 'more than convenient housing for working equipment and [. . . played] a part themselves in the distributive processes of reception, distribution and discharge'.

Any grain silo now would have to meet another test. As a structure, it would not normally be able to qualify as plant (CAA 2001, s. 22, List B, item 7). The only exception would be expenditure on 'silos provided for temporary storage' or on 'storage tanks' (CAA 2001, s. 23, List C, item 28).

Cross-references

The following headings from this A to Z Chapter may be relevant in particular cases where this type of expenditure is being considered. See also the Chapter headed 'Meaning of Plant', which begins at 180-000.

- Buildings (260-150)
- Structures (262-590)

260-950   Greenhouses

Legislation: CAA 2001, s. 23 (List C, item 17)

Cases: *Gray v Seymours Garden Centre Horticulture* [1993] BTC 213

HMRC material: CA 22090, CA 23785

Commentary

A greenhouse will only qualify as plant if it has sophisticated mechanisms for providing the correct growing environment.

Most greenhouses are 'structures'. Authority for this view can be found in the *Seymours Garden Centre* case where a 'planteria' (a type of greenhouse) was clearly held to be premises. As the judge ruled: 'the highest it can be put is that it functions as a purpose-built structure. But . . . that is not enough to make the structure plant.'

If it could be said to be a building, a greenhouse would initially be disqualified from being plant by virtue of CAA 2001, s. 21 and as a structure, by virtue of s. 22.

Nevertheless, an exception is made (CAA 2001, s. 23, List C, item 17) for a glasshouse 'which is constructed so that the required environment (namely, air, heat, light, irrigation and temperature) for the growing of plants is provided automatically by means of devices forming an integral part of its structure'. The Act does not specifically say that such a greenhouse will qualify as plant. However, it will be outside the restrictions contained within CAA 2001, s. 21 and 22. By implication, it is therefore likely that such a greenhouse would qualify as plant.

The HMRC manuals instruct inspectors to accept that a greenhouse is plant if all of certain listed conditions are met, as follows:

(1)   the structure and the associated equipment must have been designed as a single unit which operates as one entity;

(2)   it must include extensive computer-controlled equipment;

(3)   the computer-controlled equipment must be essential to achieving an optimum artificial growing environment for whatever crops are being grown;

(4)   the equipment must have been permanently installed when the greenhouse was constructed; and

(5)   there must be computer systems which control boilers and piped heating systems, temperature, humidity, automatic ventilation and automatic thermal or shade screens.

The HMRC instructions go on to say that other equipment may include a mechanism for carbon dioxide enrichment, a hydroponic culture, mobile benching or transport tables and/or artificial lighting systems.

The reference at (3) above to computer-controlled equipment is of interest. Many greenhouses have automatic devices that existed long before computer-controls were introduced for such items. There is nothing in the legislation to insist that they should be computer controlled – the only requirement is that the environment should be 'provided automatically by means of devices'. The HMRC interpretation is thus open to challenge.

HMRC will normally expect a greenhouse to be used for year-round growing of high value crops if it is to qualify as plant. Specifically, they will be seeking evidence that the specially created growing environment extends the natural growing season.

If an argument is to be held with HMRC on a borderline case, it is likely that reference should be made to the dry-dock case (*Barclay, Curle* – see 260-540) or the grain silo case (*Schofield v Hall* – see 260-940). Those two cases are examples of cases where the assets were premises but where it was held that the premises themselves functioned as plant.

HMRC published details of an industry specific agreement, negotiated with the National Farmers' Union (NFU), which deals with glasshouses in the context of long-life assets. The relevant text was found in Revenue *Tax Bulletin*, June 1998, p. 552 , though that article is now marked as 'no longer current'. The manuals comment as follows:

'An agreement was made with the NFU that sophisticated greenhouses which qualify for allowances as machinery and plant ... are not long-life assets. It says that such glasshouses built to current designs have a useful economic life not exceeding 25 years and will not therefore be long-life assets for the purposes of Capital Allowances. The agreement includes only expenditure incurred up to 31 December 2005 because designs and technology will not stand still. If glasshouses are developed before then which have a useful economic life exceeding 25 years, they will necessarily be outside this agreement.'

There is no updated guidance relating to this issue on the HMRC website or in the manuals at the time of writing.

Cross-references

The following headings from this A to Z Chapter may be relevant in particular cases where this type of expenditure is being considered. See also the Chapter headed 'Meaning of Plant', which begins at 180-000.

- Buildings (260-150)
- Land (261-300)
- Structures (262-590)

261-020 Human body

Legislation: none

Cases: *Norman v Golder* (1945) 26 TC 293; *Bourne v Norwich Crematorium Ltd* (1967) 44 TC 164

HMRC material: none

Commentary

The *Norman v Golder* case provides brief but simple authority for the view that the human body is not plant. In the Court of Appeal, Lord Greene commented: 'Your own body is not plant . . . I have never heard it suggested by anybody that the taxpayer's own body could be regarded as plant. In fact the point has only, I think, to be stated.'

Accountancy Age in 1998 referred to an Egyptian belly dancer who had won her case for tax relief on her belly on the grounds that it was a depreciating asset! The suggestion was made that 'one could argue that a belly is plant and equipment used by the taxpayer to carry on business'. Unfortunately, the *Norman v Golder* case above would seem to take precedence for the purpose of UK tax law.

Incidentally, it is also established that human remains are not 'goods or materials' for the purposes of claiming IBAs (*Bourne v Norwich Crematorium*).

Cross-references

The following heading from this A to Z Chapter may be relevant in particular cases where this type of expenditure is being considered. See also the Chapter headed 'Meaning of Plant', which begins at 180-000.

Animals (260-060)

261-100   Insulation

Legislation: CAA 2001, s. 23(4) (list C, item 7), 27, 28, 63(5)

Key case law: none

Revenue material:

> CA 21010
> CA 22030
> CA 22220

Commentary

Special rules apply to treat as plant the cost incurred by a person in insulating a building or structure against heat loss. There is also a deeming provision to ensure that the plant or machinery is treated as belonging to the trader. In the event of a disposal, the disposal value is treated as nil. The HMRC view is that the rules apply only to existing buildings, and not to new ones, and this principle is well established even though the wording of the legislation is not entirely clear on the point.

Expenditure incurred before 1 or 6 April 2008 (for corporation tax and income tax respectively) qualified under this heading only if it was for insulation of an *industrial* building. That qualifying condition was removed from April 2008. The scope of the provision was also widened from the same date to cover any qualifying activity, though still subject to the usual restrictions in relation to a dwelling house (see 165-100).

There is no definition in the legislation of the concept of 'insulation against loss of heat' but HMRC instructions to Inspectors are to give that term its ordinary meaning. Thus, the term will include 'things like roof lining, double glazing, draft exclusion and cavity wall filling'. If expenditure is incurred to insulate against both noise and loss of heat then HMRC do not object to this as long as it is clear that insulation against loss of heat is one of the reasons for incurring the expenditure.

CAA 2001, s. 28(2) extends this special relief to the lessor of any commercial building. Once more, the scope of this provision, which previously applied only to an industrial building, was widened from April 2008, but the restriction on expenditure on a dwelling house remains. No further relief is due under these capital allowance rules, however, if a deduction is available under either ITTOIA 2005, s. 312 or CTA 2009, s. 251 (deductions for expenditure on energy-saving items): see below.

The definition of industrial building (relevant, for these purposes, only for expenditure incurred before April 2008) is given in CAA 2001, Pt. 3, Ch. 2. This part is considered in detail in the Chapter headed 'Industrial Buildings Allowances', which begins at 300-000. In brief, an industrial building or structure is one used for the purposes of a trade carried on in a factory or similar premises. Certain types of building are specifically excluded, including offices and retail premises.

Where the special legislation regarding thermal insulation does not apply, for example because the insulation is against the loss of cold air rather than warm air (eg for a warehouse in which food is stored) (or, prior to April 2008, because the building was not an industrial building or structure) then it is necessary to consider the provisions of CAA 2001, s. 21–23 and of case law generally. Once this is relied on, the position is not so good. Insulation will often be incorporated into a building and may also be excluded by virtue of CAA 2001, s. 21, list A, item 1 as being a wall, floor, ceiling or whatever. The only specific relief given in list C is for 'sound insulation provided mainly to meet the particular requirements of the qualifying activity'. This type of expenditure is therefore not specifically excluded but would have to be considered on ordinary case law principles. Even then, the expenditure cannot be saved by list C if 'its principal purpose is to insulate or enclose the interior of a building or to provide an interior wall, floor or ceiling which (in each case) is intended to remain permanently in place' (CAA 2001, s. 23(4)). On the other hand, there will often be insulation which could not in an ordinary use of English be said to be incorporated into a building – for example, a roll of foam that is put down in an attic area and which could be easily removed.

On the face of it, there is a clear contradiction between item 7 in list C (providing possible relief for sound insulation in some circumstances) and CAA 2001, s. 23(4) which excludes an item whose principal purpose is to insulate the interior of a building. The way the note is worded is ambiguous so it is not clear whether the expression 'intended to remain permanently in place' applies to an asset with the principal purpose of insulating or enclosing the interior of the building. Certainly, the grammar does not work well if the two expressions are linked together. However, if the 'intended to remain permanently in place' qualification does not apply, then any asset with the principal purpose of insulating or enclosing the interior of the building will be excluded from list C, and in this case it is difficult to see what possible purpose can be served by item 7 of list C in CAA 2001, s. 23.

This is a difficult area to reconcile with any sense. Furthermore, the HMRC manuals say absolutely nothing on the subject of sound insulation. A common-sense approach would seem to be that list C, item 7 must be there for a purpose and that therefore, in normal circumstances, relief should be available for the cost of sound insulation provided mainly to meet the particular requirements of the trade.

Expenditure by landlords on energy-saving items

There is a potential overlap between the rules at CAA 2001, s. 28 (thermal insulation) and those at CTA 2009, s. 251 and at ITTOIA 2005, s. 312 (deduction given to landlords for capital expenditure on energy-saving items).

The latter provisions give full relief for certain expenditure incurred by landlords, but only where no relief is due under the capital allowances rules. Equally, however, the thermal insulation rules at CAA 2001, s. 28 do not (since April 2008) apply if a deduction is allowable under those other provisions (CAA 2001, s. 28(2B) and (2C)). The mechanics of dealing with this circular denial of relief are far from elegant but the effect of the overlapping provisions is explained as follows in the *Explanatory Notes* to the Finance Bill 2008:

'The new subsections (2B) and (2C), therefore, effectively preserve the taxpayer's entitlement to the more favourable 100 per cent deduction, under either section 31ZA of ICTA [now CTA 2009, s. 251] or s. 312 of ITTOIA (as the case might be), by excluding the expenditure from capital allowances where a deduction would be allowable under either of the two other statutory provisions.'

Once more, see ¶300-050 for a full explanation of how that outcome is achieved in statutory terms.

Cross-references

The following headings from this A to Z Chapter may be relevant in particular cases where this type of expenditure is being considered. See also the Chapter headed 'Meaning of Plant', which begins at 180-000.

- Alterations to buildings (260-040)
- Buildings (260-150)
- Central heating, etc systems (260-290)
- Curtains (260-370)
- Electrical installations and equipment (260-600)
- Shutters (262-500)
- Walls (262-910)

261-200   Kennels

Legislation: none

Cases: *Carr v Sayer* [1992] BTC 286

HMRC material: CA 22030, CA 32212–32224; Press Release, 17 December 1993

Commentary

There is only one case that has specifically looked at the tax treatment of dog kennels.

The case of *Carr v Sayer* concerned both normal and quarantine kennelling. In each case, it was held that the kennels were not plant but rather were purpose-built permanent buildings or structures which were used as such. It followed that they were 'the premises at which and in which' the business was conducted. Although they had certain features that made them specially appropriate to serve as kennels, these were 'building design features and no more'. They did not mean that the resultant structures had the character of equipment or apparatus. Incidentally, the case also established the principle that they were not industrial buildings. The taxpayer had argued that, if they were not plant, they were industrial buildings in use 'for the purposes of a trade which consists in the storage . . . of goods or materials on the arrival by sea or air into any part of the United Kingdom'.

It seems that a small dog kennel, if used for the purposes of the trade (for example, to house a genuine guard dog) could still qualify as plant. The Revenue press release dated

Plant and Machinery: A to Z

17 December 1993 specifically suggested that 'while a wooden hut large enough to contain people is likely to be a building, a small dog kennel is not'. The HMRC manuals do not specifically comment on whether a kennel is a structure. It may well be a question of size and of whether or not the kennel can be moved. If it is permanently fitted then HMRC is perhaps more likely to argue that it is a structure. If such an argument were to be successful, then the kennel could not qualify as plant because of CAA 2001, s. 22, List B, item 7.

Quarantine kennels were refused IBAs in *Carr v Sayer*.

Cross-references

The following headings from this A to Z Chapter may be relevant in particular cases where this type of expenditure is being considered. See also the Chapter headed 'Meaning of Plant', which begins at 180-000.

- Animals (260-060)
- Buildings (260-150)
- Poultry houses (262-230)
- Structures (262-590)

261-300   Land

Legislation: CAA 2001, s. 22(1)(b), 23 (List C, item 22), 24, 273

Cases: *IR Commrs v Barclay, Curle and Co Ltd* (1969) 45 TC 221; *Benson v The Yard Arm Club Ltd* (1979) 53 TC 67; *Melluish v BMI (No. 3) Ltd* [1995] BTC 381

HMRC material: CA 22040

Commentary

CAA 2001, s. 24 makes it clear that land cannot qualify as plant: 'For the purposes of this Act expenditure on the provision of plant or machinery does not include expenditure on the acquisition of an interest in land.'

This piece of legislation clearly overrides the words of Lord Justice Templeman in the Court of Appeal hearing of the *Yard Arm Club* case. Lord Templeman gave his view that 'if land, premises or structures operate as the means by which a trading operation is carried out, then they rank as plant'. Whilst this may remain true of premises or structures, as discussed elsewhere in this manual, it must now be incorrect to apply that principle to land in view of the legislation quoted above.

There is a separate and important issue relating to fixtures and this is dealt with in the Chapter headed 'Industrial Buildings Allowances', which begins at 300-000.

There is another separate issue in relation to expenditure on a site in preparation for the installation of plant or machinery. The expenditure may not qualify in its own right as expenditure on plant or machinery but, in this case, IBAs may be due under CAA 2001, s. 273. This provision is not limited to Enterprise Zone cases but applies generally under the IBA scheme.

Cross-references

The following headings from this A to Z Chapter may be relevant in particular cases where this type of expenditure is being considered. See also the Chapter headed 'Meaning of Plant', which begins at 180-000.

- Amusement parks (260-050)
- Buildings (260-150)
- Car parks (260-250)
- Demolition costs (260-510)
- Football grounds (260-790)
- Golf courses (260-930)
- Professional fees and preliminary costs (262-240)
- Roads, etc (262-320)
- Structures (262-590)

261-310   Letter boxes

Legislation: none

Cases: none

HMRC material: none

Commentary

There is no specific guidance in the legislation or elsewhere on whether or not letter boxes can qualify as plant.

It is suggested that the actual flap built in as part of a door or wall would be excluded by virtue of CAA 2001, s. 21, List A, item 1 which prohibits expenditure on walls and doors from qualifying as plant. Also, in such a case, HMRC would undoubtedly argue that the letter flap is an asset incorporated into the building or 'of a kind normally incorporated into buildings'.

It is possible, however, that an argument could successfully be made for treating as plant an actual box which has quite possibly been supplied separately and which is moveable and if necessary, replaceable.

Plant and Machinery: A to Z

Cross-references

The following headings from this A to Z Chapter may be relevant in particular cases where this type of expenditure is being considered. See also the Chapter headed 'Meaning of Plant', which begins at 180-000.

- Doors (260-550)
- Fixtures (260-760)
- Gates (260-920)

261-320   Lifts, escalators and walkways

Legislation: CAA 2001, s. 21 (List A, item 5), 23, 25, 33A

Cases: *Macsaga Investment Co Ltd v Lupton* (1967) 44 TC 659; *Lupton v Cadogan Gardens Developments Limited* (1971) 47 TC 1; *Schofield v R & H Hall Ltd* (1975) 49 TC 538; *Cole Brothers Ltd v Phillips* [1982] BTC 208; *Stokes v Costain Property Investments Ltd* [1984] BTC 92; *Melluish v BMI (No. 3) Ltd* [1995] BTC 381

HMRC material: CA 21190, CA 21230, CA 22010

Commentary

As noted above, the tax treatment of lifts has been considered in a large number of cases. In practice, however, the treatment is usually clear-cut, though an element of doubt about the correct treatment has arisen since the introduction in the *Finance Act* 2008 of the rules on integral features (see, generally, 247-000ff.). Lift shafts are included in the expression 'building' (CAA 2001, s. 21, List A, item 5) and cannot normally qualify as plant. The exclusion covers 'shafts or other structures in which lifts, hoists, escalators and moving walkways are installed'.

Lifts

The definition of 'integral features' at CAA 2001, s. 33A(5) includes 'a lift, an escalator or a moving walkway'. In other words, a distinction is drawn between the lift shaft (which will not normally qualify, but see below) and the lift itself, with parallel rules for escalators, etc (which will qualify, as integral features).

But is the position as simple as that? Ignore, for a moment, the rules relating to integral features. List C at CAA 2001, s. 23 contains numerous items that are protected from the restrictive effects of CAA 2001, s. 21. Before April 2008, the position could therefore be summarised as follows:

- a lift is incorporated into a building and allowances are therefore denied, initially, by s. 21(3)(a);
- the treatment of a lift was previously rescued by item 6 in List C at s. 23;
- it was therefore necessary to consider whether, on ordinary case law principles, a lift was plant or machinery;

- case law principles would lead clearly to the conclusion that a lift would indeed qualify as such.

At first glance, the position has changed now that the wording of item 6 at List C has been amended. In its revised format, that item refers only to hoists. The apparent intention of the legislation is therefore that lifts should qualify only as integral features. However, this does not take account of item 1 at List C which refers to 'machinery'. HMRC's *Capital Allowances* manual, at CA 21190, states uncontroversially that 'lifts and escalators are machinery'. The point is debatable, and is considered in more detail at 247-100.

The dispute relates only to the heading under which allowances can be claimed for lifts – it is absolutely clear that they qualify one way or the other. But the point is not merely academic, as the route followed will determine whether or not any writing-down allowances need to be restricted to the lower rate.

The HMRC manuals at CA 21190 tell inspectors that they should 'treat expenditure on the provision of the wiring which operates a lift or escalator as part of the expenditure incurred on the provision of the lift or escalator'.

Lift shafts

Although the costs of a lift shaft do not normally qualify, they will do so in some cases under CAA 2001, s. 25, concerned with building alterations that are connected with the installation of plant or machinery. This short section arises 'if a person carrying on a qualifying activity incurs capital expenditure on alterations to an existing building incidental to the installation of plant or machinery for the purposes of the qualifying activity'. Where those conditions are met, s. 25 deems the expenditure to be on plant or machinery. There is therefore an apparent contradiction between CAA 2001, s. 21, which says that expenditure on the provision of plant or machinery does not include any expenditure on lift shafts, and s. 25 which, in some circumstances, may provide relief for such expenditure. The correct reading of these two sections of the *Capital Allowances Act* 2001 is that s. 25 overrides s. 21. The reason for this is that s. 21 says that the lift shaft (for example) is not plant, but s. 25 effectively says that it is nevertheless treated as if it were part of the cost of the lift itself.

This interpretation is confirmed in the HMRC manuals at CA 21190. The instructions there say that 'the lift shaft itself is not plant or machinery. However, expenditure on installing a lift shaft in an existing building should qualify under CAA 2001, section 25 ... as expenditure on alterations to an existing building incidental to the installation of plant or machinery.'

In summary, therefore, the cost of lifts, escalators, etc will normally qualify as plant without problem. The cost of installing a lift shaft in a new building will not qualify (though the provision of wiring for the lift will). The cost of installing a lift shaft in an existing building will normally qualify, by virtue of CAA 2001, s. 21.

Plant and Machinery: A to Z

441

There would not appear to be any material distinction when the lift shaft is erected on the outside of the building. If it is in a new building it will not qualify. If it is in an existing building, it will be incidental to the installation of the lift.

Cross-references

The following headings from this A to Z Chapter may be relevant in particular cases where this type of expenditure is being considered. See also the Chapter headed 'Meaning of Plant', which begins at 180-000.

- Alterations to buildings (260-040)
- Demolition costs (260-510)
- Electrical installations and equipment (260-600)
- Machinery (262-000)
- Plant rooms (262-210)
- Professional fees and preliminary costs (262-240)
- Stairs (262-560)

261-330   Lighting

Legislation: CAA 2001, s. 21 (List A, item 2), 23 (List C, items 25 and 26), 33A

Cases: *J Lyons & Co Ltd v Attorney General* (1944) 170 LT 348; *Lancashire Electric Power Company v Wilkinson* (1947) 28 TC 427; *IR Commrs v Scottish & Newcastle Breweries Ltd* [1982] BTC 187; *Cole Brothers Ltd v Phillips* [1982] BTC 208; *Wimpy International Ltd v Warland* [1989] BTC 58 (item 3); *Hunt v Henry Quick Ltd* [1992] BTC 440; *King v Bridisco Ltd* [1992] BTC 440

HMRC material: CA 21160–21180, CA 22030

Commentary

This is obviously an important category of expenditure which needs to be considered whenever a property is bought, sold or refurbished. The position has been much clearer since the introduction of the rules relating to integral features (see, generally, 247-000ff.). Those rules replace the earlier treatment for expenditure incurred from 1 or 6 April 2008 (for corporation tax and income tax respectively). Lighting systems are specifically included as integral features and qualify as such under those rules, but any writing-down allowances will be at the lower 'special rate' of 10 per cent.

The starting point is CAA 2001, s. 21. List A, item 2, says that 'mains services, and systems, for water, electricity and gas' are to be included in the term 'building' and that such items therefore fail to qualify as plant unless they are within the exemptions in List C. The key exemption of relevance to lighting expenditure used to be the one applying for 'electrical systems (including lighting systems) provided mainly to meet the particular requirements of the trade, or to serve particular plant or machinery used for the purposes of the trade'. That item was removed by the *Finance Act* 2008 but that Act also introduced the concept of integral features and ensures that lighting systems can qualify under those rules.

An issue that can arise in practice is that of whether the lighting installation is to be considered as one single item of plant or whether it should be broken down and each component part considered on its own merits. In the leading case on this topic, that of *Cole Brothers Ltd v Phillips*, the company failed in its attempt to persuade the courts to consider the whole of the expenditure as being on a single item of plant or machinery.

For a general discussion about the circumstances in which HMRC will accept that an electrical installation should be treated as a single entity, see 260-600.

By 2007, HMRC had published, but without otherwise drawing attention to it, some guidance on 'when can lighting qualify for capital allowances' and this seemed to allow a rather more generous interpretation than previously of the allowances that might be due. The guidance suggested, for example, that relief for the whole lighting system might be due where 'a new supermarket is built containing a lighting system that has been designed to help display the goods throughout the shop to their best advantage'. Again, relief might be due if 'a trader commissions a new office for its business, and specifies anti-glare lighting throughout so that staff can use their computers effectively'.

The HMRC view differed, however, in the case of a business that expanded into premises that already contained a lighting system, arguing that the system 'was not installed to meet the particular requirements of the trader's business'.

In some cases, part of a lighting system may qualify. The HMRC guidance in respect of such expenditure was as follows but these items were based on item 2 of List C at CAA 2001, s. 23 (lighting provided to meet the particular requirements of the trade or to serve particular plant and machinery). That item was omitted by the *Finance Act* 2008 and no longer applies to lighting or other electrical systems:

- lighting in display cabinets, or in those parts of a building used as sales areas, may qualify if the lighting is specifically designed to encourage the sale of goods on display;
- this can include the public areas in businesses such as banks and building societies;
- lighting can qualify if installed specifically to supply light to particular items of plant or machinery (eg lighting designed for use with computer equipment);
- lighting specifically installed to provide ambience in a hotel or restaurant may qualify (see 260-500: décor);
- lighting may qualify if it is installed to illuminate sports pitches, but not general lighting in changing rooms and areas available to the general public.

Cross-references

The following headings, mostly from this A to Z Chapter, may be relevant in particular cases where this type of expenditure is being considered. See also 180-250 which deals specifically with the treatment of lighting in the case of *J Lyons & Co Ltd v Attorney General*. Above all, see now 270-000ff. (integral features).

Plant and Machinery: A to Z

- Buildings (260-150)
- Electrical installations and equipment (260-600)
- Electricity substations (260-610)
- Fire safety (see 160-500)
- Floodlighting (260-770)
- Machinery (262-000)
- Plant rooms (262-210)
- Professional fees and preliminary costs (262-240)

261-370 Loose tools

Legislation: ITTOIA 2005, s. 68; CTA 2009, s. 68

Cases: *Hinton v Maden & Ireland Ltd* (1959) 38 TC 391

HMRC material: none

Commentary

Tax relief is given for expenses incurred on replacing or altering any tool used for the purposes of the trade if relief would otherwise be denied solely on the basis that the costs constitute capital expenditure. The term 'tool' is defined to include any implement, utensil or article. (This is a rare example of twinned legislation, as the wording is the same in the income tax and corporation tax legislation, in each case at s. 68 of the relevant act.)

The ordinary treatment of such items, therefore, will not involve capital allowances.

Occasionally, it may be preferable to treat them as plant and this should be acceptable provided that they have a working life of at least two years. The two-year test is not based on statute but is derived from the 'permanent employment in the business' test first propounded in *Yarmouth v France* (see the Chapter headed 'Meaning of Plant', which begins at 180-000). The point was specifically considered in the *Maden & Ireland* case where knives and lasts with an average life of three years were held by a three to two majority in the House of Lords to be plant.

Cross-references

The following headings from this A to Z Chapter may be relevant in particular cases where this type of expenditure is being considered. See also the Chapter headed 'Meaning of Plant', which begins at 180-000.

- Consumables (260-340)
- Containers (260-350)

262-000   Machinery

Legislation: CAA 2001, s. 23 (List C, item 1)

Cases: none

HMRC material: CA 21010; CG 76901ff

Commentary

To qualify for capital allowances under CAA 2001, Pt. 2, expenditure must have been incurred 'on the provision of plant or machinery' (CAA 2001, s. 11). It follows that an item of machinery qualifies for capital allowances in its own right – it is not necessary to demonstrate that a machine is plant.

Whilst there is great uncertainty over the meaning of plant, it is usually clear whether or not an asset can be said to be machinery.

The HMRC manuals comment briefly on the definition of 'machinery' and specify that 'machinery includes machines and the working parts of machines'. They expand this slightly by adding that 'a machine usually has moving parts'. The examples quoted are motor vehicles, lathes and computers (CA 21010).

The word 'machinery' is also significant for capital gains tax purposes and, in this context, the Revenue gave some further guidance on its interpretation in *Tax Bulletin* 13 (October 1994), though that article is 'no longer current'. The guidance, now broadly at CG 76901ff, defined a machine as 'any apparatus which applies mechanical power' and quote further examples as including 'antique clocks and watches such as "Tompion" clocks', 'trawlers, fishing vessels, tankers and other vessels propelled by engines' and 'railway locomotives and tramway engines ... irrespective of the method of propulsion'. HMRC would not accept as machinery, on the other hand, 'vessels propelled by sail or oars'. It is possible, of course, that such vessels would qualify as plant.

Finally, it should be noted that machinery is not affected by the restrictions imposed by CAA 2001, s. 21 (buildings) or by s. 22 (structures) as s. 23, List C, item 1 specifically exempts 'any machinery (including devices for providing motive power) '.

Cross-references

See the Chapter headed 'Meaning of Plant', which begins at 180-000.

262-030   Milking parlours

Legislation: CAA 2001, s. 23 (List C)

Cases: none

HMRC material: none (regarding plant and machinery)

Commentary

A milking parlour will normally correctly be treated as the building within which the milking operations are carried out. There will doubtless be much in the way of plant within the building but it is difficult to envisage many circumstances in which the building as a whole would qualify as plant.

To obtain treatment of such a building as plant it would be necessary to show that it fell within one of the exemptions in CAA 2001, s. 23, List C. It is not at all clear that any of the exemptions could apply to a milking parlour. Agricultural Buildings Allowances (see 425-000) will in principle be available.

The best option will therefore normally be to make a very precise analysis of the expenditure incurred on the milking parlour. All machinery and equipment should qualify as plant, as well as electrical wiring, etc serving that machinery and equipment.

The position may be different, however, if the parlour is separately installed in an existing building. In this case, first principles would dictate that it is plant rather than part of the building. Similarly, it is understood that portable milking parlours exist. In the Swiss mountains, for example, it is reported that farmers living in rather basic accommodation move some rather grander milking parlours around the countryside. It may also be that similar items are used for agricultural shows and so on. Such parlours would presumably qualify.

Cross-references

The following headings from this A to Z Chapter may be relevant in particular cases where this type of expenditure is being considered. See also the Chapter headed 'Meaning of Plant', which begins at 180-000.

- Buildings (260-150)
- Structures (262-590)

262-040   Mirrors

Legislation: none

Cases:

Jarrold v John Good & Sons Ltd (1963) 40 TC 681
Lupton v Cadogan Gardens Developments Limited (1971) 47 TC 1

HMRC material: none

Commentary

In normal circumstances, mirrors should qualify as plant. They were included in the assets claimed as plant in the *Jarrold v Good* case. As they were not the subject of debate in front of the commissioners it can be taken that they were accepted as plant. Again, in the *Cadogan Gardens Developments* case expenditure on mirrors was accepted as qualifying for plant and machinery allowances.

Cross-references

The following headings from this A to Z Chapter may be relevant in particular cases where this type of expenditure is being considered. See also the Chapter headed 'Meaning of Plant', which begins at 180-000.

- Buildings (260-150)
- Fixtures (260-760)
- Furniture and furnishings (260-820)

262-100   Number plates

Legislation: none

Cases: none

HMRC material: CA 21250, CA 23510

Commentary

In the case of personalised or ordinary number plates, it is necessary to distinguish between the physical plate consisting of a piece of metal or whatever with a combination of numbers and letters, and the right to use a particular registration mark. In the case of specialised number plates, most of the value lies in this intangible right.

The physical plate itself may well qualify as an item of plant or machinery, though with the caveat that it 'is a chattel that does not become plant or machinery unless and until it is attached to a car which is itself plant or machinery' (CA 21250).

However, the HMRC view (which is undoubtedly correct) is that expenditure on the intangible right cannot qualify as expenditure on plant or machinery. Nevertheless, instructions to inspectors are that they 'should accept that the price of a car etc which includes the cost of registering the car with a "normal" number can all be qualifying expenditure'.

As regards the employee tax consequences where such a number plate is made available for a director or employee, see the book *P11D: Tax-Efficient Benefits and Expenses*, also published by CCH.

Plant and Machinery: A to Z

Cross-references

The following heading from this A to Z Chapter may be relevant in particular cases where this type of expenditure is being considered. See also the Chapter headed 'Meaning of Plant', which begins at 180-000.

Cars (260-240)

262-150   Panelling

Legislation: CAA 2001, s. 21 (List A, item 1)

Cases: *IR Commrs v Scottish & Newcastle Breweries Ltd* [1982] BTC 187; *Wimpy International Ltd v Warland* [1989] BTC 58; *J D Wetherspoon plc v R & C Commrs* (2007) Sp C 657

HMRC material: CA 21140

Commentary

The treatment of wall panelling is a difficult area, with seemingly contradictory case law.

Walls in themselves do not qualify as plant, as they are clearly caught by item 1 in List A at CAA 2001, s. 21. Special rules apply if the panelling can clearly be linked to thermal insulation (CAA 2001, s. 28; see 160-400), and decorative assets will in some circumstances qualify as plant and machinery (see 260-500).

In the *Wimpy* case, wall panelling was used to line all interior walls to the areas where customers sat. The panels were normally made of blockboard fitted on to battens attached to the wall, from which they could be lifted off but on occasions, because of fire regulations, were made of a special non-combustible material and screwed to the wall to avoid the use of wooden battens. They were fitted partly to cover imperfections in the wall but mainly, it was claimed, to create an environment suited to the company's assessment of the public's current taste. Their 'design life' was estimated at about five years.

The commissioners considered that the treatment of these items was borderline, noting that 'the creation of atmosphere must, in the nature of things, be less important in Wimpy's trade than in an hotel or a restaurant where customers will be expected to linger over their meals, but we do not think that the concept is wholly incompatible with the conduct of a fast food restaurant'. The commissioners could not ignore the evidence that the wall panels were chosen to create the right environment for the particular trade. Nor could it be said that the claim in respect of the panels was so extreme as to fall outside the scheme of capital allowances for commercial premises. The commissioners decided that, on balance, they should qualify as plant 'under the general description of embellishments'.

In the *Wetherspoons* case, by contrast, the company failed to convince the commissioners that the wooden panelling, despite being affixed to the property, had retained a separate identity. As the decorative panelling effectively turned the premises from an unpanelled into a mainly panelled room, it was more appropriately described as part of the premises rather than having a separate identity.

The commissioners in *Wetherspoons* referred to the *Scottish & Newcastle Breweries* case which made it clear that an embellishment to a pub could be plant provided that it had not become part of the premises but had retained a separate identity. The commissioners accepted that the panelling was an embellishment to create ambience for the purposes of the Appellant's trade but went on to consider the weight to be given to the fact that the panels were fixed to the wall and formed part of the premises:

> 'The structure of the rooms was clearly not incomplete without the panelling. A substantial part of the walls was not panelled and the panelling was fixed to the walls. The panelling was clearly capable of being removed; indeed similar panelling had been removed from a pub at Gatwick Airport and reused. There is no reason to believe that removal of the battens would cause more than surface damage to the plaster. However we find that the panelling was not likely to be removed after only a short period since this would obviously involve substantial refurbishment during which period the pub would have to be closed, although periodic redecoration of the interior would clearly be needed from time to time and no doubt consideration would be given to whether the panelling should remain. There was no suggestion that the panelling was a necessary embellishment to the pub, in view of the history of the premises as a theatre. Since the panelling only covered part of the walls we conclude that it did appear visually to retain a separate identity.

> ...

> ... it seems to us that we are being asked whether the decorative panelling is more appropriately described as part of the premises in which the pub's trade is carried on or instead as an embellishment used to enhance the atmosphere of those premises.

> A factor ... which seems to us to be helpful to consider in the context of the decorative panelling is the extent to which the panelling can be regarded as an unexceptional component which would not be an unusual feature of premises of the type to which the Appellant is inviting the public. If an item is or becomes such an unexceptional component of the premises into which it is introduced, that, in our view, is a factor tending to the conclusion that it does not retain a separate identity for relevant purposes. The relevance of this factor is, we consider, supported by the treatment in para. 1(2) of Schedule AA1 of any asset in a building which is not incorporated into the building but is of a kind normally incorporated into buildings, as effectively, part of the building, and also the exclusion from this treatment, by item 14 of Column 2 of Table 1 in Schedule AA1, of 'decorative assets provided for the enjoyment of the public in the hotel, restaurant or similar trades'.

> Because the decorative panelling in the Prince of Wales effectively turns the premises, or that part of them to which it is applied, from an unpanelled room into a room which is mainly panelled, we consider that it is an unexceptional component of the type of premises, in contradistinction, for example, to the fixed but not easily removable metal sculpture, which was held, in Scottish & Newcastle Breweries, to be plant.

> Balancing all the above matters, we conclude that the panelling is more appropriately described as having become part of the premises than as having retained a separate identity. Therefore it does not qualify as plant.'

Cross-references

The following heading from this A to Z Chapter may be relevant in particular cases where this type of expenditure is being considered. See also the Chapter headed 'Meaning of Plant', which begins at 180-000.

- Buildings (260-150)
- Walls (262-910)

262-200   Partitions

Legislation: CAA 2001, s. 23 (List C, item 13)

Cases: *Jarrold v John Good & Sons Ltd* (1963) 40 TC 681; *Lupton v Cadogan Gardens Developments Limited* (1971) 47 TC 1

HMRC material: CA 21120–21140, CA 22030

Commentary

Partitions will normally qualify as plant where they are moveable and where there is an intention to move them 'in the course of the qualifying activity'. In the *John Good* case, it was held that partitions which met these criteria were apparatus with which the company carried on its trade.

HMRC do not accept that all moveable partitions are plant. Inspectors are instructed (at CA 21120) to check 'whether they need to possess mobility as a matter of commercial necessity'. Inspectors are also asked to check whether they have in fact ever been moved.

The legislation governing partitions is in CAA 2001, s. 21–23. If they can be said to be 'walls' or otherwise to be incorporated into the building or of a kind normally incorporated into buildings then they will not qualify, unless they are within the specific exemption in CAA 2001, s. 23, List C. This exemption (at item 13) is for 'partition walls, where moveable and intended to be moved in the course of the qualifying activity'. If they do come within this category then it does not necessarily follow that they qualify but they then need to be considered on ordinary case law principles. In the *John Good* case, it was accepted that the partitions qualified as plant on the grounds that the company,

> 'instead of having internal walls in its office building, needs to have, and does have, for the special requirements of its business, moveable partitioning, by means of which it can, in response to changing volumes of business in its departments or to the cessation of departments or the emergence of new departments, rapidly and cheaply and without much interruption of business alter the subdivisions of its office building.'

It should be noted that the *John Good* decision has received subsequent approval, as, for example, in the House of Lords in the case of *Barclay, Curle*.

Sometimes partitions are papered over so that they become disguised and start to look like any other wall. This is not necessarily fatal to the claim to treat them as plant but is likely to prejudice the inspector's view against an acceptance of the point. At the least, such treatment could give the inspector ammunition for trying to demonstrate that they were not 'intended to be moved in the course of the trade'.

Partitions were also accepted as plant in the *Cadogan Gardens Developments* case.

Cross-references

The following headings from this A to Z Chapter may be relevant in particular cases where this type of expenditure is being considered. See also the Chapter headed 'Meaning of Plant', which begins at 180-000.

- Buildings (260-150)
- Screens (262-430)
- Walls (262-910)

262-210   Plant rooms

Legislation: CAA 2001, s. 21 and 22

Cases: *Wimpy International Ltd v Warland* [1989] BTC 58

HMRC material: none

Commentary

Sometimes when plant is bought or constructed the business will need to build a plant room to house the plant or machinery. The question then arises as to whether the cost of the plant room itself qualifies as plant.

Such expenditure will rarely qualify. This is because the plant room will have become part of the premises and would in any case be a building or structure which would therefore be disqualified by CAA 2001, s. 21 or 22.

In the *Wimpy* case, which appears to be the only one where the issue of a plant room was specifically considered, the commissioners allowed the cost of the plant room to qualify as plant. The Revenue did not appeal on that point so there is no view from the courts. Any such decision would in any case have been overruled by the introduction of the legislation now at CAA 2001, s. 21 and 22.

Cross-references

The following headings from this A to Z Chapter may be relevant in particular cases where this type of expenditure is being considered. See also the Chapter headed 'Meaning of Plant', which begins at 180-000.

Plant and Machinery: A to Z

- Buildings (260-150)
- Structures (262-590)

262-230   Poultry houses

Legislation: none

Cases: *O'Srianian v Lakeview Limited* [1984] TL(I) 125; *Carr v Sayer* [1992] BTC 286; *Attwood v Anduff Car Wash Ltd* [1997] BTC 454

HMRC material: CA 22110

Commentary

Poultry houses are unlikely to qualify as plant in most cases. It is true that in the Irish case involving the company *Lakeview Limited*, it was held in the Irish High Court that a prefabricated poultry house was plant, on the grounds that it played a part in the egg production process of the taxpayer. However, the judge in the recent case of *Anduff Car Wash* disagreed with the decision in the Irish case, commenting that 'I have considerable doubt whether the premises test was properly satisfied in that case'.

The HMRC view is that 'most poultry houses/chicken shacks are buildings or structures and so are excluded from plant or machinery allowances. (. . .) They are not plant even if they are used in intensive poultry production and contain automated systems for ventilation, heating, food and water. (. . .) Similarly, the fixed chicken cages inside a poultry house should not be accepted as plant' (CA 22110).

For a general discussion of the issues, see under temporary buildings at 262-740.

On the other hand, there may well be cases where the poultry house is smaller and moveable. In such a case, it will not be a structure as it is not fixed (CAA 2001, s. 22(3)(a)), and there will be a better argument for treating it as plant. Similarly, there seems no reason why cages should not qualify in some circumstances, though it will be necessary to bring out a contrast with the kennels in the *Carr v Sayer* case.

Cross-references

The following headings from this A to Z Chapter may be relevant in particular cases where this type of expenditure is being considered. See also the Chapter headed 'Meaning of Plant', which begins at 180-000.

- Animals (260-060)
- Buildings (260-150)
- Kennels (261-200)
- Structures (262-590)
- Zoo cages (263-000)

262-240   Professional fees and preliminary costs

Legislation: none

Cases: *Jarrold v John Good & Sons Ltd* (1963) 40 TC 681; *Wimpy International Ltd v Warland* [1989] BTC 58 (items 13, 14); *J D Wetherspoon plc v R & C Commrs* (2007) Sp C 657

HMRC material: CA 20070

Commentary

HMRC accept that professional fees can be treated as expenditure on the provision of plant 'if they relate directly to the acquisition, transport and installation of the plant or machinery'.

Often, an overall fee will be paid in respect of a building project. The taxpayer will normally want to apportion professional costs in the same ratio as the expenditure itself is apportioned between plant and other items. However, HMRC resist this approach as they take the view that the value of professional services relating to plant is likely to be lower than that relating to other parts of the project. Whether or not this is reasonable will depend on the circumstances. One can certainly envisage cases where the work in respect of fixtures and fittings may be at least as complex as the work in respect of the basic building itself. It may be helpful to obtain a letter from the professionals involved giving some details of any particularly complex issues in relation to the fixtures and fittings.

HMRC apply identical principles to the preliminary costs of a building project, which they define as including 'site management, insurance, general purpose labour, temporary accommodation and security' incurred over the duration of a project.

Any argument by HMRC that the *Ben-Odeco* principles can be applied so as to disallow the costs of professional fees should be resisted (*Ben-Odeco Limited v Powlson* (1978) 52 TC 459). (For a discussion of the *Ben-Odeco* issue, see 260-720.) As the commissioners in the *Wimpy* case said, professional fees can normally be treated as part of the capital expenditure incurred in the installation of plant ('we think that they can properly be included in the claim for an allowance'). The same commissioners went on to say that planning fees are distinguishable from *Ben-Odeco* type costs (finance costs, etc). Planning fees could not be excluded in principle from expenditure on plant, though the actual amount qualifying in each case would have to be determined on the facts.

The question of preliminary costs was considered in the case of *J D Wetherspoon plc v R & C Commrs* (2007) Sp C 657. It was held in that case that preliminary costs could be apportioned in part to incidental building alterations qualifying under what is now CAA 2001, s. 25 (see 260-040). The case also made the point that projected overheads should be apportioned rateably over all the measured work. It could not have been the intention of Parliament that if a taxpayer was to be entitled to include preliminaries in capital

Plant and Machinery: A to Z

expenditure claimed it should be necessary to enter into a detailed assessment in order to allocate the preliminaries. Where a relatively small amount of work and record-keeping would give substantially greater accuracy, it would be reasonable and proportionate that the work should be done, but not otherwise.

Cross-references

The following headings from this A to Z Chapter may be relevant in particular cases where this type of expenditure is being considered. See also the Chapter headed 'Meaning of Plant', which begins at 180-000.

- Alterations to buildings (260-040)
- Demolition costs (260-510)
- Finance costs (260-720)

262-250   Public address systems

Legislation: none

Cases: *Cole Brothers Ltd v Phillips* [1982] BTC 208

HMRC material: CA 21230

Commentary

In their letter to the Football League written in January 1991, the Revenue accepted that 'public address equipment – microphones, amplifiers and loudspeakers' would normally qualify as plant or machinery (CA 21230).

In the *Cole Brothers* case, the public address system costs were listed under the heading of 'expenditure not in dispute', ie as qualifying as plant. The hearing in the Court of Appeal and again in the House of Lords made it clear that the public address system was indeed to be treated as plant.

Cross-references

The following headings from this A to Z Chapter may be relevant in particular cases where this type of expenditure is being considered. See also the Chapter headed 'Meaning of Plant', which begins at 180-000.

- Electrical installations and equipment (260-600)
- Telecommunication systems (262-710)
- Telephones and fax machines (262-720)
- Televisions and videos (262-730)

262-300 Removal costs

Legislation: none

Cases: *Nuclear Electric Plc v Bradley* [1996] BTC 165

HMRC material: CA 21190; BIM 42530

Commentary

Where plant is moved from one business site to another it may be that the costs will be allowable as a trading deduction. If they are not so allowed, inspectors are instructed that they should 'treat those costs as expenditure on plant and machinery and give capital allowances on them' (CA 21190). Similarly, the Revenue manuals at old CA 1504 used to instruct inspectors that 'transportation and installation costs should be regarded as expenditure on the provision of plant or machinery'.

A word of caution is needed. HMRC (at BIM 42530) make the following distinction so as to disallow the expenses of moving plant and machinery in certain circumstances:

> 'The expenses of removal of machinery and plant including the cost of dismantling and re-erection, should be allowed except where the removal was essentially part of a scheme for expansion of the business, as distinct, for example, from a removal merely to re-site the machinery or plant to secure greater efficiency within the scope of an existing, even though increasing, trade.'

The distinction between 'a scheme for expansion' on the one hand and 'greater efficiency within the scope of an existing, even though increasing, trade' on the other clearly allows plenty of room for argument. Hopefully, HMRC will normally simply accept in these circumstances that allowances are due.

The distinction between revenue costs on the one hand and capital costs on the other was touched upon in the Court of Appeal judgment given by Millett LJ in the *Nuclear Electric* case.

Cross-references

The following heading from this A to Z Chapter may be relevant in particular cases where this type of expenditure is being considered. See also the Chapter headed 'Meaning of Plant', which begins at 180-000.

Professional fees and preliminary costs (262-240)

262-310 Reservoirs, etc

Legislation: CAA 2001, s. 22 (List B, item 4), 23 (List C, item 27)

Plant and Machinery: A to Z

Cases: *Margrett v Lowestoft Water & Gas Company* (1935) 19 TC 481; *IR Commrs v Barclay, Curle and Co Ltd* (1969) 45 TC 221

HMRC material: CA 22020–22030

Commentary

Reservoirs, dams and barrages do not normally qualify as plant. List B, item 4 specifies that any such item is to be treated as a 'structure or other asset' which is therefore prevented from qualifying as plant.

An exception is given for a reservoir which is 'incorporated into a water treatment works' or for a service reservoir where it is supplying treated water to a specific housing estate or 'other particular locality'. The *Lowestoft Water & Gas* case lends credence to the HMRC view that reservoirs are not generally to be treated as plant. The point was not specifically addressed but the clear implication of the case was that it was not to be treated as an item of plant.

The question of dams was considered in the *Barclay, Curle* case. Lord Reid felt that a dam would not normally qualify as plant but went on to say, 'I could imagine circumstances in which a dam would be such an integral part of the means required for a trading operation that it should be regarded as plant'. In the House of Lords, though, Lord Donovan said that the item in question (a dry dock) 'differs from a dam, which, for the moment at least, I regard more as a storehouse for water'. In the context of that sentence, the implication is that a dam would be unlikely to qualify as plant but it is not specifically stated in that manner.

Cross-references

The following headings from this A to Z Chapter may be relevant in particular cases where this type of expenditure is being considered. See also the Chapter headed 'Meaning of Plant', which begins at 180-000.

- Structures (262-590)
- Water supplies and water tanks (262-920)
- Water towers (262-940)

262-320   Roads, etc

Legislation: CAA 2001, s. 22 (List B, item 2), 23 (List C, item 31)

Cases: none

HMRC material: CA 22100

Commentary

Roads do not qualify as plant. CAA 2001, s. 22, List B, item 2 disqualifies 'any way, hard standing (such as a pavement), road, railway, tramway, a park for vehicles or containers, or an airstrip or runway'. The provision of rails themselves, together with sleepers and 'ballast for a railway or tramway' is, however, outside the exclusion (List C, item 31).

Cross-references

The following headings from this A to Z Chapter may be relevant in particular cases where this type of expenditure is being considered. See also the Chapter headed 'Meaning of Plant', which begins at 180-000.

- Car parks (260-250)
- Car wash apparatus (260-260)
- Land (261-300)
- Tunnels (262-780)

262-400   Safes and strongrooms

Legislation: CAA 2001, s. 23 (lLst C, item 12)

Cases: *Carr v Sayer* [1992] BTC 286

HMRC material: CA 22030

Commentary

Safes are specifically not caught by table 1 of CAA 2001, s. 21 and 22 – see List C, item 12. As such, there is no statutory reason why a safe should not qualify as plant. It follows that it must be considered on ordinary case law principles.

The *Carr v Sayer* case, concerned with the tax treatment of dog kennels, contained the following observation by Sir Donald Nicholls:

'One of the functions of a building is to provide shelter and security for people using it and for goods inside it. That is a normal function of a building. A building used for those purposes is being used as a building. Thus a building does not partake of the character of plant simply, for example, because it is used for storage by a trader carrying on a storage business. This remains so even if the building has been built as a specially secure building for use in a safe-deposit business ... Again, I say nothing about particular fixtures within such a building.'

Although 'strongrooms in bank or building society premises' are similarly within the List C, item 12 exemption, such rooms will always need to be looked at on their own merits to see whether they in fact qualify as plant on ordinary case law principles. As the words quoted above make clear, it will not necessarily be the case that a whole strongroom will qualify as plant.

Cross-references

The following headings, mostly from this A to Z Chapter, may be relevant in particular cases where this type of expenditure is being considered. See also the Chapter headed 'Meaning of Plant', which begins at 180-000.

- Buildings (260-150)
- Electrical installations and equipment (260-600)
- Fire safety (see 160-500)
- Security systems (262-450)
- Shutters (262-500)
- Structures (262-590)

262-420 Sanitary ware

Legislation: CAA 2001, s. 23 (List C, item 2 (formerly, but see now the integral feature rules) and 5); s. 33A

Cases: *Lupton v Cadogan Gardens Developments Limited* (1971) 47 TC 1; *Wimpy International Ltd v Warland* [1989] BTC 58

HMRC material: CA 21200, CA 21230, CA 22030, CA 22100

Commentary

Sanitary ware generally qualifies as plant. CAA 2001, s. 23, List C, item 5 specifically exempts 'washbasins, sinks, baths, showers, sanitary ware and similar equipment'. As such, these items are to be considered on ordinary case law principles, which favour their treatment as plant.

HMRC officers are instructed (at CA 21200) that they should accept that baths, washbasins and toilet suites are plant. In a letter to the Football League written in January 1991, the Revenue indicated that 'toilet sanitary ware, sinks and basins, baths and showers whether for staff or public (but not the mains water supply)' would normally qualify as plant. Similarly, inspectors are instructed to allow as plant the cost of temporary huts moved from one site to another by builders, contractors, etc to provide toilet facilities (CA 22110).

Finally, hot-water systems will invariably qualify as plant (CA 21200) on normal case law principles, but since April 2008 will be treated as integral features. Cold-water supplies would in the past only qualify where provided mainly to meet the particular requirements of the trade or to serve particular plant or machinery used for the purposes of the trade (former List C, item 2). They too will now qualify as integral features (see CAA 2001, s. 33A).

Cross-references

The following headings from this A to Z Chapter may be relevant in particular cases where this type of expenditure is being considered. See also the Chapter headed 'Meaning of Plant', which begins at 180-000.

- Buildings (260-150)
- Furniture and furnishings (260-820)
- Structures (262-590)
- Water supplies and water tanks (262-920)

262-430   Screens

Legislation: none

Cases: *Leeds Permanent Building Society v Proctor* [1982] BTC 347; *Wimpy International Ltd v Warland* [1989] BTC 58

HMRC material: CA 21120–21140, CA 22090, CA 23140

Commentary

It has been held that decorative screens used for window displays qualify as plant. This was the decision in the *Leeds Permanent Building Society* case. The purpose of the screens was to attract the attention of passers-by. The screens were designed specially for the Building Society and, indeed, frequently for the actual branch in which they were situated.

The Revenue put forward some fairly bizarre arguments to prove that they should not qualify as plant but the arguments were decisively rejected in the High Court. For example, the Revenue tried to argue that the attracting of customers was 'not of itself a sufficient business function to stamp an article as plant'.

It was also incorrect to argue that the screens formed part of the premises or setting. They were not 'part of or inseparably annexed to' the office and were incapable of use for any other business unless they were considerably modified. As such, it was clear that the screens were part of the furniture with which the trade was carried on.

In the *Wimpy* case, screens were installed between many of the tables for the purposes of privacy and so on. The screens were held to be an integral part of the seating equipment in the restaurants and therefore to qualify as plant. It was immaterial whether the screens were attached to the tables or fixed to the floor.

Cross-references

The following headings from this A to Z Chapter may be relevant in particular cases where this type of expenditure is being considered. See also the Chapter headed 'Meaning of Plant', which begins at 180-000.

Plant and Machinery: A to Z

- Buildings (260-150)
- Counters and checkouts (260-360)
- Décor (260-500)
- Display equipment (260-530)
- Entertaining-related expenditure (260-630)
- Fixtures (260-760)
- Furniture and furnishings (260-820)
- Partitions (262-200)
- Shutters (262-500)

262-440   Seats

Legislation: none

Cases: *Munby v Furlong* (1977) 50 TC 491; *Brown v Burnley Football and Athletic Co Limited* (1980) 53 TC 357; *IR Commrs v Scottish & Newcastle Breweries Ltd* [1982] BTC 187; *Wimpy International Ltd v Warland* [1989] BTC 58

HMRC material: CA 21230, CA 22240–22260

Commentary

Chairs or other forms of seating will normally qualify as plant without any problem. In the *Wimpy* case, for example, the commissioners said that the chairs were amongst the items which plainly formed part of the plant. Similarly, in the *Munby v Furlong* case, a dentist's chair was referred to in passing as an example of an item obviously qualifying as plant.

Seating in sports arenas, etc however, was the subject of dispute in the *Burnley Football and Athletic* case.

Expenditure on seats at a sports ground will not normally qualify under CAA 2001, s. 30–33 (expenditure on safety at sports grounds). However, it will often qualify under general principles.

The HMRC view appears to be that seating which is no more than an integral part of a football ground stand will not qualify as plant. However, HMRC go on to say that 'most modern types of seats are likely to qualify as plant or machinery, both plain plastic tip-up seats and more luxurious types of seat' (CA 21230). The cost of altering an existing building will qualify as plant where that cost is incidental to the installation of the plant.

Cross-references

The following headings from this A to Z Chapter may be relevant in particular cases where this type of expenditure is being considered. See also the Chapter headed 'Meaning of Plant', which begins at 180-000.

- Alterations to buildings (260-040)

- Buildings (260-150)
- Fixtures (260-760)
- Furniture and furnishings (260-820)
- Sports grounds (safety) (262-550)
- Structures (262-590)

262-450 Security systems

Legislation: CAA 2001, s. 23 (List C, item 8, 11 and 12), 27, 33 and 63(5)

Cases: *Cole Brothers Ltd v Phillips* [1982] BTC 208; *Carr v Sayer* [1992] BTC 286; *Bradley v London Electricity plc* [1996] BTC 95; *Lord Hanson v Mansworth (HMIT)* (2004) Sp C 410

HMRC material: CA 21200, CA 22270; EIM 21811

Commentary

This heading is divided into two categories. The reason for this is that special, and strict, rules apply to certain expenditure on personal security measures. Where these special rules do not provide tax relief then the expenditure must be considered on general principles.

Personal security
The special rules are given under CAA 2001, s. 33. Security expenses come within the special rules where all of the following conditions are met:

(1) a 'relevant qualifying activity' (see 150-000) is being carried on by an individual or partnership (not a company);

(2) the individual or partnership incurs the expenditure in connection with the provision of a security asset – see below;

(3) if the special rules did not apply, no tax relief would otherwise be due either in calculating the income from the qualifying activity or under the capital allowances legislation (CAA 2001, s. 27(1));

(4) the asset is provided or used to meet a special threat to the individual's personal physical security;

(5) that threat arises wholly or mainly because of the relevant activity; and

(6) the sole object of incurring the expenditure is to meet that threat.

Only certain assets are able to qualify under this special legislation and, in this respect, the following points are to be noted:

(1) the asset must be provided to improve *personal* security;

(2) it must not be a car, ship or aircraft;

(3) it can be an item of equipment or a structure (such as a wall);

(4) it must not be a 'dwelling'. HMRC say that 'a flat used as a residence, including a flat above business premises, is a dwelling but a block of flats is not a single dwelling' (CA 22270);

(5) it must not be 'grounds appurtenant to a dwelling' and for these purposes HMRC follow the private residence 'half a hectare' rules (regarding which see TCGA 1992, s. 222 and Revenue manuals at CG 64350ff).

HMRC list alarm systems, bullet-resistant windows, reinforced doors and windows, and perimeter walls and fences as examples of items that may qualify as security assets (CA 22270).

HMRC have issued guidance on a number of related issues, as follows:

(1) HMRC head office will take the decision as to whether there is a threat to physical security, but the amount of any allowance due will be decided at district level (CAA 2001, s. 33(6)(b)).

(2) The fact that an asset has to be attached to land or a building will not prevent it from being a security asset.

(3) Similarly, the fact that an asset improves the personal physical security of another member of the trader's family or household will not disqualify it, as long as it is also there to protect the trader's own personal physical security (CAA 2001, s. 33(4)).

(4) If an asset is intended solely to improve personal physical security but there is another use for the asset which arises incidentally, then the whole of the expenditure will still qualify for capital allowances. For example, bullet-proof glass may have the incidental effect of keeping the house warm.

(5) On the other hand, if an asset is provided partly to improve personal physical security and partly for other reasons then only the appropriate proportion of the expenditure will qualify for relief. This proportion is defined as 'the proportion of the expenditure attributable to the intended use to improve personal physical security'. This must surely be one of the most bizarre concepts to pin down anywhere in the Taxes Acts. One can hardly imagine an individual at threat from a terrorist organisation telling HMRC that he had installed large bullet-proof windows 75 per cent to prevent a terrorist attack and 25 per cent because they were guaranteed to have low maintenance for 10 years!

Where all of the above conditions are met, the expenditure is treated as if it were on plant or machinery and the asset is deemed to belong to the individual or partnership as a result of the expenditure being incurred. In the event of an asset giving rise to a disposal for capital allowances purposes, the security asset is deemed to be disposed of for nil consideration (CAA 2001, s. 63(5)).

HMRC take a strict line on the interpretation of this special legislation. There will be relatively few cases where HMRC will accept both that there is a genuine personal security risk and that it arises from the nature of the trade. The legislation is a close parallel to that which concerns employees and which is found at ITEPA 2003, s. 377.

That employee-related legislation is discussed in the HMRC manuals at EIM 21811, where HMRC specify that the deduction is for individuals whose work 'exposes them to a very real threat to their physical safety from terrorists, extremists and others who may resort to violence'. A case was heard in 2004 involving the late Lord Hanson. The special commissioner ruled that Lord Hanson was entitled to tax relief under the employment income legislation as there was a special employment-related threat to his personal physical security. The decision was based on a factual finding that Hanson was a potential terrorist target by virtue of his role as executive chairman of Hanson plc. It was also found that the sole object of the company in providing the security services was to meet that threat. (For an in-depth review of the employee tax position, see the publication *P11D: Tax-efficient Benefits & Expenses* (produced by the same author and publishers as this book) at section 8.46. The publication can be ordered from Wolters Kluwer (UK) Limited by telephoning 0870 777 2906.)

Other security measures

Where the special rules outlined above do not apply, any security costs will fall to be considered on general principles.

To the extent that assets are part of the building then they will not qualify unless they are exempted by CAA 2001, s. 23, List C. List C does provide a number of exemptions, including the following:

- computer, telecommunication and surveillance systems (including their wiring or other links) (item 8);
- burglar alarm systems (item 11);
- strongrooms in bank or building society premises (item 12);
- safes (again, item 12).

The items listed immediately above do not necessarily qualify but there is a good chance they will do. Their treatment must be considered on general principles and case law precedents. However, HMRC do accept that alarm and sprinkler systems qualify as plant (CA 21200).

Where an item forms part of an electrical system, then it will qualify under the rules relating to integral features if it fails to do so under any of the other provisions.

Cross-references

The following headings from this A to Z Chapter may be relevant in particular cases where this type of expenditure is being considered. See also the Chapter headed 'Meaning of Plant', which begins at 180-000.

- Alterations to buildings (260-040)
- Buildings (260-150)
- Cameras (260-200)
- Doors (260-550)
- Electrical installations and equipment (260-600)
- Fencing (260-700)

Plant and Machinery: A to Z

- Gates (260-920)
- Floodlighting (260-770)
- Professional fees and preliminary costs (262-240)
- Telecommunication systems (262-710)
- Telephones and fax machines (262-720)
- Televisions and videos (262-730)
- Windows (262-960)

262-460   Sewerage

Legislation: CAA 2001, s. 21 (List A, item 3 and 4), 22 (List B, item 6), 23 (List C, items 2 and 29)

Cases: *Bridge House (Reigate Hill) Limited v Hinder* (1971) 47 TC 182

HMRC material: CA 21170–21180

Commentary

Waste disposal systems, and sewerage and drainage systems, are not normally able to qualify as plant as they are specifically included in the expression 'building' (List A). An exception is made for sewerage systems which are either provided mainly to meet the particular requirements of the trade or are to serve particular plant or machinery used for those purposes (List C, item 2).

Similarly, a drainage ditch is not able to qualify (List B, item 6) although expenditure on 'the provision of slurry pits or silage clamps' is outside the scope of the exclusion (List C, item 29).

Where a complex sewerage system is installed, the first step taken by HMRC would be to consider whether it should be treated as a single installation or broken down into its component parts. For a detailed discussion of this principle, see under electrical installations and equipment at 260-600. The HMRC view, however, is that most systems should not be looked at as a single entity but rather should be broken down and looked at in piecemeal fashion.

In practice, a system is only likely to qualify if it can be demonstrated that the sewerage system is of a scale or nature that is dictated by the requirements of the particular trade. For example, a factory producing sewerage needing special treatment before entering the mains system might well be able to demonstrate that the whole of that system was 'provided mainly to meet the particular requirements of the trade'.

Cross-references

The following headings from this A to Z Chapter may be relevant in particular cases where this type of expenditure is being considered. See also the Chapter headed 'Meaning of Plant', which begins at 180-000.

- Caravans and caravan sites (260-230)
- Electrical installations and equipment (260-600)
- Reservoirs, etc (262-310)
- Sanitary ware (262-420)
- Slurry storage facilities (262-530)
- Structures (262-590)
- Water supplies and water tanks (262-920)

262-470 Shelves

Legislation: CAA 2001, s. 21(3)

Cases: *Hunt v Henry Quick Ltd* [1992] BTC 440

HMRC material: CA 21230

Commentary

In a letter to the Football League in January 1991 (reproduced at 180-400), the Revenue included 'racking, shelving, cupboards and furniture' as items 'which would normally qualify as plant or machinery'.

In general, there should be no doubt that shelving qualifies as plant. There can, however, be borderline cases where mezzanine floors are installed for storage purposes (see, for example, the *Henry Quick* case). This issue is discussed in more detail under the heading of floors and flooring materials at 260-780.

In practice, there should never be any problem with free-standing shelves. The position is not quite so clear, however, once shelves are fixed in a building. HMRC would have a possible argument in such a case that they are an asset incorporated into the building which would therefore be precluded from qualifying by virtue of CAA 2001, s. 21. It may be necessary to encourage the architect to leave some of the shelf planning until the building has been completed – HMRC's hand will be strengthened if the architect's drawings clearly identify the shelving as part of the building.

Cross-references

The following headings from this A to Z Chapter may be relevant in particular cases where this type of expenditure is being considered. See also the Chapter headed 'Meaning of Plant', which begins at 180-000.

- Alterations to buildings (260-040)

- Buildings (260-150)
- Counters and checkouts (260-360)
- Décor (260-500)
- Display equipment (260-530)
- Fixtures (260-760)
- Floors and flooring materials (260-780)
- Furniture and furnishings (260-820)
- Storage equipment (262-570)
- Structures (262-590)

262-480   Ships

Legislation: CAA 2001, Pt. 2, Ch. 12, s. 127–158

Cases: *John Hall Junior & Co v Rickman* (1906) 1 KB 311; *The South Metropolitan Gas Company v Dadd* (1927) 13 TC 205; *Benson v The Yard Arm Club Ltd* (1979) 53 TC 67

HMRC material: CA 21215, CA 22050, CA 22270; CG 76908ff

Commentary

In most cases, it will be clear that a ship or boat qualifies as plant where it is used for the purposes of a trade. This is so even though the only tax case specifically concerned with a ship decided that it did not qualify as plant.

In the case concerned, that of *The Yard Arm Club*, an old ship had been converted for use as a floating restaurant. It was held that no capital allowances were due as the ship had become the structure within which the restaurant trade was carried on. It was not apparatus with which the business was conducted. As the judge said in the Court of Appeal, there was no obvious distinction between a restaurant on the Thames and a fish and chip shop in Bethnal Green. Both were acting as premises in which the trades were carried on:

> 'The fact that a ship or hulk could be used as plant in many businesses does not enable a taxpayer to claim capital allowances for a ship or hulk which performs no function in the business actually carried on by the taxpayer Company, other than the function of premises providing accommodation for that business.'

There could be a possible argument with a very large ship that it was equivalent to a hotel or other building. At the time of writing this element of this manual, the author has recently read about proposals for a vast ship that would effectively become the permanent home of many people as it travels around the world. Possible arguments about whether such a ship could qualify as plant can be imagined. It is thought, however, that in the vast majority of cases a boat or ship used for the purposes of the trade will indeed qualify.

HMRC's *Capital Gains* manual, at CG 76908ff, contains some useful pointers in connection with CGT issues and the following principles should apply equally for capital allowance purposes:

- a yacht or other vessel which is propelled only by sail is not regarded as machinery [though the question of whether it is plant needs to be separately considered];
- large racing or ocean-going yachts which are fitted with auxiliary engines should be regarded as machinery;
- trawlers, fishing vessels, tankers and other vessels which are propelled by engines are regarded as machinery.' In most cases, this type of vessel will be used in a business and will qualify for capital allowances.'

The special legislation at CAA 2001, Pt. 2, Ch. 12 applies where a ship owner incurs expenditure on the provision of a ship for the purposes of a qualifying activity.

Pontoons

HMRC accept that floating pontoons should be treated as plant 'even if they are attached to a pile or other fixed structure'. Fixed pontoons, on the other hand, are not accepted as plant (CA 21215).

Cross-references

The following headings from this A to Z Chapter may be relevant in particular cases where this type of expenditure is being considered. See also the Chapter headed 'Meaning of Plant', which begins at 180-000.

- Docks (including dry docks) (260-540)
- Structures (262-590)

262-490   Shop fronts

Legislation: CAA 2001, s. 21, 22

Cases: *Wimpy International Ltd v Warland* [1989] BTC 58 (item 6)

HMRC material: CA 21140, CA 22110; BIM 46904

Commentary

Shop fronts were the subject of a claim for plant or machinery allowances in the *Wimpy* and *Associated Restaurants* cases. However, the special commissioners disallowed the claim and the disallowance was confirmed in the courts. In the High Court, the judge commented that there appeared to be a finding of fact by the commissioners that the shop fronts were part of the premises. The judge felt that this was a view 'to which the Commissioners were entitled to come', particularly as the commissioners had contrasted the shop fronts (not qualifying) on the one hand with the advertising fascia boards (qualifying) on the other. In reaching their decision, the commissioners noted that shop fronts were, in the English climate, a necessary part of the premises.

The Court of Appeal's approval of the decision of the commissioners regarding the shop fronts was stronger, Fox LJ commenting that they had properly concluded that 'the shop

Plant and Machinery: A to Z

fronts and doors were not plant'. This was the case even though they were designed to attract customers and had a relatively short life span.

The HMRC view on the treatment of shop fronts is clear-cut with instructions to inspectors saying 'you should not give plant or machinery allowances on shop fronts. They are not plant or machinery' (CA 22110). The guidance does go on to say, however, that a showcase associated with a shop front but distinct from it should be treated as fixtures and fittings (and presumably therefore should be allowed as plant).

HMRC will normally allow the cost of replacing a shop front as an item of revenue expenditure unless there are particular reasons to regard it as capital in nature (BIM 46904).

Cross-references

The following headings from this A to Z Chapter may be relevant in particular cases where this type of expenditure is being considered. See also the Chapter headed 'Meaning of Plant', which begins at 180-000.

- Buildings (260-150)
- Display equipment (260-530)
- Doors (260-550)
- Furniture and furnishings (260-820)
- Gates (260-920)
- Shelves (262-470)
- Shutters (262-500)
- Storage equipment (262-570)
- Structures (262-590)
- Windows (262-960)

262-500   Shutters

Legislation: CAA 2001, s. 21 (List A, item 1)

Cases: *Cole Brothers Ltd v Phillips* [1982] BTC 208

HMRC material: none

Commentary

Shutters do not generally qualify as plant, because of item 1 of List A.

This would appear to apply even where shutters are added to an existing building for the specific purposes of the trade.

There are a few possible exclusions provided by CAA 2001, s. 23. Thus, shutters might be able to qualify as plant if they could be said to be furniture and furnishings (item 5), to provide sound insulation provided for the particular requirements of the trade (item 7), to be equipment designed for containing fire (item 10) or to serve as decorative assets 'provided for the enjoyment of the public in the hotel, restaurant or similar trades' (item 14).

Even if the shutters do fall within one of these exemptions, it will be necessary to show that their principal purpose is not to insulate or enclose the interior of a building (per CAA 2001, s. 23(4)).

If all of the above hurdles are successfully jumped then shutters are to be considered on ordinary case law principles and may stand a good chance of qualifying. In the Court of Appeal in the *Cole Brothers* case, one judge commented that, 'I would have thought that the blinds fitted to shop windows to protect the goods displayed there from excessive sunlight were as much "plant" as the heating system which prevents them from freezing'.

Cross-references

The following headings, mostly from this A to Z Chapter, may be relevant in particular cases where this type of expenditure is being considered. See also the Chapter headed 'Meaning of Plant', which begins at 180-000.

- Alterations to buildings (260-040)
- Buildings (260-150)
- Curtains (260-370)
- Electrical installations and equipment (260-600)
- Insulation (see 160-400)
- Screens (262-430)
- Shop fronts (262-490)
- Structures (262-590)
- Windows (262-960)

262-510 Silage clamps

Legislation: CAA 2001, s. 23 (List C, item 29)

Cases: none

HMRC material: none

Commentary

Anybody seriously interested in the treatment of silage clamps as plant would do well to read the amusing article by Trevor Johnson in *Taxation* magazine dated 27 November 1997, as well as the paragraphs in the same magazine dated 8 January 1998 in the Feedback section.

Trevor Johnson referred to what is now CAA 2001, s. 23, List C and quoted Revenue guidance as follows:

Plant and Machinery: A to Z

'It is therefore clear that a silage clamp can qualify for capital allowances but to do so it must be regarded as plant or machinery. There are no specific guidelines to set out what form the silage clamp must take in order to qualify as plant or machinery. Each case must be decided on its merits and a decision reached taking into account existing case law.'

The article made the point that it obviously is possible for a silage clamp to qualify as plant but there is no guidance from HMRC on when it will do so.

The response in January 1998 was provided by a Mr John Ward and referred to a case in Northallerton which was apparently reported in the *Darlington and Stockton Times* on 7 March 1992. It appears that the Revenue lost a case in front of the general commissioners. The accountants had described the silage clamp in question as having three bays each of which held 650 tonnes of silage. Also, there was an underground effluent tank which was attached to the bays and was capable of holding over 10,000 gallons.

The accountant had successfully resisted a Revenue argument that there needed to be an extensive amount of operating machinery and successfully argued that the silage clamp and also the effluent tank were apparatus qualifying for allowances as plant.

If unsuccessful, it may well be that an alternative claim could be made to agricultural buildings allowances but, of course, the rate of tax relief will then be much lower (and the allowances will cease altogether from April 2011).

Cross-references

The following headings from this A to Z Chapter may be relevant in particular cases where this type of expenditure is being considered. See also the Chapter headed 'Meaning of Plant', which begins at 180-000.

- Buildings (260-150)
- Land (261-300)
- Machinery (262-000)
- Sewerage (262-460)
- Slurry storage facilities (262-530)
- Structures (262-590)

262-530   Slurry storage facilities

Legislation: CAA 2001, s. 23 (list C, item 29)

Key case law: none

Revenue material: HMRC Brief 66/08

Commentary

Waste disposal systems, and sewerage and drainage systems, do not normally qualify as plant as they are specifically included in the expression 'building' (list A). An exception is made for sewerage systems which are either provided mainly to meet the particular requirements of the trade or are to serve particular plant or machinery used for those purposes (list C, item 2). Similarly, a drainage ditch is not able to qualify (list B, item 6) although expenditure on 'the provision of slurry pits or silage clamps' is outside the scope of the exclusion (list C, item 29).

At the end of 2008 (in HMRC Brief 66/08), HMRC issued guidance on various capital allowance issues, including the treatment of slurry storage facilities. The guidance was linked to the *Nitrate Pollutions Prevention Regulations*, which came into force on 1 January 2009. HMRC use the law as it applies in England and Wales to define a slurry storage system as including:

'● a slurry storage tank, whether above or below ground
● any reception pit and any effluent tank used in connection with the slurry storage tank
● any channels and pipes used in connection with the slurry storage tank, and reception pit or any effluent tank '

According to HMRC, a ' "slurry storage tank" includes a lagoon, pit (other than a reception pit) or tower used for the storage of slurry'.

HMRC accept that 'slurry storage systems located anywhere in the UK, which are used for the temporary storage of slurry, qualify as plant or machinery for the purposes of the capital allowances legislation'. By contrast, allowances will not be given for 'any building or structure which is part of a slurry storage facility'. This follows normal principles and, in interpreting the legislation, HMRC apply the principles of *Attwood v Anduff Car Wash Ltd* [1997] BTC 454 considered in detail at 260-260.

By way of illustration, HMRC have given an example of a slurry storage facility at a farm. The facility includes an above ground circular store, a reception pit and 'an open sided shed which provides shelter to the tank, preventing rainwater from falling into the store – the circular store is situated inside the shed'. HMRC state that:

'In this example the circular store and the reception pit are plant or machinery and qualify for capital allowances. Any channels or pipes associated with them also qualify. However, the shed is a structure and is therefore specifically excluded from being plant or machinery.'

As a general principle, the HMRC guidance states that:

'Officers of HMRC should, in general, accept claims for plant and machinery allowances in respect of slurry storage systems. Enquiries should be limited to significant claims for systems which appear to differ from the components described above, or facilities which include buildings or structures.'

Enhanced capital allowances

Enhanced allowances may be available for 'small scale slurry and sludge dewatering equipment': see 185-550.

Cross-references

The following headings from this A to Z Chapter may be relevant in particular cases where this type of expenditure is being considered. See also the Chapter headed 'Meaning of Plant', which begins at 180-000.

- Buildings (260-150)
- Land (261-300)
- Sewerage (262-460)
- Silage clamps (262-510)
- Structures (262-590)

262-540   Spare parts

Legislation: none

Cases: none

HMRC material: none

Commentary

Spare parts for items of plant or machinery will normally be part of the cost of repairing such plant or machinery and will not be capital in nature. As such, the expenditure will not qualify for capital allowances but a deduction will normally be available as part of the computation of trading profits.

In some circumstances, however, HMRC will require spare parts to be capitalised. They give as an example the case of an aircraft bought together with a spare engine and a set of spares, the whole thing being acquired as a single package. In this case, instructions to inspectors of taxes used to be to treat the whole cost as capital expenditure incurred on the provision of plant (old CA 1567). The circumstances in which HMRC would require such spare parts to be capitalised were when they are 'held more or less permanently on standby for substitution as and when required while repairs are being carried out on the parts replaced to make those parts replaced either fit for return to the original plant or machinery, or to be held on standby in their turn'.

The newer capital allowances manual is silent on the matter but it is not thought that there has been any change of practice.

Cross-references

The following heading from this A to Z Chapter may be relevant in particular cases where this type of expenditure is being considered. See also the Chapter headed 'Meaning of Plant', which begins at 180-000.

- Consumables (260-340)

262-550   Sports grounds (safety)

Legislation: CAA 2001, s. 27(1), (2), 30–32 and 63(5)

Cases: *Brown v Burnley Football and Athletic Co Limited* (1980) 53 TC 357

HMRC material: CA 21230, CA 22030, CA 22240–22260

Commentary

The 1994 legislation which is now broadly at CAA 2001, s. 21 and 22 does not apply to certain expenditure on safety at sports grounds (CAA 2001, s. 23(1) and (2)). Instead, such safety measures are governed by CAA 2001, s. 30–32 which provides relief in certain circumstances where no allowance or deduction would otherwise be due.

A number of specialist terms are introduced in CAA 2001, s. 30–32 with cross references to Part III of the *Fire Safety and Safety of Places of Sport Act* 1987 and to the *Safety of Sports Grounds Act* 1975.

The importance of this special legislation should not be missed. It is quite conceivable that works on a sports stadium will qualify as to 20–30 per cent under the 'ordinary' rules of what constitutes plant, and that at least as much again will qualify under these special rules.

Reference should always be made to the 'Green Guide' ('Guide to Safety at Sports Grounds') which is the bible for sports ground safety issues. The Guide is the product of years of research into the safety issues at sporting venues and in particular takes account of the lessons learnt from the Hillsborough tragedy of 1989, and from the Taylor report that followed that event.

The Guide has no direct statutory force but no sports stadium is likely to be issued with a safety certificate under the *Safety of Sports Grounds Act* 1975 or the *Fire Safety and Safety of Places of Sport Act* 1987 unless the recommendations of the Guide are followed rigorously. This therefore brings it directly into relevance as far as the *Capital Allowances Act* 2001 is concerned.

Many HMRC officers are not aware of the existence (never mind the significance) of the Guide and it may well be necessary to educate a local inspector to appreciate what is involved.

Plant and Machinery: A to Z

The extent of the Guide's significance can perhaps be appreciated from a comment in the HMRC manuals on the question of police control rooms which are considered in two different places in the HMRC manuals, at CA 21230 and again at CA 22240. The conclusion is that if the local authority take the view that they have the power to require the installation of a police control room under the provisions of the *Safety at Sports Grounds Act* 1975, then the expenditure will indeed qualify under CAA 2001, s. 30–32. This is so even though 'the construction of a building or structure does not normally qualify' under that section. This principle, if correctly understood and applied, can have a very wide application.

A number of other points are worthy of particular mention.

First, as a general observation, it is clear that if a claim is being made for expenditure not covered by these sections, it will have to satisfy the conditions of CAA 2001, s. 21–33 and of existing case law principles. In this respect, some caution needs to be taken with the *Burnley Football and Athletic* case, where the company failed to obtain capital allowances on the cost of the stand. See in this respect 180-400 for Revenue commentary in the light of that case.

The HMRC manuals (at CA 22240) make a specific point about seats and their covers. These cannot, in HMRC's opinion, be covered by the Local Authority Safety Certificate and therefore do not fall within the provisions of CAA 2001, s. 30–32. The manual goes on to say, however, that in any case 'expenditure on seats is likely to qualify as expenditure on plant in the normal way'.

Finally, it should be noted that the plant or machinery is deemed to belong to the person incurring the expenditure and thus satisfies one of the conditions needed for capital allowances to be due. Also, if there is any disposal then the value is taken to be nil (CAA 2001, s. 63(5)).

Cross-references

The following headings, mostly from this A to Z Chapter, may be relevant in particular cases where this type of expenditure is being considered. See also the Chapter headed 'Meaning of Plant', which begins at 180-000.

- Alterations to buildings (260-040)
- Buildings (260-150)
- Cameras (260-200)
- Demolition costs (260-510)
- Electrical installations and equipment (260-600)
- Fencing (260-700)
- Fire safety (see 160-500)
- Floodlighting (260-770)
- Football grounds (260-790)
- Professional fees and preliminary costs (262-240)
- Public address systems (262-250)
- Seats (262-440)

- Structures (262-590)
- Televisions and videos (262-730)
- Walls (262-910)

262-560   Stairs

Legislation: CAA 2001, s. 21 (List A, item 1)

Cases: *Wimpy International Ltd v Warland* [1989] BTC 58

HMRC material: CA 22010

Commentary

Stairs do not normally qualify as plant. They are precluded from so doing by CAA 2001, s. 21, List A, item 1.

The legislation in CAA 2001, s. 21 confirms the finding in the *Wimpy* case in which the company failed to obtain plant or machinery allowances on staircases.

It is worth bearing in mind that to be within table 1, the asset must be 'in or connected with the building' (CAA 2001, s. 21(3)(c)). It follows that if there is a staircase which is clearly not 'in or connected with' a building then it could still qualify as plant. It is possible, for example, that stairs which formed part of a theatrical stage might qualify. Another example might be outside stairs which lead not into a building but up to some outdoor feature, for example, a swimming pool.

The treatment of escalators follows that of lifts and is therefore dealt with under the heading of lifts, escalators and walkways at 261-320 above.

Cross-references

The following headings may be relevant in particular cases where this type of expenditure is being considered. See also the Chapter headed 'Meaning of Plant', which begins at 180-000.

- Buildings (260-150)
- Fire safety (see 160-500)
- Lifts, escalators and walkways (261-320)

262-570   Storage equipment

Legislation: CAA 2001, s. 23 (List C, item 4 and 28)

Cases: *Wimpy International Ltd v Warland* [1989] BTC 58 (item 16); *Hunt v Henry Quick Ltd* [1992] BTC 440; *King v Bridisco Ltd* [1992] BTC 440

HMRC material: CA 22030

Plant and Machinery: A to Z

Commentary

Storage equipment is specifically exempted from the provisions of CAA 2001, s. 21 and 22 (List C, item 4).

As such, it is to be considered on the basis of ordinary principles and case law decisions. In the *Wimpy* case, built-in storage units and dispensers were considered by the Revenue to be plant if they constituted equipment used for the purposes of the trade. Such equipment will normally qualify as plant.

Storage equipment can, of course, come in various guises. As far as mezzanine floors are concerned, see under floors and flooring materials at 260-780. As regards builders' huts used for storage purposes, see under temporary buildings at 262-740.

List C, item 28 provides an exemption from the provisions of CAA 2001, s. 21 and 22 for expenditure on 'the provision of silos provided for temporary storage, or on the provision of storage tanks'.

Cross-references

The following headings from this A to Z Chapter may be relevant in particular cases where this type of expenditure is being considered. See also the Chapter headed 'Meaning of Plant', which begins at 180-000.

- Buildings (260-150)
- Cold rooms (260-310)
- Counters and checkouts (260-360)
- Display equipment (260-530)
- Fixtures (260-760)
- Floors and flooring materials (260-780)
- Furniture and furnishings (260-820)
- Plant rooms (262-210)
- Shelves (262-470)
- Structures (262-590)
- Temporary buildings (262-740)
- Water supplies and water tanks (262-920)

262-590   Structures

Legislation: CAA 2001, s. 22 and 23 (List B, item 7, note 3 and List C generally)

Cases: *IR Commrs v Smyth* (1914) 3 KB 406; *Cardiff Rating Authority v Guest Keen Baldwin's Iron and Steel Co Ltd* (1949) 1 KB 385; *St John's School v Ward* (1974) 49 TC 524; *Dixon v Fitch's Garage Ltd* (1975) 50 TC 509; *Schofield v R & H Hall Ltd* (1975) 49 TC 538; *Benson v The Yard Arm Club Ltd* (1979) 53 TC 67; *Brown v Burnley Football and Athletic Co Limited* (1980) 53 TC 357; *IR Commrs v Scottish & Newcastle Breweries Ltd*

[1982] BTC 187; *Wimpy International Ltd v Warland* [1989] BTC 58; *Hunt v Henry Quick Ltd* [1992] BTC 440

HMRC material: CA 21230, CA 22050–22060, CA 31110

Commentary

Fixed structures do not qualify as plant (CAA 2001, s. 22(1) and (3)). The only exceptions are those items in List C at CAA 2001, s. 23 or otherwise exempted in CAA 2001, s. 22 or 23.

The question then arises of what is meant by a structure. For these purposes, HMRC still look to a definition provided in a 1914 case, that of *IR Commrs v Smyth*, in which the judge said that a structure 'is something which has been artificially erected or constructed and which is distinct from the earth surrounding it'. The HMRC manuals (at CA 31110) then include a lengthy quotation from the judgment in that case. Elsewhere, HMRC have defined a structure as 'any substantial man-made asset'.

For IBA purposes, it will be beneficial to demonstrate that an asset is a structure. For the purposes of claiming allowances on plant and machinery, on the other hand, it will generally be necessary to demonstrate that an asset does not come within that definition. However, it will be to no avail if an asset is shown not to be a structure but the expenditure on it is nevertheless on the acquisition of an interest in land. In such a case, allowances would still be prohibited by virtue of CAA 2001, s. 24.

One point that is important to notice is that a structure does not come within the prohibitions of CAA 2001, s. 22 unless it is fixed. This is because of the definition given in subs. 3(a) which says that a structure means 'a fixed structure of any kind, other than a building'. Any item that is moveable is therefore not a structure for those purposes. Where an asset is within List C at CAA 2001, s. 23 then it does not follow that it necessarily qualifies as plant. It does mean, however, that it can be considered on ordinary principles including established case law. Thus, the possible exemptions include dry docks, towers, supporting floodlights, silos and a variety of other assets. The HMRC manuals (at CA 22050) contain the following paragraph:

> 'The cases where a structure was held to be plant show that a building or structure can be plant if and only if it is apparatus for carrying on the business or employed in the business rather than being the premises or place in which the business is carried on.'

It is the author's opinion that this interpretation is not quite correct. The words 'rather than' are too much in HMRC's favour. If an asset functions both as the apparatus and as the premises then the case law principles would suggest that it can qualify as plant. For a more detailed discussion of the issues involved, see the Chapter headed 'Meaning of Plant', which begins at 180-000.

Plant and Machinery: A to Z

Cross-references

Many of the other categories listed in this A to Z Chapter may need to be individually considered. See, for example, the special rules relating to greenhouses (260-950) on the one hand or security systems (262-450) on the other.

262-600   Swimming pools

Legislation: CAA 2001, s. 23 (List C, item 16)

Cases: *Cooke v Beach Station Caravans Ltd* (1974) 49 TC 514; *Boys' and Girls' Welfare Society* (MAN/96/1041 15274) (a VAT case)

HMRC material: CA 22050–22060

Commentary

Although a swimming pool is arguably a structure, it is specifically outside the scope of CAA 2001, s. 22. CAA 2001, s. 23, List C, item 16 excludes from those provisions 'swimming pools (including diving boards, slides and structures on which such boards or slides are mounted) '.

It follows from this that a swimming pool can be considered on its own merits in the light of general case law principles. The only direct tax case that has specifically considered whether or not a swimming pool should qualify as plant is that of *Cooke v Beach Station Caravans*. In that case, the judge held that the pools were 'part of the means whereby the trade is carried on, and not merely the place at which it is carried on'. The two pools in that case had the function of providing 'pleasurable and safe buoyancy'.

HMRC accept that swimming pools will qualify as plant where they are provided for the trades of 'hotelier, caravan park operator, holiday camp operator, etc' (CA 22060). Qualifying expenditure will include the cost of excavation as well as the pool construction and any terracing.

HMRC view is that the cost of changing rooms and sun lounges has to be excluded. This is probably correct, although it should be possible to isolate part of the expenditure on such rooms as being on plant. Where the pool is an indoor pool then the HMRC view is that the building housing the pool is not plant. This would also appear to be correct, but see the comments immediately below about insulation materials.

Anybody arguing with HMRC on the application of the *Beach Station Caravans* case would do well to have a look too at the *Welfare Society* case heard by a VAT Tribunal and reported in March 1998. The case concerned the installation of a hydrotherapy pool and was concerned with the issue of whether the pool could be described as 'equipment or appliances'. The VAT legislation is very different and the facts of the case were specific, the pool having been designed quite clearly for use by handicapped people. The Tribunal found that 'the pool itself (including the adjacent pedestrian area used for access to the water) and the environmental control system form in our view an integral piece of equipment for use by the handicapped'. It is also interesting to note the Tribunal's comment on the building within which the pool was housed: 'We draw a distinction between on the one hand the structural walls of the building, with their cavity filling and on the other hand the applied thermal and acoustic lining round the walls of the pool room, which we regard as part of the pool installation itself.'

Cross-references

The following headings from this A to Z Chapter may be relevant in particular cases where this type of expenditure is being considered. See also the Chapter headed 'Meaning of Plant', which begins at 180-000.

- Amusement parks (260-050)
- Caravans and caravan sites (260-230)
- Entertaining-related expenditure (260-630)
- Structures (262-590)

262-700   Taxi licence plates

Legislation: none

Cases: none directly relevant but see *Lyon v Pettigrew* [1985] BTC 168 (a CGT case) for related issues

HMRC material: CA 21250

Commentary

In considering the tax treatment of a taxi licence plate, a distinction has to be made between the physical asset (the plate itself) and the right conferred by ownership of that asset (ie the right to operate a taxi). The former is an item of plant but the latter is not.

In practice, this means that only a nominal amount of the cost will qualify as plant (CA 21250).

Cross-references

The following headings from this A to Z Chapter may be relevant in particular cases where this type of expenditure is being considered. See also the Chapter headed 'Meaning of Plant', which begins at 180-000.

- Cars (260-240)
- Number plates (262-100)
- Spare parts (262-540)

Plant and Machinery: A to Z

262-710 Telecommunication systems

Legislation: CAA 2001, s. 22 (List B, item 7(c)), 23 (List C, item 8)

Cases: none

HMRC material: CA 22030, CA 23130

Commentary

Amongst the items unaffected by the legislation in CAA 2001, s. 21 and 22 are 'computer, telecommunication and surveillance systems (including their wiring or other links)' (item 8 in List C in CAA 2001, s. 23).

Such items will normally qualify as plant.

CAA 2001, s. 22, List B, item 7(c) makes it clear that structures used for the provision of telecommunication, television or radio services are not caught by the provisions of CAA 2001, s. 22. As such, they are to be considered on their own merits based on case law principles.

Cross-references

The following headings from this A to Z Chapter may be relevant in particular cases where this type of expenditure is being considered. See also the Chapter headed 'Meaning of Plant', which begins at 180-000.

- Alterations to buildings (260-040)
- Buildings (260-150)
- Electrical installations and equipment (260-600)
- Public address systems (262-250)
- Software (260-330)
- Telephones and fax machines (262-720)
- Televisions and videos (262-730)

262-720 Telephones and fax machines

Legislation: CAA 2001, s. 23 (List C, item 8)

Cases: *Hampton v Fortes Autogrill Ltd* (1980) 53 TC 691; *Cole Brothers Ltd v Phillips* [1982] BTC 208

HMRC material: CA 21180–21200, CA 21230

Commentary

These clearly qualify as plant.

Similarly, the cost of wiring for such items will qualify. Under the heading of 'electrical installations' HMRC instructions tell inspectors to accept as plant 'wiring, control panels and other equipment installed specifically to supply equipment which is plant or machinery' (CA 21180).

In the *Cole Brothers* case, the trunking for the telephone system (costing over £60,000) was accepted by the Revenue as plant.

The following Revenue instruction to inspectors (CA 21200) is helpful in relation to costs associated with the installation of telephone systems:

> 'If you receive a capital allowance claim for an underground cable system (including television, telecommunications, or electricity supply systems) the costs of installing the cables will include the costs of excavating the land and providing ducting that houses the cables. The cabling and the ducting may be recognised as separate components of the asset in the claimant's accounts (so that they are depreciated at different rates). Where the ducting is installed as a direct incident of the installation of the cabling, the costs of the ducting and the associated excavation are, for capital allowance purposes, part of the costs incurred on the provision of the cabling regardless of the treatment in the accounts.'

The HMRC manuals recognise a specific set of circumstances in which a farmer may contribute towards the cost of a telephone installation where a railway crosses farmland. The manuals confirm that if the farmer makes a contribution towards such installation costs he is to be given capital allowances on his contribution as being expenditure on plant or machinery.

Cross-references

The following headings from this A to Z Chapter may be relevant in particular cases where this type of expenditure is being considered. See also the Chapter headed 'Meaning of Plant', which begins at 180-000.

- Electrical installations and equipment (260-600)
- Public address systems (262-250)
- Telecommunication systems (262-710)
- Televisions and videos (262-730)

262-730   Televisions and videos

Legislation: none

Cases: *Cole Brothers Ltd v Phillips* [1982] BTC 208; *Salt v Golding* (1996) Sp C 81

HMRC material: CA 21200–21230; Press Release 15 March 1984

Commentary

As long as they are used for the purposes of a qualifying activity, televisions and videos should normally qualify without problem as plant and machinery. In the *Salt v Golding* special commissioners' case, it had been accepted that they would so qualify but the appellant was (unsuccessfully) claiming scientific research allowances on them so as to obtain a faster rate of tax relief.

As always, it is necessary to look not only at the nature of the item itself but also at its function within any particular business. A slight note of caution was sounded in this respect in the *Cole Brothers* case. In the High Court, Justice Vinelott commented that 'the courts may yet have to consider whether expenditure on the provision of enticing amenities – for instance, piped music or television to entertain customers whilst their cars are filled with petrol or washed ... can be said to be expenditure on the provision of plant'.

In the ordinary way, however, where such items are used for security purposes, for training purposes or in other circumstances where they are clearly functioning as apparatus within the trade, there should be no doubt about the availability of plant or machinery allowances.

Where cable television is installed, the Revenue manuals used to accept explicitly that the entire cable network should be treated as a single entity qualifying for capital allowances as plant or machinery, including the costs of any plastic ducting which contains the actual cables (old CA 1575). The HMRC manuals no longer contain such an explicit statement, but further detail of this aspect was given in a Revenue press release on 15 March 1984. In that press release, the Revenue accepted, following Counsel's advice, that the full cost of cable systems would be allowed as expenditure on the provision of plant or machinery, including even the cost of cutting and covering trenches in which the cable ducting is to be laid in the ground.

Cross-references

The following headings from this A to Z Chapter may be relevant in particular cases where this type of expenditure is being considered. See also the Chapter headed 'Meaning of Plant', which begins at 180-000.

- Electrical installations and equipment (260-600)
- Telecommunication systems (262-710)
- Telephones and fax machines (262-720)

262-740   Temporary buildings

Legislation: CAA 2001, s. 21, 23 (List C, items 20 and 21 (and possibly other items))

Cases: *O'Srianian v Lakeview Limited* [1984] TL(I) 125; *Attwood v Anduff Car Wash Ltd* [1997] BTC 454; *St John's School v Ward* (1974) 49 TC 524

HMRC material: CA 22110

Commentary

This is an important category which arises quite frequently in practice and where the amounts of expenditure involved can be substantial.

The starting treatment is now in CAA 2001, s. 21(1) which states that expenditure on the provision of plant or machinery does not include any expenditure on the provision of a building. A temporary building is nonetheless a building and so, on first principles, cannot qualify as plant.

However, CAA 2001, s. 23, List C, item 21 says that the exclusion of buildings does not apply 'to any moveable building intended to be moved in the course of the qualifying activity'. For such moveable buildings, therefore, it is necessary to look at general principles, including those established in case law.

There is one leading case on the subject of temporary buildings, that of *St John's School v Ward*. The school failed in its appeal to the High Court and to the Court of Appeal. The judge said that 'at first blush and at last blush the laboratory and gymnasium appear to me to be buildings or premises and not plant'. He concluded that 'education is not carried out with these particular buildings but in these particular buildings'.

On the basis of the *St John's School* case, the HMRC view is that 'prefabricated buildings are not plant even if they can be taken down and re-erected somewhere else'. The only exception recognised by HMRC is for builders' huts. Inspectors are instructed to treat such huts as plant if they 'are moved from one site to another and used by builders and contractors to provide canteen and toilet facilities or as storage sheds' (CA 22110).

Ignoring the treatment of builders' huts, can HMRC justify their view that prefabricated buildings are not plant 'even if they can be taken down and re-erected somewhere else'? There is clearly an analogy here with the partitions which were held to qualify as plant in the *John Good & Sons* case (see 262-200). In the *St John's School* case, however, counsel for the school had given evidence that the layout of the gymnasium and laboratory, which were the temporary buildings concerned, could be changed by rearranging some panels, 'for example, division of the laboratory space so as to produce two separate laboratories might be carried out by three inexperienced persons in four days'. The reaction of the judge was to ask 'So what?'. He explained, the fact that:

> 'a building can be taken down by inexperienced workmen and put up in a different way, or that the interior can be changed from two small rooms to one large one, or something of that kind, does not seem to me to alter the basic question of what is the structure, and if the structure is a building or premises it remains a building or premises.'

In summary, the position is somewhat tantalising. The legislation at CAA 2001, s. 23 recognises that a building that is moveable and intended to be moved may possibly qualify as plant. Case law is not generally favourable, though the *John Good & Sons* case provides a chink of light. With the exception of huts used by builders, HMRC seem set against allowing as plant any temporary buildings even if they are genuinely moved for the purposes

Plant and Machinery: A to Z

of the trade. Nevertheless, there must in some trades be instances of buildings being used in a way that is broadly analogous to the use by builders of their huts. It may well be that, in such cases, a claim for treatment as plant could be properly justified. An example might be the use of temporary public toilet facilities, as, for example, at sporting and similar events.

List C, item 20 specifically exempts 'buildings provided for testing aircraft engines run within the buildings' from the CAA 2001, s. 21 provisions. Such aircraft buildings would therefore need to be considered on ordinary case law principles.

Cross-references

The following headings from this A to Z Chapter may be relevant in particular cases where this type of expenditure is being considered. See also the Chapter headed 'Meaning of Plant', which begins at 180-000.

- Buildings (260-150)
- Caravans and caravan sites (260-230)
- Structures (262-590)

262-780   Tunnels

Legislation: CAA 2001, s. 22 (List B, item 1), 23 (List C, item 25)

Cases: none

HMRC material: none

Commentary

Tunnels do not qualify as plant. Together with bridges, viaducts, aqueducts, embankments and cuttings, they are classified as structures by CAA 2001, s. 22, which means that they are unable to qualify.

The only exception, provided by List C, item 25, is for expenditure on 'the provision of pipelines or underground ducts or tunnels with a primary purpose of carrying utility conduits'.

Cross-references

The following headings from this A to Z Chapter may be relevant in particular cases where this type of expenditure is being considered. See also the Chapter headed 'Meaning of Plant', which begins at 180-000.

- Car parks (260-250)
- Roads, etc (262-320)
- Structures (262-590)

262-900   Wallpaper designs and pattern books

Legislation: none

Cases: *Rose & Co (Wallpaper & Paints) Ltd v Campbell* (1968) 44 TC 500; *McVeigh v Arthur Sanderson & Sons Limited* (1969) 45 TC 273

HMRC material: none

Commentary

In the *Rose & Co* case, the company created wallpaper pattern books which were successful in generating wallpaper sales. It was held that these books were not plant. The reason for this was that the expenditure was not considered to be capital in nature. The judge felt that this view, taken by the commissioners, was reasonable.

The *Arthur Sanderson* case was rather different, involving expenditure incurred in producing or acquiring designs for use in manufacturing wallpaper. The Revenue conceded that the expenditure in that case was capital in nature but there was disagreement over whether it was plant. Various issues were conceded by the Revenue so the remaining point in dispute was the expenditure on the acquisition of designs. The Revenue argued that no part of the design costs should be allowed but this was rejected by the judge who therefore decided in favour of the company.

Cross-references

The following headings from this A to Z Chapter may be relevant in particular cases where this type of expenditure is being considered. See also the Chapter headed 'Meaning of Plant', which begins at 180-000.

- Books (260-110)
- Consumables (260-340)
- Designs and patterns (260-520)

262-910   Walls

Legislation: CAA 2001, s. 21 (List A, items 1 and 5), 22 (List B, item 6), 23 (List C, items 7, 12 and 13)

Cases: *Wangaratta Woollen Mills v Commissioner of Taxation of the Commonwealth of Australia* (1969) 43 ALJR 324; *Wimpy International Ltd v Warland* [1989] BTC 58 (items 2, 17, 19)

HMRC material: CA 22220, CA 22270

Plant and Machinery: A to Z

Commentary

In the ordinary way, a wall will be part of the building and will not qualify as plant. This is clearly true on ordinary case law principles and is reinforced by List A, item 2, at CAA 2001, s. 21. Sea walls are similarly excluded by virtue of List B, item 6.

Where the wall forms part of a shaft or other structure for a lift, escalator, etc then the prohibition is under table 1, column 1, item E.

There are certain exceptions listed in List C at CAA 2001, s. 23. These concern sound insulation which is provided mainly to meet the particular requirements of the trade, a wall which forms part of a strongroom in a bank or building society premises or a partition wall in certain circumstances. For this last item, see under partitions (moveable) at 262-200.

None of the exemptions mentioned in the paragraph above apply if the purpose of the asset is to provide an interior wall which is intended to remain permanently in place (CAA 2001, s. 23(4)).

Where the exemptions do apply, it is necessary to consider whether the wall should qualify as plant on ordinary principles and on the basis of established case law. In the *Wimpy* case, wall tiles were not allowed as plant but wall panels were accepted, even though the commissioners felt they were 'near the borderline'. It had been accepted as a fact that the wall panels were provided mainly to create a suitable environment for the trade. In most cases, the panels were removable.

The HMRC manuals comment on two specific instances in relation to walls. First, expenditure on cavity wall filling is to be treated as expenditure on thermal insulation and so will qualify as plant if the building is within the definition of an industrial building or structure (but for expenditure incurred from 1 or 6 April 2008, the *Finance Act* 2008 removed the requirement that the building should be an industrial building). In this respect, see under insulation at 261-110 (CA 22220).

Second, the manuals make it clear that a wall may qualify as a security asset. For details of this category of expenditure, see under security systems at 262-450.

Cross-references

The following headings from this A to Z Chapter may be relevant in particular cases where this type of expenditure is being considered. See also the Chapter headed 'Meaning of Plant', which begins at 180-000.

- Advertising hoardings (260-010)
- Alterations to buildings (260-040)
- Buildings (260-150)
- Ceilings and canopies (260-280)
- Demolition costs (260-510)
- Doors (260-550)

- Fencing (260-700)
- Gates (260-920)
- Lifts, escalators and walkways (261-320)
- Panelling (262-150)
- Partitions (moveable) (262-200)
- Professional fees and preliminary costs (262-240)
- Screens (262-430)
- Shop fronts (262-490)
- Structures (262-590)
- Windows (262-960)

262-920 Water supplies and water tanks

Legislation: CAA 2001, s. 21 (List A, item 2), 23 (List C, former items 2 and 3), 33A

Cases: *Margrett v Lowestoft Water & Gas Company* (1935) 19 TC 481; *Cattermole v Corporation of Reigate* (1941) 24 TC 359; *IR Commrs v Barclay, Curle and Co Ltd* (1969) 45 TC 221; *Cole Brothers Ltd v Phillips* [1982] BTC 208; *Wimpy International Ltd v Warland* [1989] BTC 58 (item 10)

HMRC material: CA 21180–21200, CA 21230, CA 22100

Commentary

This is an important topic which arises frequently in practice.

The starting point is found in CAA 2001, s. 21. List A item 2 says that 'mains services, and systems, for water, electricity and gas' are to be included in the expression 'building' and that such items therefore fail to qualify as plant unless they are within exemptions listed in CAA 2001, s. 23, now including integral features (discussed in depth at 247-000ff.). This is on the assumption that the assets concerned are 'in, or connected with' the building (CAA 2001, s. 21(3)(c)).

For expenditure incurred before April 2008, the main CAA 2001, s. 23 exemption was for water systems that are either provided mainly to meet the particular requirements of the qualifying activity or are provided to serve particular plant or machinery used for the purposes of the qualifying activity. This exemption, at item 2 of List C, was withdrawn from April 2008. Water heating systems were also specifically exempted (at item 3) but once more that exemption has now disappeared. Both cold water systems and water heating systems now attract plant and machinery allowances on the grounds that they specifically qualify as integral features.

The tax treatment of water supplies mirrors very closely that of electrical installations and it would be advisable to refer to the section on electrical installations and equipment at 260-600. As in that case, one issue to consider would be what HMRC call the 'entity' test. It is necessary to decide whether a water system should be treated as a single functioning item of plant or whether it needs to be broken down into its component parts and each part considered separately. The HMRC view is that 'most cold-water systems, etc should not be looked at as a single entity' and so inspectors are instructed to adopt a piecemeal approach (CA 21180). This instruction, though, predated the integral features rules, which give a different slant to the whole question of whether an entity should be looked at as a whole or as a collection of individual parts.

In practice, HMRC made a distinction before April 2008 between hot-water systems (allowable – see CA 21200) and cold-water systems, the cost of which was not normally allowed unless they were specific to the trade. This treatment was referred to in the *Cole Brothers* case, where counsel for the company commented on:

> 'the Crown's practice based on the views expressed by the courts over the years whereby, for example, expenditure on cold-water piping is regarded as part of the cost of the building and therefore as not qualifying for capital allowances, while relief was given on the cost of apparatus to provide hot water and central heating and of all hot water pipes.'

This distinction is of no continuing relevance, however – the *Finance Act* 2008 removed both items 2 and 3 from List C, respectively covering (inter alia) cold water systems that were trade-specific and hot water systems generally. In both cases, relief would be due now under the integral features provisions only.

In the *Lowestoft Water & Gas Company* case it was held that a tower supporting a water tank was a structure and was therefore not plant. However, this view was considered incorrect in the *Barclay, Curle* decision, in which one of the judges in the House of Lords commented, 'the tank certainly was plant, and if the cost of the foundations necessary to support plant at ground level is part of the costs of the plant, then I think that this tower must be treated in the same way as foundations below ground level'. Again, in *St John's School v Ward* (1974) 49 TC 524, the treatment of a water tank as plant was confirmed. It was in the *Wimpy* case, however, that the most specific consideration was given to the treatment of cold-water tanks, two 500-gallon tanks having been installed at the insistence of the water authority. The need for the tanks arose specifically because there was a perception that there would be a high demand for water because of the nature of the trade. The commissioners were confident in their view that the tanks were to be treated as part of the apparatus used in the company's trade: 'Water pipes are to be judged on the same basis as electric wiring. In so far as the installations which they serve are plant they too are plant. But if they form part of a general water supply such as any occupier would need they are not.'

The commissioners reached a similar view in the case that was heard alongside *Wimpy*, that of *Associated Restaurants Limited v Warland*:

> 'As a general principle we think that if [the company] installs water tanks of a size or description which is specifically related to the conduct of its trade they could properly be regarded as apparatus of the trade and qualify as plant but if they are tanks such as any occupier of the premises would use they should be regarded as part of the reticulation of central services and not plant.'

The HMRC manuals are silent on the tax treatment of a water-storage tank, other than in the very different context of an investigation where inspectors are instructed to be on the lookout for the 'water-storage tank' that turns out to be a swimming pool (EM 2022)! It seems clear, however, that such tanks would now at least qualify as part of the 'cold water system' so as to qualify for allowances as integral features.

Cross-references

The following headings, mostly from this A to Z Chapter, may be relevant in particular cases where this type of expenditure is being considered. See also the Chapter headed 'Meaning of Plant', which begins at 180-000 and the commentary on 'integral features' beginning at 247-000ff.

- Alterations to buildings (260-040)
- Buildings (260-150)
- Electrical installations and equipment (260-600)
- Fire safety (see 160-500)
- Reservoirs, etc (262-310)
- Sewerage (262-460)
- Structures (262-590)
- Water towers (262-940)

262-940   Water towers

Legislation: CAA 2001, s. 22 and 23 (List C, items 27 and 28)

Cases: *Margrett v Lowestoft Water & Gas Company* (1935) 19 TC 481 (but see also *IR Commrs v Barclay, Curle and Co Ltd* (1969) 45 TC 221)

HMRC material: none

Commentary

The question of whether a water tower can qualify as plant has caused much agonising in the courts. In the *Lowestoft Water & Gas Company* case heard in the 1930s, the judge overruled the decision of the commissioners and decided that the water tower could not qualify as plant. The case was the subject of much debate in the *Barclay, Curle* case heard in 1969. Whilst there was not unanimity, a majority in the House of Lords in the *Barclay, Curle* case decided that the *Lowestoft Water & Gas Company* decision had been wrong and the water tower should indeed have qualified as plant. As Lord Guest put it: 'the water tower came within the definition of ... "apparatus" used for the purpose of the business of supplier of water. It was the harnessing of the natural element of gravity ... to perform a trade function.'

Now, however, we also have to consider the effect of CAA 2001, s. 22, which says that a structure is not to qualify as plant or machinery unless it is within one of the exemptions in

CAA 2001, s. 23. List C, item 27, provides a glimmer of help, offering an exemption for 'expenditure on the provision of silos provided for temporary storage, or storage tanks'. The term 'storage tank' would not appear to be a comfortable description of a water tower. Item 27 provides a possible reprieve for a 'reservoir incorporated into a water treatment works' and for a service reservoir for treated water used to supply a housing estate 'or other particular locality'. None of these possible exemptions would clearly apply to a water tower. The HMRC manuals provide no guidance either way.

Cross-references

The following headings from this A to Z Chapter may be relevant in particular cases where this type of expenditure is being considered. See also the Chapter headed 'Meaning of Plant', which begins at 180-000.

- Buildings (260-150)
- Sewerage (262-460)
- Structures (262-590)
- Water supplies and water tanks (262-920)

262-950   Windmills

Legislation: CAA 2001, s. 21–23

Cases: *Cardiff Rating Authority v Guest Keen Baldwin's Iron & Steel Co Ltd* (1949) 1 KB 385; *Dixon v Fitch's Garage Ltd* (1975) 50 TC 509; *IR Commrs v Scottish & Newcastle Breweries Ltd* [1982] BTC 187

HMRC material: none

Commentary

There is authority from a non-tax case to treat a windmill as a structure. In *Cardiff Rating Authority v Guest Keen Baldwin's Iron & Steel Co*, Lord Denning defined a structure as:

> 'something of substantial size which is built up from component parts and intended to remain permanently on a permanent foundation; but it is still a structure even though some of its parts may be moveable, as, for instance, about a pivot. Thus, a windmill or a turntable is a structure.'

As a structure, it would appear at first glance that no capital allowances can be due on a windmill as plant. Item 7 of List B of CAA 2001, s. 23 catches 'any structure' not caught under a more specific provision. However, CAA 2001, s. 22 is subject to List C at CAA 2001, s. 23 (CAA 2001, s. 22(4)). This raises the question, therefore, of whether a windmill could be said to be 'machinery (including devices for providing motive power)'. It is the author's view that a windmill would be said to come within this definition of machinery. If this view is correct then there is nothing within either table of CAA 2001, s. 21 or 22 to prevent a windmill from qualifying as plant.

Given that there are no direct case law precedents, it would then be necessary to consider whether a windmill would qualify as plant on ordinary principles. Again, the author's view would be that it could indeed so qualify, particularly if it is still being used as a windmill rather than as a tourist attraction.

There is one possible complication. In the *Scottish & Newcastle Breweries* case, Lord Lowry was considering the precedent provided by *The Yard Arm Club* case in which a ship used as a restaurant was held not to be plant. Lord Lowry commented that:

> 'the ship, with all its novelty and atmosphere, could no more be called plant then a restaurant consisting of an Elizabethan manor house, a thatched cottage, a barn or a converted windmill, although like all those buildings, it could be embellished and adorned with "plant" suitable to the surroundings and to the purposes of the trade.'

It would not appear, however, that that case presents any particular problems for the treatment of a windmill if it is genuinely being used as such. What it may well mean, however, is that a windmill that has become a tourist attraction but no longer functions actively as a windmill may no longer qualify.

Cross-references

The following headings from this A to Z Chapter may be relevant in particular cases where this type of expenditure is being considered. See also the Chapter headed 'Meaning of Plant', which begins at 180-000.

- Buildings (260-150)
- Structures (262-590)

262-960   Windows

Legislation: CAA 2001, s. 21 (List A, item 1)

Cases: *Cole Brothers Ltd v Phillips* [1982] BTC 208

HMRC material: CA 22010, CA 22220, CA 22270

Commentary

Normally, windows do not qualify as plant. This is because they are included in the expression 'building', per CAA 2001, s. 21 (List A, item 1).

Window panels, lighting and sockets were allowed by the special commissioners in the *Cole Brothers* case and the Crown did not appeal against the treatment of those items.

Double glazing may qualify under CAA 2001, s. 28 (thermal insulation of a building – see 261-110): 'double glazing may be installed to insulate against both noise and loss of heat. The expenditure will qualify under s. 28 provided that it is clear that insulation against loss of heat is one of the reasons for its being incurred' (CA 22220).

Plant and Machinery: A to Z

Reinforced windows may qualify as a security asset under CAA 2001, s. 33. This is confirmed in the HMRC manuals at CA 22270. As regards security assets generally, see 262-450.

Cross-references

The following headings, mostly from this A to Z Chapter, may be relevant in particular cases where this type of expenditure is being considered. See also the Chapter headed 'Meaning of Plant', which begins at 180-000.

- Buildings (260-150)
- Display equipment (¶260-530)
- Fire safety (see 160-500)
- Partitions (moveable) (262-200)
- Screens (262-430)
- Security systems (262-450)
- Shutters (262-500)

263-000 Zoo cages

Legislation: CAA 2001, s. 23 (List C, item 33)

Cases: *Carr v Sayer* [1992] BTC 286

HMRC material: CA 22030

Commentary

Although a zoo cage may well be a structure (and therefore potentially caught by CAA 2001, s. 22), any expenditure on the provision of fixed zoo cages is saved by the provisions of CAA 2001, s. 23 (List C, item 33).

It is not clear to the author what triggered this particular exemption. There is no case law concerning zoo cages.

Zoo cages come in many varieties and each case will need to be considered on its merits. Factors that may assist a claim would include the following:

(1) Smaller, more mobile cages will be more in the nature of plant than larger, permanent ones. If they are mobile, they fall outside the definition of 'structure' which is defined to be a *fixed* structure (CAA 2001, s. 22(3)).

(2) Any features that have a function beyond that of providing shelter from the elements should be emphasised. This may include security mechanisms or display features.

An essential quality of zoo cages is that, in addition to housing animals, etc they have the function of displaying them safely to the public. This distinguishes them from, for example, the quarantine kennels in the *Carr v Sayer* case, a distinction brought out specifically in the HMRC manuals at CA 22030.

Cross-references

The following headings from this A to Z Chapter may be relevant in particular cases where this type of expenditure is being considered. See also the Chapter headed 'Meaning of Plant', which begins at 180-000.

- Animals (260-060)
- Buildings (260-150)
- Security systems (262-450)
- Structures (262-590)
- Temporary buildings (262-740)

INDUSTRIAL BUILDINGS ALLOWANCES

Introduction and general principles

300-000   Industrial buildings allowances: overview

The IBA rules give tax relief for the cost of construction of factories and certain other industrial buildings. The mechanism was in the past to give relief for the cost over a 25-year period. However, the allowances are now being phased out and their real value is far less significant than it used to be.

Phasing out of allowances

In a wholly unexpected announcement in the March 2007 Budget, the Chancellor announced that IBAs (and ABAs – see 425-000ff.) were to be phased out over a four-year period. According to the *Explanatory Notes* accompanying the subsequent Finance Bill 2007, the allowances 'are to be withdrawn because they are anachronistic and poorly targeted'. Thus a form of tax relief that dates back, effectively, at least as far as the 1919 Finance Act is now perceived to have served its purpose. Legislation in the *Finance Act* 2008 confirms that the IBA legislation ceases to apply in relation to expenditure incurred from 1 April 2011 (for corporation tax purposes) or 6 April 2011 (for income tax), and that the value of the allowances is to be phased out over the years leading up to their final abolition. This is achieved by reducing the value of the allowances by 25 per cent in 2008–09 (or for the financial year beginning on 1 April 2008 (FY 2008)) 50 per cent in 2009–10 (or FY 2009); and 75 per cent in 2010–11 (or FY 2010). As explained in the 2007 *Explanatory Notes*, 'expressing the transitional provisions in this manner also caters for the phasing-out in the case of recalculated allowances on a sale or acquisition'.

The *Finance Act* 2007 contained provisions that applied for most disposals made from 21 March 2007 and that prevented from that date the making of any balancing adjustments on disposals of industrial buildings (with the exception of disposals of buildings in enterprise zones). Details are given below at 305-200ff. and the transitional arrangements are considered at 305-225.

Legislation: FA 2007, s. 36

Capital gains

Normally, the giving of IBAs does not have any bearing on any capital gains tax (CGT) computations, or on the calculation of a capital gain for corporation tax purposes, except that a CGT loss may be restricted where IBAs have been given (see 310-550).

Previous and transitional rules

Before the changes referred to above started to apply, allowances were given at four per cent on a straight line basis, but at a different rate for a subsequent owner. The law was very much more complex when a building was sold within 25 years of first use:

- if it was sold at a profit, the owner would typically suffer a balancing charge at the point of sale to claw back any tax relief that had been given in earlier years;
- no such balancing adjustment was normally made, however, more than 25 years after the date on which the building was first used;
- this provided some important tax planning considerations. The grant of a long lease, for example, was not treated as a sale and so did not produce a balancing adjustment, though the parties were able to elect for alternative treatment;
- a person selling the factory, etc at a loss within that 25-year period would normally have obtained tax relief for that loss, but adjusted for periods during which the building did not qualify;
- a subsequent buyer, if he continued to use the building for qualifying purposes, could obtain relief for the balance of the original expenditure; and
- the rules had some odd results in practice, not least in the way that the purchaser of a used building was treated. A person buying a building that was nearly 25 years old, for example, would often enjoy a very rapid rate of tax relief.

All of this has now changed.

300-100   Conditions for obtaining IBAs

The three main conditions that need to be met if IBAs are to be obtained are as follows, and these conditions remain true during the four year run-off period before IBAs are finally withdrawn:

(1)   expenditure must be incurred on the construction of a building or structure.

This is considered in depth at 300-500 but the key principle is to note that IBAs are generally given on construction expenditure, not necessarily on the amount paid to buy a building. The treatment of expenditure on buying an existing building is addressed at 305-200;

(2)   the building must either be in use for a qualifying trade (see 301-500) or fall within one of the following definitions:

(a)   a qualifying hotel (see 315-000);
(b)   a qualifying sports pavilion (see 315-500); or
(c)   a commercial building or structure in relation to qualifying enterprise zone expenditure (see 320-000).

The term 'industrial building' is specifically defined as any building or structure that is in use for the purposes of a qualifying trade or that falls within one of these other three listed categories.

Buildings outside the UK are excluded unless the profits of the trade for which the building is used are assessable in accordance with the rules that apply to calculate trading profits for income tax or corporation tax purposes.

Certain trades that would qualify on first principles are specifically excluded (see 302-600).

Certain roads on industrial estates are treated as if they were industrial buildings (see 300-650);

(3)   the expenditure must be 'qualifying expenditure' (see 304-000).

No allowances are due unless a claim is made in a tax return (see 101-000).

To determine who is entitled to any allowances, it is necessary to identify the person with the 'relevant interest' in the building (see 304-500).

Legislation: CAA 2001, s. 271, 282

Other material: CA 32850

300-150   Exclusion of double allowances

To the three conditions numbered above can be added the fact that no double allowances may be claimed. Specifically, no IBAs can be claimed on any expenditure that has qualified for:

- agricultural buildings allowances (see 425-000);
- assured tenancies allowances (see 625-000);
- dredging allowances (see 600-000);
- flat conversion allowances (see 475-000);
- mineral extraction allowances (see 500-000);
- plant and machinery allowances (see 150-000);
- research and development allowances (see 525-000); or
- scientific research allowances (see 525-000).

Sometimes, a taxpayer will be able to choose between two types of allowance. For example, a cold store may qualify under either the IBA rules or as plant or machinery. Once the choice has been made, HMRC will not allow the taxpayer to switch in later years. Such choices therefore need careful consideration, taking account (for example) of the possible effects of the long-life asset rules (for certain plant and machinery) and of the different treatments of disposals of assets under the two regimes (including, for example, the fact that there can now be no balancing charge under the IBA regime). It is also now necessary, of course, to take account of the gradual withdrawal of IBAs such that no further allowances will be given from 1 April 2011.

Legislation: CAA 2001, s. 7

Other material: CA 31800

Giving effect to allowances and charges

300-200   Overview

The legislation identifies four sets of rules to determine how allowances are to be given or balancing charges made, as follows:

- for trades;
- for lessors and licensors;
- for buildings temporarily out of use; and
- for buildings for miners, etc – carrying back balancing allowances.

There is a general rule that, for income tax purposes, allowances and charges are to be given effect in calculating income for a chargeable period. For corporation tax purposes, they are to be taken into account in calculating profits for a chargeable period.

The length of a chargeable period does not affect the amount of any initial allowance (or, before their abolition, the amount of any balancing allowance or balancing charge) but it may affect the amount of any writing-down allowance.

A company not resident in the UK may be within the charge to both corporation tax and income tax. In this case, allowances relating to a source that is chargeable to corporation tax must be given against corporation tax; those relating to a source chargeable to income tax must be given against income tax.

Legislation: CAA 2001, s. 2(1), 566; CAA 2001, Pt. 3, Ch. 11

300-250   Trades

For a trader, any allowance due under the IBA rules is treated as a trading expense in calculating the profits of the trade. Similarly, any balancing charge (arising under the transitional rules, or before such charges were abolished) is or was treated as a trading receipt.

The same treatment is given to any person entitled to an allowance in respect of a commercial building if that person occupies the building in the course of a profession or vocation. This will in practice apply only to buildings in enterprise zones.

Legislation: CAA 2001, s. 352

Highway undertakings

The carrying on of a highway undertaking (see 302-050) is treated for these purposes as a trade.

Legislation: CAA 2001, s. 341(1)

300-300   Lessors and licensors

The abolition of balancing events, and the related transitional provisions, apply for lessors as for traders (see 305-200ff.). The following paragraphs should now be read in the light of those changes.

The following rules apply where a person is entitled to an allowance or liable to a balancing charge for a particular chargeable period, and where his interest in the building is subject to a lease or a licence at the relevant time.

If the building is an asset of either a UK or an overseas property business, then any allowances are to be treated as expenses, and any charges as receipts, of that business.

If no property business is being carried on, then the legislation creates the pretence of such a business. In this case, allowances are to be treated as expenses, and charges as receipts, of the imaginary business.

Some clarification of this was given in the Explanatory Notes to the *Capital Allowances Act 2001*, explaining the development of the legislation from its 1990 predecessor Act:

> 'Section 9 of CAA 1990 does not deal expressly with the situation where the person is carrying on an overseas property business as well as a Schedule A [now, UK property] business. Section 353(2) to (4) resolves what is supposed to happen in this situation by requiring the allowance to be given effect in connection with the business of which the lease is an asset.
>
> It is thought that this merely brings out what is implicit in CAA 1990.'

(Explanatory Notes, Annex 2, note 47.)

For all of the above, the interest in the building must be subject to a lease or licence 'at the relevant time'. This is defined as follows:

(1)   for an initial allowance, the period from the time the expenditure was incurred to the time when it is first used for any purpose;

(2)   for a writing-down allowance, the end of the chargeable period; and

(3)   for a balancing allowance or balancing charge, the time immediately before the event giving rise to that allowance or charge.

Legislation: CAA 2001, s. 353

300-350   Buildings temporarily out of use

General principle

Where a building falls temporarily out of use, the treatment is not the same as would apply if the building ceased altogether to be used. If it has qualified as an industrial building

499

immediately before the period of temporary disuse, it is treated as if it continued to qualify during the period of temporary disuse.

Legislation: CAA 2001, s. 285, 354

Hotels

For qualifying hotels, the period of temporary disuse cannot extend beyond the second anniversary of the end of the chargeable period in which the temporary use begins.

Legislation: CAA 2001, s. 317(4)

Other buildings

For any other building that has qualified for IBAs, there is no statutory time limit on the length of a period of temporary disuse. However, HMRC does apply guidelines. Instructions to inspectors are that they should accept the concept of temporary disuse if a building is 'capable of being used for something'. It is not a requirement that it should be capable of being used for a qualifying trade. On the other hand, if it is not capable of any further use, then it will not be treated as only temporarily disused.

HMRC offers the following further guidelines on how they will interpret this section:

- if a taxpayer consciously lets the building fall into disrepair because he has redevelopment plans in mind, then this will not, according to HMRC, amount to temporary disuse; and
- temporary disuse should occur between two periods of use. HMRC gives the view that: 'it is implicit that the benefit of treating the building as being in temporary disuse is only available provided that the building is, in fact, used again. So a building will not be temporarily disused where, say, it is left empty for three years and then demolished'.

A period of disuse may come within the definition of 'temporary disuse' if the next period of use is by a new owner. HMRC will not resist the granting of allowances for what appears to be genuine temporary disuse, even if circumstances subsequently change to make the disuse permanent. In such a case, any allowances given were previously liable to be clawed back by virtue of a balancing charge (or reduced balancing allowance) when the disuse becomes permanent, though this is no longer the case since the changes introduced in 2007 (albeit still conceivably subject to transitional provisions).

Where disuse of a building is accepted as being temporary, the following rules apply for giving effect to allowances and charges:

- if the building was last in use as an industrial building for the purposes of a trade that has since been permanently discontinued, the person entitled to the allowances should be treated as if he were carrying on a property business. Allowances and (where still applicable) charges should then be treated as, respectively, expenses or receipts of that property business; and

- the same treatment is given where the relevant interest was previously subject to a lease or a licence that has since come to an end.

Where the first of these applied (building last in use as an industrial building for the purposes of a trade that has since permanently ceased) tax relief was potentially available against any balancing charge arising (ie for such charges as arise under the transitional rules applying from March 2007 or as arose before the changes introduced from that date). The deductions to be made against the balancing charge were the same as those that are available to be offset against post-cessation receipts under ITTOIA 2005, s. 254 or CTA 2009, s. 196. Broadly, this covers losses, expenses or debits, not arising from the discontinuance itself, that would have been allowable if the business had continued.

This treatment, which has no effect on any deductions allowed under any other provisions, is only applied where there is an actual cessation. It does not apply to a deemed cessation under either ITTOIA 2005, s. 18 or CAA 2001, s. 577(2A) (respectively: income tax effect of a change in the ownership of a trade, etc and deemed commencement and cessation of a trade for corporation tax purposes).

Legislation: CAA 2001, s. 354(2)(a)

Other material: CA 32800

300-400   Buildings for miners, etc – carrying back balancing allowances

Special rules apply to trades that consist of, or include, the working of a source of mineral deposits (as defined at 301-850). In such a trade, a balancing allowance may (before 21 March 2007) have arisen when the mine, etc ceased to be worked or where the foreign concession came to an end. Where the relevant conditions were met, any balancing allowance that exceeded the profits of the last chargeable period could be carried back against the profits of earlier periods. The allowance had to be set first against the current year, then against the previous year and then backwards in order.

Allowances could only be given for chargeable periods amounting in total to five years. A proportionately reduced allowance could be given if part of one chargeable period is needed to make up the full five years. An accounting period had to be counted towards the five-year period even if there were insufficient profits in that accounting period to absorb any of the balancing allowance. No allowance could be given so as to create or increase a loss in any accounting period.

A claim for loss relief under ICTA 1988, s. 393A(1) (relief for company trading losses) took precedence over a claim under this CAA 2001, s. 355. Any loss therefore had to be offset first, with any remaining profits to be relieved by the balancing allowance carried back.

To qualify under this heading, all of the following conditions had to be met:

- the trade had to consist of or include the working of a source of mineral deposits;
- the balancing allowance had to arise in the last chargeable period in which the trade was carried on;
- the event triggering the balancing allowance had to be either the ending of the foreign concession or the fact that the source of mineral deposits had ceased to be worked;
- the allowance must have been in relation to expenditure on a building that was constructed for occupation by, or for the welfare of, people who were employed at or in connection with the working of the mineral deposits; and
- the profits of the final chargeable period had to be insufficient to absorb in their own right the balancing allowance.

Legislation: CAA 2001, s. 355

Expenditure on the construction of a building or structure

300-500 Introduction

The legislation does not attempt to define the concept of expenditure on the construction of a building or structure. Instead, it specifies certain types of expenditure that are specifically to be included or excluded. These categories are expanded by published HMRC guidance. The following paragraphs therefore show the different treatments of various sorts of expenditure, with the justification in each case.

300-550 Meaning of 'building'

The term 'building' is not defined – other than to include a structure – but HMRC says that 'anything with four walls and a roof' should be treated as a building if it is 'of reasonably substantial size'. Something too small to constitute a building is likely to be a structure.

Legislation: CAA 2001, s. 271(2)(a)

Other material: CA 31050

300-600 Meaning of 'structure'

In a non-tax case, Lord Denning defined a structure as 'something of substantial size which is built up from component parts and intended to remain permanently on a permanent foundation; but it is still a structure even though some of its parts may be movable, as, for instance, about a pivot'. The judge then went on to mention a windmill or a turntable as an example of a structure (*Cardiff Rating Authority v Guest Keen Baldwin's Iron and Steel Co Ltd*).

In deciding what constitutes a structure, HMRC relies on an even older case, that of *IR Commrs v Smyth*. In that case, Scrutton J attempted the following definition:

> 'I think a structure is something artificially erected, constructed, put together, of a certain degree of size and permanence, which is still maintained as an artificial erection, or which, though not so maintained, has not become indistinguishable in bounds from the natural earth surrounding. What degree of size and permanence will do is a question of fact in every case.'

On the basis of the above definition, the judge contrasted the 'modern earth banks of a reservoir, recently erected and continually repaired' (a structure) with 'huge earthworks, long ago constructed and repaired, but now become part of the original earth' (not a structure).

HMRC says that something should be treated as a structure 'if it has been artificially erected or constructed and is distinct from the earth surrounding it' and go on to list the following as examples of structures:

- roads;
- car parks with a hard concrete or asphalt surface;
- concrete surfacing;
- tunnels and culverts;
- walls;
- bridges;
- aqueducts;
- dams;
- hard tennis courts; and
- fences.

Cases: *IR Commrs v Smyth* [1914] 3 KB 406; *Cardiff Rating Authority v Guest Keen Baldwin's Iron and Steel Co Ltd* [1949] 1 All ER 27

Other material: CA 31110, 31120

300-650   Expenditure that is treated as being on the construction of a building

As long as all other conditions are met, eg that the building is in use for a qualifying trade or other qualifying activity, the following will qualify for IBAs as if they constituted expenditure on the construction of a building:

- capital expenditure on repairs to part of a building. This specifically includes proper trading expenditure on repairs to a building where that expenditure is disallowed in computing trading profits on the grounds that it is capital in nature;
- capital expenditure on improvements, additions or alterations to an existing building;
- the costs of demolishing an existing building in order to construct a new building; and
- professional fees relating to the design and construction of an industrial building, as long as the construction of the building goes ahead. Where the project is abandoned, the HMRC view is that no allowances will be due ('that kind of expenditure is not

Industrial Buildings

expenditure on the construction of a building because no building is constructed and so it does not qualify for IBA').

Expenditure may qualify for IBAs if it is incurred on preparing a site for the installation of plant or machinery. IBAs may be claimed where:

- capital expenditure has been incurred in 'preparing, cutting, tunnelling or levelling' land;
- that work has been carried out for the purpose of preparing the land as a site on which plant or machinery is to be installed; and
- no IBAs or plant or machinery allowances would otherwise be given.

Where these conditions are met, IBAs can be claimed as if the purpose of the expenditure were to prepare the site for the construction of a building, and as if the installed plant or machinery were a building.

Note that the section does not deem the expenditure to be on an industrial building – only on a building. It would seem to follow that the plant or machinery must meet the other IBA conditions if allowances are to be given. In particular, it should be in use for the purposes of a qualifying trade.

Legislation: CAA 2001, s. 272–273

Other material: CA 31400

300-700   Roads on industrial estates

A road on an industrial estate may qualify as an industrial building. It follows from this that the landlord of an industrial estate can claim IBAs on the cost of constructing a road on the estate, even though he is not himself carrying on a qualifying trade.

Relief will be available if the buildings on the estate are wholly or mainly industrial buildings, as defined for capital allowance purposes. In the absence of any definition, it is assumed that 'wholly or mainly' must mean that more than half of the buildings qualify, though HMRC could apply a different interpretation.

Legislation: CAA 2001, s. 284

Other material: CA 32340

300-750   Non-qualifying expenditure

The following expenditure does not qualify as being on the construction of a building:

- the cost of land or rights over land.
  Where necessary, an apportionment must be made to exclude the cost of land (CAA 2001, s. 356). See also the case of *Bostock and Ors v Totham (HMIT)* regarding the manner in which an apportionment is to be made.

The cost of a freehold for an industrial building will always include land, so an apportionment is necessary in all cases. Similarly, an apportionment will be needed if a premium is paid for the leasehold interest in an industrial building.

Again, an apportionment may be needed if the building includes other assets that are the subject of a separate capital allowances claim. For the interaction of IBAs and allowances due on plant or machinery, see 310-500;

- the costs of obtaining planning permission.
  HMRC will not in practice disallow part of a builder's quotation where that quotation includes the cost of obtaining planning permission;
- capitalised interest;
- the costs of a public inquiry;
- the cost of draining or reclaiming land;
- landscaping;
- legal expenses;
- architect's fees where the project does not go ahead (see above); and
- most expenditure met directly or indirectly by somebody else. See under 'Contributions to capital expenditure' at 301-000.

Sometimes, allowances are based not on the construction expenditure as such but on the (lower) figure of capital expenditure incurred by the purchaser. For these purposes, the HMRC manuals state that legal fees, surveyors' fees and stamp duty 'but nothing else' should be included in the buyer's capital expenditure.

Legislation: CAA 2001, s. 272(1), 532–536

Cases: *Bostock v Totham (HMIT)* [1997] BTC 257

Other material: CA 14100–14300, CA 31305–31310, 31400, 33520

300-800   Capital expenditure

Meaning of capital expenditure

In several places, this Division refers to 'capital expenditure'. The legislation applies various principles that are of relevance to IBAs:

- capital expenditure excludes any expenditure that may be deducted by the person concerned in calculating the profits or gains of his trade, etc;
- in relation to the recipient of the expenditure, the term excludes any amount that has to be added in calculating those profits or gains; and
- in relation to either a recipient or a person incurring the expenditure, the term excludes any expenditure for which a deduction can be made as an annual payment or re certain royalties (under ITA 2007, Pt. 15, Ch. 6 or ITA 2007, s. 906).

The IBA legislation draws a frequent distinction between the meaning of capital expenditure on the construction of a building and capital expenditure incurred by a purchaser on buying a building. The HMRC manuals make it clear that legal and similar costs cannot be included in the construction costs of a building. Where, however, a buyer incurs legal fees, surveyor fees or stamp duty, then these costs ('but nothing else') may be included in calculating his capital expenditure.

For a more detailed discussion of what constitutes capital expenditure generally, see 102-000.

Legislation: CAA 2001, s. 4

Other material: CA 31400, 33520

Date expenditure incurred – general rule

The legislation also addresses the question of the date on which capital expenditure is treated as incurred. This is important for a number of reasons; including, fundamentally, the fact that one of the conditions for the giving of writing-down allowances for any period is that 'expenditure has been incurred'.

The question of when expenditure is incurred is considered at 102-000. The general rule is that expenditure is treated as incurred 'as soon as there is an unconditional obligation to pay it', even if the expenditure does not fall due for payment until a later date.

Legislation: CAA 2001, s. 5, 309(1)(a)

VAT

The above rules do not apply where expenditure is treated as incurred as a result of a person incurring an additional VAT liability. For the treatment of such a liability, see 305-300.

Contributions to capital expenditure

301-000   Tax position of the recipient

There is a general rule that no IBAs are due if the cost of the construction is to be met by someone else. The question of whether the contribution is capital or revenue in nature is not relevant. Nor does it matter whether the contribution is paid before or after the expenditure is incurred.

There are three circumstances in which a contribution received does not have to be deducted for IBA purposes from expenditure incurred:

(1)   the general rule can be ignored if the expenditure is met by a grant made under Northern Ireland legislation and 'declared by the Treasury by order to correspond to a grant under Part II of the *Industrial Development Act* 1982'. The HMRC manuals refer to one 'exception to this exception' as follows (at CA 14200):

'The grant is still deducted from the expenditure in line with the general rule if it is "netted off" by Para. 8, Sch. 3 *Oil Taxation Act* 1975 for the purposes of arriving at expenditure for petroleum revenue tax (PRT) relief. If part of expenditure met by the grant would have qualified for PRT relief and part would not, apportion the grant so the part which relates to expenditure which would be netted off is deducted from the capital expenditure for capital allowances purposes and the remainder is not.'

(2)   where money is received by way of insurance or compensation for an asset that has been 'destroyed, demolished or put out of use' then this too is not treated as falling within the restriction. Therefore, if the compensation received is applied in constructing a new industrial building, the full cost of the building can still be allowed. However, the compensation may need to be brought into account as disposal proceeds of the old asset (see 305-700). (Given that no balancing charge can be made more than 25 years after the building is first used, the treatment of compensation as disposal proceeds may be more beneficial than offsetting the compensation against the cost of a new building.);

(3)   a contribution can be ignored by the recipient if it is made by somebody who cannot claim tax relief on it, except where the contributor is a public body. The contributor must not be claiming relief either:

(a)   in relation to a trade or other qualifying activity; or

(b)   as a contribution allowance (see below) under CAA 2001, s. 537.

If a grant is made but the recipient then repays it, there is no strict basis for reversing the denial of tax relief. By concession, tax relief will be given in some circumstances. ESC B49 reads as follows:

'Where some or all of the expenditure on the provision of an asset has been met by the Crown, any Government, or any other public or local authority, s. 532–536 CAA 2001 [previously CAA 1990, s. 153] prevent capital allowances from being given on that expenditure. By concession, where the grant is later repaid in whole or in part, the amount repaid will be treated as expenditure on which capital allowances may be given.

Capital allowances are also restricted where expenditure on an asset is met by a person other than the Crown or public body who is entitled to capital allowances or a trading deduction on that amount.

Where a grant which has been deducted from expenditure qualifying for capital allowances under this rule is later repaid in whole or in part, the Inland Revenue will treat the amount repaid as expenditure on which capital allowances may be given provided the repayment falls to be taxed on the person who made the grant through a balancing adjustment or as a trading receipt.'

In any other case, relief will be denied even if the grant or other contribution is returned:

'These are the only cases where a person repaying all or part of a grant may be given capital allowances on the amount repaid. In all other cases you should refuse to give capital allowances on a grant repaid because there is nothing in the legislation to give them' (CA 14300).

Revenue instructions to inspectors are that they should:

'. . . treat a non-returnable grant of money given by way of gift, that is, not in return for anything, as a contribution if there is a clear connection between the receipt of the grant and the incurring of the expenditure. The grant should be specifically related to the capital expenditure on the provision of capital assets.'

If, on the facts, the payment is a loan, then it should not be treated as a contribution.

Legislation: CAA 2001, s. 532–536

Other material: CA 14100–14300; ESC B49

Formalising the concession

In November 2008, HMRC presented draft legislation for the purpose of enacting around 20 extra statutory concessions. However, the enactment of ESC B49 concerning repaid grants has proved difficult in practice. In an e-mail dated 3 March 2009 to members of the Corporation Tax Operational Consultative Committee, HMRC commented as follows:

'A scoping study of ESC B49, undertaken to see whether it could successfully be legislated, has shown that the required legislation will be complex, and also needs to take into account recent developments in the way capital allowances are given which were not envisaged when the ESC was first drafted, eg the Annual Investment Allowance. Additionally there is the possibility that some of the scenarios the ESC potentially addresses might never arise in practice, and providing for them would significantly increase the length and complexity of the legislation.'

As such, HMRC raised eight questions for discussion. Once responses have been received to those questions, HMRC will consider further whether and how to enact the principles currently enshrined in the concession.

301-050   Tax position of the contributor

The rules granting relief to a person contributing to capital expenditure on an industrial building are given in CAA 2001, s. 537 and 539. The first of these gives the 'general conditions' that apply to all types of capital allowance. The later section gives the rules as they specifically apply to industrial buildings allowances.

CAA 2001, s. 539 is omitted, and s. 537 adapted accordingly, from April 2011, from which time the IBA rules cease to apply (FA 2008, Sch. 27, para. 6).

The conditions for a contributor (C) to obtain allowances are as follows:

- C must have contributed a capital sum to expenditure on the provision of an asset;
- without the contribution, the expenditure would have been treated as incurred by the recipient of the contribution (R) such that R would have been entitled to capital allowances;
- C and R must not be connected persons; and
- C's contribution must be made for the purposes of a trade or relevant activity that

qualifies for IBA purposes and that is carried on, or to be carried on, either by C himself or by a tenant of land in which C has an interest.

Where these conditions are met, C is treated as if the contribution were expenditure incurred by him on the provision, for the purposes of the particular trade or relevant activity, of an asset similar to that provided by means of his contribution. The asset is then deemed at all material times to be in use for the purposes of the trade or relevant activity.

A further issue arises if C has been entitled to an allowance by virtue of a contribution made for the purposes of a trade or relevant activity carried on by a tenant of land in which C had an interest. If there is a subsequent transfer of ownership of the interest that was held by C at the time the contribution was made, then the new owner will obtain the benefit of writing-down allowances. These will first arise to the new owner for the chargeable period in which he acquires the relevant interest.

On the other hand, C's contribution may have been made for the purposes of his own trade or relevant activity. If this is the case, and if the whole or a part of the trade, etc is subsequently transferred, the entitlement to the allowances is passed to the new owner of the trade. The year of transfer does not give rise to an apportionment – the whole allowance goes to the new owner if the transfer of the whole activity has taken place by the day before the end of the chargeable period. If, though, only a part of the trade or relevant activity has been transferred, then allowances are made to the transferee 'to the extent that they are properly referable to the part transferred'.

For these purposes, the rules relating to the relevant interest (see 304-500) apply ('with any necessary modifications') to the contribution just as they apply to expenditure incurred on the construction of an industrial building. However, the rules in CAA 2001, s. 311 (relating to the calculation of allowances after the sale of a relevant interest – see 305-200) are specifically disapplied by CAA 2001, s. 539(6).

Legislation: CAA 2001, s. 537ff.

Qualifying trades

301-500   Overview and tables

As summarised at 300-050, one of the three main IBA conditions is that the building should be in use for a specified purpose. This purpose may be a qualifying trade (covered here) or use as a hotel (see 315-000), a sports pavilion (315-500), or a commercial building in an enterprise zone (320-000).

The term 'trade' does not generally include a profession or vocation for IBA purposes.

The definition of 'qualifying trade' is given by providing two tables. As long as it is not caught by any specific exclusion (see 302-600) the trade will qualify if it is:

- 'a trade of a kind described in Table A,'; or
- 'an undertaking of a kind described in Table B, if the undertaking is carried on by way of trade'.

It follows that the only distinction between the tables is the need to ensure that 'undertakings' within Table B are 'carried on by way of trade'.

Tables A and B are as follows, and commentary is added after the tables:

Table A

TRADES WHICH ARE 'QUALIFYING TRADES'

1	Manufacturing	A trade consisting of manufacturing goods or materials.
2	Processing	A trade consisting of subjecting goods or materials to a process.
		This includes (subject to s. 276(3)) maintaining or repairing goods or materials.
3	Storage	A trade consisting of storing goods or materials:
		(a) which are to be used in the manufacture of other goods or materials;
		(b) which are to be subjected, in the course of a trade, to a process;
		(c) which, having been manufactured or produced or subjected, in the course of a trade, to a process, have not yet been delivered to any purchaser; or
		(d) on their arrival in the United Kingdom from a place outside the United Kingdom.
4	Agricultural contracting	A trade consisting of:
		(a) ploughing or cultivating land occupied by another;
		(b) carrying out any other agricultural operation on land occupied by another; or
		(c) threshing another's crops. For this purpose 'crops' includes vegetable produce.
5	Working foreign plantations	A trade consisting of working land outside the United Kingdom used for:
		(a) growing and harvesting crops;
		(b) husbandry; or
		(c) forestry.
		For this purpose 'crops' includes vegetable produce and 'harvesting crops' includes the collection of vegetable produce (however effected).
6	Fishing	A trade consisting of catching or taking fish or shellfish.
7	Mineral extraction	A trade consisting of working a source of mineral deposits. 'Mineral deposits' includes any natural deposits capable of being lifted or extracted from the earth, and for this purpose geothermal energy is to be treated as a natural deposit.
		'Source of mineral deposits' includes a mine, an oil well and a source of geothermal energy.

Table B

UNDERTAKINGS

1 Electricity	An undertaking for the generation, transformation, conversion, transmission or distribution of electrical energy.
2 Water	An undertaking for the supply of water for public consumption.
3 Hydraulic power	An undertaking for the supply of hydraulic power.
4 Sewerage	An undertaking for the provision of sewerage services within the meaning of the *Water Industry Act* 1991.
5 Transport	A transport undertaking.
6 Highway undertakings	A highway undertaking, that is, so much of any undertaking relating to the design, building, financing and operation of roads as is carried on: (a) for the purposes of; or (b) in connection with the exploitation of highway concessions.
7 Tunnels	A tunnel undertaking.
8 Bridges	A bridge undertaking.
9 Inland navigation	An inland navigation undertaking.
10 Docks	A dock undertaking. A dock includes: (a) any harbour; and (b) any wharf, pier, jetty or other works in or at which vessels can ship or unship merchandise or passengers, other than a pier or jetty primarily used for recreation.

Legislation: CAA 2001, s. 274

301-550   Manufacturing

The concept of 'a trade consisting of manufacturing goods or materials' should present few difficulties in practice, despite the lack of a statutory definition. HMRC has provided the following guidance:

'You should have no difficulty in deciding whether a trade consists of manufacturing goods or materials. Basically, it should consist of making things that are goods or materials. A factory will have a trade which consists of manufacturing goods or materials.

There is not a statutory definition of manufacturing so you should give it its normal meaning. Manufacturing is the making of articles, especially in a factory. It also includes the assembly of goods from component parts manufactured somewhere else. For example, you should treat a computer assembly plant as manufacturing.'

Before the capital allowances legislation was consolidated and rewritten in the *Capital Allowances Act* 2001, there was a specific reference to 'a trade carried on in a mill, factory or other similar premises'. This reference has been omitted in the new legislation but there is no intention to change the effect:

'This Act does not include this. These words add nothing which is not covered by s. 18(1)(e) [CAA 1990], "a trade which consists in the manufacture of goods or materials or the subjection of goods or materials to any process" (note 970 from *Explanatory Notes to CAA 2001).*'

A Court of Appeal judge in the *Vibroplant* case, considered below, gave a concise summary in saying that 'it seems to me that a factory makes an article and a mill processes an article'. Other buildings held to be within the definition of a mill or similar premises include cold storage premises *Ellerker v Union Cold Storage Co Ltd* and grain elevators *IR Commrs v Leith Harbour and Docks Commrs.*

In view of the assurance that the new wording encompasses all trades that were previously carried on in 'a mill, factory or other similar premises', it remains relevant to consider the case law decisions applying to the previous wording. In the *Ellerker* case, Macnaghten J provided the following insights into how these terms should be understood (paragraph breaks added for clarity):

'What then do the words "factory" and "mill" mean according to the common understanding of mankind? I take it that a factory is a building used for the manufacture of goods and equipped with machinery, and that the word is generally understood in that sense. It is a building where goods are made.

The meaning of the word "mill" is also, I think, plain enough. A mill is a building where goods are subjected to treatment or processing of some sort and machinery is used for that purpose. The miller in his corn mill grinds wheat into flour, or oats into oatmeal. So, too, at a scutching mill the miller scutches the flax, to prepare it for spinning. The saw mill, the rolling mill, the flatting mill, the puffing mill and the cotton mill are all buildings where goods are treated or subjected to some process. I was told in the course of the argument that in Lancashire no one in the trade would call a building where cotton cloth is woven a cotton mill. The expression "cotton mill" is confined to those buildings where spinning takes place. The buildings in which the yarn is woven into cloth are called, and properly called, factories.

Mills and factories – though they differ in this respect, that in the former goods are treated or processed and in the latter goods are manufactured or made – have this in common, that both are equipped with machinery worked in former days by wind or water and nowadays by steam or electricity or some other power.'

The case itself concerned cold stores, which are now clearly accepted as qualifying as industrial buildings ('Cold stores are industrial buildings'). Often, they may also qualify as plant and the business can then choose which type of allowance to claim. The treatment as plant will almost invariably be preferred but the possibility should not be overlooked that the store might be subject to the long-life asset rules. If there is a chance that it will eventually be sold, then it may also be appropriate to consider the different rules that apply to sales under the two parts of the capital allowances regime. This is all the more relevant if the store may be sold more than 25 years after it was first constructed.

See 302-600 for specific exclusions (for offices, retails shops, etc) that may deny allowances in certain cases.

Cases: *Ellerker v Union Cold Storage Co Ltd* (1938) 22 TC 195); (*IR Commrs v Leith Harbour and Docks Commrs* (1941) 24 TC 118

Other material: CA 32210ff.

301-600   Processing goods and materials

The concept of 'a trade consisting of subjecting goods or materials to a process' has been the subject of case law on two fronts. First, it is necessary to consider the meaning of 'goods or materials' and secondly, the more difficult issue needs to be addressed of what is meant by 'subjecting . . . to a process'.

Once more, see 302-600 for specific exclusions (for offices, retail shops, etc) that may deny allowances in certain cases that would otherwise qualify as processing trades.

Goods or materials

There is no statutory definition of this expression for tax purposes but various guidelines have emerged from capital allowance case law and elsewhere.

HMRC accepts that 'materials' can mean more than raw materials: 'materials that have been manufactured may be used in the manufacture of other products'. HMRC also comments that in the absence of a statutory definition, the word 'materials' should be given its ordinary meaning.

The HMRC manuals refer to the *Sale of Goods Act* 1979, which gives a statutory definition of 'goods'. As interpreted at CA 32212:

> '"Goods" includes all personal chattels other than things in action and money; and in particular "goods" includes emblements, industrial growing crops, and things attached to or forming part of the land which are agreed to be severed before sale or under the contract of sale and includes an undivided share in goods.'

Other material: CA 32212

Land

Land does not come within the definition of 'goods or materials'. This seems self-evident and is in any case confirmed at CA 32212. It follows that site preparation cannot qualify as the subjection of goods to a process. See, however, 300-650 for the treatment of site preparation prior to the installation of plant or machinery.

Other material: CA 32212ff.

Money, cheques and related documents

The question of whether money can be 'goods or materials' was considered in *Buckingham v Securitas Properties Ltd*. In that case, coins and notes were sorted into wage packets but the IBA claim was refused on the grounds that the money did not constitute goods or materials:

> 'The word "goods" in this context is intended to bear its ordinary dictionary meaning of "merchandise" or "wares". I cannot think that the Legislature, in employing the word "goods" in either phrase, was intending to include money in the sense of currency that can be offered in the payment of the price on the sale of the merchandise or wares'.

The exclusion applies only to money used as currency. So (from the same case): 'there is … little difficulty in regarding antique coins and notes that are bought and sold in retail shops as "goods" according to legal terminology'. This concept is now recognised in the HMRC manuals ('Coins held as trading stock by a jeweller who incorporates them into jewellery that is made are goods or materials').

The same case quoted with approval an *Oxford English Dictionary* definition of 'goods' as 'merchandise; wares; now chiefly manufactured articles.' The definition of 'merchandise' was similarly quoted, as including 'the commodities of commerce; moveables which may be bought and sold'.

Similar issues were considered in *Girobank plc v Clarke (HMIT)*. The case concerned a data processing centre used by a bank. The reasoning (but not the ultimate decision) of the commissioners was overruled in the High Court but reinstated in the Court of Appeal. The case is useful in the way it defines the limitations of what may qualify as goods or materials. The items that were said to be subjected to a process consisted of pouches, envelopes, containers and documents. As the commissioner said:

> 'They are certainly all tangible items. They have all probably at some time been bought and sold by someone as goods in the course of trade. They are certainly capable of being sold in that way. But it seems clear to me that the transaction documents are not received at the Wigan Centre as goods. They are received as pieces of paper carrying information, instructions or requests. They carry messages and that is their value to the business. They are not held as stock-in-trade or inventory of the business. They are not sold on by Girobank. While they may once have been goods and conceivably they could be sold as goods, that is not why they are there and submitted to the activities at the centre … Once the stationery is used in the procedures it is used as fresh medium for carrying internal messages and is no longer held as goods.'

This was quoted with approval in the Court of Appeal.

Cases: *Buckingham v Securitas Properties Ltd* [1980] 53 TC 292; *Girobank plc v Clarke (HMIT)* [1998] BTC 24

Other material: CA 32212

People

In *Bourne v Norwich Crematorium Ltd*, the question was considered of whether a crematorium could qualify for allowances on the grounds that it was subjecting goods or materials to a process.

The High Court judge was unable to accept that human remains constituted 'goods or materials':

> 'I can only say that although the human body is no doubt material in the same sense that all things visible are material, there is in my judgment something in the word "materials", in the plural, which forbids the construction of the phrase "goods and materials" which is urged upon me. In my judgment it would be a distortion of the English language to describe the living or the dead as goods or materials.'

Cases: *Bourne v Norwich Crematorium Ltd* (1967) 44 TC 164

Animals

In the case of *Carr (HMIT) v Sayer*, the Revenue argued that 'dogs and cats do not fall within the definition of "goods" which expression is limited to inanimate objects'. The HMRC stance has subsequently softened, however, accepting that animals other than dogs and cats 'may be goods'. In particular, inspectors are instructed to accept that 'rodents bred for experimental purposes are capable of being goods where the objective is to produce animals of a standard weight and size that meet other pre-determined criteria such as being germ-free and so are saleable products'.

In the *Sayer* case, the commissioners had accepted the Revenue view that dogs and cats were not within the meaning of 'goods or materials' but the High Court judgment – though going in favour of the Revenue – was less clear-cut on the particular point. Referring to the wording of the *Capital Allowances Act* 1990, the judge commented that:

> 'Live animals do not fall within the (undefined) expression "goods or materials" as used elsewhere in s. 7(1): for example, para. (e) is concerned with a trade consisting of the manufacture of goods or materials. Whether the same is true of para. (f)(iv) is more debatable'

The *Bourne v Norwich Crematorium Ltd* case made reference to the *Metropolitan Police Courts Act* 1839. The word 'goods' in that Act was held, in *R v Slade*, to include dogs.

Cases: *R v Slade* [1888] 21 QBD 433; *Bourne v Norwich Crematorium Ltd* (1967) 44 TC 164; *Carr (HMIT) v Sayer* [1992] BTC 286

Other material: CA 32212

Subjecting to a process

For a building to qualify under the 'processing' heading, a second test needs to be met: that of whether the goods or materials are 'subjected to a process'. This section considers the way in which this concept has developed in case law, and the interpretation applied in practice by HMRC.

The HMRC manuals take the view that the question is one of fact and distil this concept to two questions, such that the 'subjected to a process'' test will be met if:

'there is a substantial measure of uniformity of treatment, or
there is a continuous and regular action or succession of actions taking place or carried on in a definite manner.'

HMRC instructions encourage inspectors of taxes to visit the site if they 'have problems' with the question of whether goods are being subjected to a process.

For further guidance, HMRC makes reference to five cases where the concept has been tested:

Kilmarnock Equitable Co-operative Society Ltd v IR Commrs (1966) 42 TC 675;
Buckingham v Securitas Properties Ltd (1980) 53 TC 292;
Vibroplant Ltd v Holland (HMIT) (1982) 54 TC 658;
Girobank plc v Clarke (HMIT) [1998] BTC 24 (CA); and
Bestway (Holdings) Ltd v Luff (HMIT) [1998] BTC 69.

One of the key principles to emerge from these (and other) cases is that the concept of 'subjecting to a process' does not have to imply any alteration to the nature of the material itself.

The *Kilmarnock* case, which the Revenue lost, concerned a process of cleaning coal and packing it in small paper bags. Lord Migdale ruled that 'subjected to' means that it went through a process, and 'process' means 'some course of operations'. The coal:

'started this operation or series of operations as a stream of dirty coal but it ended up as clean coal in an attractive wrapping. The nature of the material remained the same but it had been made more marketable and would probably attract a higher price for the same weight than if it had been sold unscreened in a large and dirty sack.'

In the same case, Lord Cameron put the matter in these terms:

'The word "process" in its ordinary connotation seems to me to mean no more than the application of a method of manufacture or adaptation of goods or materials towards a particular use, purpose or end, while "to subject" means no more than to treat in some manner or other.'

In the words of the Lord President (Clyde):

'an industrial building may connote something other than a place where goods or materials are manufactured: it may include within the category of an industrial building a place where goods or materials are subjected to a process which falls short of the manufacturing of a new article.'

The *Securitas* case concerned a building used for the purposes of 'storage and wage-packeting large sums of cash'. The Revenue was successful in this case, but on the grounds (discussed above) that the cash did not constitute goods or materials. The Revenue did not win its argument that there was no 'subjecting to a process'.

The company claimed that it was carrying out a process:

'breaking down bulk coins and notes into individual wage-packets, which had to be prepared to the specific requirements of respective employers and had to exclude torn or defaced notes or foreign coins.'

The Revenue unsuccessfully argued that 'the operations did not constitute "the subjection of goods to any process" ... because nothing was done to the notes and coins to enhance their value or make them more marketable, or to alter their substance'. The courts would have none of it. As Slade J put it:

'the coins and notes came into the security area in bulk form and left it reduced to individual wage-packets, after being dealt with through the activities of a staff, requiring numeracy and accuracy, who had to take care that each wage packet contained the right amount and selection of notes and coins, broken down according to the employer's specifications. I am inclined to think that these activities did involve the subjection of the coins and notes to a "process", within the ordinary meaning of words and within the meaning of the subsection, even though it could not be said that their texture, substance or value was altered by such activities'.

HMRC summarises the decision as follows:

'In that case the subjection of goods to a process was held to be

- a continuous and regular action or succession of actions taking place or carried on in a definite manner; or
- a continuous (natural or artificial) operation or series of operations.'

Counsel for the company used this dictionary definition, and the company was successful on this particular point. The definition was quoted with approval in the *Vibroplant* case, considered below.

The *Girobank plc* case referred to above was lost on the basis that the documents were not goods or materials, as discussed above. In this respect, the Court of Appeal restored the view of the commissioners, overturning the opinion of the High Court. As such, the question of whether the items were subjected to a process did not need to be considered by the Court of Appeal. Nevertheless, the judge referred briefly to the matter and commented that 'I think it is a difficult point. As at present advised, I rather prefer the view of the judge'.

On this basis, the view of the High Court on the question of subjecting goods to a process remains valid. The judge in fact had much to say on the matter and several of the paragraphs are worth quoting in full:

'In my view s. 18(1)(e) [CAA 1990 – now broadly items 1 and 2 of Table A at CAA 2001, s. 274(1)] must be interpreted in its entirety. Thus the alternative of "the subjection of goods or materials to any process" has to be read in context with the earlier reference to "a trade which consists in the manufacture of goods or materials". This conjunctive reading of the sub-paragraph as opposed to the disjunctive reading submitted by Mr Powrie seems to me to be clearly correct for at least two reasons.

The first reason for reading the two parts together is that the two expressions are both contained in the one sub-paragraph [no longer the case in CAA 2001].

The second reason is that it seems to me that industrialists would consider that there is a close relationship between manufacture and processing and that the two expressions can be readily understood together. In my judgment goods are commonly said to be processed, but not necessarily to the extent that new goods have been manufactured, when some process, treatment or procedure is applied to them which adds value to them, or prevents value from being lost from them, as items in the chain of production of goods as components, products, finished goods or similar items for sale. Processing thus has a common meaning as a step in or towards the manufacture and sale of something. A particular process may be the first, an intermediate or the last stage in preparing a product for sale. It may be carried out by someone different from the final manufacturer or assembler. The person carrying out the process will then be adapting or treating goods for sale by himself. This adaptation may result in something less than would normally be described as manufacturing a new material or item of goods for sale. Hence the need for the alternative words in s. 18(1)(e).

From a plain reading of s. 18(1)(e) I would not normally expect that a process would fall within s. 18(1)(e) unless it is a process of the kind I have described.'

After a review of the legislation and the earlier case law, the Judge in that case went on to give a wide definition of 'process' for these purposes:

'Drawing together the legislature and these authorities, I find nothing that limits the very broad width of "any process" to processes only of an "industrial" character, if by that is meant that something has to be made by the process, or that the operations have to be carried out only or chiefly by machines. Nor is it required of a process that it alters the goods and materials subjected to it in any way but rather it may suffice of a process that it should clean, sort or package the goods or materials fed into it.'

One caveat needs to be added. In the *Bestway (Holdings)* case, the special commissioners commented on the paragraph just quoted: 'We venture to suggest that this passage may be expressed too widely'. It was held that the various operations carried on by Bestway did not amount to the subjection of goods or materials to a process:

'We do not believe that the various operations described above treat Cash & Carry's goods with the substantial measure of uniformity of treatment or system of treatment required to enable the operations to become a process. Some goods are unpacked, others are not. Some goods are relabelled, others are not. Some goods do not have product codes on their arrival, although the majority do.

Having observed some of the operations described above at both Abbey Road and Luton, we have come to the conclusion that those operations do not constitute processes. We find as a fact that the goods and materials of the Bestway group are not subjected to a process.'

In a further case, that of *Crusabridge Investments Ltd v Casings International Ltd*, it was held that the marking of defects on tyres did not amount to a subjection of the tyres to a process:

'There is, in my judgment, no process to which the tyre is subjected. It is the very same tyre before the examination and after the examination. Nothing has happened to it that alters its nature or indeed effects any kind of change in the tyre. I cannot regard the marking of the defects with yellow chalk as constituting such an alteration of the tyre as to indicate that it has been subjected to a process'.'

Cases: *Kilmarnock Equitable Co-operative Society Ltd v IR Commrs* (1966) 42 TC 675; *Crusabridge Investments Ltd v Casings International Ltd* (1979) 54 TC 246; *Buckingham v Securitas Properties Ltd* (1980) 53 TC 292; *Vibroplant Ltd v Holland (HMIT)* (1982) 54 TC 658; *Girobank plc v Clarke (HMIT)* [1998] BTC 24; *Bestway (Holdings) Ltd v Luff (HMIT)* [1998] BTC 69

Other material: CA 32213

Maintenance and repairs

The qualifying trade of 'processing' is specifically extended in Table A to include 'maintaining or repairing goods or materials'. However, this is subject to CAA 2001, s. 276(3), which states that such activities will not qualify if:

- the goods or materials are employed in a trade or an undertaking;
- the person employing the goods or materials is the same as the person who carries out the maintenance or repair; and
- the trade or undertaking is not a qualifying trade in its own right.

The case of *Vibroplant Ltd v Holland* pre-dated a change in legislation (in 1982) but remains important in determining the meaning of 'subject to a process'. The definition of 'processing' in Table A above now includes, subject to one caveat, 'maintaining or repairing goods or materials'. As this extended meaning did not apply in 1974, the period to which the *Vibroplant* case related, the case was argued on the question of whether the company was subjecting goods or materials to a process.

Vibroplant claimed IBAs on structures in which plant was cleaned, serviced and repaired after hiring out to the public. The claim failed because each item passing through the system was treated individually. By contrast, a process connoted 'a substantial measure of uniformity of treatment or system of treatment'. The judge used two analogies to reinforce the point:

> 'It seems to me that an ordinary garage where cars are serviced and repaired according to their particular requirements does not involve subjecting goods or materials to any process. Similarly, a doctor's surgery where individuals are treated for their individual ailments does not involve the subjection of people to any process.'

See below, however, for the question of car repairs, following amended legislation.

The view was confirmed in the Court of Appeal, where a further ground for rejecting the claim was established. As Templeman LJ put it:

> '... the allowances now in question are intended to encourage manufacturing, processing, producing, importing and allied trades. In our judgment a building used for the purpose of cleaning, servicing and repairing vehicles and other articles belonging to a taxpayer whose trade consists of hiring out those articles for reward is not similar to a mill or factory because nothing similar to manufacture or processing is involved at any stage. The distinction is confirmed by the authorities.'

When the legislation was subsequently updated to include repair work in the list of qualifying trades, this distinction was retained. As such, the maintaining or repairing of goods or materials can now in principle qualify, whether the goods or materials are subsequently used by the repairing person or by a third party. If they are to be used by the person carrying out the repair, however, the building will only qualify (as explained above) if the trade for which the goods are used is itself a qualifying trade. HMRC illustrates this with the following helpful example:

'Cassandra runs a taxi business. It is a qualifying trade because it is a transport undertaking. She has a workshop in which she repairs and maintains the taxis. The workshop qualifies for IBA because the goods that are repaired and maintained there are used by Cassandra in a qualifying trade.

If Cassandra gets bored with the taxi business and starts to hire out the cars without drivers her business stops being a transport undertaking and is no longer a qualifying trade. At that point the workshop stops qualifying for IBA because it is used by Cassandra to repair cars which she uses in a non-qualifying trade.'

Legislation: CAA 2001, s. 276(3)

Cases: *Vibroplant Ltd v Holland* 54 TC 658

Other material: CA 32220

Subjecting to a process – summary of principles

The *Bestway* case goes further than any other in summarising the key principles that apply to determine whether the 'subjected to a process' condition is met. In a useful judgment by Lightman J, the following guidelines are given:

- the phrase 'subjection of goods to any process' must be considered as a whole;
- it is not sufficient that 'anything is done to goods'. Thus the mere conveyance of goods is not enough: some form of treatment is necessary;
- the treatment may fall short of manufacturing a new article or making any alteration whether in the nature or size of the goods or materials;
- it is not necessarily insufficient that what is done is a preliminary to something else being done, and in particular to the trade of selling. But the fact that a particular activity is a preliminary to something else being done may be relevant in considering whether that activity constitutes the subjection of goods to a process;
- subjection to a process means a treatment (or course of operations) involving the application of a method of manufacture or adaptation of goods or materials towards a particular use, purpose or end;
- for a trade or part of a trade to consist in the subjection of goods or materials to a process, it is not sufficient that individual items or defects are treated individually. There is required a substantial measure of uniformity of treatment or system of treatment. Thus the servicing and repair of plant or a car is not within the original meaning of subjection to a process, as each plant or car is treated individually. (But see now the extended definition which includes repairs and maintenance in some circumstances, as explained below);

- the process need not be industrial or complex;
- the views expressed in *Girobank plc* need to be considered (even though the legal status of those views is not entirely satisfactory – see above); and
- not every treatment of goods or materials constitutes a subjection to a process. A uniform treatment or system of treatment of some real significance is postulated.

To this list should be added the treatment of repairs and maintenance, as considered above.

Subjecting to a process – specific activities
HMRC has stated that the following activities would specifically not qualify as subjecting goods or materials to a process:

- site preparation – see above;
- testing and inspecting cars for MOTs, on the grounds that looking at a car is not subjecting it to a process. See below, however, for the treatment of vehicle repair workshops;
- taking photographs. The HMRC view is that 'the operation of the camera is not itself a process because all that it does is allow light to be admitted'. The authority for this view is unclear; and
- acceleration of the normal process of growth, for example plants in greenhouses or chickens in broiler houses.

Subjecting to a process – television and radio companies
The Revenue reached an agreement with the television industry in the 1960s regarding the treatment of a television company's trade for IBA purposes. A television trade as a whole does not qualify but the part of the trade that consists of making videotapes is a qualifying trade, with the result that studio buildings used for that part of the trade may attract IBAs.

HMRC instructions to tax officers apply the agreement as follows:

'Under the agreement the following buildings qualify for IBA on the basis that the activities in those areas are reflected in the production of videotapes:

- studio areas;
- control rooms;
- production facilities;
- videotape processing rooms, etc;
- technical areas, including workshops;
- film processing studios;
- scenery construction workshops.

Rooms or buildings, including transmission stations, where no production of programme material takes place do not qualify for IBA. Transmission aerials qualify for plant and machinery allowances.

You should treat an IBA claim from a radio company in the same way as you would treat an IBA claim from a television company. Treat its recording studios like television studios.'

Other material: CA 32217

Subjecting to a process – vehicle repair workshops

Most vehicle repair shops will not qualify for IBAs. Although vehicle maintenance and repair constitute the subjection of goods or materials to a process (within the extended definition given above) allowances will normally be denied because of the rules relating to 'excepted use'. The term 'excepted use' does not appear in the legislation but is a Revenue term that serves well enough to summarise the various restrictions within CAA 2001, s. 277 (offices, retails shops, etc). The HMRC view is thus that relief will be denied in relation to most vehicle repair workshops on the grounds that they are 'a retail shop, or premises of a similar character where a retail trade or business (including repair work) is carried on'.

Other material: CA 32221

Other trades

The restriction for retail and various other trades is considered in depth at 302-600.

301-650   Storage

Storage trades generally

The question of whether there is a qualifying storage trade has similarly been the subject of case law, with several tax cases helping to define how the rules are to be applied in practice. One such case – that of *Bestway Holdings Ltd v Luff (HMIT)* – caused the Revenue to take a harder line than it had done previously.

The judge in that case held that within the context of the IBAs legislation, '"storage" … means keeping in storage as a purpose and end in itself, and does not extend to such storage as is merely a necessary and transitory incident of the conduct of the business …'.

The HMRC understanding of the implications of the case was summarised in Revenue *Tax Bulletin*, Issue 44, December 1999 (IRInt. 204). This statement is fundamental to the interpretation of the relevant section of the legislation and is therefore reproduced in full below. See further below, however, for details of the *Maco Door & Window Hardware (UK) Ltd v R & C Commrs* case, which has challenged some of the thinking in this statement:

'INDUSTRIAL BUILDINGS ALLOWANCE – TRADE WHICH CONSISTS OF THE STORAGE OF GOODS OR MATERIALS PART OF A TRADE

The decision of the High Court in the case of "Bestway (Holdings) Ltd v Luff" [1998] BTC 69 has altered our view on the meaning of "part of a trade" and a "trade which consists in the storage of goods or materials" in relation to industrial buildings allowances.

Part of a trade

To qualify for IBA the building or structure must be in use for the purposes of a qualifying trade. The qualifying trade does not need to be the whole of the trade carried on, it can be a part of the trade (s. 18(2) CAA 1990 [now CAA 2001, s. 276]).

We previously took the view that anything done in the course of a trade is a part of the trade for this purpose.

Bestway shows that this view was too wide. The court held that although the activities in question do not need to be self-contained, they must be a significant, separate and identifiable part of the trade carried on.

A trade which consists in the storage of goods or materials

A building or structure in use for the purposes of "a trade which consists in the storage of goods or materials" will qualify for IBA if one of the further conditions in s. 18(1)(f)(i) to (iv) [now CAA 2001, s. 274(1) Table A, item 3] is satisfied.

Although we did not previously try to define what is meant by this phrase, we said that the main test was whether the further conditions in s. 18(1)(f)(i) to (iv) [now CAA 2001, s. 274(1) Table A, item 3] were satisfied, for instance a warehouse used by a steel stockholder to store its stock would qualify for IBA if the goods stored would subsequently be used in the manufacture of other goods or materials.

The decision in *Bestway* clarifies the meaning of this phrase. The court held that the determining factor in deciding whether the goods are stored is the purpose for which they are kept or held. A building is only used for storage if the purpose of keeping goods there is their storage as an end in itself. There is no such use for storage if the goods are kept there for some other purpose. Storage which is merely a necessary and transitory incident of the conduct of the business is not sufficient. The decision in *Crusabridge Investments Ltd v Casings International* (54 TC 246) [see below] was distinguished as the collection and storage of tyres was an essential part of the business in that case.

Consequences of the decision in Bestway

The main impact is likely to be on [those] wholesale trades where we have previously accepted, in the particular circumstances of the case, that there was a qualifying part trade of storage of goods or materials which would be used in the manufacture of other goods or materials or subjected in the course of a trade to a process. In order for the building or structure to continue to qualify for IBA, the storage must form a significant, separate and identifiable part of the trade and be conducted as a purpose and end in itself, not just a necessary and transitory incident of the conduct of the wholesale business.

Each case will have to be considered on its own facts. The sort of business which may be affected by the *Bestway* decision is a builder's merchant where it has previously been accepted that a building or structure in use for the purposes of the trade which consists in the storage of building materials that are to be used in the manufacture of other goods or materials would qualify. Depending on the facts, such storage may no longer qualify the building or structure for IBA.

Where claims to IBA have been accepted for previous periods in accordance with our previous prevailing practice and IBA ceases to be due as a result of the revised view of the meaning of "part of a trade" and a "trade which consists in the storage of goods or materials", the revised view should be applied to claims of that taxpayer for chargeable periods ending after 31 December, 1999. Claims for periods ending on or before 31 December, 1999 in respect of the expenditure that has been agreed as qualifying for IBA under our previous prevailing practice will be allowed subject to any other changes in the nature and conduct of the trade that may affect entitlement to IBA for those periods, such as the admission of retail customers or the outsourcing of supplies.'

523

The extended quotation above refers to the earlier case of *Crusabridge Investments Ltd v Casings International*. It is genuinely difficult to reconcile fully the two decisions, though the judge in the later case was fully aware of the tension between his ruling and that of *Crusabridge*. His explanation was that in the earlier case there was 'a finding that the collection and storage of tyres was "an essential part" of the business'. Perhaps the true explanation is that he would in fact have reached a different decision in the *Crusabridge* case anyway: 'in any event I do not think that that decision should stand in the way of what is clearly the correct answer in this case'.

Legislation: CAA 2001, s. 276

Cases: *Crusabridge Investments Ltd v Casings International* (1979) 54 TC 246; *Bestway Holdings Ltd v Luff (HMIT)* [1998] BTC 69

The Maco Door & Window case

The difficulty in reconciling the *Bestway* and *Crusabridge* cases was explored in *Maco Door & Window Hardware (UK) Ltd v R & C Commrs*, and again in the subsequent Chancery Division appeal. This case concerned a building that was used to house goods manufactured by the appellant's Austrian parent company. The UK company sold the goods to wholesalers in the UK for manufacturing purposes.

For the purposes of its UK trade, the company needed to hold substantial levels of stock because orders had to be in minimum sizes and because of the difference between the delivery time required by its customers of 7 to 10 days, and the order time from the parent company of six weeks or more.

HMRC contended that the UK company's trade was not that of storage but was rather one of buying and selling products wholesale. Furthermore, storage was not part of the trade but was rather something inherent in wholesaling.

The progress of the case through the courts was a tortuous one. The company succeeded in front of the commissioner; HMRC won its appeal in the Chancery Division, where the judge took the view that the *Crusabridge* case had been wrongly decided; the company was then successful by a majority verdict in the Court of Appeal. However, the company finally lost its case, by a narrow majority, in the House of Lords in 2008. There was an important distinction between a trade and an activity undertaken in the course of a trade. The concept of 'part of a trade' implied that the part must have the same sort of characteristics as the trade as a whole: the activity would have to be a viable section of a composite trade – in other words, a section that would still be a recognisable trade if separated from the composite whole. In this case, the storage activities were carried out to support the taxpayer's wholesale trading operation; they weren't trading or commercial activities in themselves.

These decisions between them can be seen as determining whether there is a 'trade consisting of storing goods or materials'. If that hurdle is successfully negotiated, it is then necessary to see whether the trade falls within the four permitted categories of storage. It will do so if it consists of storing goods or materials meeting any of the following criteria:

- if the goods or materials are to be used in the manufacture of other goods or materials;
- if they are to be subjected, in the course of a trade, to a process;
- if having already been manufactured or produced or subjected, in the course of a trade, to a process, they have not yet been delivered to any purchaser; or
- if the goods or materials are being stored on their arrival in the UK from a place outside the UK.

Each of these is considered in turn below.

Cases: *Saxone Lilley & Skinner (Holdings) Ltd v IR Commrs* (1967) 44 TC 122; *R & C Commrs v Maco Door and Window Hardware (UK) Ltd* [2008] BTC 486

Goods or materials to be used in the manufacture of other goods or materials

The HMRC interpretation of this is that the goods must be used as raw materials or components for the new goods or materials. In the HMRC view, machinery used in the manufacturing process, and consumable stores such as new bits for drilling machines, are not within the wording.

There is no requirement, however, that the person storing the goods or materials will use them in his own trade. HMRC gives an example of a warehouse used by a steel stockholder to store steel. This will qualify for IBAs as long as the person who buys the steel either uses it in the manufacture of goods or materials or subjects it to a process.

Other material: CA 32224

Goods or materials to be subjected, in the course of a trade, to a process

This category does not include the storage of machinery used to subject other goods or materials to a process.

Other material: CA 32224

Goods or materials not yet delivered to any purchaser

The Northern Irish case of *Dale (HMIT) v Johnson Brothers* makes it clear that, in this context, 'the word "any" is a word importing wide generality'. As the judge put it, 'One looks, not for a "true" purchaser but for "any" purchaser'.

The HMRC manuals restate this – less elegantly but more clearly – as follows:

> 'Goods in "c" [ie goods which have been manufactured or processed or subjected to a process but have not yet been delivered to any purchaser] are goods that still belong to the person who manufactured or produced them or subjected them to a process. Goods that belong to the

person storing them are not in "c" because the person storing them will have purchased them and so they will have been delivered to a purchaser.'

Cases: *Dale (HMIT) v Johnson Brothers* (1951) 32 TC 487

Other material: CA 32224

Goods or materials stored on their arrival in the UK

Some care is needed with the interpretation of this part of the legislation. The two leading tax cases both give the impression of distorting the natural interpretation of the legislation so as to reach a result that is perceived to be fair.

HMRC rewords the condition as a requirement to meet three tests:

- the goods or materials have been imported;
- they are being stored for the first time since their arrival in the UK; and
- they are still in transit, ie they have not yet arrived at their final destination in the UK (though the building in which the goods are stored does not need to be in the port, etc area where they entered the UK).

The condition that the goods must still be in transit is not easy to understand on the basis of the legislation itself. The explanation for HMRC view, however, lies in the case of *Copol Clothing v Hindmarch (HMIT)*, a case which the Revenue won almost by accident, having unsuccessfully argued a different technical point. The company owned a warehouse in Manchester that was used for warehousing and storage. The judgment appears to be based on the fact that the legislation, if read naturally, would give an unfair advantage to a wholesaler importing foreign goods over one selling UK produce. As Fox LJ stated it (paragraph breaks added for clarity):

'It is necessary, it seems to me, to consider the reason for the storage. The words "goods or materials on their arrival by sea or air into any part of the United Kingdom" leave upon me the impression that what subpara. (iv) is dealing with is goods in transit. Storage "on arrival" in the United Kingdom suggests some temporary storage before onward transmission. The sub-paragraph, I think, is dealing with goods which have reached the United Kingdom but not their ultimate destination and are stored meanwhile.

In the present case the goods, when they reach the warehouse in Manchester, are not in transit at all. They have reached the consignee (the Company) who is in fact the purchaser. I do not think it is the purpose of the statute to give the allowance merely in respect of a building which is used to store manufactured goods which have been purchased from outside the United Kingdom and delivered to the purchaser. Certainly, as the judge pointed out, no such allowance is given in respect of goods manufactured in the United Kingdom which have been delivered to the purchaser (sec. 7(1), subpara. (f)(iii)).

The allowance under subpara. (iv) is given to encourage the provision of storage for goods which have just arrived in the United Kingdom and before their onward transit. The storage in the present case is not that at all – it is merely the storage that any wholesaler wants for his goods. That situation seems to me to be a far cry from the storage of goods "on their arrival by sea or air into the United Kingdom". The storage, at this point, really bears no relation to the arrival by sea or air into the United Kingdom. It is merely storage by an owner of goods until he disposes of them.'

A claim for IBAs in respect of quarantine kennels (*Carr [HMIT] v Sayer*) similarly failed to impress the judges. Partly this was because of an unease at describing cats and dogs as 'goods or materials' (see 301-600) but the claim also ran into trouble on the issue of storage. Looked at in isolation, it was arguable that the required wording of the legislation was met:

'However, when one stands back, the end-product envisaged by the several ingredients combined into para. (f)(iv) seems to me to be of a different order from the facility provided by the taxpayers. Quarantine kennels exist to provide for owners the means of complying with statutory requirements of animal isolation for periods of weeks or months on public health grounds. The provision of such a facility does not fall naturally within the scope of an enactment concerned to encourage the provision of storage facilities in support of ports. The taxpayers' service is provided to meet a need which exists, not as part of the ordinary process of physical transportation, but because of statutory restrictions on the conditions in which animals must live for a lengthy period when they come into this country. The service is the means by which animal owners can comply with these statutory restrictions. That is not a facility which can at all happily be described as "the storage of goods ... on their arrival by sea or air" into this country.'

Cases: *Copol Clothing v Hindmarch (HMIT)* [1984] BTC 35; *Carr [HMIT] v Sayer* [1992] BTC 286

Other material: CA 32224

301-700 Agricultural contracting

This fourth category of qualifying trade in Table A lies improbably within the context of industrial buildings. The trade will qualify if it consists of:

'(a) ploughing or cultivating land occupied by another,
(b) carrying out any other agricultural operation on land occupied by another, or
(c) threshing another's crops. For this purpose "crops" includes vegetable produce.'

The key point to note is the occurrence of the word 'another' in each line; the relief is not available for a farmer occupying his own land. HMRC gives the example of a man who owns farm equipment that is used to provide services for other farmers. IBAs would then be due on the cost of construction of a building used to store his combine harvesters, and so on.

301-750 Working foreign plantations

IBAs are due on a building for a trade of working foreign plantations, defined in the legislation (Table A, item 5) as follows:

'A trade consisting of working land outside the United Kingdom used for:

(a) growing and harvesting crops,
(b) husbandry, or
(c) forestry.

For this purpose "crops" includes vegetable produce and "harvesting crops" includes the collection of vegetable produce (however effected).'

Legislation: CAA 2001, s. 274

301-800   Fishing

The sixth activity listed in Table A as a qualifying trade is 'a trade consisting of catching or taking fish or shellfish'. Simply, this enables those in the fishing industry to claim IBAs on buildings used for their trade.

Legislation: CAA 2001, s. 274

301-850   Mineral extraction

The trade of mineral extraction enjoys its own capital allowance regime – CAA 2001, Pt. 5, 'Mineral Extraction Allowances' (see the Chapter headed 'Mineral Extraction Allowances', which begins at 500-000). Most mining buildings qualify for allowances under that other regime.

For IBA purposes, the trade of mineral extraction is defined as follows (Table A, item 7):

- '● A trade consisting of working a source of mineral deposits.
- ● "**Mineral deposits**" includes any natural deposits capable of being lifted or extracted from the earth, and for this purpose geothermal energy is to be treated as a natural deposit.
- ● "**Source of mineral deposits**" includes a mine, an oil well and a source of geothermal energy.'

The HMRC manuals explain the interaction of the two types of capital allowance in the following terms:

'Most mining buildings qualify for MEA. The inclusion of a trade of mineral extraction as a qualifying trade for IBA lets IBA be given on buildings which would not qualify for MEA. The sort of buildings covered are buildings used for subjecting the raw material which is mined to any other process, for example an oil refinery.'

Some further light was cast on this concept in the Explanatory Notes to the rewritten *Capital Allowances Act* 2001. The 1990 Act had referred to geothermal energy 'whether in the form of aquifers, hot dry rocks or otherwise' but the words in inverted commas have now been omitted. The authors of the new legislation have given their view – after some technical explanations – that the words were more of a hindrance than a help and that 'omitting the words does not change the legal effect'. (Explanatory Notes, Annex 2, note 46 – see www.legislation.hmso.gov.uk/acts/en/annex2.pdf for full details.)

As regards buildings used for the welfare of those employed in mineral extraction trades, see 302-600.

Other material: CA 32228

301-900   Electricity undertakings

The first activity listed within Table B is defined as 'an undertaking for the generation, transformation, conversion, transmission or distribution of electrical energy'.

There is no directly associated case law and no commentary within the HMRC manuals. The old case of *Lancashire Electric Power Company v Wilkinson* touched on the rules applying before the introduction of modern capital allowances.

As regards the treatment of an electricity substation as an item of plant, see *Bradley (HMIT) v London Electricity plc* – the claim for such treatment failed.

Cases: *Lancashire Electric Power Company v Wilkinson* (1947) 28 TC 427; *Bradley (HMIT) v London Electricity plc* [1996] BTC 95

301-950   Water, hydraulic power, sewerage

These definitions have so far proved uncontroversial. The HMRC manuals contain no commentary on any of the three terms. See the specific definitions in Table B at 301-500.

Legislation: CAA 2001, s. 274

302-000   Transport

The meaning of 'a transport undertaking' has been the subject of HMRC guidance. This is because the legislation itself offers no further definition of what is meant by the term.

The key point is that the provision of transport must be an end in itself – note the parallel here with the treatment of storage trades, as discussed above. In HMRC's view, therefore, 'an undertaking is a transport undertaking if its primary activity is the provision of transport'. The transport may involve goods or passengers and 'it does not matter . . . how the transportation is done'.

HMRC goes on to give a number of useful pointers as to what, in its view, will or will not constitute a transport undertaking:

- a transport undertaking will normally be carried on by 'a person acting as a common carrier';
- such a person is likely to hold himself out 'as providing a service of transporting goods or passengers to any person wishing to use' the services in question;

- operators of taxi, railway or bus services are likely to be carrying on a transport undertaking;
- airport operators are also likely to come within the definition, but buildings will only attract allowances if they are used for qualifying activities. Shopping facilities within an airport, for example, will not qualify;
- to the extent that an organisation like the Post Office is providing a service of transporting mail, that will qualify;
- a wholesaler using a fleet of vehicles to collect and deliver his trading stock is not carrying on a transport undertaking, as the transport is merely ancillary to the primary activity;
- a person hiring out cars or other vehicles, without a driver, is not carrying on a transport undertaking; and
- the operator of a toll bridge, tunnel or road will not qualify.

In several cases, the Revenue have accepted that particular activities constitute a transport undertaking, though in each of these the company concerned lost its argument on other grounds. These include *Buckingham (HMIT) v Securitas Properties Ltd* , *Sarsfield (HMIT) v Dixons Group plc* and the special commissioners' decision of *West Somerset Railway plc v Chivers (HMIT)*.

Legislation: CAA 2001, s. 274

Cases: *Buckingham (HMIT) v Securitas Properties Ltd* (1980) 53 TC 292; *West Somerset Railway plc v Chivers (HMIT)* (1995) Sp C 1; *Sarsfield (HMIT) v Dixons Group plc* [1998] BTC 288

Other material: CA 32230

302-050   Highway undertakings (tolls, etc)

This item in Table B is qualified by a note which leads to sections 341–344, which contain various definitions. See also the HMRC manuals beginning at CA 38050.

The carrying on of a highway undertaking is automatically treated as the carrying on of an undertaking by way of trade. The legal effect of this is that, throughout most of the IBAs legislation, references to a trade can be interpreted as if they include references to a highway undertaking, as defined. There is one exception, however. The statutory trick of treating part of a trade or undertaking as a separate trade in its own right (see 302-250) does not apply to highway undertakings limiting the effect of the highway undertaking rules to exclude CAA 2001, s. 276).

A person carrying on a highway undertaking is treated as occupying, for the purposes of that undertaking, any road in relation to which it is carried on.

The concept of 'highway undertaking' is defined in Table B, item 6. As such, allowances can be claimed in respect of :

'so much of any undertaking relating to the design, building, financing and operation of roads as is carried on:

(a)   for the purposes of, or
(b)   in connection with,

the exploitation of highway concessions.'

The term 'highway concession', in relation to a road, is itself defined. Where the road is, or will be, used by the general public, then the concession means the right to receive sums from the relevant authority. If, on the other hand, the road is a toll road, then a highway concession is the right to charge tolls in respect of the road.

For the above purposes, the 'relevant authority' means any of the following:

- the Secretary of State;
- the Scottish Ministers;
- the National Assembly for Wales; or
- the Department for Regional Development in Northern Ireland.

It will be seen from the above that IBAs are given where roads are constructed and operated by a person in the private sector. Typically, this may be capital expenditure incurred on public highways under the Government's Design, Build, Finance and Operate (DBFO) initiative. Under the initiative, private companies will be paid fees for taking responsibility for the design, building, financing and operating of major public highways. Typically, the fees paid will be based on the level of use of the road, but also taking into account factors such as safety and availability.

Legislation: CAA 2001, s. 274, s. 341ff.

Other material: CA 38050

The relevant interest

For the purposes of determining where the relevant interest (see 304-500) lies, a highway concession is not initially treated as an interest in the road. However, the highway concession is treated as the relevant interest in relation to expenditure incurred by a person on the construction of the road if:

- he was not entitled to an interest in the road when he incurred the expenditure; but
- he was at that time entitled to a highway concession in relation to the road.

The effect of this is that a person who is entitled to a highway concession, and who then builds a road, can claim IBAs on the construction expenditure.

Other material: CA 38200

Balancing adjustment

Where the relevant interest has been a highway concession in accordance with the above rules, the ending of the concession will be a balancing event unless the concession is treated as extended. The proceeds from the balancing event will consist of any insurance money received by the person entitled to the highway concession in so far as it relates to qualifying expenditure. Any compensation received should also be included, to the extent that it consists of a capital sum.

A highway concession is treated as being extended if the person entitled to the concession takes up a renewed concession in respect of either the whole or part of the road. Similarly, it is treated as extended if that person (or a person connected with him) takes up a new concession in respect of the whole or part of the road, or of a road that includes the whole or part of the road.

There is a limitation on the extension. The concession is treated as being extended only insofar as the old concession and the new one relate to the same road, and only for the period of the new (or renewed) concession. It does not matter whether or not the new concession is on the same terms as the old one. For the above purposes, a person is treated as taking up a new or renewed concession if he is given the opportunity to be granted the renewed or new concession and takes advantage of that opportunity. The question of whether the arrangements are legally enforceable is not relevant.

Where, under these rules, a highway concession is treated as extended, apportionments should be made on a just and reasonable basis for the purposes of calculating any balancing adjustment. This will be necessary when there are differing periods relating to different parts of the road in relation to which the concession has been granted.

Legislation: CAA 2001, s. 344

302-100   Tunnels, bridges, inland navigation

Once more, there is nothing in the HMRC manuals to expand on any of the three terms. See the specific definitions in Table B.

Legislation: CAA 2001, s. 274

302-150   Docks

The HMRC manuals clarify that the meaning of this expression 'is not intended to be restrictive'. Marinas will normally qualify, as will any structure where it is possible for vessels to load or unload, whether or not the structure is in fact used in that way (if it is not so used, however, it may fail to meet other criteria needed for allowances to be granted).

A pier, etc will not qualify as a dock undertaking if it is used for entertainment. HMRC gives Southend Pier as an example of a structure for which allowances will not be given.

Legislation: CAA 2001, s. 274

Other material: CA 32232

302-200   Welfare buildings

Without special legislation, a building used for the recreational or other welfare purposes of employees would not qualify for allowances. The legislation therefore makes special provision for such a building. Relief will be due where a building is provided:

- by a person carrying on a qualifying trade; and/or
- for the welfare of workers employed in that qualifying trade.

Relief will still be denied, however, if the building is caught under the exclusions for retail shops, etc as considered below. HMRC gives the example of a grocery shop provided for factory workers who cannot otherwise get to the shops during working hours: relief will be denied by virtue of CAA 2001, s. 277.

Buildings listed by HMRC as potentially qualifying under this heading are canteens, day nurseries, garages, hard tennis courts, hostels and indoor sports halls.

HMRC draws an odd distinction between 'workers' and 'employees generally', stating that 'workers are employees who are directly engaged in the productive, manufacturing or processing sides of a business. Office staff and management are not workers for the purposes of this legislation'. In the author's view, this is an inaccurate interpretation, but the outcome is broadly correct. The point is that the extension of IBAs to welfare buildings applies only where the building is in use for the welfare of workers employed in a qualifying trade. The correct understanding of the section would therefore seem to be that 'employees generally' are still workers but that they are not employed in the qualifying trade.

The outcome of this is illustrated by the following example given by HMRC: 'a canteen provided for assembly line workers will qualify for IBA while a canteen provided for office staff will not'. A welfare building used for mixed purposes will qualify 'provided that the use by workers is not negligible'.

Legislation: CAA 2001, s. 275

Other material: CA 32320

302-250   Parts of trades and undertakings

It is quite possible that one part of a trade or undertaking would qualify under the definitions outlined at 301-550 to 302-200 above but another would not. In this case, allowances may still be claimed, but only on those buildings or structures that are in use for the qualifying part of the trade.

An example of this used by HMRC is an airport containing a shopping precinct. Those buildings in use for the purposes of the transport undertaking itself will qualify for relief. The parts of the airport used as shops will not attract IBAs.

The *Bestway* case (discussed at 301-600) draws a distinction between part of a trade and activities that are mere preliminaries to a trade: 'to qualify for the allowances, the activities in question must be a significant, separate and identifiable part of the trade carried on'. The company had claimed allowances on buildings used for such activities as checking, sorting, unpacking and labelling. However, these were held to be mere preliminaries to its main trade as wholesaler – the activities did not amount to a separate part trade of subjecting goods or materials to a process.

HMRC provides guidance on how it interprets this:

> 'A part of a trade does not need to be a self-contained part. It should, however, be a significant, separate and identifiable part of the trade carried on. The expression "part of a trade" does not mean any activity undertaken in the course of a trade.'

In the *Crusabridge* case, also referred to above, it was held on the facts that the storage of remoulded tyres was a qualifying part trade of storage.

Legislation: CAA 2001, s. 276

302-300   Mixed use

A separate issue arises where a building is used for two purposes simultaneously. In such cases, allowances will normally be due in full. The point was addressed in the case of *Saxone, Lilley & Skinner (Holdings) Ltd v IR Commrs*:

> 'The Crown's main argument was that "in use for the purposes of a trade" or of a part of a trade means wholly or mainly in use for such purposes. But that involves writing in words which are not there, and I can see nothing in the context to make that necessary. Moreover, it requires no feat of imagination in a draftsman to see that cases may arise where the same building or the same part of it is being used for two purposes, and if it were intended to exclude such cases I would expect that to be made clear. The Act does deal with the case where one part of a building is used for one purpose and another part is used for a different purpose, but it contains no machinery for dealing with dual use of the same part. Of course there can be cases where the use for a statutory purpose is only intermittent or small and such cases could not reasonably be brought within the Act; but here the use for a statutory purpose was regular and substantial.'

HMRC now accepts that in such cases, full allowances should be given unless the qualifying use is less than ten per cent of the total. This is subject to the issue of excluded activities considered below. In the HMRC view, 'any use for the purposes of a retail shop etc prevents IBA being given no matter how small the excepted use is'.

Cases: *Saxone, Lilley & Skinner (Holdings) Ltd v IR Commrs* (1967) 44 TC 122

Other material: CA 32310ff.

302-350   Parts of a building

The above paragraphs consider one scenario where part of a trade qualifies and a second scenario where the same building is in use for more than one purpose at the same time. A third possibility is that part of the building will be in use for a qualifying purpose whilst a separate part of the same building will be in use for non-qualifying purposes.

The legislation addresses this issue by providing that any reference to a building or structure includes a reference to part of that building or structure. As such, each part of the building should be looked at in isolation and allowances claimed accordingly, albeit subject to the 25 per cent *de minimis* rule (CAA 2001, s. 283, described at 303-500).

This principle applies unless 'the context otherwise requires'.

Legislation: CAA 2001, s. 571

Other material: CA 32650

302-400   Building used by more than one licensee

Special rules apply to buildings occupied under licence, rather than under the terms of a lease. A building occupied by several licensees will not qualify for IBAs unless the building, or an identifiable part of the building, is used by all licensees for the purposes of a qualifying trade. Where only part of the building is so used, then allowances will be restricted to that part. See 302-500, however, for the treatment of small workshops.

The word 'lease' and related expressions are defined at CAA 2001, s. 360. The HMRC manuals explain the distinction between a licence and a lease in the following terms:

'A lease creates an interest in land but a licence does not. Normally a licence does not give exclusive possession and so it is possible for there to be several licensees of the same building. For example, one licensee may have the right to use the building in the morning on weekdays, another the right to use it on weekday afternoons and a third at weekends.'

Legislation: CAA 2001, s. 278, 360

Other material: CA 32350

302-500   Small workshops

Special IBA rules used to apply to small, and very small, workshops. For expenditure incurred since 27 March 1983, this is no longer the case.

A practical issue can still arise, however, in relation to industrial workshops constructed for separate letting to small businesses. A Revenue Statement of Practice issued on 26 March 1980 offers some practical help on the matter:

> *'Industrial buildings allowance: Industrial workshops constructed for separate letting to small businesses*
>
> Under the industrial buildings allowance rules (Part 1 CAA 1990) a building only qualifies for relief if it is in use as an industrial building or structure as defined in Section 18. Where a number of small workshops which are to be industrial buildings are constructed for separate letting to small businesses, it is thus necessary for the owner of the relevant interest to establish in each case that the tenant is carrying on a qualifying trade. He must also establish, in each case, how much, if any, of the building is used for non-qualifying purposes, such as for offices. These requirements can be burdensome, particularly where tenants change frequently, and further information on these points has to be obtained to establish that each workshop continues to be used in full as an industrial building.
>
> The Inland Revenue have decided that, in future, they will normally be prepared to deal with industrial buildings allowance claims for estates consisting of small industrial workshops on a global instead of individual basis. Where, therefore, individual workshops units of 2,500 square feet or less intended for separate letting as industrial buildings to small businesses are constructed as an estate, the Inspector will normally be satisfied with a general description of the uses to which the units will be put and, unless the circumstances suggest the need for further enquiry, will not ask for particulars of the trades carried on by individual tenants or details of the uses to which these premises are put. For the purpose of writing-down allowances, the whole of any estate built at one time (or part of an estate where it is constructed in phases) will be regarded as having been brought into use when the first workshop begins to be used.
>
> A sale of the relevant interest in the estate would also be dealt with on a global basis so far as possible, but when only part of the estate is sold, separate computations would normally be necessary to establish the balancing adjustments and the successor's allowances.
>
> This practice is intended to simplify the administration of the industrial buildings allowance rules as they apply to most industrial workshop estates built for letting as separate units to small businesses. It will not apply where, exceptionally, several units in one estate are let to the same tenant or connected tenants; where the estate is to a significant extent used for trades which do not attract industrial buildings allowance; and in any other circumstances where the relief available would be significantly lower on a strict application of the industrial building allowances rules.'

Other material: HMRC Statement of Practice SP 4/80

Excluded activities

302-600   Overview of excluded activities

Even where an activity constitutes a qualifying trade, allowances are denied if the building is in use 'as, or as part of, or for any purpose ancillary to' the purposes of a number of specified types of premises. Five such forbidden categories are listed:

- a dwelling-house;
- a retail shop, or premises of a similar character where a retail trade or business (including repair work) is carried on;
- a showroom;
- a hotel; and
- an office.

Allowances in respect of such premises will only be available if the expenditure on the prohibited part is less than 25 per cent of the total expenditure – see 303-500.

There are exceptions in relation to certain workers in the field of mineral extraction, or workers on foreign plantations – see below.

Legislation: CAA 2001, s. 277

302-650   Dwelling-houses

There is no statutory definition of dwelling-house for IBA purposes, so the term must be given its ordinary meaning. The definition at CAA 2001, s. 531(1), picking up the meaning used in the *Rent Act* 1977, applies only for the purposes of Assured Tenancy Allowances and in theory has no significance for IBA purposes. Nevertheless, the HMRC view is that for IBA purposes, the meaning should be 'read in the same way'.

As such, the HMRC opinion of how the term is to be interpreted used to be as follows:

'A dwelling-house is a building, or part of a building, which is a person's home. A person's second or holiday home is a dwelling-house as is a flat which is used as a residence. A block of flats is not a dwelling-house although the individual flats within the block may be. A university hall of residence, accommodation used for holiday letting, a hospital, a nursing home or a prison are not dwelling-houses.'

At the end of 2008, however, HMRC changed their view in relation to properties such as university residences: see 165-100.

A recent VAT case offers a perspective on the concept that the definition of a dwelling-house depends not on the structure of a building but on its use. The point was made, but not specifically determined by the judge, in the following terms in the case of *C & E Commrs v Zielinski Baker and Partners Ltd*:

Industrial Buildings

'It is obvious that dwelling is the act of use of a building. An example is a firm of accountants who use a house in town. If they moved out and no alteration was made and a family moved in, what had been a business premises would now be a dwelling-house which it had not been before'

It should be emphasised that this quotation does not provide a binding precedent. Nevertheless, the case may be worth reviewing if any arguments are needed on the definition of 'dwelling-house'. It should also be noted, however, that Customs appealed successfully to the House of Lords.

Legislation: CAA 2001, s. 277

Cases: *C & E Commrs v Zielinski Baker and Partners Ltd* [2004] BTC 5,249

Other material: CA 11520

302-700 Retail shops

This exclusion covers a retail shop as such but also 'premises of a similar character where a retail trade or business (including repair work) is carried on'.

In the *Kilmarnock* case, Lord Cameron drew a distinction between a retail business and a retail shop, suggesting that the latter has a narrower meaning. The purposes of a retail shop were 'to enable members of the public to resort to a place where they may see and purchase goods or materials by retail and to serve as a place of exhibition and sale of a shopkeeper's wares'. In the present case, there was no resort by the public to the premises to buy packaged coal; the premises were not contiguous or adjacent to a retail shop, far less to any retail shop owned by the appellants.

The packaging of the coal did indeed assist the retail business but could not fairly be said to be 'ancillary, ie, subordinate or subservient, to the purposes of a retail shop'. As Lord Guthrie put it in the same case: 'the development of a wholesale and retail trade in a commodity is a bigger and broader conception than the mere furtherance of the purposes of a retail shop'.

The meaning of a retail shop has also been considered in a number of rating cases. The concept of 'shop' has a wider meaning than merely premises where physical goods are sold over the counter. HMRC quotes buildings occupied by 'laundrettes, banks, undertakers, jobbing builders and shoe repairers' as other examples of shops. In the context of the IBA legislation, the meaning of 'shop' is in any case extended to include premises of a similar kind.

Care is needed with the concept of 'retail'. The HMRC view on this is expressed as follows:

'Trade customers are not the public and so a building which serves only trade customers is not a retail shop. A wholesaler's premises are not a retail shop if all the customers are trade customers. If, however, the public are allowed to shop at a wholesaler's premises it will be a retail shop even if most of the customers are trade customers.'

Most vehicle repair workshops are, in the HMRC view, unable to qualify for IBAs. This is because they are 'premises ... where a retail trade or business (including repair work) is carried on'. HMRC takes the line that a vehicle repair workshop will qualify only if all the following conditions are met:

- the area is completely separated from the rest of the motor dealer's premises. This does not have to involve a separate building as long as the workshop 'occupies a distinguishable part of the building' and is not used to any significant extent for purposes other than vehicle repair;
- the workshop does not include the reception area for cars; and
- ordinary retail customers are discouraged from having access to the area concerned. This condition will also cause many tyre and exhaust businesses to lose out on IBAs – if customers inspect the work in the workshop itself, then the building will not qualify.

See below for the meaning of 'ancillary to' – especially in the context of retail shops.

Legislation: CAA 2001, s. 277

Cases: *Kilmarnock Equitable Co-operative Society Ltd v IR Commrs* (1966) 42 TC 675

Other material: CA 32221, 32311

302-750   Showrooms

There is relatively little guidance on the meaning of 'showroom' and nothing of interest on the matter in the HMRC manuals. The *Bestway* case, however, did touch on the issue. The commissioners in that case struggled with the concept:

'There appears to be no authority as to what constitutes a showroom and we were therefore referred to dictionary definitions which we have not found to be very helpful.

In the last resort the decision as to what is and what is not a showroom must be one of impression and having inspected both ... premises we are of the opinion that neither of those premises can be called a showroom. Although there are attempts at certain displays of goods at both premises and although it is true that [one site] possesses a small internal-display window, these are matters which are very much de minimis in our judgment.'

The inspector in that case accepted a finding by the commissioners that the buildings in question were not showrooms. This was, in the words of the judge, on the grounds that 'the steel racking on which goods available to customers were placed was not designed to display goods to their best advantage, but to facilitate the speedy disposal of goods to educated purchasers who knew precisely what they wanted to purchase.'

Legislation: CAA 2001, s. 277

Cases: *Bestway (Holdings) Ltd v Luff (HMIT)* [1998] BTC 69

302-800　Hotels

Once more, there is little guidance as to the interpretation of a hotel for these purposes. Some care is needed, though, to understand how the structure of the legislation works here.

The starting point is that 'a building is not in use for the purposes of a qualifying trade if it is in use as, or as part of, or for any purpose ancillary to the purposes of ... a hotel'. The excluding section makes no reference to the fact that certain hotels qualify for IBAs (see 300-500).

To understand this, it must be noted that a qualifying hotel qualifies for IBAs in its own right and not because a hotel trade is a qualifying trade: indeed, although certain hotels qualify for allowances they are never within the definition of qualifying trades.

It follows that a building in use for purposes ancillary to those of a qualifying hotel will – strictly – qualify for relief only if it is part of the qualifying hotel itself. A separate building will not qualify in its own right as a hotel and will still be excluded from the definition of a qualifying trade by reason of the 'ancillary to the purposes' rule.

It is possible that HMRC does not take this point in practice. The capital allowances manual appears to imply that a building separate from the qualifying hotel, but in use for purposes ancillary to it, may still qualify for relief: 'Examples of buildings which are used for purposes ancillary to the purposes of a retail shop [include] ... a hotel laundry which serves a group of hotels unless the hotels are qualifying hotels.'

If what is envisaged here is a separate building housing the laundry, not part of any of the hotels operated by the group, then HMRC appears to be making a generous interpretation of the rules. Incidentally, the wording 'ancillary to the purposes of a retail shop' in this quotation should presumably read 'ancillary to the purposes of a retail shop or hotel'.

Legislation: CAA 2001, s. 277(1)(c)

Other material: CA 32313

302-825　Offices

The meaning of 'office' for these purposes has been considered in two tax cases.

Back in 1950, it was established that a drawing office attached to a factory was not an office for the purposes of the IBA rules (*IR Commrs v Lambhill Ironworks Ltd*). Lambhill Ironworks were structural engineers and it was held that its drawing office was an industrial building or structure. The Revenue had sought to disallow allowances, partly by reference to the exclusion of retail shops, offices, etc. The judges would have none of it, however. The Lord President (Cooper) referred to the various types of building that are excluded from qualifying for allowances and commented that 'the genus to which the enumerated species all belong is manifestly non-industrial'. Finding the Revenue position 'almost unarguable', he went on to say that for most firms of structural engineers or shipbuilders, the drawing office was 'to all outward semblance and in real substance an integral, and indeed a vital part of the industrial premises and devoted to the industrial operations carried on therein'. The drawing office was neither an office in itself nor used for a purpose ancillary to the purposes of the general office.

Lord Keith, in the same case, agreed: 'An office must be something which clearly has not got anything of an industrial character or is not directly ancillary to the industrial operations conducted in the rest of the works'.

The meaning of office was again considered in the case of *Girobank plc v Clarke (HMIT)*. Although the company lost the case on other grounds, the court held that the premises under consideration could not be described as an office. In this aspect of the decision, the Court of Appeal overruled the High Court judgment and restored the view of the commissioners. The building in question was occupied for the purpose of various processing activities and these involved no administrative functions other than certain limited managerial functions that had been specifically identified. It was a data-processing centre and the commissioner came to the view that it was like a modern light industrial building. His opinion that the building was therefore not an office was justifiable on the basis of the facts as he had stated them. The case referred back to a non-tax case of *Carter v The Standard Ltd*. In that earlier case, McKeown J said:

'The only proper and safe way to construe the statute, in my judgment, is to confine the meaning of the term "office" to what is ordinarily meant by that expression, ie the place where the central management emanates and where the manager and his staff do their work.'

Pulling all the above principles together, it will be clear that it is the activities carried on in a building that are important, rather than the name given to the building. In the HMRC view:

'you decide whether a building is an office by looking at the activities carried out in it. A building or part of a building which is directly involved in a manufacturing operation or the subjection of goods to a process will not normally be an office. A building occupied by managerial staff or concerned with marketing or administration will be.'

The HMRC view is that accommodation occupied by any of the following will be offices for IBA purposes and so will not qualify for allowances:

- the board and senior executive;
- planning and administration;
- personnel;
- works, planning and control;
- works manager and staff dealing with costing and despatch;
- wages offices; and
- purchasing and sales departments.

On the other hand, HMRC accepts that accommodation used for the editorial staff of a newspaper will not normally constitute an office. This is on the grounds that their activities will form an integral part of the production of the paper.

Similarly, HMRC accepts that 'buildings which house staff engaged in time and motion study in a factory, progress chasing, factory layout and management, costing, training of factory staff, factory fire precautions, etc are not offices for the purposes of the IBA legislation'.

Legislation: CAA 2001, s. 277

Cases: *Carter v The Standard Ltd* [1915] 30 DLR 492; *IR Commrs v Lambhill Ironworks Ltd* (1950) 31 TC 393; *Girobank plc v Clarke (HMIT)* [1998] BTC 24

Other material: CA 32312

302-850   Meaning of 'ancillary to'

The meaning of 'ancillary to' was considered in the case of *Kilmarnock Equitable Co-operative Society Ltd v IR Commrs* and again in the case of *Sarsfield (HMIT) v Dixons Group plc*. The two cases bring out some fine distinctions.

In *Kilmarnock*, the company sold coal and claimed allowances on a depot which was used to screen and pack the coal in paper bags. The Revenue had argued that the building was in use for a purpose ancillary to the purposes of a retail shop. The judge (the Lord President (Clyde)) ruled that the use to which the product was eventually put was not relevant. It was only necessary to consider the purpose for which the premises themselves were used. The building was used to package coal. It was of no importance that this was a preliminary operation which preceded some other trading operation. The purpose of the use of the building was a quite separate and independent purpose in itself, 'just as the purpose of the use of a building for constructing something from a raw material cannot be described as ancillary to the purposes of a retail shop where the finished product is sold to the public'. The judge went on to say:

> 'In neither case is the purpose of the use of the building ancillary or subservient to the purpose of the retail shop where the product from the building may ultimately be sold. They are independent purposes the one from the other.'

Lord Migdale considered the point further in the same case:

> 'Counsel for the Crown contended that the purpose of a retail shop was to sell goods over the counter. The purpose of the operation carried on in this building was to prepare the coal so that it could be sold over the counter in a retail shop. It was found in the case that the bulk of these packages were in fact sent to retail shops, so it could be truly said that the purpose of the use of the building was ancillary to the purpose of the retail shop. I find it difficult to accept this argument. It confuses the purpose of the use of the building with the ultimate destination of those goods. The goods were intended for ultimate retail sale. It was to that end that the coal

was put into small packets. The building was in that sense used to produce goods which could be retailed. To be ancillary to the purpose of a shop the purpose of the use of the building would have to be subservient or subordinate to retail selling. It could be said to be subservient only in the sense that both look to the retail buyer but that can be said of nearly all manufacturing operations.'

The point was further tested by the *Dixons* group, who won in the High Court but ultimately lost in the Court of Appeal. The group had a subsidiary company that received, stored and delivered goods bought for sale in the group's retail shops. It was accepted that the buildings were in use for the purposes of a transport undertaking. Nevertheless, IBAs were denied to the subsidiary, on the grounds that the use of its warehouses was ancillary to the purposes of a retail shop: 'the purpose of the warehouse was exclusively that of receiving, storing and distributing to the retail shops the goods necessary for those shops to operate as retail shops'. This reasoning was summarised by Morritt LJ as follows:

'The use of the warehouse serves no other purpose. It is not the case of a warehouseman or distributor with a variety of customers for whom he receives, stores and distributes goods. In such a case the role of the warehouseman or distributor and the purpose of the use to which he puts his building is indeed separate from and independent of the purposes of the shops he supplies. But in this case the retail shops of Dixons Ltd are the only shops for which the warehouse is used for the reception, storage and distribution of goods. In such a case, in my view, the use of the warehouse is subservient and subordinate and therefore ancillary to the purposes of the retail shops for it has no other.'

The company was not saved by the fact that the transport and warehousing activities were carried on by a separate undertaking that was independent of the retail shops: 'the fact that the undertaking is separate and its purpose preliminary to that of some other trading operation in a retail shop is not of itself inconsistent with the purpose of the use to which it puts its building being ancillary to the purposes of the shop.'

In commenting on the above decisions, HMRC gives the following example:

'A bakehouse which produces bread is not in use for purposes ancillary to the shop where the bread is sold because making the bread is not ancillary to selling it. If, however, the bakehouse is actually part of the retail shop no IBA is due because use as a retail shop is excluded use. A bakehouse in a separate building or in a separate extension at the back of the shop is not part of the shop and can qualify for IBA.'

HMRC goes on to give the following examples of buildings that are excluded as being ancillary to the purposes of a retail shop:

- '● a printing works used solely for the printing requirements of a multiple shop concern;
- ● a garage for the delivery vans of a multiple shop concern;
- ● a workshop used by the maintenance staff of a retail shop for the repair and maintenance of the shop fittings, and
- ● a hotel laundry which serves a group of hotels unless the hotels are qualifying hotels.'

The exclusion relating to retail shops, etc applies where a building is in use for any purpose ancillary to the various other listed purposes. A literal interpretation of this would deny relief where the building is used partly for prohibited purposes and partly for other purposes.

HMRC does not take this view, however, accepting that allowances will normally be preserved if the building is apparently ancillary to more than one activity:

'If a warehouse is not only used to store goods for delivery to retail shops but also for wholesale goods the mixed use of the building will prevent it from being ancillary to the retail shops. This follows from the Kilmarnock case where it was held that an activity could only be ancillary to one thing. If it supports two activities it is ancillary to neither.'

A similar point is made where it is stated that 'a building can only be ancillary to one purpose. This means that if a building is used for two purposes it is not in use for purposes ancillary to either'. By way of example, 'a wholesale distribution warehouse that supplies goods to retail shops owned by a connected person and to arms length customers is not in use for purposes ancillary to either'.

Legislation: CAA 2001, s. 277

Cases: *Kilmarnock Equitable Co-operative Society Ltd v IR Commrs* (1966) 42 TC 675; *Sarsfield (HMIT) v Dixons Group plc* [1998] BTC 288

Other material: CA 32313

302-900 Exceptions

Excluded activities – exceptions

The legislation lists two exceptions from the exclusions. In other words, there are two categories of building that may qualify for relief even though they would otherwise be caught by the exclusion applying to retail shops, offices, etc.

The first exception relates to working land outside the UK used as a foreign plantation (as defined in Table A, item 5 – see 301-500). The second relates to buildings used in connection with working a source of mineral deposits (per Table A, item 7 – see 301-850). To qualify for either exemption, the building must be constructed for occupation by, or for the welfare of, people employed in the specified trades.

These buildings will not be precluded from qualifying for relief if either:

- the building is likely to be of little or no value to the person carrying on the trade when the land or source is no longer worked; or
- the building will cease to be owned by that person on the ending of a foreign concession under which the land or source is worked.

For the above purposes, a foreign concession is defined as 'a right or privilege granted by the government of, or any municipality or other authority in, a territory outside the United Kingdom'.

The reference to 'little or no value' is to be read as meaning that the property will have little or no value for any purpose. The National Coal Board lost a claim for IBAs in relation to houses built for and occupied by colliery workers (*IR Commrs v National Coal Board*). The houses were capable of use by people other than colliery workers and so no allowances were due. As Lord Radcliffe put it:

> 'The question to be asked, in order to see whether it qualifies for allowance now, is whether ... the capital expenditure incurred in respect of the building would be likely to have any appreciable residual value for the owner. If the answer is "Yes", then the expenditure does not qualify for industrial buildings allowance: if the answer is "No", it does.'

Legislation: CAA 2001, s. 277(2)

Cases: *IR Commrs v National Coal Board* (1957) 37 TC 264

Non-industrial parts of buildings

303-500   Introduction

It will often happen that part of a building would qualify as an industrial building and part would not. Typically, this will arise in a factory block that also contains offices – the factory qualifies but the offices are excluded as described at 302-825. As long as the qualifying expenditure (see 304-000) relating to the non-industrial part is no more than one-quarter of the total qualifying expenditure, then allowances can be claimed in full, without any restriction. This deceptively simple rule can give rise to a number of complications in practice.

The 25 per cent test specifically relates to expenditure. A simple apportionment of surface area of a building will not be appropriate if, on the facts, some parts of the building were more expensive than others.

It is quite possible that a non-industrial part of a building will qualify at certain times but not at others.

> ### *Example*
>
> A factory is built at a total cost of £2 million. It is agreed that the cost relating to the offices is £600,000. As this exceeds 25 per cent of the total construction expenditure, no allowances are due on the offices (see 303-500).
>
> A year later, the factory part of the building is extended at a further cost of £1 million. No further costs are incurred on the offices. As such, the total expenditure has now risen to £3 million, of which £2.4 million relates to the factory and £600,000 to the offices. The non-industrial part of the building is now less than 25 per cent and allowances can from this point on be claimed on the whole building.

> The same rule applies in reverse. If, therefore, additional expenditure on offices, etc takes the non-industrial part of the total expenditure from below 25 per cent to above 25 per cent, then allowances will be restricted from that point on.

Legislation: CAA 2001, s. 283

303-550   Building not premises

The legislation refers to 'part of a building', rather than to part of the overall premises, so the 25 per cent test must be applied to each building individually. This therefore raises the question of what constitutes 'a building' for the purposes of the 25 per cent test.

This point was considered in the case of *Abbott Laboratories Ltd v Carmody (HMIT)*. The company claimed capital allowances on the whole of a factory site, including a chemical block, a pharmaceutical block, a maintenance block and an administrative block. This last building was at a distance of 25 yards from the pharmaceutical block and connected to it by a covered passage. The Revenue successfully contended that the administrative block was a separate building which was used as an office and which did not qualify for IBAs.

It is worth noting that this case does not in fact provide a satisfactory precedent. Although the company lost, this was on the basis of the finding by the commissioners. It was held in the High Court that their decision was justified but the judge specifically did not address the general point of law of whether premises consisting of individual blocks within a factory could ever be regarded as a single unit for capital allowances purposes.

The HMRC view is that two buildings linked by an overhead bridge or covered corridor should be treated as separate buildings if the link could be removed easily. Inspectors are also likely to consider whether the different buildings share common supplies (of water, power, heat, etc). If they do, that will be an argument in favour of treating the units as a single unified structure. Similarly, they may be treated as one overall structure if it would be impossible to demolish part of the factory, etc without seriously damaging the other parts.

The question of what constitutes an entity, or a building, is one of the notoriously grey areas of tax law. Given the substantial amounts of money that can be at stake, it is perhaps surprising that there have not been more capital allowance cases on this topic. In cases of doubt, it may well be appropriate to make reference to some of the precedents arising from treatment of capital expenditure, repairs and so on. Cases that could be worth considering would include the following:

- *Bullcroft Main Collieries Ltd v O'Grady* (1932) 17 TC 93;
- *Samuel Jones & Co (Devonvale) Ltd v IR Commrs* (1952) 32 TC 513;
- *Phillips v Whieldon Potteries Ltd* (1952) 33 TC 213;
- *Wynne-Jones v Bedale Auction Ltd* (1976) 51 TC 426; and
- *Brown (HMIT) v Burnley Football and Athletic Co Ltd* (1980) 53 TC 357.

The above list is far from exhaustive but does contain some of the key cases in which the matter has been considered.

HMRC also refers to the case of *Lancashire Electric Power Company v Wilkinson*, in which the power house of a generating station was held to be a single industrial building.

It should be noted that the concept of the 'entity' or 'building', for the purposes of applying the 25 per cent test, is a different concept from that of how each part of the overall expenditure is to be treated. HMRC has expressed very clearly the view that each 'block of expenditure' should be treated separately, even where incurred by the same person at different times. If, therefore, the owner of a factory builds an extension, there will be two separate issues:

(1) the question of whether the extension should be taken into account in calculating the 25 per cent test for the building as a whole; and

(2) the issue of how relief is given for the two separate amounts including, for example, the timing of the expenditure to be written off.

In the example above, therefore, the lifetime of the £2 million expenditure will run from the original date of construction. Allowances on the extension will run for 25 years from the time it is first brought into use.

Cases: *Lancashire Electric Power Company v Wilkinson* (1947) 28 TC 427; *Abbott Laboratories Ltd v Carmody (HMIT)* (1968) 44 TC 569

Other material: CA 31600, 32750

303-650   Interaction with plant and machinery allowances

As regards the way this 25 per cent rule works when plant and machinery allowances are claimed on fixtures, see 310-500.

Qualifying expenditure

304-000   Overview

Industrial Buildings Allowances are given by reference to qualifying expenditure, defined initially as 'the expenditure incurred on the construction of the building or structure, or other expenditure'.

In the straightforward case of a building that has been constructed by a trader and has not been sold, the allowances will generally be a percentage of the qualifying expenditure. In other cases, the concept of qualifying expenditure will remain relevant but will merely form a part of a more complex calculation. See 305-200 for a summary of the way allowances are calculated when there has been a sale of the relevant interest.

Expenditure may be treated as qualifying expenditure under any of the following headings:

(1) capital expenditure on the construction of a building (CAA 2001, s. 294 – see 304-050);

(2) where a building is bought unused without the involvement of a developer (CAA 2001, s. 295 – see 304-100);

(3) where a building is bought unused from a developer (CAA 2001, s. 296 – see 304-100);

(4) where expenditure is incurred on the construction of a building within an enterprise zone and where the relevant interest in the building is bought within a two-year period beginning with the date on which the building was first used, where either:

(a) all of the expenditure is qualifying enterprise zone expenditure (CAA 2001, s. 301 – see 320-000; or

(b) part only of the expenditure is qualifying enterprise zone expenditure (CAA 2001, s. 303 – see 320-300).

Legislation: CAA 2001, s. 271(1)(c), 292

304-050   Capital expenditure on construction

In most cases, the qualifying expenditure will simply be the capital expenditure incurred on the construction of a building. This will apply where either:

- the relevant interest in the building has not previously been sold; or
- it has been sold, but only after the first use of the building.

> ### Example
>
> Abacus Ltd buys some freehold land for £1 million. It spends £1.5 million on the construction of a factory. The qualifying expenditure is £1.5 million.
>
> Abacus Ltd later sells the land and factory for £5 million, of which £2 million is treated as the cost of land and £3 million as the payment for the factory. The sale is to Calculator Ltd. The price paid by Calculator Ltd does not affect the qualifying expenditure which remains at £1.5 million.
>
> It does not necessarily follow, though, that Calculator Ltd can claim allowances on £1.5 million. See 305-200 for the way in which allowances are calculated after a sale of the relevant interest. As regards the treatment of sale and purchase costs, etc, see 300-750. For the question of apportioning expenditure between sums that do and sums that do not qualify for allowances, see 305-600.

Developer involved – building used before first sale

A developer may construct a building that is used before it is sold. During a period where the market is not buoyant, for example, the developer may choose to let the property out until he finds a purchaser.

A technical difficulty arises because this scenario does not fit within any of the four categories listed by the legislation (under CAA 2001, s. 292). The general rule described above cannot apply as (for the builder) the expenditure incurred on the construction of the building is not capital but revenue expenditure. Nor will the purchase be of an unused building (see below).

To resolve the issue, the legislation creates a fiction whereby:

- the expenditure on the construction of the building is treated as if it were qualifying expenditure;
- it is assumed that all appropriate writing-down allowances have been made to the developer; and
- any appropriate balancing adjustment is deemed to have been made at the point of sale.

These special rules apply to the purchaser where the relevant interest (see 304-500) is sold by the developer in the course of the development trade. (The rules do not affect the tax treatment of the developer, for whom the building is likely to remain as trading stock until the date of sale. Assuming this is the case, then the builder can obviously not claim IBAs. These rules applying to developers have their own definitions – see 304-100. One condition for the rules to apply is that the developer sells the building in the course of the trade that consists in the construction of buildings with a view to their sale. If, as a fact, the building changes its status from trading stock to fixed asset for the builder, then these rules relating to developers will not apply. Any IBAs will be dealt with under ordinary principles.)

Legislation: CAA 2001, s. 294, 297

304-100   Purchase of unused building

Different rules apply where:

- expenditure is incurred on the construction of a building;
- the relevant interest in the building is sold before the building is first used; and
- a capital sum is paid by the purchaser for the relevant interest.

There are two possible outcomes, the treatment depending on whether or not a developer is involved, ie the test is whether the relevant interest in an unused building is being sold:

(1)   by a developer in the course of his development trade; or

(2)   by somebody else.

No developer involved

In some circumstances, the sale of the interest in the building will not be by a developer. This will normally mean that the property will not have become part of the developer's trading stock. In this case, the qualifying expenditure will be the lower of:

- the capital sum actually paid for the purchase of the relevant interest; and
- the expenditure incurred on the construction of the building.

It is possible that the relevant interest will be sold more than once before the building is ever actually used. In such a case, the qualifying expenditure will be the lesser of the construction cost and the amount paid by the person who first brings the property into use. Any amounts paid by previous purchasers are ignored. HMRC gives the following example to illustrate the above.

> ### Example
>
> David incurs capital expenditure on constructing a building. He does not bring it into use and sells it to Stephen. Stephen decides that it is not suitable for his business and sells it, still unused, to Graham who pays a capital sum to Stephen. The qualifying expenditure is the lower of David's construction expenditure and the price Graham pays Stephen. The price Stephen paid to David is ignored.

The qualifying expenditure is treated as incurred by the purchaser when the capital sum becomes payable.

Legislation: CAA 2001, s. 295

Other material: CA 33520

Developer involved

Where a developer has owned an interest in the building, which is then sold in the course of the developer's trade, the capital sum paid by the purchaser for the relevant interest will normally be the qualifying expenditure.

Again, however, a restriction applies in cases where a building has been constructed by a property developer and has changed hands more than once before it is brought into use. In this case, the qualifying expenditure will be the lower of the price paid by the final purchaser and the price paid on its original sale by the developer.

In either case, the qualifying expenditure is treated as incurred by the purchaser at the time when the capital sum became payable by him. If a deposit is paid, followed by the balance on completion, the whole amount is treated as incurred on the date of completion.

Legislation: CAA 2001, s. 296

Other material: CA 33520

Developers – definition of terms

For the purposes of defining qualifying expenditure, a developer is a person carrying on a trade that consists wholly or partly in the construction of buildings with a view to their sale. The fact that a company subcontracts the actual construction expenditure does not prevent the company from being a developer.

A developer is treated as selling an interest in a building in the course of his development trade if he sells it in the course of the trade (or part trade) that consists in the construction of buildings with a view to their sale.

Legislation: CAA 2001, s. 293

Other material: CA 33520

Relevant interest

304-500   Significance

The concept of the relevant interest is fundamental for determining who is entitled to IBAs.

The starting point is a definition of the relevant interest in relation to any qualifying expenditure. This is stated to be 'the interest in the building to which the person who incurred the expenditure on the construction of the building was entitled when the expenditure was incurred'. There may well be more than one relevant interest in any given building.

Example 1

Nick owns the freehold of some land. He builds a factory on the land. Nick's relevant interest in the factory will be the freehold interest. He then leases the factory to Sue.

Sue pays for the construction of an extension. The relevant interest in the cost of the extension is Sue's leasehold interest. Nick continues to claim IBAs on the main part of the factory and Sue claims IBAs on the cost of the extension.

After five years, Sue assigns her leasehold interest to her company Sue Ltd. From that point, Sue Ltd owns the relevant interest in the extension. Nick continues to own the relevant interest in the original part of the factory.

Legislation: CAA 2001, s. 286(1)

Other material: CA 31600

More than one interest

It is possible that the person incurring construction expenditure on the building will have more than one interest in the building. In this case, where one interest is reversionary on all the others then the relevant interest will be that reversionary interest.

For capital allowance purposes, the meaning of 'leasehold interest' is given as 'the interest of a tenant in property subject to a lease'. The term 'lease' is defined to include a tenancy and also, if the term to be covered by the lease has begun, an agreement for a lease. A mortgage is not a lease.

A reversionary interest is 'the interest of the landlord in the property subject to the leasehold interest or lease'. Put simply, the reversionary interest is the one that will survive the longest.

Example 2

A freeholder grants a lease to a tenant. The freeholder then requires space for a small factory and is granted a sublease by the tenant, on which he incurs construction costs. The relevant interest in those costs will be the freehold interest as this is reversionary on the leasehold interest.

Legislation: CAA 2001, s. 360

Other material: CA 31600

Other interests

The relevant interest will normally be a freehold or leasehold interest. The HMRC manuals acknowledge, however, that various other interests may constitute the relevant interest. For example:

- for the purposes of the IBA rules, a lease includes an agreement for a lease, as long as the term to be covered by the lease has begun. As such, an agreement for a lease may be the relevant interest;
- a tenancy at will is a lease and can therefore be the relevant interest; and
- an equitable interest can also be the relevant interest.

The HMRC manual also states that 'a property dealer may buy an industrial building as part of its trading activities. If it does, it acquires the relevant interest in the building and can claim WDA provided that the building continues to be in use as an industrial building'. At first glance, it might be thought that this could only apply if the property dealer buys the property as a fixed asset rather than as trading stock. However, on a strict interpretation of the legislation this does not seem to be the case. Indeed, the HMRC manual specifically states that:

'A person who buys a used industrial building may incur revenue rather than capital expenditure. For example, the building may be bought by a property developer as trading stock.

If the building is in qualifying use after the sale the person may claim IBA. The reason is that the WDA of a person who buys a used building is based on the residue of qualifying expenditure after sale ... and this is the same whether the buyer's expenditure is capital or revenue.'

A freeholder with the relevant interest may grant a lease under which the tenant has an option to buy the relevant interest. In this case, the relevant interest remains with the freeholder until the option is actually exercised.

A building may be bought by several people as tenants in common. Where this happens, Revenue instructions to inspectors are that they 'should look through to all the tenants in common who have a beneficial interest in the building for the purposes both of assessing the income from the building and giving IBAs'.

Legislation: CAA 2001, s. 360(1)(a)

Other material: CA 33040ff., 34510

304-550   Interest acquired on completion of construction

A person incurring expenditure on the construction of a building may have an agreement that he will acquire an interest in the building only after the construction is completed. Where his entitlement to an interest in the building arises 'on or as a result of the completion of the construction', then he will be deemed to have had that interest at the time the expenditure was incurred.

For example, a company may pay for the construction of a factory with an agreement that a long lease will be granted to the company once the construction is complete. The lease granted in accordance with that agreement will be the relevant interest in the factory.

Legislation: CAA 2001, s. 287

304-600   Creation of subordinate interest

The general rule is that the creation of a subordinate interest in the building will not affect ownership of the relevant interest. For example, the freeholder of a parcel of land may pay for a building to be constructed on that land. If he subsequently grants a lease to a third party, the freeholder will nevertheless retain the relevant interest in the building. The freeholder, and not the leaseholder, therefore continues to obtain allowances, even if a premium is paid by the leaseholder. This is subject to a possible election where a lease exceeds 50 years (see 304-750).

This principle was briefly tested in the case of *Woods v R M Mallen (Engineering) Ltd.* In that case, the person incurring the expenditure on the construction of the industrial building had a lease for 99 years. A sublease was granted for 99 years, less three days. It was claimed that the subtenant thereby had the relevant interest. In what should have been a straightforward appeal, the commissioner reached the wrong decision, which was swiftly overturned by the High Court. The meaning of the relevant legislation was clear: the grant of the sublease was not a disposal of the relevant interest.

Legislation: CAA 2001, s. 288(1)

Cases: *Woods v R M Mallen (Engineering) Ltd* (1969) 45 TC 619

304-650   Merger of leasehold interest

A leasehold interest may cease to exist either because it is simply surrendered or because the person entitled to the leasehold interest acquires the interest that is reversionary on it. In either case, the interests will merge and the interest into which the leasehold interest merges will become the relevant interest. See 304-700 for the different rules that apply when a lease is terminated.

> ### Example
>
> Alpha Ltd owns the freehold of a large warehouse. Alpha Ltd grants a long lease to Beta Ltd. Beta Ltd incurs expenditure on extending the factory. Alpha Ltd will have the relevant interest in the original expenditure and Beta Ltd will have the relevant interest in the cost of the extension.
>
> If Beta Ltd acquires the freehold from Alpha Ltd, then the leasehold and freehold interests will merge. From that point, Beta Ltd has the relevant interest in the whole of the expenditure.

Legislation: CAA 2001, s. 289

304-700   Termination of lease

The above paragraphs have considered the rules that apply when a leasehold interest is extinguished either on being surrendered or because the person entitled to the interest acquires the interest that is reversionary on it. Different rules apply where a lease is terminated. The legislation outlines four scenarios and provides the tax treatment for each:

(1)   on termination of the lease, the lessee may (with the consent of the lessor) remain in possession of the building, even though no new lease is actually granted to him. In this case, the lease is treated as continuing for as long as the lessee remains in possession. As such, there is no balancing event;

(2)   on termination of the original lease, a new one may be granted to the lessee as a result of the exercise by him of an option which he had under the terms of the first lease. Here, the second lease is treated as a continuation of the first. As such, there is no balancing event;

(3) on termination of the lease, the lessor may pay a sum to the lessee in respect of a building comprised in the lease. In this case, the lease is treated as terminating by virtue of the lessee surrendering it in return for the sum received from the lessor. In this case, there will be a balancing event; or

(4) when the original lease terminates, a new lease may be granted to a different lessee, in which case the new lessee may pay a sum to the previous lessee. In such a case, the two leases are treated as if they were one and the same, having been assigned by the earlier lessee to the new one in consideration of the payment. In this case, too, there will be a balancing event.

As to the treatment of balancing events generally, see 305-500.

Legislation: CAA 2001, s. 359

304-750   Election to treat grant of long lease as sale of the relevant interest

As discussed at 304-600, the grant of a lease out of the relevant interest normally has no effect for IBA purposes. The person holding the relevant interest at the time the expenditure was incurred normally continues to receive IBAs.

The only exception is if the lessor and lessee jointly elect to treat the grant of the long lease as the sale of the relevant interest. This provision allows those who are not entitled to IBAs (eg pension funds or local authorities) to pass on the benefit of the allowances to their tenants, though the practical effect of this was considerably reduced by the changes introduced in the *Finance Act* 2007 under which there have normally been no balancing adjustment for events occurring from 21 March 2007.

For an election to be made, the duration of the lease must exceed 50 years. The effect of the election is that the grant of the lease will be treated as if it were a sale of the relevant interest by the lessor to the lessee. The date of the sale is the date from which the lease takes effect. Any premium (or other capital sum) paid by the lessee in consideration for the grant of the lease is treated as the sale and purchase price. The interest out of which the lease was granted is treated as ceasing to exist and the interest acquired by the lessee therefore becomes the relevant interest. In the past, a balancing adjustment would (if appropriate) have been made on the lessor and the lessee would have been entitled to IBAs.

As in other circumstances, any part of the premium relating to the land on which the building stands should be excluded. The election will cover all the construction expenditure and all buildings in relation to which the original interest (ie out of which the lease is granted) is the relevant interest. An election must be made within two years from the date on which the lease takes effect; a late election will be accepted only if 'there is a clear in-date indication in the papers or in the correspondence that an election will be made', or if 'everyone concerned has submitted claims, computations etc on the basis that an election has been or will be made'.

Various anti-avoidance provisions apply. First, no election can be made if the sole or main benefit to the lessor from the granting of the lease and the making of the election is likely to be the obtaining of a balancing allowance.

Secondly, no election may be made where the lessor and lessee are connected persons. The only exception to this is where the lessor is a statutory body and the lessee is a company over which it has control.

Whilst the question of the duration of the lease will normally be clear cut, the property income rules (ITTOIA 2005, s. 303 and CTA 2009, s. 243) apply in cases that are less straightforward. HMRC summarise these rules as follows:

> 'Broadly, a lease is treated as being shorter than the term specified in the lease agreement if it looks unlikely that it will last that long. Conversely, a lease is treated as being longer than the term specified if the lessee may become entitled to a further lease when the original lease ends. In that case the original lease is treated as continuing until the further lease ends.'

The duration of a lease is determined without regard to the fact that a new lease may be granted as a result of the exercise of an option available under the terms of an earlier lease.

Where the anti-avoidance rules did not present problems in a particular case, the option to make an election did provide an important tax planning opportunity. In the case of a 999-year lease, for example, the freeholder effectively had the option either of retaining the capital allowances or of passing them on to the leaseholder. Depending on the tax position of both landlord and tenant, there could be significant differences in the overall tax result.

Legislation: CAA 2001, s. 290–291

Other material: CA 33100

Initial and writing-down allowances

305-000   Overview

Three types of allowance have historically been available in relation to qualifying expenditure:

- an initial allowance – see 305-050;
- writing-down allowances – considered in detail from 305-100; and
- balancing allowances (and also charges), though these are withdrawn in most cases from 21 March 2007 – see 305-500.

If there was a sale of the relevant interest during the first 25 years, then the following was a typical summary of how allowances would in the past have been calculated, but this has all changed since 21 March 2007:

- initial allowances (if any) would be given;

- writing-down allowances were at first given at four per cent per year (now reducing by one percentage point per year from April 2008);
- a balancing event would occur at the time of the sale, which was likely to give rise to either a balancing charge or a balancing allowance, though these balancing adjustments now only apply in transitional cases;
- if the building continued to qualify as an industrial building after the sale, writing-down allowances would in the past have been given on a different basis from the date of the sale until the 25th anniversary of the first use of the building, whereas since 21 March 2007 the new owner broadly inherits the tax position of the previous owner and takes over the remaining allowances; and
- each subsequent sale of the relevant interest during the 25-year period would in the past give rise to a further balancing event and to a recalculation of the writing-down allowances due (if any) for the remainder of the original 25-year period, but this no longer applies except in transitional cases.

305-050   Initial allowances

Initial allowances are now restricted to qualifying enterprise zone expenditure (see 320-000). Expenditure incurred during the year to 31 October 1993 qualified for a 20 per cent initial allowance, as long as the building was in use by 31 December 1994. Various transitional rules applied.

Other material: CA 34300

305-100   Writing-down allowances: first principles

The basic rule is that a writing-down allowance is given to a person for a chargeable period if:

- qualifying expenditure has been incurred on a building;
- the person concerned has the relevant interest in the building in relation to that expenditure at the end of the chargeable period for which an allowance is claimed; and
- the building is in use as an industrial building at the end of that chargeable period.

There used to be two very different ways in which writing-down allowances had to be calculated, the method depending on whether or not there had ever been a 'relevant event' (normally, a sale of the relevant interest in the building after it had at some time qualified as an industrial building, but see 305-200).

See 305-225 for examples illustrating the calculation of allowances due for periods from April 2008.

Legislation: CAA 2001, s. 309

305-150 Writing-down allowances before any relevant event

Where there has been no relevant event, the writing-down allowance given for any chargeable period is normally four per cent of the qualifying expenditure, though this figure is reduced from April 2008, as explained at 305-225 below. Allowances are then given until the expenditure is exhausted.

This will apply typically to a new building.

Example 1

A Ltd has paid £1 million for the construction of a factory it uses for its trade. Writing-down allowances will be given to A Ltd of £40,000 per year for 25 years, though this is now subject to the phasing out of IBAs and to their complete withdrawal from 2011. This is referred to as a 'straight line basis'; the IBA rules do not borrow from the plant and machinery regime the concept of the annually-reducing balance.

See also 305-225 for examples illustrating the calculation of allowances due for periods from April 2008.

The allowances due for the accounting period do not depend on the timing of the expenditure within the period.

If full allowances were not claimed for some periods, the writing-down allowances could continue for more than 25 years from the date of first use. This is the effect of the way the legislation is structured and is confirmed at CA 34510 ('a WDA may be made for a chargeable period more than 25 years after the building was first used provided that there is still qualifying expenditure to write off and the building is in qualifying use'), though this will now rarely be of more than academic interest.

A similar approach would also apply after a building has been sold if it has not previously qualified as an industrial building. This is because a relevant event can never now arise and, in the past, would only have arisen when the building was an industrial building or after it had ceased to be one.

A person buying a used building that has never previously qualified will therefore simply claim allowances from the chargeable period in which it is first used as an industrial building. As explained below, however, the total amount on which allowances will be available will eventually be restricted because of the earlier period of non-industrial use, though this ceases to be relevant for new buildings as IBAs will have been completely abolished long before the 25th anniversary.

Legislation: CAA 2001, s. 310, s. 314(1)

Other material: CA 34510

There are numerous exceptions to the general 4 per cent rule, as shown in the example below. In particular, the allowance is proportionately increased or reduced if the chargeable period is more or less than one year. See below for the meaning of 'chargeable period'.

Example 2

A warehouse is built at a cost of £2 million (excluding land costs) and IBAs are claimed on the expenditure. The company that constructed the building draws accounts up to 31 July each year but then decides to change its accounting date. It therefore has a short chargeable period of eight months to 31 March.

Subject to any other factors, the allowance due for the nine-month accounting period will be £40,000, calculated as:

$$£2,000,000 \times 4\% \times 75\% \times 8/12$$

The following points may need to be considered:

- if the construction expenditure was incurred before 6 November 1962, the annual writing-down allowance is two per cent, rather than four per cent;
- the figure of four per cent is reduced to three per cent from 1 April 2008 (so 4% × 75% in this example), to two per cent from 1 April 2009, and to one per cent from 1 April 2010, with no further allowances due thereafter (see 305-225);
- the amount of the allowance is always restricted to what is known as the residue of qualifying expenditure (see 305-250). The residue is to be ascertained immediately before the writing-down allowance is given at the end of any chargeable period. This rule has the effect that the total allowances due in relation to any qualifying expenditure cannot exceed the amount of that expenditure;
- the person claiming the writing-down allowance may require the allowance to be reduced or entirely disclaimed for any given period; or
- in the case of qualifying enterprise zone expenditure, the rate of allowance is normally 25 per cent, rather than four per cent or less (see 320-200).

Very different rules used to apply if there has been a relevant event, though the rules were radically changed with effect from 21 March 2007 – see 305-200.

Legislation: CAA 2001, s. 309–314; Sch. 3, para. 66

Other material: CA 34510

Meaning of 'chargeable period'

For the purposes of quantifying the writing-down allowances that are due, it will be necessary to know when a chargeable period is more or less than one year. The capital allowances legislation contains its own definition.

For corporation tax purposes, the term 'chargeable period' is synonymous with 'accounting period' (CAA 2001, s. 6(1)). This latter term is in turn defined at CTA 2009, s. 9ff. An accounting period can never exceed 12 months and it will always end at an (official) accounting date of the company.

For income tax purposes, a chargeable period is synonymous with a period of account. To define this term, it is necessary to draw a distinction between (on the one hand) someone claiming allowances in calculating the profits of a trade, profession or vocation and (on the other) any other person entitled to claim allowances.

Legislation: CAA 2001, s. 6

Traders

For a person who is entitled to an allowance in calculating the profits of a trade, profession or vocation, the period of account (and therefore the chargeable period) will normally be the period for which the business accounts are drawn up. This is subject to the following exceptions.

(1) if two periods overlap, the common period is treated as belonging to the first period of account only;

(2) similarly, if one period of account includes another, the common period is treated as belonging to the first period of account only;

(3) if there is a gap between two periods of account, the gap is treated as belonging to the first period of account only;

(4) a period of account cannot, for these purposes, exceed 18 months. If it would otherwise do so, the period must be divided into separate periods of account. In this case:

(a) the first period of account is to begin with the start date of the original period; and
(b) each subsequent period of account is to begin with an anniversary of that date.

It will follow that none of the periods of account will exceed 12 months.

Legislation: CAA 2001, s. 6(2)(a)

Others

For all other persons entitled to claim capital allowances, the period of account – and therefore the chargeable period – will be the tax year ended 5 April.

Legislation: CAA 2001, s. 310

305-200   Writing-down allowances following a relevant event

As already explained, the Chancellor unexpectedly announced in the Budget of March 2007 that IBAs (and ABAs) were to be phased out over a four-year period. As a first step towards this goal, provisions were introduced that prevented, for most disposals made from 21 March 2007, the making of any balancing adjustments on disposals of industrial buildings (with the exception of disposals of buildings in enterprise zones).

The principles described in the previous paragraphs used to be greatly modified where a building had at some point been an industrial building and there had been a subsequent sale of the relevant interest. The purchaser of a used building, particularly one that was nearing the 25th anniversary of its construction, was often able to obtain much more rapid relief than the person who incurred the original construction costs. The 2007 changes prevent the making of any further balancing adjustments, other than in transitional cases, with the effect that the rules described in this paragraph no longer apply. The transitional rules are explained at 305-225.

Before the 2007 changes, the different calculation of WDAs operated when there had been a 'relevant event'. This normally meant simply the sale of the relevant interest in the building that constituted a balancing event and that therefore triggered a balancing adjustment for the vendor. The definition also included, however:

- the incurring, by a person with the relevant interest in qualifying expenditure, of an additional VAT liability in respect of that expenditure (CAA 2001, s. 347 – see 305-300); or
- the making, to a person with the relevant interest in qualifying expenditure, of an additional VAT rebate in respect of that expenditure (relevant interest in qualifying expenditure, of an additional VAT liability in respect of that expenditure (CAA 2001, s. 349 – see 305-300).

As explained at 305-150, there could be no relevant event if the building has never qualified for IBAs before the date of the sale.

To calculate the annual writing-down allowances for somebody who had bought a used industrial building, the legislation applied a formula as follows:

$$\text{RQE} \times \text{A/B}$$

where:

RQE   was the residue of qualifying expenditure (see 305-250) immediately after the event;
A   was the length of the chargeable period for which allowances are being claimed; and
B   was the length of the period that:

- started with the date of the event; and
- ended with the 25th anniversary of the day on which the building was first used (such that the date (or dates) on which the expenditure was incurred would cease to be relevant after the qualifying event).

See also 305-225 for details of the transitional rules applying for periods from April 2008.

Legislation: CAA 2001, s. 311; FA 2007, s. 36

305-225   Phasing out of IBAs

Introduction and overview

As already indicated, the Chancellor announced in the Budget of March 2007 that IBAs (and Agricultural Buildings Allowances) were to be phased out over a four-year period.

The phasing out is put into effect in different ways:

- the *Finance Act* 2007 provided that no IBA balancing adjustment is to be made for balancing events occurring (broadly) from 21 March 2007. This is explained in greater detail below;
- the *Finance Act* 2008 confirms that the annual IBA writing-down allowance is reduced to three per cent from April 2008 and by a further one per cent per year thereafter, until the allowances are finally withdrawn from 1 April 2011.

Different rules apply to qualifying enterprise zone expenditure (see 320-000).

No further balancing adjustments

The vendor of an industrial building is no longer subject to a balancing charge at the time of disposal (and is not able to obtain a balancing allowance if selling at a loss). Exceptions are made for contracts that were already agreed before the amended rules were announced (a 'pre-commencement contract': see below) and for enterprise zone expenditure, which is subject to its own transitional rules.

Pre-commencement contracts

To avoid catching transactions that were already in the pipeline at the time the rules were introduced, the former rules continue to apply where the balancing event occurs before 1 April 2011 'in pursuance of a relevant pre-commencement contract'. A contract will be treated as such where all of the following conditions are met:

- the contract was made in writing before 21 March 2007;
- either that contract was unconditional or its conditions had been satisfied before that date;
- no terms remained to be agreed on or after that date; and
- the contract has not been varied in a significant way on or since that date.

Where any one or more of these conditions is breached, then the disposal or other relevant event is described as a 'post-commencement balancing event' and there can be no balancing adjustment.

The basic rule

The legislation provides detailed rules for calculating writing-down allowances for a 'transitional chargeable period'. This is defined as a period that begins on or after 1 April 2008 (corporation tax) or 6 April 2008 (income tax) (FA 2008, s. 85).

The rules are simpler where the whole of a chargeable period falls within a financial year (CT) or tax year (income tax). This would arise, for example, where a company draws its accounts up to 31 March each year. In this case, the allowances are calculated by multiplying the WDA that would otherwise have been available by the specified percentage for the year. This percentage is 75 per cent for the year ended 31 March or 5 April 2009, reducing annually thereafter to 50, 25 and zero per cent.

The same formula is used whether or not there has been an earlier relevant event. This first example illustrates the position where there has been no previous transfer of the relevant interest in the building.

Example 1

A Ltd draws accounts up to 31 March each year. The company incurred expenditure of £1 million in the construction of an industrial building in the year 2000 and brought the building into use on 28 February 2001, claiming allowances of £40,000 per year from that time.

For the year to 31 March 2009, the company can claim allowances of £30,000 (£40,000 × 75 per cent). For the following year, it can claim £20,000. In the year to 31 March 2011, it can claim £10,000. No further allowances are then due.

Suppose, instead, that A Ltd has sold the building to B Ltd. This can be illustrated as follows.

Example 2

A Ltd incurred expenditure of £1 million in the construction of an industrial building in the year 2000 and brought the building into use on 28 February 2001, claiming allowances of £40,000 per year from that time. A Ltd sold the building to B Ltd for £1,200,000 on 1 July 2007 under a contract made that month. Both companies have a 31 March year-end.

A Ltd cannot claim allowances for the year ended 31 March 2008 as the company does not have the relevant interest in the building at the end of the accounting period. Its final WDA claim is therefore for the year ended 31 March 2007 and there is no balancing charge at the time of the sale.

A Ltd has claimed a total of £280,000 and the residue before sale is therefore £720,000. This figure is now also the residue after sale as far as B Ltd is concerned. The RQE × A/B formula (see 305-200) still applies and so it is necessary to calculate the period from 1 July 2007 to 28 February 2026 (ie the 25th anniversary of the date on which the building was first used) (per CAA 2001, s. 311), a duration of 224 months. B Ltd can therefore claim allowances for the year to 31 March 2008 of £38,572 (£720,000 × $^{12}/_{224}$). This then reduces year by year, using the same percentages as above, to give figures of £28,929, £19,286 and £9,643 respectively for the final three years before IBAs are finally withdrawn.

Writing-off of expenditure

Expenditure is written off as if full allowances were being given (FA 2008, s. 85(8)). This can make a difference where the 25th anniversary of the building's first use falls in the transitional period.

Industrial Buildings

Example 3

C Ltd draws accounts up to 31 March each year. On 1 October 2006, the company bought a building which had first been used on 1 February 1985. The residue after sale was £400,000. Using the same RQE $\times$ $^A/_B$ formula, the company originally calculated that there were 40 months from the date of purchase (1 October 2006) to the 25th anniversary of the first use (1 February 2010). As such, it claimed £120,000 for the year to 31 March 2007 (£400,000 $\times$ $^{12}/_{40}$) and the same for the following year.

For the year ended 31 March 2009, the claim is restricted to £90,000 but the residue is calculated as £40,000 (rather than £70,000). In the year to 31 March 2010, allowances are therefore initially calculated as £60,000 (ie 50 per cent of the allowances that would have been due before the application of the phasing-out rules) but this figure is further capped at £40,000, at which point all allowances are exhausted.

Rules for chargeable periods not coinciding with financial or tax years

The calculation is more complex where the chargeable period straddles the end of the financial or tax year. In this case, it is necessary to calculate separately the 'apportioned writing-down allowance' for each financial or tax year in which the chargeable period falls, and then to aggregate the resulting figures. For each of those periods, the 'apportioned writing-down allowance' is given (FA 2008, s. 85(5)) by the formula

$$(DCPY/DCP) \times WDA \times P$$

where:

DCPY   is the number of days in the chargeable period which fall in the financial or tax year in question;

DCP   is the number of days in the chargeable period;

WDA   is the writing-down allowance to which the person would otherwise be entitled for the chargeable period; and

P   is the specified percentage for the year in question (100, 75, 50 or 25 per cent – as explained above).

Example 4

D Ltd draws accounts up to 31 December each year. The company incurred expenditure of £1 million in the construction of an industrial building in 2000 and brought the building into use on 28 February 2001, claiming allowances of £40,000 per year from that time.

For the year to 31 December 2008, it is necessary to split the year into two parts:

- For the period from 1 January to 31 March 2008, the calculation is $(^{91}/_{366}) \times £40,000 \times 100$ per cent, giving a figure of £9,945.
- For the period from 1 April to 31 December 2008, the calculation is $(^{275}/_{366}) \times £40,000 \times 75$ per cent, giving a figure of £22,541.

These figures are then aggregated to give the IBAs due for the whole year as £32,486.

Exactly the same principles are used where there has been a relevant event. Once more, it will be necessary to restrict the allowances where the 25th anniversary of first use falls within the transitional period.

Example 5

E Ltd draws accounts up to 30 April each year. On 1 October 2006, the company bought a building which had first been used on 1 February 1985. The residue after sale was £400,000. Using the same RQE $\times$ $^A/_B$ formula, the company originally calculated that there were 40 months from the date of purchase (1 October 2006) to the 25th anniversary of the first use (1 February 2010). As such, it claimed £120,000 for the year to 30 April 2007 (£400,000 $\times$ $^{12}/_{40}$).

For the year ended 30 April 2008, the claim is calculated as follows:

- For the period from 1 May 2007 to 31 March 2008, the calculation is $(^{336}/_{366})$ $\times$ £120,000 $\times$ 100 per cent, giving a figure of £110,164.
- For the period from 1 April to 30 April 2008, the calculation is $(^{30}/_{366})$ $\times$ £120,000 $\times$ 75 per cent, giving a figure of £7,377.

These figures are then aggregated to give the IBAs due for the whole year as £117,541. The residue of expenditure remaining, however, is calculated as if the full £120,000 has been given for the year, and is therefore £160,000.

For the year to 30 April 2009, the claim is as follows:

- For the period from 1 May 2008 to 31 March 2009, the calculation is $(^{335}/_{365})$ $\times$ £120,000 $\times$ 75 per cent, giving a figure of £82,603.
- For the period from 1 April to 30 April 2009, the calculation is $(^{30}/_{365})$ $\times$ £120,000 $\times$ 50 per cent, giving a figure of £4,932.

These figures are then aggregated to give the IBAs due for the whole year as £87,535. The residue of expenditure remaining, however, is once more calculated as if the full £120,000 has been given for the year, and is therefore £40,000.

For the year to 30 April 2010, the claim will initially be calculated as follows:

- For the period from 1 May 2009 to 31 March 2010, the calculation is $(^{335}/_{365})$ $\times$ £120,000 $\times$ 50 per cent, giving a figure of £55,068.
- For the period from 1 April to 30 April 2010, the calculation is $(^{30}/_{365})$ $\times$ £120,000 $\times$ 25 per cent, giving a figure of £2,466.

These figures are then aggregated to give a figure of £57,534. In this case, however, the claim is restricted to the residue brought forward of £40,000. All allowances are then exhausted.

Anti-avoidance

Legislation at CAA 2001, s. 313A aims 'to prevent connected parties from seeking to obtain multiple writing-down allowances by transferring a building qualifying for industrial buildings allowances (IBAs) to a series of owners in quick succession' (per the *Explanatory Notes* to the 2008 Finance Bill). The legislation applies for IBAs only and, in the rare circumstances in which it will apply, limits the amount of WDA that a buyer may claim in the chargeable period in which the buyer acquires the relevant interest. The rules apply where:

(1) there is a sale of the relevant interest in the building which is a balancing event to which s. 314 applies;

(2) the buyer and seller have different chargeable periods;

(3) the control test (within the meaning of s. 567) is met (see 307-050); and

(4) the purpose, or one of the main purposes, of the sale is the obtaining of a tax advantage by the buyer under the IBA rules.

The amount of WDA to which the buyer is entitled in the chargeable period in which the sale takes place is calculated according to the formula:

$$(DI/CP) \times WDA$$

where:

DI   is the number of days in the chargeable period for which the buyer is entitled to the relevant interest;

CP   is the number of days in the chargeable period; and

WDA   is the writing-down allowance to which the buyer would otherwise be entitled.

The restriction applies to any sale (as widely defined for IBA purposes) of the relevant interest that occurs from 12 March 2008, except for one that is made in pursuance of a 'relevant pre-commencement contract'. This latter concept is defined to mean a contract that meets all of the following conditions:

- it was a written contract made before 12 March 2008;
- either the contract was unconditional or its conditions had been satisfied before that date;
- no terms remained to be agreed on or after that date; and
- it was not varied in any significant way on or after that date.

305-250   Residue of qualifying expenditure

This concept is important for various reasons. First, the writing-down allowance for any period can never exceed the residue of qualifying expenditure; this principle overrides any other.

Example 1

IBAs are claimed on a bridge that cost £300,000 to build. The residue of qualifying expenditure is £10,000 (possibly, but not necessarily, because allowances have already been received totalling £290,000). Whatever calculations take place to work out the allowance due for the current period, the amount will be capped at £10,000.

Legislation: CAA 2001, s. 312

Secondly, the concept is always needed to calculate a balancing adjustment; for example, on the sale of the relevant interest, and to work out writing-down allowances following such an event.

In the simplest case, the residue of qualifying expenditure is the construction cost of a building, less all allowances already given. In practice, the calculation is more complex. The term 'residue of qualifying expenditure' is defined as 'the qualifying expenditure that has not yet been written off in accordance with Chapter 8'. CAA 2001, Pt. 3, Ch. 8 – entitled 'Writing Off Qualifying Expenditure' – determines both the extent to which qualifying expenditure is to be written off and the time at which such write-off takes place, as follows:

When initial allowances are made

When initial allowances are made, the amount of the initial allowance is to be written off at the time when the building is first used. This may be later than the time at which the allowance is made, as initial allowances can be made before a building is first brought into use – confirmed at CA 34700.

When a writing-down allowance is made

When a writing-down allowance is made, the amount of the allowance is written off at the end of the chargeable period for which the allowance is made. If a balancing event occurs at the end of this chargeable period, then the writing-down allowance is deducted in calculating the residue of qualifying expenditure immediately before the balancing event. This will therefore have a bearing on the amount of the balancing adjustment to be made (though this no longer applies other than in relation to qualifying enterprise zone expenditure or under the transitional rules described at 305-225 above).

Example 2

A storage warehouse cost £600,000, excluding any element relating to land. It has been in use as an industrial building since it was built. It qualified for an initial allowance of £120,000. In 10 periods, a writing-down allowance of £24,000 per year has been given. In one period, a reduced writing-down allowance of £16,000 was made (because of a change of accounting date).

Total allowances given therefore amount to £376,000. The residue of qualifying expenditure is therefore £224,000 (£600,000 minus £376,000). This figure would in the past have been relevant for calculating any balancing allowance or charge for the owner if he disposed of the relevant interest in the warehouse (for example, by selling it).

Legislation: CAA 2001, s. 313, 333–334

Other material: CA 34700

When a research and development allowance is made

When a research and development allowance is made:

Industrial Buildings

(1) again, the amount of the allowance is written off at the end of the chargeable period for which the allowance is made (CAA 2001, s. 335). The point here is that a building that has qualified for research and development allowances (RDAs) may start to be used as an industrial building. No clawback of the RDAs is made at the time it started to be used as an industrial building, so they must be taken into account in calculating the residue of qualifying expenditure. In effect, the RDAs enjoyed by the business would therefore in the past have been recovered by HMRC as an IBA balancing charge, though this will no longer apply other than for cases dealt with by the transitional provisions (see 305-225).

(2) once more, if a balancing event (see 305-600) occurs at the end of this chargeable period, then the writing-down allowance is deducted in calculating the residue of qualifying expenditure immediately before the balancing event (CAA 2001, s. 335(2)). This would therefore in the past have had a bearing on the amount of the balancing adjustment to be made.

When the building is not an industrial building

When the building is not an industrial building:

(1) at certain times, it is necessary to write off notional writing-down allowances (CAA 2001, s. 336). This will apply for any periods, from the time the building was first used for *any* purpose, during which it did not qualify as an industrial building. This provision is more complex than it seems at first glance.

(2) the notional writing-down allowances are defined as the allowances that would have been made if the building had been an industrial building for the period or periods in question. The rate of such allowances may be at four per cent but will be at a different rate if, for example, there had previously been a sale of the relevant interest and therefore a balancing adjustment.

Example 3

A factory unit is built at a cost (excluding land) of £600,000 and is first used on 1 July 1994. It is in use as an industrial building until 30 September 2002. It is used for purposes that do not qualify for IBAs until 1 February 2004. It is then in qualifying use again until it is sold for £1m on 1 July 2007. The business draws up accounts to 30 April throughout.

Full writing-down allowances are given for the years ended 30 April 1995–30 April 2002. No allowances are due for the year ended 30 April 2003, as the building is not in use for a qualifying purpose at the end of that year. For the year ended 30 April 2004, on the other hand, a full writing-down allowance is due. Writing-down allowances are also given for the years ended 30 April 2005, 2006 and 2007.

It might be assumed that notional allowances need to be given for one year only, being the missed year for which allowances were denied. This is not, however, what the legislation actually dictates. Notional allowances have to be taken into account if the building is not an industrial building for certain periods. An industrial building is one that is (for example) in use for the purposes of a qualifying trade. In this example, there is a

---

16-month period (1 October 2002–31 January 2004) during which the building is not an industrial building.

In this example, therefore, the notional allowances to be written off will be £32,000 (£600,000 × 4% × $^{16}/_{12}$. Assuming that allowances of £24,000 per year have been claimed and given for each of the 12 years that do qualify, the total expenditure to be written off will be £320,000 (calculated as notional £32,000 plus actual £288,000 (£24,000 × 12)). The residue of qualifying expenditure is therefore £280,000.

See 300-350 for the treatment of periods of temporary disuse.

When a balancing adjustment is made

This applies where the relevant interest in the building is sold (CAA 2001, s. 337(1)) and where a balancing adjustment is made (now only possible under the transitional provisions). In such a case:

(1)   where a balancing allowance is made, the excess of the residue of qualifying expenditure before the sale over the net sale proceeds is written off at the time of the sale; and

(2)   where a balancing charge is made, the amount of the residue of qualifying expenditure is increased by the amount of the charge at the time of the sale. But if the charge is made under s. 319(6) then the residue after the sale is limited to the net proceeds of the sale.

Example 4

Continue with the Example above, which ended with a residue before sale of £280,000. Suppose that the factory unit is sold for £250,000 (excluding any land element). The excess of £30,000 is written off at this time and the residue therefore becomes £250,000. As such, the purchaser's allowances are capped at the figure of his own expenditure.

Example 5

Continuing as before, suppose now that the factory unit is sold for £800,000 rather than for £250,000. The residue before sale was £280,000. Under the rules applying before 21 March 2007, the balancing charge would have been such as to recapture all the allowances given, so £288,000. The residue immediately after the sale would therefore have been £568,000. (This may be seen as representing the original construction cost, less the £32,000 notional allowances written off.)

This is a case of 'let the buyer beware!'. The purchaser would here have paid more than the original construction cost but his allowances would have been restricted by reference to events – a period of non-qualifying use – that took place before he acquired the property.

If the balancing charge had been made under CAA 2001, s. 319(6) (difference between net allowances given and the adjusted net cost – see 305-800) then the residue after the sale would have been limited to the net proceeds of the sale.

> Under the provisions generally applying for disposals made from 21 March 2007, the residue after sale is equal to the residue before sale, so £288,000 in this example.

When capital value is realised

This applies when there is a balancing adjustment on realisation of capital value in accordance with CAA 2001, s. 328. This is an anti-avoidance rule that relates only to enterprise zone expenditure. It is discussed in detail at 320-350.

Crown, or certain others, entitled to allowances

This applies where the Crown, or other person who is not within the charge to tax, has at any time been entitled to the relevant interest in a building (see 310-150).

Legislation: CAA 2001, s. 328, 338; FA 2007, s. 36

Demolition costs

The residue of qualifying expenditure immediately before the sale may in the past have needed to be increased where demolition costs were incurred.

The rule applied where a building was demolished and the person incurring the cost of the demolition was either claiming a balancing allowance or receiving a balancing charge. In such a case, the 'net cost of the demolition' was to be added to the residue of qualifying expenditure immediately before the demolition.

The net cost of the demolition was defined as any amount by which the cost of the demolition exceeded any money received for the remains of the property.

Where the demolition costs were treated in this way, the demolition costs were not taken into account as part of the expenditure on any replacement property.

Legislation: CAA 2001, s. 340

305-300   VAT: rebates and additional charges

VAT and direct tax generally

The interaction of VAT and direct taxes was addressed in Statement of Practice B1, the text of which was first issued by the Revenue on 7 May 1973.

VAT and IBAs – background

A complication can arise for IBA purposes where an additional VAT liability arises or where a rebate is due. The legislation addressing this issue is concerned with an 'additional VAT liability' and an 'additional VAT rebate'.

Various key definitions are important for applying the special rules. The HMRC manuals (CA 39050) explain the background to this issue as follows:

'The VAT payable on the purchase of a capital asset is broadly determined by the first use of that asset. Generally all the VAT incurred on the purchase of the asset can be claimed back by a VAT registered business on its next VAT return if it is to be used for business purposes to make taxable supplies.

The VAT Capital Goods Scheme adjusts this recovery of VAT if broadly the use of certain capital assets changes later on. If the proportion of use changes later on from taxable (for VAT) to exempt (for VAT) additional VAT is payable by the purchaser. If the proportion of use changes from exempt (for VAT) to taxable (for VAT) additional VAT is repaid by Customs.

The VAT Capital Goods scheme applies to land and buildings worth £250,000 or more. It can result in additional VAT consequences for up to ten years.

An additional VAT liability is the further VAT payable to Customs if the proportion of use of an asset covered by the VAT Capital Goods scheme changes from taxable to exempt.

An additional VAT rebate is VAT repayable by Customs when the proportion of use of an asset covered by the VAT Capital Goods scheme changes from exempt to taxable.

The relevant VAT interval is the period used to make the computation which gives rise to the additional VAT payable or the additional VAT rebate.

An additional VAT liability is incurred and an additional VAT rebate arises on the last day of the relevant VAT interval.'

Where an apportionment has been made in relation to any qualifying expenditure, the same apportionment is to be made of any additional VAT liability or rebate.

Additional VAT liabilities

On the basis of the above, a person holding the relevant interest in an industrial building may incur an additional VAT liability in relation to that expenditure. In such circumstances, the extra VAT falling due is treated as further qualifying expenditure on the asset. In this case, the residue of qualifying expenditure is treated as increased, at the time the additional liability accrues, by the amount of that additional liability (CAA 2001, s. 347).

Any initial allowance made on such an additional VAT liability is treated as written off at the time the liability accrues (CAA 2001, s. 348).

For writing-down allowance purposes, the incurring of the additional VAT liability is a 'relevant event' (see 305-200). The event is treated as occurring at the time the liability accrues (CAA 2001, s. 347(3)).

The effect of the above is that writing-down allowances are re-calculated in the same way as following a sale of the building. The new figure for the residue of qualifying expenditure is spread over the remaining period using the same formula (RQE × A/B) as discussed at 305-200.

Example 1

Elgar 1 Ltd constructs a factory for £1 million (excluding any land cost) and brings it into use on 1 March 2000. It draws accounts up to 30 September.

Allowances are claimed at £40,000 per year for each of the seven years to 30 September 2006. Due to a partial change of use, an additional VAT liability of £12,000 is incurred on 1 December 2006.

What writing-down allowances are due for the year ended 30 September 2007?

The residue of qualifying expenditure immediately before the event is £720,000 (£1 million less seven amounts of £40,000).

The residue of qualifying expenditure immediately after the event is £732,000 (£720,000 plus £12,000 additional VAT).

The length of the chargeable period is 12 months.

The length of the period from the date of the event (1 December 2006) to the 25th anniversary of the date on which the building was first used (1 March 2025) is 18 years and three months (219 months).

Using the formula of RQE $\times$ A/B, the allowances for the year (and for subsequent years) are calculated as follows:

$$£732,000 \times 12/219 = £40,110.$$

It should be noted that the timing of the VAT event within the year has an impact on the allowances due from that point on. If, in the above example, the event had occurred later within the same accounting period, say on 1 September 2007, the allowances due for that period (and the following periods) would have been:

$$£732,000 \times 12/210 = £41,829.$$

VAT rebates

The same principles apply in reverse if a VAT rebate accrues to a person who is entitled to the relevant interest in an industrial building.

Depending on how the figures work out, receipt of a VAT rebate may reduce ongoing writing-down allowances. In the past, it might have created a balancing charge, but this is no longer the case.

Where, immediately before the rebate accrues, the residue of qualifying expenditure is more than, or equal to, the rebate, then the effect would simply have been to reduce the amount of writing-down allowances from that time on (CAA 2001, s. 349).

Restating but reversing the above example, this can be illustrated as follows:

Example 2

Elgar 2 Ltd constructs a factory for £1 million (excluding land) and brings it into use on 1 March 2000. It draws accounts up to 30 September.

Allowances are claimed at £40,000 per year for each of the seven years to 30 September 2006. Due to a partial change of use, a VAT rebate of £12,000 is made to Elgar 2 Ltd on 1 December 2006.

What writing-down allowances are due for the year ended 30 September 2007?

The residue of qualifying expenditure immediately before the event is £720,000 (£1 million less seven amounts of £40,000).

The residue of qualifying expenditure immediately after the event would under the old rules have been £708,000 (£720,000 less £12,000 rebated VAT).

The length of the chargeable period is 12 months.

The length of the period from the date of the event (1 December 2006) to the 25th anniversary of the date on which the building was first used (1 March 2025) is 18 years and three months (219 months).

Using the formula of RQE × A/B, the allowances for the year would therefore have been calculated as follows under the old rules:

$$£708,000 \times {}^{12}/_{219} = £38,795.$$

Where, immediately before the rebate accrues, the residue of qualifying expenditure was less than the amount of the rebate, a balancing charge would in the past have been made equal to the excess. If there was no residue at that point, the balancing charge would have been equal to the amount of the rebate (CAA 2001, s. 350), and no further writing-down allowances would be due.

If a balancing charge was made under the above rules, the 'starting expenditure' for the purposes of calculating a balancing adjustment (see 305-500) may have needed to be reduced by the amount of the balancing charge (CAA 2001, s. 350(5)).

An amount equal to the VAT rebate is written off at the time when the rebate accrues (CAA 2001, s. 351). It appears that this is intended to be for the purposes of calculating the residue of qualifying expenditure for the purposes of CAA 2001, s. 313, though perhaps there is a glitch in the legislation here. Section 313 refers to the writing-off of expenditure in accordance with CAA 2001, Ch. 8 but this s. 351 is not within that Chapter. This apparent anomaly did not arise under the 1990 Act.

Balancing adjustments: principles

305-500   Overview

A balancing adjustment may be required if qualifying expenditure has been incurred on a building and there is a balancing event either whilst the building is still an industrial building or after it has ceased to be one. The balancing adjustment may be either a balancing allowance or a balancing charge.

Legislation: CAA 2001, s. 314

Changes applying from March 2007

The *Finance Act* 2007 introduced rules that apply, subject to transitional provisions, to disposals made from 21 March 2007, and that prevent from that date the making of any balancing adjustments on most disposals of industrial buildings (with the exception of disposals of buildings in enterprise zones). Details are given at 305-200ff.

Other than in relation to:

- qualifying enterprise zone expenditure (see 250-950);
- disposal events that are subject to the transitional provisions (see 249-725); or

the rules do not therefore apply for disposals made from 21 March 2007. See earlier editions of this book for full details of the rules previously applying.

Anti-avoidance rules

306-500   Overview

General anti-avoidance principles, as developed in such cases as *WT Ramsay Ltd v IR Commrs* and *Furniss (HMIT) v Dawson*, are beyond the scope of this book. Nevertheless, their effects should be considered in appropriate circumstances, such as where artificial steps are inserted into a series of otherwise commercial transactions, or where a series of transactions is 'pre-ordained'.

In relation to capital allowances generally, and IBAs in particular, there are various statutory anti-avoidance provisions, including:

- arrangements having an artificial effect on pricing (CAA 2001, s. 357);
- restricted balancing allowances where a sale is subject to a subordinate interest (CAA 2001, s. 325); and
- avoidance affecting the proceeds of a balancing event (CAA 2001, s. 570A).

Most of these provisions are unlikely to have any practical effect since the abolition of balancing adjustments for IBA purposes, and the commentary in this book has been cut back accordingly (but see earlier editions if necessary).

The treatment of capital value received in relation to a building in an enterprise zone (CAA 2001, s. 328) is addressed at 320-350. HMRC's power (under CAA 2001, s. 562(2)) to impose a different apportionment on the different elements of a transaction is discussed at 305-700. Various restrictions on the ability to treat the grant of a long lease as a sale of the relevant interest (CAA 2001, s. 291) are considered at 304-750. The requirement, in certain circumstances, to substitute market value for actual proceeds (CAA 2001, s. 568) is addressed at 307-100. Anti-avoidance rules relating to the transfer of a UK trade to a company in another member state are touched on at 310-000.

Cases: *WT Ramsay Ltd v IR Commrs* (1983) 54 TC 101, *Furniss (HMIT) v Dawson* [1984] BTC 71

306-550 Arrangements having an artificial effect on pricing

A person may buy a building at an artificially inflated price.

> ### Example
>
> A Ltd may pay a reverse premium to B to encourage B to enter into a lease. This may be a normal commercial arrangement but may be part of an artificial series of transactions. Suppose that in return B agrees to pay an inflated rent under the lease. Once A Ltd has secured the rental stream, it can sell the relevant interest to C at an artificially high price. C can then claim higher allowances than would otherwise have been the case.

Circumstances where the rules apply

The HMRC manuals give examples of transactions that may be caught under these provisions. Their list of examples, which is not likely to be comprehensive, includes details of schemes involving reverse premiums, lease-backs, construction leases and rental guarantees.

See also the case of *R v IR Commrs, ex parte Matrix Securities Ltd* for an illustration of the circumstances that led to this anti-avoidance legislation.

The special rules apply where:

- there is a sale of the relevant interest in a building;
- 'related arrangements' (see below) have been entered into, by the time the sale price is fixed, that have had the effect of increasing the value of the relevant interest; and
- the arrangements contain a provision that 'has an artificial effect on pricing' (see below).

Legislation: CAA 2001, s. 357

Industrial Buildings

Cases: *R v IR Commrs, ex parte Matrix Securities Ltd* [1994] BTC 85

Other material: CA 39620

Effect of applying the rules

In these circumstances, the amount treated for IBA purposes as paid for the acquisition of the relevant interest is reduced to what it would have been without the arrangements having the artificial effect. Any excess expenditure does not qualify for IBAs.

Legislation: CAA 2001, s. 357(1)

Definitions

The term 'related arrangements' is defined to cover arrangements between two or more persons that relate to an interest in, or right over, the building, or else to other arrangements that are made with respect to such an interest or right.

Arrangements are treated as containing a provision having an artificial effect on pricing 'to the extent that they go beyond what could reasonably have been regarded as required in comparable commercial transactions by the market conditions prevailing when the arrangements were entered into'.

The term 'comparable commercial transactions' is in itself defined to mean transactions that are made at arm's length in the open market and that involve interests in, or rights over, buildings that are similar to the one to which the arrangements relate.

Legislation: CAA 2001, s. 357

Sales treated as being for alternative amount

307-000 Introduction

Given that no balancing adjustments are generally made for balancing events from 21 March 2007, much of the legislation described in the following paragraphs would now appear to have no further practical effect. The commentary has therefore been cut back, but see earlier editions of this book for full details.

The legislation uses the heading 'sales treated as being for alternative amount' to cover both an anti-avoidance rule and a tax planning opportunity. The overall effect of the legislation can be summarised as follows (but subject to the more precise details given after the summary):

- first, there are tax avoidance rules that require market value to be substituted for actual proceeds where certain transactions are designed primarily to reduce a person's tax liability;

- secondly, there is a requirement to substitute market value for the actual proceeds figure in certain transactions between (broadly) connected parties; and
- thirdly, where there is a transfer between such connected parties, but there is no tax avoidance motive, there is a chance to elect to transfer the relevant interest in an industrial building at such a value as ensures that no balancing adjustment is triggered (though this will now in most cases be unnecessary, following changes introduced from March 2007).

Legislation: CAA 2001, s. 567(5)

307-050   Definitions

To operate these rules correctly, two primary definitions are given.

Control test

First, there is the concept of 'the control test'. This test is said to be met if the buyer and seller are connected persons or if:

- the buyer is a body of persons over whom the seller has control;
- the seller is a body of persons over whom the buyer has control; or
- both the seller and the buyer are bodies of persons and both are under the control of another person.

This definition of the control test gave rise to a number of subsidiary definitions.

Tax advantage test

The second main definition that is needed for these purposes is of the concept of 'the tax advantage test'. This is said to be met if the sole or main benefit that might be expected to accrue from the sale is the obtaining of a tax advantage by all or any of the parties concerned. The tax advantage must be the obtaining of an allowance or an increased allowance, or the avoidance or reduction of a balancing charge, under any part of the *Capital Allowances Act* 2001 except the plant or machinery rules.

The HMRC manuals acknowledge that 'it is difficult to use the main benefit provisions if the taxpayer can come up with good commercial reasons for the transaction'. Furthermore, the definition needs to be seen in the context of the changes introduced from 21 March 2007 which prevent the making of any balancing adjustment in most circumstances.

Legislation: CAA 2001, s. 567(4), 577(4)

Other material: CA 13100

307-100 Market value

Market value had to be substituted for the actual sale proceeds if either the control test or the tax advantage test was met. This was, however, subject to any possible election under CAA 2001, s. 569.

Legislation: CAA 2001, s. 568(1)

Other material: CA 13100

307-150 Election for alternative amount

The following paragraph now needs to be read in the context of the general rule applying from 21 March 2007 that prevents the making of any balancing charge or allowance for transactions from that date.

The parties to a property transaction may in principle elect for the sale to be treated as taking place 'for the alternative amount' if:

- either the control test is met (eg the purchaser and seller are connected); or
- the transfer of the relevant interest is not in fact a sale but is merely treated (under CAA 2001, s. 573 – see 305-600) as being a sale at market value.

Any election must be made by both parties to the transaction, and submitted within two years from the date of the sale. HMRC insists that the election should be signed by the person or persons with control at the time the election is made:

> 'An election signed by a person who had control at the time of sale but who no longer has control when the election is made is not valid. For example, an election signed by a former director after ceasing to be a director is not valid, even if that person was a director at the time of the sale'

Once the election is made, all necessary assessments or adjustments are to be made to give it effect. Thereafter, any balancing charge that would have fallen on the vendor will instead be imposed on the purchaser.

However, no election was possible in certain specified circumstances.

The effect of the legislation was that a transaction between connected parties would never take place at its purported value (unless that value happens to be the same as either the market value or the figure of the residue before the sale). If no election was made, market value would be substituted. If the parties to the transaction did make a valid election then the figure used would be the one that produced no balancing allowance or charge.

Legislation: CAA 2001, s. 569, CAA 2001, s. 570(5)

Miscellaneous provisions

310-000 Transfer of UK trade to a company in another member state

Under the capital gains tax legislation, a company resident in one EU member state may be able to transfer the whole or part of a UK trade to a second company resident in a different member state, without producing any liability on the gain; the gain is treated as transferred on a no gain, no loss basis. There are numerous conditions applying which are beyond the scope of this Chapter. One particular condition, however, is that both parties to the transaction must make a claim.

Where all those conditions are met, so that TCGA 1992, s. 140A applies, the transfer will not give rise to any balancing allowance or balancing charge for IBA (or for other capital allowance) purposes. The transferee company will be treated as stepping into the shoes of the transferor company.

There is anti-avoidance legislation that can prevent the CGT relief from applying. Where this happens, the capital allowances relief will similarly be denied. In the broadest terms, the anti-avoidance legislation takes effect if the transfer of the trade is not made for bona fide commercial reasons or if it is part of a scheme that has tax avoidance as a main purpose. The tax avoidance may relate to capital gains tax, capital allowances or any other kind of taxation. The HMRC view is that 'a commercial scheme may be caught if tax avoidance is one of the main purposes of the deal'. A statutory clearance procedure is available.

Where necessary, expenditure should be apportioned in a just and reasonable manner between assets that are transferred and those that are retained. However, HMRC makes the point that industrial buildings should each have their own residue of qualifying expenditure so that an apportionment should be unnecessary.

Where these rules apply, the rules under ICTA 1988, s. 343(2) (effect of a company reconstruction without a change of ownership) specifically do not apply.

Legislation: TCGA 1992, s. 140A; CAA 2001, s. 561

Other material: CA 15560; see also the HMRC Manual, *Capital Gains Tax*, CG 45700

310-050 Apportionments: appeals

Various references have been made in the above Chapters to the need to apportion figures in particular circumstances.

Where two or more parties to a transaction are affected by an apportionment, there are procedural rules for deciding how the tribunal proceedings are to be conducted.

Legislation: CAA 2001, s. 563–564

310-100   Requisitioned land

If the Crown requisitions land, it is treated for IBA purposes as being in possession of that land by virtue of a lease during the period of requisition. As a result, this does not represent a transfer of the relevant interest. References in the IBA legislation to the surrender of a lease, to the extinguishment thereof on the person entitled to the lease acquiring the reversionary interest, or to the merger of a leasehold interest, are construed accordingly.

Any payment to the Crown, in respect of any building constructed on requisitioned land, by the person entitled to possession of the land is treated as paid in consideration of the surrender of that notional lease.

Persons authorised by the Crown to occupy all or part of the land during the period of requisition are treated as if they had been granted a sublease by the Crown.

A 'period of requisition' means a period in respect of which compensation is, or, but for any agreement to the contrary, would be, payable under the *Compensation (Defence) Act* 1939, s. 2(1)(a) by reference to the rent which might reasonably be expected to be payable under a lease granted immediately before the beginning of that period.

Legislation: CAA 2001, s. 358

Other material: CA 39550

310-150   Crown (or other person outside the charge to tax) holds relevant interest

Special rules apply in relation to the writing-off of qualifying expenditure if the relevant interest has been held by the Crown or by some other person not within the tax to charge.

In such circumstances, it is necessary to write off all the writing-down allowances and balancing adjustments that could have been made if the relevant interest had been held by a person within the charge to tax.

The write-offs take place using certain assumptions; broadly, that all things done by or to the Crown, (etc) in relation to the building were done by a person within the charge to tax. Any sale of the relevant interest by the Crown, (etc) is treated as made in connection with the termination of a trade carried on by the notional person within the charge to tax. There are rules to determine the timing of the notional periods of account.

Legislation: CAA 2001, s. 339

Other material: CA 34700

310-200   Extended meaning of 'sale of property'

For capital allowance purposes, a sale of property is held to include the exchange of one property for another.

It also includes the surrender of a leasehold interest (in Scotland, the interest of the tenant in property subject to a lease) for valuable consideration.

To give effect to these provisions:

- references to 'net proceeds of sale' or to 'price' are taken to include any consideration given for the exchange or surrender; and
- references to any capital sum that is either included in the net proceeds of sale, or paid on a sale, are taken to include 'so much of the consideration for the exchange or surrender as would have been a capital sum if it had been a money payment'.

Legislation: CAA 2001, s. 572

310-250   Time of sale

Any reference to the time of a sale is to be read as a reference to the earlier of:

- the time of completion; or
- the time when possession is given.

Legislation: CAA 2001, s. 572(4)

310-300   Partnership changes

As a general principle, partnership capital allowances are made to the partners who are for the time being carrying on the relevant trade, property business, profession or vocation.

The amount of any allowance or charge is to be calculated as if the present partners had at all times been carrying on the relevant activity. Anything done by their predecessor partners in carrying on the relevant activity is therefore treated as done by the present partners.

This will be the case where there has been a partnership change but with at least one partner carrying on the relevant activity after that change.

Legislation: CAA 2001, s. 558

310-350 Successions

Where one person succeeds to the trade or other relevant activity carried on by someone else, this does not in itself constitute a cessation of the trade. Nevertheless, the trade will be treated as discontinued if all of the persons carrying it on before the succession permanently cease to carry it on. It may also be treated as permanently ceasing under ITTOIA 2005, s. 18 or 362 (company starting or ceasing to be within charge to income tax) or may be treated as discontinued under CTA 2009, s. 41 (effect of company ceasing to trade) or 289 (effect of company starting or ceasing to be within charge to corporation tax).

Where the trade, etc is treated in this way as ceasing, any industrial building that was used for the purposes of the discontinued trade, etc and that is not in fact sold, will be deemed to be sold at market value to the successor if it is then immediately used for the purposes of the new trade, etc. No initial allowance may be claimed by the successor.

If there is a discontinuance, but the building is sold, then a balancing adjustment would before 21 March 2007 have been made in the normal way. If the parties were connected, market value would apply but subject to a possible election (under CAA 2001, s. 569 – see 307-150) to transfer the building at the figure of its residue before sale.

If the succession is not treated as a discontinuance, this must be by virtue either of the partnership change rules (see above) or of the rules relating to company reconstructions (ICTA 1988, s. 343(2)). In the case of company reconstructions, allowances and charges are made to or on the successor as if everything done by the predecessor had in fact been done by the successor.

Legislation: CAA 2001, s. 559

310-400 Definitions

Wherever possible, relevant definitions have been given in context in this Chapter.

CAA 2001, s. 577 defines various terms as used for capital allowances purposes.

CAA 2001, Sch. 1, Pt. 2 provides an alphabetical list of definitions contained within the Act, together with the appropriate section numbers.

310-450   Transitional provisions

When the *Capital Allowances Act* 1990 was re-written under the tax law rewrite process, it reappeared as the *Capital Allowances Act* 2001. Various transitional provisions were at that point relegated to CAA 2001, Sch. 3. CAA 2001, Sch. 3, Pt. 5 relates specifically to IBAs.

310-500   Interaction with plant and machinery allowances

Introduction

The basic principles of how IBAs interact with Plant and Machinery ('P&M') allowances are straightforward. To the extent that allowances are claimed under one regime, no claim can be made under the other.

Sometimes, a person will have a choice of regime under which to claim allowances. An example often arising in practice is of a cold store or other temperature-controlled premises, touched on at 300-050 and 301-550. As discussed at those sections, the issues to consider where there is a genuine choice will include the speed at which allowances can be claimed, the possibility of long-life asset restrictions under the P&M regime and the extent to which allowances may be clawed back in the event of a future sale of the asset. The proposed abolition of the IBA regime will now also have a bearing on that decision.

Where the purchase price of a building includes other assets, a just apportionment will need to be made. This can apply where part of the cost is land but will equally apply where part of the cost is plant or machinery on which P&M allowances have been claimed.

As regards the preparation of sites for the installation of plant or machinery (CAA 2001, s. 273) see 300-650.

Allowances may be available under the P&M regime for expenditure on heat insulation for an industrial building (CAA 2001, s. 28).

Legislation: CAA 2001, s. 7, 562

Other material: CA 31310

Effect of past claims

Once an asset has been the subject of a claim under one regime, it will retain that status and allowances cannot subsequently be claimed by the same owner under the other regime.

A change of ownership, however, may give the chance for the treatment to be reappraised. In the case of fixtures, this is made explicit in the legislation. The effect of the legislation is to limit the allowances given on a fixture to its original cost. This is done by imposing a cap on the maximum expenditure that can be taken into account for P&M purposes. This cap is given by the formula:

$$F/T \times R$$

Where:

F   represents the part of the consideration for the transfer by the past owner that is attributable to the fixture;

T   is the total consideration for the transfer; and

R   is the residue of qualifying expenditure attributable to the relevant interest immediately after the transfer. This is to be calculated on the assumption that the transfer was a sale of the relevant interest.

One effect of this is that the new owner's qualifying expenditure for P&M purposes can never exceed the original construction costs.

Legislation: CAA 2001, s. 186

Other material: CA 26450

Interaction with the 25 per cent rule

A point of interest arises concerning the practical application of the rule that allows allowances to be claimed on the whole of a building if the expenditure on non-qualifying parts is less than 25 per cent of total expenditure on the building (see 303-500).

The point can be illustrated with the following simplified example. A business pays for the construction of a building at a total cost (excluding land) of £1m. The trade itself is a qualifying trade. The expenditure can be broken down as follows:

	Factory £(1000s)	Offices £(1000s)	Total £(1000s)
Main expenditure	650	230	880
Fixtures	105	15	120
Total	755	245	1,000

The fixtures form a part of the building for IBA purposes and it is open to the business to claim IBAs on the cost inclusive of those fixtures. If this is done, no P&M allowances can be claimed on the same expenditure (CAA 2001, s. 7).

If no P&M claim is made, it then seems that the gross figures above can be considered for the purposes of applying the 25 per cent rule. The expenditure on the offices (£245,000) is less than a quarter of the total expenditure on the factory (£1 million). In statutory terms, the qualifying expenditure relating to the non-industrial part is no more than 25 per cent of the qualifying expenditure relating to the whole building. Therefore the *de minimis* rule applies, so that the whole of the building is treated as an industrial building.

But what if P&M allowances are claimed on the fixtures? Given that the remaining expenditure of £230,000 is more than one quarter of the total remaining expenditure of

£880,000, does it follow that no allowances are due on the £230,000 and that the IBA claim must be restricted to £650,000?

On a practical level, the expenditure is likely to be split and two computations will be prepared, one for P&M allowances and one for IBAs. This is likely to lead to a decision to disallow the expenditure of £230,000 on the offices. But is this correct? The technical analysis would seem to be as follows:

- the whole building is, on a natural interpretation of the words, in use for the purposes of the qualifying trade (CAA 2001, s. 271(1)(b));
- this is then overridden, however, by the rule that states that an office is not to be treated as a building in use for the purposes of a qualifying trade (CAA 2001, s. 277);
- this exclusion does not apply (per CAA 2001, s. 284, as above) if the qualifying expenditure relating to the non-industrial part is no more than 25 per cent of the qualifying expenditure relating to the whole of the building;
- 'qualifying expenditure' is simply capital expenditure on the construction of the building (CAA 2001, s. 294), without any reference to how the building is used; and
- no IBA is to be made in relation to the expenditure on the fixtures as allowances have been claimed under the P&M regime (CAA 2001, s. 7). There is nothing in that section to say, however, that the expenditure ceases to be qualifying expenditure – the structure is rather to say 'this is qualifying expenditure but, for other reasons, no allowances can be claimed'.

It is suggested that there is no reason in these circumstances to restrict the allowances to exclude the office element. It should be emphasised, however, that this is not an 'official' view – the HMRC manuals are silent on the matter and the author has been unable to find any precedent or commentary to back up his interpretation. It is perhaps surprising that a real case has not come to light on the matter, as there must be circumstances where the issue would arise in practice.

Legislation: CAA 2001, s. 283ff.

Other material: CA 26450

310-550   Interaction with capital gains tax

Introduction

One of the areas that can be misunderstood in relation to capital allowances generally is the interaction with capital gains tax (CGT). This paragraph addresses the issue.

Disposal proceeds and allowable costs

The general rule is that the granting of capital allowances does not have any bearing on the computation of a capital gain for CGT (or corporation tax) purposes. Specifically, the fact that an allowance has been made does not affect either the allowable expenditure or the disposal consideration for CGT purposes, whether or not that allowance is subsequently recaptured by a balancing charge. This is discussed in the Chapter headed 'Plant and Property' (which begins at 250-000) but the comments that follow relate specifically to CGT and industrial buildings allowances.

If, for example, a factory is bought for £1 million and sold for £1.5 million, the capital gain will (subject to costs, indexation, etc) be £500,000. It is likely that IBAs will have been given to relieve some or all of the expenditure. The computation of the gain as £500,000 will apply whether the building is sold after (say) 24 years, in which case a balancing charge would in the past almost certain have been made, or after (for example) 26 years in which case there will be no balancing adjustment (see 305-600).

The only exception is if the building is sold at a loss. In this case, the loss is restricted to take account of capital allowances given. For the purposes of calculating a capital gain, the legislation works by excluding from the allowable cost any expenditure that has been the subject of a capital allowance. This will have the effect of reducing or eliminating the capital loss; it will not convert a loss into a gain.

There are provisions (TCGA 1992, Sch. 3, para. 3) to apply the rules in cases where gains have been 'rebased' to March 1982.

The HMRC Manual, *Capital Gains*, contains various examples illustrating the effects of these rules for capital gains tax purposes (see, for example, CG 16902).

> ### Example
>
> A factory is bought for £1 million and sold some years later for £780,000. It has qualified as an industrial building throughout. After making any balancing adjustments, net allowances are given of £220,000. The allowable base cost is therefore restricted by the £220,000, which produces a net result of no taxable gain or allowable loss.

In practice, there may still be a loss arising. First, there will almost certainly be acquisition and disposal costs. Secondly, any amount relating to land should be isolated. No IBAs will be due on the land element, and it follows that a capital loss may arise to that extent.

The restriction of losses by reference to capital allowances is modified where companies have acquired assets in 'relevant circumstances' – typically, a no gain/no loss acquisition.

For a case where the interaction of CGT and capital allowances was considered in relation to an enterprise zone property unit trust, see *St C Smallwood v R & C Commrs*.

Legislation: TCGA 1992, s. 41, 174

Cases: *St C Smallwood v R & C Commrs* (2005) Sp C 509

Other material: HMRC Manual, *Capital Gains* CG 15410, 45922

Qualifying hotels

315-000   Overview

The rules giving allowances for certain hotels were introduced from 1978 to encourage the hotel trade. If a building falls within the definition of 'qualifying hotel', then it qualifies for IBAs in its own right; it is not necessary to consider further the nature of the trade carried on.

The rules granting IBAs in relation to hotels apply only to expenditure incurred from 12 April 1978. In relation to a hotel acquired after that date, expenditure will not qualify if the original construction expenditure was incurred before 12 April 1978 (CAA 2001, Sch. 3, para. 58). There is, however, nothing to stop allowances being given for new expenditure incurred on an hotel that was originally constructed before that date. In such a case, an apportionment will be required if the hotel is subsequently sold, ensuring that the proceeds are apportioned between the parts that have qualified for allowances and those that have not.

Legislation: CAA 2001, s. 271(1)(b)(ii); Sch. 3, para. 58

315-050   Meaning of 'hotel'

The legislation does not define 'hotel' for these purposes. The HMRC manuals do, however, provide some clear guidelines. Referring to the *Hotel Proprietors Act* 1956, the manuals suggest that a hotel should be interpreted as:

> 'an establishment held out by the proprietor as offering food and drink and, if so required, sleeping accommodation, without special contract, to any traveller presenting himself who appears able and willing to pay a reasonable sum for the services and facilities provided and who is in a fit state to be received.'

HMRC accepts that a guest house or holiday camp will be within the definition of hotel and will therefore qualify for IBAs if all the relevant conditions are met. On the other hand, HMRC goes on to list many types of establishment that do not, in its opinion, qualify: 'self catering holiday accommodation, pubs and farmhouses with a few rooms to let, seaside and other lodging houses, residential homes, convalescent and nursing homes, health farms, etc'.

HMRC accepts that a hotel can consist of more than one building or structure. As such, they will allow relief for various amenities of the hotel, even if non-residents are also permitted to use them. By way of example, the HMRC manuals refer to squash courts, tennis courts, a swimming pool and a car park.

Staff accommodation also qualifies for allowances as part of the hotel, whether it is in the main building or elsewhere.

Other material: CA 32402

315-100   Conditions

The legislation lists five main conditions for a hotel to qualify, as follows:

(1)   the accommodation must be of a permanent nature;

(2)   it must be open for at least four months of the year between April and October inclusive;

(3)   when open, it must have at least 10 letting bedrooms;

(4)   the sleeping accommodation must consist wholly or mainly of letting bedrooms; and

(5)   the services provided for guests must normally include breakfast, an evening meal, the making of beds and the cleaning of rooms.

For these purposes, a 'letting bedroom' is specifically defined as 'a private bedroom available for letting to the public generally and not normally in the same occupation for more than one month'. It is on the basis of this definition that establishments such as residential homes will normally be disqualified; bedrooms in such establishments are normally in the same occupation for more than one month at a time.

Revenue Statement of Practice SP 9/87 addressed the question of the provision of meals. HMRC has indicated that it will regard the meals test as satisfied 'where the offering of breakfast and dinner is a normal event in the hotel's carrying on of its business. HMRC will not regard it as satisfied where the service of meals is exceptional, eg if either breakfast or an evening meal is available only on request'.

Legislation: CAA 2001, s. 279

315-150   Reference period

One of the more difficult technical issues in relation to qualifying hotels arises from the concept of the 'reference period'. The difficulty arises from the interaction of the 'April to October' rule referred to above and the accounting period of the company. It may be necessary to consider the opening periods of the hotel in two consecutive calendar years.

HMRC gives the example of a business with a 30 June accounting date. If accounts are drawn up to 30 June 2006, then it will be necessary to consider the months of July to September 2005 and also April to June 2006 to determine whether or not the hotel is a qualifying hotel during the year ended 30 June 2006. This is the normal rule that applies where the hotel is in use for the purposes of the trade throughout the 12-month period.

If the hotel starts to be used during the accounting period, then the reference period will be the 12-month period beginning with the date on which the hotel was first used for the trade. If the business with the 30 June 2006 year-end only started to use the hotel from 1 January 2005, for example, it will be necessary to look at the whole of the calendar year to determine whether or not the hotel qualifies during the accounting period to 30 June. Similarly, if the hotel has not previously qualified for relief because it had fewer than 10 letting bedrooms, but additional rooms are constructed, the reference period will be the 12-month period beginning with the date on which it had enough bedrooms.

If the hotel ceases altogether to be used, then it will cease to be a qualifying hotel from that moment. Subject to this, a change of use before the end of the chargeable period, or a period of temporary disuse, will not prevent the building from qualifying. As the HMRC manuals put it, 'once a hotel has satisfied the conditions for being a qualifying hotel for a chargeable period, it continues to be a qualifying hotel until the end of that chargeable period unless it ceases altogether to be used'.

Legislation: CAA 2001, s. 279

Other material: CA 32403

315-200   Accommodation for hotel workers

Staff accommodation qualifies for allowances as long as the hotel itself so qualifies. The legislation simply treats such accommodation as part of the hotel, whether or not in fact in the same building. On the other hand, domestic accommodation provided for the business proprietor (sole trader or partner), or for members of his family or household, will not qualify. If the proprietor's accommodation is part of the main hotel, then it may in practice give rise to IBAs by virtue of the 25 per cent rule (see 303-500). If it is in a separate building, then it can never qualify.

Legislation: CAA 2001, s. 279(7)

315-250   Excluded activities

The exclusions relating to dwelling-houses, retail shops, etc do not apply to qualifying hotels. As such, a retail shop inside a hotel will still qualify for allowances as long as it is part of the amenities of the hotel itself.

Other material: CA 32403

Qualifying sports pavilions

315-500   Qualifying sports pavilions

A qualifying sports pavilion is defined as a building that is occupied by a person carrying on a trade and used as a sports pavilion for the welfare of workers employed in that trade. The trade does not have to be one that qualifies in its own right as one that would give rise to IBAs.

HMRC applies the test of whether the building exists primarily for the convenience of the players or whether it is mainly for spectators. Only the former will qualify. As such, a sports pavilion will normally be adjacent to a playing-field, pitch or track and will be a place where the players can change, bathe, shower, obtain refreshments and so on. Buildings existing primarily for spectators will not qualify. Nor will church halls, social centres, etc, as these are not considered to exist primarily for the convenience of the players.

The above interpretation is in accordance with the HMRC manuals. Arguably, HMRC's interpretation is slightly stricter than the legislation in fact requires. Certainly, there is nothing within the *Capital Allowances Act* 2001 to define a sports pavilion in these terms.

If a sports centre that includes non-qualifying accommodation also includes accommodation that is provided primarily for the convenience of the players, then HMRC accepts that an apportionment of the expenditure should be made.

Legislation: CAA 2001, s. 280

Other material: CA 32500

Enterprise zones

320-000   Background

Special rules for buildings in enterprise zones were introduced in the *Finance Act* 1980. The stated intention of the legislation was to stimulate development in specified areas that had become run down. The areas that were to benefit from the legislation were to be designated by the Secretary of State for the Environment or, as the case may be, by the Secretaries of State for Scotland and Wales, or by the Department of the Environment for Northern Ireland. As such, enterprise zones have ranged geographically from (for example) Belfast and Londonderry to Glasgow, Dundee and parts of Lanarkshire, to Lower Swansea Valley, parts of Sunderland, parts of the East Midlands, the Isle of Dogs and parts of Northwest Kent. Between them, these examples give some idea of the geographical spread.

The designation of an enterprise zone lasts for 10 years. Construction expenditure will qualify for the special IBA rules if it is qualifying expenditure on a site in an enterprise zone. It must be incurred within 10 years of the designation of the zone, or within 20 years if it is incurred under a contract that was entered into within 10 years of the designation.

320-050   Main tax effects: overview

The enterprise zone rules form part of the overall IBA legislation. Unless otherwise specified, therefore, qualifying expenditure on an enterprise zone building will be treated for IBA purposes in the same way as any other qualifying expenditure discussed elsewhere in this Chapter.

Nevertheless, there are some key differences, including in particular the following:

- the abolition of most balancing adjustments for events occurring from 21 March 2007 does not apply for enterprise zone expenditure, but IBAs will be withdrawn even for enterprise zone expenditure from April 2011;
- at the time of abolition of IBAs, there will be a seven-year run-off period during which taxpayers may still face balancing charges (see below);
- a wider range of buildings, specifically to include commercial buildings, can qualify under the enterprise zone rules than under the general IBA rules;
- an initial allowance is available for enterprise zone expenditure;
- if a full (100 per cent) initial allowance has not been taken, expenditure qualifies for writing-down allowances at a much faster rate;
- the tax treatment differs from the main IBA rules where buildings are bought that have already been used; and
- in view of the attractive tax benefits, the enterprise zone rules are subject to their own anti-avoidance legislation.

As indicated above, commercial buildings may be included in the list of buildings qualifying under the enterprise zone rules. For the avoidance of doubt, however, the other tax benefits just listed are not restricted to commercial buildings. All the tax advantages can apply equally to industrial buildings and qualifying hotels, as long as they fall within a designated enterprise zone and the expenditure is incurred within the specified time limits.

Phasing out of IBAs

As mentioned above, IBAs have been phased out since April 2007 and will be completely abolished from April 2011. As a general principle, this will apply for qualifying enterprise zone expenditure as it does for all other allowances under the IBA code.

For enterprise zone expenditure only, balancing adjustments can still be made. Furthermore, it will still be possible for a person to incur a balancing charge up to 5 April 2018 in relation to such expenditure (FA 2008, Sch. 27, para. 31). More specifically, the balancing charge will (from April 2011) arise if:

- an initial allowance or writing-down allowance has been made under the enterprise zone rules;
- an event occurs which would have given rise to a balancing charge under those rules; and
- a balancing event occurs within seven years of the date on which the building for first used.

Similarly, an initial allowance for qualifying enterprise zone expenditure will be withdrawn if:

- an event occurs which would have caused the allowance to be withdrawn if (from April 2011), CAA 2001, s. 307 had not been withdrawn; and
- a balancing event occurs within seven years of the end of the chargeable period for which the allowance was made.

For chargeable periods that start before 1 or 6 April 2011 (the 'relevant date' for corporation tax and income tax respectively), but end after that date, any writing-down allowances will only be given for the part of the period falling before that date. This is achieved (per FA 2008, s. 86(2)) by calculating the allowance for that period according to the following formula:

$$(DCPB/DCP) \times WDA$$

where:

DCPB is the number of days in the chargeable period which fall before the relevant date;

DCP is the number of days in the chargeable period; and

WDA is the writing-down allowance to which the person would otherwise be entitled for the chargeable period.

320-100 Extended meaning of industrial building or structure

The main IBA legislation lists four types of property that may qualify for IBAs. In practice, the one most often considered is a building or structure that is in use for the purposes of a qualifying trade. The second category is a qualifying hotel and the third a qualifying sports pavilion. The fourth type of qualifying expenditure is on a building or structure that is, in relation to qualifying enterprise zone expenditure, a commercial building or structure.

For these purposes, the term 'commercial building' is defined as a building that is used for the purposes of a trade, profession or vocation, or as an office or offices (whether or not for the purposes of a trade, profession or vocation). There is an exclusion for any building in use as, or as part of, a dwelling-house.

This immediately throws up two further key differences from the treatment of buildings in use for a qualifying trade:

- first, the extension to use for a profession or vocation applies for enterprise zone purposes but does not apply for other IBA purposes; and
- secondly, for enterprise zone buildings the exclusion relates only to a dwelling-house. Buildings that qualify under the other IBA rules are excluded not only if they are in use as a dwelling-house but also if they are a retail shop, a showroom, a hotel or an office.

The legislation uses the term 'EZ building' to mean a 'building on a site in an enterprise zone'. The term 'qualifying enterprise zone expenditure' is then defined as capital expenditure that is incurred on the construction of an EZ building within the specified time limit.

Legislation: CAA 2001, s. 271, 281, 298–299

Ten-year rule

If expenditure is incurred within 10 years after the site was first included in the zone, then it will be clear that the expenditure falls within the specified period. If the expenditure is incurred within 20 years of the original date, but under a contract entered into within 10 years of that date, then in principle it will still qualify.

See SI 1996/2435 for an example of a statutory instrument designating an enterprise zone. The instrument shows the date it was made, the date it was laid before Parliament and the date it comes into force. It is the last of these dates that is taken into account for setting the 10-year rule (see para. 4 of the statutory instrument – 'Period of Designation').

Using that example, the designated date is 21 October 1996. It follows that any expenditure incurred up to 20 October 2006 will automatically fall within the time limit. In practice, however, it may be possible to claim under the enterprise zone rules for expenditure incurred up to 20 October 2016. This is subject to changes introduced in *Finance Act* 2007, however: although those changes do not apply to enterprise zone expenditure, it does appear to be the case that all IBAs (ie including those relating to enterprise zones) are to be abolished from April 2011. In practice, there would have been very few claims after that date anyway.

HMRC will check for abuse of this rule. It gives an example of a contract that was made for an industrial estate but that is changed into one for a large factory. The HMRC view is that 'a substantial change of this nature could result in an entirely new contract'. If that new contract was made more than 10 years after the zone was designated, then it will not be possible to claim IBAs under the enterprise zone rules. HMRC does acknowledge, however, that this is a grey area. It goes on to say that 'variation clauses in a contract may … permit considerable changes to be made without invalidating the contract. Small changes, which do not go to the root of the bargain between the parties, may also constitute a mere variation of the original contract'.

The following paragraphs assume, except where stated otherwise, that all the expenditure is incurred within the designated 10- (or 20-) year period.

Other material: CA 37150

320-150   Initial allowances

Overview and first principles

The main attraction of the enterprise zone rules is the availability of a 100 per cent initial allowance for qualifying EZ expenditure. In other words, a person incurring construction costs can for tax purposes write off the whole of those costs at the start. The initial allowance is normally made for the chargeable period in which the qualifying expenditure is incurred. If, however, it is incurred for a trade, profession or vocation by a person who is about to carry it on then it is treated as if it had been incurred on the first day on which the

Industrial Buildings

person actually carries on that trade, profession or vocation. A person claiming an initial allowance may require the amount of the allowance to be reduced to a lower amount.

To qualify for the initial allowance, a person must have incurred qualifying enterprise zone expenditure. The building in question must be intended to be an industrial building that would either be occupied by that person, occupied by a qualifying lessee or used by a qualifying licensee. For initial allowances, there is no condition that the building should actually have been brought into use.

For the above purposes, the term 'qualifying lessee' is defined as 'a lessee under a lease to which the relevant interest is reversionary'. The term 'qualifying licensee' is defined as either:

- a licensee of the person who incurs the qualifying expenditure; or
- a licensee of a lessee of the person incurring the expenditure.

Given that the legislation grants initial allowances 'if the building … is to be an industrial building', it follows that a mechanism is needed to withdraw the initial allowance if, in the event, the building never becomes an industrial building. Therefore, the legislation allows for such an initial allowance to be withdrawn if, when the building is first used, it is not an industrial building. This might apply if, for example, the building was in the event used as a dwelling-house. HMRC is empowered to raise or amend assessments as necessary to give effect to this.

If the person to whom the initial allowance is made sells the relevant interest before the building is first used, then the initial allowance is to be withdrawn. Again, HMRC can raise assessments as necessary.

Legislation: CAA 2001, s. 305ff

Grants received

To the extent that expenditure is taken into account for the purposes either of a relevant grant or of a relevant payment made towards the expenditure, no initial allowance is to be made. If such a grant or relevant payment is made after the initial allowance has been given, the allowance is to be withdrawn 'to that extent'.

If the amount of the grant or payment is repaid to the grantor by the grantee, whether in whole or in part, then the grant or payment is treated (to that extent) as never having been made.

Once more, HMRC is empowered to made such assessments, or adjustments to assessments, as are necessary to give effect to these provisions.

For these purposes, a grant or payment is relevant if it falls into one of the following categories:

- a grant that is made under the *Transport Act* 1968, s. 32 34 or 56(1);

- a payment made under s. 56(2) of that same Act; or
- a grant made under the *Greater London Authority Act* 1999, s. 101.

In each of the above cases, it will only be a relevant grant or payment if it is declared by the Treasury by order to be relevant for the purposes of the withholding of initial allowances.

Legislation: CAA 2001, s. 308

Additional VAT

For the interaction between VAT and IBAs generally, and for the definition of relevant terms, see 305-300.

A person with the relevant interest in an EZ building may incur additional VAT in respect of qualifying enterprise zone expenditure. If certain conditions are met, such a person is entitled to a 100 per cent initial allowance (or, by claim, a reduced figure) on an additional VAT liability. The allowance is made for the chargeable period in which the additional VAT liability accrues.

The following conditions apply:

(1) a person must have been entitled to an initial allowance in respect of qualifying enterprise zone expenditure;

(2) the person entitled to the relevant interest in relation to that expenditure (whether the same person or not) must incur an additional VAT liability in respect of that expenditure;

(3) when the additional VAT liability is incurred, the building must, or must be intended to be, an industrial building that is either:

    (a) occupied by the person who is entitled to the relevant interest;
    (b) occupied by a qualifying lessee (see above); or
    (c) used by a qualifying licensee (again, see above); and

(4) the additional VAT liability must be incurred within 10 years of the date on which the site of the building was first included in the enterprise zone.

Legislation: CAA 2001, s. 346

320-200 Writing-down allowances

If a full 100 per cent initial allowance has been given, then clearly the same person will not be entitled to any writing-down allowances. If, however, the initial allowance has been partially disclaimed, then writing-down allowances are available on a straight line basis at a rate of 25 per cent of the qualifying enterprise zone expenditure (rather than the four per cent available for industrial buildings outside an enterprise zone).

Industrial Buildings

> **Example**
>
> A property company incurs expenditure of £1 million on a property that qualifies for enterprise zone allowances. Taking account of its overall tax and commercial position, it claims only 60 per cent as an initial allowance in year one. As long as the building qualifies as an industrial building by the end of year two, the company will be able to claim allowances of a further £250,000 in that year. The balance of £150,000 may be claimed in year three.

Different rules apply where a used building has been bought – see 320-250.

Legislation: CAA 2001, s. 310(1)(a)

320-250 Purchase of used buildings

When an EZ building is bought after it has first been used, the tax treatment depends on whether or not the transaction takes place within two years of first use. In all cases, it should be remembered that the general withdrawal of balancing adjustments from 21 March 2007 (see 249-700ff.) does not apply for expenditure in enterprise zones.

Building bought after more than two years

If a building is bought more than two years after the date on which it was first used, no initial allowance will be available to the purchaser; an initial allowance is available only to 'a person who has incurred qualifying enterprise zone expenditure'. It follows that, without special legislation to the contrary, initial allowances can only ever be available to the person who actually incurs the original construction expenditure.

The vendor of the building will, assuming that the relevant interest has been transferred, be subject to a balancing adjustment. The purchaser is then entitled to writing-down allowances. In this case, however, allowances are given as for any other industrial building. The accelerated rate of 25 per cent per year is not available. (Again, this is not spelt out in the legislation. However, the availability of the 25 per cent rate is given by CAA 2001, s. 310(1)(a). CAA 2001, s. 310 does not apply if s. 311 applies (CAA 2001, s. 310(3)). CAA 2001, s. 311 does apply after a sale of the relevant interest. The point is confirmed in the HMRC manuals.)

> **Example**
>
> A person incurring expenditure of £1 million and claiming a 100 per cent initial allowance sells the property for £1.2 million after exactly five years. He will incur a balancing charge on the full amount of the £1 million. The purchaser will obtain writing-down allowances by spreading the £1 million over the remaining 20 years. Subject to any

Industrial Buildings

adjustments for varying lengths of the chargeable period, etc (see 305-150), the purchaser will claim allowances at a rate of £50,000 per year.

Legislation: CAA 2001, s. 305(1)

Other material: CA 37375

Building bought within two years of first use

Different rules come into play if:

- expenditure has been incurred on the construction of an EZ building;
- the building has been brought into use;
- the relevant interest is sold within a period of two years beginning with the date of that first use; and
- the sale is the first one since the building was brought into use.

From the vendor's point of view, any balancing adjustment is made in the ordinary way. From the purchaser's side, however, the concept of the residue of qualifying expenditure immediately after the sale is disregarded.

The legislation then creates a fiction whereby:

- the purchaser is treated as having incurred qualifying enterprise zone expenditure; and
- all the IBA rules are then applied as if the building were first used on the date of the sale.

This is an attractive outcome for the purchaser, as the treatment offers the possibility of an initial allowance (up to 100 per cent) or of writing-down allowances of up to 25 per cent per year.

Where these rules apply, the general principle is that the qualifying enterprise zone expenditure will be the lesser of:

- the capital sum paid in this transaction for the purchase of the relevant interest; and
- the amount of expenditure actually incurred on the construction of the building.

Different rules apply, however, if the expenditure on the construction of the EZ building was incurred by a developer who then sold on the relevant interest in the course of his development trade.

Where this is the case, and assuming that the sale by the developer is the relevant sale, then the amount of the qualifying enterprise zone expenditure is the amount paid by the purchaser for the relevant interest. The effect of this is that the purchaser can obtain allowances on a sum that includes the developer's profit margin.

> ## Example
>
> A developer spends £1 million constructing a factory, lets it out for 18 months whilst the market is quiet, and then sells it for £1.2 million, excluding any land value. The purchaser can claim allowances on the full amount of £1.2 million.
>
> It is possible that a third party will be involved, so that the sale by the developer is not the relevant sale. In this case, the amount of qualifying expenditure will be the lower of:
>
> - the capital sum paid by the purchaser to acquire the relevant interest on the relevant sale; and
> - the price that was paid to the developer for his original sale of the relevant interest.
>
> This again has the effect that a profit made by the developer can be included as part of the construction cost. A profit made by a middle man, however, is excluded.
>
> In all the above cases, the qualifying expenditure is treated as incurred at the time the capital sum becomes payable by the purchaser.

Legislation: CAA 2001, s. 301

320-300   Expenditure only partly incurred within time limit

Given the nature of the rules relating to enterprise zone expenditure, it is quite possible that part of the cost will be incurred within the 10-year time limit and part at a later date. For the person incurring the original expenditure, the treatment is straightforward – the expenditure qualifies as enterprise zone expenditure only if it is incurred within the time limits.

If a person buys an EZ building more than two years after it was first used, the treatment is again clear-cut. No EZ rules apply to the purchaser – see 320-250.

The position can be more complicated if a building that was constructed only partly within the time limits is bought unused or within two years of first use. In all cases, the result of the legislation is to work out what proportion of the expenditure was incurred within the time limits and to apportion accordingly the expenditure that would have qualified under the rules described above. The legislation uses a series of formulae to determine the tax treatment in these cases. For the purposes of these formulae, the following meanings apply:

(1)   QE is the amount of the qualifying expenditure;

(2)   E is the part of the expenditure on the construction of the EZ building that is incurred within the time limit;

(3)   T is the total expenditure on the construction of the building;

(4)   L is the lesser of:

    (a)   the capital sum paid for the relevant interest on the relevant sale; and
    (b)   the expenditure incurred on the construction of the building

(5)   C is the capital sum paid for the relevant interest by the purchaser; and

(6)   D is the lesser of:

(a)   the price paid for the relevant interest on its sale by the developer; and

(b)   the capital sum paid for the relevant interest on the relevant sale

Legislation: CAA 2001, s. 299–304

General principle – building sold unused

The general principle is that where only a part of the expenditure is incurred within the time limit then, on a subsequent sale, only that part is treated as qualifying enterprise zone expenditure. The part of the qualifying expenditure that is qualifying enterprise zone expenditure is therefore given by the formula:

$$QE \times E/T$$

In other words, the qualifying expenditure is apportioned on the basis of the proportion of the construction expenditure that was incurred within the time limits.

This will apply where the building is bought unused (whether or not a developer is involved).

Legislation: CAA 2001, s. 302(1)

Used building sold within two years

The legislation then addresses the position where a used building that was partly constructed within the EZ time limits is sold within two years. For these rules to apply, that sale (referred to as 'the relevant sale') must be the first sale since the building was brought into use (see 320-350 if it is not). The purchaser must be paying a capital sum to acquire the relevant interest on the relevant sale.

As under the ordinary rules described at 320-250, any balancing adjustment to be made on the vendor is made as normal. Again, the residue of qualifying expenditure immediately after the relevant sale has to be disregarded.

The exact treatment will depend on whether or not a developer is involved. He will be treated as involved where he has incurred expenditure on the construction of the building and has sold the relevant interest in the building in the course of his development trade.

The intention and effect of the legislation is to split the qualifying expenditure so that the new buyer can claim allowances under the enterprise zone rules only to the extent that the original expenditure qualified as enterprise zone expenditure. Any remaining part will be dealt with under the normal IBA rules, in which case allowances may be denied altogether (eg because a commercial building will not qualify under the general rules) or will be given at a much slower rate.

No developer involved

Where there is no developer involved, the part that is to be treated as qualifying enterprise zone expenditure (referred to in the legislation as 'Z') is given by the formula:

$$Z = L \times E/T$$

The purchaser will also be treated as incurring qualifying expenditure which is not qualifying enterprise zone expenditure. This figure ('N') will be calculated as:

$$N = L - Z$$

ie the balance of L as above. It does not necessarily follow that any allowances will be due on this amount (N), as explained in the Example below.

Example

A building was constructed for £700,000, of which £500,000 was within the 10-year limit and the balance was later. A purchaser pays £650,000 for the building 18 months after it is first brought into use.

As the capital sum paid is less than the original expenditure, the purchaser can only claim allowances of any sort on that lesser sum. The sum then has to be split to show how much qualifies as enterprise zone expenditure. The amount so qualifying will be:

$$£650,000 \times £500,000/£700,000 = £464,286$$

The balance of £185,714 is still 'qualifying expenditure' for general IBA purposes. It will only qualify for IBAs, though, if it is on an industrial building (within the narrower, non-EZ sense). It is clear from CAA 2001, s. 271 that the test of what is 'qualifying expenditure' is different from that of whether the building qualifies as an industrial building.

Developer involved

The above rules are modified where a developer is involved. In this case, the amount of the qualifying enterprise zone expenditure ('Z') is given by the formula:

$$Z = C \times E/T$$

In other words, the cost of construction incurred by the developer is not relevant. Instead, the apportionment is applied to the price paid to the developer by the purchaser, thus taking account of any profit margin made by the developer. (Again, the apportionment relates to the question of whether the cost was incurred within the enterprise zone time limits.)

The qualifying expenditure that is not qualifying enterprise zone expenditure ('N') will be given by the formula:

$$N = L - (L \times E/T)$$

Again, this is subject to the caveat given in the example above.

Position where there has been an intermediate transaction

The formulae immediately above are on the assumption that the sale by the developer is actually the relevant sale, (ie there has not been an intermediate transaction). If there has been such an intermediate transaction, it is necessary to introduce one final formula. In this case, the qualifying expenditure ('Z') is calculated:

$$Z = D \times E/T$$

The qualifying expenditure that is not qualifying enterprise zone expenditure ('N') is calculated using the formula:

$$N = D - Z$$

Legislation: CAA 2001, s. 303–304

When expenditure is treated as incurred

Strangely, the HMRC manuals – or at least, the parts that are made available for public consumption – contain no commentary on (or even mention of) CAA 2001, s. 303 and 304, as considered in the above paragraphs.

One area where clarification would have been welcome is in relation to the timing of expenditure.

CAA 2001, s. 303(5) states that 'any qualifying expenditure arising under this section or s. 304 is to be treated as incurred when the capital sum on the relevant sale becomes payable'.

CAA 2001, s. 303 and 304 are those that apply the rules, described in the above paragraphs, where expenditure on a building was incurred only partly within the time limits and where that building is sold within two years.

At first glance, the quoted subsection seems to be saying that it is the date of the relevant sale that needs to be checked against the ten-year time limit. However, it is the author's view that this cannot be the correct interpretation. The only expenditure that arises under CAA 2001, s. 303 and 304 is the expenditure that the purchaser is treated as incurring. In other words, the 25-year rule (for example, see 305-600) will run from the date the capital sum became payable. For the purpose of determining the extent to which the construction expenditure was incurred within the 10-year time limit, normal principles must apply to determine when that expenditure was incurred. HMRC effectively confirms this, albeit in a close context rather than directly in relation to CAA 2001, s. 303(5) when they write:

> 'You may get a claim for EZ allowances from a person who buys an unused building in an enterprise zone. If you do you should check the date on which the construction expenditure was

incurred because it is the date on which the construction expenditure was incurred and not the date of purchase that matters in deciding whether EZ allowances are available.'

Other material: CA 37450

320-350   Anti-avoidance: realisation of capital value

Introduction

The chance to obtain a full write-off for tax purposes of substantial capital expenditure is an attractive prize. It follows that HMRC will be particularly sensitive to any abuses of the system.

In 1994, legislation was introduced to close what was perceived as a loophole in the rules. Although these anti-avoidance principles could have been applied to IBAs generally, the decision was taken to impose them only in relation to buildings in enterprise zones. The legislation was introduced following the *Matrix Securities* case referred to at 306-550.

The perceived abuse consisted of realising the value of a property by disposing of the commercial substance of the interest whilst retaining the relevant interest itself. In other words, a person was able to realise his investment in the property but to retain the capital allowances in full. The HMRC manuals suggest that the two commonest methods were as follows:

(1)   a long lease could be granted out of the relevant interest for a premium and a ground rent. In such a case, the lessor and lessee may jointly elect for the granting of the lease to be treated as the sale of the relevant interest (see 304-750). If they do not do so, however, the transaction will not produce any balancing event.

As such, a person could incur expenditure of, for example, £1 million and obtain immediate tax relief on the full amount of the £1 million. A 999-year lease could then be granted to a third party in return for a premium of £1 million and a nominal rent. Following first principles as discussed at 304-600, this does not constitute a disposal of the relevant interest. The person who originally incurred the expenditure can therefore retain the full benefit of the tax allowances; and

(2)   the lessee under the terms of a long lease might agree to pay a capital sum in exchange for reduced future rentals.

Other material: CA 37705

Overview of provisions

Provisions were therefore introduced to attack such schemes insofar as they related to qualifying enterprise zone expenditure. The effects of the legislation are as follows:

• where 'capital value' (a defined term) is realised, this is treated as a balancing event whether it occurs while the building is an industrial building or after it has ceased to be one (CAA 2001, s. 328(1));

- no balancing allowance is given as a result of such a deemed balancing event (CAA 2001, s. 328(2));
- the amount of capital value realised is treated as proceeds from the balancing event (CAA 2001, s. 328(3));
- the 'starting expenditure' for the purposes of CAA 2001, s. 319 (see 305-800) is reduced by the amount of capital expenditure realised (CAA 2001, s. 328(4)(a));
- if the other anti-avoidance provisions of CAA 2001, s. 325 (restriction of balancing allowances) apply to increase the net proceeds of sale (see 306-600) then the amount of capital value is deducted from that increased figure (CAA 2001, s. 328(4)(b)); and
- an amount equal to any capital value realised is written off at that time for the purposes of calculating the residue of qualifying expenditure (CAA 2001, s. 313 and 338).

Example

EZ Ltd has the relevant interest in a building in an enterprise zone. Qualifying expenditure amounted to £1 million. Although 100 per cent initial allowances could have been claimed, a writing-down allowance was claimed instead. The residue of qualifying expenditure is £600,000. A long lease is granted in return for a premium and a nominal rent.

If the premium is of £1 million (or more), there will be a balancing charge of £400,000. EZ Ltd still has the relevant interest but is entitled to no further allowances.

If the premium is £500,000, there is no balancing allowance. EZ Ltd still has the relevant interest and can continue to claim writing-down allowances. However, the residue of qualifying expenditure is reduced by the £500,000 received and future allowances will be restricted on ordinary principles (ie under CAA 2001, s. 312 – see 305-200).

Legislation: CAA 2001, s. 327

Conditions

The two fundamental conditions that must apply if the anti-avoidance rules are to have effect are as follows:

(1) the qualifying expenditure must have qualified for enterprise zone allowances (CAA 2001, s. 327); and

(2) the capital value that is paid must be attributable to a subordinate interest to which the relevant interest is subject now or will be subject in future (CAA 2001, s. 328(5)).

A further condition (CAA 2001, s. 330) is that the rules will not normally apply unless the payment is made within seven years from the date on which the agreement was made under which the qualifying expenditure was incurred. If the original agreement for incurring the qualifying expenditure was conditional, then the seven-year deadline runs from the time when it became unconditional. If a payment of capital value is made after more than seven years, but under an agreement that was itself made, or itself became unconditional, within that seven-year period, then the anti-avoidance legislation still has effect.

In certain circumstances, there will be no seven-year time limit. In these cases, the anti-avoidance rules can apply any time within the normal 25-year period. This will be the case where arrangements under which the relevant interest was acquired, or made in connection with its acquisition, include certain provisions. These provisions are such as either require, or make substantially more likely, any of the following:

- the subsequent sale of the relevant interest;
- the subsequent grant of an interest in land out of the relevant interest; or
- any other event triggering the payment (or deemed payment) of capital value attributable to the subordinate interest.

HMRC gives an example of a builder who is having difficulty selling his newly-constructed office block. He finds a purchaser but has to give a guarantee that he will take back a long lease of the office block after eight years if the purchaser is unable to let it out to a third party. A premium paid by the builder after the eight-year period under the terms of the guarantee will still be caught, because it is paid under arrangements made when the purchaser originally acquired the building.

Legislation: CAA 2001, s. 327ff.

Other material: CA 37760

Main definitions

This legislation requires a number of definitions. The concept of 'capital value' broadly means a capital sum. Any amount that would have been a capital sum if it had been a money payment is to be treated as a capital sum for these purposes. Any premium taxable as rent under ITTOIA 2005, s. 277 to 281 or CTA 2009, s. 217 to 221 is, however, to be excluded.

The term 'interest in land' is for these purposes defined to include any of the following:

- a leasehold estate in the land, whether in the nature of a head lease, sub-lease or under-lease;
- an easement or servitude; or
- a licence to occupy land.

Legislation: CAA 2001, s. 331(1)

Capital value attributable to subordinate interest

The legislation defines the basis on which any capital value will be treated as attributable to the subordinate interest. It will be so treated if it is paid in any of the following circumstances:

- in consideration of the grant of the subordinate interest (CAA 2001, s. 329(1)(a)). If any premium given in consideration of the grant of the subordinate interest is less than a commercial premium, and if no commercial rent is payable in respect of that interest, then capital value will be attributable under this heading. The amount attributable will be calculated as if a commercial premium had been paid and as if it were in consideration of the grant of the subordinate interest (CAA 2001, s. 329(2));

- instead of any rent payable by the person entitled to the subordinate interest (CAA 2001, s. 329(1)(a)). Capital value will be attributed under this heading if any value given instead of any rent payable by the person entitled to the subordinate interest is less than the commercial amount. In this case, the calculation will be made as if the commercial amount had been paid (CAA 2001, s. 329(3));
- in consideration of any such rent being assigned (CAA 2001, s. 329(1)(a)). Capital value will be attributed under this heading if rent payable in respect of the subordinate interest is assigned but any value given in consideration of the assignment is less than the commercial amount. The capital value will then be attributable as if the commercial amount had been given (CAA 2001, s. 329(4));
- in consideration of the surrender of the subordinate interest (CAA 2001, s. 329(1)(d)). Capital value is attributable under this heading if the subordinate interest is surrendered and if any value given in consideration of the surrender is less than the commercial amount. In this case, capital value is attributable as if the commercial amount had been given (CAA 2001, s. 329(5)); and
- in consideration of the variation or waiver of any of the terms on which the subordinate interest was granted (CAA 2001, s. 329(1)(d)(ii))). Capital value is attributed under this heading if any of the terms on which the subordinate interest was granted are varied or waived but any value given in consideration of the variation or waiver is less than the commercial amount. Once more, capital value is attributable as if the commercial amount had been given in consideration of the variation or waiver (CAA 2001, s. 329(5)).

If the grant of a long lease is treated as a sale, by election under CAA 2001, s. 290, as a sale then no capital value is attributed to the subordinate interest if paid in consideration of the grant of such a lease. In determining whether capital value is attributable to the subordinate interest, the following further terms are defined:

- the 'commercial amount' is the amount that would have been given had the transaction been at arm's length;
- a 'commercial premium' means the amount of the premium that would have been given had the transaction been at arm's length;
- the term 'commercial rent' is defined as 'such rent as may reasonably be expected to have been required in respect of the subordinate interest (having regard to any premium paid in consideration of the grant of the interest) if the transaction had been at arm's length'; and
- as far as Scottish Law is concerned, references to an assignment are to be taken as references to an assignation.

Legislation: CAA 2001, s. 329

320-400   Enterprise zones – miscellaneous provisions

Buildings straddling boundaries

Given that an enterprise zone building is defined as a 'building on a site in an enterprise zone', it follows that a building may fall partly inside and partly outside such a zone. Revenue instructions to inspectors are to give enterprise zone allowances on so much of the building as falls within the zone. The remaining part of the building should be dealt with under the normal IBA rules.

Obviously, this would necessitate some sort of apportionment of the expenditure. No specific guidance is given in the HMRC manuals on how that apportionment should be made.

Legislation: CAA 2001, s. 298(2)

Roads on industrial estates

For IBA purposes generally, this issue is addressed at 300-650.

In relation to qualifying enterprise zone expenditure, the term 'industrial estate' is defined to include an area, such as a business park, which 'consists wholly or mainly of commercial buildings'.

Legislation: CAA 2001, s. 284(2)

Change of use

Revenue instructions are that any change of use, after a building has qualified for EZ allowances, should be ignored if the building is either an industrial building, a commercial building or a qualifying hotel after the change of use.

The same paragraph of the HMRC manual comments on the position where somebody buys a building that qualified under the enterprise zone rules but that is now outside the 10-year designation period. Such a person may claim writing-down allowances in the usual way that applies to expenditure on non-EZ buildings. If the transaction takes place within 25 years from the date of first use, the vendor will be subject to a balancing adjustment and the purchaser may claim writing-down allowances over the balance of the 25-year period.

Other material: CA 37400

EZPUTs

An enterprise zone property unit trust is a type of collective investment scheme through which investors may buy an interest in land or buildings in an enterprise zone. The HMRC manuals provide the following comments:

'Where the EZPUT invests in an industrial building it is the individual investors rather than the scheme itself who are entitled to the IBAs. Similarly, it is the individual investors who are responsible for any balancing charge which may arise.'

Special legislation in ICTA 1988, s. 469 may need to be considered, as well as Regulations under the *Income Tax (Definition of Unit Trust Scheme) Regulations* 1988 (SI 1988/267).

Other material: CA 39700

BUSINESS PREMISES RENOVATION ALLOWANCES

Overview

400-000   Overview

Business Premises Renovation Allowances (BPRAs) apply to expenditure incurred in the five-year period from 11 April 2007. The allowances offer 100 per cent up-front tax relief for the costs of renovating or converting certain unused business property in any of the 2,000 or so areas of the UK that are designated as disadvantaged. Allowances can be claimed by an individual or company incurring capital expenditure on bringing qualifying business premises back into business use. The allowances are available both to landlords and to businesses occupying their own properties.

The scheme of allowances offers full tax relief where, without the special rules, allowances might have been available at:

- 20 or 10 per cent (plant and machinery);
- 4 per cent, reducing eventually to zero (industrial buildings); or
- 0 per cent – ie no allowances due for the bulk of the expenditure on certain offices and other commercial premises.

Allowances are due only to the person incurring the expenditure. They can be clawed back if there is a sale or other 'balancing event' within seven years from the date on which the premises are first brought back into use (or on which they are first made suitable and available for letting). A subsequent purchaser of the property has no entitlement to allowances.

Entitlement to BPRAs depends on three conditions:

- a person must incur qualifying expenditure (see 400-500);
- that expenditure must be on a qualifying building (see 400-600); and
- the person must have the relevant interest in that building (see 401-100).

Legislation: CAA 2001, s. 360A; FA 2005, s. 92, Sch. 6, *(Appointed Day) Order* 2007, SI 2007/949

400-050   Giving effect to allowances and charges

Allowances are generally treated as an expense of the trade, profession or vocation and any balancing charge is treated as a trading, etc receipt.

This rule is varied if a person's interest in the building is subject to a lease or a licence at any time in the chargeable period in question. If the building is an asset of a property business carried on by him, then any allowance will be treated as an expense of that business and any charge as a receipt. In any other case, which will be exceptional, the person is treated as if he were carrying on a property business, and allowances are given as if they were an expense of that business, and charges as if they were a receipt of the business.

Legislation: CAA 2001, s. 360Z

Qualifying expenditure

400-500 Overview

Qualifying expenditure must be capital expenditure that is incurred before the fifth anniversary of the scheme coming into effect, so by 11 April 2012 (though this date may be extended by Treasury regulations).

The expenditure must be incurred in connection with one of the following:

- the conversion of a qualifying building (see below) into qualifying business premises (see below);
- the renovation of a qualifying building that is (or will become) qualifying business premises; or
- repairs to a qualifying building (or to the building of which the qualifying building forms part) to the extent that the repairs are incidental to the above-mentioned conversion or renovation work.

For these purposes, repairs are treated as capital expenditure to the extent that they are not tax deductible in calculating the profits of a trade, etc or of a property business.

Exclusions

The following expenditure, however, will *not* qualify:

- the acquisition of land or of rights in or over land;
- the demolition of existing buildings;
- the extension of a qualifying building (except as required to provide access to the qualifying business premises);
- the development of land adjoining or adjacent to a qualifying building; or
- the provision of plant and machinery, except for fixtures (as defined at CAA 2001, s. 173(1)).

HMRC guidance makes it clear, for example, that the cost of adding another storey or a basement to a qualifying building would not constitute qualifying expenditure.

Legislation: CAA 2001, s. 360B

Other material: CA 45300

400-600   Qualifying buildings

A qualifying building can be a building or structure, or part of either. It must meet all of the following conditions:

- on the date on which the conversion or renovation work begins, it must be situated in a disadvantaged area (see below);
- it must have been unused for at least the 12 months leading to the date on which the renovation, etc work began;
- it must last have been used either for the purposes of a trade, vocation or profession or as an office or offices (for whatever purposes); and
- it must not last have been used as (or as part of) a dwelling.

A further rule applies in the case of a part of a building or structure. The part must not, on the date on which the renovation, etc work began, have last been occupied and used in common with any other part of the building or structure. However, this rule can be ignored if the other part was last used as a dwelling or if the other part was unused for at least the 12 months leading to the date on which the renovation, etc work began.

HMRC has illustrated the rules relating to part of a building as follows:

> 'Jim owns and runs the Morrison hotel. He decides to move to Paris and lets the hotel become disused. He lets all the floors above the ground floor to Leonard, who wants to run it as a hostel. After the ground floor has been unused for two years Alice says that she is looking for restaurant premises. Jim leases the ground floor to Alice who converts it into a restaurant. Alice's conversion expenditure qualifies for BPRA.'

Legislation: CAA 2001, s. 360C

Other material: CA 45300

Designated area

By default, this term covered any area designated as disadvantaged for the purposes of FA 2003, Sch. 6 (stamp duty land tax – disadvantaged areas relief). The Treasury has power, however, to designate different areas for the purposes of this capital allowances relief, and has chosen to exercise that power with effect from 11 April 2007, the date on which the BPRA rules start to apply (see 400-000). This being the case, the stamp duty areas have never in practice applied for these purposes (as the legislation states that the stamp duty rules apply only where no regulations have been made). As such, the following areas are designated for these purposes:

- The whole of Northern Ireland.
- Any other area of the UK that is specified as a development area by the Assisted Areas Order 2007 (SI 2007/107).

According to government guidance on the Office of Public Information website:

'Assisted Areas are those areas where regional investment aid can be granted in accordance with European Union (EU) legislation. Regional aid is used to promote the economic development of certain disadvantaged areas within the EU.'

Where the postcode is known, it is possible to see whether or not a building lies within an assisted area using the site at www.dtistats.net/regional-aa/aa2007.asp.

A building may lie on the border of a designated area. In this case, a just and reasonable apportionment has to be made to determine how much of the overall expenditure is attributable to the part located in the disadvantaged area.

Legislation: CAA 2001, s. 360C; *Business Premises Renovation Allowances Regulation 2007 SI 2007/945*

Other material: www.opsi.gov.uk/si/em2007/uksiem_20070945_en.pdf

400-650   Qualifying business premises

The conditions for qualifying business premises overlap with the requirements listed above in relation to a qualifying building. Specifically, premises must:

- constitute a building or structure (or part of a building or structure);
- be a qualifying building;
- be used (or available and suitable for letting for use) either for the purposes of a trade, vocation or profession or as an office or offices (for whatever purposes);
- not be used (or available for use) as a dwelling or as part of a dwelling; and
- not be used, or (broadly) owned, for the purposes of a disqualified trade sector (see below).

Premises do not cease to be qualifying business premises if they are temporarily unsuitable for use or letting, as long as they were qualifying business premises immediately beforehand. HMRC illustrates this with an example of a property damaged by water leakage.

Legislation: CAA 2001, s. 360D

Disqualified trade sectors

To meet EU regulations, and thus enable BPRA to be available to other sectors, certain types of trade are disqualified for relief under the BPRA rules. More specifically, a building will not be qualifying business premises if either of the following applies:

- the person with the relevant interest (see 401-100) in the premises is carrying on a relevant trade; or
- the premises are wholly or partly used for the purposes of such a trade.

The term 'relevant trade' is defined to mean 'a trade in any sector in relation to which Commission Regulation (EC) No 1628/2006 on the application of Articles 87 and 88 of the Treaty to national regional investment aid does not apply by virtue of paragraph 2 of Article

1 of that Regulation.' According to the *Explanatory Notes* issued with SI 2007/945, now replicated at CA 45300, the trades affected are:

- fisheries and aquaculture;
- shipbuilding;
- the coal industry;
- the steel industry;
- synthetic fibres;
- the primary production of certain agricultural products; and
- the manufacture and marketing of products which imitate or substitute for milk and milk products.

A trade is for these purposes defined to include a part of a trade.

Legislation: Legislation: CAA 2001, s. 360D; SI 2007/945

Relevant interest

401-100   Relevance

Allowances are given under the BPRA scheme only to the person who:

- incurred the expenditure (and not, therefore, to any subsequent owner); and
- holds the relevant interest in the qualifying building.

The term 'relevant interest' is defined in CAA 2001, s. 360E and 360F. It is also subject to s. 360Z3. The rules for determining the relevant interest are very similar to those for flat conversion allowances, which in turn mirror the IBA rules.

Generally, the relevant interest is the interest in the qualifying building held by the person when the expenditure was incurred. This will normally be a freehold or leasehold interest in the property.

If a person has more than one interest in a qualifying building, and one of the interests is reversionary on all the others, (ie superior – for example, a freehold or a head lease over subleases) then the superior lease is the relevant interest.

An interest does not cease to be the relevant interest just because of the creation of a new interest to which it is subject. So, for example, a freeholder who has the relevant interest will not lose that interest just because he grants a lease. No writing-down allowance is given, though, if the person has granted a long lease for a capital sum.

A leasehold interest may be extinguished if the person entitled to it acquires the interest which is reversionary on it. For example, Abel (as freeholder) may have granted a lease to Cain. If Cain then acquires the freehold, the leasehold interest is extinguished (as, in simple terms, Cain cannot have a lease with himself). In such circumstances, the interest into which the leasehold interest merges (the freehold interest, in this example) becomes the relevant interest.

A person who does not have the relevant interest at the time he incurs the conversion or renovation expenditure may claim the allowances provided he is entitled to an interest in the qualifying building as a result of the conversion.

The purchaser of the relevant interest in a qualifying building is not entitled to claim BPRAs, even if the vendor is required to bring in a disposal value. The system of giving BPRAs is in this way like the code for flat conversion allowances but differs from other parts of the capital allowances code in this respect.

Legislation: CAA 2001, s. 360A(2), 360E-I

402-000   Termination of leases

The issue of when a lease terminates is important for the definition of 'relevant interest'. The rules (exactly mirroring those applying for the purposes of flat conversion allowances) apply as follows:

- if a person remains in possession of a qualifying building after the termination of a lease without a new lease being granted to that person (but with the lessor's consent) then the old lease is treated as continuing until the lessee remains in possession of the qualifying building;
- if a person is granted a new lease as a result of exercising an option available to that person under the old lease, then the new lease is treated as a continuation of the old;
- where lessors pay a sum to the lessee on termination of the lease, the lease is treated as coming to an end by surrender – with the payment treated as the consideration for the surrender; and
- where, on the termination of a lease, another lease is granted to a third party and – in connection with the transaction – the new lessee pays a sum to the original lessee, then the two leases are treated as the same lease (assigned by the original lessee to the new lessee in consideration for the payment).

The word 'lease' has the same meaning here as for the purposes of flat conversion allowances (see 477-000).

Legislation: CAA 2001, s. 360Z3, 360Z4

Initial and writing-down allowances

403-000   Initial allowances

Subject to the question of grants received (see 403-200), the treatment of initial allowances is the same as the treatment of those allowances for the purposes of flat conversion allowances (476-500).

The person incurring the qualifying expenditure is entitled to an initial allowance equal to 100 per cent of the expenditure for the chargeable period in which the expenditure is incurred. The person may choose to claim a lesser amount, in which case the balance of relief is given by means of writing-down allowances in subsequent periods.

Planning point

The availability of full relief for expenditure incurred makes this an attractive proposition for somebody keen to invest in property, albeit subject to the seven-year clawback rule as described at 403-400. Relief can effectively be taken twice: first, as capital allowances and again as expenditure to offset when calculating any future capital gain (see TCGA 1992, s. 41).

However, an initial allowance is not available if, at the relevant time, they do not constitute qualifying business premises (see 400-650).

Any initial allowance made (when the expenditure was incurred) but no longer available must be withdrawn and assessments amended as a result. This will be necessary if, at the relevant time (see below):

- the qualifying building does not constitute qualifying business premises; or
- if the person to whom the allowance was made has sold the relevant interest in the qualifying building before the relevant time.

The 'relevant time' for the above purposes means the time when the business premises are first used by the person with the relevant interest (or, if they are not so used, the time when they are first suitable for letting for the purposes of a trade, etc or for letting as an office).

Legislation: CAA 2001, s. 360G, 360H

403-200   Writing-down allowances

Subject to the question of grants received (see below), the treatment for BPRAs is again the same as the treatment for flat conversion allowances.

The amount of the writing-down allowance is 25 per cent per year on a straight line basis but:

- a lesser amount may be claimed;

Business Premises Renovation

- the 25 per cent figure is increased or decreased proportionately for chargeable periods that are longer or shorter than one year; and
- the amount of a writing-down allowance is capped at the residue of qualifying expenditure, the amount of which is to be calculated 'immediately before writing off the writing-down allowance at the end of the chargeable period'. The residue of expenditure is the qualifying expenditure not yet written off.

The 25 per cent figure is *not* affected by the reduction to 20 per cent of most plant and machinery writing-down allowances.

Writing-down allowances may only be claimed where, at the end of the chargeable period, the claimant has a relevant interest in a qualifying building and has not granted a long lease on the building, ie one that exceeds 50 years. The rules in ITTOIA 2005, s. 303 apply to determine the length of a lease and the provisions of CAA 2001, s. 360Z3(3) (new lease acquired following the exercise of an option under the old lease) are for these purposes ignored.

Legislation: CAA 2001, s. 360I, 360J

Grants received

The general provisions relating to contributions do not apply to business premises renovation allowances. However, no initial or writing-down allowance is to be made to the extent that the expenditure is taken into account for the purposes of a relevant grant or a relevant payment towards the expenditure.

The grant or payment is 'relevant' if it is a State aid that has been notified to and approved by the European Commission. It is also 'relevant' if declared to be so for these purposes by Treasury order.

If a relevant payment or grant is made after an initial or writing-down allowance has been made then the allowance is to be withdrawn to that extent; assessments are to be made or adjusted as necessary (but within three years of the end of the chargeable period) to implement this.

Legislation: CAA 2001, s. 360L, 537(1)

Balancing events

403-400   Overview

Once more, the rules here are a close parallel to those applying for the purposes of flat conversion allowances.

If a balancing event takes place within seven years of the date on which the premises were first used, or were first suitable for letting for the purposes of a trade, etc or as an office, then a balancing adjustment will be made. A balancing charge will recover excess allowances that have been given and a balancing allowance will give further tax relief.

If more than one balancing event occurs, it is only the first that gives rise to a balancing allowance or charge.

No balancing allowance is available, or charge made, if the balancing event occurs more than seven years after the time the premises were first used, or were first suitable for letting for the purposes of a trade, etc or as an office.

Legislation: CAA 2001, s. 360M

403-500   Balancing events and proceeds

A statutory table lists the possible balancing events and the proceeds – received or receivable by the person who incurred the expenditure – which are deemed to arise from each event, as follows:

Balancing event	Proceeds
Sale of relevant interest	Net sale proceeds
Grant of a long lease for a capital sum	The higher of: ● the capital sum paid; and ● the commercial premium that would have been paid in an arm's length transaction
End of lease if a connected person has a superior interest	The market value at the time the lease ends
Death of person who incurred qualifying expenditure	The residue of qualifying expenditure immediately before the death
Demolition or destruction of the qualifying building	Net amount for the remains, plus any insurance money received, plus any other capital sums received as compensation
Qualifying building ceases to be qualifying business premises	The market value at the time

The definition of 'sale' is broadened in CAA 2001, s. 573, and this applies for business premises renovation allowances.

HMRC has confirmed that temporary disuse is not a balancing event.

Legislation: CAA 2001, s. 360O

Other material: CA 45300

Business Premises Renovation

403-600   Calculation of balancing adjustments

CAA 2001, s. 360P determines the amount of any balancing adjustment and whether it should be treated as a balancing charge or a balancing allowance. Broadly, it considers the difference between the 'residue of qualifying expenditure' and the proceeds from the balancing event.

The residue is defined as the amount of qualifying expenditure that has not yet been written off in accordance with s. 360Q–360S. The proceeds are determined in accordance with the table at 403-500.

If there are no proceeds or there is no residue, then the figure is nil for the purposes of calculating the difference.

If the proceeds exceed the residue, then there is a balancing charge equal to the difference. However, the balancing charge may not exceed the total allowances (initial or writing-down) made to the person in respect of the qualifying expenditure.

If the residue exceeds the proceeds, then there is a balancing allowance equal to the difference.

There is a special rule where the balancing event is the end of a lease. The statutory table shows proceeds equal to the market value of the relevant interest. However, this only applies if there is a person with a superior interest to the relevant interest and who is connected to the person with the relevant interest. Although the legislation does not explicitly provide for this, it is assumed that in other cases the lease ending will give rise to nil proceeds.

Legislation: CAA 2001, s. 360K, 360O

403-700   Residue of qualifying expenditure

The residue of qualifying expenditure needs to be ascertained to ensure that the total of initial and writing-down allowances given do not exceed the qualifying expenditure. Similarly, it is needed to determine the type and amount of any balancing adjustment on a balancing event occurring within the first seven years.

The residue can be expressed as:

$$QE + DEM - IA - WDA$$

where

QE   = the qualifying expenditure;
DEM   = net demolition costs (see below);
IA   = the initial allowance made in respect of the qualifying expenditure; and
WDA   = the total writing-down allowances made in respect of the qualifying expenditure.

It is also necessary to know when the residue has to be adjusted to reflect any allowances made. This is required to ensure that any comparison with the proceeds (when calculating the balancing adjustment) is correctly made.

An initial allowance reduces the residue at the time that the qualifying business premises are first used, or first suitable for letting, for the purposes of a trade, etc or as an office. A writing-down allowance reduces the residue at the end of the chargeable period for which it is made.

If:

- a balancing event occurs at the end of a chargeable period; and
- a writing-down allowance is made for that chargeable period in respect of the qualifying expenditure,

then the residue should be calculated after deducting the writing-down allowance.

Legislation: CAA 2001, s. 360J(3), s. 360P, 360R

403-800   Demolition of the qualifying building

A special rule applies if the qualifying building is demolished. In practice, this will only be relevant if the qualifying building is demolished during the first seven years (and, by being demolished, ceases to be a qualifying building). This is because writing-down allowances are only available for chargeable periods at the end of which the property is a qualifying building (see 400-600).

If the person who incurred the qualifying expenditure incurs the cost of demolition, then the net cost of demolition is added to the residue. The result of this is that the net cost of demolition will be relieved as a balancing allowance or will reduce the impact of a balancing charge.

The net cost of demolition is defined as the cost of demolition, less the cost of any proceeds for the sale of the remains of the qualifying building.

It would appear that on a strict reading of the legislation, this could lead to a double tax charge if there are both demolition costs and proceeds for the remains.

> ### Example
>
> Suppose that demolition costs amount to £10,000 and the remains fetch £4,000 (although removal costs reduce this to a net figure of £3,000).
>
> The net cost of demolition would equal £6,000, (ie £10,000 − £4,000). This would be added to the residue. However, when considering the proceeds, the taxpayer must consider the 'net amount received'. This would equal the £4,000 received (less, presumably, the £1,000 removal costs). In either event, the £4,000 receipts would be taken into account twice.

It is unlikely that the point would be taken by HMRC; furthermore, the wording follows that of other parts of the capital allowances legislation, but this is something of which people should be aware if the amounts involved are significant.

Finally, the legislation ensures that the demolition costs should not be used both to increase the residue and also to make up qualifying expenditure (under any Part of the *Capital Allowances Act* 2001) in respect of any replacement property.

Legislation: CAA 2001, s. 360S

403-900   Anti-avoidance

The anti-avoidance rules in CAA 2001, s. 567–570 (but not the election under s. 569(1)) apply to business property renovation allowances as to industrial buildings allowances. These rules provide for market value if sales are between connected persons or are transactions to obtain a tax advantage. The rules are described in detail at 306-500 (IBAs). However, no election under s. 569 (alternative amount to be taken in respect of a sale) is available in respect of business property renovation allowances.

Legislation was introduced in 2003 to counter an abuse relating to balancing allowances. Businesses were entering into artificial transactions that depressed the market value of the asset prior to a sale to a connected person. The business selling the asset could then obtain accelerated relief by means of an early balancing allowance. The rules apply for business property renovation payments as they do for industrial buildings allowances, and are described in detail at 306-600.

Legislation: CAA 2001, s. 570, 570A

404-000   Apportionments

Sale receipts which relate partly to buildings subject to business premises renovation allowances and partly to other assets are to be apportioned on a just and reasonable basis. This equally applies to other proceeds arising from balancing events, but subject to the other rules in the *Capital Allowances Act* 2001 providing for apportionments.

Legislation: CAA 2001, s. 360Z2

Additional VAT liabilities and rebates

405-000   Additional VAT liabilities and rebates

Additional VAT liabilities and rebates may be taken into account for the purposes of giving allowances or making balancing charges.

Various terms used here are as defined at 120-200 above: additional VAT liability (and timing of when incurred); additional VAT rebate (and timing of when made); timing of when the liability or rebate accrues. Having defined these terms, the following rules apply.

Initial allowance

An initial allowance is given where a person who has been entitled to an initial allowances incurs an additional VAT liability in respect of the qualifying expenditure. The additional liability must be incurred at a time when the building is, or is about to be, qualifying business premises.

Subject to any claim to reduce it, the initial allowance is 100 per cent of the additional VAT liability and is made for the chargeable period in which the additional liability accrues.

If an initial allowance is made in respect of an additional VAT liability that is incurred after first use of the premises for a qualifying purpose then the amount of the allowance is written off at the time the liability accrues.

Legislation: CAA 2001, s. 360T–360W, 547–549

Writing-down allowances

A person who has the relevant interest in relation to qualifying expenditure may incur an additional VAT liability in respect of that expenditure.

The additional liability is then treated as qualifying expenditure, thereby increasing the residue of qualifying expenditure at the time the liability accrues. The increase is the amount of that liability.

Legislation: CAA 2001, s. 360V

Rebates and balancing adjustments

An additional VAT rebate may be made – in respect of qualifying expenditure – to a person who is entitled to the relevant interest in relation to that expenditure.

This constitutes a balancing event but no balancing allowance can ever be made as a result. A balancing charge may be made, however:

- if there is no residue of qualifying expenditure immediately before the time at which the rebate accrues, then the balancing charge will be the amount of the rebate; and
- if there is such a residue, then the balancing charge will be the amount by which the rebate exceeds that residue.

If an additional VAT rebate is made in respect of qualifying expenditure, an amount equal to that rebate is written off at the time the rebate accrues.

Legislation: CAA 2001, s. 360X, 360Y

Business Premises Renovation

AGRICULTURAL BUILDINGS ALLOWANCES

Overview

425-000   Overview

Phasing out of allowances

Agricultural buildings allowances (ABAs) provide tax relief for capital expenditure incurred on constructing agricultural buildings or other works (CAA 2001, s. 361(1)).

In a wholly unexpected announcement in the March 2007 Budget, the Chancellor announced that ABAs (and IBAs – see 300-000ff.) were to be phased out over a four-year period. According to the *Explanatory Notes* accompanying the subsequent Finance Bill 2007, the allowances 'are to be withdrawn because they are anachronistic and poorly targeted'. Thus a form of tax relief that has existed for many decades is now perceived to have served its purpose.

Legislation in the *Finance Act* 2008 confirmed that the ABA legislation ceases to apply in relation to expenditure incurred from 1 April 2011 (for corporation tax purposes) or 6 April 2011 (for income tax), and that the value of the allowances is being phased out over the years leading up to their final abolition. This is achieved by reducing the value of the allowances by 25 per cent in 2008–09 (or for the financial year beginning on 1 April 2008 (FY 2008)), 50 per cent in 2009–10 (or FY 2009) and 75 per cent in 2010–11 (or FY 2010). As explained in the 2007 *Explanatory Notes*, 'expressing the transitional provisions in this manner also caters for the phasing-out in the case of recalculated allowances on a sale or acquisition'.

The *Finance Act* 2007 contained provisions that applied for most disposals made from 21 March 2007 and that prevented from that date the making of any balancing adjustments on disposals of agricultural buildings.

First principles

Subject to the above comments, allowances are normally given at four per cent on a straight line basis.

Agricultural buildings allowances (ABAs) provide tax relief for capital expenditure incurred on constructing agricultural buildings or other works (CAA 2001, s. 361(1)).

Expenditure must be 'qualifying expenditure' (see ¶426-200) incurred by a person who has an interest in land in the UK. That land must be occupied wholly or mainly for the purposes of husbandry (see 425-500), and the expenditure must be incurred for the purposes of husbandry on that land. A building overseas cannot be an agricultural building for ABA purposes.

Similarities to IBAs

Many features of the ABA system are similar to the Industrial Buildings Allowance (IBA) rules, including the following:

- allowances are made to the person with the relevant interest (see 427-000) in the qualifying expenditure (see 426-200);
- no allowances are given on the cost of the land on which a building stands; and
- relief is normally given on a straight line basis at an annual rate of 4 per cent (see 428-000), but reducing annually from April 2008 up to the date of final abolition in April 2011.

Differences from IBAs

But other features of ABA are different from the IBA system, including (but not restricted to) the following:

- ABAs are given according to the time at which the expenditure is incurred, whether or not the building has been brought into use at that time;
- as long as the *first* use of the building is for the purposes of husbandry, allowances will continue to be given even if the use of the building changes;
- where there is a transfer of the relevant interest, the normal treatment has been that allowances simply continue for the new owner, without any balancing adjustment (see 428-000) (ie even before the changes announced in the March 2007 Budget);
- an election was necessary (but is now no longer generally possible) to secure a balancing allowance, or for a purchaser to obtain allowances on his expenditure (see 428-000); and
- allowances may be due on dwelling houses (such as farmhouses and cottages) and sometimes on shops (see 425-500).

Legislation: CAA 2001, s. 361(2)

425-025   Phasing out of ABAs

Introduction and overview

As indicated at 425-000, the Chancellor announced in the Budget of March 2007 that ABAs (and Industrial Buildings Allowances) were to be phased out over a four-year period. The phasing out is put into effect in different ways:

- The *Finance Act* 2007 provided that no ABA balancing adjustment is to be made for balancing events occurring (broadly) from 21 March 2007. (This is explained in greater detail below.)
- The *Finance Act* 2008 confirmed that the annual ABA writing-down allowance was to be reduced to 3 per cent from April 2008 and by a further 1 per cent per year thereafter, until the allowances are finally withdrawn from 1 April 2011.

No further balancing adjustments

The vendor of an agricultural building is no longer subject to a balancing charge at the time of disposal (and is not able to obtain a balancing allowance if selling at a loss). Exceptions are made for contracts that were already agreed before the amended rules were announced (ie 'pre-commencement contracts' – see below).

The basic rule

The legislation provides detailed rules for calculating writing-down allowances for a 'transitional chargeable period'. This is defined as a period that began from 1 April 2008 (corporation tax) or 6 April 2008 (income tax) (*Finance Act* 2008, s. 85).

The rules are simpler where the whole of a chargeable period falls within a financial year (CT) or tax year (income tax). This would arise, for example, where a company draws its accounts up to 31 March each year. In this case, the allowances are calculated by multiplying the WDA that would otherwise have been available by the specified percentage for the year. This percentage is 75 per cent for the year ending 31 March or 5 April 2009, reducing annually thereafter to 50, 25 and 0 per cent.

The same formula is used whether or not there has been an earlier relevant event. This first example illustrates the position where there has been no previous transfer of the relevant interest in the building.

Example 1

A Ltd draws accounts up to 31 March each year. The company incurred expenditure of £1 million in the construction of an agricultural building in 2000 and has been claiming allowances of £40,000 per year from that time.

For the year to 31 March 2009, the company can claim allowances of £30,000. For the following year, it can claim £20,000. In the year to 31 March 2011, it can claim £10,000. No further allowances are then due.

If, for whatever reason, A Ltd or a successive owner were claiming a lower amount of allowance, then that lower amount would simply be reduced by one-quarter for the year to 31 March 2009.

Writing-off of expenditure

Expenditure is written off as if full allowances were being given (*Finance Act* 2008, s. 85(8)). This can make a difference where the 25th anniversary of the original expenditure falls in the transitional period. In the example above, for instance, £40,000 will be written off even in the year in which only £30,000 can actually be claimed.

Agricultural Buildings

Rules for chargeable periods not coinciding with financial or tax years

The calculation is more complex where the chargeable period straddles the end of the financial or tax year. In this case, it is necessary to calculate separately the 'apportioned writing-down allowance' for each financial or tax year in which the chargeable period falls, and then to aggregate the resulting figures. For each of those periods, the 'apportioned writing-down allowance' is given (*Finance Act* 2008, s. 85(6)) by the formula:

$$(RDCPY/RDCP) \times WDA \times P$$

where:

RDCPY   is the number of relevant days in the chargeable period which fall in the financial or tax year in question;

RDCP   is the number of relevant days in the chargeable period;

WDA   is the writing-down allowance to which the person would otherwise be entitled for the chargeable period; and

P   is the specified percentage for the year in question (100, 75, 50 or 25 per cent – as explained above).

This formula differs from that used for IBA purposes as it includes the concept of 'relevant days', defined to mean the days within any chargeable period for which the person was entitled to the relevant interest in relation to the qualifying expenditure.

Example 2

D Ltd draws accounts up to 31 December each year. The company incurred expenditure of £1 million in the construction of an agricultural building in 2000 and has been claiming allowances of £40,000 per year from that time.

Reduced allowances were available for the year to 31 December 2008. For the following year, allowances will be calculated as follows:

- For the period from 1 January to 31 March 2009, the calculation is $(^{91}/_{365}) \times £40,000 \times 75$ per cent, giving a figure of £7,480.
- For the period from 1 April to 31 December 2009, the calculation is $(^{275}/_{365}) \times £40,000 \times 50$ per cent, giving a figure of £15,068.

These figures are then aggregated to give the ABAs due for the whole year as £22,548.

WDAs following a relevant event – comparison with IBA rules

The withdrawal of the balancing adjustment represents a less radical change to the system of ABAs than to that of industrial buildings allowances, as balancing adjustments were the exception rather than the rule under the ABA scheme. The effect is that allowances can now broadly be given to the purchaser of an agricultural building only as a continuation of the allowances that were previously given to the vendor. In technical terms, 'the amount of the residue of qualifying expenditure immediately after a post-commencement relevant event is taken to be the amount of the residue of qualifying expenditure immediately before that event'.

Post-commencement balancing events

The changes to the system of ABA balancing events, and allowances following a sale or other relevant event, apply in principle to any event from 21 March 2007 (Budget day of that year). However, to avoid catching transactions that were already in the pipeline at that date, the former rules continue to apply where the balancing event occurs before 1 April 2011 'in pursuance of a relevant pre-commencement contract'. A contract is treated as such where all of the following conditions are met:

- the contract was made in writing before 21 March 2007;
- either that contract was unconditional or its conditions had been satisfied before that date;
- no terms remained to be agreed on or after that date; and
- the contract has not been varied in a significant way on or since that date.

Where any one or more of these conditions is breached then the disposal or other relevant event is described as a 'post-commencement balancing event' and there can be no balancing adjustment.

425-050   Giving effect to allowances and charges

A trader gives effect to allowances in calculating the profits of the trade. So:

- any allowance is treated as an expense of the trade; and
- any balancing charge is treated as a trading receipt, though such charges can now only arise under the transitional provisions described at 425-025 above.

A person who is not carrying on a trade, but is carrying on a UK property business (see ITA 2007, s. 989 or ICTA 1988, s. 832(1)), similarly gives effect to allowances in calculating the profits of the business.

If a person is carrying on neither a trade nor a UK property business then an allowance or charge is given effect in calculating the profits of a UK property business that he is deemed to be carrying on.

Legislation: CAA 2001, s. 391–392

Agricultural buildings

425-500 Introduction

ABAs are given by reference to capital expenditure on the construction of an 'agricultural building'. The expenditure must be 'qualifying expenditure' (see 426-200) and allowances are given to the person with the 'relevant interest' (see 427-000) in that expenditure.

The legislation provides a curiously imprecise definition of 'agricultural building'. CAA 2001, s. 361(1)(a) refers to expenditure incurred 'on the construction of a building (such as a farmhouse, farm building or cottage) or on the construction of fences or other works'. CAA 2001, s. 361(2)(a) then defines 'agricultural building' as 'a building, fence or other works referred to in subsection (1)(a)'.

If the inclusion of the term 'other works' seems to leave the definition wide open, it is curtailed considerably by a second key condition. ABAs are given only where expenditure is incurred by a person with an interest in land in the UK that is occupied for the purposes of husbandry and the expenditure must also be incurred for such purposes. The person occupying the land and the person incurring the expenditure may, however, be different. Thus a landlord may be entitled to ABAs on expenditure he incurs even though the land is 'occupied' by a tenant farmer.

The term 'related agricultural land' is used to describe the land in which the person incurring the construction expenditure has a freehold or leasehold interest. The significance of this is explained at 427-000.

Legislation: CAA 2001, s. 361(2), 369(1)(a)

425-550 Husbandry

As noted above, ABAs are given only where qualifying expenditure (see 426-200) is incurred by a person with an interest in land in the UK that is occupied for the purposes of husbandry. The expenditure must also be incurred for such purposes. If there is an intention to use it for husbandry but the asset is in fact first used for other purposes, the expenditure is then excluded and any allowance already made (whether or not it has taken effect) is withdrawn.

The term 'husbandry' is defined to include 'any method of intensive rearing of livestock or fish on a commercial basis for the production of food for human consumption'. It also includes the cultivation of 'short rotation coppice' (considered below).

Buildings devoted, for example, to the rearing of horses cannot qualify for agricultural buildings allowances, since they are not (presumably) used for the production of food for human consumption. However, the HMRC manuals confirm that agricultural buildings allowances are also available for horticulture and market gardening. In this respect, the position may be contrasted with the statutory definition of farming for other tax purposes, where market gardening is specifically excluded.

HMRC instructions tax officers are to 'treat land as occupied for the purposes of husbandry if the trade or business carried on by the person occupying the land depends to a material extent on the fruits (natural or commercial) of that land'. As regards poultry farming, see *Watson Brothers v Hornby* (in which the hatchery was held to be outside the definition of 'husbandry').

The question as to whether a particular activity amounts to husbandry is one of fact. In *IR Commrs v William Ransom & Son Ltd* a company traded as a manufacturing chemist and herb grower. It occupied a farm on which it grew herbs for treatment in its factory. The Revenue argued that the company did not occupy the farm for husbandry. Sankey J held that it did. He said that:

> 'though I am not prepared to hold that a man who tills and cultivates the soil is in all circumstances a husbandman or a man engaged in husbandry, I can see no distinction between a man who does so in order to produce food for human consumption and a man who does so in order to produce medicines or drugs, also for human consumption. Beyond that, the question is very much [one] of fact . . . '

Nevertheless, it should be noted that the capital allowance definition of husbandry, as given above, specifically requires that the activity should be for the production of food for human consumption.

Legislation: CAA 2001, s. 362, 374, 577(3)

Cases: *IR Commrs v William Ransom & Son Ltd* (1930) 12 TC 21; *Watson Brothers v Hornby* (1942) 24 TC 506

Other material: *Property Income Manual* PIM 3030

425-600   Short rotation coppice

As noted above, 'husbandry' specifically includes 'the cultivation of short rotation coppice' which for ABA purposes is defined to mean 'a perennial crop of tree species planted at high density, the stems of which are harvested above ground level at intervals of less than ten years'.

HMRC's *Business Income Manual* gives the following assistance in understanding what is meant by this term:

> 'Short rotation coppice [. . .] is a way of producing fuel for "green" power stations which burn non-fossil fuels. Poplars or willows are planted at high density. The roots (or stools) are not

Agricultural Buildings

disturbed and send up shoots which are cut down to ground level every three years or so and used for fuel.'

Legislation: FA 1995, s. 154(3)

Other material: BIM 55205; *Property Income Manual* PIM 3030

425-650   Farmhouses

The word 'farmhouse' is not defined. In the leading case on the subject, *Lindsay v IR Commrs*, the business of a Scottish sheep farm was conducted on behalf of the tenant (who resided abroad) by his agents, who were solicitors. There was only one dwelling-house on the farm, and it was occupied by the head shepherd. The tenant incurred expenditure in providing a new scullery for the house and claimed capital allowances in respect of it. The Revenue contended that the house was not a 'farmhouse' because the tenant did not live on the farm, and so no capital allowances were available.

The court agreed with the general commissioners that the farmhouse did not cease to be such merely because the person conducting the farm business is not the farmer himself but a person to whom he delegates the duty of running the farm business, such as, in this case, the shepherd employed to run it. Correspondingly, a building occupied by the proprietor is not necessarily a farmhouse if the farm is in fact run from some other building (see *IR Commrs v John M Whiteford & Son* below).

HMRC's view is now that 'a farmhouse is the building that a farm is run from. When you decide whether a building is a farmhouse you should look at the duties of the occupant rather than who the occupant is'. A farm may have more than one farmhouse.

Cases: *Lindsay v IR Commrs* (1953) 34 TC 289; *IR Commrs v John M Whiteford & Son* (1962) 40 TC 379

Other material: CA 40100

425-700   Farm buildings

According to HMRC, 'a farm building is a structure like a barn, a cowshed, a chicken shack, a milking parlour or a stable'. HMRC will look at the use to which a building is put, and take the line that 'a building used by a farmer as a retail shop is an agricultural building to the extent that it sells farm produce. It is not an agricultural building to the extent that it sells bought-in produce or products'.

Other material: CA 40100

425-750   Cottages

The word 'cottage' is also not defined. In the leading case, *IR Commrs v John M Whiteford & Son*, a farmer and son farmed in partnership. Originally they both lived in the farmhouse on one of the two holdings which they farmed as a single unit. In 1958 the son married and built a house on the farm for his own occupation. The Revenue contended that:

- the new house was not a cottage because it was too large and expensive and also because it was occupied by one of the partners; and
- it was not a farmhouse either, because it is not possible to have two farmhouses on one farm.

The Court of Session held that the house was indeed a cottage. The Lord President said (at p. 384) that:

'On the Crown's argument, if the ... house [in question] was occupied by a tractor man it would become a cottage ... but if it happened to be occupied by someone engaged in the management of the farm it would by some mysterious sleight of hand be converted from a cottage into something else. In my view the status or employment of the occupier of the premises is not a test, and the proper criterion is the purpose of the occupation of the premises in question. Here, indubitably, the purpose of the occupation of this ... house is husbandry, or under the partnership agreement the son for whom it was built and who occupies it must give his whole time and attention to the business of the partnership. Upon that test, therefore, it seems to me clear that the ... house in question is an agricultural cottage ... '

In HMRC's view:

'The dictionary defines a cottage as a small dwelling house and that is the definition you should use. If a building is so large or costly that it cannot reasonably be regarded as a cottage it will not be a cottage for ABA purposes. A building occupied by the owner of a farm will be a cottage rather than a farmhouse if it satisfies the definition of cottage and the farm is run from some other building. If, however, the owner of the farm lives in a mansion and the farm is run from some other building the mansion is not an agricultural building because it is not a cottage or a farmhouse and so no ABA is due.

Cottages occupied by retired farm workers and buildings constructed to provide welfare facilities for farm employees are agricultural buildings.'

Cases: *IR Commrs v John M Whiteford & Son* (1962) 40 TC 379

Other material: CA 40100

425-800   Other works

HMRC accepts that the expression 'other works' will include any of the following:

- '• 'Drainage and sewerage works
- Water and electricity supply installations
- Walls
- Planting shelter belts of trees

- Silos
- Farm roads
- Reclamation of former agricultural land
- Removal of trees or hedges that are dead, diseased or obstruct agricultural operations.'

Other material: CA 40100

Qualifying expenditure

426-200   Overview

Three main conditions need to be met for expenditure to be qualifying expenditure for ABA purposes:

(1)   a person must have incurred capital expenditure (see 426-250) on the construction of an agricultural building (see 425-500);

(2)   the expenditure must have been incurred for the purposes of husbandry (as described at 425-500); and

(3)   the relevant interest (see 427-000) must not have been sold (or has been sold only after the first use of the building).

Legislation: CAA 2001, s. 369

426-250   Capital expenditure

Capital expenditure

As to the meaning of 'capital expenditure' generally, see 102-000.

HMRC accepts that the following types of expenditure constitute capital expenditure on the construction of a farmhouse or other agricultural building:

- expenditure on repairs which is not allowable as a revenue deduction;
- capital expenditure on improvements to, or the reconstruction of, the building;
- demolition costs where the demolition is a preliminary to replacing a building; and
- architects' fees.

Where the building is constructed from stone or gravel from a quarry on the agricultural estate, or from timber grown on the estate, the proportion of the working costs of the quarry or the pit attributable to the stone, etc used may be treated as expenditure qualifying for agricultural buildings allowances, unless it is allowable as a deduction for a property business.

Other material: CA 40200

426-300 Farmhouses

Farmhouses

In the case of a farmhouse (see 425-500), the expenditure qualifying for ABAs is restricted to a maximum of one-third of the expenditure in question.

The maximum one-third is allowed as qualifying expenditure if 'the accommodation and amenities of the farmhouse are proportionate to the nature and extent of the farm'.

Where they are not proportionate then 'only such part of the expenditure as is just and reasonable (and not exceeding one-third) is to be taken into account'. HMRC gives an example of a farmhouse with a private cinema and a jacuzzi, where 10 per cent of the expense might be allowed. Each case will need to be considered on its merits but the extreme nature of this example may illustrate that reductions below the one-third level should be rare.

The one-third restriction applies only to farmhouses. For all other agricultural buildings, full relief may be due. However, only a proper proportion of the expenditure qualifies for ABAs where 'the building is to be used partly for the purposes of husbandry on the related agricultural land and partly for other purposes'.

HMRC gives an example of a shop which may qualify for ABAs to the extent that it sells items produced on the farm or market garden.

Planning point

It may not always be clear whether or not a building constitutes a farmhouse (see 425-500). If it can be demonstrated that it is not then the one-third cap will not apply (though there may be a restriction to the extent that it is not used for business purposes).

Legislation: CAA 2001, s. 369

Other material: CA 40100, 40200

426-350 Land

Land

Where expenditure on the construction of a building also includes expenditure on the acquisition of land, or of rights in or over land, then that element is excluded for the purpose of computing allowances.

Legislation: CAA 2001, s. 363

Agricultural Buildings

Relevant interest

427-000 Relevant interest: significance and meaning

Significance

ABAs are given to the person who, at the given time, has the relevant interest in the qualifying expenditure.

Legislation: CAA 2001, s. 361(3)

Meaning

The 'relevant interest' is defined as the freehold or leasehold interest in agricultural land, being the interest to which the person who incurred construction expenditure was entitled when that expenditure was incurred.

The ABA rules differ from the IBA legislation in this respect: for IBA purposes, the relevant interest is in the building constructed. For ABAs, the interest is not in the building itself but rather in the related agricultural land.

The HMRC manual lists types of interest that may qualify (the freehold interest; an agreement to acquire the freehold interest; the Scottish equivalents of either of these; a lease; an agreement to acquire a lease). The manual adds that 'an interest such as a licence, grazing or commons rights, rent of grass keep, etc cannot be a relevant interest'.

For ABA purposes, the freehold interest in any land means the fee simple estate in the land, or an agreement to acquire the fee simple estate. In Scotland, it means the interest of the owner or an agreement to acquire that interest.

If a person who incurs the construction expenditure has more than one interest in the related agricultural land, the relevant interest is the one that is reversionary on the others. Put simply, the reversionary interest is the one that will survive the longest (eg the freehold rather than the leasehold interest).

Where any land is conveyed or assigned by way of security (eg by mortgage or charge), for as long as a right of redemption subsists, the person in whom the right of redemption is vested is deemed to hold any interest in fact held by the creditor. HMRC illustrates this as follows:

> 'A farmer who builds an agricultural building may use the related agricultural land as security for a loan, for example by mortgaging the farm. If the farmer does that, the title to the land will be transferred to the person who made the loan but the relevant interest in relation to the agricultural building will stay with the farmer. You should only see a case like that if the farmland is in Ireland.'

> **Example**
>
> Adam acquires the freehold of Blackacre farm. He enters into an agreement with Brian to grant him a lease of the farmhouse at some future date. He grants an agricultural tenancy of part of the farm to Christy, and a grazing agreement of a paddock to Darren. He then mortgages the whole farm, subject to the various subordinate interests, to the bank. Finally he enters into a binding contract with Edwin to sell him the farmhouse, subject to Brian's right to a lease.
>
> Adam has a relevant interest as owner of the freehold. Adam's bank has no major interest, any interest in fact held by it being deemed to be held by Adam.
>
> Christy has a relevant interest as the owner of a lease. Edwin has a relevant interest as he has the benefit of an agreement to acquire the freehold estate.
>
> Neither Brian nor Darren has a relevant interest. An agreement to acquire a lease where the term has not yet begun is not a relevant interest, and a grazing agreement does not constitute a lease.

Legislation: CAA 2001, s. 364–366, 393

Other material: CA 41000

427-200   Leases

A lease does not cease to be the relevant interest merely because of the creation of a new interest to which it is subject. The person to whom the subordinate interest is granted does not thereby acquire the relevant interest that was already in existence.

If the relevant interest is a lease which is extinguished by surrender, or by merger on the lessee acquiring the immediate reversion, then the interest into which the lease merges becomes the relevant interest, unless a fresh lease is granted on extinguishment of the former lease.

> **Example**
>
> Amos is the freehold owner of a farm. Ben is his immediate tenant. Ben has sub-let part to Claude. Ben surrenders his lease to Amos who immediately grants him a new lease on different terms. Claude then surrenders his lease to Ben but takes no new lease. Ben then purchases the freehold reversion from Amos.
>
> Assuming Ben's old lease to be a relevant interest, his new lease will continue to be a relevant interest when granted following surrender of the old. Ben's new lease will become the relevant interest in place of Claude's lease when Claude surrenders it, as no new lease is granted. Finally, when Ben acquires the freehold reversion from Amos, the freehold will become the relevant interest in place of Ben's lease which merges into it.

Agricultural Buildings

A relevant interest which is a lease may come to an end other than by surrender or merger (eg because the lease reaches the end of its term), or may be surrendered or may merge on the granting of a new lease. In such a case, the person with the reversionary interest in respect of the old lease (or, in Scotland, the landlord in the property subject to the lease) is treated as acquiring the relevant interest, and the rules relating to transfer of relevant interests operate accordingly; the old lease and the reversionary interest are treated as the same interest. There are two exceptions to this rule:

(1)   if a new lease is granted, and the new lessee makes any payment to the former lessee in respect of assets on which the expenditure attracting allowances has been incurred, the old and new leases are treated as the same interest; the incoming lessee is treated as acquiring the old lease from the outgoing lessee;

(2)   the old and new leases are also treated as one and the same if a new lease is granted to the original lessee.

Legislation: CAA 2001, s. 365–368

Definitions

A 'lease' includes an agreement for a lease where the term to be covered by the lease has begun and also embraces 'any tenancy', but does not include a mortgage; 'lessee', 'lessor' and 'leasehold interest' are construed accordingly.

In applying the law to Scotland, the term 'leasehold interest' means the tenant in property subject to a lease and the reversionary interest denotes the interest of a landlord in property subject to a lease.

Legislation: CAA 2001, s. 393(3)

427-300   Purchase of relevant interest before first use

Expenditure may be incurred on the construction of an agricultural building for the purposes of husbandry but, before that building is used, the relevant interest may be sold for a capital sum. In such a case, the qualifying expenditure is the lesser of the actual construction expenditure incurred and the capital sum paid by the purchaser. The qualifying expenditure is then treated as incurred when the capital sum becomes payable.

For the purposes of calculating the capital expenditure incurred on construction of a farmhouse, the cost is restricted as explained at 426-200.

Where appropriate, an apportionment must be made to exclude from the amount of the capital sum paid, (ie by the purchaser for the relevant interest) any amount attributable to non-qualifying assets.

If there is more than one sale of the relevant interest before the building is first used, it will be necessary to compare the construction cost with the capital sum paid by the final purchaser.

> ### Example
>
> Archer erects farm buildings at a cost of £10,000. Before they are used he sells them to Helen for £12,000. Helen allows them to fall into disrepair and finally sells them to Ian, without having put them to any use, for £8,000.
>
> Archer is not entitled to any writing-down allowances in respect of his expenditure. Helen is not entitled to writing-down allowances in respect of the expenditure on construction (£10,000).
>
> Ian is entitled to claim writing-down allowances on the smaller of the construction expenditure (£10,000) and the purchase price he paid (£8,000) – ie £8,000.

Legislation: CAA 2001, s. 370

427-400   Different relevant interests

A person may be entitled to different relevant interests in different parts of the land. In this case, a just and reasonable apportionment is to be made, the ABA rules applying 'as if the person had incurred the expenditure apportioned to each part separately'.

Legislation: CAA 2001, s. 371

Allowances and charges

428-000   First principles

Writing-down allowances may be available for qualifying expenditure. No first year (or initial) allowances are given for ABA purposes and balancing allowances and charges ceased to be given or made from 21 March 2007, subject to the transitional provisions described at 425-025.

For a person to claim writing-down allowances, three principal conditions must be met:

(1)   qualifying expenditure must have been incurred;

(2)   the person claiming the allowance must, at some time in the chargeable period, be entitled to the relevant interest in relation to the qualifying expenditure; and

(3)   that time must fall within the writing-down period (see below).

Agricultural Buildings

The writing-down period is calculated by reference to the chargeable period (see 106-100) of the person who incurred the qualifying expenditure. The period runs for 25 years from the first day of that person's chargeable period in which the expenditure was incurred.

> ### Example
>
> John draws up farming accounts to 31 March and incurs qualifying expenditure in January 2005. The writing-down period begins on 1 April 2004 and ends on 31 March 2029. However, allowances are restricted from April 2008 and no further allowances are given after April 2011.

An annual writing-down allowance of four per cent of expenditure is given on a straight-line basis. However, this is subject to the following points:

- The figure of 4 per cent is reduced year by year from 2008, so that the figure becomes 3, 2 and 1 per cent respectively for periods from 1 or 6 April 2008, 2009 and 2010, before the allowances are abolished in April 2011.
- The figure of 4 per cent is proportionately increased or decreased if the chargeable period is not of exactly one year.
- The person claiming the allowance may require it to be reduced to a specified amount, though this may well result in a failure to claim full relief over the 25-year period.
- The writing-down allowance is limited to the residue of qualifying expenditure.
- The final writing-down allowance may be of a different amount.
- No writing-down allowance is given if, when the building was first used, it was not used for the purposes of husbandry, even if it was subsequently used for the purposes of husbandry. (Conversely, if when the building was first used, it was in fact used for the purposes of husbandry, it would continue to qualify for agricultural buildings allowances for the full 25-year period, even if use of the building subsequently changed, with the result that it was no longer used for the purposes of husbandry.
- No writing-down allowance is given if the person is entitled to a balancing allowance, or is subject to a balancing charge, in the chargeable period in relation to the same qualifying expenditure, though this can now only happen subject to the transitional rules applying from 21 March 2007.
- The rules may be modified if there has been an acquisition of the relevant interest after first use of the building.

Legislation: CAA 2001, s. 372–378

Other material: *Property Income Manual*, PIM 3030

428-100   Final writing-down allowance

The 'final writing-down allowance' is the allowance made to the person holding the relevant interest in qualifying expenditure when the 25-year writing-down period comes to an end. If the writing-down allowance would be less than the residue of qualifying expenditure at the time the allowance is to be made, the allowance is increased to that higher amount.

However, this is subject to an important caveat: when calculating the residue for the purpose of applying this rule, it is assumed that everyone who has been entitled to the relevant interest during the writing-down period has been entitled to allowances, and also that everyone has claimed allowances in full (ie even if the allowances have in part been disclaimed).

The effect of the rule is to tidy up the allowances where, for example, there has been a sale of the relevant interest without an election to have a balancing event, as discussed below.

Legislation: CAA 2001, s. 379

428-200   Allowances following a sale – no balancing event

Even before the changes introduced in 2007, the sale of a property (or – strictly – a sale of the relevant interest) did not automatically trigger a balancing event (though it could do so by election – see 429-500). In this way, the calculation of ABAs differs from the IBA rules.

Where there was no election to create a balancing event (and now such an election is not possible), allowances simply continue for the new owner as they would have done for the old owner if there had been no disposal. This applies whether the relevant interest has been acquired 'by transfer, by operation of law or otherwise'.

For the year of transfer, an apportionment is made between allowances for the vendor and allowances for the purchaser. Both the vendor and the purchaser are to claim 'an appropriate part of any writing-down allowance' for the chargeable period in which the transaction occurs.

What does this mean in practice? If both businesses have a common year end, it seems straightforward.

Example

Suppose that the sale is from Company A to Company B and takes place on 1 October, and that both companies draw accounts up to 31 December. Suppose that the qualifying expenditure is £1 million and that no election is made for a balancing event.

If Company A had not sold, it would have claimed allowances of £40,000. As it is, it can claim allowances of £30,000 ($^9/_{12}$ of the normal allowance) and Company B can claim allowances of £10,000 ($^3/_{12}$ of the normal allowance).

But often, the chargeable periods of the parties to the transaction will not coincide. In such cases, both the new owner and the previous owner will still be entitled to an 'appropriate part' of the allowance for their chargeable periods in which the transaction takes place.

Agricultural Buildings

> ### *Example*
>
> Company A (as above) still has a 31 December year end but Company B draws accounts up to 31 July.
>
> Company A can still claim allowances of £30,000.
>
> In this example Company B can claim allowances of £33,333 ($^{10}/_{12}$ of the normal writing-down allowance) as there are 10 months from the date of acquisition to the accounting date.
>
> In the following accounting period, Company A can claim no further allowances but Company B can claim full allowances of £40,000.

This, it is suggested, is the only sensible application of the wording of CAA 2001, s. 375. The HMRC manuals contain no examples to illustrate the interpretation of the section.

As illustrated above, the coincidence of acquisition dates and chargeable periods may result in the previous owner and the new owner, between them, acquiring more than four per cent writing-down allowances in the overlapping period. In such a case, an adjustment would then be made at the end of the writing-down period to ensure that the aggregate amount of the allowances given over the period was equal to the expenditure incurred.

Conversely, if the process results in the total allowances claimed being less than the total expenditure incurred, then the new owner (or his successor) can normally claim the outstanding balance in the last chargeable period of the 'writing-down period'. These adjustments are explained above.

Where only part of the land in question changes hands, the allowance is apportioned and the above rules are applied to that part of the allowance which is referable to the land being transferred, which is dealt with as though it were a separate allowance.

Legislation: CAA 2001, s. 375–379

Balancing events

428-500 Types of event

There are three possible types of balancing event:

(1) a sale of the relevant interest (only a balancing event if the vendor and purchaser sign a joint election to that effect);

(2) the demolition or destruction of the building (only a balancing event if the owner elects for it to be one); or

(3) the fact of the building ceasing altogether to be used (without being demolished or destroyed) (again, only a balancing event if the owner elects for it to be such).

See earlier editions of this book for details of how balancing adjustments were calculated under the old rules.

Legislation: CAA 2001, s. 381–382; FA 2007. s. 36

428-700   Apportionments

Proceeds received are apportioned between assets attracting allowances and other assets. More specifically, where the proceeds relate to a farmhouse, on which a maximum one-third of expenditure qualifies for allowances (see 426-200), only a similar proportion of those monies will be added to the residue of expenditure. Likewise, where expenditure is incurred on assets which serve partly the purpose of husbandry and partly other purposes, and is apportioned between the two (see 426-200), the proceeds are similarly apportioned.

Again, where the transfer which constitutes the balancing event is of only part of the land in which the relevant interest subsists, or if the balancing event is the destruction or demolition, etc of part only of an asset, the expenditure is apportioned, and that portion which is 'properly attributable' to the part sold, destroyed, etc is treated as a separate item of expenditure from the rest. However, whenever there is a sale between connected parties, or persons under common control, or in circumstances in which a tax advantage could be obtained, market value is invariably substituted for the price actually passing for the purposes of applying the rules on agricultural buildings allowances (see 430-500).

Legislation: CAA 2001, s. 384, 388

428-800   Anti-avoidance rules

Deemed sale at market value

Any transfer of the relevant interest otherwise than by sale, (eg by exchange) is treated as a sale at market value. Thus, if A gives B a plot of land containing cowsheds, and B gives A a barn in exchange, for the purposes of determining allowances (or charges), both the cowsheds and the barn will be deemed to have changed hands at their open market value.

Legislation: CAA 2001, s. 573

429-000   Time limits

In certain circumstances, it was possible to make an election to trigger a balancing event. Such an election had to be made by notice in writing to HMRC:

- for corporation tax purposes, no later than two years from the end of the accounting period in which the event took place; or
- for income tax purposes, on or before the first anniversary of the 31 January following the tax year in which ended the period of account in which the event took place.

Agricultural Buildings

429-100   Exclusion of election

No election could be made if either person who should make it (which included both the former owner and the new owner in the case of a transfer) was not within the charge to UK tax.

Further, the election could not be made if it appeared, in the case of a transfer, that the sole or main benefit which might have been expected to accrue to any of the parties to the transaction was the obtaining of a balancing allowance, or of a greater allowance than might otherwise have been obtained. This anti-avoidance provision applies not only to the transaction in respect of which the allowance is claimed, but also where that transaction is one of a number of transactions in which the obtaining of an allowance constituted the sole or main benefit accruing to a party.

Legislation: CAA 2001, s. 382

Other issues

430-500   Sales treated as being for alternative amount

The anti-avoidance rules in CAA 2001, s. 567–570 equally apply to agricultural buildings allowances. These rules provide for market value if sales are between connected persons or are transactions to obtain a tax advantage. The rules are described in detail at 307-000 (IBAs). However, no election under CAA 2001, s. 569 (alternative amount to be taken in respect of a sale) is available in respect of agricultural buildings allowances.

430-600   Successions to a trade, etc

The provisions of CAA 2001, s. 558, 559 and ICTA 1988, s. 343(2) relating to successions to a trade where there is no discontinuance apply to agricultural buildings as they apply to industrial buildings (see 310-350), as do the provisions relating to discontinuances with and without sale of assets. However, in the case of a discontinuance without sale of assets, it should be noted that a balancing event only arises where the taxpayer so elects (see 429-500), and such an election may not be made if it appears that the sole or main benefit expected to accrue to the parties is the obtaining of an allowance (or greater allowance). In any case, no balancing adjustment is normally made (subject to transitional provisions) for events occurring on or after 21 March 2007.

Legislation: CAA 2001, s. 382(2)–(5)

430-700   Contributions and subsidies

Expenditure is not regarded as having been incurred by any person insofar as it has been, or is to be, met directly or indirectly by subsidies, etc or contributions from third parties, subject to the exceptions in CAA 2001, s. 535, 536(1)–(3) (see 429-500).

However, where a person contributes towards expenditure for the purposes of a trade carried on by him, or by a tenant of land in which he has an interest, capital allowances may be made to the contributor as if his expenditure had been incurred on the provision, for the purposes of that trade, of a similar asset. This may be applicable in circumstances where the expenditure would, apart from CAA 2001, s. 536, be treated as wholly incurred by another person.

> ### *Example*
>
> Andrew acquires an asset for £100,000, ie he incurs expenditure of £100,000.
>
> Ian subsequently contributes £30,000. If CAA 2001, s. 532(1) did not apply, the expenditure would be treated as wholly incurred by Andrew.
>
> However, since s. 532(1) does apply, Andrew is able to claim allowances based on expenditure of only £70,000 and Ian can claim allowances on expenditure of £30,000.

For it to be taken into account, the person incurring it must be entitled to a 'relevant interest' in the agricultural land in respect of which it is incurred.

CAA 2001, s. 540 is omitted from April 2011, from which time the ABA rules cease to apply.

Legislation: CAA 2001, s. 540; FA 2008, Sch. 27, para. 10

Agricultural Buildings

FLAT CONVERSION ALLOWANCES

Overview

475-000   Overview

Flat conversion allowances (FCAs) are 'intended to encourage the conversion of empty or underused space above shops and other commercial premises to residential use'. Elsewhere, HMRC has stated that the rules 'target the scheme on properties in traditional shopping streets and similar locations'.

To this end, FCAs are given in relation to qualifying flats (see 475-700), which must be held for the purposes of short-term letting.

To qualify for FCAs, key conditions are as follows:

- a person must incur qualifying expenditure – broadly, capital expenditure on defined conversion or renovation work (see 475-500);
- that person must hold the 'relevant interest' in the flat (see 475-800);
- the work must be in respect of a flat (see 475-700);
- the property in which the flats are situated must have been built before 1980 and, at the time of construction, the upper floors must have been intended for residential use (see 475-600);
- the part of the building which is to be converted must have been either unused or used only for storage for at least a year before the conversion or renovation work began (see 475-500); and
- the flats to be created must not be 'high value' (see 475-700).

As with other allowances, relief is given by treating the allowances as business expenses. The treatment is explained in detail at 475-050.

An initial allowance is available of up to 100 per cent of the qualifying expenditure, ie full tax relief from the start on the cost of such expenditure (see 476-500).

Where, for whatever reason, full relief is not given by way of an initial allowance, writing-down allowances may be claimed of up to 25 per cent of the qualifying expenditure. Such allowances are given on a straight line basis, not by reference to the reducing balance though this is subject to various possible causes of variation (again, see 476-600). The 25 per cent figure was *not* reduced in line with the reduction of the writing-down allowances given for plant and machinery from April 2008.

A balancing adjustment (allowance or charge) is made if a balancing event (see 476-700) takes place within seven years of 'the time when the flat was first suitable for letting as a dwelling'.

Flat Conversion

Where there is a transfer of the relevant interest, the person to whom it is transferred cannot claim FCAs, even if the vendor has suffered a balancing charge. This represents a major difference from most other types of capital allowance.

Legislation: CAA 2001, s. 393Aff.

Other material: CA 43100

475-050 Giving effect to allowances and charges

The property in respect of which the allowance is claimed will normally be part of a person's UK property business. Allowances are treated as an expense of that business, while balancing charges are treated as receipts of the business (CAA 2001, s. 393T(2)). The term 'UK property business' is as defined in CTA 2009, s. 205 (for corporation tax purposes) or ITTOIA 2005, s. 264 (per ITA 2007, s. 989) (for income tax purposes) (CAA 2001, Sch. 1, Pt. 2). There are no special rules for claiming the allowances, which will simply form part of the self-assessment return.

Exceptionally, the flat may not be an asset of a person's UK property business during the chargeable period in which the qualifying conversion or renovation expenditure is incurred. This will normally apply if a person carries out the conversion or renovation, but does not hold other properties for letting. In this case, the person is treated as if he or she were carrying on a UK property business, and allowances are given as if they were an expense of this business, and charges as if they were a receipt of the business.

These rules allow the person to gain immediate access to the initial allowances, before he or she starts to hold the property out for letting and begins a UK property business. The allowances can be withdrawn if the business never actually begins; for example, because the finished flat is not used for letting. In this case, the flat would not be a qualifying flat.

Legislation: CAA 2001, s. 393T, Sch. 1, Pt. 2

Excess allowances

As capital allowances are now given as a business expense, excess allowances form a loss of that business, and are treated as follows.

For income tax purposes, they form part of the loss of a property business. They are carried forward and set against future profits of that business. Alternatively, the person may, on a claim, set excess net capital allowances of a UK property business (but not other elements of a loss incurred on such a business) sideways against his or her general income of the chargeable period in which the capital allowances are made, or general income of the following chargeable period.

For corporation tax purposes, excess capital allowances are first set against the company's total profits of the accounting period in which they are made. Any excess losses are carried forward and treated as a loss of the succeeding period. Alternatively, the company can, on a claim, surrender the excess losses, including the capital allowances, to a group company under the group relief rules.

Legislation: ICTA 1988, s. 392A, 402; ITA 2007, s. 120ff.

Other material: CA 43650

Definitions

475-500   Qualifying expenditure

Qualifying expenditure is capital expenditure incurred in connection with:

- the conversion of a qualifying building or part of a qualifying building into a qualifying flat or flats (see 475-700); or
- the renovation of a flat in a qualifying building to create a qualifying flat.

Only capital expenditure will qualify, so that routine repairs will not qualify. However, repairs to a qualifying building, to the extent that they are incidental to the conversion or renovation, will qualify.

Helpfully, the legislation states that any repairs to a building will be treated as capital expenditure 'if it is not expenditure that would be allowed to be deducted in calculating the profits of a UK property business for tax purposes'.

Conversion or renovation expenditure only qualifies if the part of the building which is to be converted was either unused or used only for storage for at least a year before the conversion or renovation work began.

This 'empty flat' requirement may lead to premises being deliberately left empty so as to allow renovation or conversion expenditure to qualify for allowances, thus leaving the area to suffer unnecessarily (albeit temporarily) – a somewhat anomalous result considering the purpose of the legislation. The legislation is silent on what is meant by 'unused', as are the HMRC guidance notes on this legislation. It is unclear, for example, whether a property deliberately left unused for a year, but consequently occupied by squatters, would have its clock reset.

If part of the upper floors satisfy the test then it may be possible to apportion the expenditure and to claim relief on part of it only. HMRC quotes the following example on its website:

> 'A shop may have three floors above the ground floor that were primarily for residential use when the property was constructed. If two of those floors had been unoccupied for 2 years before conversion work began and one had been used as an office, you should apportion any conversion expenditure that relates to all three floors.'

The HMRC manual lists the following examples of capital costs that would qualify:

Flat Conversion

- dividing up a single property to create flats;
- building dividing walls;
- installing a new kitchen or bathroom;
- inserting or removing walls, windows, or doors;
- installing and upgrading plumbing, gas, electricity or central heating;
- re-roofing incidental to the conversion/renovation;
- providing access to the flat(s) separate from the commercial premises, including extensions to the building to contain this access, if required; or
- providing external fire escapes where regulations require.

The capital expenditure must be made 'in connection with' the conversion or renovation of the building or flat. The HMRC manual confirms that an architect's or surveyor's fees incurred in connection with the conversion would normally qualify. Further guidance on the HMRC website confirms that:

> 'Expenditure incurred in connection with the conversion or renovation of a flat may include costs outside the direct boundary of the new or renovated flat such as the creation of stairwells within the building or provision of extension, solely to provide access to the new flats. It may also include architect's and surveyor's fees.'

Legislation: CAA 2001, s. 393B

Other material: CA 43150; www.hmrc.gov.uk/specialist/flatsovershops.htm

Non-qualifying expenditure

The legislation lists certain types of expenditure that cannot be qualifying expenditure. Such excluded expenditure is that incurred on or in connection with:

- the acquisition of land;
- the acquisition of rights over land;
- the development of land adjoining or adjacent to a qualifying building (unless, presumably, it is itself a qualifying building);
- the extension of a qualifying building, except to the extent required for the purpose of providing a means of access to a qualifying flat (see 475-700); and
- the provision of chattels, (eg furniture) or furnishings.

The Treasury can make further provisions by regulation as to what does or does not constitute qualifying expenditure.

As noted above, the conversion of the building into one or more qualifying flats must not extend beyond the confines of the build as it existed before the conversion starts. Any extension to the existing building will not be qualifying expenditure. However, an extension is permitted if its only function is to provide access to the ground level as a means to get to and from the flat without using the business premises on the ground floor.

Legislation: CAA 2001, s. 393B

Other material: CA 43150

475-600   Qualifying buildings

A number of conditions must be met if the building is to qualify:

(1)   all or most of the ground floor (see below) must be authorised for business use;

(2)   when the building was constructed, it must appear that the floors above the ground floor were primarily for residential use (see below);

(3)   the property must not have more than four storeys above the ground floor; an attic will count towards this total if it has been or could be lived in; and

(4)   the property must have been built before 1 January 1980, and any subsequent extensions must have been completed by 31 December 2000.

The definition may be amended by Treasury order.

The original use of the ground floor is not relevant; it may have been residential, commercial or of mixed use.

Legislation: CAA 2001, s. 393C

Definitions of floors, etc

The meaning of 'ground floor' is not defined. The HMRC manual (at CA 43200) comments:

'It should normally be clear which floor is the ground floor from the appearance of the building. You may have a case where this is less clear, for example the building may be built into a considerable slope. Normally you should treat the floor that contains the main entrance to the shop as the ground floor.'

The number of storeys does not include an attic or loft unless it can be lived in before the conversion starts. The HMRC manual states:

'Do not count the attic when you consider the number of storeys unless it can be lived in. An indication of this would be windows in the roof and proper stair access. An attic or loft that is not suitable for living in does not count as a storey, even if it can be used for storage.'

HMRC will not necessarily expect proof of the original intention with regard to the upper floors, commenting:

'The upper floors must have been originally primarily for use as dwellings. Normally the original use should be clear from the design and appearance of the building. However, you may not be able to determine the original use with absolute certainty. In that case you should treat a building as a qualifying building if it appears that the upper floors were constructed primarily for use as a dwelling or dwellings.'

Nor will HMRC insist on exclusive residential use (for the legislation refers to use 'primarily' as one or more dwellings):

'There may have been some business use in the upper floors. For example there may have been storerooms, offices or workshops or, indeed, the shop may have extended above the ground

Flat Conversion

649

floor. A building will be a qualifying building provided the greater part of the storeys above the ground floor were for use primarily as dwellings. For example, a four-storey building could qualify if it was built with a showroom or office on the first floor, provided that it appears that the original purpose of the second and third floors was residential.'

Legislation: CAA 2001, s. 393C(3)

Other material: CA 43200

Business use

As noted above, a condition of relief is that all or most of the ground floor must be 'authorised for business use'. This expression is defined by reference to the definitions in rating legislation. The actual legislation depends on the location of the building as given in the following table:

Table 9.1   Authorised for business use

Location of building	*Authority for use and class of use*
England or Wales	Class A1, A2, A3, B1 or D1(a) as specified in the Schedule to the Town and Country Planning (Use Classes) Order 1987 (SI 1987/764)
Scotland	Either:
	Class 1, 2, 3 or 4 as specified in the Schedule to the Town and Country Planning (Use Classes) (Scotland) Order 1997 (SI 1997/3061), or
	Article 3(5)(j) of the Town and Country Planning (Use Classes) (Scotland) Order 1997 (SI 1997/3061), or
	Authorised for use for the provision of medical or health services – other than from premises attached to the residence of the consultant or practitioner
Northern Ireland	Either:
	Class 1, 2, 3, 4 or 15(a) as specified in the Schedule to the Planning (Use Classes) (Northern Ireland) Order 1989 (SR 1989/290), or
	Article 3(5)(b), (c) or (h) of the Planning (Use Classes) (Northern Ireland) Order 1989 (SR 1989/290).

In broad terms, the classes of business use are:

- retail shops;
- premises for the provision of financial and professional services;
- premises for the sale of food and drink;
- other offices and premises for R&D activities and industrial processes which can be carried out in residential areas; and

- premises for medical and health services, such as doctor's surgeries and dental practices.

Legislation: CAA 2001, s. 393C(2)

Other material: CA 43200

475-700   Qualifying flats

Definition of flat

A flat is a dwelling which is a self-contained set of premises, which forms part of a building, and which 'is divided horizontally from another part of the building'. The term 'dwelling' is in its turn defined to mean 'a building or part of a building occupied or intended to be occupied as a separate dwelling'.

The horizontal division ensures that converting a property into semi-detached or terraced 'houses' would not qualify. It would seem that maisonettes (with separate entrances) would not necessarily qualify if the entrances are on the same level, though HMRC has confirmed that 'the rules do not require a qualifying flat to occupy only a single floor within the building'. In borderline cases, architects will need to take care to ensure that allowances are not forgone unnecessarily.

Legislation: CAA 2001, s. 393A(3), (4)

Other material: CA 43250; www.hmrc.gov.uk/specialist/flatsovershops.htm

Definition of qualifying flat

A qualifying flat is one which meets all the following conditions, namely that it:

- is in a qualifying building;
- is suitable for letting as a dwelling (see below);
- is held for the purpose of short-term letting (see below);
- is accessible without using the part of the ground floor that is authorised for business use;
- has no more than four rooms, excluding kitchen and bathroom (however big) and any 'closet, cloakroom or hallway not exceeding five square metres in area';
- is not a high value flat (see below);
- is not created as part of a scheme involving one or more high value flats (so 'affordable housing' flats incorporated into a conversion involving some luxury flats will not be qualifying flats); and
- is not let to a person connected with the person who incurred the expenditure on the renovation or conversion.

The definition may be amended by Treasury order.

Flat Conversion

HMRC has commented that 'generally speaking, a lounge/diner, a through living room, a kitchen/diner or kitchen/living room will comprise one room'.

Legislation: CAA 2001, s. 393D

Other material: CA 43250; www.hmrc.gov.uk/specialist/flatsovershops.htm

Suitable for letting

The HMRC manual confirms that there is no requirement that the flat is actually let, as long as it is being actively marketed and a tenant is being sought.

The legislation deals with temporary unsuitability of flats for letting. If a flat is a qualifying flat before such a period, then it is to be treated as a qualifying flat during that period. The HMRC manual states that a flat would not cease to be a qualifying flat because it is being redecorated between tenancies.

Legislation: CAA 2001, s. 393D(4)

Other material: CA 43250

Short-term letting

The statutory definition of short-term letting is 'letting as a dwelling on a lease for a term (or, in Scotland, period) of not more than five years'.

The HMRC manual states that: 'a letting under an assured shorthold tenancy will be short-term letting provided that any initial fixed-term lease does not exceed 5 years. The potential for a period of statutory periodic tenancy after the expiry of the fixed term does not alter this'.

The manual goes on to make the point that the letting that counts is that to the occupying tenant, and 'the length of a lease to an intermediate lessor does not matter'. As a result, the person claiming allowances for the conversion costs may lease the property to a tenant for a period of, say, ten years. As long as the tenant sub-lets it on a short-term let, allowances may be due.

Legislation: CAA 2001, s. 393D(2)

Other material: CA 43250

High value flats

A flat is a high value flat if its 'notional rent' exceeds specific limits, which are set out in a statutory table as follows:

Limits for notional rents

Number of rooms in flat	*Flats in Greater London*	*Flats elsewhere*
One or two rooms	£350 per week	£150 per week
Three rooms	£425 per week	£225 per week
Four rooms	£480 per week	£300 per week

As above, kitchens and bathrooms are ignored in calculating the number of rooms. So too is any 'closet, cloakroom or hallway not exceeding five square metres in area'.

The notional rent is the rent that could reasonably be expected for the flat on the date the expenditure is first incurred, making the following assumptions:

- the conversion or renovation is complete;
- the flat is let furnished;
- no premiums are payable to the landlord or any person connected with the landlord;
- the tenant is not connected with the person incurring the expenditure on the conversion or renovation;
- for a flat in England or Wales, it is let on an assured shorthold tenancy; and
- for a flat in Scotland, it is let on a short assured tenancy.

The high value test operates only at the date on which expenditure is first incurred on the conversion or renovation work. A flat does not become a high value flat if, at some time after the conversion or renovation expenditure is first incurred, the rent it could or does achieve exceeds these limits.

HMRC has confirmed that 'the test operates independently of any future movements in the property letting market'.

Treasury regulations may amend the limits in the above table.

Legislation: CAA 2001, s. 393E

Other material: CA 43250

475-800   Relevant interest

Allowances are given under the FCA scheme only to the person who:

- incurred the expenditure (and not, therefore, to any subsequent owner); and
- holds the relevant interest in the flat.

The term 'relevant interest' is defined in CAA 2001, s. 393F and 393G. It is also subject to CAA 2001, s. 393V. The rules for determining the relevant interest are similar to those for industrial buildings allowances (see 304-500). Generally, the relevant interest is the interest in the flat held by the person when the expenditure was incurred. This will normally be a freehold or leasehold interest in the property.

Flat Conversion

653

If a person has more than one interest in a flat, and one of the interests is reversionary on all the others (ie superior – for example, a freehold or a head lease over subleases) then the superior lease is the relevant interest.

An interest does not cease to be the relevant interest just because of the creation of a new interest to which it is subject. So, for example, a freeholder who has the relevant interest will not lose that interest just because he grants a lease. No writing-down allowance is given, though, if the person has granted a long lease (see 476-600) for a capital sum (CAA 2001, s. 393J(1)).

A leasehold interest may be extinguished if the person entitled to it acquires the interest which is reversionary on it. For example, Abel (as freeholder) may have granted a lease to Cain. If Cain then acquires the freehold, the leasehold interest is extinguished (as, in simple terms, Cain cannot have a lease with himself). In such circumstances, the interest into which the leasehold interest merges (the freehold interest, in this example) becomes the relevant interest.

A person who does not have the relevant interest at the time he incurs the conversion or renovation expenditure may claim the allowances provided he is entitled to an interest in the flat as a result of the conversion.

The purchaser of the relevant interest in a qualifying flat is not entitled to claim flat conversion allowances, even if the vendor is required to bring in a disposal value (CAA 2001, s. 393J(1)). Flat conversion allowances differ from other parts of the capital allowances code in this respect.

Legislation: CAA 2001, s. 393A(2), CAA 2001, s. 393F–J

Termination of leases

The issues of when a lease terminates is important for the definition of 'relevant interest'. The matter is addressed in the legislation as follows:

- if a person remains in possession of a flat after the termination of a lease without a new lease being granted to that person (but with the lessor's consent) then the old lease is treated as continuing until the lessee remains in possession of the flat;
- if a person is granted a new lease as a result of exercising an option available to that person under the old lease, then the new lease is treated as a continuation of the old;
- where lessors pay a sum to the lessee on termination of the lease, the lease is treated as coming to an end by surrender – with the payment treated as the consideration for the surrender;
- where, on the termination of a lease, another lease is granted to a third party and – in connection with the transaction – the new lessee pays a sum to the original lessee, then

the two leases are treated as the same lease (assigned by the original lessee to the new lessee in consideration for the payment).

Legislation: CAA 2001, s. 393V

Other material: CA 43300, 43600

475-900   Definition of lease

The term 'lease' is defined to be a tenancy and includes any agreement for a lease once the lease term has begun. A mortgage is not a lease.

In Scotland, 'leasehold interest' means the interest of a tenant in a property subject to a lease.

Legislation: CAA 2001, s. 393W

Calculation of allowances and charges

476-500   Initial allowances

The person incurring the qualifying expenditure is entitled to an initial allowance equal to 100 per cent of the expenditure for the chargeable period in which the expenditure is incurred (whether or not the flat is let during that period). The person may choose to claim a lesser amount (CAA 2001, s. 393H), in which case the balance of relief is given by means of writing-down allowances in subsequent periods.

The availability of full relief for expenditure incurred makes this an attractive proposition for somebody keen to invest in property, albeit subject to the seven-year clawback rule as described at 476-700. Relief can effectively be taken twice: first, as capital allowances and again as expenditure to offset when calculating any future capital gain (see TCGA 1992, s. 41).

However, an initial allowance is not available if, when the flat is first suitable for residential letting, it is not a qualifying flat (see 475-700).

Any initial allowance made (when the expenditure was incurred) but no longer available must be withdrawn and assessments amended as a result. This will be necessary if, when the flat is first suitable for residential letting:

- it is not a qualifying flat; or
- it has been sold by the person to whom the initial allowance was made.

Flat Conversion

> **Example**
>
> Zoe carries out work on renovating a flat during the year to 5 April 2009, and claims 100 per cent tax relief on the costs in 2008–09. She obtains a tax refund as a result.
>
> Costs rise and Zoe cannot fund the remaining work. She therefore sells the property in November 2009, before the flats are ready for letting. The initial allowance is withdrawn and her 2008–09 tax liability is re-calculated accordingly.

Legislation: CAA 2001, s. 393H–I

Other material: CA 43350

476-600   Writing-down allowances

The amount of the writing-down allowance (ie if a full initial allowance has not been claimed) is 25 per cent per year on a straight line basis but:

- a lesser amount may be claimed;
- the 25 per cent figure is increased or decreased proportionately for chargeable periods that are longer or shorter than one year; and
- the amount of a writing-down allowance is capped at the residue of qualifying expenditure, the amount of which is to be calculated 'immediately before writing off the writing-down allowance at the end of the chargeable period'.

The 25 per cent rate is *not* reduced to 20 per cent from April 2008.

Writing-down allowances may only be claimed where, at the end of the chargeable period, the claimant has a relevant interest in a qualifying flat and has not granted a long lease on the flat, ie one that exceeds 50 years. The rules in ICTA 1988, s. 38 apply to determine the length of a lease. (CAA 2001, s. 393J(3)(b) ensures, however, that CAA 2001, s. 393V(3) – which treats a new lease acquired following the exercise of an option under the old lease as a continuation of that old lease – does not affect the calculation of the 50 years.)

Legislation: CAA 2001, s. 393J–L

Other material: CA 43400

476-700   Balancing allowances and charges

If a balancing event takes place within seven years of the time when the flat was first suitable for letting, then a balancing adjustment will be made. A balancing charge will recover excess allowances that have been given and a balancing allowance will give further tax relief.

If more than one balancing event occurs, it is only the first that gives rise to a balancing allowance or charge. No balancing allowance is available, or charge made, if the balancing event occurs more than seven years after the flat was first suitable for letting.

A table at CAA 2001, s. 393O lists the possible balancing events and the proceeds – received or receivable by the person who incurred the expenditure – which are deemed to arise from each event, as follows:

Balancing events and proceeds

Balancing event	*Proceeds*
Sale of relevant interest	Actual sale proceeds
Grant of a long lease (see 254-525) for a capital sum	The higher of: • the capital sum paid; and • the commercial premium that would have been paid in an arm's length transaction
End of lease if a connected person has a superior interest	The market value at the time the lease ends
Death of person who incurred qualifying expenditure	The residue immediately before the death
Demolition or destruction of flat	Net amount for the remains, plus any insurance money received, plus any other capital sums received as compensation
Flat otherwise ceases to be a qualifying flat	The market value at the time

The definition of 'sale' is broadened in CAA 2001, s. 573, and this applies for flat conversion allowances.

Legislation: CAA 2001, s. 393M

Calculation of balancing adjustments

To determine the amount of any balancing adjustment, it is necessary to consider the difference between the 'residue of qualifying expenditure' and the proceeds from the balancing event.

The residue is defined in CAA 2001, s. 393L as the amount of qualifying (or demolition) expenditure that has not yet been written off in accordance with CAA 2001, s. 393R and 393S. The proceeds are determined in CAA 2001, s. 393O, as shown above.

If the proceeds exceed the residue, then there is a balancing charge equal to the difference. However, the balancing charge may not exceed the total allowances (initial or writing-down) made to the person in respect of the qualifying expenditure.

If the residue exceeds the proceeds, then there is a balancing allowance equal to the difference.

Flat Conversion

There is a special rule where the balancing event is the end of a lease. The table in CAA 2001, s. 393O shows proceeds equal to the market value of the relevant interest. However, this only applies if there is a person with a superior interest to the relevant interest and who is connected to the person with the relevant interest. Although the legislation does not explicitly provide for this, it is assumed that in other cases the lease ending will give rise to nil proceeds.

Legislation: CAA 2001, s. 393P

Other material: CA 43450

476-800 Residue of qualifying expenditure

The residue of qualifying expenditure needs to be ascertained to ensure that the total of initial and writing-down allowances given do not exceed the qualifying expenditure (CAA 2001, s. 393K(3)). Similarly, it is needed to determine the type and amount of any balancing adjustment on a balancing event occurring within the first seven years of the flat first being available for letting (CAA 2001, s. 393M(5)).

The residue can be expressed as:

$$QE + DEM - IA - WDA$$

where

QE   is the qualifying expenditure;
DEM is the net demolition costs (see below);
IA   is the initial allowance made in respect of the qualifying expenditure; and
WDA is the total writing-down allowances made in respect of the qualifying expenditure.

It is also necessary to determine when the residue is adjusted to reflect the allowances made. This is required to ensure that any comparison with the proceeds (when calculating the balancing adjustment) is correctly made.

An initial allowance reduces the residue at the time that the flat is first suitable for letting as a dwelling. A writing-down allowance reduces the residue at the end of the chargeable period to which it relates.

If:

- a balancing event occurs at the end of a chargeable period; and
- a writing-down allowance is made for that chargeable period in respect of the qualifying expenditure,

then the residue should be calculated after deducting the writing-down allowance.

Legislation: CAA 2001, s. 393P, CAA 2001, s. 393R

Other material: CA 43400

Demolition of the flat

A special rule applies if the flat is demolished. In practice, this will only be relevant if the flat is demolished during the first seven years after which it is first suitable for letting as a dwelling (and, by being demolished, ceases to be a qualifying flat). This is because writing-down allowances are only available for chargeable periods at the end of which the flat is a qualifying flat (see 475-700).

If the person who incurred the qualifying expenditure incurs the cost of demolition, then the net cost of demolition is added to the residue. The result of this is that the net cost of demolition will be relieved as a balancing allowance or will reduce the impact of a balancing charge.

The net cost of demolition is defined as the cost of demolition, less the cost of any proceeds for the sale of the remains of the flat.

It would appear that on a strict reading of the legislation, this could lead to a double tax charge if there are both demolition costs and proceeds for the remains.

Example

Suppose that demolition costs amount to £10,000 and the remains fetch £4,000 (although removal costs reduce this to a net figure of £3,000).

The net cost of demolition would equal £6,000 (ie £10,000 − £4,000). This would be added to the residue. However, when considering the proceeds, the taxpayer must consider the 'net amount received'. This would equal the £4,000 received (less, presumably, the £1,000 removal costs). In either event, the £4,000 receipts would be taken into account twice.

It is unlikely that the point would be taken by HMRC; furthermore, the wording follows that of other parts of the capital allowances legislation, but this is something of which people should be aware.

Demolition costs may not be used both to increase the residue and also to make up qualifying expenditure (under any Part of the *Capital Allowances Act* 2001) in respect of any replacement property.

Legislation: CAA 2001, s. 393S

Other material: CA 43500

Flat Conversion

Other issues

477-000 Contributions and subsidies

The general provisions relating to contributions (see 115-000) do not apply to flat conversion allowances.

Legislation: CAA 2001, s. 537(1)

477-100 Apportionments

Sale receipts which relate jointly to flats subject to flat conversion allowances and other assets are to be apportioned on a just and reasonable basis. This equally applies to other proceeds arising from balancing events, but subject to the other rules in CAA 2001 providing for apportionments.

Legislation: CAA 2001, s. 393U

Other material: CA 43550

477-200 Anti-avoidance

The anti-avoidance rules in CAA 2001, s. 567–570 (but not the election under CAA 2001, s. 569(1)) apply to flat conversion allowances as to industrial buildings allowances. These rules provide for market value if sales are between connected persons or are transactions to obtain a tax advantage. The rules are described in detail at 307-000 (IBAs). However, no election under CAA 2001, s. 569 (alternative amount to be taken in respect of a sale) is available in respect of flat conversion allowances.

Further legislation is intended to counter an abuse relating to balancing allowances. Businesses were entering into artificial transactions that depressed the market value of the asset prior to a sale to a connected person. The business selling the asset could then obtain accelerated relief by means of an early balancing allowance. The rules apply for flat conversion allowance payments as they do for industrial buildings allowances, and are described in detail at 306-650.

Legislation: CAA 2001, s. 570(1), CAA 2001, s. 570A

MINERAL EXTRACTION ALLOWANCES

Overview

500-000   Overview

Mineral Extraction Allowances (MEAs) are available in respect of capital expenditure incurred in connection with mineral extraction.

To qualify for relief, a person must be carrying on a mineral extraction trade (see 500-100) and must incur qualifying expenditure (see 500-150). Relief is not available to lessors of land containing minerals.

The relief applies to mineral extraction activities carried on worldwide, including sand and gravel extraction, hard rock mining, the oil sector and geothermal energy.

Expenditure qualifying for MEAs includes expenditure on exploration, access to a source, acquisition of the source, construction of certain works in connection with the source, the working of the source itself, and restoration of the site after work has ceased. Expenditure attributable to the value of land, rather than to the value of the mineral deposits, is excluded. Other items which do not generally qualify include processing plants, buildings for employees' accommodation or welfare, and offices.

The normal rate of allowance is 25 per cent per annum on a reducing balance basis. In respect of the acquisition of a 'mineral asset', ie the mineral deposits or rights over them, the rate is 10 per cent per annum on a reducing balance basis. Certain first-year allowances are available, but only for expenditure incurred by a company for the purposes of a ring-fence trade (see 500-200).

Each asset is written down individually: there is no 'pooling' as for plant and machinery (but see 500-200). On the disposal or destruction of an asset in respect of which allowances have been given, a balancing allowance or charge will be made.

Where an asset is sold to a person who in turn carries on a trade of mineral extraction, the purchaser may claim allowances for his acquisition costs to the extent that they do not exceed the residue of expenditure which qualified for allowances in the hands of the seller.

Allowances are available in respect of a part of, or a share in, an asset of any description as they are for the asset itself, so long as the asset is used for the purposes of a trade.

Legislation: CAA 2001, s. 394ff., 435

Other material: CA 50110

500-050   Giving effect to allowances and charges

A person carrying on a mineral extraction trade gives effect to allowances in calculating the profits of that trade. So:

- any allowance is treated as an expense of the trade; and
- any balancing charge is treated as a trading receipt.

Legislation: CAA 2001, s. 432

Other material: Other material: CA 50410

Definitions

500-100   Mineral extraction trade

This is defined as a trade which consists of or includes the working of a source of mineral deposits of a wasting nature. A 'source of mineral deposits' specifically includes:

- a mine;
- an oil well; and
- a source of geothermal energy.

Legislation: CAA 2001, s. 394

Other material: CA 50120

500-150   Qualifying expenditure

The category into which expenditure falls may determine the extent of allowances available. In particular, expenditure on the acquisition of a mineral asset (see below) attracts writing-down allowances at a rate of only 10 per cent, compared to a rate of 25 per cent for other qualifying expenditure.

Expenditure incurred by a person about to carry on a mineral extraction trade is treated as incurred on the day that the person does first carry it on.

Original expenditure is distinguished from second-hand costs, the qualifying expenditure being determined differently in relation to each.

The legislation lists four types of qualifying expenditure, each of which has different definitions and rules, and then adds two provisos.

The four types of qualifying expenditure are as follows:

- capital expenditure on mineral exploration and access (see below) which is incurred for the purposes of a mineral extraction trade (see 500-100);
- capital expenditure on acquiring a mineral asset (see below) which is incurred for the purposes of a mineral extraction trade (see 500-100);
- expenditure which is treated as qualifying expenditure on mineral exploration and access under CAA 2001, s. 407(5) (acquisition of mineral asset owned by previous trader – see below) or CAA 2001, s. 408(2) (acquisition of oil licence from non-trader – see below); and
- expenditure which is qualifying expenditure under CAA 2001, Ch. 5 (expenditure on works likely to become valueless; contribution to buildings or works for benefit of employees abroad; expenditure on restoration within three years of ceasing to trade (see below)).

The provisos are that expenditure is not qualifying expenditure if:

- it is excluded from being such by CAA 2001, s. 399 (see below); or
- it is caught by any of the provisions of CAA 2001, Ch. 4 that limit the amount of qualifying expenditure (see below).

Legislation: CAA 2001, s. 418(1)

Other material: CA 50200

Excluded expenditure

The legislation lists various types of expenditure that are excluded from being qualifying expenditure:

- expenditure on plant and machinery (except for certain pre-trading expenditure qualifying under CAA 2001, s. 402);
- works constructed wholly or mainly for subjecting the raw product of a source to any process, other than for preparing the raw product for use as such. (Thus, for example, a smelting plant is disqualified, but a crusher for breaking down ore into a usable size is not);
- buildings or structures for occupation by, or for the welfare of, workers (which may, however, qualify for industrial buildings allowance: see 300-000 onwards). This restriction is subject to possible relief under CAA 2001, s. 415 (contributions to buildings, etc for the benefits of workers abroad);
- buildings constructed wholly for use as offices; and
- buildings constructed partly for use as offices, unless 10 per cent or less of the capital expenditure is attributable to office use.

Legislation: CAA 2001, s. 399

Other material: CA 50320

Qualifying expenditure on mineral exploration and access

Another main purpose of the code of MEAs is to give allowances for the cost of mineral exploration and access. This category covers capital expenditure (see 102-000) on mineral exploration and access, incurred for the purposes of a mineral extraction trade.

The concept of 'mineral exploration and access' is defined as:

- searching for or discovering and testing the mineral deposits of a source; or
- winning access to such deposits.

For these purposes, expenditure on an unsuccessful application for planning permission is regarded as expenditure on mineral exploration and access, and qualifies for allowances. This includes not only the cost of the application, but also the cost of pursuing an appeal against refusal.

Qualifying expenditure on mineral exploration and access incurred by a person carrying on a trade of mineral extraction is treated as incurred for the purposes of the trade, whether the expense is incurred before or after commencement of the trade. This applies whether or not the exploration relates to the same mineral source, or even the same mineral; a tin-mining company wishing to diversify may be eligible for allowances for exploration of sources of silver, oil or geothermal energy.

Any results obtained from a search, exploration or inquiry are treated as assets representing the expenditure on the search, etc. Thus, for example, a balancing charge would arise if such results were sold for more than the tax written-down value of the exploration costs.

Certain types of exploration expenditure may qualify for allowances for research and development allowances (see 525-000), potentially offering a more rapid rate of tax relief than MEAs. In particular, expenditure on searching for, discovering and testing new petroleum deposits is regarded by HMRC as expenditure on research and development, up to the point at which the existence of oil in commercial quantities is proved. The point used to be explicitly stated at former CA 26235, but the same point is now broadly made in the *Oil Taxation* manual at OT 26017 and OT 26236.

Legislation: CAA 2001, s. 396, 400, 409(3)

Other material: OT 26017, OT 26236

Pre-trading expenditure

Expenditure incurred by a person about to carry on a trade is generally treated as incurred on the day on which that person begins to carry on the mineral extraction trade. But pre-trading expenditure on mineral exploration and access qualifies only if it falls within the categories of:

- pre-trading exploration expenditure – see below; or
- pre-trading expenditure on plant or machinery – again, see below.

Where relief is due under one of these headings, it is given by way of a balancing allowance rather than a writing-down allowance. As such, relief is given in full on the day the trade begins.

Legislation: CAA 2001, s. 400, 409(3), 426

Other material: CA 50240ff.

Plant and machinery

With one exception, expenditure on plant or machinery is not qualifying expenditure for mineral extraction purposes. Instead, where a person carrying on a trade of mineral extraction incurs expenditure in connection with that trade on plant or machinery for mineral exploration and access, it will be taken to be incurred on the provision of plant or machinery wholly and exclusively for the purposes of that trade.

Pre-trading expenditure on 'plant or machinery' qualifies for MEAs (as mineral exploration and access) if it is sold, demolished, destroyed or abandoned before a 'mineral extraction trade' (see 500-100) is begun. (Other pre-trading expenditure, not abandoned, etc is treated for plant and machinery allowances as incurred on the first day of trading.)

The expenditure must have been incurred for mineral exploration and access (see above) and the plant or machinery must have been used in connection with that exploration and access at a source.

The cost of the asset, after deduction of any sale proceeds, insurance, salvage or compensation received for it, is treated as qualifying expenditure incurred on the first day of the trade. If the mineral exploration and access at the source in connection with which the plant or machinery was used has ceased before the trade commences, then expenditure incurred more than six years before the date of commencement is excluded from allowances.

Legislation: CAA 2001, s. 161, 399(1), 402

Other material: CA 50240ff.

Other pre-trading expenditure

Pre-trading expenditure on mineral exploration and access, other than on plant or machinery, qualifies for allowances where either:

- mineral exploration and access is continuing at the source in question at the date on which a 'mineral extraction trade' commences; or
- mineral exploration and access has ceased at the source in question, but the expenditure was incurred within six years before the trade commenced elsewhere.

In either case, allowances will be given for the excess of the pre-trading expenditure over any capital sum that is received by the claimant before trade commenced and is 'reasonably attributable' to the incurring of the expenditure at the source in question.

Legislation: CAA 2001, s. 401

Qualifying expenditure on acquiring a mineral asset

This category covers capital expenditure (see 102-000) on acquiring a mineral asset, incurred for the purposes of a mineral extraction trade. A mineral asset is defined as:

* any mineral deposits or land comprising mineral deposits; or
* any interest in, or right over, such deposits or land.

In each case, the deposits must be of a wasting nature, which presumably means that although expenditure on winning access to such sources of geothermal energy as hot rocks *is* allowable, the cost of the rocks themselves is not because they are not of a wasting nature.

This definition of mineral assets is subject to an exclusion for the undeveloped market value of the land (see below) and to a reduction where premium relief has previously been allowed (see below).

Subject to CAA 2001, Ch. 4 (second-hand assets – see below), the following are treated as expenditure on acquiring a mineral asset (and not as expenditure on mineral exploration and access), with the result that they attract allowances at the lower rate only (see 500-200):

* the acquisition of, or of rights over, the site of a source of mineral deposits; and
* the acquisition of, or of rights over, mineral deposits.

The HMRC manual states that 'expenditure on non mineral bearing land acquired to give access to adjacent mineral deposits is not qualifying expenditure even though the access land may have been bought at a premium over its existing use value'.

Legislation: CAA 2001, s. 394(4), 397-400

Other material: CA 50220

Undeveloped market value

Without further refinement of the legislation, relief would be available for the whole cost of the land. However, the intention of the legislation is that allowances should not be available in respect of land as such, but only in respect of the mineral deposits which it contains. Accordingly, qualifying expenditure does not include the 'undeveloped market value' of an interest in land, whether in the UK or elsewhere.

The 'undeveloped market value' means the consideration which the land might reasonably be expected to fetch on a sale in the open market at the time of actual acquisition, on the assumptions:

* that there is no source of mineral deposits on or in the land; and

- that it is and will continue to be unlawful to carry out any development other than anything which has been or has begun to be lawfully carried out, or for which planning permission has been granted by a general development order, at the time when the land is acquired.

In other words, allowances are not available in respect of the land in the state of development or non-development in which it stands at the time of the acquisition. If there are buildings or structures already erected on the land, they too are excluded from allowances.

Example

Ann, who carries on a trade of mining, acquires an area of land in the UK for the purpose of mining silver. At the time of acquisition the land is used for farming, and has a number of farm buildings, wind pumps, etc erected on it. Ann pays £500,000 for the land. Its value on the assumptions that it contains no mineral deposits and that further development would be unlawful is £350,000, of which £80,000 is attributable to the buildings and erections on it. Ann makes no use of the buildings, etc for any purpose.

Ann will be unable to claim allowances in respect of the undeveloped value, except insofar as attributable to the abandoned buildings. Hence £270,000 of Ann's expenditure is disqualified (£350,000 less £80,000 for the unused buildings).

(Note that it is irrelevant whether the person who sold the land to Ann has obtained any allowances, eg agricultural buildings allowance, on the buildings, etc in question.)

If the buildings or structures cease permanently to be used for any purpose only at a later date, then allowances become available in respect of them at that later time, after subtracting any allowances previously given to the claimant for them as industrial buildings, plant, mineral assets, etc. The legislation uses the formula:

$$V - (A - B)$$

where:

V   is the value of the buildings or structures at the date of acquisition (disregarding any value attributable to the land);

A   is the amount of capital allowances (except any Assured Tenancy Allowances) made to the buyer in respect of the buildings or structures (or assets within them); and

B   is the amount of any balancing charges suffered by the buyer in respect of those buildings, structures or assets.

Any question whether development has been or is being carried out lawfully is determined by reference to the law of the territory in which the land is situated. Any question whether development is of a character for which planning permission is granted by a general development order is determined as if the land were situated in England or Wales.

'Development', 'development order' and 'planning permission' are construed according to either the *Town and Country Planning Act* 1990, s. 336(1), the *Town and Country Planning*

(Scotland) Act 1997, s. 277(1), or the *Planning (Northern Ireland) Order* 1991 (SI 1991/1220), art. 2(2), depending upon where the land is situated.

The exclusion does not apply if a valid election is signed under CAA 2001, s. 569 (sales treated as being for an alternative amount – see 500-500).

Legislation: CAA 2001, s. 404–405, 422(4), 436

Other material: CA 50330

Premiums: prevention of double deduction

Where a claimant qualifies for allowances in respect of land for which relief has already been given by way of deduction in respect of part of any chargeable premium, (ie under ITTOIA 2005, s. 60 to 67 or CTA 2009, s. 62 to 67) in a previous chargeable period, a deduction of the amount of relief given must be made from the claimant's expenditure.

The amount of qualifying expenditure is reduced using the formula:

$$D \times (E/T)$$

where:

D   is the total of deductions made under ITTOIA 2005, s. 60 to 67 or CTA 2009, s. 62 to 67;

E   is the amount of capital expenditure that would have qualified for MEAs if the buyer had been entitled to allowances in the earlier chargeable periods; and

T   is the total capital expenditure incurred on acquiring the interest in the land.

Legislation: CAA 2001, s. 406

Other material: CA 50370

Qualifying expenditure – second-hand assets

Assets reflecting expenditure on mineral exploration and access

Where a person who carries on a trade of mineral extraction ('the purchaser') buys an asset which has previously attracted capital allowances, the extent to which the purchaser can claim allowances is restricted. Broadly, the 'capital expenditure' incurred by the purchaser on acquiring the asset qualifies for relief only up to the residue of the expenditure which qualified for allowances in the hands of a former owner.

The circumstances in which the restrictions operate are these. A person carrying on a mineral extraction trade (see 500-100) incurs capital expenditure in acquiring an asset. Either the immediate vendor, or a previous owner ('the previous trader'), has incurred capital expenditure on acquiring the asset, or bringing it into existence, in connection with a trade of mineral extraction carried on by him.

The restrictions do not apply where the asset in question is a mineral asset (see above) situated in the UK (see above), and the capital expenditure incurred by the purchaser of the asset consists of the payment of sums under a contract which he entered into before 16 July 1985, the date on which the consultative paper '*Mines and Oil Wells Allowances*' was published.

Legislation: CAA 2001, s. 407 and Sch. 3, para. 87

Expenditure in respect of the 'purchased asset'

An asset which has previously been acquired, etc by a mineral extraction trader is referred to in the legislation as 'asset X'. Asset X can include two or more assets which together make up the one purchased asset, and the asset (or assets) from which the purchased asset is derived.

The 'buyer's expenditure' is the capital expenditure he incurred, less any amount disqualified as qualifying expenditure under CAA 2001, s. 404 (undeveloped market value – see above) in relation to the acquisition of land.

Sometimes, part of the value of the mineral asset (see above) acquired by the purchaser will be referable to expenditure incurred by the previous trader on mineral exploration and access (see above) rather than on mineral extraction. Expenditure on that part of the asset's value qualifies in the purchaser's hands for the higher (25 per cent) allowance given on expenditure on mineral exploration and access, to the extent that it does not exceed the equivalent part of the previous trader's expenditure. The balance is treated as expenditure on the purchase of a mineral asset, and qualifies for 10 per cent allowances.

Example

Angus purchases an area of land for £50,000, spends a further £60,000 on constructing a well and sinking a shaft for exploration and access, and then sells the whole to Basil for £150,000. Basil can claim the 25 per cent allowance on £60,000 of his own expenditure.

The question of whether research and development allowances were made to the previous trader has no bearing on the determination of his qualifying expenditure on the purchased asset. But where expenditure incurred by the previous trader has already been deducted as a trading expense, MEAs are not available on any of the attributable purchase cost.

Legislation: CAA 2001, s. 407, 411(1)

Assets formerly owned by non-traders, etc

Where a person incurs expenditure on assets for the purpose of mineral exploration and access, but does not carry on any trade of mineral extraction, and he sells the assets to another person who does, that other person's qualifying expenditure is limited to the amount of expenditure which the vendor incurred on the assets.

In the case of an oil licence being acquired from a person not carrying on a mineral extraction trade, a just and reasonable apportionment may need to be made. This will arise where part of the value of the interest is attributable to expenditure incurred ('E1') by the seller on mineral exploration and access. The buyer's qualifying expenditure will then be the lower of E1 and E2, where E2 is that part of the buyer's expenditure that it is reasonable to attribute to that part of the interest.

Legislation: CAA 2001, s. 408, 409(1)

Qualifying expenditure limited by reference to historic costs

UK oil licences

Where a person acquires a UK oil licence or an interest in such a licence, that person's qualifying expenditure cannot exceed the amount paid to the Secretary of State (or, in Northern Ireland, the Department of Enterprise, Trade and Investment) by the person to whom the licence was granted. A UK oil licence is defined, for these purposes, to mean a licence under Part I of the *Petroleum Act* 1998 or under the *Petroleum (Production) Act (Northern Ireland)* 1964.

Where only an interest in an oil licence is purchased, the purchaser's qualifying expenditure is restricted to such portion of the original payment as it is 'just and reasonable' to attribute to the interest.

Legislation: CAA 2001, s. 410, 552(2)

Limit to previous trader's residue of qualifying expenditure

Where the expenditure of the previous trader, (ie the last one to incur expenditure on acquiring the asset or bringing it into existence) related to an asset or assets from which the purchased asset is derived, then his qualifying expenditure will be apportioned on a 'just and reasonable' basis and that part which is attributable to the purchased asset will be treated as his qualifying expenditure for the purpose of determining the 'purchaser's qualifying expenditure'.

Example

Amos carries on a trade of mineral extraction. He incurs capital expenditure of £100,000 in the purchase of a mineral asset. £90,000 was qualifying expenditure for the purposes of allowances. He later grants a lease of the asset to Bob at a premium of £60,000. The proportion of Amos's qualifying expenditure to be attributed to the purchased asset, (ie the lease) will be a just and reasonable apportionment of his qualifying expenditure, ie

$$£90,000 \times \frac{£60,000}{£100,000} = £54,000.$$

The purchaser's qualifying expenditure depends upon the allowances claimed by the previous trader. Where the previous trader did not become entitled to an allowance or liable to balancing charges in respect of his qualifying expenditure, then the purchaser can claim as qualifying expenditure so much of 'his own expenditure' as does not exceed the amount of 'the previous trader's qualifying expenditure'. On the other hand, where the previous trader has claimed allowances or incurred balancing charges, the purchaser's qualifying expenditure is so much of his expenditure as is equal to the residue of the previous trader's qualifying expenditure: that is, such trader's qualifying expenditure, less allowances made to him in respect of it, plus the amount on which any balancing charge was made.

Where the previous trader's qualifying expenditure is apportioned on a just and reasonable basis, then his balancing charges and allowances are similarly apportioned.

Legislation: CAA 2001, s. 411

Intra-group transfers: transferee's qualifying expenditure

Restrictions apply when a mineral asset is transferred between companies in the same group. For these purposes, a group exists where the transferor company controls the transferee, or vice-versa, or where both companies are under the control of a third person. 'Control' means power over the affairs of a company, directly or indirectly, by virtue of voting power or regulatory documents.

Where a company acquires a mineral asset from another company in the group, its qualifying expenditure is restricted to the capital expenditure incurred by the transferor company in acquiring the asset. Where the transferee company acquires only an interest in a mineral asset acquired by the transferor, its qualifying expenditure is determined by a 'just apportionment' of the total expenditure incurred by the transferor. This does not apply where the mineral asset in question is a UK oil licence (see above), or where the acquisition is a sale in respect of which an election is in force to substitute residue of expenditure for open market value in a sale between connected persons (see 500-650).

If the transferee company's expenditure relates to the acquisition of land in such a manner that its undeveloped market value on acquisition generally falls to be excluded from qualifying expenditure, and the transferee company carries on a trade of mineral extraction, any reference to the time of acquisition of the interest in land means the time at which it was acquired by the transferor, or where there is a sequence of transactions the first transferor in the sequence.

Where the undeveloped market value of an interest in land thereby unrelieved includes the value of buildings or structures, expenditure on which is treated as qualifying on permanent disuse, and there is a sequence of transactions within the group, then the latest transferee is deemed to have incurred the qualifying expenditure on those buildings or structures.

Legislation: CAA 2001, s. 412, 413, 574

Qualifying expenditure – works likely to become valueless

Capital expenditure by a person on the construction of 'works' in connection with the working of a source of mineral deposits may be qualifying expenditure. This will be the case where the works are likely to be of little or no value to the last person working the source, (ie whoever works it immediately before the source ceases to be worked).

Similarly, qualifying expenditure includes the construction of works in connection with the working of a source of mineral deposits under a foreign concession (a right or privilege granted by an authority of a foreign territory), which are likely to become valueless to the person working the source immediately before the concession comes to an end.

The term 'works' is not defined, but 'can include railway lines, roads and jetties at the site of mineral extraction'.

Other material: CA 50230

Buildings, etc for the benefit of employees abroad

Under some foreign concessions the land (and buildings erected on it) will revert to a public authority without compensation. In such circumstances the claimant may also have been required to contribute capital sums to the cost of:

- buildings to house employees;
- water, gas or electricity supplies to such buildings; or
- works to be used in provision of services or facilities for employees or their dependants.

The types of buildings which qualify for MEAs are limited. The definition of an 'industrial building or structure' includes a building in use for the purposes of a trade which consists in the working of any mine, oil well or other source of mineral deposits (see 301-850). Industrial buildings allowances are specifically extended to certain buildings, etc constructed for occupation by, or for the welfare of, employees (see 302-600). This can include dwelling houses, etc despite the usual prohibition on IBAs for such expenditure, but only if the building is likely to have little or no value when the source is worked out or if it will cease to be owned by the person in question when a foreign concession comes to an end.

MEAs may be claimed in respect of contributions to buildings which will become valueless to the person working the source when a foreign concession ends. Allowances extend to such expenditure, except in so far as it results in the acquisition of an asset or qualifies for any allowance other than under the mineral extraction provisions.

Legislation: CAA 2001, s. 415

Restoration of land

MEAs are extended to certain expenditure incurred on the restoration of a site of mineral extraction, including any land used in connection with the working of the source, after the trade has ceased. The expenditure:

- must be incurred within three years after the last day on which the trade was carried on;
- must not have been deducted for income or corporation tax purposes in relation to that or any other trade; and

- must be such as would have been qualifying expenditure (or an allowable deduction in computing profits) if the trade had still been carried on.

The expenditure is deemed to be incurred on the last day of trading. Relief is still available if the trade has ceased.

'Restoration' includes landscaping, and any work required in connection with the grant of planning permission (or an equivalent foreign condition) for the mining development.

The allowance is given in respect of the 'net cost' of the restoration, ie the cost of the restoration work after deducting any receipts, eg for spoil or tipping rights, during the three-year period after the trade ceases.

Expenditure on such restoration as qualifies under this heading is not deductible in computing profits for income or corporation tax irrespective of whether it constitutes qualifying expenditure. Receipts which are deducted in calculating the 'net cost' of restoration are not chargeable to tax as income.

Adjustments by means of discharge or repayment of tax will be made as necessary to give effect to these provisions.

Legislation: CAA 2001, s. 416

Calculation of allowances and charges

500-200   General principles

Unlike the plant and machinery code of allowances, expenditure on mineral extraction is not 'pooled'. Each item of qualifying expenditure is written down separately, and only disposal proceeds relating to that particular item are set against the expenditure. Having said this, HMRC will not in practice object to pooling where 'assets are grouped together for computational convenience' as long as:

- individual sources are separated; and
- assets qualifying for relief at 10 per cent are kept separate from those qualifying at 25 per cent.

The HMRC manuals accept that where this is done, there is normally 'no objection to the practice of deducting the disposal receipt from the balance of qualifying expenditure'. However, the manual does warn that 'in exceptional circumstances it may be necessary to reconstruct separate computations for individual items where a disposal receipt arises or a balancing allowance is due'. It explains that 'a separate computation in respect of individual assets will be required where there are disposals to a mineral extraction trader and it is necessary to apply the second-hand cost restriction rules in s. 410'.

On balance, therefore, separate computations are advisable.

Writing-down allowances are given on a reducing balance basis. The figure on which allowances are calculated in respect of any expenditure is based on the qualifying expenditure (in the year or brought down from the previous period) less any disposal receipts. The legislation uses the terms 'UQE' (for 'unrelieved qualifying expenditure') and 'TDR' (for 'the total of any disposal receipts to be brought into account').

Legislation: CAA 2001, s. 416D

Other material: CA 50410, 50470

Unrelieved qualifying expenditure

The amount of unrelieved qualifying expenditure is defined differently for the year in which the expenditure is incurred, and for subsequent years.

For the chargeable period in which qualifying expenditure is incurred, the whole amount is unrelieved qualifying expenditure, unless it qualifies for first-year allowances (see below).

For subsequent chargeable periods, the unrelieved qualifying expenditure incurred is reduced by any allowances given and by the amount of any disposal receipts taken into account in earlier periods.

Legislation: CAA 2001, s. 419

Demolition costs

The net cost of demolishing a building which qualifies for allowances may be added to the qualifying expenditure in calculating the balancing charge or allowance relating to the demolition. The 'net cost' means the excess of the cost of demolition over receipts for the remains. The cost or net cost of demolition cannot then be allowed again as expenditure incurred on provision of a replacement.

Legislation: CAA 2001, s. 433

Other material: ICAEW Technical Release TR 233

Total of any disposal receipts

Where a person has incurred qualifying expenditure on providing assets, he must bring a disposal value into account if any such asset is disposed of or if it permanently ceases to be used for the purposes of a mineral extraction trade.

Example

Cyril carries on a trade of mining, and in the course of that trade acquires an area of land, together with the mineral deposits contained therein. Cyril claims capital allowances for the mineral deposits, to which a value of £150,000 is attributed. Two years later, Cyril sells off an area of land, together with minerals, for a price of which £60,000 is attributable to the minerals.

Cyril is entitled to allowances as follows:

	Qualifying expenditure £	Writing-down allowance at 10% £	Unrelieved qualifying expenditure £
Year 1	150,000	15,000	135,000
Year 2	135,000	13,500	121,500
Year 3 (£121,500 − £60,000)	61,500	6,150	55,350

A disposal value is also to be brought into account if an asset begins to be used in a way which constitutes development (other than lawful development begun, or for which planning permission has been granted, when the asset was acquired, or development that is carried out for the purposes of the person's mineral extraction trade). For definitions (lawful development, etc) see 500-150.

Except when partly attributable to land (see below) 'disposal value' is defined as in relation to the plant and machinery code of allowances (see 190-600), varying according to the nature of the disposal, as follows.

Legislation: CAA 2001, s. 421, 423

Sale of the asset

As would be expected, the basic rule is that if an asset is sold then the disposal value equals the net proceeds of that sale. There is no definition of 'net proceeds' but a common-sense approach means that it is the amount of proceeds after deducting any costs of sale.

The legislation does say that in addition to these net proceeds there must be brought in any insurance received for any event that has affected the price obtainable on the sale of the asset. Similarly, any other capital compensation received for the same reason must be brought into account.

Legislation: CAA 2001, s. 423

Sale of the asset at less than market value

There is a general principle that where an asset is sold below its market value then it is necessary to bring in the market value figure. There are, however, certain exceptions. If the disposal gives rise to a charge to tax as earnings from an employment – for example because it is given to an employee or sold to him at less than its market value – then only the actual proceeds (if any) need to be brought into account. This is the case even if no tax is actually payable by the director or employee because of the £30,000 exemption applying to certain payments on the termination, etc of an employment.

Similarly, market value does not have to be substituted if the buyer can claim capital allowances on the asset as plant or machinery or under the scientific research allowance

675

rules (though this exemption does not apply if the buyer is a dual resident investing company connected with the seller, even if the buyer and seller are connected with each other.

If the asset is sold for more than its market value then any balancing charge will be restricted by reference to the historic cost of the asset (see below).

Legislation: CAA 2001, s. 423

Other material: CA 23250

The demolition or destruction of the asset

If the asset is totally demolished then three elements need to be added together to produce the proceeds figure for capital allowance purposes:

(1)   the net proceeds of sale of the remains of the asset; plus

(2)   any insurance payment made in respect of the demolition or destruction; plus

(3)   any other compensation which is capital in nature and which is received in respect of the demolition or destruction.

Legislation: CAA 2001, s. 423

Other material: CA 50500

The permanent loss of the asset

An asset may be lost even though it has not been demolished or destroyed (though this seems unlikely in the context of MEAs). In this case, the principle is identical to that under the above heading (demolition or destruction) except that there will obviously not be any sale proceeds for the remains of the machinery or plant.

Legislation: CAA 2001, s. 423

The permanent discontinuance of the trade

It may be that the trade is brought to an end before any of the above events. If the permanent discontinuance is followed by one of the events outlined in the above paragraphs then the disposal value is still the amount specified for whichever event duly occurs. Thus, if the trade ceases and the asset is then sold, the proceeds will be calculated on the basis of the first of the above headings.

Legislation: CAA 2001, s. 423

Any other event

If a disposal value needs to be brought into account, but none of the events envisaged in the preceding paragraphs has taken place, then the open market value is to be brought into account as the disposal value. However, the disposal value of an oil licence may in certain circumstances be treated as nil.

It will not always be the case that an asset is treated as disposed of, etc when a capital sum is received (so as to represent a disposal receipt). For example, a mining company may receive a lump sum payment in exchange for agreeing not to work a source, or part of a source. If such a payment is a capital sum which could be 'reasonably attributed' to any expenditure then it must be brought into account as a disposal receipt in the same way as a sum received for an asset.

The HMRC manual makes the point that 'permanent cessation of use includes the case where a company ceases to be resident in the UK through a branch or agency'.

Legislation: CAA 2001, s. 423–425, 553(2)

Other material: CA 50420

Disposal receipts partly attributable to land

Where part of a disposal receipt is attributable to land which did not qualify for allowances, that part is disregarded, and does not form part of the disposal receipts to be deducted before calculating subsequent allowances. More particularly, the amount taken into account as a disposal receipt is only so much of the disposal value as exceeds the 'undeveloped market value' of the interest in land. For the meaning of undeveloped market value, see 500-150.

Legislation: CAA 2001, s. 424

500-250   Balancing charges

If TDR exceeds UQE (broadly, receipts and qualifying expenditure respectively, but see above for the precise meaning of these terms) then the person will be subject to a balancing charge. The amount of the charge will be the excess, but capped at the allowances already given in relation to the expenditure in question, less any balancing charges already made in respect of the same expenditure.

Legislation: CAA 2001, s. 418(4)

Other material: CA 50450

500-300   Writing-down allowances

If UQE exceeds TDR then the person will be entitled to a writing-down allowance or (in various specified circumstances – see below) to a balancing allowance.

The rate of any writing-down allowance depends upon the nature of the expenditure:

- For expenditure on the acquisition of a 'mineral asset' (see 500-150), the rate is 10 per cent.
- For other qualifying expenditure, the rate is 25 per cent.

The 10 or 25 per cent rate may be varied as follows:

- The rate increases or reduces for chargeable periods (see 106-100) that are longer or shorter than one year.
- The 10 or 25 per cent reduces proportionately if the mineral extraction trade is carried on for only part of the chargeable period.
- The person claiming the allowance may require it to be reduced to a specified amount.
- No writing-down allowance is given if a balancing allowance is available.

Legislation: CAA 2001, s. 417(4), 418

500-350   Balancing allowances

The legislation lists various circumstances in which the entitlement is to a balancing allowance rather than to a writing-down allowance, as explained under the following headings. In all cases, there will only be a balancing allowance if there is an excess of unrelieved qualifying expenditure over any disposal receipts that need to be brought into account (see above).

As regards balancing allowances for pre-trading expenditure, see 500-150. Other balancing allowances are given under the following headings.

Permanent discontinuance of trade

A person will be entitled to a balancing allowance, rather than a writing-down allowance, if the mineral extraction trade is permanently discontinued in the chargeable period.

Legislation: CAA 2001, s. 431

Other material: CA 50460ff.

Disposal or loss of asset

A person will be entitled to a balancing allowance if he has incurred qualifying expenditure on mineral exploration and access, and:

(1)   the asset is lost;

(2)   it permanently ceases to be used for the purposes of the mineral extraction trade;

(3)   the person loses possession of the asset in circumstances where it is reasonable to assume that the loss is permanent;

(4)   the asset in question ceases to exist as such (eg because it has been destroyed or dismantled); or

(5)   the asset begins to be used wholly or partly for purposes other than those of the person's mineral extraction trade.

Legislation: CAA 2001, s. 430

Other material: CA 50500

Giving up exploration, etc

A person will be entitled to a balancing allowance if:

* he has incurred qualifying expenditure on mineral exploration and access;
* he gives up the exploration, search or inquiry to which the expenditure related; and
* he does not (whether at that time or later) carry on a mineral extraction trade that includes the working of mineral deposits to which the expenditure related.

The allowance will be due for the chargeable period in which the person gives up the exploration.

Legislation: CAA 2001, s. 427

Ceasing to work mineral deposits

A person will be entitled to a balancing allowance if:

(1)   he permanently ceases to work particular mineral deposits; and

(2)   the qualifying expenditure was incurred:

(a)   on mineral exploration and on access that related only to those deposits; or

(b)   on acquiring a mineral asset (see 500-150) that consisted of those deposits or part of them.

Where two or more mineral assets which at any time were comprised in (or otherwise derived from) a single mineral asset, then no balancing allowance is given until the person permanently ceases to work the deposits comprised in all the mineral assets concerned.

Legislation: CAA 2001, s. 428

Buildings ceasing to be used

A person will be entitled to a balancing allowance if the expenditure was qualifying expenditure under CAA 2001, s. 415 (contributions to buildings or works for benefit of employees abroad – see 500-150), and those buildings or works cease permanently to be used for the mineral extraction trade in question.

The allowance will be due for the chargeable period in which the buildings or works cease to be used.

Legislation: CAA 2001, s. 419

500-400   Ring-fence trades – first-year allowances

First-year allowances (at 100 per cent) are available for qualifying expenditure on mineral exploration and access (see 500-150) in a ring-fence trade.

CAA 2001, s. 416B sets out the general qualifying conditions for this mineral exploration and access expenditure (which, for this purpose, includes seismic data or similar mineral access results), clarifying that it must be incurred by a company wholly for use in a ring-fence trade chargeable under ICTA 1988, s. 501A. The expenditure must not fall within the following exclusions:

* acquisition of a mineral asset; or
* acquisition of an asset from a connected company.

To avoid giving unintended first-year allowances, certain provisions relating to the timing of expenditure are specifically disapplied for the purposes of determining whether first-year allowances are due. These are the provisions of CAA 2001, s. 400(4) (pre-trading expenditure) and s. 434 (mineral exploration and access expenditure where commencement of trade is imminent).

The entitlement to 100 per cent first-year allowances is for the chargeable period in which the claimant company incurs qualifying mineral exploration and access expenditure. In this case, there is specific provision which allows the claim for first-year allowances to be for either part or all of the qualifying mineral and exploration access expenditure.

There are specific restrictions to exclude certain expenditure on mineral exploration and access from the 100 per cent first-year allowance category. This is a broadly-framed anti-avoidance provision which disallows first-year allowance claims in circumstances where arrangements relating to a transaction are entered into wholly or mainly for a disqualifying purpose. The term 'arrangements' is widely drawn and it is notable that such arrangements do not have to be legally enforceable to come within the scope of the restriction here. Arrangements have a disqualifying purpose if their whole or main object is to enable a person to claim a first-year allowance or a greater first-year allowance than would otherwise arise.

Writing-down allowances for qualifying expenditure incurred prior to 17 April 2002 are given on a reducing balance basis at 25 per cent, except on mineral assets which are given at a rate of 10 per cent. Balancing adjustments are required in a number of circumstances, such as the disposal of an asset, the abandonment of a field or the cessation of trading.

Legislation: CAA 2001, s. 416A–416E

Other issues

500-500   Sales treated as being for alternative amount

The legislation uses the heading 'sales treated as being for alternative amount' to cover both an anti-avoidance rule and a tax planning opportunity. The overall effect of the legislation can be summarised as follows (but subject to the more precise details given after the summary).

- First, there are tax avoidance rules that require market value to be substituted for actual proceeds where certain transactions are designed primarily to reduce a person's tax liability.
- Second, there is a requirement to substitute market value for the actual proceeds figure in certain transactions between (broadly) connected parties.
- Third, where there is a transfer between such connected parties, but there is no tax avoidance motive, there is a chance to elect to transfer the relevant interest in an industrial building at such a value as ensures that no balancing adjustment is triggered.

In other words, there is both a danger area and a tax planning opportunity. The structure of the legislation is as follows:

- Introduction and definitions (CAA 2001, s. 567).
- Sales that have to be treated as taking place at market value (CAA 2001, s. 568).
- Election to treat sales as being for an alternative amount (CAA 2001, s. 569).
- Supplementary provisions (CAA 2001, s. 570).

These rules do not apply where CAA 2001, s. 561 (transfer of a UK trade to a company in another member State) applies (CAA 2001, s. 567(5)).

The rules apply in an identical fashion for the purposes of mineral extraction allowances as they do for industrial buildings allowances. As such, they are covered in depth in the Chapter headed 'Industrial Buildings Allowances', which begins at 300-000.

500-550   Finance leases – lump sums

The two Finance Acts of 1997 introduced a range of provisions aimed at countering situations where finance lessors could obtain tax advantages by manipulating certain reliefs and allowances. Anti-avoidance measures are aimed at leasing arrangements which provide for low initial rental payments and a compensating capital payment later on, and at those which defer the rental payments to the back end of the lease.

These rules apply for MEAs purposes as they apply to plant and machinery, and are considered in depth at 220-400ff.

500-600 Avoidance affecting proceeds of balancing event

Anti-avoidance legislation targets tax avoidance schemes that artificially depress the value of the proceeds figure so as to create or increase a balancing allowance. The rules apply for MEAs as for Agricultural Buildings Allowances (for example) and are described in detail at 429-500.

Legislation: CAA 2001, s. 570A

500-650 Transactions between connected persons

The rules applicable for IBA purposes (see 307-100) are also applicable for the purposes of MEAs. If an election under CAA 2001, s. 569 is made, the transfer takes place at an amount equal to the excess of qualifying expenditure over any allowances already made to the seller and any disposal receipts already brought into account.

500-700 Successions to trade

The provisions of CAA 2001, s. 559 and ICTA 1988, s. 343(2) (see 310-350) similarly apply for the purposes of MEAs as they apply for IBA purposes. If there is a discontinuance with sale of assets, market value will be applied if buyer and seller are connected persons or under common control (as for IBA purposes). In other cases, the sale will generally be subject to the normal rules.

If there is a discontinuance without sale of assets, there will be a deemed sale at the date of the succession at market value if the predecessor and successor are connected persons or under common control, subject to the election to avoid a balancing charge which is applicable as for IBA purposes (see 310-350). If the predecessor and successor are not so connected, etc there will be a deemed sale at the date of the succession at market value.

Legislation: CAA 2001, s. 559

500-750 Subsidies, etc

The rules denying relief where expenditure is met by others apply for MEAs purposes as for many other capital allowances, including IBAs. For a detailed description of those rules, see 301-000.

Legislation: CAA 2001, s. 532–536

500-800   Contributions to capital expenditure

Relief may be given to a person contributing to capital expenditure on mineral extraction. The first of these gives the 'general conditions' that apply to all types of capital allowance. The later section gives the rules as they specifically apply to MEAs.

The conditions for a contributor (C) to obtain allowances are as follows:

- C must have contributed a capital sum to expenditure on the provision of an asset;
- without the contribution, the expenditure would have been treated as incurred by the recipient of the contribution (R) such that R would have been entitled to capital allowances;
- C and R must not be connected persons; and
- C's contribution must be made for the purposes of a trade that is carried on, or to be carried on, either by C.

Where these conditions are met, C is treated as if the contribution were expenditure incurred by him on the provision, for the purposes of his trade, of an asset similar to that provided by means of his contribution. The asset is then deemed at all material times to be in use for the purposes of C's trade.

It is possible that C's contribution may have been made for the purposes of his own trade. If this is the case, and if the whole or a part of the trade, etc is subsequently transferred, the entitlement to the allowances is passed to the new owner of the trade. The year of transfer does not give rise to an apportionment – the whole allowance goes to the new owner if the transfer of the whole activity has taken place by the day before the end of the chargeable period. If, though, only a part of the trade or relevant activity has been transferred then allowances are made to the transferee 'to the extent that they are properly referable to the part transferred'.

Legislation: CAA 2001, s. 537–542

500-850   Interaction with capital gains legislation

Any excess of proceeds over historic cost may give rise to a chargeable gain. Any net allowances given may restrict any capital loss.

In the case of a disposal of land, any capital gains computation will bring in the undeveloped market value excluded from the MEA computations.

Legislation: TCGA 1992, s. 41(2); CAA 2001, s. 407, 427

RESEARCH AND DEVELOPMENT ALLOWANCES

Overview

525-000 Research and development allowances: overview

Research and development allowances (RDAs) are available for certain capital expenditure on research and development. Separate relief, not under the capital allowances code, is available for qualifying revenue expenditure. Both the capital allowance relief and the revenue relief are generous compared to reliefs for other types of expenditure.

The treatment of revenue expenditure is beyond the scope of this book, which is concerned entirely with the allowances available for capital expenditure. These are given where a person incurs 'qualifying expenditure' (see 525-300) on 'research and development' (see 525-200).

RDAs are given at 100 per cent and balancing charges can arise where an asset is sold, demolished or destroyed. Ceasing to use an asset for research and development purposes does not trigger a balancing charge.

RDAs are available only for traders, not for those carrying on a profession or vocation.

Legislation: CAA 2001, s. 437ff; ITTOIA 2005, s. 87; CTA 2009, s. 87

Other material: CA 60100ff.

525-100 Giving effect to allowances and charges

An allowance in respect of qualifying expenditure is treated as a trading expense. A balancing charge in respect of such expenditure is treated as a trading receipt.

RDAs are given for the chargeable period in which the expenditure is incurred, but if incurred before the trade was set up, then in the chargeable period beginning with the commencement.

Legislation: CAA 2001, s. 441(2), 447(3), 450

Definitions

525-200   Meaning of 'research and development'

Overview

The capital allowance legislation used to state that the term 'research and development' was to be defined by reference to ICTA 1988, s. 837A, but 'includes oil and gas exploration and appraisal'. However, CAA 2001, Sch. 1, Pt. 2 (which contains 'defined expressions' for capital allowance purposes) has since 6 April 2007 pointed to CAA 2001, s. 437. Although the s. 437 definition only applies 'in this Part' (i.e. for the purposes of research and development allowances and not, for example, where there are references to the concept in the IBA legislation), there now appears to be no statutory justification for looking at ICTA 1988, s. 837A for capital allowance purposes. This is because the ICTA legislation specifically applies only 'for the purposes of, and subject to, the provisions of the Corporation Tax Acts which apply this section' and there is now nothing in CAA 2001 to apply that section.

Broadly, the concept is based on generally accepted accounting practice, but subject to certain statutory provisions that can override such practice.

Expenditure on research and development includes both expenditure for carrying out research and development as such, and also the cost of providing facilities for carrying out such work. Examples of capital expenditure which may qualify for allowances include expenditure on the provision of laboratories, pilot plant and other research equipment. There is no requirement that the plant should be fixed so the provision of a car for an employee involved in research work may qualify for allowances.

However, the term excludes expenditure incurred on acquiring rights in, or rights arising out of, research and development. Thus the cost of acquiring patent rights, for example, is excluded.

No allowance is given in respect of expenditure on land, except such proportion as is attributable to existing buildings or structures already on that land, or plant or machinery which has become a fixture. Nor is an allowance given in respect of expenditure on a dwelling; where, however, less than one-quarter of the capital expenditure on a building is attributable to a part-use as a dwelling, the whole building may qualify.

In applying this 25 per cent test, any additional VAT liability or rebate (see 525-700) is to be ignored.

Legislation: CAA 2001, s. 438–440

Other material: CA 60300

Accounting practice

Research and development is initially defined to mean 'activities that fall to be treated as research and development in accordance with generally accepted accounting practice' (ie generally-accepted accounting practice with respect to accounts of UK companies – incorporated or formed under UK law – that are intended to give a true and fair view.

The meaning of 'generally accepted accounting practice' varies according to whether or not accounts are prepared in accordance with international accounting standards (IAS). For IAS accounts, the term means generally accepted accounting practice with respect to such accounts. In any other case, it means UK generally accepted accounting practice, ie generally accepted accounting practice with respect to accounts of UK companies (other than IAS accounts) that are intended to give a true and fair view. It has the same meaning in relation to the accounts of other persons, entities and foreign companies as it has for UK companies. This, effectively, grants statutory authority (for taxation purposes) to the current accounting standard covering Research and Development (Statement of Standard Accounting Practice 13).

Before 24 July 2002, 'normal accounting practice' was the term used instead of 'generally accepted accounting practice', the former expression being that which applied to the accounts of UK-registered companies (former ICTA 1988, s. 837A(5)). This formulation also effectively gave statutory authority to SSAP 13.

Legislation: ICTA 1988, s. 836A, 837A; FA 2004, s. 50

Regulations and guidelines

The Treasury is then empowered to issue regulations to override accountancy practice, so that certain activities may be declared to constitute, or not to constitute, research and development for tax purposes. These regulations may refer to (and thus enact) guidelines issued by the Secretary of State for Trade and Industry and may also include provisions that are considered 'necessary or expedient'. Such regulations have duly been issued, stating that:

'(a) activities that fall to be treated as research and development in accordance with the "Guidelines on the Meaning of Research and Development for Tax Purposes" issued by the Secretary of State for Trade and Industry on 5 March 2004, are research and development; and

(b) activities that do not fall to be treated as such in accordance with those guidelines are not research and development.'

Two sets of such guidelines have been issued by the Secretary of State for the Department of Trade and Industry for these purposes. Both sets are reproduced in full in HMRC's *Corporate Intangibles Research and Development* manual. The newer guidelines (dated 5 March 2004) are at CIRD 81900; these are intended to be simpler than the predecessor

Research and Development

guidance rather than changing the law. The newer guidelines also emphasise that R&D relief may apply to development work as well as to research expenditure.

Legislation: ICTA 1988, s. 837A(3), (4); SI 2004/712

Other material: CIRD 81900

HMRC guidance

Regrettably, HMRC has backtracked on the extent to which it is prepared to offer guidance on the meaning. The older guidelines (from the year 2000) provided a useful summary view of HMRC's interpretation of the term. But what is the legal status of those guidelines now? They are still published in the manual but the commentary on the newer (2004) guidelines states that:

> 'The 2004 guidelines are not intended to extend or restrict the activities that qualify as R&D for the purposes of the relief when compared to the 2000 guidelines. They draw on the 2000 guidelines, the commentary on those guidelines, and practical experience of those using them since the introduction of the guidelines.
>
> The clearer structure of the 2004 guidelines, and our desire to only have one authoritative text means that an extensive commentary, of the type that accompanied the 2000 guidelines, is not appropriate.'

Nevertheless, the older guidelines remain useful in practice and extracts are therefore reproduce below, with the justification (as above) that 'the 2004 guidelines are not intended to extend or restrict the activities that qualify'.

2000 guidelines (still reproduced at CIRD 81990)

Science

> 'Science is the systematic study of the nature and behaviour of the material and physical universe, and technology is the practical application of science, especially in industry and commerce. The process by which new scientific and technological information is discovered, gathered and used involving theoretical conjecture, observation, experiment, measurement and deduction, is referred to as "research and development".'

Research and development

The same paragraph of the HMRC guidance goes on to provide a copy of the DTI *Guidelines on the meaning of research and development for tax purposes*, which includes the following:

> 'The overarching definition of R&D for tax purposes follows that used for the purposes of normal accountancy practice for UK companies in Accounting Standard SSAP13. The definition in SSAP13 is itself based on the definition developed by the OECD for the purposes of statistical surveys of R&D (commonly referred to as "Frascati"). Frascati defines R&D as comprising "creative work undertaken on a systematic basis in order to increase the stock of knowledge ... and the use of this stock of knowledge to devise new applications". But the humanities are excluded because they do not fall within the fields of science or technology.
>
> ...

SSAP13 lists various activities which would normally be included in R&D:

- experimental, theoretical or other work aimed at the discovery of new knowledge, or the advancement of existing knowledge;
- searching for applications of that knowledge;
- formulation and design of possible applications for such work;
- testing in search for, or evaluation of, product, service or process alternatives;
- design, construction and testing of pre-production prototypes and models and development batches;
- design of products, processes, services or systems involving new technology or substantially improving those already produced or installed;
- construction and operation of prototypes and pilot plants.

SSAP13 lists various activities that would normally be excluded from R&D:

- testing analysis either of equipment or product for the purposes of quality or quantity control;
- periodic alterations to existing products, services or processes even though these may represent some improvement;
- operational research not tied to specific research and development activity;
- cost of corrective action in connection with break-downs during commercial production;
- legal and administrative work in connection with patent applications, records and litigation and the sale or licensing of patents;
- activity, including design and construction engineering, relating to the construction, relocation, rearrangement or start-up of facilities or equipment other than facilities or equipment whose sole use is for a particular research and development project;
- market research.'

The guidelines contain much additional material to which reference should be made in cases of doubt.

In the case of *BE Studios Ltd v Smith & Williamson Ltd*, it was held that recruitment fees did not constitute staffing costs (as defined for R&D purposes) and did not form part of the cost of ancillary activities. They were prevented from qualifying as such by the exclusion applying to 'administration and other supporting services not directly related to the R&D activity'. Indeed, the company had failed to show that it was carrying on qualifying activities of research and development at all. In the opinion of the judge, management services did not qualify for R&D tax relief because managers were not 'directly and actively engaged in such research and development'. Even if that conclusion had been wrong, there was no evidence that the relevant staff were engaged in qualifying R&D.

Legislation: ICTA 1988, s. 837A(3), (4); SI 2004/712

Cases: *BE Studios Ltd v Smith & Williamson Ltd* [2005] BTC 361

Other material: CIRD 81900, 81990

525-300   Qualifying expenditure

The following conditions must be met if expenditure is to be qualifying expenditure:

- a person must incur capital expenditure (see 102-000) on research and development (see 525-200);
- the expenditure must be undertaken directly by the person incurring the expenditure, or undertaken on his behalf (see below);
- if he is already carrying on a trade when the expenditure is incurred, then the research and development must relate to that trade ('the relevant trade'); or
- in any other case, he must – after incurring the expenditure – set up a trade (again, 'the relevant trade') that is connected with the research and development.

Where capital expenditure is incurred that qualifies in part under these conditions, a just and reasonable apportionment is to be made. The same expenditure is not to be taken into account for more than one trade.

See 525-700 for a discussion of the interaction of research and development allowances with the VAT Capital Goods Scheme.

'On his behalf'

The second bullet point above refers to the requirement that research and development must be directly undertaken by the claimant or on his behalf.

This issue was considered in *Gaspet Ltd v Elliss*. The Court of Appeal held that for research to be directly undertaken 'on behalf' of a claimant, an agency relationship (or something 'akin thereto') had to exist between the person(s) 'directly undertaking' the research and the claimant, though the relationship did not necessarily have to be contractual.

Kerr LJ thought that the person(s) 'directly undertaking' the research include those 'who, having decided that the research should be done, take steps to ensure that it is done' and 'the persons who have undertaken direct responsibility for the research and procured it to be carried out'. In this case, a company which was a member of two oil production syndicates entered into an agreement with the taxpayer company (then called Saga UK) whereby Saga UK would fund the exploration and development, and in return receive the syndicate member's share of the petroleum produced. It was common ground that expenditure on exploration for oil qualified for scientific research allowances, but it was held that Saga UK's expenditure was not incurred on research undertaken directly by Saga UK or on its behalf, and that no allowance was available.

Legislation: CAA 2001, s. 439

Cases: *Gaspet Ltd v Elliss* [1987] BTC 218

'Related to the trade'

The concept of research and development related to a trade is specifically defined to include 'research and development which may lead to or facilitate an extension of that trade'. It also includes 'research and development of a medical nature which has a special relation to the welfare of workers employed in that trade'.

As regards medical costs generally, the HMRC view is that:

'Medical research which qualifies for RDA does not include research undertaken for the benefit of the community as a whole. However, medical research undertaken for the benefit of the community as a whole may qualify for RDA as R&D which may lead to or facilitate an extension of the trade. For example, medical research undertaken by a drug company for the purpose of its trade may qualify because it is related to its trade of manufacturing drugs.'

In *Salt v Golding (HMIT)*, an author contended that in carrying on a trade of publishing works written by others, he satisfied the necessary conditions by incurring capital expenditure on research and development related to that trade. The expenditure related to computer and recording equipment.

The taxpayer was employed to lecture or teach at a film school. In his spare time, he conducted research into the technical aspects of film-making and published a book containing the result of his research. In 1994, the taxpayer published another book, not written by him but consisting of a lecture given by one Bronson Howard, who died in 1911, so that the work was out of copyright. The subject of that book was the construction of plays, which he believed to be relevant to his research on film-making.

The special commissioner said that he could not see how any of the taxpayer's research could be related to the publication of a lecture given before 1911; merely using the equipment for printing the lecture was not using it for research. Consequently, all the taxpayer's research in the year to 5 April 1994 was attributable to his profession as an author. Plant and machinery allowances were due but not scientific research allowances.

Legislation: CAA 2001, s. 439

Cases: *Salt v Golding (HMIT)* (1996) Sp C 81

Other material: CA 60400

Calculation of allowances and charges

525-400 Allowances

In contrast to the other capital allowance regimes, the research and development legislation recognises none of the following concepts:

- initial allowances;
- first-year allowances;
- writing-down allowances; or
- balancing allowances.

Instead, allowances (unnamed) are given of 100 per cent of the qualifying expenditure, less any disposal value that has to be brought into account in the same period for the same expenditure. Allowances are due for the chargeable period in which the expenditure is incurred, or – for pre-trading expenditure – for the first chargeable period in which the trade is carried on.

A person may claim a reduced allowance of any amount between zero and 100 per cent but it is not then possible to claim the remaining allowances in a subsequent chargeable period, as no writing-down or balancing allowances are given.

Planning point

On the face of it, it can never make sense to disclaim part of the 100 per cent allowance, as no further relief will be given at a later date for the same expenditure.

The catch, though, relates to balancing charges (see 525-500). These are restricted by reference to allowances claimed. If a lower allowance has been claimed, any balancing charge may accordingly be lower. Once account is taken of different tax rates, of available trading losses and perhaps of group relief claims, it may therefore make sense in certain circumstances to restrict the allowances claimed.

Legislation: CAA 2001, s. 441

525-500 Balancing charges

A balancing charge may arise if a trader has claimed research and development allowances and then makes a disposal related to the same expenditure, in a later chargeable period. (If the disposal is in the same period, it will simply reduce the allowance claimed in the first place.)

See 525-600 for the special rules relating to oil licences and 525-700 for the extension of the rules to VAT rebates received.

Balancing charges are not made if a charge is made in respect of the disposal under the provisions relating to industrial buildings (see the Chapter headed 'Industrial Buildings Allowances', which begins at 300-000) or plant and machinery (see the Chapter headed 'Plant and Machinery: Detailed Provisions', which begins at 185-000). The reference to IBAs is removed with effect from April 2011 by virtue of FA 2008, Sch. 27, para. 6.

The amount of the balancing charge is defined as the excess of the disposal value (see below) over the unclaimed allowance, but capped at the allowances made in respect of that expenditure.

Example

Researcher Ltd pays £1 million for a laboratory (excluding the part allocated to land).

Although very profitable, it benefits from group relief and is therefore able to restrict its claim to £800,000, ie leaving £200,000 unclaimed. The laboratory is sold (again, excluding the land value) for £900,000 three years later.

The balancing charge is £700,000, calculated as the excess of proceeds (£900,000) over unclaimed allowances (£200,000).

If, instead, the sale price at the later date was £1.2 million, the balancing charge would initially be calculated as £1 million, but this would be capped at £800,000, being the amount of allowances claimed in relation to the expenditure in question.

Legislation: CAA 2001, s. 442, 443(3)

Disposal events and values

A disposal value has to be brought into account if the person ceases to own the asset in question or if it is demolished or destroyed. The disposal value to be brought into account is as follows:

- if the disposal is a sale for an amount which represents at least full market value, the disposal value is the figure of net sale proceeds;
- if the asset is demolished or destroyed, the disposal value is the amount of any compensation or insurance monies received, together with any amount received for the remains of the asset; and
- in any other case, the disposal value is the open market value of the asset (except that the disposal value of an oil licence may in certain circumstances be treated as nil.

Legislation: CAA 2001, s. 443(4), 553(2)

Costs of demolition

If the person incurs demolition costs, the disposal value is to be reduced accordingly.

If the demolition costs exceed the disposal value, then the person is treated as incurring qualifying expenditure equal to the excess. This extra relief is available as long as, immediately before the demolition, the asset had not started to be used for purposes other than research and development related to the trade.

Example

Research and development expenditure of £300,000 is incurred by Scifi Ltd on the provision of research laboratories.

18 months later, the building is demolished at a cost of £120,000. Parts of the demolished building are sold for £50,000. The company continues to trade.

An allowance of £300,000 is given for the earlier accounting period.

On demolition, a further allowance of £70,000 becomes due, ie the cost of demolition of £120,000, less the proceeds of sale of £50,000. This allowance is given in charging the profits of the later accounting period.

Legislation: CAA 2001, s. 442

Research and Development

693

Other issues

525-600   Disposal of oil licences

Background

Without corrective legislation, expenditure might have been relieved twice. Both research and development allowances and mineral extraction allowances could have been made, without recapture of the former, for the same outlay. To avoid this, a disposal, including any past disposal, of an oil licence is deemed to be an event that gives rise to a clawback of research and development allowances.

An interest in an oil field consists typically of a share in the relevant licence and in the plant, etc used to extract and transport the oil or gas to a processing facility (platforms, pipelines, etc). Oil companies regularly trade these interests as they review their activities in any given oil region.

A company which has carried out exploration and appraisal work on a licensed area will have been entitled to research and development allowances for the expenditure incurred in that activity. HMRC have always believed that the licence therefore became 'an asset representing allowable research and development expenditure'; and that any sale of the licence should result in the clawback of the research and development allowances.

The oil companies take a different view. A licence, in their opinion, is a set of rights which are not altered simply because oil is discovered in the ground which is subject to those rights. The asset which does represent the research and development expenditure is the knowledge gained from the exploration and appraisal.

Where a company disposes only of part of its interest in a field, it does not part with this asset at all, although it allows its new co-owner to review the scientific data. If it disposes of its entire interest in a field, it does transfer title in the data to the buyer, but much of this data will have become publicly available under the licensing arrangements with the Department of Trade and Industry. The buyer is unlikely to pay the seller much for information which it has already acquired free of charge. As the amount of the research and development allowances clawback must equal the proceeds of the sale of the asset representing the research and development expenditure (CAA 2001, s. 443(4), 577(1)), and those proceeds will necessarily be very small, the research and development allowances clawback will be negligible or zero, in most cases.

Even though a seller of an oil field should suffer no clawback of research and development allowances, the buyer might still have a claim to mineral extraction allowances (see the Chapter headed 'Mineral Extraction Allowances', which begins at 500-000) for the seller's expenditure on exploration and appraisal. For while the licence may not 'represent' the exploration and appraisal expenditure, the value of the rights conferred by the licence will be attributable to the value of the oil in the ground covered by the licence. The discovery of these reserves will in turn be attributable to the seller's 'expenditure . . . on mineral exploration and access' (CAA 2001, s. 407(3): see 500-150), ie the exploration and appraisal expenditure.

While the oil industry was aware of this apparent asymmetry, it was, by consensus, not exploited. Sale and purchase documentation would provide that the buyer would only claim mineral extraction allowances if the seller was prepared to suffer a clawback of research and development allowances. Relief for the same expenditure was thus not claimed twice and the parties to the sale of any field had the flexibility to accommodate their respective tax positions in the sale price. The Revenue apparently acquiesced in this approach as any loss of tax was a matter of timing only and it facilitated a market in oil fields, which is felt to be in the public interest.

It is a reasonable inference that the need for the change to the rules was attributable to a breakdown in the consensus between the oil companies and that the Revenue had been exposed to some double claims.

Accordingly, any disposal of an interest in an oil licence, past or future, whose value is attributable to expenditure eligible for research and development allowances, is deemed to be an occasion on which an asset representing research and development expenditure ceases to belong to the seller (CAA 2001, s. 408(1), 443(2), 552, 555). As a result, s. 441(1) (see 525-400) will require the seller to include in its computation of trading income a trading receipt equal to the value of the licence attributable to the expenditure eligible for research and development allowances. Typically, this value is agreed between the parties and recorded in the sale and purchase documents. The rule applies to licences anywhere in the world.

For sales taking place on or after 13 September 1995, mineral extraction allowances are not given on an amount greater than that for which research and development allowances were allowed (CAA 2001, s. 408).

Legislation: CAA 2001, s. 408, 443

Election for research and development allowances not to be recaptured

Parties who had treated a transfer of an oil licence entered into before 13 September 1995 as not involving a clawback of research and development allowances for the seller may elect to preserve that treatment. The transferor must give notice, with the consent of the transferee, to the Board of the amount of the value given for the interest in the licence which 'is attributable to allowable exploration expenditure incurred by the transferor'.

That amount, which can be any figure including nil, will be subject to a research and development allowances clawback on the transferor and available to the transferee for a mineral extraction allowances claim. The amount shown in the notice cannot be less than any trading receipt already included in respect of the transfer by the transferor in any computation of trading profits submitted to HMRC, unless the Board agree. HMRC can allow as mineral extraction allowances a lower figure than that shown in the notice: presumably to prevent inflated claims where there is no immediate cost to the transferor whose research and development allowances clawback is covered by trading losses.

Should the transferee not consent to the notice, the tribunal may nevertheless give effect to it if they are satisfied that the parties had entered into the transfer on the 'mutual understanding' that the amount shown in the notice did reflect a part of the value of the licence attributable to the transferor's allowable exploration expenditure. For this purpose, the rules on procedure for apportionments (CAA 2001, s. 562) are extended to cover research and development allowances.

An election, once made, is irrevocable and cannot be varied. Detailed rules apply to determine whether or not the transfer did occur before 13 September 1995. This covers the situation where the parties have agreed unconditionally to a transfer which nevertheless requires, before it can proceed, the approval of the Department of Trade and Industry or of the transferor's joint venture partners.

Legislation: CAA 2001, Sch. 3, para. 91

525-700 Sales between connected persons

Where the seller and buyer are connected persons or are under common control, a sale of research and development expenditure is taken at market value for the purposes of any balancing adjustment, even if the sale is at an undervalue or overvalue.

To the extent that capital expenditure on research and development is not already covered by 100 per cent allowances, where there is no significant element of gaining a tax advantage, the transferor and transferee may generally elect by notice in writing to the inspector to treat the sale as taking place at the tax written-down value, if that is lower than market value. The election also has the effect of treating the buyer and the seller as one continuous owner as regards any balancing charge for events after the date of the sale, ie in determining allowances to be clawed back, etc.

Where it appears with respect to a sale (or with respect to transactions of which the sale is one) that the sole or main benefit which might have been expected to accrue to any of the parties was the obtaining of certain tax advantages, the provisions which apply for industrial buildings allowances purposes (see the Chapter headed 'Industrial Buildings Allowances', which begins at 300-000) apply equally for the purposes of research and development expenditure.

Legislation: CAA 2001, s. 567–569

525-800   Interaction with capital goods scheme

A person may incur allowable research and development expenditure and incur an additional VAT liability while he still owns the asset representing such expenditure. That liability is capital expenditure incurred on the research and development (CAA 2001, s. 447(1), (2)).

The whole of a dwelling is for research and development if not more than one-quarter of the capital expenditure is justly apportioned to the construction or acquisition of the dwelling (CAA 2001, s. 438(3)–(5)). The one-quarter test disregards any additional VAT liability or rebate (s. 438(6)).

Any VAT rebate, which arises while the person still owns the asset, is taxed as a trading receipt for the period in which the rebate is made, unless it is brought into account in making an allowance or charge (CAA 2001, s. 443(6), 448). If the person no longer carries on the trade, the rebate accrues for tax purposes immediately before the trade ceased.

Any VAT rebate, which arises while the person still owns the asset and which is taxed as a trading receipt under CAA 2001, s. 448, reduces the amount of the expenditure and allowance for the purposes of CAA 2001, s. 442 (s. 449).

When deciding if an asset ceased to belong to a person on or after or before the period for which an allowance is given, an allowance due to an additional VAT liability under CAA 2001, s. 447(2) is disregarded for the purpose of s. 441(1), 442(1)–(3), 443(1). However, this disallowance does not affect the amount of the expenditure or allowance for those same subsections.

See 120-200 for the meaning of 'additional VAT liability' and 'additional VAT rebate'.

Legislation: CAA 2001, s. 446

Research and Development

KNOW-HOW ALLOWANCES

Overview

550-000   Overview

The term 'know-how' is defined for capital allowance purposes to mean certain industrial information and techniques. See 550-100 for a full definition.

Know-how allowances are not given for expenditure incurred by companies from 1 April 2002. Such expenditure is instead dealt with under the *Finance Act* 2002 rules relating to intellectual property.

Subject to these points, capital allowances are available under CAA 2001, Pt. 7 where a person incurs qualifying capital expenditure on the acquisition of know-how. The allowances are only available to traders.

Allowances are given in calculating the profits of a trade (see 550-050). The calculation of allowances and charges used (broadly) to mirror the rules applying for plant and machinery writing-down allowances, but when the rate of writing-down allowances reduced for plant and machinery purposes from April 2008, the changes did not have effect for the calculation of know-how allowances. See 550-250 for full details.

Know-how is specifically stated to be property for capital allowance purposes. As such, references in the *Capital Allowances Act* 2001 to the purchase and sale of property include the acquisition and disposal of know-how.

Legislation: CAA 2001, s. 453ff.

Other material: CA 70001, 70020, 74500

550-050   Giving effect to allowances and charges

A trader gives effect to allowances in calculating the profits of the trade. So:

- any allowance under the know-how code is treated as an expense of the trade; and
- any balancing charge is treated as a trading receipt.

Legislation: CAA 2001, s. 463

Definitions

550-100   Definition of know-how

The term 'know-how' is defined to mean:

'any industrial information and techniques likely to assist in:

- manufacturing or processing goods or materials;
- working a source of mineral deposits (including searching for, discovering or testing mineral deposits or obtaining access to them), or
- carrying out any agricultural, forestry or fishing operations.'

Although they are not specifically applied for know-how purposes, the provisions and case law referring to the manufacture or processing of goods and materials for IBA purposes (see the Chapter headed 'Industrial Buildings Allowances', which begins at 300-000) may be of interest in relation to the first part of this definition.

For these purposes:

'"mineral deposits" include any natural deposits, including geothermal energy, capable of being lifted or extracted from the earth. A source of mineral deposits includes a mine, oil well or source of geothermal energy. Searching for, discovering or testing mineral deposits or obtaining access to them are working a source of mineral deposits.'

Legislation: CAA 2001, s. 452

Other material: CA 70010

Exclusion of commercial know-how

HMRC take the view that allowances are available only on industrial and technical, but not commercial, know-how, as originally explained in a *Revenue Interpretation* (IR Int. 46):

'The terms of this definition accordingly restrict allowances to capital expenditure incurred in acquiring information relevant only to industrial or technical processes. Information relevant to commercial processes is not included.

Our view is that know-how which does not assist directly in the manufacturing and processing operations is commercial know-how. Examples include information about marketing, packaging or distributing a manufactured product. Such information does not assist directly in the manufacture of that product. Rather it is concerned with selling the product once it has been manufactured.

As such it is not in our view within the definition of know-how in [s. 452(2)] and so cannot qualify for allowances under [that section].'

A similar point is now made in HMRC's *Capital Allowances* manual:

'Things like market research, customer lists and sales techniques are commercial know-how. They do not assist directly in manufacturing or processing operations. Rather, they are concerned with selling goods or materials once they have been manufactured. They are not industrial information or techniques likely to assist in the manufacture of goods or materials or in the working of a mine or in agricultural operations. This means that commercial know-how is not within the definition of know-how in CAA and so it does not qualify for capital allowances.

You may get a claim from a person who pays for a franchise agreement that capital allowances are due because all or part of the payment is for know-how. All or part of the payment may be for know-how but it is not likely to be the type of know-how that qualifies for capital allowances. A franchise agreement is essentially a licence to operate a business. Any know-how that is transferred by a franchise agreement is more likely to be commercial know-how than industrial information and techniques. If so it will not qualify for capital allowances.'

Legislation: CAA 2001, s. 452

Other material: CA 70030

550-150 Qualifying expenditure

Capital expenditure (see 102-100) is qualifying expenditure for these purposes if it is incurred on the acquisition of know-how by a person:

- who is carrying on a trade at the time of the acquisition and who acquires the know-how for use in that trade;
- who acquires the know-how and subsequently sets up and commences a trade in which it is used;
- who acquires the know-how together with the trade (or part of a trade) in which it was used and the parties to the acquisition make an election under ITTOIA 2005, s. 194 or CTA 2009, s. 178 (consideration for know-how on disposal of trade to be treated as payment for goodwill unless parties otherwise elect – see 525-300); or
- who acquires the know-how together with the trade (or part of a trade) in which it was used and the trade in question was, before the acquisition, carried on wholly outside the UK (again, see 525-300).

A person incurring expenditure on know-how before setting up and commencing the trade in which it is used is treated as incurring it on that setting up and commencement.

Legislation: CAA 2001, s. 454

550-200 Excluded expenditure

Expenditure is not qualifying expenditure to the extent that it is already deductible for tax in some other way.

Expenditure is not qualifying expenditure in certain instances where there is a connection between the buyer and the seller of the know-how. Specifically, no allowances are given 'where the seller controls the buyer or the buyer controls the seller or some other person controls both the buyer and the seller'.

If a person disposes of a trade or part of a trade together with know-how used in that trade, any consideration received by him is normally treated (for both the buyer and seller) as a payment for goodwill by virtue of ITTOIA 2005, s. 194(3) or CTA 2009, s. 178(3). Where this is the case, such expenditure is not taken into account for capital allowances purposes.

There are two exceptions (ITTOIA 2005, s. 194(4), (5), CTA 2009, s. 178(4), (5)) to the general rule, as follows:

- the rule does not apply if a joint election is made by both persons concerned within two years of the disposal; and
- the rule does not apply to the buyer if the trade was, before the acquisition, carried on wholly outside the UK.

Where either of these exceptions applies, the expenditure can qualify under the know-how capital allowances rules.

Legislation: CAA 2001, s. 452(2), 454–455

Other material: CA 71000

Calculation of allowances and charges

550-250   Pooling

Overview

No first-year allowances are given for know-how expenditure.

All qualifying expenditure must be put into a single pool, but with a separate pool for each trade. The plant and machinery concepts of short and long-life assets do not apply for know-how expenditure.

Writing-down allowances are given based on a pool of qualifying expenditure. The method of calculating allowances may be summarised as follows:

- allowances are normally given each year at 25 per cent of the value of the pool, on a reducing balance basis;
- a balancing charge will arise if a disposal value to be brought into account exceeds the expenditure left in the pool;
- a balancing allowance arises only on permanent discontinuance of the trade; and

- unlike the system for plant and machinery allowances, the disposal value is not restricted to original cost.

Legislation: CAA 2001, s. 456

Detail

The technical detail underlining this summary is given below.

Allowances are calculated by comparing – for each pool of qualifying expenditure – the values of 'AQE' and 'TDV' (these abbreviations being used in the legislation) where:

- AQE is the amount of 'available qualifying expenditure' in the pool for the period in question; and
- TDV is the 'total of any disposal values' that must be brought into account in the pool for the period in question (see below).

AQE consists of two elements:

- any unrelieved qualifying expenditure that is brought forward in the pool from the previous chargeable period; plus
- any qualifying expenditure properly allocated to the pool in the period in question.

Unrelieved qualifying expenditure will arise where, in the previous period, AQE exceeded TDV. The figure of unrelieved expenditure will be the amount of that excess, less the writing-down allowance (if any) given in that earlier period (CAA 2001, s. 461). (No amount of unrelieved qualifying expenditure is carried forward from the final chargeable period, defined to mean the chargeable period in which the trade is permanently discontinued (s. 457(5).)

Qualifying expenditure is allocated to the pool as long as:

- it has not been taken into account in determining qualifying expenditure of an earlier period; and
- the expenditure has been incurred by the end of the chargeable period. (See 102-000 for details of when expenditure is treated as incurred.)

TDV is the total of any disposal values to be brought into account. A person must bring a disposal value into account for the chargeable period in which he sells know-how on which (whether in that or any earlier chargeable period) he has incurred qualifying expenditure. The disposal value for these purposes is the figure of net sale proceeds, so far as they consist of capital sums.

In the case of know-how allowances, the disposal value is not restricted to cost.

No disposal value needs to be brought into account if the sale consideration is treated as a goodwill payment under ITTOIA 2005, s. 194 or CTA 2009, s. 178 (disposal as part of disposal of the whole or part of the trade).

Know-How

If AQE exceeds TDV, then the person is entitled to a writing-down allowance of 25 per cent; but:

- the 25 per cent increases or reduces for chargeable periods that are longer or shorter than one year;
- the 25 per cent reduces proportionately if the trade is carried on for only part of the chargeable period;
- the person claiming the allowance may require it to be reduced to a specified amount; and
- no writing-down allowance is given in the final chargeable period.

Example

Zeus has a pool of qualifying expenditure brought down from the previous chargeable period, amounting to £20,000.

He incurs capital expenditure on know-how of £10,000 in the year.

His maximum claim for the current year will be £7,500 ((£20,000 + £10,000) × 25%).

However, he knows that in the following year he will be a higher-rate taxpayer and so he decides to restrict his allowances this year to just £2,000. As such, his computation will be as follows:

	£
Unrelieved qualifying expenditure b/fwd	20,000
Qualifying expenditure in year	10,000
AQE	30,000
Allowance (restricted)	(2,000)
Unrelieved qualifying expenditure c/fwd	28,000

Assuming that there is neither an acquisition nor a disposal of know-how in the following year, Zeus will be able to claim allowances next year of £7,000. If he had claimed maximum allowances this year, the unrelieved qualifying expenditure carried forward would have been £22,500 and the maximum relief next year would have been £5,625.

In the final chargeable period, a balancing allowance is given if the qualifying expenditure for that period exceeds any disposal value to be brought into account.

If TDV exceeds AQE, the person is subject to a balancing charge. This applies equally in the final chargeable period as in any other period.

Legislation: CAA 2001, s. 457–462

Other material: CA 71300

550-300   Capital or revenue

As noted above, only capital expenditure is qualifying expenditure for capital allowance purposes. Similarly, disposal values need to be brought into account – for the purposes of calculating TDV – only 'so far as they consist of capital sums'. It follows that the distinction between capital and revenue expenditure is an important one.

The term 'capital expenditure' is defined for capital allowance purposes generally at CAA 2001, s. 4(2) (see 102-000).

The HMRC *Capital Allowances* manual contains useful commentary on the question of whether know-how expenditure is revenue or capital, including the following:

- payments or royalties received for imparting or disclosing know-how that has been accumulated in the course of a trade should normally be treated as trading receipts, whether one-off or recurring. This category would cover, for example, manufacturing techniques, technical knowledge and secret processes. See the House of Lords decision in *Jeffrey v Rolls-Royce Ltd*;
- similarly, payments made to acquire know-how wholly and exclusively for the purposes of a trade are normally revenue deductions allowable under the normal rules for calculating business profits;
- a payment for know-how that is made in shares may nevertheless be properly classified as a revenue receipt. See *Thomsons (Carron) Ltd v IR Commrs*;
- know-how may give rise to a capital receipt if 'disposed of as one element of a comprehensive arrangement under which a trader effectively gives up an established business in a particular territory'. See, for example, *Evans Medical Supplies Ltd v Moriarty* ;
- a know-how agreement may contain a 'keep out covenant' whereby the seller of the know-how gives an undertaking which protects the buyer against competition from the vendor or from other licensees. Any payment received for such an undertaking (whether or not legally valid) is treated as part of the consideration for the know-how (ITTOIA 2005, s. 192(3), (4), CTA 2009, s. 176(3), (4)). Such a payment is normally treated as capital expenditure (CA 73000, based on *Associated Portland Cement Manufacturers Ltd v IR Commrs* (1945) 27 TC 103);
- by contrast, know-how disposed of in the course of a continuing trade will normally produce a trading receipt. If taxable under neither the capital allowance rules nor as a trading receipt, such proceeds will be taxed by virtue of ITTOIA 2005, s. 583 or (for corporation tax purposes) CTA 2009, s. 910.

Cases: *Associated Portland Cement Manufacturers Ltd v IR Commrs* (1945) 27 TC 103; *Evans Medical Supplies Ltd v Moriarty* (1958) 37 TC 540; *Jeffrey v Rolls-Royce Ltd* (1962) 40 TC 443; *Thomsons (Carron) Ltd v IR Commrs* (1976) 51 TC 506

Other material: CA 72000ff.

Other issues

550-350   Partnership changes and successions to a trade

Special rules apply to deal with partnership changes and successions to a business. These apply for know-how purposes as they do for the purposes of calculating IBAs. The rules are described in detail at 310-350.

Legislation: CAA 2001, s. 557–559

550-400   Non-residents

Payments made by a non-resident to a person carrying on a trade in the UK for the use of UK intellectual property may in law be payments the source of which is in the UK, but nevertheless are treated, for double taxation relief purposes, as foreign source income, except to the extent that they represent consideration for services (other than merely incidental services) rendered in the UK by the recipient to the payer.

Other material: ESC B8

550-450   Divers

As a result of an agreement between the Revenue and the Association of Offshore Diving Contractors, certain costs of training divers will qualify as expenditure on know-how.

Other material: CA 74000

PATENT ALLOWANCES

Overview

575-000 Overview

Capital allowances are available when a person incurs qualifying expenditure (see 575-250) on the purchase of 'patent rights' (see 575-100).

The legislation is contained in CAA 2001, Pt. 8.

Technically, patent allowances are available for both income tax and corporation tax purposes. However, corporation tax relief for such expenditure incurred by companies since 1 April 2002 will in practice be given instead under the regime applying for expenditure on intangible assets.

The system of giving patent allowances is in essence similar to that for plant and machinery, in that:

- expenditure is normally pooled; and
- allowances are given at an annual rate of 25 per cent on a reducing balancing basis.

Allowances are only made to a person if he is carrying on a trade or if any income from the rights would be otherwise liable to income tax or corporation tax.

A separate form of relief is available for costs incurred, (eg by an inventor) in obtaining a patent, including both patent fees and related expenses.

575-050 Giving effect to allowances and charges

Allowances and charges for traders

An allowance in respect of qualifying trade expenditure (see 575-250) is treated as a trading expense. A balancing charge in respect of such expenditure is treated as a trading receipt.

Legislation: CAA 2001, s. 478

Allowances and charges for non-traders – income tax

Allowances for qualifying non-trade expenditure are deducted from or set off against the person's income from patents for the year, and are given effect at Step 2 of the calculation in ITA 2007, s. 23. Any excess allowances are carried forward to be set against such income of future years.

Patent

Any balancing charge in respect of qualifying non-trade expenditure is assessed to income tax.

Legislation: CAA 2001, s. 479

Allowances and charges for non-traders – corporation tax

As already noted, corporation tax relief for expenditure incurred by companies since 1 April 2002 on patents will normally be given under the regime applying for expenditure on intangible assets, rather than by way of capital allowances. Allowances may still be available, however, for expenditure incurred before that date.

Allowances for qualifying non-trade expenditure are deducted from the company's income from patents for the accounting period in question. Any excess allowances are carried forward to be set against such income of future years, and must be used as soon as there is income from patents against which they can be set.

Any balancing charge in respect of qualifying non-trade expenditure is taxed as income from patents.

Legislation: CAA 2001, s. 480

Definitions

575-100 Patent rights

Patent rights

The term 'patent rights' is defined as 'the right to do, or authorise the doing of, anything which would, but for that right, be an infringement of a patent'.

Legislation: CAA 2001, s. 464

Future patent rights

Where a person incurs expenditure on obtaining a right to acquire future patent rights, this is treated as if it were expenditure incurred on the actual purchase of patent rights.

If a person incurs expenditure on obtaining a right to acquire future patent rights, and subsequently does acquire those rights, then the expenditure is treated as if it were on the purchase of those rights.

For these purposes, 'a right to acquire patent rights' means 'a right to acquire in the future patent rights relating to an invention in respect of which a patent has not yet been granted'.

Legislation: CAA 2001, s. 465

575-150 Licences

A person who acquires a licence in respect of a patent is treated as purchasing patent rights.

Similarly, a person who grants a licence in respect of a patent is treated as selling part of the patent rights, except that where a person (entitled to patent rights) grants an exclusive licence; this will be treated as selling the whole of those rights.

For these purposes, an exclusive licence is 'a licence to exercise those rights to the exclusion of the grantor and all other persons for the period remaining until the rights come to an end'.

When the Crown or a foreign government uses a patent, it is treated as using it under a licence. Sums paid in respect of such use are treated as paid under licence.

Legislation: CAA 2001, s. 466; 482

575-200 Income from patents

The term 'income from patents' is defined to include:

- any royalty or other sum paid in respect of the use of a patent;
- any balancing charges to which the person is liable; and
- any amounts on which tax is payable under ITTOIA 2005, s. 587, 593 or 594, or under CTA 2009, s. 912 or 918 (taxation of receipts from sale of patent rights).

Legislation: CAA 2001, s. 483

575-250 Qualifying expenditure

To qualify for patent allowances, expenditure must be either 'qualifying trade expenditure' or 'qualifying non-trade expenditure'.

Legislation: CAA 2001, s. 467

Qualifying trade expenditure

Qualifying trade expenditure is defined as capital expenditure (see 102-000) that is incurred by a person on the purchase of patent rights (see 575-100) for the purposes of a taxable trade carried on by that person. The same expenditure cannot be taken into account for the purposes of more than one trade.

Patent

Expenditure incurred for the purposes of a trade by a person about to carry it on is treated as incurred on the first day on which he does carry it on, unless before that time he has sold the patent rights.

Legislation: CAA 2001, s. 468

Qualifying non-trade expenditure

Qualifying non-trade expenditure is capital expenditure which a person incurs on the purchase of patent rights where:

- the expenditure is not qualifying trade expenditure; but
- any income that the person receives in respect of the rights is liable to tax.

Legislation: CAA 2001, s. 469

Calculation of allowances and charges

575-300   Overview

No first-year allowances are given for patent expenditure.

To calculate capital allowances, and any balancing charge, qualifying expenditure is pooled.

All of a person's non-trade expenditure goes into one pool. Qualifying trade expenditure goes into a separate pool with, as appropriate, a different pool for each trade.

Allowances are then calculated separately for each pool. The concepts of short- and long-life assets do not apply for the purposes of calculating patent allowances.

The method of calculating allowances may be summarised as follows:

- allowances are normally given each year at 25 per cent of the value of the pool, on a reducing balance basis;
- a balancing charge will arise if a disposal value to be brought into account exceeds the expenditure left in the pool, but subject to a cap; and
- a balancing allowance arises only on permanent discontinuance of the trade.

The technical detail underlining this summary is given below.

Allowances are calculated by comparing – for each pool of qualifying expenditure – the values of 'AQE' and 'TDR' (these abbreviations being used in the legislation) where:

- AQE is the amount of 'available qualifying expenditure' in the pool for the period in question: (see below); and

- TDR is the 'total of any disposal receipts' that must be brought into account in the pool for the period in question (see below).

Legislation: CAA 2001, s. 470, 471

575-350   Allowable qualifying expenditure

Allowable qualifying expenditure

AQE consists of two elements:

- any unrelieved qualifying expenditure that is brought forward in the pool from the previous chargeable period; plus
- any qualifying expenditure properly allocated to the pool in the period in question.

Unrelieved qualifying expenditure will arise where, in the previous period, AQE exceeded TDR. The figure of unrelieved expenditure will be the amount of that excess, less the writing-down allowance (if any) given in that earlier period. (No amount of unrelieved qualifying expenditure is carried forward from the final chargeable period.)

Qualifying expenditure is allocated to the pool as long as:

- it has not been taken into account in determining qualifying expenditure of an earlier period;
- the expenditure has been incurred by the end of the chargeable period (see 102-000 for details of when expenditure is treated as incurred);
- the rights have not come to an end, without being revived, before the accounting period in question; and
- the rights have not been disposed of before the accounting period in question.

Legislation: CAA 2001, s. 473–475

575-400   Total disposal receipts

Total disposal receipts

TDR is the total of any disposal receipts to be brought into account. There are two different types of receipt that may need to be taken into account for these purposes, but subject to a limit on the overall amount of the disposal value (see below).

First, a person must bring a disposal value into account for the chargeable period in which he sells the whole or any part of any patent rights on which he has incurred qualifying expenditure.

Secondly, an amount may need to be brought into account by virtue of FA 1997, Sch. 12, para. 11 (finance lease or loan: receipt of major lump sum) (see 575-550).

Patent

The disposal value for these purposes is the figure of net sale proceeds, so far as they consist of capital sums.

The aggregate disposal value in relation to any particular rights cannot exceed the expenditure incurred by the taxpayer or, in relation to a purchase from a 'connected person' (see 120-200), that incurred by such person if greater (or the greatest in relation to a chain of such purchases). This is simply illustrated by the following HMRC example:

> 'David, Stephen and Graham are connected. David buys patent rights for £11,000. He sells them to Stephen for £10,000 who then sells them to Graham for £9,000. If Graham sells the rights for £12,000 the limit on his disposal value is £11,000, the amount David paid for the rights. It is not £9,000, the amount Graham paid to Stephen for the rights.'

Where the disposal value does exceed the expenditure incurred by the taxpayer, the excess may be chargeable to tax under ITTOIA 2005, s. 587 or CTA 2009, s. 912: see 575-600. Once more, this is well illustrated with a simple HMRC example:

> 'Eric spends £10,000 on buying patent rights and claims capital allowances. He grants a licence to Geoff for £6,000. He has to bring a disposal value of £6,000 to account then. If Eric grants a licence next year to Jack for £6,000 the disposal value which he has to bring to account is £4,000. The original capital expenditure was £10,000 and £6,000 was treated as disposal value when Eric granted the licence to Geoff. This means that any later disposal value is restricted to £4,000 (= £10,000 − £6,000). The remaining £2,000 he received when he granted the licence to Jack is assessed to income tax.'

Legislation: CAA 2001, s. 476–477

Other material: CA 75120, 75200

575-450   Writing-down allowances

Writing-down allowances

If AQE exceeds TDR, then the person is entitled to a writing-down allowance of 25 per cent, but:

- the 25 per cent increases or reduces for chargeable periods (see 106-100) that are longer or shorter than one year;
- the 25 per cent reduces proportionately if, in the case of qualifying trade expenditure (see 575-250) the trade is carried on for only part of the chargeable period;
- the person claiming the allowance may require it to be reduced to a specified amount; and
- no writing-down allowance is given in the final chargeable period.

Planning point

It may make sense to restrict allowances in one year if a higher rate of tax relief will be available in the later year, or if there are unused personal allowances in the earlier year.

Example

Apollo has a pool of qualifying expenditure brought down from the previous chargeable period, amounting to £20,000.

He incurs capital expenditure on patents of £10,000 in the year.

His maximum claim for the current year will be £7,500 ((20,000 + 10,000) × 25%).

However, he knows that in the following year he will be a higher rate taxpayer and so he decides to restrict his allowances this year to just £2,000. As such, his computation will be as follows:

	£
Unrelieved qualifying expenditure b/fwd	20,000
Qualifying expenditure in year	10,000
AQE	30,000
Allowance (restricted)	(2,000)
Unrelieved qualifying expenditure c/fwd	28,000

Assuming that there is neither an acquisition nor a disposal of patent rights in the following year, Apollo will be able to claim allowances next year of £7,000. If he had claimed maximum allowances this year, the unrelieved qualifying expenditure carried forward would have been £22,500 and the maximum relief next year would have been £5,625.

Legislation: CAA 2001, s. 471(4), 472

575-500   Balancing allowances and charges

Balancing allowances and charges

In the final chargeable period, a balancing allowance is given if AQE exceeds TDR, ie if the qualifying expenditure for that period exceeds any disposal value to be brought into account.

If TDR exceeds AQE, the person is subject to a balancing charge equal to the excess. This applies equally in the final chargeable period as in any other period.

The 'final chargeable period', for a pool to which qualifying trade expenditure (see 575-250) has been allocated, means the chargeable period in which the trade is permanently discontinued.

Patent

713

For a pool to which qualifying non-trade expenditure is allocated, the 'final chargeable period' is defined as the chargeable period in which the last of the patent rights on which the person has incurred qualifying non-trade expenditure either comes to an end (without those rights being revived) or is wholly disposed of.

Legislation: CAA 2001, s. 471, 472

575-550　Major lump sum (finance lease or loan)

Where any 'major lump sum' is paid in respect of certain leasing arrangements, a balancing charge arises equal to the smaller of the major lump sum or the capital allowances given.

A 'major lump sum' is one which, while not itself rent, falls for accounting purposes, in accordance with normal accountancy practice, to be treated partly as repayment of a finance lease or loan, and partly as a return on investment. The leasing arrangements affected are, broadly, finance leases as understood according to SSAP 21. This provision forms part of a set of rules designed to align the tax liability of the lessor under a finance lease with the accountancy treatment, on the basis that a finance lease is in essence a loan secured on the leased asset.

An identical rule applies where allowances have been claimed related to plant or machinery (see 575-300) or to mineral extraction.

Legislation: FA 1997, Sch. 12, para. 11(8).

Other material: *Finance Leasing* manual FLM 35.17ff.

Other issues

575-650　Successions to a trade

Where there is a succession which is not a discontinuance by virtue of the rules regarding partnership changes or company reconstructions without significant change of ownership, capital allowances are calculated as if the persons carrying on the trade before and after the transfer were the same persons.

Legislation: CAA 2001, s. 557ff.

575-700　Sales between connected persons and tax-structured transactions

Where there is a sale of patent rights between connected persons, or where it appears that the sole or main benefit expected to accrue to the parties was the obtaining of writing-down allowances or balancing allowances, the amount of expenditure to be brought into account by the buyer is limited as follows:

(1) where a disposal value is brought into account by the seller for capital allowances purposes, that disposal value;

(2) where the seller is taxed on a sum under ITTOIA 2005, s. 587 or CTA 2009, s. 912, that sum; and

(3) in any other case, the smallest of:

    (a) the price which the rights would have fetched if sold in the open market;

    (b) the amount of capital expenditure incurred by the seller on acquiring the rights; or

    (c) if capital expenditure was incurred by a person connected with the seller on acquiring the rights, that capital expenditure.

Legislation: CAA 2001, s. 481

DREDGING ALLOWANCES

Overview

600-000   Overview

Dredging allowances are available for certain dredging work that is 'done in the interests of navigation'.

Relief may be available under CAA 2001, Pt. 9 where two conditions are met:

(1)   a person carries on a qualifying trade (see 600-150); and

(2)   qualifying expenditure (see 600-150) has been incurred on dredging.

Writing-down allowances are normally given at a rate of four per cent on a straight line basis (see 600-250 for more details).

Balancing allowances are given in certain circumstances (see 600-300). There are no balancing charges.

There are no first-year or initial allowances.

Allowances may be restricted where there are contributions or subsidies (see 600-350). Conversely, a person who makes a capital contribution to dredging expenditure may be able to claim dredging allowances (see 600-350).

Legislation: CAA 2001, s. 484

600-050   Giving effect to allowances and charges

A trader gives effect to allowances in calculating the profits of the trade. So any writing-down or balancing allowance is treated as an expense of the trade.

Legislation: CAA 2001, s. 489

Definitions

600-100   Dredging

For capital allowance purposes, the term 'dredging' does not include anything done other than in the interests of navigation.

Subject to this qualification, dredging includes 'the removal of anything forming part of, or projecting from the bed of, the sea or of any inland water'. It does not matter what means are used for the removal. Nor does it matter if the thing that is removed was wholly or partly above water.

The term 'dredging' also covers the widening of inland waterways.

The HMRC interpretation of the definition is that dredging includes 'the deepening or .widening of a channel for the passage of ships, whether in tidal waters or in an inland waterway. Dredging does not include normal maintenance work on an existing channel'.

Legislation: CAA 2001, s. 484

Other material: CA 80200

600-150   Qualifying expenditure

Qualifying expenditure is capital expenditure (see 102-000) incurred for the purposes of a qualifying trade by the person carrying on that trade, but only where one of the following conditions is met:

- the dredging is for the benefit of vessels coming to, leaving or using a dock or other premises occupied by the person for the purposes of the qualifying trade; or
- the person carries on a qualifying trade within CAA 2001, s. 484(2)(a) (the maintenance or improvement of the navigation of a harbour, estuary or waterway – see below).

Where capital expenditure is incurred partly for the purposes of a qualifying trade and partly for other purposes, a 'just and reasonable apportionment' must be made to determine how much of the expenditure is treated as qualifying for these purposes.

Where dredging is carried on only as part of a trade or undertaking, then that part is treated as a separate trade for the purposes of making such an apportionment.

Dredging carried on by a harbour authority for the purposes of keeping its channels clear for navigation is generally considered as revenue expenditure (see *Whelan v Dover Harbour Board*).

Legislation: CAA 2001, s. 485

Cases: *Whelan v Dover Harbour Board* (1934) 18 TC 555

600-200   Qualifying trade

A 'qualifying trade' is a trade or undertaking which (or part of which) either:

(1) consists of the maintenance or improvement of the navigation of a harbour, estuary or waterway (CAA 2001, s. 484(2)(a)); or

(2) is listed in Table A or B of CAA 2001, s. 274 (qualifying trades for IBA purposes – see 301-500) (CAA 2001, s. 484(2)(b)).

For the purposes of determining what constitutes qualifying expenditure, it may be necessary to distinguish between the expenditure under (1) and that under (2), as explained above.

HMRC accepts that the operation of a marina will normally fall within the definition of a 'dock undertaking' (see 301-500) for IBA purposes. In such a case, the trade will qualify for the purposes of claiming dredging allowances.

HMRC gives the example of a furniture manufacturer who occupies a dock which is used to import materials and to export finished products. As the manufacture of furniture is a qualifying trade for IBA purposes, capital expenditure incurred on deepening the dock can qualify for dredging allowances.

A further Revenue example concerns a ship operator. The operator uses the ship partly for transporting goods (a qualifying trade for IBA purposes) and partly for providing pleasure cruises (not a qualifying trade). Expenditure on dredging the dock would have to be apportioned between the two parts of the trade, and allowances would be given only on the qualifying part.

Legislation: CAA 2001, s. 484(2)

Other material: CA 80500

Calculation of allowances and charges

600-250   Writing-down allowances

To claim writing-down allowances, the person must at some time in the chargeable period be carrying on the qualifying trade for which the qualifying expenditure was incurred.

Capital expenditure incurred before the start of trading, but with a view to carrying on a trade, is treated as incurred on the day the trading actually begins.

Capital expenditure incurred in connection with a dock or other premises not yet occupied by the taxpayer for the purposes of a qualifying trade (but with a view to so occupying the premises) is similarly treated as incurred on the first day on which he both carries on the trade and occupies the dock, etc.

An annual writing-down allowance of four per cent of expenditure is given on a straight-line basis. However, this is subject to the following points:

- a lower figure of two per cent was given for expenditure incurred before 6 November 1962. As a result, there may still be open claims in relation to expenditure incurred in (for example) 1960, but not for expenditure incurred in (say) 1970;
- the figure of four (or two) per cent is proportionately increased or decreased if the chargeable period is not of exactly one year;
- the person claiming the allowance may require it to be reduced to a specified amount;
- the writing-down allowances must not in total exceed (whether for the same person or for two or more persons) the amount of the expenditure;
- no writing-down allowances can be given from 25 years after the start of the first day of the chargeable period in which the expenditure was incurred (50 years for expenditure incurred before 6 November 1962; and
- no writing-down allowance is given if the person is entitled to a balancing allowance in the same chargeable period in relation to the same expenditure.

Planning point 1

Reducing a claim may have the effect that not all expenditure will be relieved. Indeed, this will nearly always be the case, unless there is eventually a balancing allowance (but see the second planning point, below). This is because allowances will continue to be given at four per cent per year but will eventually cease because of the rule that restricts allowances after 25 years.

Example 1

Joshua's company draws up accounts to 31 December each year. The company incurred expenditure of £100,000 in March 1983 and claimed allowances of £4,000 each year. As the company was making losses, a decision was taken in 1998 to disclaim the allowances for two years.

On 31 December 2007, the writing-down period comes to an end. Allowances of £92,000 (23 × £4,000) have been given. The balance of £8,000 must be written off.

Where there has been a change of accounting date, and no allowances have been disclaimed, an apportionment of the final period will be required to ensure that the total allowances given do not exceed the expenditure incurred.

Example 2

Tanya's company also draws up accounts to 31 December each year. The company also incurred expenditure of £100,000 in March 1983 and claimed allowances of £4,000 each year. No allowances have been disclaimed but the accounting date is changed to 30 September in 2006 by virtue of a nine-month accounting period (for which allowances of just £3,000 will have been due).

In the accounts to 30 September 2008, the allowances would be restricted to £1,000. This is on the grounds that of the 12-month accounting period to 30 September 2008; three months fall within the 25-year writing-down period (so $3/12$ of the normal allowance of

£4,000 gives the final writing-down allowance of £1,000). Total allowances given will equal the expenditure incurred of £100,000.

Planning point 2

It seems that disclaimed allowances may be partially recovered by having a change of accounting date.

Suppose that Tanya's company (in Example 2 above) had disclaimed allowances totalling £8,000 in earlier years.

Based on the wording of the legislation, it would appear to be possible to argue that full writing-down allowances are available for the final year. If £4,000 can be claimed for that year, then this will effectively recapture £3,000 of the allowances that were not claimed previously.

The matter is not entirely free from doubt and, to the author's knowledge, has not been tested, but it appears to him to be justified on a strict interpretation of the legislative wording.

Legislation: CAA 2001, s. 486–487; Sch. 3, para. 103

600-300   Balancing allowances

A balancing allowance may be given for the chargeable period in which a qualifying trade is sold or permanently discontinued.

The amount of the allowance will be the total of the qualifying expenditure incurred, less all allowances already given (including any initial allowance or writing-down allowance under predecessor legislation and irrespective of whether effect has been taken of any allowance against profits, etc).

The term 'permanent discontinuance' does not include a deemed discontinuance under ITTOIA 2005, s. 18 or under CAA 2001, s. 577(2A) (companies beginning or ceasing to carry on trade).

The HMRC manual also adds the following instruction to Revenue officers:

'You should treat a sale of the trade as a permanent discontinuance unless

- the trade is treated as continuing under s. 343(2) ICTA (company reconstruction without change of ownership) or
- the trade is treated as continuing under section 561 CAA (transfer of UK trade to another EU company) or
- the sale is a connected person sale or a sole or main benefit sale [discussed below].'

Legislation: CAA 2001, s. 488

Other material: CA 81600

Anti-avoidance measures

A sale does not, for this purpose, include certain sales between connected persons. The test is identical to the control test used for IBA purposes (see 307-050).

Similarly, a sale does not for this purpose include a transaction that fails the 'sole or main benefit test'. Once more, this is identical to that used for IBA purposes (see 307-050). However, as HMRC acknowledges: 'it is difficult to use the main benefit provisions if the taxpayer can come up with good commercial reasons for the transaction'.

Other material: CA 13100

Other issues

600-350   Contributions and subsidies

The general provisions relating to contributions and subsidies (see 115-000) do not apply to dredging.

A person is not treated as having incurred expenditure for the purposes of any trade insofar as it is met directly or indirectly by the Crown, or by any government or public or local authority in or outside the UK. Similarly, a person's expenditure is to be reduced by any capital sums contributed by another person for purposes other than those of the recipient's trade. Any such amount received by the trader is therefore to be deducted before calculating dredging allowances.

A person who contributes a capital sum to another person's expenditure on dredging is treated as having incurred capital expenditure on dredging and is, therefore, entitled to allowances if he is carrying on a qualifying trade.

Legislation: CAA 2001, s. 532, 543

600-400   Successions to trades

The provisions which ensure that, where there is a partnership change or company reconstruction without change of ownership, capital allowances are calculated as if the persons carrying on the trade before and after were the same person (see 120-000) apply for the purposes of dredging allowances as they apply for IBA purposes.

Legislation: ICTA 1988, s. 343(2); CAA 2001, s. 557–559

ASSURED TENANCY ALLOWANCES

Overview

625-000   Overview

Relief under this scheme is available only for expenditure incurred (or treated as incurred) before 1 April 1992. Allowances are still given under the code, however, and the way this works is therefore considered in more depth at 625-100.

Allowances are given by reference to construction costs.

A qualifying dwelling-house must have been let under an assured tenancy, but not all dwelling-houses which are let on an assured tenancy are qualifying dwelling-houses (see 625-150).

A dwelling-house may be a flat or a maisonette contained in a larger building. The relevant interest in a dwelling-house which is part of a larger building is the part of the relevant interest in the larger building which subsists in the dwelling-house. For example, the relevant interest in a flat contained in a block of flats whose relevant interest is the freehold, is the freehold interest in that flat.

Many of the principles are similar to those applying for IBA purposes, including the idea of the 'relevant interest' (see 625-150) and the 25-year cut-off period for making any allowances or charges. Unlike IBAs, however, allowances under this code are not being phased out.

Legislation: CAA 2001, s. 491(1)

Other material: CA 85500

625-050   Giving effect to allowances and charges

A person who is carrying on a UK property business gives effect to allowances in calculating the profits of that business. So:

- any allowance is treated as an expense of the business; and
- any balancing charge is treated as a business receipt.

If a person is not carrying on a UK property business, then an allowance or charge is given effect in calculating the profits of such a business that he is deemed to be carrying on.

Legislation: CAA 2001, s. 529

625-100   Historical background

The assured tenancy scheme enables certain approved bodies to let newly-built property at rents not restricted by the provisions of the Rent Acts. The scheme was introduced by the *Housing Act* 1980 and applies to buildings which have at all times been occupied under an assured tenancy.

A special regime of capital allowances for dwelling-houses let on assured tenancies was introduced in 1982. The law is now found in CAA 2001, Pt. 10. Under this regime, allowances are available where an approved body incurs capital expenditure on the construction of a building which is to be or to include a qualifying dwelling-house.

This system of allowances was effectively brought to an end by the *Housing Act* 1988. However, there are measures to protect allowances given and to ensure that allowances continue for companies which were approved at 15 March 1988. If the tenancy falls to be regarded as an assured tenancy for the purposes of the *Housing Act* 1988 (irrespective of whether it fell previously within the definition of an assured tenancy in the *Housing Act* 1980, s. 56), relief by way of writing-down allowances or balancing allowances (and any balancing charge) is only available (or made) in respect of expenditure:

- incurred or contracted for before 15 March 1988 by an 'approved company' or by a person selling the 'relevant interest' (see 625-150) in the building to an approved company before any of the dwelling-houses come into use; or
- incurred by an approved company before 1 April 1992 where the approved company bought or contracted to buy the relevant interest in the building before 15 March 1988.

Legislation: CAA 2001, s. 491

Definitions

625-150   Qualifying dwelling-house

Allowances are available by reference to certain capital expenditure on 'qualifying dwelling-houses'. Subject to the matters below, a 'qualifying dwelling-house' means a dwelling-house let on a tenancy which is for the time being an assured tenancy within the meaning of the *Housing Act* 1980, s. 56 or the *Housing Act* 1988 (but not an assured shorthold tenancy).

A dwelling-house which has been a qualifying dwelling-house will be regarded as a qualifying dwelling-house at any time when:

- it is for the time being subject to a regulated tenancy or a housing association tenancy (as defined in the *Rent Act* 1977); and
- the landlord under that tenancy either is an approved body (for the purposes of the *Housing Act* 1980, s. 56(4)) or was an approved body but has ceased to be such for any reason.

A dwelling-house will only be a qualifying dwelling-house if the landlord is a company and either is, for the time being, entitled to the 'relevant interest' (see below) in the dwelling-house or is the person who incurred the capital expenditure on the construction of the building in which the dwelling-house is comprised.

It will not be a qualifying dwelling-house if any of the following applies:

- the landlord is an approved housing association or is a self-build society;
- the landlord and the tenant are connected persons (see 120-200);
- the tenant is a director of a company which is, or is connected with, the landlord;
- the landlord is a close company and the tenant is a participator in that company or an associate of such a participator; or
- the tenancy is entered into as part of an arrangement between the landlords (the owners) of different dwelling-houses under which one landlord takes a person as a tenant in circumstances where, if that person was the tenant of a dwelling-house let by the other landlord, that dwelling-house would not be a qualifying dwelling-house by virtue of the connected persons or close company provisions above.

Legislation: CAA 2001, s. 490, 505, 531

Temporary and permanent disuse

The occurrence of a dwelling-house ceasing altogether to be used is an event giving rise to a balancing adjustment.

A dwelling-house will not be regarded as ceasing altogether to be used when it falls temporarily out of use. Where, immediately before any period of temporary disuse, it is a qualifying dwelling-house, it will be regarded as continuing to be a qualifying dwelling-house during the period of temporary disuse.

If a dwelling-house ceases to be a 'qualifying dwelling-house' otherwise than by reason of a sale or transfer of the 'relevant interest', the relevant interest will be treated as having been sold, at the time the dwelling-house ceases to be a qualifying dwelling-house, for the price it would have fetched if sold in the open market.

Although the commencement of non-qualifying use of a dwelling-house following qualifying use results in a balancing adjustment, there may be non-qualifying use before qualifying use. This affects the calculation of any such adjustment on a later event (see below).

Legislation: CAA 2001, s. 506

625-200   Relevant interest

The term 'relevant interest' is used in relation to writing-down allowances and to certain events crystallising a balancing adjustment. The 'relevant interest' means:

Assured Tenancy

- in relation to any expenditure incurred on the construction of a building, the interest in that building to which the person who incurred the expenditure was entitled when he or she incurred it; and
- in relation to a dwelling-house comprised in such a building, that interest, to the extent that it subsists in the dwelling-house, which is the relevant interest in relation to the capital expenditure incurred on the construction of that building.

Where a body is entitled to two or more interests in the building, when it incurs expenditure on the construction of the building, and one of those interests is reversionary on all the others, that interest will be the relevant interest. See 304-500 for a discussion of what is meant by reversionary interest.

A person who incurs expenditure on constructing a building, and who is entitled to an interest in the building on or as a result of that construction, is treated as having that interest at the time the expenditure is incurred, even though – at the time – there is no completed building as such.

Where a lease is created out of the relevant interest, that interest will not cease to be the relevant interest merely because of the creation of the lease. A 'lease' includes an agreement for a lease where the term to be covered by the lease has begun, or a tenancy. Where the relevant interest is a leasehold interest (or, in Scotland, the interest of a tenant in property subject to a lease) and is extinguished because of its surrender or on the body entitled acquiring the interest which is reversionary on it, the interest into which that leasehold merges (or, in Scotland, the interest of the landlord in the property which is the subject of the lease) will thereupon become the relevant interest.

Legislation: CAA 2001, s. 495–500, 531

625-250   Qualifying expenditure

Allowances are made by reference to the capital expenditure incurred on the construction of a building (or part of a building, incorporating an appropriate dwelling-house. Capital expenditure may be treated as having been incurred on construction in certain cases in which a building is bought unused.

Expenditure incurred on the acquisition of land or rights in or over land does not form part of the construction expenditure.

Expenditure on repairs may be treated as construction expenditure.

Legislation: CAA 2001, s. 493, 501, 571

Qualifying expenditure attributable to a dwelling-house

A building will often be sub-divided into flats, etc particularly in the assured tenancy market. This provides difficulty as to the allocation of expenditure between parts of the building. Rules determine a statutory basis for the allocation.

Subject to the timing of expenditure, below, the 'capital expenditure attributable to a dwelling-house' is as follows:

(1) if the building is a 'single qualifying dwelling-house', all the capital expenditure is attributable to that dwelling-house; and

(2) in the case of a 'dwelling-house which forms part of a building', and subject to the relevant limit (see below), the aggregate of:

    (a) that proportion of the capital expenditure which is properly attributable to the construction of the dwelling-house; and

    (b) where there are common parts of the building, such proportion of the capital expenditure on those common parts as it is just and reasonable to attribute to the dwelling-house and which does not exceed 10 per cent of that proportion of the capital expenditure referred to in (a) above.

The 'relevant limit' is £60,000 if the dwelling-house is in Greater London and £40,000 if it is elsewhere.

'Common parts' means common parts of the building which:

- are not intended to be in a separate occupation (whether for domestic, commercial or other purposes); but
- are intended to be of benefit to some or all of the qualifying dwelling-houses included in the building.

The capital expenditure on any such parts of the building is so much of the expenditure as it is just and reasonable to attribute to those parts.

The appropriate capital expenditure is limited to that incurred or treated as incurred (on acquisition of an unused building: see below) between 10 March 1982 and 31 March 1992.

Legislation: CAA 2001, s. 491(1), 511

Buildings bought unused

Where expenditure is incurred on the construction of a building and the 'relevant interest' (see 625-150) is sold (or otherwise transferred) before use of any dwelling-house, the purchaser will be deemed to have incurred, on the date when the price becomes payable, the actual expenditure on construction incurred or the net price paid by him for the interest, whichever is the less. If the relevant interest is sold more than once before use, then the preceding provision will have effect only in relation to the last of those sales.

The expenditure actually incurred on construction is left out of account for the purpose of allowances to or charges on the constructor.

The person acquiring the relevant interest is entitled to writing-down allowances equal to four per cent of the capital expenditure, proportionately reduced or increased for a 'chargeable period' of less or more than one year.

Acquisitions from developers

If the vendor is in the trade of constructing and selling buildings, and sells the interest in the course of that trade, the purchaser will obtain allowances based on the net purchase price if the builder sells the 'relevant interest' before the building is used. If there are intervening purchasers before the building is brought into use, the ultimate purchaser will obtain allowances based on the lesser of the price paid by him and the price paid by the first purchaser.

HMRC illustrates this with the following example:

'Example

Keith Plc is a property developer.

It builds a block of flats for letting under the assured tenancy scheme on land which it owns for £2 million. Before any of the flats have been used it sells the block to Sam Ltd for £2.5 million excluding the cost of the land. Sam Ltd sells the block to Tony Plc for £2.7 million excluding the cost of the land. Tony Plc decides that it does not want to be a landlord and sells the block to Paul Ltd for £2.6 million excluding the cost of the land.

Paul's qualifying expenditure is £2.5 million because that is the lower of the price paid to Keith Plc (£2.5 million) and the price Paul Ltd paid (£2.6 million).'

Legislation: CAA 2001, s. 502, 503

Other material: CA 85250

Calculation of allowances and charges

625-300   Writing-down allowances

A person holding the 'relevant interest' (see 625-150) in relation to certain expenditure on a building may be entitled to capital allowances in respect of any qualifying dwelling-houses incorporated within it.

A writing-down allowance for a 'chargeable period' is made where:

- qualifying expenditure has been incurred on a building;
- a person, who is or has been an approved body, is entitled to the relevant interest in that expenditure at the end of that chargeable period; and

- at the end of that chargeable period, the building is or includes a 'qualifying dwelling-house' or two or more qualifying dwelling-houses.

Legislation: CAA 2001, s. 507(1)

Writing-down allowances before a sale of the relevant interest

The writing-down allowance is made to that body for that chargeable period. Where there has been no sale of the relevant interest, the allowance is normally equal to four per cent of the qualifying expenditure attributable to the dwelling-house, but:

- for an accounting period of less or more than a year, that percentage will be proportionately reduced or increased;
- in no case may the amount of the writing-down allowance exceed the unexpired 'residue of expenditure' (see below); and
- a person may choose to claim a reduced allowance.

Legislation: CAA 2001, s. 507–510

Writing-down allowances following a sale of the relevant interest

Where the relevant interest in a building incorporating a qualifying dwelling-house is sold or otherwise transferred, and the sale gives rise to a balancing allowance or balancing charge, future writing-down allowances for the purchaser are calculated as follows.

The new owner will be allowed writing-down allowances on the residue of expenditure (see below) immediately after the sale, spread over the number of years remaining until the 25th anniversary of first use. For those familiar with the IBA regime, the principle is the same. For any chargeable period, the allowance can be worked out by using the following formula:

$$\text{Residue of expenditure (RQE)} \times \frac{\text{length of chargeable period (A)}}{\substack{\text{length of unexpired period of 25 years} \\ \text{from first use (B)}}}$$

In no case may the writing-down allowance exceed the unexpired 'residue of expenditure' (see below). As before, a person may choose to claim a reduced allowance.

Legislation: CAA 2001, s. 507–510

625-350 Balancing adjustments

Overview

A balancing allowance or charge may be made where any of the events listed below occur while it is a qualifying dwelling-house. The allowance or charge will be made to or on the

Assured Tenancy

person entitled to the 'relevant interest' immediately before the event occurs and will be made for the chargeable period in which the event occurs.

The events referred to above are:

- where the relevant interest in the dwelling-house is sold or transferred;
- where that interest, being a leasehold interest (or, in Scotland, the interest of a tenant in property subject to a lease) or interest under an agreement for lease (where the term to be covered by the lease has begun) or tenancy, comes to an end otherwise than on the person entitled to it acquiring the interest of the landlord in property subject to a lease (though special provisions apply to leases held over); or
- where the dwelling-house is demolished or destroyed or, without being demolished or destroyed, ceases altogether to be used.

No balancing allowance is available, or charge made, where the event occurs more than 25 years after the dwelling-house was first used.

Legislation: CAA 2001, s. 513–514

Sale proceeds

The level of proceeds (for convenience, collectively referred to below as 'sale proceeds') to be taken into account is determined by the nature of the balancing event, as follows.

Sale of the relevant interest

As would be expected, the basic rule is that if an asset is sold, then the disposal value equals the net proceeds of that sale. There is no definition of 'net proceeds' but a common-sense approach means that it is the amount of proceeds after deducting any costs of sale.

The demolition or destruction of the dwelling-house

If the dwelling-house is totally demolished, then three elements need to be added together to produce the proceeds figure for capital allowance purposes:

- the net proceeds of sale of the remains of the dwelling-house; plus
- any insurance payment made in respect of the demolition or destruction; plus
- any other compensation which is capital in nature and which is received in respect of the demolition or destruction.

The dwelling-house ceases altogether to be used

In this case, the proceeds figure is taken to be the amount of any capital compensation, of whatever description, received by the person in question in respect of the event.

Legislation: CAA 2001, s. 515 – Table

Qualifying dwelling house throughout period of ownership

The rules are relatively straightforward where the dwelling-house has been a qualifying dwelling-house throughout the 'relevant period of ownership' (see below).

A comparison is made between the sale proceeds figure (if anything) and the residue of qualifying expenditure immediately before the event.

If the residue exceeds any proceeds figure, then there is a balancing allowance equal to the difference. Conversely, any excess of proceeds over residue will produce a balancing charge, but subject to an overall limit on the amount of that charge.

The amount on which a balancing charge is made may not exceed the amount of any initial allowance, together with any writing-down allowances made. Such allowances are taken as made for chargeable periods which end on or before the date of the event giving rise to the charge.

Legislation: CAA 2001, s. 516, 518

Not a qualifying dwelling house throughout period of ownership

Different rules apply where the property has not been a qualifying dwelling-house throughout the 'relevant period of ownership' (see below).

Where the sale proceeds are not less than the 'starting expenditure attributable to the dwelling-house' (see below), a balancing charge will be made and the amount on which it is made will be an amount equal to the 'relevant allowances'.

Where there are no sale proceeds, or where those proceeds are less than the starting expenditure attributable to the dwelling-house (see below), then:

- if the adjusted net cost of the dwelling-house exceeds the relevant allowances, a balancing allowance will be made equal to the excess; and
- if the adjusted net cost of the dwelling-house is less than the relevant allowances, a balancing charge will be made equal to the shortfall.

'The relevant period of ownership' here means the period beginning at the time when the dwelling-house was first used for any purpose and ending with the event giving rise to the balancing allowance or balancing charge. However, where there has been a sale of the dwelling-house after first use and before that event, the relevant period will begin on the day following that sale or, if there has been more than one such sale, the last such sale.

'The starting expenditure' here means:

- where the adjustment applies to the person incurring the expenditure (or deemed to have incurred it on the purchase of an unused building): the capital expenditure incurred (or deemed to have been incurred) on the construction of the dwelling-house; or
- where the person to or on whom the balancing allowance or balancing charge falls to be made is not the person who incurred (or is deemed to have incurred) that expenditure: the residue of that expenditure (see below) at the beginning of the relevant period (see above),

together (in either case) with any amount to be added to the residue of that expenditure in respect of the net cost of demolition.

The 'adjusted net cost' is the expenditure incurred in respect of the dwelling-house, less any sale, insurance, salvage or compensation received, time-apportioned to reflect the period of qualifying use during the whole of the relevant period, ie:

$$(S - P) \times \frac{I}{R}$$

where

S is the starting expenditure attributable to the dwelling-house;
P is the proceeds from the balancing event;
I is the number of days in the relevant period of ownership on which the dwelling house was a qualifying dwelling-house; and
R is the number of days in the whole of the relevant period of ownership.

HMRC illustrates this with the following example:

'Example

A dwelling house cost £30,000 to buy unused in 1985:

It was brought into use on 1 January 1986 but it only became a qualifying dwelling house on 1 January 1988.

It was a qualifying dwelling house until it was sold, for £6,000, on 31 December 2001, that is for 14 years out of the 16 years of ownership.

The adjusted net cost is (£30,000 − £6,000) £24,000 × 14/16 = £21,000.'

The provisions relating to non-qualifying use do not override those relating to a sale between connected persons or person under common control if it is deemed to be made of an amount equal to the residue of expenditure (see below).

Legislation: Legislation: CAA 2001, s. 517, 520–522, 569(5)

Other material: CA 87000

625-400   Residue of expenditure

Any 'expenditure attributable to a qualifying dwelling-house' (see 625-250) will be treated as written off to the extent and as at the time specified below, and references to the residue of any such expenditure are construed accordingly.

Any initial allowance made is treated as written-off when the qualifying dwelling-house is first used and any writing-down allowance made for any chargeable period will be treated as written-off at that time.

Where a writing-down allowance is made for any chargeable period and at the same time an event occurs which gives rise or may give rise to a balancing allowance or balancing charge, the writing-down allowance is deducted before computing any balancing adjustment. It therefore reduces the residue of expenditure immediately before the balancing event.

Where, at any time after the date of first use of the building, there has been a period for which the whole or part of the building was not a qualifying dwelling-house, notional writing-down allowances for that period are deducted in arriving at the residue of expenditure.

Where a balancing allowance is made on a sale, there will be treated as written off as at the time of the sale the amount by which the residue of the expenditure before the sale exceeds the net proceeds of the sale.

Where a balancing charge is made on a sale, the residue of the expenditure will be deemed to be increased as at the time of sale by the amount on which the charge is made. The residue immediately after the sale is restricted to the net proceeds of sale, if less. This can only occur where the provisions of CAA 2001, s. 526 have been applied.

Where the demolition of a dwelling-house gives rise, or might give rise, to a balancing allowance or charge, the excess of any cost of demolition to the person incurring it over any monies received for the remains will be added to the residue, immediately before the demolition, of the expenditure attributable to the dwelling-house; where this provision applies, the cost or net cost will not be treated as expenditure incurred in respect of any other property by which that property is replaced.

Legislation: CAA 2001, s. 512, 524–528

Other issues

625-450   Termination of leases

Subject to the matters below, the termination of a lease will result in a balancing adjustment on the person who had the interest under the lease.

Where, with the consent of the lessor, a lessee of any building remains in possession after the termination of the lease without a new lease being granted to him, that lease will be deemed to continue as long as he remains in possession.

Similarly, where, on the termination of a lease, a new lease is granted to the lessee in pursuance of an option available to him under the terms of the first lease, the provisions relating to dwelling-houses will have effect as if the second lease were a continuation of the first lease. These continuation provisions may be relevant in relation to any construction expenditure (including repairs) incurred by the lessee and, in particular, events giving rise to balancing adjustments in respect thereof.

Assured Tenancy

Where, on the termination of a lease, the lessor pays any sum to the lessee in respect of a building comprised in the lease, the provisions regarding dwelling-houses will have effect as if the lease had come to an end by reason of its surrender in consideration of the payment.

Where, on the termination of a lease, another lease is granted to a different lessee and, in connection with the transaction, that lessee pays a sum to the person who was the lessee under the first lease, the provisions regarding dwelling-houses will have effect as if both leases were the same lease and there had been an assignment thereof by the lessee under the first lease to the lessee under the second lease in consideration of the payment. This will clearly affect the allowances available to the second lessee.

These provisions apply to any agreement for a lease where the term to be covered by the lease has begun, or to any tenancy, as they apply to a lease.

Legislation: CAA 2001, s. 499, 571

625-500   Apportionments

A just and reasonable apportionment is to be made if the sum paid for the sale of the relevant interest in a building is attributable partly to assets qualifying for relief under the Assured Tenancy Allowances scheme, and partly to other assets, (eg for the land on which the dwelling stands). Proceeds from balancing events, eg insurance proceeds on destruction of the property, are also to be apportioned in this way.

Legislation: CAA 2001, s. 530

625-550   Transfers treated as sales

Any transfer of the relevant interest in a dwelling-house, otherwise than by way of sale, will normally be treated as a sale of that interest at market value.

Legislation: CAA 2001, s. 573

625-600   Successions to trades, etc

Effects of successions

Where a person ceases to carry on activities relating to a trade, another person may begin to carry on those activities.

The effect on the first person may be such that he is regarded as having ceased a trade, whilst the effect on the second person may be that he is regarded as commencing a trade. Either party may be regarded as continuing to carry on the same trade as he did previously, notwithstanding the depletion in its activities or the increase in its activities. If the second person previously carried on a trade, that trade may be treated as ceasing with the addition of the new activities.

Alternatively, the effect may be that there is merely a change in the persons carrying on a trade or part of a trade: the second person succeeds to the trade (or part) previously carried on by the first person. The second person may carry on the trade (or part) as a separate trade or as part of a larger trade. Whether there is a succession will clearly depend upon the facts and circumstances.

A succession does not involve a cessation of a trade and a commencement of a trade but may be treated for certain purposes as if it did so. For example, a transfer of a trade from one company to another company (a succession by implication) is normally treated as a deemed discontinuance and commencement but will not be so treated if there is no significant change of ownership.

If there is a partnership succession which is not a discontinuance, capital allowances in respect of the majority of categories of assets are generally calculated as if the persons carrying on the trade before and after the transfer of trade were the same persons. However, in relation to dwelling-houses let on assured tenancies, no specific provisions are given in relation to successions.

Where there is a company reconstruction without significant change of ownership, capital allowances are calculated as if the persons carrying on the trade before and after the transfer were the same persons unless the successor is a dual-resident investing company.

Legislation: ICTA 1988, s. 343(2)

Discontinuance with sale of assets

Where there is a discontinuance with a sale of assets, different rules apply, depending on whether buyer and seller are connected:

- if the buyer and seller are connected persons or are under common control, market value will be applied, subject in certain cases to a possible election to avoid any balancing charge arising; and
- if the buyer and seller are not so connected, etc or if no election is possible, provided it is not a tax-structured transaction (sole or main benefit test: see below), the sale will be subject to normal rules for calculating any balancing charge or allowance.

Discontinuance without sale of assets

Where there is a discontinuance without a sale of assets, the treatment again depends on whether the predecessor and successor are connected persons:

- if the predecessor and successor are connected persons or under common control, there will be a deemed sale at the date of the succession at market value if there is a transfer, other than a sale, of the 'relevant interest' in the dwelling-house but subject to a possible election to avoid any balancing charge arising by reference to the deemed sale; and

735

- if the predecessor and successor are not so connected, etc, there will be a deemed sale at the date of the succession at market value if there is a transfer, other than a sale, of the relevant interest in the building, etc. However, an election may be made to avoid any balancing charge arising, since the transfer is treated as if it fell within; ie as if it were a transaction between connected persons or persons under common control. This is subject to the proviso that the transfer does not involve the obtaining of a tax advantage.

Legislation: CAA 2001, s. 567–568, 573–574

625-650   Sales, etc between persons under common control

Sales between connected persons, etc

A sale of a dwelling-house, where the buyer and the seller are connected persons, is taken at market value for the purposes of any balancing adjustment, even if the sale is at an undervalue or overvalue. Transfers of the 'relevant interest' in dwelling-houses otherwise than at open market value are treated as sales for these purposes.

Where there is no significant element of obtaining a tax advantage, the transferor and transferee may elect, by notice in writing to the inspector, to treat the sale as taking place at an amount equal to the residue of expenditure immediately before sale, if that is lower than market value. In the case of a qualifying dwelling-house, no election may be made unless both the seller and the buyer are approved bodies (see 625-150). An election also cannot be made where the transferee is a dual-resident investing company.

Legislation: CAA 2001, s. 567–573

Sales, etc between persons under common control

A sale of a dwelling-house where the seller and the buyer are under 'common control' is taken at market value even where the sale is at an undervalue or overvalue.

In this context, the term 'common control' is taken to refer to the 'control' of one body of persons by another person or of two bodies of persons by another person: for a body corporate, by reference to the influence on its affairs through shares, votes or regulatory documents or, for a partnership, by reference to the rights to the greater part of the assets or income. In most cases, such control will also be an indication that the persons are connected.

Legislation: CAA 2001, s. 568(1)(a), 574

625-700   Tax avoidance provisions

Tax advantage

Special provisions apply where it appears with respect to a sale (or with respect to transactions of which the sale is one) that the sole or main benefit which might have been expected to accrue to any of the parties was the obtaining of an allowance, the obtaining of a deduction, the obtaining of a greater allowance or deduction or the avoidance or reduction of a charge.

It should be noted that motive does not form part of this test, ie it is not strictly a tax avoidance provision.

Although reference is specifically made to sales and not to other transfers, transfers of the 'relevant interest' in dwelling-houses are treated as sales.

In such a case, a transfer of a dwelling-house is taken at market value, even where it is sold at a price other than the open market price. However, no election may be made to transfer at an amount equal to the residue of expenditure immediately before the sale.

Legislation: CAA 2001, s. 567–569, 573

Other provisions

Further anti-avoidance legislation is aimed at tax avoidance schemes that artificially depress the value of the proceeds figure so as to create or increase a balancing allowance.

For these purposes, a 'tax avoidance scheme' is defined as 'a scheme or arrangement the main purpose, or one of the main purposes, of which is the obtaining of a tax advantage by the taxpayer'.

Where, as a result of such a scheme, the proceeds figure to be brought into account is less than it would otherwise have been, the taxpayer is not entitled to any balancing allowance at all. In other words, the legislation does not merely prevent an abuse but also imposes a penalty. Furthermore, the residue of expenditure immediately after the event is calculated as if the balancing allowance had been given.

Legislation: CAA 2001, s. 570A

Assured Tenancy

Case Table

(References are to paragraph numbers)

	Paragraph
A	
Abbott v Albion Greyhounds (Salford) Ltd (1945) 26 TC 390	260-060
Abbott Laboratories Ltd v Carmody (1968) 44 TC 569	260-700; 303-550
Anchor International Ltd v IR Commrs [2005] BTC 97; (2003) Sp C 354 . . .	260-790; 260-930
Anglo-Persian Oil Co Ltd v Dale [1932] 1 KB 124; (1931) 16 TC 253	102-100
Associated Portland Cement Manufacturers Ltd v Kerr (1946) 27 TC 103	550-300
Associated Restaurants Ltd v Warland [1989] BTC 58	260-280; 260-780
Atherton v British Insulated and Helsby Cables Ltd [1926] AC 205; 10 TC 155	102-100
Attwood v Anduff Car Wash Ltd [1996] BTC 44	260-250; 260-260; 260-540; 260-610; 260-700; 262-230; 262-530; 262-740

	Paragraph
B	
Baldwins Industrial Services plc and Barr Ltd (TCC December 2002)	185-150
Barclays Mercantile Industrial Finance Ltd v Mawson [2003] BTC 81	155-100; 160-000
Barclays Mercantile Industrial Finance Ltd v Melluish [1990] BTC 209	220-000
Ben-Odeco Ltd v Powlson (1978) 52 TC 459	260-720; 262-040
Benson v Yard Arm Club Ltd (1979) 53 TC 67	180-100; 180-300; 261-300; 262-480; 262-590; 262-950
BE Studios Ltd v Smith & Williamson Ltd [2005] BTC 361	525-200
Bestway (Holdings) Ltd v Luff [1998] BTC 69	260-310; 301-600; 301-650; 302-750
BMBF (No. 24) Ltd v IR Commrs [2003] BTC 178	220-200
Bostock v Totham [1997] BTC 257 . . .	300-750

	Paragraph
Bourne v Auto School of Motoring (Norwich) Ltd (1967) 44 TC 164 . . .	200-060; 260-240
Bourne v Norwich Crematorium Ltd (1967) 44 TC 164	261-020; 301-600
Boys' and Girls' Welfare Society MAN/96/1041	262-600
Bradley v London Electricity plc [1996] BTC 95	260-610; 262-450; 301-900
Bridge House (Reigate Hill) Ltd v Hinder (1971) 47 TC 182	262-460
Brown v Burnley Football & Athletic Co Ltd (1980) 53 TC 357	160-600; 210-150; 260-790; 262-440; 262-550; 262-590; 303-550
Buckingham v Securitas Properties Ltd (1979) 53 TC 292	301-600; 302-000
Bullcroft Main Collieries Ltd v O'Grady (1932) 17 TC 93	303-550

	Paragraph
C	
Cardiff Rating Authority v Guest Keen Baldwin's Iron and Steel Co Ltd (1949) 1 KB 385	262-590; 262-950; 300-600
Carr v Sayer [1992] BTC 286	260-150; 260-610; 260-740; 261-200; 262-230; 262-400; 262-450; 263-000; 301-600
Carter v Standard Life [1915] 30 DLR 492	302-825
Cattermole v Corporation of Reigate (1941) 24 TC 481	262-920
Chambers (GH) (Northiam Farms) Ltd v Watmough (1956) 36 TC 711	201-120
Clark v Perks [2001] BTC 336	235-100
Cole Bros Ltd v Phillips (1982) 55 TC 188; [1982] BTC 208	160-500; 180-050; 180-150; 180-250; 180-300; 210-150; 260-060; 260-280; 260-300; 260-600; 260-630; 260-900; 261-320; 261-330; 262-250; 262-450; 262-500; 262-720; 262-730; 262-920; 262-960
Cooke v Beach Station Caravans Ltd (1974) 49 TC 514	260-030; 260-050; 260-290; 260-790; 260-900; 262-600

Paragraph

Copol Clothing v Hindmarch [1984]
BTC 35   301-600
Crusabridge Investments Ltd v Casings
International Ltd (1979) 54 TC
246 . . . .   301-600;
301-650; 302-250
C & E Commrs v Shaklee International
(1981) 1 BVC 444   165-500
C & E Commrs v Zielinski Baker and
Partners Ltd [2004] BTC 5,249   302-650
Cyril Lord Carpets Ltd v Schofield
(1966) 42 TC 637   115-000

D

Dale v Johnson Bros (1951) 32 TC
487   301-600
Daphne v Shaw [1926] 11 TC 256 . . . .   180-200;
260-110; 260-520
Decaux (JC) (UK) Ltd v Francis (1996)
Sp C 84   260-170
Delta Finance Newco v IR Commrs
(2002) Sp C 316   220-200
Derby (Earl) v Aylmer [1915] 3 KB
374; (1915) 6 TC 665   260-060
Dixon v Fitch's Garage Ltd (1975) 50
TC 509 . . . .   180-300;
260-020; 260-280; 262-590; 262-950

E

Edwards v Bairstow and Harrison
[1956] AC 14; (1955) 36 TC 207 . . .   260-600
Ellerker v Union Cold Storage (1938)
22 TC 195 . . . .   260-310;
301-550
Ensign Tankers (Leasing) Ltd v Stokes
[1992] BTC 110 . . . .   185-010;
260-710
Evans Medical Supplies Ltd v Moriarty
(1957) 37 TC 540   550-300

F

Family Golf Centres Ltd v Thorne
(1998) Sp C 150 . . . .   260-790;
260-930
Fitton v Gilders and Heaton (1955) 36
TC 233   250-080
Fleming v Associated Newspapers Ltd
[1973] AC 628; (1972) 48 TC
382   260-630
Frazer v Trebilcock (1964) 42 TC
217   185-150
Furniss v Dawson [1984] AC 474;
(1984) 55 TC 324; [1984] BTC
71 . . . .   220-000;
306-500

Paragraph

G

Gaspet Ltd v Elliss (1987) 60 TC 91;
[1987] BTC 218   525-300
Girobank plc v Clarke [1996] BTC
241 . . . .   301-600;
302-825
Gray v Seymours Garden Centre
(Horticulture) [1993] BTC 213;
[1995] BTC 320 . . . .   260-610;
260-950
Gurney v Richards (1989) 62 TC 287;
[1989] BTC 326   200-060

H

Hampton v Fortes Autogrill (1979) 53
TC 691 . . . .   260-280;
262-720
Hancock v General Reversionary &
Investment Co Ltd [1919] 1 KB 25;
7 TC 358   102-100
Hanson (Lord) v Mansworth (2004) Sp
C 410 . . . .   160-700;
262-450
Hinton v Madden & Ireland Ltd (1959)
38 TC 391 . . . .   180-100;
180-200; 180-300; 260-350; 261-370
Hunt v Henry Quick Ltd [1992] BTC
440 . . . .   260-600;
260-780; 261-330; 262-470; 262-570;
262-590

I

IR Commrs v Barclay, Curle & Co Ltd
(1968) 45 TC 221 . . . .   180-200;
180-300; 260-040; 260-540; 260-790;
260-920; 260-950; 261-300; 262-310;
262-920; 262-940
IR Commrs v John M Whiteford &
Son (1962) 40 TC 379 . . . .   425-650;
425-750
IR Commrs v Lambhill Ironworks Ltd
(1950) 31 TC 393   302-825
IR Commrs v Leith Harbour and Docks
Commrs (1941) 24 TC 118   301-550
IR Commrs v National Coal Board
(1957) 37 TC 264   302-900
IR Commrs v Scottish & Newcastle
Breweries Ltd (1982) 55 TC 252;
[1982] BTC 187 . . . .   180-100;
180-150; 180-250; 260-280; 260-370;
260-500; 260-600; 260-770; 260-780;
260-790; 260-820; 261-330; 262-150;
262-440; 262-590; 262-950

Cop

Paragraph

IR Commrs v Smyth (1914) 3 KB
406 . . . . 262-590;
300-600
IR Commrs v William Ransom & Son
Ltd (1930) 12 TC 21 425-550

J

Jarrold v John Good & Sons Ltd
(1963) 40 TC 681 . . . . 180-200;
180-250; 260-030; 260-150; 260-290;
260-370; 262-040; 262-200; 262-240
Jeffrey v Rolls Royce Ltd (1962) 40
TC 443 550-300
John Hall Junior & Co v Rickman
(1906) 1 KB 311 262-480
Jones (Samuel) & Co (Devondale) Ltd
v IR Commrs (1952) 32 TC 513 303-550

K

Kilmarnock   Equitable   Co-operative
Society Ltd v IR Commrs (1966) 42
TC 675 . . . . 301-600;
302-700; 302-850
King   v   Bridisco   Ltd   [1992]   BTC
440 . . . . 260-600;
260-780; 261-330; 262-570

L

Lancashire   Electric   Power   Co   v
Wilkinson (1947) 28 TC 427 . . . . 260-600;
261-330; 301-900; 303-550
Leeds Permanent Building Society v
Proctor (1982) 56 TC 293; [1982]
BTC 347 . . . . 180-250;
260-150; 260-500; 262-430
Lindsay v IR Commrs (1953) 34 TC
289 425-650
Lupton   v   Cadogan   Gardens
Developments Ltd (1971) 47 TC
1 . . . . 160-500;
261-320; 262-040; 262-200; 262-420
Lyon v Pettigrew [1985] BTC 168 262-700
Lyons (J) & Co Ltd v A-G [1944] Ch
281 . . . . 180-250;
260-150; 260-600; 261-330

M

McKinney   v   Hagans   Caravans
(Manufacturing) Ltd [1997] BTC
402 115-000
Macsaga Investment Co Ltd v Lupton
(1967) 44 TC 659 261-320
McVeigh v Arthur Sanderson & Sons
Ltd (1969) 45 TC 273 . . . . 260-110;
260-520; 262-900

Paragraph

Maco Door & Window Hardware (UK)
Ltd v R & C Commrs [2006] BTC
829; (2005) Sp C 508 301-650
Margrett v Lowestoft Water and Gas
Co (1935) 19 TC 481 . . . . 262-310;
262-920; 262-940
Mason v Tyson (1980) 53 TC 333 260-820
Matrix Securities Ltd, ex parte [1994]
BTC 85 . . . . 306-550;
320-350
Melluish v BMI (No. 3) [1995] BTC
381 . . . . 260-030;
260-040; 260-290; 260-760; 261-300;
261-320
Mitchell v BW Noble Ltd [1927] 1 KB
719; (1927) 11 TC 372 102-100
Morris v R & C Commrs [2006] BTC
861 200-040
Munby   v   Furlong   [1977]   Ch   359;
(1977) 50 TC 491 . . . . 180-100;
260-110; 260-320; 260-520; 262-440

N

Netlogic Consulting Ltd v R & C
Commrs (2005) Sp C 477 165-500
Norman   v   Golder   (1945)   26   TC
293 . . . . 260-060;
261-020
Nuclear Electric plc v Bradley [1996]
BTC 165 262-300

O

O'Srianian   v   Lakeview   Ltd   [1984]
TL(I) 125 . . . . 262-230;
262-740

P

Phillips v Whieldon Sanitary Potteries
Ltd (1952) 33 TC 213 303-550

R

R v IR Commrs, ex parte Matrix
Securities Ltd [1994] BTC 85 . . . . . . 306-550;
320-350
R v Slade [1888] 21 QBD 433 301-600
R & C Commrs v Maco Door &
Window Hardware (UK) Ltd [2008]
BTC 486; [2006] BTC 829; (2005)
Sp C 508 301-600
Ramsay   (WT)   Ltd   v   IR   Commrs
[1982]   AC   300;   (1981)   54   TC
101 . . . . 185-010;
306-500
Robson v Dixon (1972) 48 TC 527 260-040

Paragraph

Rose & Co (Wallpapers & Paints) Ltd
v Campbell (1968) 44 TC 500   262-900
RTZ Oil and Gas Ltd v Elliss [1987]
BTC 359   237-200

S

St John's School v Ward (1974) 49 TC
524 . . . .   180-300;
260-900; 262-590; 262-740
Salt v Golding (1996) Sp C 81 . . . .   262-730;
525-300
Sarsfield v Dixons Groups plc [1997]
BTC 127 . . . .   302-000;
302-850
Saxone, Lilley & Skinner (Holdings)
Ltd v IR Commrs (1967) 44 TC
122 . . . .   301-600;
302-300
Schofield v R & H Hall Ltd (1974) 49
TC 538 . . . .   260-940;
260-950; 261-320; 262-590
Shove v Lingfield Park 1991 [2003]
BTC 422   260-790
Smallwood v R & C Commrs (2005)
Sp C 509   310-550
Southern v Borax Consolidated Ltd
[1941] 1 KB 111; (1940) 23 TC
597   102-100
South Metropolitan Gas Co v Dadd
(1927) 13 TC 205   262-480
Stokes v Costain Property Investments
Ltd [1984] BTC 92 . . . .   245-000;
260-760; 261-320

T

Thomas v Reynolds (1987) 59 TC 502;
[1987] BTC 147 . . . .   260-280;
260-770
Thomsons (Carron) Ltd v IR Commrs
(1976) 51 TC 506   550-300
Tower MCashback LLP1 v R & C
Commrs [2008] BTC 805; (2007)
Sp C 619   105-000
Tucker v Granada Motorway Services
Ltd (1979) 53 TC 92   102-100

Paragraph

V

Vallambrosa Rubber Co Ltd v Farmer
(1910) 5 TC 529   102-100
Vibroplant Ltd v Holland (1982) 54 TC
658 . . . .   301-550;
301-600

W

Wangaratta Woollen Mills Ltd v
Commr of Taxation of the
Commonwealth of Australia [1969]
43 ALJR 324 . . . .   260-570;
262-910
Watson Bros v Hornby (1942) 24 TC
506   425-550
West Somerset Railways plc v Chivers
(1995) Sp C 1 . . . .   260-760;
302-000
Wetherspoon (JD) plc v R & C
Commrs (2007) Sp C 657 . . . .   180-250;
260-040; 262-150; 262-450
Whelan v Dover Harbour Board (1934)
18 TC 555   600-150
White v Higginbottom [1983] BTC
46   155-800
Wimpy International Ltd v Warland
(1988) 61 TC 51; [1989] BTC 58 . . .   160-500;
180-200; 180-250; 260-030; 260-040;
260-150; 260-280; 260-290; 260-500;
260-550; 260-600; 260-780; 261-330;
262-210; 262-240; 262-420; 262-430;
262-440; 262-490; 262-560; 262-570;
262-590; 262-910; 262-920
Wood (t/a A Wood & Co) v Provan
(1968) 44 TC 701   250-080
Woods v R & M Mallen (Engineering)
Ltd (1969) 45 TC 619   304-600
Wynne-Jones v Bedale Auction Ltd
(1976) 51 TC 426   303-550

Y

Yarmouth v France (1887) 19 QBD
647 . . . .   180-200;
180-250; 260-000; 260-060; 260-150;
260-820; 261-370

Legislation Finding List

(References are to paragraph numbers)

Provision	Paragraph
Assisted Areas Order 2007	
(SI 2007/107)	400-600
Business Premises Renovation Allowances	
Regulations 2007 (SI 2007/945)	400-600; 400-650
Capital Allowances Act 1968	100-100
Capital Allowances Act 1990	
18(1)(e)	301-600
18(1)(f)(i)–(iv), (2)	301-650
38A(4), 38C, 38D	210-150
42	220-200
42(1)–(3)	220-200
67A	215-400
75(1)	220-420
76(2)	220-420
153	301-000
Sch. AA1	260-150
Capital Allowances Act 2001	
See generally	100-000
1(1)	102-000
2(1)	106-100; 152-000; 300-200
2–23	260-790
3	101-000
4	102-000; 102-100; 300-800
4(2)	550-300
5	105-000; 185-350; 300-800
5(4)	105-100
5(5)	105-200; 200-620
5(6)	105-300
5(7)	105-400
6	106-200; 205-150; 210-250; 230-225; 305-150
6(1)	106-300; 305-150
6(1)(b)	205-150
6(2)(a)	305-150
6(6)	190-200
7	106-500; 300-150; 310-500
8	106-500
8(4)	190-700
9	106-500
9(1)	190-700
10(1)	102-100
10(1)(a)	102-100; 190-200
Pt. 2	262-000
11	105-000; 150-000; 245-000; 262-000
11(4)	160-000; 190-700; 205-000; 247-150
11(4)(b)	161-200; 215-000; 245-000
12	105-000; 152-700; 181-000
13	160-800
13A	160-900

Provision	Paragraph
14	161-000; 240-520
15(1)	155-000; 155-100
15(1)(d)	155-400
15(1)(f)	155-500
15(1)(g)	155-600
16	155-200
17	155-300
18	155-600
19	155-700
19(5)	152-600
20(1), (3)	155-800
Pt. 2, Ch. 3	160-000; 260-260; 260-280
21–33	160-600; 262-550
21–26	160-100; 180-400
21–25	260-150
21–24	260-760
21–23	180-000; 261-100; 262-200; 262-950
21	10-200; 110-100; 160-500; 185-050; 247-000; 247-100; 260-020; 260-130; 260-150; 260-200; 260-270; 260-280; 260-310; 260-320; 260-330; 260-360; 260-370; 260-540; 260-550; 260-570; 260-600; 260-610; 260-760; 260-780; 260-800; 260-820; 260-900; 260-920; 260-940; 261-100; 261-310; 261-320; 261-330; 262-000; 262-150; 262-210; 262-400; 262-460; 262-470; 262-490; 262-500; 262-550; 262-560; 262-570; 262-740; 262-910; 262-920; 262-950; 262-960
21(1)–(3)	260-020
21(1)	262-740
21(3)	250-220; 262-470
21(3)(a)	247-100; 261-320
21(3)(c)	262-560; 262-920
22	110-100; 160-600; 247-000; 260-100; 260-150; 260-200; 260-210; 260-250; 260-270; 260-280; 260-310; 260-320; 260-330; 260-360; 260-370; 260-540; 260-570; 260-580; 260-610; 260-700; 260-940; 261-200; 262-000; 262-210; 262-310; 262-320; 262-400; 262-460; 262-490; 262-550; 262-570; 262-590; 262-600; 262-710; 262-780; 262-910; 262-940; 262-950; 263-000
22(1)	262-590
22(1)(b)	261-300
22(3)	262-590; 263-000
22(3)(a)	262-230
22(4)	262-950

743

Capital Allowances Act 2001 – continued

Provision	Paragraph
23 . . . . . 10-200;	160-500; 160-600; 247-100; 250-220;
	260-000; 260-010; 260-030; 260-050;
	260-150; 260-170; 260-200; 260-230;
	260-280; 260-290; 260-310; 260-320;
	260-360; 260-370; 260-530; 260-540;
	260-550; 260-570; 260-580; 260-600;
	260-700; 260-740; 260-760; 260-770;
	260-780; 260-800; 260-820; 260-900;
	260-940; 261-100; 261-300; 261-320;
	261-330; 262-000; 262-030; 262-200;
	262-310; 262-320; 262-400; 262-420;
	262-450; 262-460; 262-500; 262-510;
	262-530; 262-570; 262-590; 262-600;
	262-710; 262-720; 262-740; 262-780;
	262-910; 262-920; 262-940; 262-950;
	263-000
23(1) 260-330; 262-550
23(2) 247-000; 260-330; 260-600; 262-550
23(3) 260-600
23(4) 247-000; 247-050; 260-280; 260-780;
	261-100; 262-910
24 262-590
24(2) 260-270
24(3) 160-100
25 . . . . 160-100; 180-400; 245-300; 250-340;
	260-040; 261-320
26 . . . . 160-200; 237-200; 260-510
26(3) 190-700
26(4) 260-510
27–33 260-200
27 . . . . 160-300; 160-500; 160-700; 261-100; 262-450
27(1) 262-450; 262-550
27(2) 190-750; 262-550
28 . . . . 247-150; 260-150; 261-100; 262-150;
	262-960; 310-500
28(2) 261-100
28(2B), (2C) 261-100
29 160-500
30–33 262-440
30–32 . . . . 160-600; 260-150; 262-550
32 180-400
33 . . . . 160-700; 260-150; 260-700; 262-450; 262-960
33(4) 262-450
33(5) 247-100
33(6)(b) 262-450
33A 10-150; 247-000; 247-050; 247-150;
	260-030; 260-150; 260-280; 260-600;
	260-760; 260-780; 261-320; 261-330;
	262-420; 262-920
33A(1) 247-000
33A(2) 160-300; 247-000; 247-100; 260-600
33A(3), (4) 247-100
33A(5) 247-000; 261-320
33A(5)(c) 260-280; 260-290
33A(7) 247-050
33B 247-000
34 165-200
34A 165-000; 230-000
35 . . . . 155-200; 165-100

Provision	Paragraph
35(2) 165-100
36 . . . . 152-300; 200-500; 201-200
36(1)(a), (b) 155-800
37 165-700
38 165-300
38A 181-000
38B 181-150; 200-300
39 . . . . 185-010; 185-350
41(1) 210-050
44 185-250
44(2) 210-050; 235-200
45A–45C 185-350; 260-260
45A 242-000
45B, 45B(5) 185-350
45C 185-350
45C(5) 185-350
45D 185-100; 200-080; 200-400
45D(2) 200-400
45D(8) 200-080
45F 185-500; 237-200
45G 185-500
45H 185-550; 242-000
45J 185-550
46 185-100
46(1) 185-350
46(2) 10-050; 160-800; 161-000; 185-150;
	200-400; 201-040; 235-200
50 105-000
51A 181-000; 181-050; 181-100
51A(5), (6), (11) 181-300
51A(11)(b) 181-000
51B 181-200; 181-300
51C 181-200; 181-300
51D 181-200; 181-300
51E 181-200; 181-300
51F 181-200
51G 181-200
51G(5), (6), (7) 181-200
51H 181-200; 181-300
51I 181-200; 181-300
51J 181-200
51J(3), (4), (5) 181-200
51K 181-300
51K(2), (3), (4), (6) 181-300
51L 181-300
51M 181-300
51M(1)(a), (8) 181-300
51N 181-300
Pt. 2, Ch. 5 235-500
52 . . . . . . 10-025; 10-100; 10-150; 185-000; 185-250;
	185-350; 185-500; 187-050; 238-000
52(1) 187-000
52(2) 101-100
52A 181-000; 181-050
54(2) 190-100
54(3) 200-200
54(4), (5) 190-100
55 190-000
55(4) 190-400

Provision	Paragraph
56 . . . . . . 10-100; 10-200; 190-200; 190-300; 235-300; 247-150	
56(1) 201-180	
56(1A) 185-500; 190-200; 237-100	
56(6) 190-500; 220-200	
56(7) 220-200	
56A 190-275	
57 190-700	
57(2), (3), (4) 190-700	
58 190-700	
58(4A)(a) 185-050	
58(6), (7) 190-750	
59 190-700	
60–63 238-100	
60(1), (1)(b) 190-750	
61 190-750	
61(1) 190-650; 242-200	
61(1)(e) 215-400	
61(1)(ee) 231-000	
61(1)(f) 215-400	
61(2) 190-750; 238-000; 245-230	
62–64 190-750	
62 . . . . 190-750; 220-470	
62(1) 237-400; 245-230; 250-480	
62(2) 238-100	
63 190-750	
63(4) 190-750	
63(5) 160-300; 160-500; 160-600; 160-700; 261-100; 262-450; 262-550	
64 190-750	
64(1) 190-750	
65 190-650	
65(1)(b) 210-050	
65(4) 220-200	
66 190-750	
67 . . . . 161-200; 215-000; 215-200	
67(1)(a) 161-200	
67(2) 260-330	
68 . . . . 190-750; 215-100	
69 215-200	
70 . . . . 215-300; 220-100	
70A 230-000; 231-150	
70B 231-250	
70C 231-300	
70C(4)–(9) 231-300	
70D 231-300	
70E 231-350; 231-355	
70E(4) 231-355	
70E(4)(a) 230-200	
Pt. 2, Ch. 6A 165-000	
70G 230-200	
70G(1)(b) 231-050	
70H 230-200	
70I 230-500	
70I(10), (12) 230-500	
70J 230-250	
70J(6) 231-000	
70K 230-300	
70L 230-350	

Provision	Paragraph
70M(3) 230-350	
70N 230-400	
70O 230-450	
70P 230-250	
70Q 230-200; 231-000	
70R 185-050; 185-100; 185-150; 230-225; 231-050	
70S 231-050	
70T 231-050	
70U 230-225; 231-100	
70V 231-000; 231-200	
70W, 70W(4)(b) 231-400	
70X 231-400	
70Y 231-450	
70YA 231-450; 232-000	
70YB, 70YB(2) 232-000	
70YC 232-000	
70YC(5) 232-300	
70YD 232-100	
70YE 190-750; 232-100	
70YF 232-300	
70YF(1), (8) 232-300	
70YG 160-900; 232-250	
70YH 232-200	
70YI 230-400; 232-050; 232-100; 232-150; 232-350; 232-400	
70YJ 230-300; 230-400	
71 . . . . 215-400; 215-400; 260-330	
72 . . . . 190-750; 215-400; 260-330	
73 . . . . 190-750; 215-400; 260-330	
74 200-620	
74(2)(a) 201-180	
Pt. 2, Ch. 8 260-240	
75 . . . . 10-200; 200-620	
75(1) 201-180	
76 . . . . 200-620; 201-060; 201-180	
77 . . . . 200-620; 201-100; 201-120	
77(1) 190-650	
77(2) 201-120	
78 . . . . 200-620; 201-140	
79 . . . . 190-750; 200-620; 201-180	
79(2), (3) 201-220	
81 201-020	
82 201-180	
82(4) 205-000; 205-050	
83 205-000	
84 . . . . 205-000; 205-100	
85 205-000	
86 . . . . 190-100; 205-150	
86(1) 238-200	
86(2) 190-650; 190-700	
86(3) 205-150	
87 205-200	
87(2) 190-650; 190-700	
88 . . . . 190-750; 205-250	
89 190-750	
89(7) 205-300	
91 210-150	
92(1) 210-150	

Capital Allowances Act 2001 – continued

Provision	Paragraph	Provision	Paragraph
93–96	210-200	126(2)	220-200
93	210-200	Pt. 2, Ch. 12	235-500; 262-480
94	185-150; 210-200; 235-200	127–158	262-480
95	185-150; 210-200	127	190-100; 235-500; 235-600
96	210-150; 210-200	127(1), (2)	235-500
97–100	210-250	128	235-600
98(3)	210-250	129	235-700
99(2)	210-250	129(1)	190-700; 235-500; 235-700
101	190-100; 210-050	130	235-200
102	10-200; 190-200; 210-050; 220-200	130(2)	235-200
103	210-150; 210-300	131	235-200
104	190-750; 210-300	131(6), (7)	235-600
Pt. 2, Ch. 10	247-150	132	190-750; 235-600
104A–104D	247-150	132(1)(a), (b)	235-600
104A	247-000; 247-150	132(2)	190-650; 190-700; 235-400
104AA	200-100; 200-600; 247-150; 260-240	132(3)	235-400
104AA(2)	200-100	133	235-400
104C	190-100; 247-000; 247-150	133(3)	190-700
104D	190-200; 247-000; 247-150	135	235-500
104D(2), (4)	247-150	135(1)	235-500
104E	210-300; 240-100; 247-150	136(b)	235-500
104F	190-000; 200-520	137	190-700; 235-500
Pt. 2, Ch. 11	220-200; 235-500	138	235-500
105	220-200	138(1)	235-500
105(2), (3), (4)	220-200	139	235-500
105(5)	220-300	140–145	235-500
106	220-300	140	235-500
106(1), (2)	220-200	141	235-500
107	190-100; 190-650	142	235-500
107(1), (2)	220-200	143	190-750; 235-500
108	190-750; 220-200; 240-100	145	235-500
109	10-200; 190-200; 205-000; 220-200	145(1)–(3)	235-500
109(1), (2), (4)	220-200	146	235-500
110	210-050; 220-200	146(3)(b)	235-500
110(2)(c)	220-300	147	235-500
111	190-750; 220-200	149	235-500
111(3)	190-700	149(1)(a)	235-500
112	220-200	150	235-500
113	220-200	151–154	235-500
114	190-750; 210-050; 220-200	154	235-500
115	220-200	155	235-500
115(1), (3)	220-200	156	235-500
116	205-000; 220-200	156(2)	235-500
117	220-200	158	235-500
117(1)–(6)	220-200	160	237-000
118–120	220-200	161	237-000; 500-150
118	220-300	161A–161D	237-100
119	220-200	161B(1)	237-200
120	220-200	161C(2)	190-700
121	220-300	163–165	160-200; 237-200; 260-510
122–125	205-000	165(3)	190-700
122	220-200	166	237-300
122(1)	220-300	166(2)	190-700
123	220-300	167–170	237-400
123(1)	235-600	167(2)	237-400
124	220-300	169	237-400
125	220-300	170	237-400
125(1), (2), (4)	220-300	171	190-750; 237-400
126	220-200	Pt. 2, Ch. 14	245-000; 245-230

Provision	Paragraph
172–204	245-000; 260-760
172(3)	245-230
172A	250-000
173	260-760
173(1)	210-200; 215-200; 245-100; 400-500
173(2)	245-100; 245-230
174	241-900
174(1)–(4)	245-100
175	160-100; 245-100
175A	245-230
176	245-230
176(2), (3)	245-230
177–180	245-200
177	245-220; 245-400
178	245-220
180A	245-230; 245-500
180A(4), (5)	245-230
181	245-240
182	245-240
182A	245-240
182A(2)	245-230
183	245-250; 245-400; 245-600; 245-700
184	245-250; 245-400
185(2)	190-700; 250-480
185(4)	250-480
185(6), (7)	245-300
186	245-300; 245-700; 310-500
186(2)	106-500; 190-700
186(3)	245-300
187	245-300; 245-700
187(2)	106-500; 190-700
188–192A	245-400
188	245-500; 245-600
188(3)	245-400
188(4)	245-400
189	245-400
190	245-600
191	245-600
192	245-230; 245-500
192(2)(a), (b), (3)	245-600
192A	245-230
192A(2)	245-230
192A(2)(a), (b)	245-230; 245-500
192A(3)	245-600
193	245-500
194	245-230; 245-500
195	245-230; 245-500
195A	245-230; 245-500
195B	245-230; 245-500
196	190-750; 245-600; 245-700
196(1), (4A)	245-230
196(5)	245-400
197	190-750; 245-600; 245-700
198–201	245-700
198	245-240; 245-700; 250-040; 250-400; 250-420; 250-460; 250-480; 250-620; 250-640
198(1)	245-700; 250-060
198(2)	245-700; 250-060; 250-400

Provision	Paragraph
199	245-700
200	245-700
201	245-700
201(3)	245-700
202–204	245-800
203(2)(b)	245-230
205	181-000
206	190-100; 200-200; 235-500
206(2)	247-150
206(3)	190-700
206(4)	190-650
207	155-900; 190-850
208	190-750
208A	200-540; 200-620
209–211	165-700
210	181-000; 187-150
211	190-100; 190-750; 205-000; 235-500; 247-150; 260-040
211(4)	190-700
Pt. 2, Ch. 17	201-220; 215-100; 238-050; 240-100; 240-520
213–218	220-500
213	220-420; 240-500
213(1)	220-470; 240-520
213(2), (3)	240-520
214–218	220-420
214	240-500; 240-540
215	160-000; 240-540
216	238-400; 240-540
217	181-000; 200-540; 205-300; 220-460; 220-500; 238-300; 240-540
218	160-800; 200-540; 205-300; 220-460; 220-500; 238-300; 240-540
218(1)	190-700
218(3)	238-500
218A	181-350
219	240-500
219(1)	220-450
220	190-700; 220-440
221–228	220-420
221	220-420; 230-350; 230-500; 240-500
221(1)(c)	230-350; 230-500
222–225	205-300
222	190-750; 220-470
222(3)	220-420
223	220-460
224	160-800; 220-420; 220-460
224(1)	190-700
225	220-430; 230-500
226	220-420
227	220-460; 230-225; 240-500
228	220-460
228(2)	190-700; 230-500
228(3), (5)	230-500
228A–228J	220-470
228A	240-500
228B	220-470
228C	220-470
228D(2), (3), (4)	220-470

Capital Allowances Act 2001 – continued

Provision	Paragraph
228E	220-470
228G	220-470
228J	220-470
228J(1)–(5), (8)	220-470
228K–228M	190-750
228K	240-500
229	190-750; 240-500
229(2)	240-560
229(3)	220-440; 240-560
229(5)	240-560
230	240-520
231	220-440; 240-500
232	220-430; 240-500
235–239	238-100
236	181-000; 238-000; 238-050; 242-000
237	238-000
238	190-750
239	190-750
240	238-200
241–245	238-400
241	220-420; 238-050; 238-300
242	238-300
242(2)	190-700
242(5), (6)	238-500
243	220-420
243(2)	190-700
247–251	152-100
252	152-200
253	152-400
255	152-500
256	152-500
258	101-000; 152-600
259–261	152-600
260(3)–(6)	152-600
260(3)(b)	101-000
261A	152-600
262	152-300
262A	242-000
263–267	120-000
263	120-000; 240-000; 240-010; 240-020
264	240-020
264(3)	190-750
265–268	240-100
265	240-100
266	240-100; 241-900
266(5), (7)	240-100
267A	240-100
268	251-000
268A	181-150; 200-020; 200-060; 200-080; 200-300; 260-240
268A(1)	200-600
268A(2)	200-020; 200-600
268B	200-400; 200-600
268C, 268C(2), (3), (4)	200-600
268D	205-050
269	155-800; 165-500; 260-630
269(3), (4)	260-630
270	100-200; 161-100

Provision	Paragraph
271	260-130; 260-150; 260-930; 300-100; 320-100
271(1)(b)	310-500
271(1)(b)(ii)	315-000
271(1)(c)	304-000
271(2)(a)	300-550
272	300-650
272(1)	300-750
273	160-100; 260-040; 261-300; 300-650; 310-500
Pt. 3, Ch. 2	261-100
274	260-130; 301-500; 301-750; 301-800; 301-950; 302-000; 302-050; 302-100; 302-150; 600-200
274(1)	301-600
275	302-200
276	301-650; 302-050; 302-250
276(3)	301-500; 301-600
277	302-200; 302-600; 302-650; 302-700; 302-750; 302-825; 302-850; 310-500
277(1)(c)	302-800
277(2)	302-900
278	302-400
279	315-100; 315-150
279(7)	315-200
280	315-500
281	20-050; 320-100
282	300-100
283	302-350; 303-500; 310-500
284	300-700; 310-500
284(2)	320-400
285	300-350
286(1)	304-500
287	304-550
288(1)	304-600
289	304-650
290	304-750; 320-350
291	304-750; 306-500
292	304-050
293	304-100
294	304-000; 304-050; 310-500
295	304-000; 304-100
296	304-000; 304-100
297	304-050
298	20-500; 320-100
298(2)	320-400
298(3)	20-050
299–304	320-300
299	320-100
301	304-000; 320-250
302(1)	320-300
303	304-000; 320-300
303(5)	320-300
304	320-300
305	20-050; 320-150
305(1)	320-250
307	320-050
308	320-150
309–314	305-150

Provision	Paragraph	Provision	Paragraph
309	305-100	360B	400-500
309(1)(a)	300-800	360C	400-600
310	305-150; 320-250	360D	400-650
310(1)(a)	320-200; 320-250	360E	401-100
310(3)	320-250	360F	401-100
311	301-050; 305-200; 305-225; 320-250	360G	403-000
312	305-250	360H	403-000
313	305-250; 305-300; 320-350	360I	403-200
313A	305-225	360J	403-200
314	305-225; 305-500	360J(3)	403-700
314(1)	305-150	360K	403-600
314(4)	575-550	360L	403-200
314(5)	575-550	360M	403-400
317(4)	300-350	360O	403-500; 403-600
319(6)	305-250	360P	403-600; 403-700
325	306-500; 320-350	360Q–360S	403-600
327	320-350	360R	403-700
328	305-250; 306-500	360S	403-800
328(1), (2), (3), (4)(a), (b), (5)	320-350	360T–360W	405-000
329(1)(a), (d), (d)(ii), (2)–(5)	320-350	360V	405-000
330	320-350	360X	405-000
331(1)	320-350	360Y	405-000
333	305-250	360Z	400-050
334	305-250	360Z2	404-000
335	305-250	360Z3	402-000
335(2)	305-250	360Z3(3)	403-200
336	305-250	360Z4	402-000
337(1)	305-250	361(1)	425-000
338	305-250; 320-350	361(1)(a)	260-700; 425-500
339	310-150	361(2)	425-000; 425-500
340	305-250	361(2)(a)	425-500
341	302-050	361(3)	427-000
341(1)	300-250	362	425-550
343(2)	430-600	363	426-350
344	302-050	364–366	427-000
346	320-150	365–368	427-200
347	305-300	369	426-200; 426-300
347(3)	305-300	369(1)(a)	425-500
348	300-800; 305-300	370	427-300
349	305-200; 305-300	371	427-400
349(1)	300-800	372–378	428-000
350	305-300	374	425-550
350(5)	305-300	375–379	428-200
351	305-300	375	428-200
Pt. 3, Ch. 11	300-200	379	428-100
352	300-250	381	428-500
353	300-300	382	428-500; 429-100
354	300-350	382(2)–(5)	430-600
354(2)(a)	300-350	384	428-700
355	101-000; 300-400	388	428-700
356	300-750	391	425-050
357	306-500; 306-550	392	425-050
357(1)	306-550	393	427-000
358	310-100	393(3)	427-200
359	304-700	393A	20-150; 475-000
360	302-400; 304-500	393A(2)	475-800
360(1)(a)	304-500	393A(3), (4)	475-700
360A	20-100; 400-000	393B	475-500
360A(2)	401-100	393C	475-600

Capital Allowances Act 2001 – continued

Provision	Paragraph	Provision	Paragraph
393C(2), (3)	475-600	418	500-300
393D	475-700	418(1)	500-150
393D(2), (4)	475-700	418(4)	500-250
393E	475-700	419	500-200; 500-350
393F–393J	475-800	421	500-200
393F	475-800	422(4)	500-150
393G	475-800	423–425	500-200
393H	476-500	423	500-200
393I	476-500	424	500-200
393J–393L	476-600	426	500-150
393J(1)	475-800	427	500-350; 500-850
393J(3)(b)	476-600	428	500-350
393K(3)	476-800	430	500-350
393L	476-700	431	500-350
393M	476-700	432	500-050
393M(5)	476-800	433	500-200
393O	476-700	434	500-400
393P	476-700; 476-800	435	500-000
393R	476-700; 476-800	436	500-150
393S	476-800	437	20-300; 525-000; 525-200
393T	475-050	438–440	525-200
393T(2)	475-050	438(3)–(6)	525-800
393U	477-100	439	525-300
393V	475-800	441	525-400
393V(3)	476-600	441(1)	525-600; 525-800
393W	475-900	441(2)	525-100
Pt. 5	301-850	442	525-500; 525-800
394	20-250; 500-000; 500-100	442(1)–(3)	525-800
394(4)	500-150	443	525-600
396	500-150	443(1)	525-800
397–400	500-150	443(2)	525-600
399	500-150	443(3)	525-500
399(1)	237-000; 500-150	443(4)	525-500; 525-600
400	500-150	443(6)	525-800
400(4)	500-400	446	525-800
401	500-150	447(1), (2)	525-800
402	237-000; 500-150	447(3)	525-100
404	500-150	448	525-800
405	500-150	449	525-800
406	500-150	450	525-100
Pt. 5, Ch. 4	500-150	Pt. 7	550-000
407	500-150; 500-850	452	20-400; 550-100
407(3)	525-600	452(2)	550-200
407(5)	500-150	453	550-000
408	500-150; 525-600	454	550-150; 550-200
408(1)	525-600	455	550-200
408(2)	500-150	456	550-250
409(1), (3)	500-150	457–462	550-250
410	500-150; 500-200	457(5)	550-250
411, 411(1)	500-150	461	550-250
412	500-150	463	550-050
413	500-150	Pt. 8	575-000
Pt. 5, Ch. 5	500-150	464	20-350; 575-100
415	500-150; 500-300	465	575-100
416	500-150	466	575-150
416A–416E	500-400	467	575-250
416B	500-400	468	575-250
416D	500-200	469	575-250
417(4)	500-300	470	575-300

Provision	Paragraph	Provision	Paragraph
471	575-300; 575-500	539(6)	301-050
471(4)	575-450	540	430-700
472	575-450; 575-500	543	600-350
473–475	575-350	544	165-600
476	575-400	545	165-600
477	575-400	547–549	405-000
478	575-050	547	120-400
479	101-000; 575-050	548	120-400
480	575-050	549	120-400
481	575-700	550	120-400
482	575-150	552	525-600
483	575-200	552(2)	500-150
Pt. 9	600-000	553(2)	500-200\525-500
484	20-200; 600-000; 600-100	555	525-600
484(2)(a), (b)	600-200	Pt. 12, Ch. 4	240-000
485	600-150	557–559	550-350; 600-400
486	600-250	557	575-550; 575-650
487	600-250	557(a)	240-020
488	600-300	558	120-000; 240-010; 310-300; 430-600
489	600-050	559	120-000; 310-350; 430-600; 500-700
Pt. 10	625-100	561	100-200; 240-100; 310-000; 500-500;
490	20-450; 625-150		600-300
491	625-100	561A	100-200
491(1)	625-000; 625-250	562	245-240; 245-700; 250-020; 250-080;
493	625-250		250-480; 310-500; 525-600
495–500	625-200	562(1)–(3)	250-480
499	625-450	562(2)	250-480; 306-500
501	625-250	562(3)	185-350; 185-550; 210-150; 250-480
502	625-250	562(3)(a), (b)	250-480
503	625-250	563	245-700; 250-080; 310-050
505	625-150	564	310-050
506	625-150	564(1)	245-700
507–510	625-300	564(2)	120-000
507(1)	625-300	566	120-100; 300-200
511	625-250	567–573	625-650
512	625-400	567–570	403-900; 430-500; 477-200
513	625-350	567–569	525-700; 625-700
514	625-350	567	305-225; 500-500; 625-600
515	625-350	567(4)	307-050
516	625-350	567(5)	307-000; 500-500
517	625-350	568	100-200; 306-500; 500-500; 625-600
518	625-350	568(1)	307-100
520–522	625-350	568(1)(a)	625-650
524–528	625-400	569	100-200; 251-000; 307-100; 307-150;
529	625-050		310-350; 403-900; 430-500; 477-200;
530	625-500		500-150; 500-500; 500-650
531	625-150; 625-200	569(1)	403-900; 477-200
531(1)	302-650	569(5)	625-350
532–536	300-750; 301-000; 500-750	570	403-900; 500-500
532	115-000; 201-060; 600-350	570(1)	477-200
534–536	115-000	570(5)	307-150
535	430-700	570A	306-500; 403-900; 477-200; 500-600;
536	115-000; 430-700		625-700
536(1)–(3)	430-700	571	100-200; 302-350; 625-250; 625-450
537–542	500-800	571(1)	161-100; 210-150; 220-200
537	115-100; 301-000; 301-050	572	100-200; 310-200
537(1)	403-200; 477-000	572(4)	310-250
538	115-000; 190-100; 201-060; 245-240	573	307-150; 403-500; 428-800; 476-700;
539	301-050		625-550; 625-600; 625-700

Capital Allowances Act 2001 – continued

Provision	Paragraph
574	500-150; 625-600; 625-650
574(2), (3)	181-200
575	120-300; 235-500; 240-100; 240-500; 247-250
575(1)	220-300; 245-230
576(1)	240-100
577	220-200; 310-400
577(1)	220-200; 525-600
577(2)	235-600
577(2A)	300-350; 600-300
577(3)	220-200; 235-700; 425-550
577(4)	307-050
Sch. A1, para. 1	242-000
Sch. A1, para. 2	242-040
Sch. A1, para. 3	242-000
Sch. A1, para. 5	242-080
Sch. A1, para. 6	242-080
Sch. A1, para. 7	242-080
Sch. A1, para. 8	242-080
Sch. A1, para. 9	242-080
Sch. A1, para. 11	242-100
Sch. A1, para. 12	242-100
Sch. A1, para. 13	242-100
Sch. A1, para. 14	242-100
Sch. A1, para. 15	242-100
Sch. A1, para. 16	242-100
Sch. A1, para. 17	242-040
Sch. A1, para. 19–22	242-150
Sch. A1, para. 18	242-060
Sch. A1, para. 21	242-150
Sch. A1, para. 22	242-150
Sch. A1, para. 23	242-000
Sch. A1, para. 24	242-500
Sch. A1, para. 24(7)	242-200
Sch. A1, para. 25	242-200
Sch. A1, para. 25(2)	242-200
Sch. A1, para. 26	242-200
Sch. A1, para. 27	242-200
Sch. A1, para. 28	242-000
Sch. 1, Pt. 2	310-400; 475-050; 525-200
Sch. 3	185-150; 310-450
Sch. 3, para. 20	210-150
Sch. 3, para. 23	220-300
Sch. 3, para. 38	250-400; 250-480
Sch. 3, para. 45	220-420
Sch. 3, para. 46(1)	238-000
Sch. 3, para. 51	220-420
Sch. 3, Pt. 5	310-450
Sch. 3, para. 58	315-000
Sch. 3, para. 66	305-150
Sch. 3, para. 87	500-150
Sch. 3, para. 91	525-600
Sch. 3, para. 103	600-250

Capital Allowances (Energy-Saving Plant and Machinery) Order 2001 (SI 2001/2541

See generally	185-350

Provision	Paragraph
art. 3, 5	185-350
art. 6	245-230

Capital Allowances (Environmentally Beneficial Plant and Machinery) Order 2003 (SI 2003/2076)

See generally	185-550
art. 5	185-550

Capital Allowances (Leases of Background Plant or Machinery for a Building) Order 2007 (SI 2007/303)

See generally	231-050
art. 1–4	231-050

Caravan Sites and Control of Development Act 1960 ... 260-230

Companies Act 2006

1161(2)	181-200

Compensation (Defence) Act 1939

2(1)(a)	310-100

Corporation Tax Act 2009

Pt. 13, Ch. 2	242-100
Pt. 14, Ch. 3	242-100
Pt. 14, Ch. 4	242-100
Pt. 15, Ch. 3	242-100
9	106-300; 305-150
10(1)(a)	181-300; 210-250
39(4)	152-200; 155-000; 155-400
41	310-350
53	102-000
54	190-750
62–67	500-150
68	261-370
106	190-750
108	190-750
109	165-300
176(3), (4)	550-300
178	550-150; 550-250
178(3)–(5)	550-200
196	300-350
205	475-050
217–221	320-350
243	304-750
251	261-100
264	155-300
277–281	320-350
289	310-350
391(3)(b)	242-100
910	550-300
912	575-200; 575-400
918	575-200
1218	155-600
1219	155-600
1223	152-400; 242-100; 242-150
1223(2)	242-080
1313(2)	220-200

Disability Discrimination Act 1995 ... 260-525

Provision	Paragraph
Disability Discrimination Act 2004	180-450
Disability Discrimination Act 2005	260-525
EC Directive 77/388	
art. 20(2)–(4)...........................	120-400
EC Directive 98/70	
art. 2	200-600
EC Regulation 2157/2001	100-200
EC Regulation 1628/2006	400-650
Finance Act 1971	100-100
Finance Act 1995	
154(3)	425-600
Finance Act 1997	
Sch. 12, para. 11 .... 190-750; 220-410;	575-400
Sch. 12, para. 11(8)	575-550
Finance Act 1998	
Sch. 18, para. 51	230-200
Sch. 18, para. 82	101-100
Sch. 18, Pt. IX	235-500
Finance Act 2000	
Sch. 22, para. 91A	230-200
Finance Act 2003	
Sch. 6	400-600
Finance Act 2004	
50....................................	525-200
134...................................	220-470
Finance Act 2005	
70....................................	230-450
Finance Act 2006	
37....................................	260-710
Sch. 4	260-710
Sch. 8, para. 15(1)	230-050
Sch. 8, para. 15(5), (6).................	231-400
Sch. 10, para. 6, 25	240-100
Finance Act 2007	
36............ 300-000; 305-200; 305-250;	428-500
37....................................	185-250
Finance Act 2008	
See generally	240-580
75(7)..................................	238-000
81(5)	190-275
85....................................	305-225
85(5)	305-225
85(6)	425-025
85(8) 305-225;	425-025
86(2)	320-050
Sch. 20	240-580
Sch. 24, para. 23	181-400
Sch. 26, para. 14	247-000
Sch. 26, para. 15	247-250
Sch. 26, para. 16	247-300
Sch. 26, para. 17	247-300

Provision	Paragraph
Sch. 27, para. 5 .... 106-500;	245-300
Sch. 27, para. 6 .... 301-050;	525-500
Sch. 27, para. 10	430-700
Sch. 27, para. 31	320-000
Finance Act 2009	
See generally	240-585
24....................................	185-050
63....................................	190-750
64....................................	190-750
122...................................	215-300
123...................................	215-300
Sch. 11, para. 26–28	200-620
Sch. 11, para. 27(3), 28(1), (2), 29(2)......	200-620
Sch. 11, para. 30, 31, 31(3)..............	200-620
Sch. 32 .... 190-750;	220-550
Sch. 61	215-300
Fire Precautions Act 1971	160-500
Fire Safety and Safety of Places of Sport	
Act 1987 .... 160-500; 160-600;	262-550
Greater London Authority Act 1999	
101...................................	320-150
Hotel Proprietors Act 1956	315-050
Housing Act 1980	
56.......................... 625-100;	625-150
56(4)	625-150
Housing Act 1988 .... 625-100;	625-150
Income and Corporation Taxes Act 1988	
13....................................	210-250
31ZA	261-100
38....................................	476-600
74(1)(a)	190-750
74(1)(f), (g)...........................	102-000
75....................................	155-600
76............ 152-500; 242-080; 242-100;	242-150
76(7).......... 242-080; 242-100;	242-150
76(12) 242-080; 242-100;	242-150
76(13)	242-100
87....................................	500-150
343............. 100-200; 240-100;	241-900
343(1) 220-200;	240-010
343(2) 120-000; 235-500; 240-010; 240-100;	
310-000; 500-700; 600-400;	625-600
343A	240-010
392A 242-080;	475-050
392A(2) 242-100;	242-150
392B 242-080;	242-150
392B(1)	242-100
393................................ 242-150	
393(1)	242-100
393A(1)...............................	300-400
393A(1)(a), (b)	242-100
393B(3)	242-100
395...................................	242-100
400...................................	242-100
402...................................	475-050

Income and Corporation Taxes
Act 1988 – continued

Provision	Paragraph
403(1)	242-100
404	215-400; 240-100
416	210-250
432AA	242-080
432AB(3)	242-080; 242-150
432AB(4)	242-080
436	152-500
436A	165-600
439B	152-500
441	152-500
469	320-400
488	242-000
489	242-000
501A	181-150; 185-500; 190-200; 500-400
502K	231-355
Pt. XII, Ch. VA	230-200
505	242-000
506	190-750
507(1)	190-750
508	242-000
524	575-700
768	220-200
774A–774G	241-900
785A	241-900
785A(5ZA)	241-900
832(1)	181-200; 425-050
836A	525-200
837A	525-200
837A(3), (4), (5)	525-200
839	190-750

Income Tax Act 1945

	100-100

Income Tax Act 2007

Provision	Paragraph
23	575-050
60–67	500-150
72	242-020
120	475-050
383	240-020
388	240-020
Pt. 15, Ch. 6	102-100; 300-800
906	102-100; 300-800
989	425-050; 475-050

Income Tax (Definition of Unit Trust
Scheme) Regulations 1988
(SI 1988/267) ... 320-400

Income Tax (Earnings and Pensions) Act
2003

Provision	Paragraph
22	155-800
26	155-800
115(1)	181-150
132	201-060
171(1)	200-600
229	200-500; 201-200
231	200-500; 201-200
377	160-700; 262-450
403(1)	190-750

Income Tax (Trading and Other Income)
Act 2005

Provision	Paragraph
12	190-750
12(4)	152-200; 155-000; 155-500
15	155-800
18	300-350; 310-350; 600-300
33	102-000
34	190-750
48(1)	201-180
68	261-370
109	190-750
110	190-750
111	165-300
Pt. 2, Ch. 10A	230-200
148I	231-355
192(3), (4)	550-300
194	550-150; 550-250
194(3)–(5)	550-200
217	190-200
254	300-350
260	165-100
264	475-050
303	304-750; 403-200
312	261-100
323	155-300
327	165-100
337(1)	300-350
362	240-100
583	550-300
587	575-200; 575-400; 575-700
593	575-200
594	575-200

Industrial Development Act 1982
Pt. II ... 115-000; 301-000

Interpretation Act 1978
Sch. 1 ... 160-100

Local Government, Planning and Land Act
1980 ... 20-050

Long Funding Leases (Elections)
Regulations 2007 (SI 2007/304)
reg. 2(2)–(6), 3, 4 ... 230-225

Merchant Shipping Act 1894
742 ... 235-100

Offshore Installations Act 1971 ... 235-200

Oil Taxation Act 1975
Sch. 3, para. 8 ... 301-000

Personal Injuries (Emergency Provisions)
Act 1939 ... 205-050; 201-180

Petroleum Act 1998
Pt. I ... 500-150

Petroleum (Production) Act (Northern
Ireland) 1964 ... 500-150

Rent Act 1977 ... 302-650; 625-150

Provision	Paragraph
Research and Development (Prescribed Activities) Regulations 2004 (SI 2004/712)	525-200
Road Traffic Act 1988	
58(1), (4)	200-600
185(1)	200-020; 200-600
Road Traffic (Northern Ireland) Order 1981 (SI 1981/154)	
art. 31A(4), (5)	200-600
Safety of Sports Grounds Act 1975	160-600; 262-550
Sale of Goods Act 1979	301-600
Social Security Contributions and Benefits Act 1992	201-180; 205-050
Social Security Contributions and Benefits (Northern Ireland) Act 1992	201-180; 205-050
Social Security (Miscellaneous Provisions) Act 1977	
12	201-180; 205-050
Taxation of Chargeable Gains Act 1992	
37(2)	251-000
38(1)(b)	250-320
41	310-550; 476-500
41(1)	250-200; 250-320; 251-000
41(2)	500-850
41(3)	251-000
41A	230-000
44	110-400
44(1)	110-300
44–47	110-300
140A	310-000
140E	100-200
140E(2)(c)	100-200
152	110-400
154	110-400
170(3)–(6)	247-300
174	310-550
222	160-700; 262-450
Sch. 3, para. 3	310-550
Taxes Management Act 1970	
9A(2)(c)	101-100

Provision	Paragraph
9ZA(2)	101-100
12AA	245-700
42(6), (7)	101-000
98	185-350; 220-200; 245-230
Town and Country Planning Act 1990	
336(1)	500-150
Town and Country Planning (Northern Ireland) Order 1991 (SI 1991/1220)	
art. 2(2)	500-150
Town and Country Planning (Scotland) Act 1990	
277(1)	500-150
Town and Country Planning (Use Classes) (Northern Ireland) Order 1989 (SI 1989/290)	475-600
Town and Country Planning (Use Classes) (Scotland) Order 1997 (SI 1997/3061)	475-600
Town and Country Planning (Use Classes) Order 1987 (SI 1987/764)	475-600
Transport Act 1968	
32, 34, 56(1), (2)	320-150
Value Added Tax Act 1994	
4(2)	120-400
24	120-400
War Damage Act 1943	180-250
Water Industry Act 1991	301-500
Extra-statutory Concessions	
B8	550-400
B16	160-500
B47	165-100
B49	301-000
C12	106-300
Statements of Practice	
B1	305-300
4/80	302-500
1/86	205-350
9/87	315-100
3/91	155-700
6/94	235-700

Index

(References are to paragraph numbers)

Paragraph

A

Abortive expenditure
. plant and machinery allowances 161-200

Accommodation
. MPs and others 165-200

Accounting practice
. leased assets 220-000
. long funding leases 231-500
. research and development 525-200

Advertising hoardings
. plant and machinery allowances 260-010

Aerials
. plant and machinery allowances 260-020

Agricultural buildings allowances
. agricultural buildings, meaning 425-500
. availability 20-000
. anti-avoidance 428-800
. balancing events 425-025; 428-200
. . apportionments 428-700
. . exclusion of election 429-100
. . phasing out allowances 425-025
. . time-limits for election 429-000
. . types of 428-500
. contributions 430-700
. cottages 425-750
. farm buildings 425-700
. farmhouses 425-650
. generally 425-000
. giving effect to allowances and
. . charges 425-050
. husbandry 425-550
. other works, meaning 425-800
. phasing out 425-000; 425-025
. post-April 2008 . . . . 100-150; 425-025
. qualifying expenditure 426-200
. . capital expenditure, meaning 426-250
. . farmhouses 426-300
. . land 426-350
. relevant interest 427-000
. . different interests 427-400
. . leases 427-200
. . purchase before first use 427-300
. sales treated as being for alternative
. . amount 430-500
. short rotation coppice 425-600
. subsidies 430-700
. successions 430-600

Paragraph

. writing-down allowances 425-050; 428-000;
                                      428-100
. writing-off of expenditure 425-025

Agricultural contracting
. industrial buildings allowances 301-700

Air conditioning systems
. plant and machinery allowances 260-030

Aircraft
. long-life assets 210-400
. protected leasing 220-300

Alterations to buildings
. disabled persons for 180-450; 260-525
. plant and machinery allowances 260-040

Alternative finance arrangements
. leased plant and machinery 215-300

Alternative finance investment bonds
. leased plant and machinery 215-300

Alum mines or works
. plant and machinery allowances 152-200;
                                      155-500

Amusement parks
. plant and machinery allowances 260-050

Animals
. plant and machinery allowances 260-060

Annual investment allowance
. amount of 181-050
. assets provided partly for business use 181-000
. claims 181-100
. cars 181-150; 200-300
. companies, restriction 181-200
. first-year allowances 181-000; 181-400;
                                      185-050
. general exclusions 181-150
. generally 100-150
. groups of companies, restriction 181-200
. integral features 247-150; 247-200
. outline 181-000
. partial depreciation subsidy 181-000
. restrictions 181-200
. . application 181-300
. . further 181-350
. scope of 181-000
. value added tax 238-050
. writing down allowances 181-400

Paragraph

Anti-avoidance provisions
. agricultural buildings allowances 428-800
. assured tenancy allowances. 625-700
. business premises renovation
  allowances 403-900
. cars 200-520; 200-540; 201-220
. dredging allowances 600-300
. enhanced capital allowances 242-000
. enterprise zones 320-350
. finance leases 220-470
. flat conversion allowances 477-200
. green technologies 240-000
. industrial buildings allowances 306-500
.. artificially inflated prices 306-550
. integral features 247-150; 247-250
. leased plant and machinery 220-000; 220-500;
  220-550
. long funding leasing, international
  leasing 231-200
. long-life assets 210-300
. mineral extraction allowances 500-600
. mining and oil activities, decommissioning
  costs 237-200
. plant and machinery allowances 240-580;
  240-585
.. finance leasing 240-560
.. hire-purchase 240-560
.. lease premiums 240-580
.. long funding leases 240-580
.. overview 240-500
.. relevant transactions 240-520
.. restrictions on allowances 240-540
.. sale and finance leasebacks 240-580
.. transfer of an entitlement to benefit 240-620
. rent factoring 241-900
. sales treated as being for an alternative
  amount 120-200
. timing of capital expenditure 105-300

Appeals
. apportionment, industrial buildings
  allowances 310-050

Apportionment
. assured tenancy allowances 625-500
. business premises renovation
  allowances 404-000
. buying and selling property – see Buying
  and selling property
. energy-saving plant and machinery 185-350
. fixtures 245-700
. flat conversion allowances 477-100
. industrial buildings allowances 310-050

Assured tenancy allowances
. anti-avoidance provisions 625-700
. apportionments 625-500
. buildings bought unused 625-250
. calculation of allowances and charges
.. balancing adjustments 625-350
.. writing-down allowances 625-300

Paragraph

. common control, sales between persons
  under 625-650
. connected persons, sales between 625-650
. generally 625-000
. giving effect to allowances and
  charges 625-050
. historical background 625-100
. qualifying dwelling-houses 625-150
. qualifying expenditure 625-250
. relevant interest 625-200
. residue of expenditure 625-400
. successions 625-600
. temporary and permanent disuse 625-150
. termination of leases 625-450
. transfers treated as sales 625-550
. writing-down allowances 20-450; 625-300

B

Balancing allowances and charges
. agricultural buildings allowances 428-200
.. apportionments 428-700
.. exclusion of election 429-100
.. phasing out allowances 425-025
.. time limits 429-000
.. types of event 428-500
. assured tenancy allowances 625-350
. business premises renovation
  allowances 403-400
.. calculation 403-600
.. demolition of qualifying building 403-800
.. proceeds 403-500
.. residue of qualifying expenditure 403-700
. disposal events 190-750
. disposal receipts 190-750
. disposal values 190-750
. dredging allowances 600-300
. flat conversion allowances 476-700
. industrial buildings allowances 305-500
.. phasing out 302-225
. mineral extraction allowances 500-250; 500-350
. overseas leasing 220-250
. patent allowances 575-500
. plant and machinery 190-400
.. available qualifying expenditure 190-700
.. balancing allowance 190-400
.. balancing charge 190-500
.. final chargeable period 190-650
.. pooling 190-100
.. reducing balance 190-000
.. total disposal receipts 190-750
. private use restriction 190-850
. research and development allowances 525-400
. sale of plant or machinery 190-750

Bicycles and bicyclists
. plant and machinery allowances 260-100

Books
. plant and machinery allowances 260-110

Paragraph

Brickfields
. plant and machinery allowances 152-200;
155-500

Bridges, tunnels etc.
. industrial buildings allowances 302-100
. plant and machinery allowances 150-200;
155-500; 260-130

Briefcases
. plant and machinery allowances 260-140

Building alterations
. disabled persons, for 180-450; 260-525
. plant and machinery allowances 260-040

Buildings
. plant and machinery allowances 260-150

Bus shelters
. plant and machinery allowances 260-170

Business entertaining expenses
. plant and machinery allowances 165-500;
260-630

Business premises renovation allowances
. balancing events 403-400
. . anti-avoidance provisions 403-900
. . apportionments 404-000
. . calculation 403-600
. . demolition of qualifying building 403-800
. . proceeds 403-500
. . residue of qualifying expenditure 403-700
. designated disadvantaged areas 400-600
. disqualified trade sectors 400-600; 400-650
. generally 400-000
. giving effect to allowances and
charges 400-050
. grants received 403-200
. initial allowances 20-100; 403-000
. qualifying building 400-600
. qualifying business premises 400-650
. qualifying expenditure 400-500
. relevant interest 401-100
. termination of leases 402-000
. value added tax liabilities and rebates 405-000
. writing-down allowances 20-100; 403-200

Buying and selling property
. allocation of proceed/purchase prices 250-020
. apportionment
. . HMRC's approach 250-100
. . just and reasonable 250-020; 250-080
. . method of 250-080
. . typical apportionment figures 250-120
. buying
. . claims by previous owners 250-400
. . elections, buyer's perspective 250-420;
250-460
. . key principles 250-400
. . legal documentation 250-400
. . no election, advising three years later,
worked example 250-480

Paragraph

. . no previous claims, worked example 250-440
. . worked examples 250-440; 250-460; 250-480
. capital gains tax 251-000
. common misconceptions 250-020
. contract wording 250-020
. fixtures election 250-040
. . apportionment 250-080–250-120
. . integral features 250-060
. furnished holiday lettings 250-140
. generally 250-000
. integral features 250-060
. newly built property
. . capital gains tax 250-200
. . principles 250-200
. . worked example 250-220
. refurbishing a property
. . incidental expenditure 250-340
. . principles 250-300
. . worked example 250-320
. residential property 250-140
. selling
. . elections, seller's perspective 250-620
. . full allowance claimed, worked
example 250-640
. . principles 250-600
. . unclaimed allowance, worked
example 250-620
. . worked examples 250-620; 250-640

C

Cameras
. plant and machinery allowances 260-200

Canals
. plant and machinery allowances 152-200;
155-500; 260-210

Canteens
. industrial buildings allowances 302-200

Capital allowances
. changes post-6 April 2008 100-150
. function of 100-100
. generally 100-000
. history 100-100
. legislation 100-000

Capital Allowances Act 2001
. structure 100-000

Capital expenditure
. case law 102-100
. contribution allowances 115-100
. . restrictions on allowances 115-000
. grants or subsidies towards, restrictions on
allowances 115-000
. meaning 102-100
. significance of 102-000
. timing of 105-000
. . additional VAT liability 105-400
. . anti-avoidance provisions 105-300

Capital expenditure – continued   **Paragraph**
. . credit period exceeding four months 105-200
. . delivery date 105-000
. . milestone contracts 105-100
. . promissory conditions 105-000

Capital gains tax
. chattels 110-300
. fixtures 110-200
. generally 110-000
. interaction with industrial buildings
   allowances 310-550
. plant, meaning 110-100
. selling property 251-000
. wasting assets 110-300

Caravans and houseboats
. plant and machinery allowances 260-230

Car parks
. disabled persons 180-450; 260-525
. plant and machinery allowances 260-250

Carpets and flooe coverings 260-780

Cars
. annual investment allowance,
   exclusion 181-150; 200-300
. anti-avoidance
. . disposal values, connected parties 200-540
. . old rules 201-220
. . special rate cars 200-520
. applicable CO2 emissions figure 200-600
. bi-fuel 200-600
. conveyance of goods or burden 200-040
. diesel 200-600
. disabled persons, hire cars 205-050
. EC certificate of conformity 200-600
. electrically propelled vehicles 200-400; 200-600
. employees 155-800; 200-500; 201-200
. estate cars 200-040
. first-year allowances 185-400; 200-400
. . electrically propelled 200-400
. . exception 200-400
. . low emissions 200-400
. hire cars, disabled persons 205-050
. long-life assets 210-200
. low emission, enhanced capital
   allowances 185-100
. main rate cars 200-100
. . meaning 200-600
. meaning 200-020; 200-600; 201-020
. modification of vehicles 200-060
. motor cycles 200-020; 200-600
. not commonly used as private vehicles and
   not suitable for use as 200-060
. off road vehicles 200-040
. old rules 10-030; 201-000
. . anti-avoidance 201-220
. . employees 201-200
. . expenditure partly met by another
    person 201-060
. . inexpensive cars 201-160

                       Paragraph
. . meaning of car 201-020
. . partial depreciation subsidy 201-140
. . purchase of expensive cars 201-040
. . qualifying hire cars 201-180
. . use for private or other purpose 201-100
. . very expensive cars 201-120
. petrol 200-600
. pick-up trucks 200-040
. plant, qualifying as 260-240
. post-April 2009 . . . . 10-030; 200-000
. . annual investment allowance 200-300
. . anti-avoidance 200-520
. . applicable CO2 emissions figure 200-600
. . bi-fuel 200-600
. . commencement and transitional
    provisions 200-620
. . comparison with old rules 200-000
. . conveyance of goods or burden 200-040
. . diesel 200-600
. . EC certificate of conformity 200-600
. . electrically propelled vehicles 200-400;
                                       200-600
. . employees 200-500
. . estate cars 200-040
. . first-year allowances 200-400
. . main rate cars 200-100
. . meaning of car 200-020; 200-600
. . modification of vehicles 200-060
. . not commonly used as private
    vehicles 200-060
. . off road vehicles 200-040
. . petrol 200-600
. . pick-up trucks 200-040
. . qualifying emissions certificate 200-600
. . road fuel gas 200-600
. . summary of new rules 200-000
. . taxis 200-080
. . transitional and commencement
    provisions 200-620
. . UK approval certificate 200-600
. . unsuitable for private use 200-060
. . vehicle scrappage scheme 200-980
. . writing-down allowances 200-200
. private use restriction 190-850
. qualifying emissions certificate 200-600
. qualifying hire cars (old rules) 201-180
. road fuel gas 200-600
. short-life assets 205-050
. taxis 200-080
. unsuitable for private use 200-060
. vehicle scrappage scheme 200-980
. writing-down allowances 200-200

Car wash apparatus
. plant and machinery allowances 260-260

Cash dispensers
. plant and machinery allowances 260-270

Ceilings and canopies
. plant and machinery allowances 260-280

Paragraph

Central heating etc. systems
. plant and machinery allowances 260-290

Cessation of trade 120-000

Chargeable period
. generally 106-100
. meaning
. . corporation tax 106-300
. . income tax 106-200

Chattels 110-300

Claims
. long-life assets 210-300
. need for 101-000
. partnerships 101-100
. reduced first-year allowances 187-050
. time-limits
. . corporation tax 101-100
. . extension of 101-100
. . income tax 101-100
. . interaction with enquiry powers 101-100

Clocks
. plant and machinery allowances 260-300

Cold rooms
. plant and machinery allowances 260-310

Commencement of trade 120-000

**Commercial buildings or structures – see
   Enterprise zones**

Computer software
. acquisition under licence 215-400
. disposals 215-400
. distinction between revenue and capital
   expenditure 215-400
. outright ownership 215-400

Computers and associated equipment
. plant and machinery allowances 260-320;
                                                              260-330

Connected persons
. assured tenancy allowances 625-650
. generally 120-300
. integral features 247-250
. mineral extraction allowances 500-650
. overseas leasing 220-200
. patent allowances 575-700
. research and development allowances 525-700
. ships 235-300
. short life assets 205-300
. value added tax 238-300

Consumables
. plant and machinery allowances 260-340

Containers
. plant and machinery allowances 260-350

Counters and checkouts
. plant and machinery allowances 260-360

Paragraph

Crown
. industrial buildings allowances
. . holding relevant interest 310-150
. . requisitioned land 310-100

Curtains
. plant and machinery allowances 260-370

Cycles and cyclists
. plant and machinery allowances 155-800;
                                                              260-100

D

Death
. sole trader 120-000

Décor
. plant and machinery allowances 260-500

Demolition costs
. industrial buildings allowances 305-300
. plant and machinery allowances 160-200;
                                                              260-510
. research and development allowances 525-400

Depreciation
. first-year allowances 187-150

Designs and patterns
. plant and machinery allowances 260-520

Disability Discrimination Act 2004
. compliance with 180-450; 260-525

Disabled persons
. adjustments and alterations for 180-450;
                                                              260-525

Display equipment
. plant and machinery allowances 260-530

Divers and diving supervisors
. plant and machinery allowances 155-800
. training, know-how allowances 550-450

Docks, dry docks and jetties
. industrial buildings allowances 302-150
. plant and machinery allowances 152-200;
                                                    155-500; 260-540

Doors and door handles
. disabled persons 180-450; 260-525
. plant and machinery allowances 260-550

Double allowances
. exclusion 106-500

Drains or levels
. plant and machinery allowances 152-200;
                                                              155-500

Dredging allowances
. anti-avoidance provisions 600-300
. balancing allowances 600-300
. contributions and subsidies 600-350

Dredging allowances – continued   **Paragraph**
. dredging, meaning 600-100
. generally 600-000
. giving effect to allowances and
    charges 600-050
. initial allowances 20-200
. qualifying expenditure 600-150
. qualifying trade 600-200
. successions 600-400
. writing-down allowances 20-200; 600-250

Dwelling-houses
. furnished lettings – see Furnished lettings
. industrial buildings allowances 302-650
. let on assured tenancies – see Assured
    tenancy allowances
. plant or machinery used in 165-100
. student accommodation 165-100

Dyehouses
. plant and machinery allowances 260-570

Dykes etc.
. plant and machinery allowances 260-580

                         E

Electrical installations and equipment
. plant and machinery allowances 260-600

Electricity substations
. plant and machinery allowances 260-610

Electricity undertakings
. industrial buildings allowances 301-900

Employees and office holders
. assets used by employees 155-800
. bicycles 155-800
. cars, use of own car 155-800
. plant and machinery allowances 155-800
. . assets used only partly for employment
    purposes 155-800
. . general restrictions 155-800
. . overseas earnings 155-800
. . particular assets used by employees 155-800
. . private use of assets 180-500

Energy-saving investments
. landlords 261-100
. plant and machinery allowances 260-620

Energy-saving plant and machinery
. apportionment 185-350
. Energy Technology Criteria List
    (Technology List) 185-100; 185-350
. Energy Technology Product List (Product
    List) 185-100; 185-350
. enhanced capital allowances 185-100
. first-year allowances 185-350
. first-year tax credits – see First-year tax
    credits
. post-6 April 2008 100-150
. revocation of certificate 185-350

                            Paragraph
Energy service providers
. fixtures 245-230

Enterprise zones
. anti-avoidance, realisation of capital
    value 320-350
. availability of allowances 20-050
. buildings straddling boundaries 320-400
. capital value, realisation 320-350
. change of building use 320-400
. enterprise zone property unit trusts 320-400
. expenditure only party incurred within time
    limit 320-300
. generally 320-000
. grants received 320-150
. industrial building or structure,
    meaning 320-100
. initial allowances 320-150
. phasing out of industrial buildings
    allowances 320-050
. purchase of used buildings 320-250
. qualifying expenditure, treatment 320-050
. roads on industrial estates 320-400
. ten-year rule 320-100
. time period 20-075
. value added tax 320-150
. writing-down allowances 320-200

**Environmentally beneficial plant and
    machinery**
. enhanced capital allowances 185-100
. first-year allowances 185-350; 185-550
. first-year tax credits – see First-year tax
    credits
. meaning 185-550
. post-6 April 2008 100-150
. Water Technology Criteria List 185-550
. Water Technology Product List 185-550

**Escalators – see Lifts, escalators and
    walkways**

European company
. formation by merger 100-200

                         F

Fairs
. plant and machinery allowances 152-200;
                                         155-500

Fencing
. plant and machinery allowances 260-700

Ferries
. plant and machinery allowances 152-200;
                                         155-500

Films, tapes and discs
. plant and machinery allowances 260-710

Finance costs
. plant and machinery allowances 260-720

Paragraph

Finance leases
. anti-avoidance provisions 220-470
. election for special treatment 220-460
. hire-purchase 220-440; 240-560
. lump sum payments 220-410
. meaning 220-450
. mineral extraction allowances 500-550
. patent allowances 575-550
. sale and leaseback 220-420
. writing-down allowances 220-440

Fire safety expenditure 160-300; 160-500

First-year allowances
. annual investment allowances, interaction
    with 181-400
. assets bought and sold in same year 187-100
. calculation 187-000
. cars 185-400
. categories of expenditure removed post April
    2008 185-010
. claiming reduced allowances 187-050
. energy saving plant and machinery 185-100;
                                                                                185-350
. enhanced capital allowances 185-100
. . hiring and leasing of assets 185-100
. environmentally beneficial
    technologies 185-100; 185-350; 185-550
. exclusions 10-050; 185-150
. first-year qualifying expenditure 185-010
. gas refueling stations 185-450
. generally 185-000
. hiring and leasing assets 185-100; 185-150
. mineral extraction, ring-fence trades 500-400
. oil or gas extraction 185-500
. partial depreciation subsidies 187-150
. post-6 April 2008 . . . . . 10-025; 100-150; 185-000;
                                                                                185-010
. private use restriction 190-850
. qualifying expenditure 185-000
. ring-fence trades 185-500
. ships 235-200
. small or medium-sized enterprises,
    expenditure incurred by 185-250
. temporary re-introduction 10-020; 185-050
. value added tax 238-000
. writing-down allowances, interaction
    with 190-300

First-year tax credits
. anti-avoidance provisions 242-000
. clawback 242-200
. companies 242-020
. . calculating the credit 242-040
. . incurring a loss in a qualifying
    activity 242-080
. . insurance companies 242-080
. . managing investments 242-080
. . overseas property business 242-080
. . Schedule A business 242-080
. . setting credit against other liabilities 242-060

Paragraph

. disposals of assets 242-200
. green technologies 242-000
. excluded companies 242-000
. relevant first-year expenditure 242-000
. restriction of losses carried forward 242-150
. surrenderable loss 242-000
. unrelieved losses
. . insurance companies 242-100
. . life assurance business 242-100
. . managing investments 242-100
. . overseas property business 242-100
. . Schedule A business 242-100
. . trades and holiday letting businesses 242-100

Fishings
. industrial buildings allowances 301-800
. plant and machinery allowances 152-200;
                                                                                155-500

Fish tanks and ponds
. plant and machinery allowances 260-740

Fixed plant and machinery
. roll-over relief 110-400

Fixtures – see also Integral features
. acquisition by assignee of energy service
    provider 245-500
. acquisition by equipment lessee 245-500
. acquisition of ownership by client 245-500
. acquisition of ownership on cessation of
    ownership 245-500
. administration 245-800
. assignment of equipment lease 245-500
. buying and selling – see Buying and selling
    property
. cessation of ownership 245-400
. disposal values 245-600
. elections to fix apportionments 245-700
. end of qualifying interest 245-400
. energy service providers 245-230
. equipment lease 245-100
. equipment lessors and lessees 245-100;
                                                                                245-220
. generally 245-000
. hotels 252-150
. incoming lessees 245-250
. integral features – see Integral features
. interest in land 245-100
. interest in relevant land 245-210
. lease 245-100
. long-life assets 210-200
. meaning 245-100
. nursing homes 252-100
. offices 252-050
. overseas buyers 245-700
. owners of 245-200
. plant and machinery allowances 260-760
. purchasers of land with fixtures 245-240
. qualifying expenditure, restrictions on 245-300
. relevant land 245-100

Fixtures – continued   **Paragraph**
. rent factoring 241-900
. residentail care homes 252-100
. retail premises 252-200
. sports centres 252-150
. termination of lease or licence 245-500

Flat conversion allowances
. anti-avoidance 477-200
. apportionments 477-100
. balancing allowances and charges 476-700
. business use 475-600
. contributions 477-000
. demolition of flat 476-800
. excess allowances 475-050
. flat, meaning 475-700
. floors, meaning 475-600
. generally 475-000
. giving effect to allowances 475-050
. high value flats 475-700
. initial allowances 20-150; 476-500
. lease, meaning 475-900
. non-qualifying expenditure 475-500
. qualifying buildings 475-600
. qualifying expenditure 475-500
. qualifying flats 475-700
. relevant interest 475-800
. residue of qualifying expenditure 476-800
. short-term letting 475-700
. subsidies 477-000
. suitable for letting 475-700
. termination of leases 475-800
. writing-down allowances 20-150; 476-600

Floodlighting
. plant and machinery allowances 260-770

Floors and flooring materials
. plant and machinery allowances 260-780

Football clubs
. plant and machinery allowances 180-400

Football grounds
. plant and machinery allowances 180-400;
                                                    260-790

Foreign plantations
. industrial buildings allowances 301-750

Fridges and freezers
. plant and machinery allowances 260-800

Furnished holiday lettings
. plant and machinery allowances 155-300
.. corporation tax definitions 155-300
.. income tax definitions 155-300
.. qualifying holiday accommodation 155-300

Furnished lettings
. wear and tear of furniture 165-100

Furniture and furnishings
. plant and machinery allowances 260-820

                                                Paragraph

G

Gas refueling stations
. first-year allowances 185-450

Gas systems
. plant and machinery allowances 152-200;
                                            155-500; 260-900

Gates
. plant and machinery allowances 260-920

Gifts
. plant and machinery allowances 161-000
.. disposal value 190-750

Glasshouses
. capital allowances 260-950

Golf courses
. plant and machinery allowances 260-930

Goods and material
. processing, industrial buildings
    allowances 301-600

Government grants and subsidies – see
    Grants and subsidies

Grain silos
. plant and machinery allowances 260-940

Grants and subsidies
. agricultural buildings allowances 430-700
. business premises renovation
    allowances 403-200
. capital expenditure 115-000
. dredging allowances 600-350
. flat conversion allowances 477-000
. mineral extraction allowances 500-750

Gravel pits
. plant and machinery allowances 152-200;
                                             155-500

Greenhouses
. capital allowances 260-950
. long-life assets 210-500

Green technologies – see **Energy-saving
    plant and machinery; Environmentally
    beneficial plant and machinery; First-
    year tax credits**

Groups of companies
. annual investment allowance
    restrictions 181-200
. integral features, intra-group transfers 247-300

H

Hand rails
. disabled persons 180-450; 260-525

Paragraph

Highway undertakings
. industrial buildings allowances 302-050

Hire-purchase
. alternative finance arrangements 215-300
. alternative finance investment bonds 215-300
. anti-avoidance provisions 240-560
. assignment of contracts 240-560
. diminishing shared ownership 215-300
. disposal values 215-100
. finance leases 220-440; 240-560
. fixtures 215-200
. generally 215-000
. lessees providing plant and machinery 215-300
. software 215-400

Hotels
. industrial buildings allowances 302-800;
. . . . 315-000
. . availability 20-000
. . conditions 315-100
. . excluded activities 315-250
. . meaning of hotel 315-050
. . phasing out 20-000
. . reference period 315-150
. . staff accommodation 315-200
. items qualifying for plant and machinery
. . . allowances 252-150

Human body
. plant and machinery allowances 261-020

Hydraulic power
. industrial buildings allowances 301-950

I

Industrial buildings allowances
. anti-avoidance provisions
. . artificially inflated prices 306-550
. . generally 306-500
. appeals, apportionment 310-050
. apportionment 310-050
. availability 20-000
. balancing adjustments 305-500
. capital gains tax, interaction with 300-000;
. . . . 310-550
. conditions for obtaining 300-100
. construction expenditure 300-500
. . building, meaning 300-550
. . capital expenditure, meaning 300-800
. . contributions to capital expenditure 301-000;
. . . . 301-050
. . date capital expenditure incurred 300-800
. . expenditure treated as being on
. . . construction 300-650
. . non-qualifying expenditure 300-750
. . roads on industrial estates 300-700
. . structure, meaning 300-600
. Crown
. . holding relevant interest 310-150
. . requisitioned land 310-100

Paragraph

. definitions 310-400
. double allowances exclusion 300-150
. enterprise zones – see Enterprise zones
. excluded activities 302-600
. . ancillary to, meaning 302-850
. . dwelling-houses, excluded activities 302-650
. . exceptions 302-900
. . hotels 302-800
. . offices 302-825
. . retail shops 302-700
. . showrooms 302-750
. fixtures on which plant and machinery
. . . allowances have been claimed 245-300
. giving effect to allowances and charges
. . buildings temporarily out of use 300-350
. . generally 300-200
. . lessors and licensors 300-300
. . mining buildings, carrying back balancing
. . . allowances 300-400
. . trades 300-250
. initial allowances 305-050
. interaction with plant and machinery
. . . allowances 310-500
. non-industrial parts of buildings 303-500
. . building not premises 303-550
. . interaction with plant and machinery
. . . allowances 303-650
. overview 300-000
. partnership changes 310-300
. phasing out 20-000; 300-000; 305-225
. post-April 2008 300-000
. qualifying expenditure 304-000
. . capital expenditure on construction 304-050
. . developers, building used before
. . . first sale 304-050
. . purchase of unused building 304-100
. qualifying trades
. . agricultural contracting 301-700
. . buildings used by more than one
. . . licensee 302-400
. . docks 302-150
. . electricity undertakings 301-900
. . fishing 301-800
. . generally 301-500
. . highway undertakings 302-050
. . list 301-500
. . maintenance and repairs 301-600
. . manufacturing 301-550
. . marinas 302-150
. . mineral extraction 301-850
. . mixed use 302-300
. . money, cheques and related documents,
. . . processing 301-600
. . parts of a building 302-350
. . parts of trades and undertakings 302-250
. . processing goods and materials 301-600
. . small workshops 302-500
. . storage 301-650
. . television and radio companies 301-600
. . transport undertakings 302-000

Industrial buildings

allowances – continued   **Paragraph**
.. tunnels, bridges, inland navigation 302-100
.. undertakings, list 301-500
.. vehicle repair workshops 301-600
.. water, hydraulic power, sewerage 301-950
.. welfare buildings 302-200
.. working foreign plantations 301-750
. relevant interest
.. acquisition on completion of
     construction 304-550
.. creation of subordinate interest 304-600
.. Crown holding 310-150
.. grant of a long lease 304-750
.. merger of leasehold interest 304-650
.. significance of 304-500
.. termination of lease 304-700
. requisitioned land 310-100
. roads on industrial estates 300-700
. sale of property 310-200
.. time of sale 310-250
. sale of property, meaning 310-200
. sales treated as being for an alternative
     amount 307-000
.. control test 307-050
.. election for alternative amount 307-150
.. market value 307-100
.. tax advantage test 307-050
. sports pavilions 315-500
. successions 310-350
. time of sale 310-250
. transfer of UK trade to company in another
     member state 310-000
. transitional provisions 310-450
. types of allowance 305-000
. value added tax rebates and additional
     charges 305-300
. writing-down allowances – see Writing-down
     allowances

Inland navigations
. industrial buildings allowances 302-100
. plant and machinery allowances 152-200;
                                        155-500

Installation of plant and machinery 160-100

Insulation expenditure 160-300; 261-100

Insurance companies
. first-year tax credits 242-080; 242-100
. plant and machinery allowances 152-500;
                                        165-600

Integral features
. annual investment allowance 247-150; 247-250
. anti-avoidance provisions 247-150; 247-250
. connected persons, sales between 247-250
. designated 10-150
. disposal value, anti-avoidance rules 247-150
. electrical installations and equipment 260-600
. exclusion from special rate pool 247-150
. intra-group transfers 247-300
. lifts, escalators and walkways 261-320

Paragraph
. lighting 261-330
. meaning 247-050
. overlap with other rules 247-100
. overview 247-000; 260-150
. qualifying items 247-050
. rate of allowances 245-000
. replacement of 247-200
. special rate expenditure 247-150
. water supplies and water tanks 262-920
. writing-down allowances 247-150

Interest in land
. plant and machinery allowances 160-100

**Investment companies and companies with
     investment business**
. plant and machinery allowances 152-400;
                                        155-600

Ironworks
. plant and machinery allowances 152-200;
                                        155-500

J

Joint lessees
. overseas leasing 220-200

K

Kennels
. plant and machinery allowances 261-200

Know-how allowances
. calculation of allowances and charges
.. capital or revenue expenditure 550-300
.. pooling 550-250
. excluded expenditure 550-200
. exclusion of commercial know-how 550-100
. generally 550-000
. giving effect to allowances and
     charges 550-050
. know-how, meaning 550-100
. partnership changes 550-350
. payments by non-residents 550-400
. qualifying expenditure 550-150
. successions 550-350
. training of divers 550-450
. writing-down allowances 20-400; 550-250

L

Land
. plant and machinery allowances 160-100;
                                        261-300

Landlords
. energy-saving items 261-100

Leased plant and machinery
. accounting practice 220-000
. aircraft 220-300

Paragraph

. anti-avoidance provisions 220-000; 220-500;
                                   220-550; 240-580
. assets leased in the UK 220-100
. designated period 220-300
. enhanced capital allowances 185-100
. exclusion from first-year allowances 185-150
. finance leases – see Finance leases
. generally 155-700; 220-000
. giving effect to allowances and charges
. . corporation tax 152-600
. . income tax 152-600
. lease purchase 220-000
. long funding leasing – see Long funding
     leasing
. overseas leasing 220-200
. protected leasing 220-300
. qualifying purposes 220-300
. rent factoring 241-900
. ships 220-300; 235-600
. short-life assets 205-200
. short-term leasing 220-300
. transport containers 220-300

Leases
. agricultural buildings allowances 427-200

Letter boxes
. plant and machinery allowances 261-310

Lifts, escalators and walkways
. disabled persons 180-450; 260-525
. plant and machinery allowances 261-320

Lighting
. disabled persons 180-450; 260-525
. machinery and plant allowances 261-330

Livestock
. plant and machinery allowances 165-300;
                                               260-060

Long funding leasing
. amount of capital expenditure
. . funding leases 231-300
. . operating leases 231-250
. anti-avoidance, international leasing 231-200
. change in accounting treatment 231-500
. commencement and transitional
     provisions 230-050
. commencement date of lease 232-350
. commencement of term 190-750
. derived leases 230-350
. disposal events and values 231-350; 231-355
. election to join scheme 230-225
. . effect of election 230-225
. . eligible leases 230-225
. . qualifying incidental leases 230-225
. . timing and method of making 230-225
. entitlement to allowances 231-150
. exclusions
. . background plant or machinery 231-050
. . right of lessor to claim capital
     allowances 231-000

Paragraph

. extension of term of lease 232-000
. finance lease test 230-400
. funding lease, meaning 230-250
. generally 165-000; 230-000
. guaranteed residual amount, increase
     in 232-100
. high value leases with a term of 5 years or
     less 232-300
. inception of a lease 232-350
. international leasing 231-200
. land, plant and machinery leased with 231-100
. lease payments test 230-450
. lease term, meaning 232-300
. long funding finance lease, meaning 230-400
. long funding lease, meaning 230-200
. long funding operating lease, meaning 230-400
. market value, meaning 232-050
. minimum lease payments, meaning 232-100
. mixed leases 230-350
. plant and machinery lease, meaning 230-300
. remaining useful economic life,
     meaning 232-400
. returns 230-200
. sale and finance leaseback 230-500
. sale and leaseback transactions 231-450
. short lease, meaning 230-500
. termination amount, meaning 232-250
. termination of lease 232-150
. termination value, meaning 232-200
. transfer and assignments by lessor or
     lessee 231-400
. use of plant or machinery previously
     under 160-900

Long-life assets
. aircraft 210-400
. anti-avoidance provisions 210-300
. businesses affected 210-100
. cars 210-200
. disposal value 210-300
. effect of application of legislation 210-050
. excluded assets 210-200
. expenditure limit not exceeded
. . companies 210-250
. . individuals 210-250
. . partnerships 210-250
. fixtures 210-200
. generally 210-000
. greenhouses 210-500
. meaning 210-150
. one large asset or many small ones 210-150
. printing equipment 210-450
. railway assets 210-200
. second-hand assets 210-150
. ships 210-200
. threshold 210-250
. useful economic life 210-150
. writing-down allowances 100-150

Paragraph

M

Maintenance and repairs
. industrial buildings allowances 301-600

Manufacturing
. industrial buildings allowance 301-550

Marinas
. industrial buildings allowances 302-150

Markets
. plant and machinery allowances 152-200;
                                      155-500

Members of Parliament and ministers
. accommodation 165-200

Mezzanine floors 260-780

Milking parlours
. plant and machinery allowances 262-030

Mineral extraction allowances
. anti-avoidance provisions 500-600
. calculation of allowances and charges 500-200
.. balancing allowances 500-350
.. balancing charges 500-250
.. demolition costs 500-200
.. first-year allowances, ring-fence
   trades 500-400
.. total of disposal receipts 500-200
.. unrelieved qualifying expenditure 500-200
.. writing-down allowances 20-250; 500-300
. capital gains tax interaction 500-850
. contributions to capital expenditure 500-800
. generally 500-000
. giving effect to allowances and
   charges 500-050
. industrial buildings allowances 301-850
. mineral extraction trade, meaning 500-100
. qualifying expenditure 500-150
.. acquiring a mineral asset 500-150
.. buildings etc. for the benefit of employees
   abroad 500-150
.. exclusions 500-150
.. mineral exploration and access 500-150
.. plant and machinery 500-150
.. premiums, prevention of double
   deduction 500-150
.. pre-trading expenditure 500-150
.. restoration of land 500-150
.. second-hand assets 500-150
.. undeveloped market value 500-150
.. works likely to become valueless 500-150
. sales treated as being for alternative
   amount 500-500
. subsidies 500-750
. successions 500-700
. transactions between connected
   persons 500-650
. writing-down allowances 20-250; 500-300

Paragraph

Mines, quarries and other concerns
. plant and machinery allowances 152-200;
                                        155-500

Mining and oil activities – see also Mineral
  extraction allowances
. qualifying expenditure 237-000
.. abandonment expenditure 237-200
.. decommissioning offshore oil
   infrastructure 237-100; 237-200
.. oil production sharing contracts 237-400
.. re-use of offshore infrastructure 237-100
.. transfer of interests in oil fields 237-300

Mirrors
. plant and machinery allowances 262-040

Money, cheques and related documents
. processing, industrial buildings
   allowances 301-600

Motor cycles
. meaning 200-020; 200-600

N

Non-resident companies 120-100

Number plates
. plant and machinery allowances 262-100

Nursing homes
. items qualifying for plant and machinery
   allowances 252-100

O

Offices
. industrial buildings allowances 302-825
. items qualifying for plant and machinery
   allowances 252-050

Oil companies
. disposal of oil licences 525-600

Oil or gas extraction – see also Mineral
  extraction allowances
. plant and machinery allowances 185-500

Overseas leasing of plant and machinery
. balancing allowances and charges 220-200
. connected persons 220-200
. final chargeable period 220-200
. generally 220-200
. joint lessees 220-200
. meaning 220-200
. non-qualifying purpose 220-200
. pooling 220-200
. recovery of excess relief 220-200
. writing down allowances 220-200

Overseas property business 155-400

Paragraph

P

Panelling
. plant and machinery allowances 262-150

Partitions
. plant and machinery allowances 262-200

Partnerships
. changes in 120-000
. . industrial buildings allowances 310-300
. . know-how allowances 550-350
. plant and machinery allowances 240-010
. . using property of partners 240-020

Parts of assets
. meaning 100-200

Patent allowances
. calculation of allowances and charges 575-300
. . allowable qualifying expenditure 575-350
. . balancing allowances and charges 575-500
. . total disposal receipts 575-400
. . writing-down allowances 20-350; 575-450
. finance lease or loan 575-550
. future patent rights 575-100
. generally 575-000
. giving effect to allowances and
     charges 575-050
. income from patents, meaning 575-200
. licences 575-150
. patent rights, meaning 575-100
. qualifying expenditure 575-250
. sales between connected persons 575-700
. successions 575-650
. writing-down allowances 520-350; 575-450

Paths
. disabled persons 180-450; 260-525

Personal security expenditure 160-300; 160-700

Plant and machinery allowances
. advertising hoardings 260-010
. aerials 260-020
. air conditioning systems 260-030
. alterations to buildings 260-040
. amusement parks 260-050
. animals 260-060
. annual investment allowance
. . amount of 181-050
. . assets provided partly for business
     use 181-000
. . claims 181-100
. . companies, restriction 181-200
. . first-year allowances 181-000; 181-400
. . general exclusions 181-150
. . generally 100-150
. . groups of companies, restriction 181-200
. . integral features 247-150; 247-200
. . outline 181-000
. . partial depreciation subsidy 181-000
. . restrictions 181-200– 181-350
. . scope of 181-000

Paragraph

. . value added tax 238-050
. . writing down allowances 181-400
. anti-avoidance provisions – see Anti-
     avoidance provisions
. available qualifying expenditure 190-000;
                                                       190-600
. balancing allowances and charges 190-400
. . available qualifying expenditure 190-700
. . balancing allowance 190-400
. . balancing charge 190-500
. . final chargeable period 190-650
. . pooling 190-100
. . reducing balance 190-000
. . total disposal receipts 190-750
. bicycles and bicycles holders 155-800; 260-100
. books 260-110
. bridges, tunnels etc. 260-130
. briefcases 260-140
. building alterations 260-040
. building alterations connected with
     installation 160-100
. buildings 160-100; 260-150
. bus shelters 260-170
. business entertainment 260-630
. buying and selling – see Buying and selling
     property
. cameras 260-200
. canals 260-210
. car parks 260-250
. car wash apparatus 260-260
. caravans and caravan sites 260-230
. cars – see Cars
. cash dispensers 260-270
. ceilings and canopies 260-280
. central heating etc. systems 260-290
. clocks 260-300
. cold rooms 260-310
. companies with investment business 152-400
. computer software 260-330
. computers 260-320
. consumables 260-340
. containers 260-350
. counters and checkouts 260-360
. curtains 260-370
. décor 260-500
. demolition costs 160-200; 260-510
. demolition or destruction of plant or
     machinery 190-750
. depreciation subsidies 165-700
. designs and patterns 260-520
. display equipment 260-530
. disposal events 190-750
. disposal receipts 190-750
. disposal values 190-750
. divers and diving supervisors 155-800
. docks, dry docks and jetties 260-540
. doors and door handles 260-550
. dyehouses 260-570
. dykes etc. 260-580
. electrical installations and equipment 260-600

Pla

Plant and machinery
allowances – continued   **Paragraph**

. electricity substations 260-610
. employees and office holders 155-800
. energy-saving investments 260-620
. entertaining-related expenditure 260-630
. excluded expenditure
. . accommodation for MPs and others 165-200
. . business entertainment 165-500
. . depreciation subsidies 165-700
. . dwelling-houses, plant used in 165-100
. . employment expenditure 165-400
. . life assurance business 165-600
. . long funding leasing 165-000
. . production animals 165-300
. farm animals 165-300; 260-060
. fencing 260-700
. films, tapes and discs 260-710
. finance costs 260-720
. first-year allowances
. . annual investment allowance, interaction
   with 181-400; 185-050
. . assets bought and sold in same year 187-100
. . calculation 187-000
. . cars 185-400
. . categories of expenditure removed post
   April 2008 185-010
. . claiming reduced allowances 187-050
. . energy saving plant and machinery 185-100;
                                 185-350
. . enhanced capital allowances 185-100
. . environmentally beneficial
   technologies 185-100; 185-350; 185-550
. . exclusions 10-050; 185-150
. . first-year qualifying expenditure 185-010
. . gas refueling stations 185-450
. . generally 185-000
. . hiring and leasing assets 185-100; 185-150
. . mineral extraction, ring-fence trades 500-400
. . oil or gas extraction 185-500
. . partial depreciation subsidies 187-150
. . post-6 April 2008 . . . . 10-025; 100-150; 185-000;
                                 185-010
. . post-April 2008 100-150
. . private use restriction 190-850
. . qualifying expenditure 185-000
. . ring-fence trades 185-500
. . ships 235-200
. . small or medium-sized enterprises,
   expenditure incurred by 185-250
. . temporary re-introduction 10-020; 185-050
. . value added tax 238-000
. . writing-down allowances, interaction
   with 190-300
. fish tanks and ponds 260-740
. fixtures – see Fixtures
. floodlighting 260-770
. floors and flooring materials 260-780
. football grounds 260-790
. fridges and freezers 260-800
. furniture and furnishings 260-820
. gas systems 260-900

                                       Paragraph

. gates 260-920
. generally 150-000
. gifts 161-000
. . disposal value 190-750
. giving effect to allowances and
   charges 152-000
. . employees and office holders 152-300
. . mines, quarries and other concerns 152-200
. . trades or business 152-100
. golf courses 260-930
. grain silos 260-940
. greenhouses 260-950
. hotels 252-150
. human body 261-020
. industrial buildings allowances, interaction
   with 303-650
. integral features – see Integral features
. interaction with industrial buildings
   allowances 310-500
. interest in land 160-100
. kennels 261-200
. land 261-300
. latent capital allowances 240-620
. leased assets – see Leased plant and
   machinery
. letter boxes 261-310
. life assurance business 152-500
. lifts and lift shafts 261-320
. lighting 261-330
. long funding lease – see Long funding
   leasing
. long-life assets – see Long-life assets
. loose tools 261-370
. machinery 262-000
. milking parlours 262-030
. mineral extraction, abandonment of plant or
   machinery 190-750
. mirrors 262-040
. MPs accommodation 165-200
. number plates 262-100
. nursing homes and fixtures in 252-100
. offices and fixtures in 252-050
. panelling 262-150
. partitions 262-200
. partnerships 240-000
. plant, meaning 180-100; 180-150; 180-200
. . apparatus or setting 180-250
. . assets used by directors or employees 180-500
. . decor 180-350
. . disabled persons, adjustments for 180-450;
                                   260-525
. . football clubs 180-400
. . functional test 180-300
. . letter to the Football League 180-400
. . plant rooms 262-210
. pooling 190-100
. . available qualifying expenditure 190-700
. . class pools 190-100
. . final chargeable period 190-650
. . single-asset pools 190-100

	Paragraph
. . small pools	190-275
. . total disposal receipts	190-750
. post-6 April 2008	150-000
. poultry houses	262-230
. preparing sites to install plant	160-100; 160-100
. pre-trading expenditure	152-700
. professional fees and preliminary costs	262-240
. public address systems	262-250
. qualifying activities	155-000
. . assets used only partly for	155-900
. . companies with investment business	155-600
. . furnished holiday lettings	155-300
. . leased plant and machinery	155-700
. . mines, transport undertakings etc.	155-500
. . offices and employments	155-800
. . ordinary property business	155-200
. . overseas property business	155-400
. . permanent discontinuance	190-750
. . trades, professions and vocations	155-100
. . use of an existing asset	160-800
. qualifying expenditure	160-000
. . buildings	160-100
. . interest in land	160-100
. . land	160-100
. . statutory restrictions, exependiture unaffected by	10-200
. . structures	160-100
. removal costs	262-300
. rent factoring	241-900
. reservoirs, dams etc.	262-310
. residential care homes and fixtures	252-100
. retail premises	252-200
. roads etc.	262-320
. safes and strong rooms	262-400
. sale of plant or machinery	190-750
. sanitary ware	262-420
. screens	262-430
. seats	262-440
. second-hand assets	210-150
. security systems	262-450
. sewerage systems	262-460
. shares in	161-100
. shelves	262-470
. shop fronts	262-490
. short-life assets – see Short-life assets	
. shutters	262-500
. silage clamps	262-510
. spare parts	262-540
. sports centres	252-150
. sports grounds safety	262-550
. stairs	262-560
. storage equipment	262-570
. structures	262-590
. successions	240-100
. swimming pools	262-600
. taxi licence plates	262-700
. telecommunication systems	262-710
. telephones and fax machines	262-720
. television and videos	262-730

	Paragraph
. temporary buildings	262-740
. tools	261-370
. total disposal receipts to be brought into account	190-000
. tunnels, bridges etc.	262-780
. value added tax liabilities and rebates	
. . connected persons	238-300
. . contracts where person may become plant owner	238-400
. . first-year allowances	238-000
. . no disposal value	238-500
. . short-life assets	238-200
. . time additional liability incurred	238-600
. . writing-down allowances	238-100
. wallpaper designs and pattern books	262-900
. walls	262-910
. water supplies and water tanks	262-920
. water towers	262-940
. windmills	262-950
. windows	262-960
. writing-down allowances	10-100; 100-150
. . annual investment allowance	181-400
. . basis periods	190-200
. . post-April 2008	100-150; 190-000
. . interaction with first-year allowances	190-300
. . integral features	247-150
. . normal rule	190-200
. . pooling	190-100
. . reducing balance	190-000
. . transitional rules	190-250
. . value added tax	238-100
. zoo cages	263-000

Plant rooms
. plant and machinery allowances	262-210

Plenum floors 260-780

Pooling machinery and plant 190-100

Portable flooring 260-780

Poultry houses
. plant and machinery allowances	262-230

Pre-trading expenditure
. mineral extraction allowances	500-150
. plant and machinery allowances	152-700

Printing equipment
. long-life assets	210-450

Processing goods and material
. industrial buildings allowances	301-600

Professional expenses and fees
. plant and machinery allowances	262-240

Professions or vocations
. qualifying activities	155-100

Property business
. furnished holiday lettings – see Furnished holiday lettings

Property business – continued   **Paragraph**
. overseas property business 155-400
. plant and machinery allowances 155-200

Public address systems
. plant and machinery allowances 262-250

Purchase and sale of plant and property
– see Buying and selling property

R

Railways and railway assets
. long-life assets 210-200
. plant and machinery allowances 152-200;
         155-500

Ramps
. disabled access 180-450; 260-525

Removal costs
. plant and machinery allowances 262-300

Rent factoring schemes
. plant and machinery 241-900

Requisitioned land
. industrial buildings allowances 310-100

Research and development
. fixtures on which plant and machinery
    allowances have been claimed 245-300

Research and development allowances
. accounting practice 525-200
. calculation of allowances and charges 525-400
. . balancing charges 525-400
. . demolition costs 525-400
. . disposal events and values 525-400
. connected persons, sales between 525-700
. disposal of oil licences 525-600
. generally 525-000
. giving effect to allowances and
    charges 525-100
. industrial buildings, use as 305-250
. on behalf of claimant 525-300
. qualifying expenditure 525-300
. related to the trade 525-300
. research and development, meaning 525-200
. value added tax capital goods scheme 525-800

Reservoirs, dams etc.
. plant and machinery allowances 262-310

Residential care homes
. items qualifying for plant and machinery
    allowances 252-100

Retail premises
. industrial buildings allowances 302-700
. items qualifying for plant and machinery
    allowances 252-200

Ring-fence trades
. plant and machinery allowances 185-500

                      Paragraph
Roads
. industrial estates
. . enterprise zones 320-400
. . industrial buildings allowances 300-700
. plant and machinery allowances 262-320

Rollover relief
. fixed plant and machinery 110-400

S

Safes and strong rooms
. plant and machinery allowances 262-400

Safety expenditure
. generally 160-300
. sports grounds 160-600

Sale of property
. meaning 100-200

Salt springs or works
. plant and machinery allowances 152-200;
         155-500

Sand pits
. plant and machinery allowances 152-200;
         155-500

Sanitary ware
. plant and machinery allowances 262-420

Screens
. plant and machinery allowances 262-430

Seats
. plant and machinery allowances 262-440

Security systems
. plant and machinery allowances 262-450

Sewerage systems
. industrial buildings allowances 301-950
. plant and machinery allowances 262-460

Shelves
. plant and machinery allowances 262-470

Ships
. balancing charges
. . amount of 235-500
. . assessments and adjustments 235-500
. . deferment 235-400
. . expenditure on new shipping 235-500
. . qualifying persons 235-500
. . qualifying ships 235-500
. . roll-over 235-500
. connected persons 235-300
. disclaimers 235-300
. discontinuance of qualifying activity 235-400
. disposal events and single ship pool 235-300
. election for single ship pool not to
    apply 235-700
. first-year allowances 235-200

Paragraph

. generally 235-000
. group relief 235-300
. jack-up drilling rigs and similar
    vessels 235-100
. leasing assets 235-600
. long-life assets 210-200
. loss relief 235-300
. meaning 235-100
. persons under common control 235-300
. plant and machinery allowances 262-480
. protected leasing 220-300
. sale/scrapping/non-qualifying activity
    use 235-400
. single ship trade 235-300
. successions 235-300
. writing-down allowances 235-300

Shop fronts
. plant and machinery allowances 262-490

Short-life assets
. connected persons 205-300
. disposals for less than market value 205-250
. election
. . conditions for 205-050
. . effect of making 205-100
. . qualifying expenditure 205-050
. . treatment denied 205-050
. four year cut-off
. . corporation tax 205-150
. . income tax 205-150
. generally 205-000
. leasing 205-200
. practical difficulties 205-350
. value added tax 238-200

Short rotation coppice
. agricultural buildings allowances 425-600

Showrooms
. industrial buildings allowances 302-750

Shutters
. plant and machinery allowances 262-500

Signs
. disabled persons 180-450; 260-525

Silage clamps
. plant and machinery allowances 262-510

Slurry storage facilities 262-460; 262-530

Small and medium-sized enterprises
. expenditure incurred by 185-250

Societas Europaea (SE) – see European
    company

Spare parts
. plant and machinery allowances 262-540

Sports centres
. items qualifying for plant and machinery
    allowances 252-150

Paragraph

Sports grounds safety
. plant and machinery allowances 160-600;
    262-550

Sports pavilions
. industrial buildings allowances 20-000; 315-500

Stairs
. plant and machinery allowances 262-560

Steps and stairs
. disabled persons 180-450; 260-525

Storage equipment
. plant and machinery allowances 262-570

Storage of goods or material
. industrial buildings allowances 301-650

Structures
. plant and machinery allowances 262-590

Student accommodation
. plant or machinery allowances 165-100

Successions
. agricultural buildings allowances 430-600
. assured tenancy allowances 625-600
. concept of 120-000
. dredging allowances 600-400
. industrial buildings allowances 310-350
. know-how allowances 550-350
. mineral extraction allowances 500-700
. patent allowances 575-650
. plant and machinery allowances 240-100
. ships 235-300

Swimming pools
. plant and machinery allowances 262-600

T

Taxis
. generally 200-080
. licence plates, plant and machinery
    allowances 262-700

Telecommunication systems
. plant and machinery allowances 262-710

Telephones and fax machines
. plant and machinery allowances 262-720

Television and radio companies
. industrial buildings allowances 301-600

Television and videos
. plant and machinery allowances 262-730

Temporary buildings
. plant and machinery allowances 262-740

Thermal insulation expenditure
. plant and machinery allowances 160-300

Time-limits
. claims 101-100

Paragraph

Time of sale
. meaning 100-200

Toilets and washing facilities
. disabled persons 180-450; 260-525

Tolls
. plant and machinery allowances 155-200;
155-500

Tools
. plant and machinery allowances 261-370

Trades or business
. giving effect to allowances and
charges 152-100
. qualifying activities 155-100

**Transfer of UK trade to company in
another member state**
. industrial buildings allowances 310-000

Transfers treated as sales
. meaning 100-200

Transport containers
. leased assets 220-300

Transport undertakings
. industrial buildings allowances 302-000
. plant and machinery allowances 152-200;
155-500

Tunnels, bridges etc.
. industrial buildings allowances 302-100
. plant and machinery allowances 152-200;
155-500; 262-780

V

Value added tax
. annual investment allowance 238-050
. business premises renovation
allowances 405-000
. capital goods scheme 120-400
. . accrual of additional VAT liabilities and
rebates 120-400
. connected persons 238-300
. contracts where person may become plant
owner 238-400
. enterprise zones 320-150
. first-year allowances 238-000
. industrial buildings allowances 305-300
. no disposal value 238-500
. research and development allowances 525-800
. short-life assets 238-200
. time additional liability incurred 238-600
. writing-down allowances 238-100

Vehicle repair shops
. industrial buildings allowances 301-600

Vehicle scrappage scheme 200-980

Videos
. plant and machinery allowances 262-730

Paragraph

W

Wallpaper designs and pattern books
. plant and machinery allowances 262-900

Walls
. plant and machinery allowances 262-910

Waste water recovery systems 185-550

Wasting assets 110-300

Water supplies and water tanks
. plant and machinery allowances 262-920

Water technologies
. plant and machinery allowances 185-550

Water towers
. plant and machinery allowances 262-940

Waterworks
. industrial buildings allowances 301-950
. plant and machinery allowances 152-200;
155-500

Wear and tear allowances
. furnished lettings 165-100

Welfare buildings
. industrial buildings allowances 302-200

Windmills
. plant and machinery allowances 262-950

Windows
. plant and machinery allowances 262-960

Working foreign plantations
. industrial buildings allowances 301-750

Workshops
. industrial buildings allowances 302-500

Writing-down allowances
. agricultural buildings allowances 20-000;
100-150; 428-000; 428-100
. assured tenancy allowances 20-450; 625-300
. business premises renovation
allowances 20-100; 403-200
. cars 200-200
. dredging allowances 20-200; 600-250
. enterprise zones 20-050; 320-200
. finance leases 220-440
. flat conversion allowances 20-150; 476-600
. industrial buildings 20-000; 100-150
. industrial buildings allowances
. . anti-avoidance 305-225
. . before any relevant event 305-150
. . chargeable period 305-150
. . chargeable period not coinciding with
financial or tax year 305-225
. . demolition costs 305-300
. . first principles 305-100
. . following a relevant event 305-200
. . phasing out 305-225

Paragraph

.. research and development
   allowances made 305-250
.. residue of qualifying expenditure 305-250
.. value added tax rebates and additional
   charges 305-300
.. writing-off of expenditure 305-225; 305-250
. integral features 247-150
. know-how allowances 20-400; 550-250
. long-life assets 100-150
. mineral extraction allowances 20-250; 500-300
. overseas leasing 220-200
. patent allowances 20-350; 575-450
. plant and machinery 10-100; 100-150
.. annual investment allowance 181-400
.. basis periods 190-200

Paragraph

.. post-April 2008 . . . . 100-150; 190-000
.. interaction with first-year allowances 190-300
.. integral features 247-150
.. normal rule 190-200
.. pooling 190-100
.. reducing balance 190-000
.. transitional rules 190-250
.. value added tax 238-100
. private use restriction 190-850

Z

Zoo cages
. plant and machinery allowances 263-000